IFIP Advances in Information and Communication Technology 558

IFIP – The International Federation for Information Processing

IFIP was founded in 1960 under the auspices of UNESCO, following the first World Computer Congress held in Paris the previous year. A federation for societies working in information processing, IFIP's aim is two-fold: to support information processing in the countries of its members and to encourage technology transfer to developing nations. As its mission statement clearly states:

IFIP is the global non-profit federation of societies of ICT professionals that aims at achieving a worldwide professional and socially responsible development and application of information and communication technologies.

IFIP is a non-profit-making organization, run almost solely by 2500 volunteers. It operates through a number of technical committees and working groups, which organize events and publications. IFIP's events range from large international open conferences to working conferences and local seminars.

The flagship event is the IFIP World Computer Congress, at which both invited and contributed papers are presented. Contributed papers are rigorously refereed and the rejection rate is high.

As with the Congress, participation in the open conferences is open to all and papers may be invited or submitted. Again, submitted papers are stringently refereed.

The working conferences are structured differently. They are usually run by a working group and attendance is generally smaller and occasionally by invitation only. Their purpose is to create an atmosphere conducive to innovation and development. Refereeing is also rigorous and papers are subjected to extensive group discussion.

Publications arising from IFIP events vary. The papers presented at the IFIP World Computer Congress and at open conferences are published as conference proceedings, while the results of the working conferences are often published as collections of selected and edited papers.

IFIP distinguishes three types of institutional membership: Country Representative Members, Members at Large, and Associate Members. The type of organization that can apply for membership is a wide variety and includes national or international societies of individual computer scientists/ICT professionals, associations or federations of such societies, government institutions/government related organizations, national or international research institutes or consortia, universities, academies of sciences, companies, national or international associations or federations of companies.

More information about this series at http://www.springer.com/series/6102

Yogesh Dwivedi · Emmanuel Ayaburi ·
Richard Boateng · John Effah (Eds.)

ICT Unbounded, Social Impact of Bright ICT Adoption

IFIP WG 8.6 International Conference on Transfer and Diffusion of IT, TDIT 2019
Accra, Ghana, June 21–22, 2019
Proceedings

Springer

Editors
Yogesh Dwivedi
Swansea University
Swansea, UK

Emmanuel Ayaburi
University of Texas Rio Grande Valley
Edinburg, TX, USA

Richard Boateng
University of Ghana
Accra, Ghana

John Effah
University of Ghana
Accra, Ghana

ISSN 1868-4238 ISSN 1868-422X (electronic)
IFIP Advances in Information and Communication Technology
ISBN 978-3-030-20673-4 ISBN 978-3-030-20671-0 (eBook)
https://doi.org/10.1007/978-3-030-20671-0

This Springer imprint is published by the registered company Springer Nature Switzerland AG
The registered company address is: Gewerbestrasse 11, 6330 Cham, Switzerland

Preface

The main goal of IFIP Working Group 8.6[1] is understanding the development, diffusion, adoption, and implementation of technology, systems, as well as the resulting information that is produced and how it is used. The 2019 IFIP Working Group 8.6 conference was held in Accra, Ghana, and was hosted by the University of Ghana. We are very grateful to the university and its members, especially the School of Business, for generously offering conference facilities at no charge.

The 2019 Conference of the IFIP WG8.6 focused on "Bright Information and Communication Technologies (ICT)." This proceedings volume examines people and organizational issues with the design, implementation, and use of Bright ICT in relation to the development of society. Bright ICT, a 2015 initiative of the Association of Information Systems introduced by Prof J. K. Lee, refers to the grand vision of a bright society enabled by ICT (Lee, 2015). The concept of Bright ICT entails the development of relevant technologies, business models, public policies, social norms, international agreements, metrics of measuring national progress, and preventing undesirable activities on the Internet. Bright ICT research involves taking a holistic view in the design of an ICT-enabled future society (Lee, 2015). The papers included in this volume present research and business models that offer opportunities to achieve the Bright ICT vision within the context of developing, transitioning, and emerging economies.

The adoption and diffusion of information technology (Dwivedi et al. 2017) have seen many dark sides such as the emergence of cyber criminals and the unethical use of ICT (Lee and Fedorowicz, 2018). This major twist from the good intention of adopting technology and Web-based services has affected developing and less developed economies. Organizations in these economies can benefit from the innovative use of ICT and the diffusion of mobile technologies within their customer base (Andoh-Baidoo, 2016). However, the less-developed economies generally lack the resources and capabilities needed to fight the negative effect of ICT (Dwivedi et al. 2015; Kamal et al. 2009). Research on ICT in the context of these economies that focuses on people and organizations is still scarce. The papers presented in the proceedings focus on proposing and testing theoretical models to address different ICT research problems.

The conference offered an opportunity for the presentation of research on the progress made in this endeavor and an opportunity to understand how the knowledge accumulated thus far translates into societal benefit. We particularly welcomed research that questioned how emerging technologies are adopted and appropriated in organizations and everyday life and the impact they are having. However, we also remained open and committed to the wider theme of the IFIP 8.6 working group. All papers were double-blind reviewed by at least two expert reviewers. We followed a constructive

1 http://ifipwg86.wikidot.com/.

reviewing process. This resulted in 30 full-length papers and four short papers from a total of 72 papers submitted. In addition, 47 doctoral consortium projects were accepted to be presented at the pre-conference doctoral consortium and they do not appear in the proceedings. The acceptance rate of the papers in the proceedings is nearly 47%. We appreciate the members of the Program Committee for helping in the reviewing and selection process and providing their comments to us in a timely manner, thereby making this event possible.

This book is organized in five parts to reflect the themes of the papers. Part I includes papers that address technology adoption, diffusion, and ubiquitous computing in government and developing countries. Part II presents papers on big data and business intelligence implementation at the firm and country levels. Part III includes papers on smart cities involving different smart technologies ranging from analytics to smart home devices. Part IV presents papers that discuss security, privacy, ethics, and misinformation. The final part includes papers that examine different concepts in social media and open computing. The papers offer insightful contributions in the context of developing economies by providing recommendations that help mitigate the dark side of the Internet and realize the potential of existing and emerging technologies.

Our sincere thanks go to all the authors, reviewers, attendees, Program Committee members, program chairs, and the University of Ghana staff who all made the 2019 IFIP WG 8.6 conference a success. Special thanks to Prof. H. R. Rao and Prof. George Kasper for helping to bring this conference to Ghana.

April 2014

Yogesh Dwivedi
Emmanuel Ayaburi
Richard Boateng
John Effah

References

Andoh-Baidoo, F.K. (2016) Organizational Information and Communication Technologies for Development, *Information Technology for Development*, 22:2, 193–204.

Dwivedi, Y. K., Rana, N. P., Jeyaraj, A., Clement, M., & Williams, M. D. (2017). Re-examining the unified theory of acceptance and use of technology (UTAUT): Towards a revised theoretical model. *Information Systems Frontiers*, 1–16. DoI: https://doi.org/10.1007/s10796-017-9774-y

Dwivedi, Y. K., Wastell, D., Laumer, S., Henriksen, H. Z., Myers, M. D., Bunker, D., … & Srivastava, S. C. (2015). Research on information systems failures and successes: Status update and future directions. *Information Systems Frontiers*, 17(1), 143–157.

Kamal, M., Good, T., & Qureshi, S. (2009). Development outcomes from IT adoption in microenterprises. In System Sciences, 2009. HICSS'09. 42nd Hawaii International Conference on (pp. 1–10). IEEE.

Lee, J. K. (2015). Research framework for AIS grand vision of the bright ICT initiative. *MIS Quarterly*, *39*(2).

Lee, J., & Fedorowicz, J. (2018). Identifying Issues for the Bright ICT Initiative: A Worldwide Delphi Study of IS Journal Editors and Scholars. *Communications of the Association for Information Systems*: 42, Article 11. DOI: https://doi.org/10.17705/1CAIS.04211

Organization

Conference Chairs

Francis Kofi Andoh-Baidoo	University of Texas Rio Grande Valley, USA
Emmanuel W. Ayaburi	University of Texas Rio Grande Valley, USA
Richard Boateng	University of Ghana, Ghana
Deborah Bunker	University of Sydney, Australia
Yogesh K. Dwivedi	Swansea University, UK
George M. Kasper	Professor Emeritus, Virginia Commonwealth University, USA
H. Raghav Rao	University of Texas at San Antonio, USA

Program Chairs

Yogesh K. Dwivedi	Swansea University, UK
Emmanuel W. Ayaburi	University of Texas Rio Grande Valley, USA
Francis Kofi Andoh-Baidoo	University of Texas Rio Grande Valley, USA
John Effah	University of Ghana, Ghana
David Asamoah	KNUST, Ghana

Organization Chairs

Emmanuel W. Ayaburi	University of Texas Rio Grande Valley, USA
John Effah	University of Ghana, Ghana

Doctoral Consortium Chair

H. Raghav Rao	The University of Texas San Antonio, USA

Conference Administrator

School of Business, University of Ghana, Ghana

Keynote Speakers

H. Raghav Rao	The University of Texas San Antonio, USA
Jae Kyu Lee	KAIST, South Korea

Current Officers of IFIP WG8.6: Transfer and Diffusion of IT

Chair

Yogesh K. Dwivedi	Swansea University, UK

Vice-chairs

Amany Elbanna	Royal Holloway University, UK
Helle Zinner Henriksen	Copenhagen Business School, UK

Secretary

Banita Lal	University of Bedfordshire, UK

Treasurer and Membership

David Wastell	Nottingham University Business School, UK

Contents

Smart Cities

Security, Privacy, Ethics and Misinformation

Social Media and Open Computing

Technology Adoption, Diffusion and Ubiquitous Computing

Neuroethics of Augmenting Human Memory Using Wearable Pervasive and Ubiquitous Technologies

Kuribachew Gizaw(✉)

Addis Ababa University, Addis Ababa, Ethiopia
kuribachewgizaw@gmail.com

Abstract. Neuroethics is a field of study that deals with the ethical and moral issues in neuroscience. Memory augmentation approaches and technologies, is rooted in the broad field of neuroscience and brings with it its own set of ethical issues. Memory augmentation is a new emergent field, where the well-being of humans is augmented using pervasive and ubiquitous technologies. Augmenting Alzheimer and dementia patients' memory with wearable pervasive computing technologies like lifelogging shows a promising memory improvement But, is it ethical to augment memory, if so what ethical issue may arise? The emergent technologies like artificial intelligence, pervasive computing and IoT (Internet of Things) are frequently used in memory augmentation. The consequence of augmentation for treating memory deficit needs a careful look. This paper will highlight the basic ethical issues related to memory augmentation technologies.

Keywords: Neuroethics · Memory augmentation ·
Wearable pervasive and ubiquitous devices

1 Introduction

Ethics related to Artificial Intelligence (AI) is about creating intelligent machines. The possible harm caused by the machines on the human race is the main ethical concern in AI. Is it morally right to lead humans into competition with machines? This is man versus machine game. On the contrary, in the human augmentation scheme, the game is man versus an augmented man. In athletics, all athletes run for a gold medal. It is obligatory for them to be away from doping to have an equal competition platform. Using doping and coming to the running track leads to sanctions. Doping is nothing but a human augmentation psychopharmacological drug that alleviates mental alertness. Such medicines are designed for treating mental illness like ADHD (Attention Deficit Hyperactivity Disorder) [1]. But now, doping is used unethically to aid study and professional competitions. Human augmentation can be done using drugs, mental-implants (brain pacemaker) and neuro-technologies. In this paper, the ethical issues on a type of neuro-technologies for augmenting human memory will be discussed.

Memory enables individuals to encode, store and retrieve (recall) information. Due to a number of factors, the human memory is not capable of accurately recalling all information that one may need with 100% accuracy. Memory augmentation is desired

Y. Dwivedi et al. (Eds.): TDIT 2019, IFIP AICT 558, pp. 3–9, 2019.
https://doi.org/10.1007/978-3-030-20671-0_1

to increase the recall capacity for individuals with and without memory deficit. For an individual with a memory failure, life will not continue to be the same as before. Based on the severity, Alzheimer and dementia patients could not be able to remember their past. They even forget information including their families, home address, their learned experience in academics and professional life. Memory is identity, without having memory life will be so difficult and treating the illness with all possible means is crucial. In the other hand, individuals with a normal memory also have a desire to increase their recall capacity. College students use doping type drugs to aid their regular study to increase their recall for an exam [1].

Wearable pervasive and ubiquitous technologies are applied to augment human memory. Wearable lifelogging technologies (a type of pervasive computing) are widely applied to augment Alzheimer and dementia patients' memory deficits. There are also ubiquitous devices designed to augment students' memory.

Neuroethics discipline has emerged to manage the advancements in neuroscience research findings. It provides neuroscientists a critical look on the potential impact of the neuro-technologies on the society [2].

There is a desire to augment human memory using wearable pervasive computing technologies. But, considering the ethical issues before starting to develop a new and adopt an existing technology is important. System developers need to be aware of the consequences of their planned technologies. The personal, societal and cultural undesired impact of memory augmentation should be assessed at first. This is a short paper to speculate on some of the major neuroethics of augmenting human memory using wearable devices. The background section present human memory and memory augmentation then the ethical issues will be discussed in the discussion section.

2 Background

2.1 Human Memory

The human memory is one of the main cognitive functions that encodes stores and retrieves information [3]. According to the SPI (Serial, Parallel, and Independent) model of memory, the human brain encodes information serially. At the same instant, thousands of input stimuli could enter the human brain. However, memory encoding happens to the stimulus that gets attention in a serial manner. Encoded information will be stored in parallel and finally retrieved independently [4]. Forgetting is unable to retrieve memories. Encoding and retrieval are the two core functions of human memory [5].

Memory Encoding starts with sensory information encoding. It is triggered when input information such as visual, tactile (Sematosensory), auditory, olfactory and gustatory stimuli strikes the brain. Memory encoding ends with making a perception (semantic description of the senses). As a perception reaches working memory/short term memory if it gets the attention it will be sent to Long-term Memory to be encoded else it will be discarded just right there [4].

Memory Retrieval results in two types of output from Long-term memory. Declarative memory output is a mental image and non-declarative memory is a motor output [6]. Declarative memory retrieval includes both recall and recognition, where recall is remembering in detail but recognition is remembering the highlight [6]. Free-recall and cued-recall are two types of recall. Free-recall is remembering the detail without having a cue and cued-recall is remembering after a cue is given [6].

2.2 Human Memory Augmentation

Augmenting memory is not only for individuals with memory deficit it also helps normal individuals develop a more effective memory [7]. Memory encoding, storage and retrieval are three functions in human memory; augmentation is used to support retrieval. Memory encoding accuracy is about the functioning of the sensory systems. Memory storage is an unconscious cognitive function. Synaptic interactions of neurons form groups of neurons for long-term memory and it occurs largely unconsciously [8]. Due to this, assisting the encoding and storage of human memory is not under the current trend of memory augmentation that this work focuses on. Augmenting memory is mainly the concern on increasing the retrieval of a memory. Once information is encoded in the human brain a human can't accurately retrieve all stored information from their past. Forgetting information is the nature of a human. This forgetting could include information which is vital to that individual.

Memory augmentation work includes the use of diaries, photos, to-do lists, calendar, address books and summarized notes to retain the past for the future. The recent trends in memory augmentation focus on using wearable cameras and life-logging technologies [3]. These tools record episodes of an individuals' life. This focus on episodic memory guards against an instance of when an individual loses his/her memory (or parts of it). These recordings of episodic memory are a collection of events that are captured in a particular time and place. It is also referred to as autobiographical memory [4, 8]. Semantic memory augmentation is also useful for human learning, decision making, and thinking.

Augmenting episodic memory can be implemented through a video recording of an individual's daily life activity using a wearable camera. Pervasive computing augmentation systems provide better assistance by generating cues from the recording and playing the cues in an unnoticeable way (e.g. as a Smartphone reminder app) [4, 8]. Research that brings together experts from neuroscience, cognitive psychology, sociology, information technology, and knowledge management disciplines has been conducted for augmenting episodic memory. It includes Forget-Me-Not [9], Memory for a life (M4L) O'Hara et al. [10] and Life-Logging [3].

Microsoft's SenseCam is the most widely known life-logging technology that is used to help patients with memory deficit by recording everyday life activities. After collecting the recordings it generates effective cues based on the context of the user (personal experiences). It also extracts thoughts, feelings and emotions from the time of the event recording. The device is used to sense the environment and record the events without human intervention. The wearer of the device can review the records using the log file as she/he requires and this improves the functioning of patients with recall problems [11].

There are also other approaches related to episodic memory augmentation. MyMemory is one such approach, it uses a mobile application to augment autobiographical memories using personal cues [12]. Odor triggered episodic memory augmentation is also available [13]. Wearable real-time face-recognition systems that use face + voice recognition to replay part of the last conversation one has with the person they are currently interacting with also helps to remember the person along with the last conversation [14]. Photos and digital libraries are used as a cue to recall episodic memory of a specific event [15, 16] and the concept of lifelogging is used to augment memory recall in work meetings [8].

Augmenting Semantic Memory is used to recall a collection of facts and general knowledge. Recall for semantic memory is the most important for learning, professional working, critical thinking and decision making [4]. Students need to have good semantic memory recall to achieve passing marks in their lessons. The most frequently reported failure in memory recall is semantic memory recall of information required during the exam (what to answer for the questions appearing in the exam) [3].

For augmenting the human semantic memory, cognitive neuroscientists recommend repetition and recency of the information. Rehearsal (repetition) during studying and reviewing the studied material before going for an exam helps a student to recall [17]. Augmentation of human semantic memory recall is addressed through using wearable devices by providing digital 'cues' [18], where a cue is a stimulus that helps to recall associated memory. The stimuli can be any of the five sensory stimuli. For example, tactile information is used as a cue in the ubiquitous memory project [18] to augment students memory. Similarly, memory palace, a device used to create contextual (personal, individuals can put what they can easily remember) cues during the encoding phase of information mapping can be used to trigger semantic memory recall later [19].

3 Discussion

3.1 Ethical Issues in Human Memory Augmentations

While talking about the ethicality of memory augmentation, what first comes to everyone mind is the manipulation of memory by others as shown in Total Recall. Total Recall is an American film in 1990 starring by Arnold Schwarzenegger that tells a story of a person with a false memory implant. According to Levy [21], there is no way for such fictions to become reality. For such fictions to be real there must be a full understanding of how memory is stored in the hippocampus and later activated to retrieve it back. Even after years in 2013 Brain initiatives have been launched around the world to understand how the brain works [20]. But still, such manipulation is far from reality. Hence, the memory encoding is a result of sensory encoding, so without the conscious involvement of the individual, memory encoding will not be realized (it will be dumping of neural circuits). In anyways if thus kinds of fictions become possible, it will be unethical and immoral to apply it. The harm caused by such technologies on the individual, in the society and as mankind will outweigh than its benefit (there could be a benefit in treating post-traumatic disorder) [21].

However, the memory augmentation types discussed in this paper to augment episodic and semantic memories are not manipulation of an individual's memory. In using wearable pervasive and ubiquitous computing devices for memory augmentation, ethical concerns can be categorized into four groups. (1) The precision of the device: as long as the pervasive and ubiquitous devices for augmenting episodic and semantic memory are accurate in functionality their aids is acceptable. If there is a little error in the systems it will lead to unintended result [1]. (2) The privacy of the individual: the privacy includes the identity of the individual like autonomy, affection, cognition and behavior. The wearable devices should be designed by considering the maximum possible privacy and optimal autonomy of the individual [20]. (3) The confidentiality and security of the memories of the individual the recorded memories and lifelogging events should be free from unauthorized access. These memories/events/knowledge are the individuals' identity while designing and implementing the systems this confidentiality should never be compromised [1]. For example, the wearable devices used by individuals with memory illness should be designed to be used by themselves, i.e. it should be in accordance with their self-efficacy and mental health situation or if their situation needs support by others these individuals should be trusted by the patients. (4) The consequences of using the device on the individual health and social life: identifying the possible unintended consequences on the social and self is very crucial for the augmentation technology. The consequence of the augmentation on the health of the individual is debated as devaluating humans' imperfection. There is a widely held view that the imperfections of a human brain do have natural balance mechanisms. Enhancing recall may cause forgetting later. Forgetting is not only memory failure it also helps to facilitate later retrieval by reducing information overload from the human brain. This type of forgetting is not forgetting all past information. It is being selective in remembering. The type and volume of memories required to be remembered needs consideration [1]. Long-term and short-term side effect on the natural self also needs to be out planned. Considering the possible societal consequences is also necessary for having culturally informed neuroethics and free from cultural bias technologies [20].

On the other hand, augmenting normal functioning memory is one of the main ethical issues raised. Drugs used to help individuals with dementia disorder like ampakine can improve the memory performance of a healthy individual. Individuals who used ampakine have shown better performance in a memory test than before [22]. Similarly, in augmenting memory using wearable pervasive and ubiquitous devices ethical issues raised in having a problem on the society. Social problems in augmenting memory: in general, augmenting could never be fairly distributed [22]. As a result, the man vs. augmented man match will create disadvantageous individuals. Individuals who are privileged and have access for the augmented technologies will be advantageous and the other individuals will be disadvantageous. The other social problem created by augmenting is life will lose its standard of normalcy [22]. Individuals with their natural ability could be considered less recaller than the individual who uses augmented technology. Here, it is good to remember that augmenting have been practised from the genesis. Even during the renaissance, in the creation of paper and printing machines, there was a debate in using the machines. It was considered that will affect humans' natural ability in recalling memories from their brain. However, it is good to consider such ethical issues while designing memory augmentation technologies. Focusing on helping the natural ability to boost recall capability is always recommended [22]. Therefore, for wearable pervasive and ubiquitous technologies to have an augmented recall throughout ones' lifetime without a drawback the characteristic of the technology matters most. Figure 1 shows the conceptual framework for including neuroethics in the design of wearable pervasive and ubiquitous technologies.

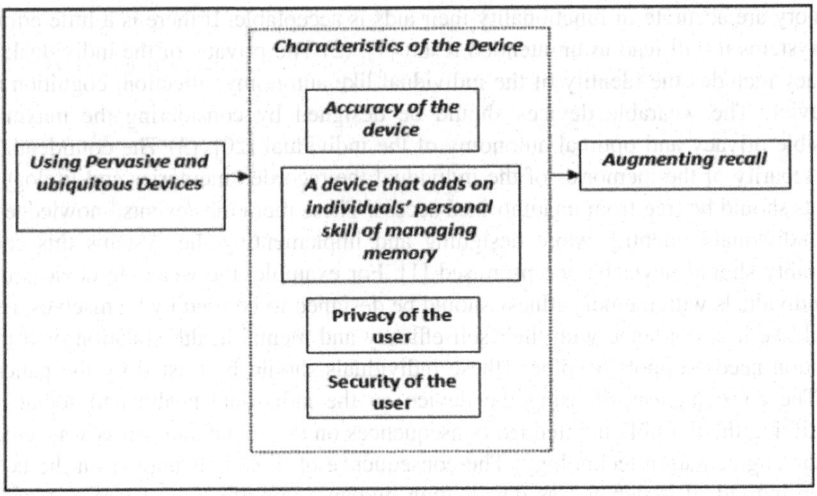

Fig. 1. Conceptual framework

4 Conclusion

The ethical issue for augmenting memory using wearable devices is highlighted in this paper. Relatively, using drugs to enhance memory is more debatable than using wearable devices. The harm caused by wearable devices will be insignificant as long as the device is precisely working and the privacy and security [23–28] of the individual are preserved. Moreover, considering societal aspects is also important to assure the ethicality of wearable devices. In augmenting healthy memories, designing technologies to boost recall by helping the natural ability is the most recommended type. This is a short paper to create an eye opener for other scholars to discuss it more.

References

1. Fuchs, T.: Emerging ethical issues in neuroscience. Nat. Neurosci. **5**(11), 1123–1129 (2002)
2. Greely, H.T., Ramos, K.M., Grady, C.: Neuroethics in the age of brain projects. Neuron **92** (3), 637–641 (2016)
3. Harvey, M., Langheinrich, M., Ward, G.: Remembering through lifelogging: a survey of human memory augmentation. Pervasive Mobile Comput. **27**, 14–26 (2016)
4. Tulving, E.: Organization of memory: QuoVadis? Cogn. Neurosci. 839–847 (1995)
5. Sprenger, M.: Memory lane is a two-way street. Assoc. Supervison Curric. Dev. **56**(3), 65–67 (1998)
6. Squire, L.R.: Declarative and nondeclarative memory: multiple brain systems supporting learning and memory. J. Cogn. Neurosci. **4**(3), 232–243 (1992)
7. Chen, Y., Jones, G.J.F.: Augmenting human memory using personal lifelogs. In: Proceedings of the 1st Augmented Human International Conference on - AH 2010 (2010)
8. Niforatos, E., Laporte, M., Bexheti, A., Langheinrich, M.: Augmenting memory recall in work meetings. In: Proceedings of the 9th Augmented Human International Conference on - AH 2018 (2018)

9. Lamming, M., Flynn, M.: "Forget-me-not" intimate computing in support of human memory. In: Proceedings of FRIEND21, 1994 International Symposium on Next Generation Human Interface (1994)
10. O'Hara, K., Morris, R., Shadbolt, N., Hitch, G.J., Hall, W., Beagrie, N.: Memories for life: a review of the science and technology. J. R. Soc. **3**, 351–365 (2006)
11. Hodges, S., et al.: SenseCam: a retrospective memory aid. In: Dourish, P., Friday, A. (eds.) UbiComp 2006. LNCS, vol. 4206, pp. 177–193. Springer, Heidelberg (2006). https://doi.org/10.1007/11853565_11
12. Chang, C., Hinze, A., Bowen, J., Gilbert, L., Starkey, N.: Mymemory: a mobile memory assistant for people with traumatic brain injury. Int. J. Hum Comput Stud. **117**, 4–19 (2018)
13. Daniels, J.K., Vermetten, E.: Odor-induced recall of emotional memories in PTSD–review and new paradigm for research. Exp. Neurol. **284**, 168–180 (2016)
14. Utsumi, Y., Kato, Y., Kuneze, K., Iwamura, M., Kise, K.: Who are you?-A wearable face recognition system to support human memory. In: 4th Augmented Human International Conference (AH 2013), pp. 1–10 (2013)
15. Lin, W., Hauptmann, A.G.: A wearable digital library of personal conversations. In: Proceedings of the Second ACM/IEEE-CS Joint Conference on Digital Libraries - JCDL 2002, p. 277 (2002)
16. Agroudy, P.E., et al.: Impact of reviewing lifelogging photos on recalling episodic memories. In: Proceedings of the 2016 ACM International Joint Conference on Pervasive and Ubiquitous Computing Adjunct - UbiComp 2016 (2016)
17. Norden, J.J., Emerita, P.: Brain areas involved in different types of memory. In: Neuroscience 14th Conference (2012)
18. Kawamura, T., Fukuhara, T., Takeda, H., Kono, Y., Kidode, M.: Ubiquitous memories: a memory externalization system using physical objects. Pers. Ubiquit. Comput. **11**(4), 287–298 (2007)
19. Harman, J.: Creating a memory palace using a computer. In: CHI 2001 Extended Abstracts on Human factors in Computing Systems - CHI 2001 (2001)
20. Amadio, J., et al.: Neuroethics questions to guide ethical research in the international brain initiatives. Neuron **100**(1), 19–36 (2018)
21. Levy, N.: Neuroethics. Cambridge University Press, New York (2007)
22. Farah, M.J.: Emerging ethical issues in neuroscience. Nat. Neurosci. **5**(11), 1123–1129 (2002)
23. Dwivedi, Y.K., Wade, M.R., Schneberger, S.L. (eds.): Information Systems Theory: Explaining and Predicting our Digital Society, vol. 1. Springer, Heidelberg (2011)
24. Hossain, M.A., Dwivedi, Y.K.: What improves citizens' privacy perceptions toward RFID technology? A cross-country investigation using mixed method approach. Int. J. Inf. Manag. **34**(6), 711–719 (2014)
25. Irani, Z., Gunasekaran, A., Dwivedi, Y.K.: Radio frequency identification (RFID): research trends and framework. Int. J. Prod. Res. **48**(9), 2485–2511 (2010)
26. Duan, Y., Edwards, J.S., Dwivedi, Y.K.: Artificial intelligence for decision making in the era of Big Data–evolution, challenges and research agenda. Int. J. Inf. Manage. **48**, 63–71 (2019)
27. Hughes, L., Dwivedi, Y.K., Misra, S.K., Rana, N.P., Raghavan, V., Akella, V.: Blockchain research, practice and policy: applications, benefits, limitations, emerging research themes and research agenda. Int. J. Inf. Manag. **49**, 114–129 (2019)
28. Gutierrez, A., O'Leary, S., Rana, N.P., Dwivedi, Y.K., Calle, T.: Using privacy calculus theory to explore entrepreneurial directions in mobile location-based advertising: Identifying intrusiveness as the critical risk factor. Comput. Hum. Behav. **95**, 295–306 (2019)

LabNet: An Image Repository for Virtual Science Laboratories

Ifeoluwatayo A. Ige(✉) and Bolanle F. Oladejo

Computer Science Department, University of Ibadan, Ibadan, Nigeria
tayo.olaolorun@gmail.com, oladejobola2002@gmail.com

Abstract. There has been recent research on image and shape storage and retrieval. Several image/shape repositories and databases of large datasets have existed in literature. However, it can be said that these repositories have generic image data content as most of them are English based images of the general world. Since they do not focus on specific field of interest while populating them, there is a high probability that they may not have a sufficient coverage for images and shapes related to specific domains or fields such as high school science-oriented images and shapes. Hence, we develop '*LabNet*'; an image repository for high school science which contains images of high school science-related subjects and laboratory courses. We use Canny's algorithm for edge detection of objects from crawled images; and then perform morphological operation algorithms for segmentation and extraction of object images. We state that our object image does not have any background and can be utilized for scene modelling and synthesis. LabNet can also be useful for high school science-based research as well as an educational tool for elementary science-based classes and laboratory exercises.

Keywords: Canny edge detection · Morphological operations · Image segmentation · Shape repository · Science laboratory

1 Introduction

Image repositories contain well annotated Computer Aided Design (CAD) shape images [1, 2], scanned object images [3], scene images [4] among others. Existing image repositories are mostly generic as not much attention was paid to relevant images peculiar to specific fields and domain. These repositories do not contain sufficient data about each domain due to their generic properties. We however intend to focus on developing a domain-based repository taking the education as our domain. We develop an open source shape image repository *LabNet;* consisting of laboratory apparatus shapes which can be easily accessible to students and teachers for easy identification, electronic learning and retrieval purposes. It can also be adopted as database platform for electronic, virtual and simulated science laboratories. This will meet the needs of those who cannot participate physically in the laboratory exercises.

Published by Springer Nature Switzerland AG 2019
Y. Dwivedi et al. (Eds.): TDIT 2019, IFIP AICT 558, pp. 10–20, 2019.
https://doi.org/10.1007/978-3-030-20671-0_2

2 Related Work

There has recently been a shift from text data to image data. This is definitely because an image easily attracts captivates its viewer's attention and mind. This in turn makes it easier for information to be passed across and assimilated by its viewers much faster than text documents [5]. There is however the need to store related and similar images together for easy accessibility and future retrieval. Image repositories contain large related image datasets. Much work has been done using image repositories and databases. [6] designed MORPH; a longitudinal face database containing human faces useful for face recognition and modelling. [7]'s work shows a color face image database for benchmarking automatic face detection algorithms. ImageNet [8] also developed a large scale ontology of images useful for visual recognition applications. [9]'s work highlighted an image database containing 3D scenes useful for training of object detection systems. [1] used Convolutional Deep Belief Network to developed ModelNet which contains a large scale 3D shapes of Computer Aided Design dataset. [10] provide a novel face database containing face images which were gotten in real-world conditions. They are useful for improvement of face recognition approaches. [11] designed 'Places' which is a database of scene photographs having scene semantic categories and attributes using Convolutional Neural Networks which could be used for scene recognition and analysis.

Specifically focusing on shape object images; [12] developed a shape database of polygonal models which provides multiple semantic labels for each 3D model. [1] also developed a shape repository that contains 3D shapes having different semantic annotations for each 3D model. Although the image data content is very largely specifically more than 3,000,000 shapes [1], they don't provide some domain specific shapes or objects for relevant field of interest. This is why domain specific image repositories have been designed for proper image processing such as face recognition repositories [7, 10], medical images repositories [13, 14] and floricultural object image purposes [15–17].

It can be noted that despite the fact that existing image repositories have large image datasets, their method of dataset collection varies. Some repositories such as [18–20] retrieved 3D models from existing Scenes; generate 3D models from existing 2D Objects [21]. Others obtain camera photographs from real life environments, use segmentation and extraction algorithms on the photographs to populate their databases [3, 10, 17]. The use of sensor tools to automatically sense objects in any given scene and image is also in literature [22]. Once the identification is done, the shapes and objects can be extracted through some object extraction techniques. Another procedure involves crawling of related images, conducting edge detection and segmentation to extract objects from images [23]. A brief critical review of image repositories in literature is shown in Table 1.

There are several edge detection algorithm such as Prewitt, Robert, Sorbel and Canny algorithms among others [24]. We however choose Canny algorithm because it performs better detection and localization than other edge detection techniques [25–28].

Image segmentation techniques also exist in literature such as region-based, feature-based, segmentation based on weakly-supervised learning in CNN [29, 30] and morphological-based techniques [31, 32]. Morphological-based segmentation has been widely used [33]. [34] used morphological image processing for weed recognition in weed and plant images. [35] applied fuzzy-canny and morphological techniques for edge detection and segmentation to some selected images for better output. We therefore present LabNet repository using canny algorithm for the detection of edges in images and morphological image processing technique for image segmentation.

Table 1. Comparative literature review of existing model/shape/image repositories

PAPER	DESCRIPTION	METHOD OF DATASET GATHERING	TECHNIQUE /ALGORITHMS	ANNOTATION METHOD	SIZE OF REPOSITORY	FORM OF SEARCH QUERY	OUTPUT IMAGE WITH OR NO BACKGROUND	ACCESSIBILITY TO REPOSITORY
Nakamura *et.al.* (2001)	Flowers Dataset	Photographs taken at Garden and parks with the use of Camera	Segmentation and Extraction	Human	230 categories	Image and Keyword	Background	Not Open Source
Shilane (2004)	Polygonal 3D model of objects	Crawl from search engines and websites	Not specified	Human	161 classes	Image	No Background	Open Source
Ricanek &Tesafaye (2006)	Adult face	Scanned images from Public records	Median Filtering and Histogram Equalization	Not Specified	515 classes	Image	Background	Not Open Source
Wah *et.al.* 2011	A dataset of Bird Species	Crawling of Bird images from online search engines	Nearest Neighbor Classification Technique	Human and web-based Annotation tool	200 bird species	Keyword	Background. Not segmented	Open Source
Liu *et.al.* (2012)	A dataset of types of 2D Dogs images	Crawling of Dog images from online search engines	Support Vector Machine and Probabilistic approaches	Human	133 Categories	Image	Background	Open source
Kumar *et.al* (2012)	A dataset of Leaves species	Images taken with the use of cameras	Nearest Neighbor Classification Technique	Human	184 trees	Image	Background	Open source
Eitz *et.al.* (2012)	A dataset of Human Sketches of objects	Human Sketches from large volunteers	Bag-of-features Sketch Representation and multi-class support vector machines for classification	Human	250 categories	Keyword	No Background	Not open source
Krause *et. al.* (2013)	A Reconstruction of 2D images of cars to 3D representations of 3D car types	Crawling of car images from online search engines	Matching of Existing 3D CAD models with 2D object through spatial pyramid matching algorithm and Bubble Bank algorithm for categorization	Human	207 categories of models	Image	Background	Not Open Source
Chang *et. al.* (2015)	A dataset of 3D Computer Aided Design (CAD) Model of objects	Crawls from online 3D model repositories	The use of Predictive algorithms for automatic annotation and rigid alignment Algorithm for Hierarchical classification	Human and Algorithmic	3135 categories	Keyword and Image	No Background	Open Source
Lenc & Kral (2015)	Face	Photograph from public records	Cropping and cleaning algorithms	Human	1135 Categories	Image	Background	Not open Source
Wu et.al. (2015)	3D CAD models of Objects	Crawls from CAD search engines	Convolutional Deep Belief networks	Human	660 categories	Image	No Background	Open Source
Martin & Harvey (2017)	Pollen Grains	Photograph of Pollen grains with the use of camera	Cropping	Human	1500 species	Keyword	Background	Open Source

3 LabNet Repository

LabNet consist of apparatus shape images categorized under each subject (physics, chemistry, biology). We categorize the images under specific exercises for each subject which enables quick search query and retrieval. Figure 1 shows a pictorial representation of how LabNet works.

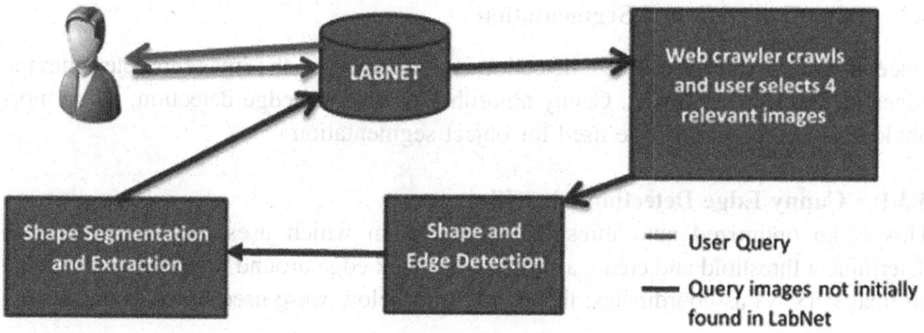

Fig. 1. LabNet design methodology

3.1 Problem Formulation

We define the apparatus shape retrieval problem as follows: given a user query as apparatus name in text as input, the output is n apparatus shapes where $n = 4$. Each apparatus shape is a pictorial representation of the apparatus text input by the user, we make the following statements

- Let a represent the apparatus shape.
- Let $\{H_n^b\}$ be a set of practical exercises under a subject category and

$$H = \{a_1,\ a_2,\ a_3,\ a_4\} \quad (1)$$

  Where a_1, a_2, a_3 and a_4 represent the practical exercises which have 4 apparatus shapes, n is the finite number of practical exercises under each subject.
- Let the sets B, C and P represent biology, chemistry and physics subjects respectively. b, c, p are used to indicate an exercise belongs to biology, chemistry or physics respectively. Then,

$$B = [\{H_1^b\}, \{H_2^b\}, \{H_3^b\}\ldots, \{H_n^b\}] \quad (2)$$

$$C = [\{H_1^c\}, \{H_2^c\}, \{H_3^c\}\ldots, \{H_n^c\}] \quad (3)$$

$$P = [\{H_1^p\}, \{H_2^p\}, \{H_3^p\}\ldots, \{H_n^p\}] \quad (4)$$

3.2 Dataset Gathering and Update

The raw images of the repository was gotten from several web-crawling from existing images on online repositories including science-based databases. A crawl is performed and the best 10 related images are shown to the user based on a web scraping technique: *Beautiful Soup* which is a python library for scraping urls and websites from the internet. Manual selection of related images is then done by specified users. Upon selection of an image, object detection and segmentation techniques are performed on the image. The extracted object is saved in the image base (Fig. 5a, b, c).

3.3 Edge Detection and Segmentation

Once an image is selected, edge detection is performed on the image to determine the edges of the detected object. Canny algorithm is used for edge detection; while morphological operations will be used for object segmentation.

3.3.1 Canny Edge Detection Algorithm

This is an optimized auto thresholding algorithm which uses localized values to determine a threshold and create a single pixel thick edge around a given image. Given an image f(x, y) as coordinates; the steps given below were used on each image

1. Gaussian kernel filter was generated using Gaussian function G(x, y)

$$G_{(x,y)} = \frac{1}{2\pi\sigma^2}\exp\left[-\frac{x^2+y^2}{2\sigma^2}\right] \tag{5}$$

   Where, 'σ' is the standard deviation of Gaussian function
2. The generated Gaussian kernel was used to blur the image and to filter noise. Smooth images $S_{(x,y)}$ were obtained using the convolution of the original image $f_{(x,y)}$

$$S_{(x,y)} = G_{(x,y)} * f_{(x,y)} \tag{6}$$

3. Next, the image gradients $M_{(x,y)}$ and direction $D_{(x,y)}$ were determined by:

$$M_{(x,y)} = \sqrt{b_x^2(x,y) + b_y^2(x,y)} \tag{7}$$

$$D_{(x,y)} = \tan^{-1}\left[b_x(x,y) * b_y(x,y)\right] \tag{8}$$

   Where b_x and b_y are the results of the filter effects $f_{(x)}$ and $f_{(y)}$ on the image $S_{(x,y)}$ along the row and column respectively.
4. Hysteresis thresholding to eliminate breaking up of edge contours [36]
5. Final edges are determined by suppressing all edges that are not connected to a very certain (strong) edge.

3.3.2 Morphological Image Segmentation

To perform any morphological operation, a given image is converted to gray scale and then to binary image. A morphological filter/mask which is a small binary array is also created. Although, there are four major operations carried out in morphological image segmentation which are dilation, erosion, opening and closing [37]. Segmentation will be done using dilation and erosion algorithms as these two operations are sufficient to effectively extract background from foreground. Dilation operation is done by systematically moving the filter over the input image to make the image bigger in size. Mathematically, Given A to be input image and B is the filter;

$$A \oplus B = \left\{ x | (\hat{B})_x \bigcap A \neq \phi \right\} \tag{9}$$

Erosion basically erodes away the boundaries of the foreground. Mathematically, dilation is given by:

$$A \ominus B = \left\{ x | (B)_x \bigcap A^c \neq \phi \right\} \tag{10}$$

3.4 Shape Annotation and Classification

Annotation of shape was done using initial search query from the user. Selected images are annotated using the search query of users. The repository is classified under strict categories. Although there are several science subjects, we restrict our database to only physics, chemistry and biology subjects. This is because these subjects are the major core and fundamental subjects in high school basic science. These subjects have laboratory practical schedule as part of their course curriculum. LabNet repository has 3 major classes, 20 subclasses and 82 categories under the subclasses. Figure 2 shows the classes, subclasses and subcategories. Figure 3 shows the visualized hierarchy of the classes, subclasses, subcategories and entities of each subcategory.

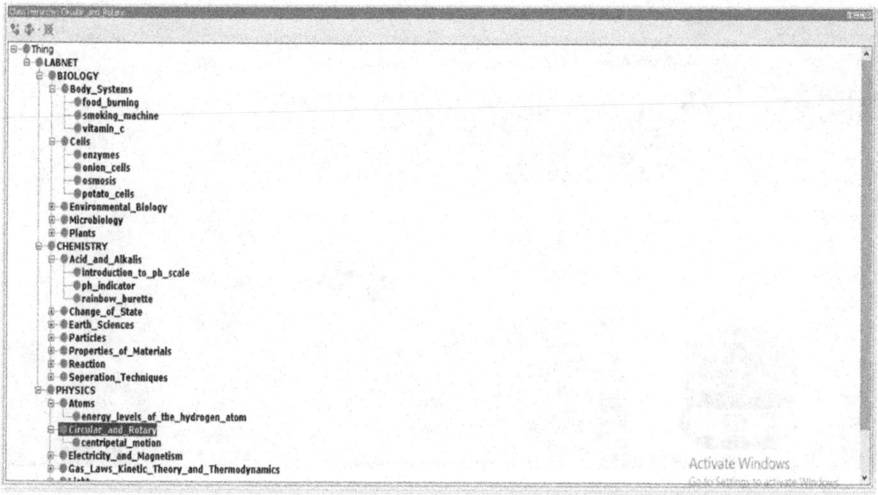

Fig. 2. A taxonomy showing the classes, sub-classes and categories under LabNet

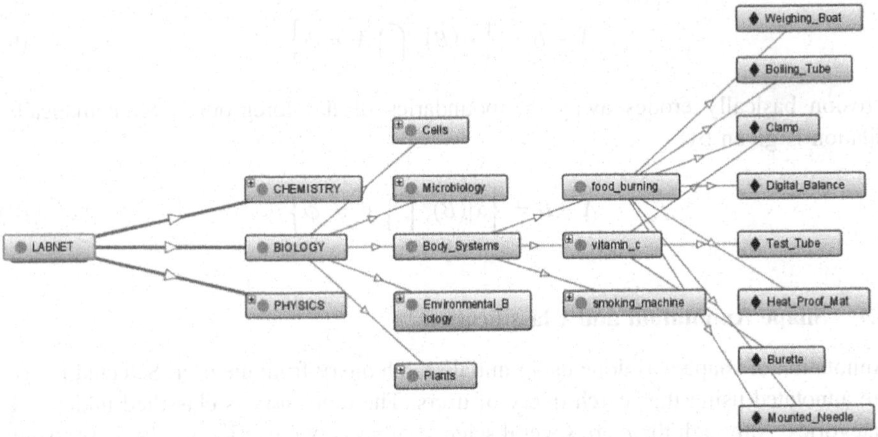

Fig. 3. A visualization of the classes, sub-classes, categories and entities (apparatus names)

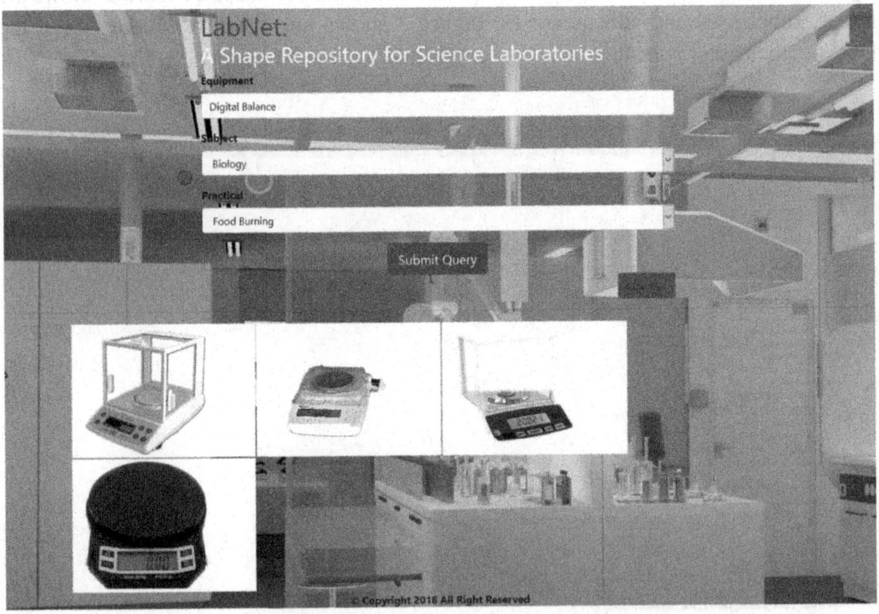

Fig. 4. User search query "cylinder" and search query result images

4 Results

The search technique is keyword-based. The user is expected to type a search query apparatus and select a subject category. Extracted keywords are matched based on annotated objects in the database. The output is shown in Fig. 4. The output images

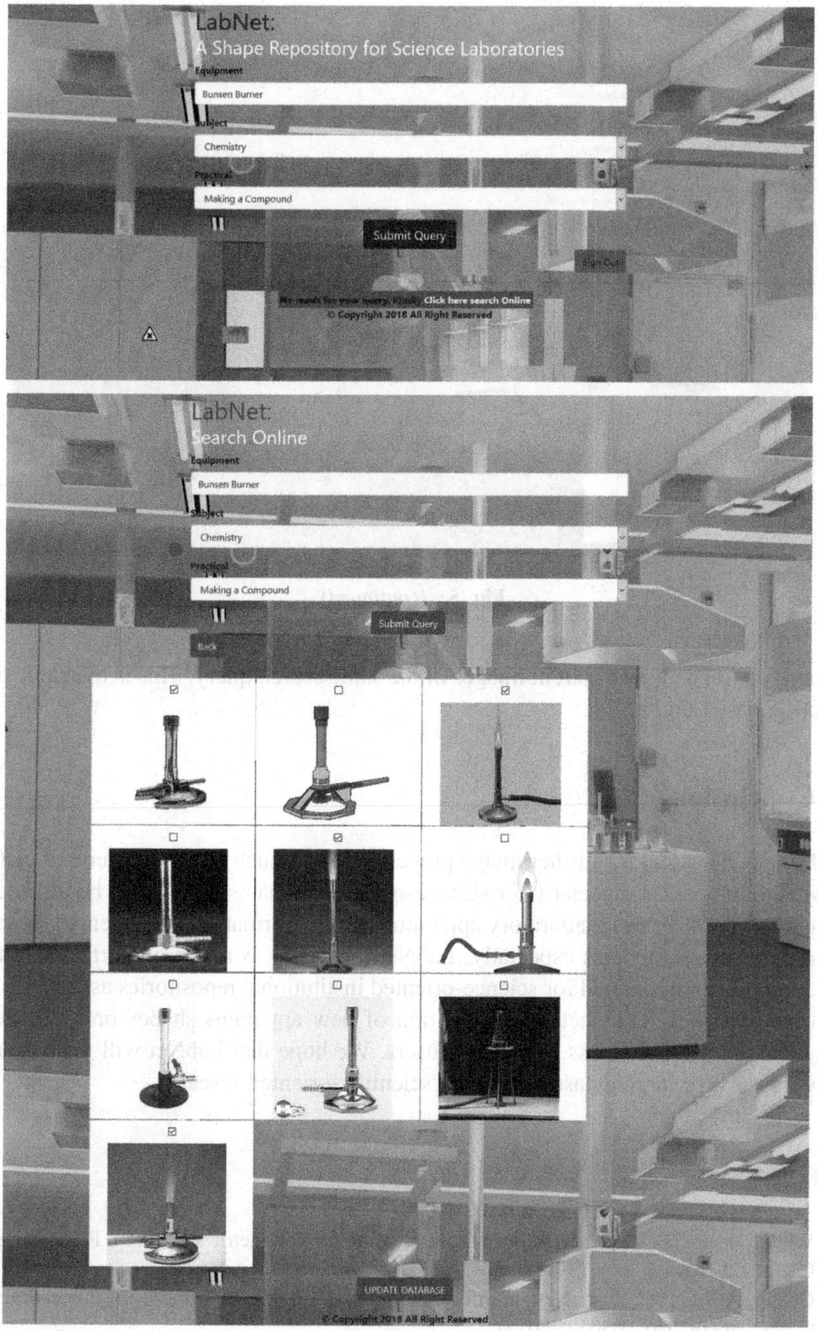

Fig. 5. (a) LabNet 'search online', (b) User selection of best image (s), (c) Search query of the same keyword and segmented object as output

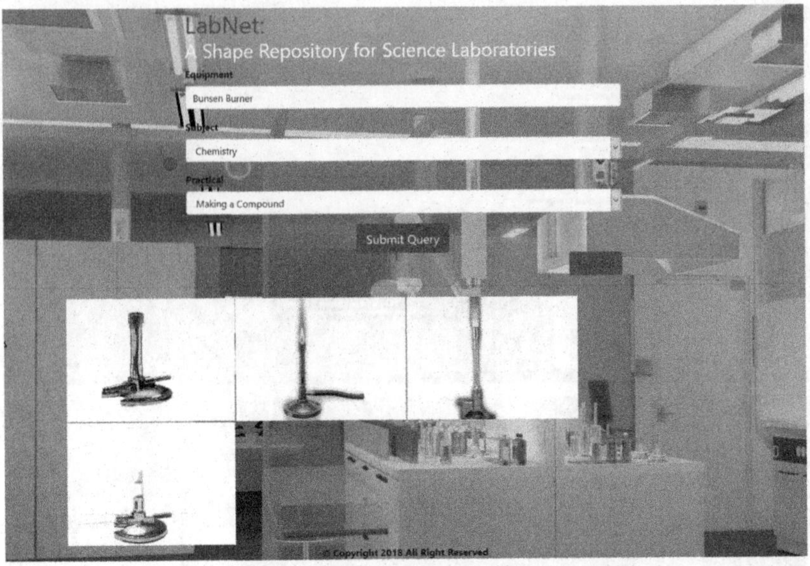

Fig. 5. (*continued*)

contain four related but different images of the same search query. This is to enable user selection based on choice.

5 Conclusion

LabNet can be useful for further image processing tasks such as text to scene or picture conversion processes especially for science-oriented domains. It can also be utilized as a teaching aid for passing laboratory apparatus based information in elementary science to primary school students especially. LabNet repository is a very important tool that can as well be incorporated for science-oriented institutional repositories as a means for electronic learning. Our method of addition of new apparatus shapes provides flexibility and the ease of access and use by users. We hope that LabNet will increase and grow into a very large dataset for wider scientific-oriented research.

References

1. Wu, Z., et al.: 3D ShapeNets: a deep representation for volumetric shapes. In: Proceedings of CVPR (2015)
2. Chang, A.X., et al.: ShapeNet: an information-rich 3D model repository. In: Proceedings of CVPR. arXiv: 1512.03012 (2015)
3. Kumar, N., et al.: Leafsnap: a computer vision system for automatic plant species identification. In: Fitzgibbon, A., Lazebnik, S., Perona, P., Sato, Y., Schmid, C. (eds.) ECCV 2012. LNCS, pp. 502–516. Springer, Heidelberg (2012). https://doi.org/10.1007/978-3-642-33709-3_36

4. Dai, A., Chang, A.X., Savva, M., Halber, M., Funkhouser, T.A.: ScanNet: richly annotated 3D reconstructions of indoor scenes. CVPR, pp. 5828–5839 (2017)
5. Dewan, P.: Words versus pictures: leveraging the research on visual communication. Partnersh.: Can. J. Libr. Inf. Pract. Res. **10**(1), 1–10 (2015)
6. Ricanek, K., Tesafaye, T.: MORPH: a longitudinal image database of normal adult age-progression. In: Proceedings of the 7th International Conference on Automatic Face and Gesture Recognition, USA, pp. 341–345 (2006)
7. Sharma, P., Reilly, R.: A color face image database for benchmarking of automatic face detection algorithms. In: Proceedings of 4th EURASIP Conference on Video/Image Processing and Multimedia Communications, 2–5 July 2003
8. Dieng, J., Dong, W., Socher, R., Li, L., Li, K., Fei-Fei, L.: ImageNet: a large-scale hierarchical image database. In: Proceedings of IEEE Conference on Computer Vision and Pattern Recognition, 20–25 June 2009
9. Russell, B., Torralba, A.: Building a database of 3D scenes from user annotations. In: Proceedings of CVPR (2009)
10. Lenc, L., Král, P.: Unconstrained facial images: database for face recognition under real-world conditions. In: Lagunas, O.P., Alcántara, O.H., Figueroa, G.A. (eds.) MICAI 2015. LNCS (LNAI), vol. 9414, pp. 349–361. Springer, Cham (2015). https://doi.org/10.1007/978-3-319-27101-9_26
11. Zhou, B., Khosla, A., Lapedriza, A., Torralba, A., Oliva, A.: Places: an image database for deep scene understanding. In: Proceedings of CoRR, abs/1610.02055 (2016)
12. Shilane, P., Min, P., Kazhdan, M., Funkhouser, T.: The princeton shape benchmark. In: Shape Modeling Applications. IEEE (2004)
13. Rifai, D., Maeder, A., Liyanage, L.: A content-based-image-retrieval approach for medical image repositories. In: Proceedings of the 8th Australasian Workshop on Health Informatics and Knowledge Management (HIKM), Sydney, Australia, 27–30 January 2015
14. Macko, M., Mikołajewska, E., Szczepańsk, Z., Augustyńska, B., Mikołajewski, D.: Repository of images for reverse engineering and medical simulation purposes. Med. Biol. Sci. **30**(3), 23–29 (2016)
15. Nakamura, S., Sawada, M., Aoki, Y., Hartono, P., Hashimoto, S.: Flower image database construction and its retrieval. In: Proceedings of the 7th Korea-Japan joint Workshop on Computer Vision, pp. 37–42 (2001)
16. Okamura, T., Toguro, M., Iwasaki, M., Hartono, P., Hashimoto, S.: Construction of a flower image database with feature and index-based searching mechanism. In: 5th International Workshop on Image Analysis for Multimedia Interactive Services (2004)
17. Martin, A.C., Harvey, W.J.: The global pollen project: a new tool for pollen identification and the dissemination of physical reference collections. Methods Ecol. Evol. **8**, 892–897 (2017)
18. Lian, Z., et al.: SHREC'11 track: shape retrieval on non-rigid 3D watertight meshes. In: Proceedings of the ACM workshop on 3D object retrieval, 3DOR 2010. ACM (2011)
19. Li, B., et al.: SHREC'12 track: generic 3D shape retrieval. In: Proceedings of Eurographics Workshop on 3D Object Retrieval, pp. 119–126 (2012)
20. Li, B., et al.: SHREC'14 track: large scale comprehensive 3D shape retrieval. In: Proceedings of 7th Eurographics Workshop on 3D Object Retrieval, 6th April, France, pp. 131–140 (2014)
21. Krause, J., Stark, M., Deng, J., Fei-Fei, L.: 3D Object Representations for Fine-Grained Categorization. In: Proceedings of the IEEE International Conference on Computer Vision Workshops (ICCVW), pp. 554–561 (2013)

22. Janoch, A., et al.: A category-level 3D object dataset: putting the kinect to work. In: Fossati, A., Gall, J., Grabner, H., Ren, X., Konolige, K. (eds.) Consumer Depth Cameras for Computer Vision, pp. 141–165. Springer, Heidelberg (2013). https://doi.org/10.1007/978-1-4471-4640-7_8
23. Chudasama, D., Patel, T., Joshi, S.: Image segmentation using morphological operations. Int. J. Comput. Appl. **117**(8), 16–19 (2015)
24. Kaur, S., Singh, I.: Comparison between edge detection techniques. Int. J. Comput. Appl. **145**(15), 15–18 (2016)
25. Kabade, A.L., Sangam, V.G.: Canny edge detection algorithm. Int. J. Adv. Res. Electron. Commun. Eng. (IJARECE) **5**(5), 1292–1295 (2016)
26. Vijayarani, S., Vinupriya, M.: Performance analysis of canny and sobel edge detection algorithms in image mining. Int. J. Innov. Res. Comput. Commun. Eng. **1**(8), 1760–1767 (2013)
27. Shokhan, M.H.: An efficient approach for improving canny edge detection algorithm. Int. J. Adv. Eng. Technol. **7**(1), 59–65 (2014)
28. Eshaghzadeh, A.: Canny edge detection algorithm application for analysis of the potential field map. In: Conference: Iran, 34th National and the 2nd International Geosciences Congress, January 2016
29. Papandreou, G., Chen, L.C., Murphy, K.: Weakly-and semi-supervised learning of a DCNN for semantic image segmentation. arXiv preprint arXiv:1502.02734 (2015)
30. Chen, L.C., Papandreou, G., Kokkinos, I.: Deeplab: semantic image segmentation with deep convolutional nets, atrous convolution, and fully connected CRFs. arXiv preprint arXiv: 1606.00915 (2016)
31. Dhore, M.P., Thakare, V.M., Kale, K.V.: Morphological segmentation in document image analysis for text document images. Int. J. Comput. Intell. Tech. **2**(2), 35–43 (2011)
32. Vartak, A.P., Mankar, V.: Morphological image segmentation analysis. Int. J. Comput. Sci. Appl. **6**(2), 161–165 (2013)
33. Sharma, R., Sharma, R.: Image segmentation using morphological operations for automatic region growing. Int. J. Comput. Sci. Inf. Technol. (IJCSIT) **4**(6), 844–847 (2013)
34. Siddiqi, M.H., Ahmad, I., Sulaiman, S.B.: Weed recognition based on erosion and dilation segmentation algorithm. In: Proceedings of International Conference on Education Technology and Computer, pp. 224–228 (2009)
35. Liu, T., Liu, R., Ping-Zeng, Pan, S.: Improved canny algorithm for edge detection of core image. Open Autom. Control Syst. J. **6**, 426–432 (2014)
36. Yeh, Y., Yang, L., Watson, M., Goodman, N., Hanrahan, P.: Synthesizing open worlds with constraints using locally annealed reversible jump MCMC. ACM Trans. Graph. **31**(4), 56 (2012)
37. Ravi, S., Khan, A.: Morphological operations for image processing: understanding and its applications. In: Proceedings of 2nd National Conference on VLSI, Signal processing and Communications NCVSComs, pp. 17–19 (2013)

Mobile App Stores from the User's Perspective

Abdullah M. Baabdullah[1](✉), Ali Abdallah Alalwan[2], Nripendra P. Rana[3], Ata Al Shraah[2], Hatice Kizgin[3], and Pushp P. Patil[3]

[1] Department of Management Information Systems, Faculty of Economics and Administration, King Abdulaziz University, Jeddah, Kingdom of Saudi Arabia
baabdullah@kau.edu.sa

[2] Amman College of Financial and Administrative Sciences, Al-Balqa Applied University, Amman, Jordan
alwan.a.a.ali@gmail.com, {Alwan_jo,Dr.atashraa}@bau.edu.jo

[3] School of Management, Swansea University, Bay Campus, Fabian Way, Swansea SA1 8EN, UK
nrananp@gmail.com, papushp@gmail.com, hatice.kizgin@swansea.ac.uk

Abstract. The use of smartphones has become more prevalent in light of the boom in Internet services and Web 2.0 applications. Mobile stores (e.g., Apple's App Store and Google Play) have been increasingly used by mobile users worldwide to download or purchase different kinds of applications. This has prompted mobile app practitioners to reconsider their mobile app stores in terms of design, features and functions in order to maintain their customers' loyalty. Due to the lack of research on this context, this study aims to identify factors that may affect users' satisfaction and continued intention toward using mobile stores. The proposed model includes various factors derived from information systems literature (i.e., usefulness, ease of use, perceived cost, privacy and security concerns) in addition to the dimensions of mobile interactivity (i.e. active control, mobility, and responsiveness). The study sets out 13 hypotheses that include mediating relationships (e.g., perceived usefulness mediates the influence of ease of use, active control, responsiveness and mobility; perceived ease of use mediates the influence of active control). As well as outlining the proposed research method, the research contributions, limitations and future research recommendations are also addressed.

Keywords: Mobile app stores · App Store · Google Play · E-Satisfaction

1 Introduction

Nowadays, various mobile applications (mobile app) are searched, purchased and installed by users using mobile stores (m-stores) as an electronic platform (Genc-Nayebi and Abran 2017). These m-stores enable users to download different kinds of applications and share their feedback as a rating or review (Iacob et al. 2013; Singh

Published by Springer Nature Switzerland AG 2019
Y. Dwivedi et al. (Eds.): TDIT 2019, IFIP AICT 558, pp. 21–30, 2019.
https://doi.org/10.1007/978-3-030-20671-0_3

et al. 2017). The rapid growth of the Internet and Web 2.0 applications has helped to increase the use of smartphones worldwide (Baabdullah et al. 2019a, 2019b). This heavy use is also due to the portability and accessibility of mobile devices. This in turn has prompted mobile app practitioners (e.g., mobile app developers) to intensively compete to maintain their market share in this competitive market (Harman et al. 2012). App Store, the first successful m-store, was launched by Apple in July 2008, and this was followed by a number of stores appearing and prospering in a growing market in the 2010s, as well as the emergence of app ecosystem studies (Roma and Ragaglia 2016). By the beginning of 2017, more than 2.2 million applications were available via App Store, and more than 2.8 million apps were distributed via Google Play store (Statista 2018a). Moreover, approximately 178.1 billion apps were downloaded and used by smartphone holders by the end of 2017 (Statista 2018b). However, only a limited number of studies have tested m-stores from the perspectives of information systems and digital marketing, which is important for effective management and avoid failure (Dwivedi et al. 2015). Therefore, this study aims to identify factors that may affect users' satisfaction and continued intention toward using m-stores. This research, which is the first of its kind, contributes to the studied context by identifying several drivers that could help mobile app practitioners to investigate the users' perception of using m-stores. In the presence of a number of mediators, a number of factors related to acceptance and use of technology were considered in addition to mobile features in order to increase the predictive power of the proposed model. This, in turn, will guide mobile app practitioners to provide a better platform in line with the users' requirements.

2 Literature Review

A search of the relevant data sets and research platforms (i.e., Google Scholar, ScienceDirect, and Emerald Insight) reveals a scarcity of studies that have examined mobile app stores from the user's perspective. This observation was made by Genc-Nayebi and Abran (2017) in their systematic review study. In fact, most studies of mobile app stores have conducted their analyses based on the technical and system features of this technology (Chandy and Gu 2012; Chen and Liu 2011; Harman et al. 2012). For example, based on the observational approach, three key features of app stores (comment features, static features, and dynamic features) were identified and analysed by Chen and Liu (2011). In their conference study, Harman et al. (2012) applied an algorithm technique to extract the most important features of m-stores, finding that features related to rating, price, and rank of downloads were the most critical.

A conference paper by Iacob et al. (2013) manually analysed the key features of app stores. The authors reported the importance of existing features such as versioning, comparative feedback, price feedback, usability, and customer support. Using the same manual method, Ha and Wagner (2013) scrutinised and categorised the reviewing reports created by users of Google Play apps. They noticed the considerable attention paid by users to quality, functionality, and aesthetics. By using the classification and regression tree (CART) method, Chandy and Gu (2012) evaluated the main features of Apple's App Store. They found that there were a number of important aspects related to reviewing, ranking, and rating statistics, along with app developer statistics (number of apps and rating mean). By adopting an experimental approach, Shen (2015) validated the moderating impact of both perceived risk and type of application on the relationship between reputation sources and attitudes toward adopting the targeted apps.

Liu et al. (2014) tested the extent to which a freemium strategy could predict sales volume and review rating. Based on data extracted from highly ranked apps, they found a positive relationship between freemium strategy, quality of Google Play apps, and volume of sales. Similarly, Roma and Ragaglia (2016) tested the relationship between three types of revenue model and sales volume of the targeted apps. They found no significant differences between paid and freemium apps in their impact on the sales performance in the case of Apple's App Store. However, as in the case of Google Play, significant differences were observed between a freemium model and a free model.

Song et al. (2014) have empirically tested key numerical and environmental features that could shape the users' satisfaction toward mobile app stores. Their results found that sufficiency, overload, and information specificity of search are the key quantity-related facilitators that predict the level of app discoverability and satisfaction. Environment-related facilitators (coherence and user-generated reviews) were also confirmed by Song et al. (2014) to have a significant impact on app discoverability. Based on data-mining extraction, Finkelstein et al. (2017) discovered a strong relationship between user rating and acceptance of the targeted m-store. They also noticed that users usually negatively rate the features of paid apps that are highly priced rather than those of free downloaded apps. Likewise, Yao et al. (2018) recently tested the main security features that could shape customer satisfaction toward using the Google Play store. Their results, which were based on the Kano Model two-dimensional questionnaire, supported the importance of privacy protection, safe browsing, and malware prevention in shaping users' satisfaction toward using the Google Play store.

Although these studies have provided clues regarding the main aspects that can shape either the success of mobile app stores or the customer perception toward using such platforms, there is a need to identify and propose a model that can capture the customer's perspective on using these stores. Indeed, such a model should first cover the main drivers that could contribute to user satisfaction with m-stores. Secondly, as these online stores are linked to mobile technology, the main mobile features have to be considered. Finally, aspects of perceived privacy and security should be addressed in any model to test the customer perspective. The conceptual model proposed in the current study is discussed in the next section.

3 Conceptual Model and Research Hypotheses

As discussed in the literature review, there is a need to propose a conceptual model that can cover the most important aspects from the user's perspective (Baabdullah 2018a, 2018b; Dwivedi et al. 2016; 2011a, b, 2017a, b; Tamilmani et al. 2017, 2018, 2019; Williams et al. 2015; Zuiderwijk et al. 2015). Therefore, different theoretical foundations have been analysed (Dwivedi et al. 2017a, b), such as the technology acceptance model (TAM) proposed by Davis et al. (1989); the theory of planned behaviour (TPB) introduced by Ajzen (1991); innovation diffusion theory (IDT) (Kapoor et al. 2014a, b; Rogers 2003); and the unified theory of acceptance and use technology (UTAUT) (Dwivedi et al. 2017a, b; Rana et al. 2016; 2017; Venkatesh et al. 2003).

As this research attempts to achieve an efficient and rigorous model, TAM was found to be suitable for the purposes of the current study. This is because TAM has been commonly and successfully adopted by prior studies on the related area of mobile technology and commerce (e.g., Alalwan et al. 2016; Alalwan et al. 2017; Lee and Han 2015; Sohn 2017). Furthermore, the two aspects of perceived usefulness and perceived ease of use have always been the focus of attention for users in relation to using new applications, especially in the related area of mobile commerce (Alalwan et al. 2016; Rana et al. 2016, 2017; Venkatesh et al. 2012).

App stores are driven by smartphone technologies. Accordingly, it is important to consider the mobile interactivity features that have been largely recognised to have an impact on customers' perception, satisfaction, and continued intention to use mobile applications (Lee 2005). Accordingly, along with TAM factors, three main dimensions of mobile interactivity were also considered in the conceptual model: active control, responsiveness, and mobility. Since using m-stores could carry user a financial cost, it was important to consider the impact of perceived financial cost. Furthermore, using m-stores, especially when purchasing freemium and paid apps, could require users to disclose their own financial and personal information; accordingly, such platforms are more likely to expose privacy and security concerns (Slade et al. 2015a, b). Thus, it was considered important to include privacy and security concerns in the current study model.

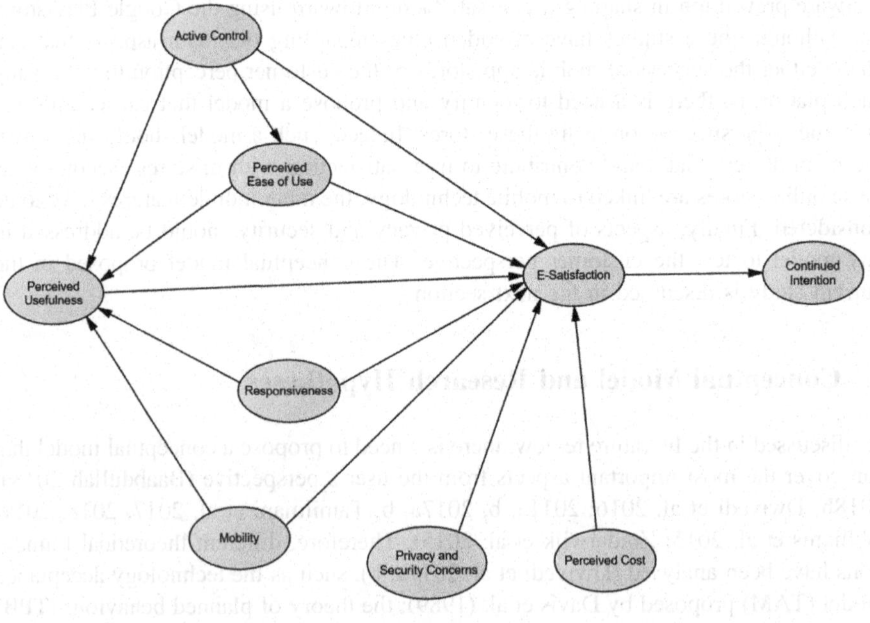

Fig. 1. Conceptual model adapted from Davis et al. (1989) and Lee (2005)

As see in Fig. 1, along with their direct impact on e-satisfaction, active control, responsiveness, and mobility were proposed to have an indirect influence via the mediating role of perceived usefulness. Active control was also suggested to have an indirect influence via the role of perceived ease of use. The instrumental impact of ease via the mediating role of usefulness was considered in the current study model as well. Both perceived cost and privacy concerns were suggested to have a negative impact on user e-satisfaction. Finally, a direct relationship between e-satisfaction and customer continued intention was proposed. All research hypotheses are presented in Table 1.

Table 1. Hypotheses summary

H#	Independent variable	Dependent variable	Hypothesis
H1	Perceived usefulness	E-satisfaction	Perceived usefulness will positively influence customer e-satisfaction toward mobile stores
H2	Perceived ease of use	E-satisfaction	Perceived ease of use will positively influence customer e-satisfaction toward mobile stores
H3	Perceived ease of use	Perceived Usefulness	Perceived ease of use will positively influence perceived usefulness of using mobile stores
H4	Active control	E-satisfaction	Active control will positively influence customer e-satisfaction toward using mobile stores
H5	Active control	Perceived usefulness	Active control will positively influence perceived usefulness of using mobile stores
H6	Active control	Perceived ease of use	Active control will positively influence perceived ease of use of using mobile stores
H7	Responsiveness	E-satisfaction	Responsiveness will positively influence customer e-satisfaction toward using mobile stores
H8	Responsiveness	Perceived usefulness	Responsiveness will positively influence perceived usefulness of using mobile stores
H9	Mobility	E-satisfaction	Mobility will positively influence customer e-satisfaction toward using mobile stores
H10	Mobility	Perceived usefulness	Mobility will positively influence perceived usefulness of using mobile stores
H11	Privacy and security concerns	E-satisfaction	Privacy and security concerns will negatively influence customer e-satisfaction toward using mobile stores
H12	Perceived cost	E-satisfaction	Perceived cost will negatively influence customer e-satisfaction toward using mobile stores
H13	E-satisfaction	Continued intention	E-satisfaction will positively influence continued intention to use mobile stores

4 Research Methodology

A quantitative research approach will be adopted for the purpose of the current study. This is because the current study model was based on a sold theoretical foundation (TAM), so the nature of the current research is to test rather than build theory. Furthermore, in order to validate the current research hypotheses, it is important to capture adequate statistical evidence from the targeted population. Thus, as it is a cost-effective data collection method, this study will run an online questionnaire survey to approach smartphone users who actually adopt and use mobile app stores (i.e., Apple's App Store and Google Play).

The main constructs in the conceptual model will be tested using measurement items extracted from the prior literature. For example, TAM factors will be measured using items proposed by Davis et al. (1989); continued intention will be measured using items from Venkatesh et al. (2012); items of e-satisfaction will be adapted from Wang et al. (2019); perceived cost will be tested using items adapted from Tsu Wei et al. (2009); items from Casaló et al. (2007) will be used to measure privacy and security concerns; the scale developed by Mallat et al. (2009) will be adapted to validate the impact of mobility; responsiveness items were derived from Zhao and Lu (2012); and Liu's (2003) scale will be used for measuring active control.

A seven-point Likert scale will be adopted to test all scale items used in the questionnaire. Before conducting the main survey, the questionnaire will be validated by a panel of experts who have specialisms in the area of digital marketing and information technology (Bhattacherjee 2012). Next, a pilot study will be conducted to ensure an adequate level of constructs' reliability (Nunnally et al. 1967). The data collected will be subjected to structural equation modelling (SEM) analyses. More specifically, a two-stage SEM approach (measurement model and structural model) was considered suitable for ensuring an adequate level of model goodness of fit, construct reliability and validity, and model predictive validity (Tabachnick et al. 2007). In this regard, it is also important to indicate that path coefficient analyses powered by AMOS will be considered for testing the research hypotheses (Hair et al. 2010).

5 Research Contributions, Limitations and Future Research Directions

This research contributes to the context of mobile devices/applications in general and m-stores in particular by identifying several drivers (i.e., perceived usefulness, perceived ease of use, active control, responsiveness, mobility, perceived cost, and privacy and security concerns) that could help mobile app practitioners to comprehensively understand the users' perception of using these electronic platforms. The proposed model in this study was developed to examine users' satisfaction and continued intention by considering a number of factors related to acceptance and use of technology in addition to mobile features. The inclusion of mobile interactivity features alongside perceived cost and privacy and security concerns in TAM would increase the predictive power of the model, especially in the presence of a number of mediators (e.g., perceived usefulness mediates the influence of ease of use, active control, responsiveness, and mobility; perceived ease of use mediates the influence of active control).

This study is the first of its kind to investigate m-stores from the user's perspective, and it is envisaged that it will pave the way for future studies to examine the validity/applicability of the proposed model and extend it with relevant factors that may have a potential influence on user satisfaction and continued intention. Future studies may also build their research on the basis of this study's discussion of relevant work in the literature review and conceptual model sections. The results of this study will help players in the mobile app market to determine the most influential factors that can shape the user's behaviours toward using m-stores. This, in turn, will guide them to launch or redesign an interactive m-store in line with the users' requirements.

In order to develop a framework that suits the user's perspective in the context of m-stores, this study analysed various information systems theories and models. However, this is considered as one of the limitations. Accordingly, future research could conduct a meta-analysis that may help to provide a systematic review as a basis for a comprehensive model. This study is also limited to conceptual model development; therefore, it is recommended that future research has empirical results that can determine the most influential factors on e-satisfaction and continued intention. Moreover, future studies are encouraged to investigate, in addition to the use behaviour, the role of different factors that were not included in the current model. Finally, the proposed conceptual model could also be applicable in other contexts related to e/m-applications and services.

References

Ajzen, I.: The theory of planned behavior. Organ. Behav. Hum. Decis. Process. **50**(2), 179–211 (1991)

Alalwan, A.A., Dwivedi, Y.K., Rana, N.P.: Factors influencing adoption of mobile banking by Jordanian bank customers: extending UTAUT2 with trust. Int. J. Inf. Manage. **37**(3), 99–110 (2017)

Alalwan, A.A., Dwivedi, Y.K., Rana, N.P., Williams, M.D.: Consumer adoption of mobile banking in Jordan: examining the role of usefulness, ease of use, perceived risk and self-efficacy. J. Enterp. Inf. Manage. **29**(1), 118–139 (2016)

Baabdullah, A.M.: Consumer adoption of mobile social network games (M-SNGs) in Saudi Arabia: the role of social influence, hedonic motivation and trust. Technol. Soc. **53**, 91–102 (2018a)

Baabdullah, A. M. (2018b). Factors influencing adoption of mobile social network games (M-SNGs): the role of awareness. Inf. Syst. Front. 1–17. https://doi.org/10.1007/s10796-018-9868-1

Baabdullah, A.M., Alalwan, A.A., Rana, N.P., Kizgin, H., Patil, P.: Consumer use of mobile banking (M-Banking) in Saudi Arabia: towards an integrated model. Int. J. Inf. Manage. **44**, 38–52 (2019a)

Baabdullah, A.M., Alalwan, A.A., Rana, N.P., Patil, P., Dwivedi, Y.K.: An integrated model for m-banking adoption in Saudi Arabia. Int. J. Bank Mark. **37**(2), 452–478 (2019b)

Bhattacherjee, A.: Social Science Research: Principles, Methods, and Practices, 2nd edn. AnolBhattacherjee, Florida (2012)
Casaló, L.V., Flavián, C., Guinalíu, M.: The role of security, privacy, usability and reputation in the development of online banking. Online Inf. Rev. **31**(5), 583–603 (2007)
Chandy, R., Gu, H.: Identifying spam in the iOS app store. In: Proceedings of the 2nd Joint WICOW/AIRWeb Workshop on Web Quality, pp. 56–59. ACM (2012)
Chen, M., Liu, X.: Predicting popularity of online distributed applications: iTunes app store case analysis. In: Proceedings of the 2011 iConference, pp. 661–663. ACM (2011)
Davis, F.D., Bagozzi, R.P., Warshaw, P.R.: User acceptance of computer technology: a comparison of two theoretical models. Manage. Sci. **35**(8), 982–1003 (1989)
Dwivedi, Y.K., Rana, N.P., Chen, H., Williams, M.D.: A Meta-analysis of the Unified Theory of Acceptance and Use of Technology (UTAUT). In: Nüttgens, M., Gadatsch, A., Kautz, K., Schirmer, I., Blinn, N. (eds.) Governance and Sustainability in Information Systems. Managing the Transfer and Diffusion of IT, vol. 336, pp. 155–170. Springer, Heidelberg (2011a). https://doi.org/10.1007/978-3-642-24148-2_10
Dwivedi, Y.K., Wade, M.R., Schneberger, S.L. (eds.): Information Systems Theory: Explaining and Predicting Our Digital Society, vol. 1. Springer, Heidelberg (2011b)
Dwivedi, Y.K., et al.: Research on information systems failures and successes: Status update and future directions. Inf. Syst. Front. **17**(1), 143–157 (2015)
Dwivedi, Y.K., Shareef, M.A., Simintiras, A.C., Lal, B., Weerakkody, V.: A generalised adoption model for services: a cross-country comparison of mobile health (m-health). Govern. Inf. Q. **33**(1), 174–187 (2016)
Dwivedi, Y.K., Rana, N.P., Janssen, M., Lal, B., Williams, M.D., Clement, M.: An empirical validation of a unified model of electronic government adoption (UMEGA). Govern. Inf. Q. **34**(2), 211–230 (2017a)
Dwivedi, Y.K., Rana, N.P., Jeyaraj, A., Clement, M., Williams, M.D.: Re-examining the unified theory of acceptance and use of technology (UTAUT): towards a revised theoretical model. Inf. Syst. Front. 1–16 (2017b). https://doi.org/10.1007/s10796-017-9774-y
Finkelstein, A., Harman, M., Jia, Y., Martin, W., Sarro, F., Zhang, Y.: Investigating the relationship between price, rating, and popularity in the Blackberry World App Store. Inf. Softw. Technol. **87**, 119–139 (2017)
Genc-Nayebi, N., Abran, A.: A systematic literature review: Opinion mining studies from mobile app store user reviews. J. Syst. Softw. **125**, 207–219 (2017)
Ha, E., Wagner, D.: Do Android users write about electric sheep? Examining consumer reviews in Google Play. In: 2013 IEEE 10th Consumer Communications and Networking Conference (CCNC), pp. 149–157. IEEE (2013)
Hair Jr., J.F., Black, W.C., Babin, B.J., Anderson, R.E.: Multivariate Data Analysis: A Global Perspective, 7th edn. Pearson Education International, Upper Saddle River (2010)
Harman, M., Jia, Y., Zhang, Y.: App store mining and analysis: MSR for app stores. In: Proceedings of the 9th IEEE Working Conference on Mining Software Repositories, pp. 108–111. IEEE Press (2012)
Iacob, C., Veerappa, V., Harrison, R.: What are you complaining about? A study of online reviews of mobile applications. In: Proceedings of the 27th International BCS Human Computer Interaction Conference, p. 29. British Computer Society (2013)
Kapoor, K.K., Dwivedi, Y.K., Williams, M.D.: Rogers' innovation adoption attributes: a systematic review and synthesis of existing research. Inf. Syst. Manage. **31**(1), 74–91 (2014a)
Kapoor, K.K., Dwivedi, Y.K., Williams, M.D.: Innovation adoption attributes: a review and synthesis of research findings. Eur. J. Innov. Manage. **17**(3), 327–348 (2014b)
Lee, E., Han, S.: Determinants of adoption of mobile health services. Online Inf. Rev. **39**(4), 556–573 (2015)

Lee, T.: The impact of perceptions of interactivity on customer trust and transaction intentions in mobile commerce. J. Electron. Commer. Res. **6**(3), 165–180 (2005)

Liu, C.Z., Au, Y.A., Choi, H.S.: Effects of freemium strategy in the mobile app market: an empirical study of Google Play. J. Manage. Inf. Syst. **31**(3), 326–354 (2014)

Liu, Y.: Developing a scale to measure the interactivity of websites. J. Advert. Res. **43**(2), 207–216 (2003)

Mallat, N., Rossi, M., Tuunainen, V.K., Öörni, A.: The impact of use context on mobile services acceptance: the case of mobile ticketing. Inf. Manag. **46**(3), 190–195 (2009)

Yao, M.-L., Chuang, M.C., Hsu, C.-C.: The Kano model analysis of features for mobile security applications. Comput. Secur. **78**, 336–346 (2018)

Nunnally, J.C., Bernstein, I.H., Berge, J.M.T.: Psychometric Theory. McGraw-Hill, New York (1967)

Rana, N.P., Dwivedi, Y.K., Lal, B., Williams, M.D., Clement, M.: Citizens' adoption of an electronic government system: towards a unified view. Inf. Syst. Front. **19**(3), 549–568 (2017)

Rana, N.P., Dwivedi, Y.K., Williams, M.D., Weerakkody, V.: Adoption of online public grievance redressal system in India: toward developing a unified view. Comput. Hum. Behav. **59**, 265–282 (2016)

Rogers, E.M.: Diffusion of Innovations. Free Press, New York (2003)

Roma, P., Ragaglia, D.: Revenue models, in-app purchase, and the app performance: evidence from Apple's App Store and Google Play. Electron. Commer. Res. Appl. **17**, 173–190 (2016)

Shen, G.C.C.: Users' adoption of mobile applications: product type and message framing's moderating effect. J. Bus. Res. **68**(11), 2317–2321 (2015)

Singh, J.P., Irani, S., Rana, N.P., Dwivedi, Y.K., Saumya, S., Roy, P.K.: Predicting the "helpfulness" of online consumer reviews. J. Bus. Res. **70**, 346–355 (2017)

Slade, E.L., Dwivedi, Y.K., Piercy, N.C., Williams, M.D.: Modeling consumers' adoption intentions of remote mobile payments in the United Kingdom: extending UTAUT with innovativeness, risk, and trust. Psychol. Mark. **32**(8), 860-873 (2015a)

Slade, E., Williams, M., Dwivedi, Y., Piercy, N.: Exploring consumer adoption of proximity mobile payments. J. Strateg. Mark. **23**(3), 209–223 (2015b)

Sohn, S.: A contextual perspective on consumers' perceived usefulness: The case of mobile online shopping. J. Retail. Consum. Serv. **38**, 22–33 (2017)

Song, J., Kim, J., Jones, D.R., Baker, J., Chin, W.W.: Application discoverability and user satisfaction in mobile application stores: an environmental psychology perspective. Decis. Support Syst. **59**, 37–51 (2014)

Statista: Mobile app usage: Statistics and Facts (2018a). https://www.statista.com/topics/1002/mobile-app-usage/. Accessed 15 Dec 2018

Statista: Number of mobile app downloads worldwide in 2017, 2018 and 2022 (in billions) (2018b). https://www.statista.com/statistics/271644/worldwide-free-and-paid-mobile-app-store-downloads/. Accessed 15 Dec 2018

Tabachnick, B.G., Fidell, L.S., Ullman, J.B.: Using Multivariate Statistics. Pearson, Boston (2007)

Tamilmani, K., Rana, N.P., Dwivedi, Y.K.: A systematic review of citations of UTAUT2 article and its usage trends. In: Kar, A.K., et al. (eds.) I3E 2017. LNCS, vol. 10595, pp. 38–49. Springer, Cham (2017). https://doi.org/10.1007/978-3-319-68557-1_5

Tamilmani, K., Rana, N.P., Dwivedi, Y.K.: Use of 'Habit' is not a habit in understanding individual technology adoption: a review of UTAUT2 based empirical studies. In: Elbanna, A., Dwivedi, Y.K., Bunker, D., Wastell, D. (eds.) TDIT 2018. IAICT, vol. 533, pp. 277–294. Springer, Cham (2018). https://doi.org/10.1007/978-3-030-04315-5_19

Tamilmani, K., Rana, N.P., Prakasam, N., Dwivedi, Y.K.: The battle of brain vs. heart: a literature review and meta-analysis of "hedonic motivation" use in UTAUT2. Int. J. Inf. Manage. **46**, 222–235 (2019)

Tsu Wei, T., Marthandan, G., Yee-Loong Chong, A., Ooi, K.B., Arumugam, S.: What drives Malaysian m-commerce adoption? An empirical analysis. Ind. Manage. Data Syst. **109**(3), 370–388 (2009)

Venkatesh, V., Morris, M.G., Davis, G.B., Davis, F.D.: User acceptance of information technology: Toward a unified view. MIS Q. **27**(3), 425–478 (2003)

Venkatesh, V., Thong, J.Y., Xu, X.: Consumer acceptance and use of information technology: extending the unified theory of acceptance and use of technology. MIS Q. **36**(1), 157–178 (2012)

Wang, Y.S., Tseng, T.H., Wang, W.T., Shih, Y.W., Chan, P.Y.: Developing and validating a mobile catering app success model. Int. J. Hosp. Manage. **77**, 19–30 (2019)

Williams, M.D., Rana, N.P., Dwivedi, Y.K.: The unified theory of acceptance and use of technology (UTAUT): a literature review. J. Enterp. Inf. Manage. **28**(3), 443–488 (2015)

Zhao, L., Lu, Y.: Enhancing perceived interactivity through network externalities: an empirical study on micro-blogging service satisfaction and continuance intention. Decis. Support Syst. **53**(4), 825–834 (2012)

Zuiderwijk, A., Janssen, M., Dwivedi, Y.K.: Acceptance and use predictors of open data technologies: Drawing upon the unified theory of acceptance and use of technology. Govern. Inf. Q. **32**(4), 429–440 (2015)

The Adoption and Diffusion of Wearables

Ton A. M. Spil(✉), Björn Kijl, and Vincent Romijnders

University of Twente, Enschede, The Netherlands
{a.a.m.spil, b.kijl}@utwente.nl,
vincentromijnders@gmail.com

Abstract. Although the sales of wearables are increasing in the last few years, it is still unknown how wearables are actually adopted and being used in everyday life by consumers. In this study, we try to identify the adoption and diffusion patterns of wearables by performing a sentiment analysis on 97 semi-structured interviews with wearables owners/users focused on relevance and requirements of and resources and resistance related to wearables. Based on this analysis we conclude that developers and manufacturers of wearables should make their devices more relevant, more reliable and easier to use. They should also address privacy issues and foster habit (using it all and every day) in order to speed up the adoption and diffusion of wearables. The theoretical contribution of this paper is that habit should be studied as a potential dependent variable for intention to use.

Keywords: Wearables · Adoption of IT · Diffusion

1 Introduction

In recent years, commercial technologies have been developed for automatically collecting data that can assist in self-regulation. The usage of wearable self-tracking technology has recently emerged as a new trend in lifestyle and personal optimization in terms of health, fitness and well-being. The proliferation of wearable technologies calls for the development of conceptual lenses to understand the drivers of their success (Benbusan 2018). We define wearables as *wrist-worn wearables for personal use, which for example monitor number of steps taken, distance travelled, speed and pace, calories burnt, heart rate, hours slept and dietary information.* Sales of wearables are rising. In the last quarter of 2016, 23 million wearables were sold worldwide and it is expected that this number will increase to 213 million by 2020.

Yet, despite wearables offering unforeseen capabilities for supporting a healthier lifestyle, market adoption of wearables is still low. Four years ago, wrist-worn wearables were supposed to be the next big thing; they were going from a nerdy dream to a mainstream reality. None of that happened. In fact, it was the opposite. The market for wearables has proved to be volatile, claiming victims much faster than we saw with the companies that went bankrupt following the introduction of the iPhone (Kovach 2016). The abandonment rate is substantial and there is no broad diffusion yet. Hence, it is important to determine factors which factors of wearables are good and not good (yet). Yet, there is still little known about how to improve the diffusion, in personal use, of

Published by Springer Nature Switzerland AG 2019
Y. Dwivedi et al. (Eds.): TDIT 2019, IFIP AICT 558, pp. 31–47, 2019.
https://doi.org/10.1007/978-3-030-20671-0_4

wrist-worn wearables. Due to this, individuals may not reap the promised health and fitness benefits, society is unable to curb widespread health problems - such as rising obesity levels - and companies may not reap the benefits of the data on which the valuation of the internet of things (IoT) industry is premised (Ledger 2014).

Hence the importance of an independent study to investigate the actual users of wearables in order to make wearables a success and give an explanation for the 'failure' so far. Our related research question is defined as follows: *How to improve the diffusion, in personal use, of wrist-worn wearables?*

2 Background

By keeping track of data about every aspect of one's life, people can gain exact knowledge of and insight into their daily lives. The collected data makes it possible to understand certain activities, habits and triggers for actions and behaviour taken. Quantifying oneself makes it able to improve a person's lifestyle and achievements with the help of measuring, analysing and comparing performances about different activities (Barcena, Wueest and Lau 2014). Due to the increase of power of processors and the miniaturization of sensors and processors, longer battery lifespan, and the opportunity of communication and data collection, one embrace the idea the possibility of using always-on devices with small effort and accurately record data with the help of smartphone apps and wearables. Next to the technological aspects, people are increasingly looking after their health (Salah, MacIntosh and Rajakulendran 2014). There are different type of wearable users; those with chronic medical conditions, sports enthusiasts who are keen to collect data about their activity performances in order to help them set goals and track their progress, persons who are interested in keeping track of certain lifestyle patterns or achieving behaviour changes, such as losing weight, having more sleep or living a healthier life (Barcena, Wueest and Lau 2014). The process of self-tracking typically involves the tracking and collection of data from an activity, followed by the comparison and analysis of the performance to the goal being desired. Based on the results, adjustments can be made and the process of quantifying one's performance aiming to reach a certain goal can be repeated.

The first generation of wearables can be seen as products that only generates revenue at the point of sale and solely run tracking and analysing software within an enclosed ecosystem provided by the wearable developers. Due to the closed ecosystem, there is no possibility of service enhancements for users by third-party providers. Where the second generation of wearables, such as the Apple Watch, has an open ecosystem for applications and services of new and traditional third-party providers, which makes it possible to create additional value beyond the pure tracking and analysis of data for the user and revenue for themselves (e.g. personalized sport and fitness support and digital health-care support) (Buchwald 2018).

Wearable defined as 'smart wristband,' 'smart bracelets,' or 'fitness tracker' are devices that track a user's physical functions and provide relatively very limited information on small interfaces. The primary goal of these devices is collection of data that a user can analyse on another device such as a pc or smartphone (Ismagilova et al. 2019). The presentation of information is relatively very limited and often do not have the possibility to install apps (e.g. Fitbit Surge). On the other side, smartwatches are larger than these more 'simple' models and often have a touchscreen. These smartwatches allow users to install different kind of apps. Smartwatches, in contrast to the more 'simple models', provide the most benefits in case they are connected to internet. Also smartwatches present other relevant information (e.g. email notifications) (Chuah et al. 2016).

3 Research Method

Myers and Newman (2007) mention that "the qualitative interview is the most common and one of the most important data gathering tools in qualitative research" (p. 3). The type of qualitative interview was a semi-structured interview, which is able to collect meaningful experiences related to the theme of the research. It is also the most used type in qualitative research in information systems (IS). In a semi-structured interview there is an incomplete script, but usually some pre-formed structure that the interviewer follows (Myers and Newman 2007). This was also the case in this research.

97 semi-structured interviews with wearable users/owners are used. These interviews are based on the USE IT method (Landeweerd et al. 2013). It is designed to determine the success of ICT innovations, and is helpful to determine the adoption process of consumers. It is based on multiple adoption and diffusion models. There has been a drilldown process to make the group more homogenous. Eventually 20 interviews are analysed, where some characteristics pop up such as the majority being high educated, experience with technology and ICT and voluntarily adopted.

The qualitative data is analysed with a sentiment analysis with the help of the coding process based on the method proposed by Miles and Huberman (1994). The analysis is divided into three different procedures: data reduction, data display and conclusion drawing/verification. This method was the base for the sentiment analysis. Coding was chosen for the data reduction due its ability for viewing the answers given by respondents and their opinions on various aspects. The responses from the respondents of the interview were assigned one of five labels, ranging from very positive (++) to very negative (− −). The data has been statistically processed in Microsoft Excel to generate an insight into the responses, and on the same time making graphical presentation possible.

For the structured literature study Wolfswinkel et al. (2015) was used and the main papers and key terms used can be found in Table 1. The content is shown in the section adoption of wearables.

Table 1. Results structured literature review

Wearables AND adoption	Rauschnabel, Brem and Ivens (2015) Chuah, Rauschnabel, Krey, Nguyen, Ramayah and Lade (2016) Spil, Sunyaev, Thiebes and Van Baalen (2017)
Continued use AND wearables	Canhoto and Arp (2017) Buchwald, Letner, Urbach and von Entress-Fuersteneck (2015) Nascimento, Oliveira and Tam (2018)
Sustained use AND health and fitness wearables	Kalantari (2017) Coorevits and Coenen (2016) Lupton (2018)
Health information AND privacy	Smith, Dinev and Xu (2011) Motti and Caine (2015) Lee, Lee, Egelman and Wagner (2016)

4 Adoption of Wearables, Privacy and Habit

First we present adoption literature to create a foundation for the interview model based on classic adoption literature followed by specific wearable adoption issues from literature and new notions on adoption.

Four determinants that describe the success of ICT innovations are derived from the domain and innovation dimensions where a distinction is present between the macro and micro level (Landeweerd et al. 2013). The micro level is related to the here-and-now situation of individual users whereas the macro level is about the group and/or longer period. The resources determinant differentiates, instead of the macro and micro level, between the material and immaterial level. It is not only clear whether ICT innovation is accepted, but also what aspects of the ICT innovation contributes to this and what aspects does not.

Relevance (relevance) is defined as the extent to which the user thinks that the innovation will solve his problems and achieve its goals. Relevance at the micro level has much in common with "expected or experienced utility" (perceived usefulness) in the Technology Acceptance Model (Davis 1989; Venkatesh and Bala 2008) and "comparative advantage" (relative advantage) of the diffusion of innovations (Kapoor et al. 2014a, b; Rogers 1995). The perceived performance is influenced by these expectations and impacts the post-usage disconfirmation of beliefs. To put relevance in the context of this report, it is refined to the degree a person believes using a wrist-worn wearable would enhance her or his personal living condition, contributing to one's health, fitness and/or well-being.

Requirements is defined as the degree to which the quality of the product fulfils the requirements of the user (Dwivedi et al. 2017). Regarding ICT innovations this mainly involves information needs and quality. The requirements determinant is related to information quality and system quality in the Information Systems Success Model (Delone and McLean, 2003; Dwivedi et al. 2011) and usability (ease of use) from the Technology Acceptance Model (Davis 1989; Venkatesh and Bala 2008). More context related research mention unreliability and/or inaccurate or inconsistent data affects discontinuance intention/sustained use/continuance intention or stopped using it (Buchwald et al. 2018; Canhoto and Arp 2017; Coorevits and Coenen 2016; Epstein et al. 2016; Kari et al. 2016; Maher et al. 2017; Nascimento et al. 2018). Shih et al. (2015) reframe data inaccuracy as a by-product of mismanagement of expectations of the device's capabilities and its expected usage.

Resources (resources) is defined as the degree to which immaterial and material resources are accessible for the design, operation and maintenance of the system. The slope for an individual to accept innovation relatively earlier than others, is positively related to perceived ease of use. Highly innovative individuals are (mostly) active information seekers, which help them to better coop with uncertainty of innovations and hence a higher adoption intention (Kapoor et al. 2017a, b; Rogers 1995). For example for certain wearables (health and wellness wearables), adopted mainly by older groups, perceived ease of use is more impactful. This due to the lower levels of technology experience and innovativeness of these older individuals. Jang Yul (2014) found, on adopting mobile fitness applications, personal innovativeness in IT as significant effect on PU and PEOU.

Finally resistance questions are asked related to the attitude (Dwivedi et al. 2017a, b; Rana et al. 2016; 2017) of the interviewees toward IT in general and wearables specifically. The technology acceptance model (TAM), diffusion of innovations (DOI) and unified theory of acceptance and use of technology (UTAUT) for IS do not incorporate privacy issues. The literature review of Kalantari (2017) reported, in the context of wearables, different authors extended the UTAUT2 model (Tamilmani et al. 2018) with for example the earlier mentioned privacy calculus theory and one author using the protection motivation theory. Whereas Kenny and Connolly (2016), in the case of health information privacy concerns, also uses the protection motivation theory to back up that individuals do appraise threats by considering media coverage, and risks associated with disclosure either to health professionals or health technology vendors. Trust can partially negate these threats (Fig. 1).

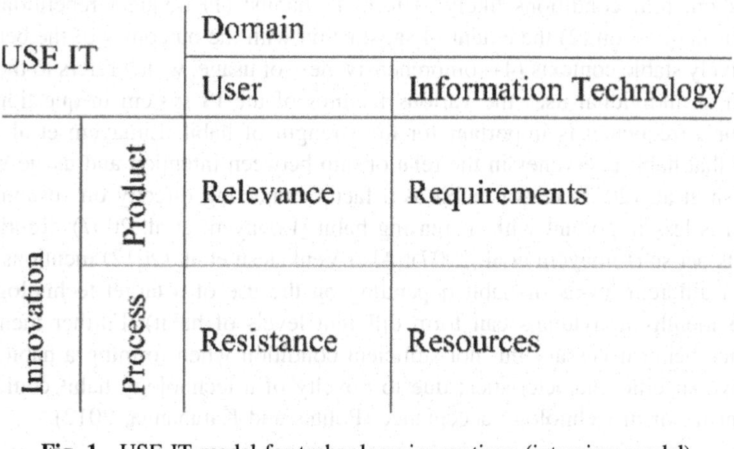

Fig. 1. USE IT model for technology innovations (interview model)

Coorevits and Coenen (2016) try to identify the key determinants from a consumer perspective leading to dissatisfaction and eventually wearable attrition. They mention that it can be assumed that considering the limited focus on user needs in wearable research development, the consumer beliefs got disconfirmed leading to avoidance. Nascimento et al. (2018) in the context of smartwatches uses confirmation and satisfaction as constructs in order to explain continuance intention, saying: "The findings of this study reveal that satisfaction is an important factor affecting a user's intention to continue using a smartwatch, especially for those users with a low level of habit. The authors also mention that selling a smartwatch that delivers on its promise or under-promises and over-delivers, will yield in a higher confirmation level, and so satisfaction (Limayem et al. 2007; Oliver 1980). Canhoto and Arp (2017), in a research of adoption and sustained use in the context of health and fitness wearables, mention consumers may have specific dietary needs that are not sufficiently captured by the wearable's dashboard. They mention it might be possible that consumers "have inflated expectations about the ability of wearables to change nutritional habits.

Buchwald et al. (2018), in the context of self-tracking devices in understanding continuance and discontinuance, does speak about satisfaction as well dissatisfaction. The authors mention, regarding to the hygiene theory of Herzberg, hygiene factors can cause dissatisfaction, but not necessarily satisfaction. For example, the presence of system unreliability fosters a discontinuance intention, whereas its absence does not contribute to the formation of a continuance intention. Kalantari (2017) mention in a literature review of wearables that "experience with technology is a key parameter in consumers' adoption" (p. 301). Kari et al. (2016) found in the context of self-tracking technology in critical experiences that either promote or hinder the adoption or lead to rejection during the implementation that previous experience on self-tracking technologies influenced the performance expectancy toward new technologies. On the other, more tailored to post-adoption and sustained use, hand experience with the target technology itself is of influence on habit and use behaviour. Where habit on its turn influence behavioural intention and use behaviour (Venkatesh et al. 2012).

Limayem et al. (2007) refers habit as "the extent to which people tend to perform behaviors (use IS) automatically because of learning" (p. 705). Limayem et al. (2007) speaks about four conditions likely to form IS habits: (1) frequent repetition of the behaviour in question (2) the extent of satisfaction with the outcomes of the behaviour (3) relatively stable contexts (4) comprehensiveness of usage, which refers to the extent to which an individual uses the various features of the IS system in question. Prior behaviour's frequency is important for the strength of habit. Limayem et al. (2007) reported that habit intervenes in the relationship between intention and usage whereas Venkatesh et al. (2012) reason habit as a factor impacting directly on sustained use. Intention is less important with increasing habit (Limayem et al. 2007). Routines are not habits per se (Limayem et al. 2007). Also Venkatesh et al. (2012) mentions people can form different levels of habit depending on the use of a target technology (e.g. within 3 months individuals can form different levels of habit). Further mentioning experience being necessary but not sufficient condition when forming a habit. Wearables have specific characteristics; due to novelty of a technology habit could be an important factor in technology acceptance (Polites and Karahanna, 2012).

Wearables and mobile phones make it possible to collect physiological data for health and wellness purposes. Users often access these data via Online Fitness Community (OFC) platforms, such as Fitbit, Strava or RunKeeper. To reap the benefits from these functionalities, users need to it habitual integrating OFC use into their everyday workout routines. However, this often fails for a longer period of time. Stragier et al. (2016) surveyed 394 (OFC) users and reported that enjoyment and self-regulatory motives indirectly predict habitual OFC use, by driving the perceived usefulness of OFCs. Prime drivers of habitual OFC use for novice users are self-regulatory motives where social motives and enjoyment are more important for experienced users.

Nascimento (2018) finds that habit was the most important feature to explain the continuance intention. Coorevits and Coenen (2016) finds, with the help of netnography, wearable fitness trackers being easy to forget one of the factors leading to attrition. One of the factors that affect the design considerations of wearables with regards to comfort is their intervention with daily behaviour and activities Coorevits and Coenen (2016) puts this under the denominator lifestyle compatibility: the change that the device requires in order to simply wear it. Users mention forgetting about the wearable when taking it off for charging or hindering during workouts. This is caused by example the unobtrusiveness and not being engaged enough to remember. Buchwald et al. (2018) reports in a study of self-tracking wearables perceived routine constraints being positively related to discontinuance intention, e.g. by wearing specific clothes. Buchwald et al. (2018) also mentions, within another constructs, individuals can also form attachments to routines or systems by affection, strengthening the individual's status quo bias. This results from the individual being comfortable and happy with the system or even when pleasure is taken in its usage, leading to a positive emotional bond. In the case of self-tracking devices, the affective-based inertia is formed during extensive every-day usage. This can have a positive effect on the continuance intention.

Kari et al. (2016) in a research the critical experiences that either promote or hinder the adoption or lead to rejection during the implementation phase in the context of self-tracking technologies, with thematic analysis of ten semi-structured interviews, mention "Effort expectancy, facilitating conditions, and habit were all based on same expectations: easy to use, easy to learn, effortless, simple, and clear functions. These were seen as essential, so that the use is easy enough (effort expectancy) and the functions support the use (facilitating conditions), and should these expectations realize, they advance the formation of habit".

Shih et al. (2015) in the context of Fitbit activity trackers mention that the wearables are tailored to remind people of the activities, but not remembering to keep the activity tracker with them. It was reported consumers having problems to keep the activity trackers with them or needing to remove it due to engaging in certain activities such as not suitable for work environment, showering, washing dishes. Also there seems to be a trade-off of the size of the wearable. A small and easy to carry with you is in a greater extent more fragile, easy to forget and less noticeable whereas a bigger wearable is being viewed as uncomfortable and bulky to wear. On the contract the respondents barely forget to take their keys, mobile phones or wallets. Shih et al. (2015) view this as the respondents might having more experiences and longer period of adoption to incorporate these other aspects into their daily (activity) routines.

Lupton et al. (2018) mention in the case of self-trackers in the context of cycling people find the devices into the everyday routines is a form of work. The people have to prepare the wearable such as charging or making sure the GPS is working properly, turning them on and remembering to bring them with them. Where some of the practice become habituated (needing little thought or attention), others on the contrary need continual vigilance.

Fritz et al. (2014) found in the context of long-term fitness tracking wearable users in three different continents that most of them integrated it deeply in their routines. The information provided by the wearables was motivating and led to long-term behaviour changes (e.g. sitting less or more walking) which led these respondents to feel frustrated and disappointed when it not being monitored/measured. They become so use to it they felt strange when they took the wearables off. But, the majority of these people however lost interest when the novelty phase moved into routine. There was a learning curve which made the respondents being to estimate their steps or calories for the day themselves and made the wearables obsolete.

5 Results

This section describes the objective data as given by the interviewees, in the next section we give a sentimental analysis and compare to literature.

5.1 Goals

The goals of using a wearable in advance are retrieved out of multiple questions. The goals for using the wearable in the first place are shown below, the upper three results are separated out of the comments in order to give a clear view of the balance between

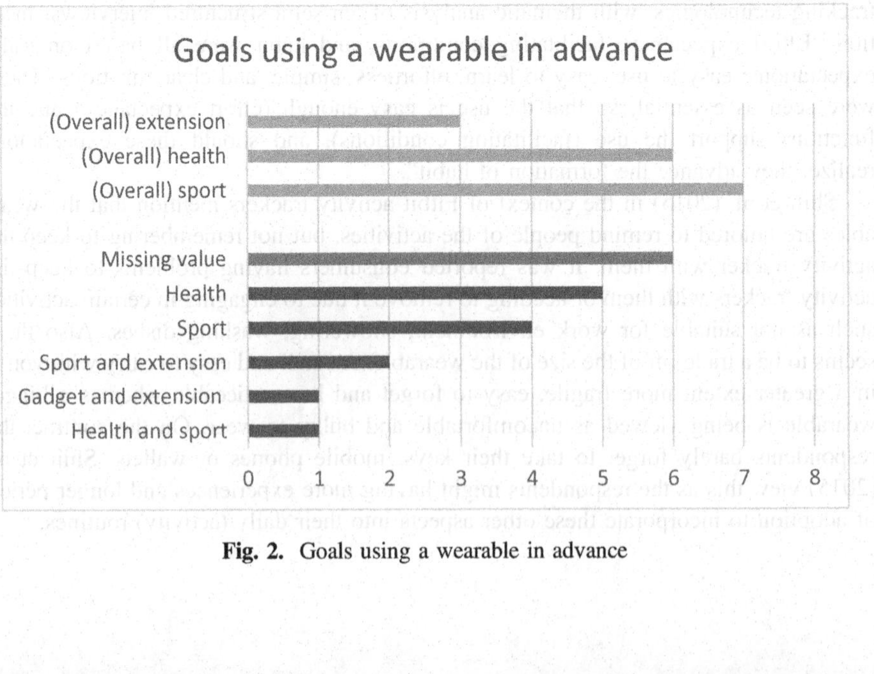

Fig. 2. Goals using a wearable in advance

the different overall goals. The half below are the original goals mentioned. As the chart shows, there is only a slight difference in the goals of using the wearable in advance: sport is at top, closely followed by health. There are no specific goals mentioned, such as losing weight, training for a marathon or quit smoking (Fig. 2).

5.2 Type of Wearable

Half of the interviewees got a smartwatch of which the brand 'Apple' the most mentioned. Twenty five percent got some sort of bracelet. Other wearables that are mentioned are pedometers, sportwatch, pebble and fitbit.

5.3 The Use of Wearables

The use of the wearables are displayed in the graph below. What stands out, is the use of the step counter and heartrate function. Where the heartrate function being used by four out seven respondents for sport/movement. Whereas running being the most mentioned sport. Sleep analysis being mentioned by three respondents, of which two mentioning the amount of sleep and one the sleep rhythm (Fig. 3).

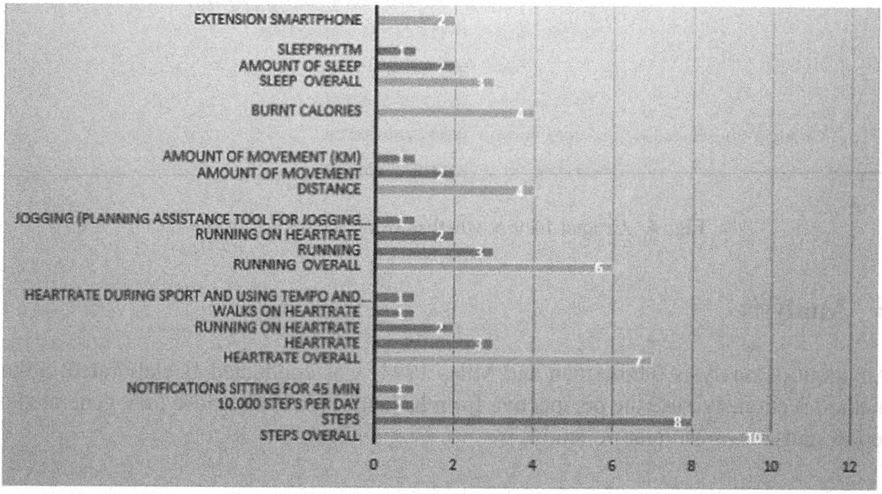

Fig. 3. The use of the wearable

5.4 Which Functions Beyond Current Possibilities

Twenty five percent of the interviewees mention they want to have an extension of their smartphone embedded in their wearable. Two respondents mention they want to have a stand-alone device by mentioning having own internet (2) and own GPS. Furthermore, respectively with a value of two (blood pressure) and one: body temperature, BMI, weight, scanning food instead of filling it in, health app giving advice about certain disease/disorder, being able to monitoring health in order to adjust and amount of alcohol in the blood are mentioned as extra options for the wearable. A Fitbit user also mentioned wanting to have more movement functions. Basically what the respondent are saying is the need for a more comprehensive and standalone device.

5.5 Crucial Factors for Whether or not to Use a Wearable

When asked what the crucial factors are to use a wearable twenty five percent of the interviewees answer the additional value and ease of use (or user friendly). Twenty percent of the interviewees mentions personal interest and reliable data. Fifteen percent mentions battery lifespan and ten percent mention health, communication, behaviour change and stand-alone device (Fig. 4).

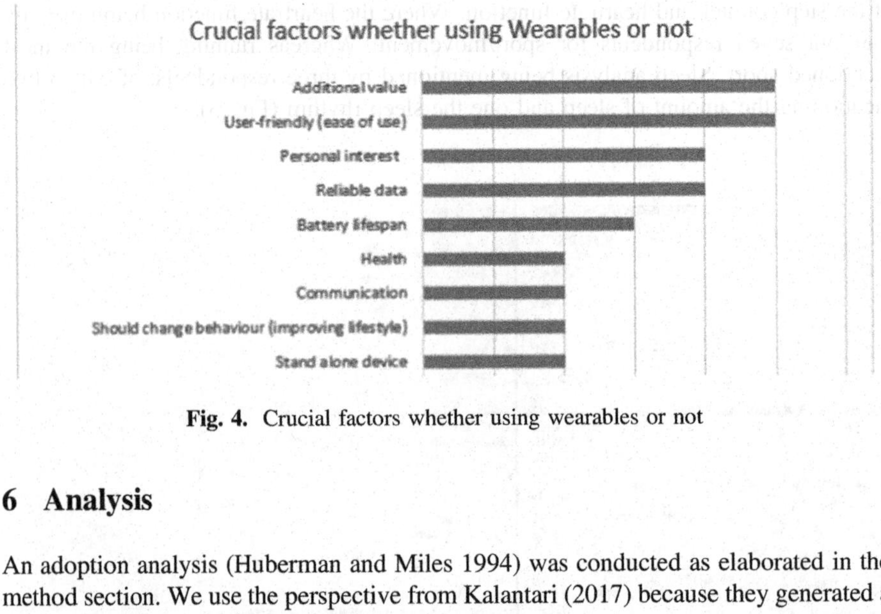

Fig. 4. Crucial factors whether using wearables or not

6 Analysis

An adoption analysis (Huberman and Miles 1994) was conducted as elaborated in the method section. We use the perspective from Kalantari (2017) because they generated a recent and relevant literature study.

6.1 Context

There is only a slight difference in the goals of using the wearable in advance, sport is at top, closely followed by health. This resembles earlier research where younger people, the appeal is to focus on fitness optimization, while older people are looking for improvement of their overall health and life extension (Canhoto and Arp 2017; Endavour 2014; Ledger 2014). As mentioned, due to the set-up of the interviews, people with wearables only for smartphone extension are left out, as such these outcomes have to be analysed. The smartwatch being the most used type of wrist-worn wearables resembles the market research report of Vliet (2017) regarding this group of age. Furthermore, Fitbit and Apple being the most mentioned brands, for respectively bracelets and smartwatches, resembles the overall market tendency in the Netherlands (Vliet 2017) and worldwide (IDC 2017). There is a difference in design between wearables, where smartwatches are more towards being designed for fashion as well as information.

6.2 Relevance

The sentiment around different relevance questions is divided. The thematic analysis also shows certain subthemes where respondents are not satisfied with certain aspects. Overall this results in a lack of relevance to a certain extent. Most respondents are being positive regarding the increase of insight and monitoring, but are divided regarding the increase of personal health with the help of their wearables. Also providing enough information for insight in personal health is being valued as well positive as negative with an overall negative sentiment mainly due to respondents people mentioning the lack of different health conditions. Especially blood pressure and diet, apart from the ones being mentioned once such as liver, body temperature and mental functions. Also wearables are not viewed as something that can give information about every aspect of health. The most mentioned comment is about some aspects that cannot be measured such as mental functions and the liver. Although the mentioned goals in advance for using a wearable are slightly more sport than health related. Positives are able to adjust their lifestyle and/or workout which in turn increases their health. Relevance/additional value is relatively a big theme of which mentioned by half of the respondents in different types of forms at multiple questions, of which multiple respondents mention it in a certain form at multiple questions which seems to amplify the importance of this theme. The continued adoption of technology is of influence by the possibility of improving oneself with the help of technology. Relevance is as well a pre- (Pfeiffer et al. 2016) as a post-adoption factor (Buchwald et al. 2018; Canhoto and Arp, 2017; Kari et al. 2016; Nascimento et al. 2018).

6.3 Reliability

The sentiment around reliability issues is tailored to the negative side and also the thematic analysis prove reliability to be an issue. Reliability is relatively a big theme of which mentioned by almost half of the respondents in different types of forms at multiple questions, of which multiple respondents mention it in a certain form at multiple questions which seems to amplify the importance of this theme. Reliability could potentially be a negative factor, due to reliability and errors are an important part of wearable due its relationship with usefulness. A lack of reliability or the presence of errors could be an important factor for discontinued use and respondents overall being negative about the errors, is in line with comparable research (e.g. Buchwald, 2018; Canhoto and Arp 2017; Epstein et al. 2016; Maher et al. 2017; Nascimento et al. 2018). Where as well software as hardware errors are mentioned as problems. Regarding consistency, people are less negative, but still divided and neutral overall. It case it was not constant, one respondent mentions he was able to clarify himself. This is in line with Lupton et al. (2018) and Fors and Pink (2017) mentioning people are continually determining the accuracy of the data, whether the metrics are influenced by other conditions, making a synergy on their own between the data from the wearable and the other conditions. A quote to illustrate this reliability subject: "No, I think that a wearable cannot give information about the full status of human health in the short term, there are already some points behind in the progress. Wearables should be in the near future focus on completing certain aspects before thinking ahead to the full health mapping". This same respondent at multiple questions speaks about data accuracy. He believes that the sensors and software are not accurate enough, especially for increasing health. Also the lack of data accuracy is mentioned as potential disabler at the 'crucial factors for wearables' question.

A small theme is about people willing to provide information, regarding health data, only when the information is reliable/correct. This could be due to that users are afraid that approximate values of the generated data could lead to incorrect allocations within tariff systems or could be used for inaccurate medical diagnoses or treatments. To put some information in context, six respondents speak about errors and systems being hacked is something common for devices and systems. Comments such as "all measuring systems are flawed" and "every system can be hacked" are present.

6.4 Ease-of-Use

The sentiment of the ease-of-use is divided between the questions and between respondents, but overall more tailored to the neutral to positive side. A side note is that the positive sentiment is more tailored to the general ease-of-use, interface and comfort factors, where there are more factors regarding ease-of-use. With the help of the thematic analysis more subthemes popped up such as the lack of a stand-alone device, compatibility, screen size and the difference between brands and type of wearables. So there is a lack of ease-of-use, but only to a certain extent and regarding certain factors.

Ease-of-use is mostly seen as a pre-adoption factor, where only one study on smartwatches found it to be a factor, by impacting satisfaction, for sustained use. The comfort is mentioned as positive aspect which is in line with e.g. Coorevits and Coenen (2016) who found, in a study with the help of netnography on wearable fitness trackers, comfort one of the factors impacting the ease of use perceptions.

The respondents of this research do have easy access to the information, with the smartphone mentioned as reinforcing aspect by retrieving and storing the information. Also easy access to information is an important pre-adoption factor in a similar research of Canhoto and Arp (2017) in the context of health and fitness wearables. Regards the ease-of-use questions, a watch is pointed out as being a positive thing. The results are somewhat skewed to the positive side due to the respondents already having experience with technology and ICT and millennials in general already being familiar with communications, media and digital technologies. Also early adopters and innovators often possess more technology innovativeness. This will help them better coop with uncertainty of new technologies and hence a higher adoption intention (Rogers 1995). Furthermore according to IS literature users gain experience with a system and resolve their PEOU concerns.

6.5 Privacy

In the race to be first to the market, security on wearables is not as seriously taken in the development by the firms as it should be, the people who wear them, or by the firms who adopt them into their existing work processes and legacy systems. Typically the legal regulatory environments lag behind several years to adapt to technological advancements. The Netherlands as specific geographical location is of interest due to differences in privacy concerns between countries. Canhoto and Arp (2016), in the context of health and fitness wearables, found different privacy concerns in Germany than a study conducted in China. Therefore, research should consider consumers in diverse geographical contexts.

Pfeiffer et al. (2016) found in the context of self-tracking devices trust to be a pre-adoption factor. Whereas Buchwald et al. (2018) found in the context of self-tracking devices trust also being a post-adoption factor, being negatively related to the discontinuance intention. Also Epstein et al. (2016) found people to stop tracking location due to concerns for data sharing, hence a post-adoption factor.

6.6 Habit

Due to novelty of a technology, habit could be an important factor in technology acceptance (Polites and Karahanna 2012; Tamilmani et al. 2018). Also do wearables have specific characteristics. Three respondents speak about not wearing the wearable the entire day, only during sport and needing enough discipline to see it as a daily routine. This is mentioned at questions such as enough information for insight personal health, increase of personal health and ease-of-use. What stands out these respondents all have more simple device such as a sport watch, Fitbit and a Pedometer. A respondent is for example saying getting more insight in personal health when she would wearing the wearable day and night. Of the three respondents mentioned earlier, one said at a different question it is easy to wear, so this is probably not the disabler. When be looked at comfort part, at questions such as ease of use for example, other respondents feel like it is easy to wear and it is easy to use (to some extent). Where a few respondents mention being a watch at the same time is an enabler. So it not exactly clear why there is a lack of forming a habit with the help of the interviews, but assumptions can be made with the help of literature and the difference between the type of wearables. Successful use of the wearable on the long-term is determined by long term integration in the daily routines, but is often hard for most consumers (Fritz et al. 2014; Stragier et al. 2016). Venkatesh et al. (2012) reason habit as a factor impacting directly on sustained use. More context related Nascimento et al. (2018) mention habit as factor for continuance intention, where Coorevits and Coenen (2016) speak about attrition. So this could be a possible disabler for continued use. Moreover, due the value of wearables is based on data, it is important for wearables to be carried with you all the time.

7 Conclusions

Wearables diffusion is hindered by lack of relevance or relative advantage to the users. Different options such as blood pressure and body temperature measurements could be added in the future to have more relevance, although this could have a negative influence on privacy mentioned later on.

For wearables to be truly effective, they need to provide information that is not just descriptive but also prescriptive.

A lack of reliability or the presence of errors could be an important factor in discontinued use. Regarding reliability, while organizations often have IT-service departments and service contracts with their vendors to solve reliability issues, within the personal ICT context it is nowadays expected that a consumer technology is working reliably and accurate since users do often not have the knowledge, time, or will for troubleshooting.

Overall people are neutral to positive (sentiment) to sharing information for diagnosis and statistical research and sharing body data, habits/addictions and living environment with the wearable. The extent depends on several factors. Also people think wearables can be hacked, but regarding privacy being at stake people are divided.

The exact reasons some people do not form the habit of using the wearable is not clear when looking at the outcomes of the interviews, but it is important. What stands out is the users of more simple models do not develop a habit of using it all day and every day.

References

Barcena, M.B., Wueest, C., Lau, H.: How safe is your quantified self. Symantech, Mountain View, CA, USA (2014)

Benbunan-Fich, R.: An affordance lens for wearable information systems. Eur. J. Inf. Syst. 1–16 (2018)

Buchwald, A., Urbach, N., von Entreß-Fürsteneck, M.: Insights into personal ICT use: understanding continuance and discontinuance of wearable self-tracking devices (2018)

Canhoto, A.I., Arp, S.: Exploring the factors that support adoption and sustained use of health and fitness wearables. J. Mark. Manag. **33**(1–2), 32–60 (2017). https://doi.org/10.1080/0267257X.2016.1234505

Chuah, S.H.W., Rauschnabel, P.A., Krey, N., Nguyen, B., Ramayah, T., Lade, S.: Wearable technologies: the role of usefulness and visibility in smartwatch adoption. Comput. Hum. Behav. **65**, 276–284 (2016)

Coorevits, L., Coenen, T.: The rise and fall of wearable fitness trackers. In: Academy of Management (2016)

Davis, F.D., Bagozzi, R.P., Warshaw, P.R.: User acceptance of computer technology: a comparison of two theoretical models. Manag. Sci. **35**(8), 982–1003 (1989)

Delone, W.H., McLean, E.R.: The DeLone and McLean model of information systems success: a ten-year update. J. Manag. Inf. Syst. **19**(4), 9–30 (2003)

Dwivedi, Y.K., Wade, M.R., Schneberger, S.L. (eds.): Information Systems Theory: Explaining and Predicting Our Digital Society, vol. 1. Springer, Heidelberg (2011). https://doi.org/10.1007/978-1-4419-6108-2

Dwivedi, Y.K., et al.: Research on information systems failures and successes: status update and future directions. Inf. Syst. Front. **17**(1), 143–157 (2015)

Dwivedi, Y.K., Rana, N.P., Janssen, M., Lal, B., Williams, M.D., Clement, M.: An empirical validation of a unified model of electronic government adoption (UMEGA). Govern. Inf. Q. **34**(2), 211–230 (2017a)

Dwivedi, Y.K., Rana, N.P., Jeyaraj, A., Clement, M., Williams, M.D.: Re-examining the unified theory of acceptance and use of technology (UTAUT): towards a revised theoretical model. Inf. Syst. Front. 1–16 (2017b). https://doi.org/10.1007/s10796-017-9774-y

Endeavour Partners: Inside wearables - part 2, July 2014. https://digitalwellbeing.org/wp-content/uploads/2015/11/2014-Inside-Wearables-Part-2-July-2014.pdf. Accessed 5 July 2018

Epstein, D.A., Caraway, M., Johnston, C., Ping, A., Fogarty, J., Munson, S.A.: Beyond abandonment to next steps: understanding and designing for life after personal informatics tool use. In: Proceedings of the 2016 CHI Conference on Human Factors in Computing Systems, pp. 1109–1113. ACM, May 2016

Fors, V., Pink, S.: Pedagogy as possibility: health interventions as digital openness (2017). http://www.mdpi.com/2076-0760/6/2/59/htm. Accessed 25 June 2018

Fritz, T., Huang, E.M., Murphy, G.C., Zimmermann, T.: Persuasive technology in the real world: a study of long-term use of activity sensing devices for fitness. In: Proceedings of the SIGCHI Conference on Human Factors in Computing Systems, pp. 487–496. ACM, April 2014

Huberman, A.M., Miles, M.B.: Data management and analysis methods (1994)

Hutchison, E.D.: Essentials of Human Behavior: Integrating Person, Environment, and the Life Course. Sage Publications, London (2016)

Ismagilova, E., Hughes, L., Dwivedi, Y.K., Raman, K.R.: Smart cities: advances in research—an information systems perspective. Int. J. Inf. Manag. **47**, 88–100 (2019)

Kalantari, M.: Consumers' adoption of wearable technologies: literature review, synthesis, and future research agenda. Int. J. Technol. Mark. **12**(3), 274–307 (2017)

Kapoor, K.K., Dwivedi, Y.K., Williams, M.D.: Rogers' innovation adoption attributes: a systematic review and synthesis of existing research. Inf. Syst. Manag. **31**(1), 74–91 (2014a)

Kapoor, K.K., Dwivedi, Y.K., Williams, M.D.: Innovation adoption attributes: a review and synthesis of research findings. Eur. J. Innov. Manag. **17**(3), 327–348 (2014b)

Kari, T., Koivunen, S., Frank, L., Makkonen, M., Moilanen, P.: Critical experiences during the implementation of a self-tracking technology. In: PACIS 2016: Proceedings of the 20th Pacific Asia Conference on Information Systems, ISBN 9789860491029. Association for Information Systems (2016)

Kenny, G., Connolly, R.: Drivers of health information privacy concern: a comparison study (2016)

Kovach, S.: Wearables are dead, 11 December 2016. https://www.businessinsider.nl/wearables-are-dead-2016-12/?international=true&r=US. Accessed 4 Feb 2018

Landeweerd, M., Spil, T., Klein, R.: The success of Google search, the failure of Google health and the future of Google plus. In: Dwivedi, Y.K., Henriksen, H.Z., Wastell, D., De', R. (eds.) TDIT 2013. IAICT, vol. 402, pp. 221–239. Springer, Heidelberg (2013). https://doi.org/10.1007/978-3-642-38862-0_14

Ledger, D.: Inside wearables - Part 2, July 2014. https://digitalwellbeing.org/wp-content/uploads/2015/11/2014-Inside-Wearables-Part-2-July-2014.pdf. Accessed 4 Feb 2018

Lee, L., Lee, J., Egelman, S., Wagner, D.: Information disclosure concerns in the age of wearable computing. In: NDSS Workshop on Usable Security (USEC), vol. 1 (2016)

Limayem, M., Hirt, S.G., Cheung, C.M.: How habit limits the predictive power of intention: the case of information systems continuance. MIS Q. **31**, 705–737 (2007)

Lupton, D., Pink, S., Heyes LaBond, C., Sumartojo, S.: Personal data contexts, data sense, and self-tracking cycling. Int. J. Commun. **12**, 647–666 (2018)

Maher, C., Ryan, J., Ambrosi, C., Edney, S.: Users' experiences of wearable activity trackers: a cross-sectional study. BMC Public Health **17**(1), 880 (2017)
Motti, V.G., Caine, K.: Users' privacy concerns about wearables. In: Brenner, M., Christin, N., Johnson, B., Rohloff, K. (eds.) FC 2015. LNCS, vol. 8976, pp. 231–244. Springer, Heidelberg (2015). https://doi.org/10.1007/978-3-662-48051-9_17
Myers, M.D., Newman, M.: The qualitative interview in IS research: examining the craft. Inf. Organ. **17**(1), 2–26 (2007)
Nascimento, B., Oliveira, T., Tam, C.: Wearable technology: what explains continuance intention in smartwatches? J. Retail. Consum. Serv. **43**, 157–169 (2018)
Prasopoulou, E.: A half-moon on my skin: a memoir on life with an activity tracker. Eur. J. Inf. Syst. **26**(3), 287–297 (2017)
Pfeiffer, J., von Entress-Fuersteneck, M., Urbach, N., Buchwald, A.: Quantify-me: consumer acceptance of wearable self-tracking devices. In: ECIS, p. ResearchPaper99, June 2016
Polites, G.L., Karahanna, E.: Shackled to the status quo: the inhibiting effects of incumbent system habit, switching costs, and inertia on new system acceptance. MIS Q. **36**, 21–42 (2012)
Porter, E., Heppelmann, E.: How smart, connected products are transforming competition, 17 March 2017. https://hbr.org/2014/11/how-smart-connected-products-are-transforming-competition. Accessed 5 Feb 2018
Rana, N.P., Dwivedi, Y.K., Lal, B., Williams, M.D., Clement, M.: Citizens' adoption of an electronic government system: towards a unified view. Inf. Syst. Front. **19**(3), 549–568 (2017)
Rana, N.P., Dwivedi, Y.K., Williams, M.D., Weerakkody, V.: Adoption of online public grievance redressal system in India: toward developing a unified view. Comput. Hum. Behav. **59**, 265–282 (2016)
Rauschnabel, P.A., Brem, A., Ivens, B.S.: Who will buy smart glasses? Empirical results of two pre-market-entry studies on the role of personality in individual awareness and intended adoption of Google glass wearables. Comput. Hum. Behav. **49**, 635–647 (2015)
Rogers, E.M.: Lessons for guidelines from the diffusion of innovations. Joint Comm. J. Qual. Patient Saf. **21**(7), 324–328 (1995)
Salah, H., MacIntosh, E., Rajakulendran, N.: Wearable tech: leveraging Canadian innovation to improve health. MaRS Discovery District, March 2014. https://www.marsdd.com/wp-content/uploads/2015/02/MaRSReport-WearableTech.pdf. Accessed 5 Feb 2018
Shih, P.C., Han, K., Poole, E.S., Rosson, M.B., Carroll, J.M.: Use and adoption challenges of wearable activity trackers. In: IConference 2015 Proceedings (2015)
Smith, H.J., Dinev, T., Xu, H.: Information privacy research: an interdisciplinary review. MIS Q. **35**(4), 989–1016 (2011)
Spil, T., Sunyaev, A., Thiebes, S., Van Baalen, R.: The adoption of wearables for a healthy lifestyle: can gamification help? (2017)
Stragier, J.: Physical activity in the digital age: an empirical investigation into the motivational affordances of online fitness communities. Doctoral dissertation, Ghent University (2017). https://doi.org/10.13140/rg.2.2.25036.21124/1
Tamilmani, K., Rana, N.P., Dwivedi, Y.K.: Use of 'Habit' is not a habit in understanding individual technology adoption: a review of UTAUT2 based empirical studies. In: Elbanna, A., Dwivedi, Y.K., Bunker, D., Wastell, D. (eds.) TDIT 2018. IAICT, vol. 533, pp. 277–294. Springer, Cham (2019). https://doi.org/10.1007/978-3-030-04315-5_19
Venkatesh, V., Bala, H.: Technology acceptance model 3 and a research agenda on interventions. Decis. Sci. **39**(2), 273–315 (2008)
Venkatesh, V., Thong, J.Y., Xu, X.: Consumer acceptance and use of information technology: extending the unified theory of acceptance and use of technology. MIS Q. **36**, 157–178 (2012)

Vliet, M.: Bezit wearables gestegen, maar nog verre van mainstream, 11 January 2017. https://www.telecompaper.com/achtergrond/bezit-wearables-gestegen-maar-nog-verre-van-mainstream–1179136. Accessed 17 Feb 2017

Wolfswinkel, J.F., Furtmueller, E., Wilderom, C.P.: Using grounded theory as a method for rigorously reviewing literature. Eur. J. Inf. Syst. **22**(1), 45–55 (2013)

Jang Yul, K.: Determinants of users intention to adopt mobile fitness applications: an extended technology acceptance model approach (2014)

Technical Support: Towards Mitigating Effects of Computer Anxiety on Acceptance of E-Assessment Amongst University Students in Sub Saharan African Countries

Kayode I. Adenuga[1(✉)], Victor W. Mbarika[2], and Zacchaeus O. Omogbadegun[1]

[1] School of ICT, ICT University (USA), Yaoundé Campus, Yaounde, Cameroon
kayodeadenuga@yahoo.ca
[2] Southern University and A&M College, Baton Rouge, LA 70806, USA

Abstract. The application of Information technology in educational context and environment has dramatically changed the pattern at which people teach and learn. Institutions of higher learning globally are increasingly adopting e-Assessment as a replacement for traditional pen on paper examination due to its cost effectiveness, improved reliability due to machine marking, accurate and timely assessment. In spite of the numerous benefits of e-assessment, it is unclear if University students in Sub Saharan African Countries are willing to accept it. The purpose of this study is to examine technical support role towards mitigating effects of computer anxiety on electronic assessment amongst University students in Nigeria and Cameroon. Therefore, the study extended Technology Acceptance Model and was validated using 102 responses collected randomly across universities in Nigeria and Cameroon. This study supports the body of knowledge by establishing that Computer Anxiety is an important factor which can affect University students regardless of their level of computer proficiency. The outcome of the proposed model indicated that when technical assistance is provided during e-Assessment, computer anxiety on majority of University students in Nigeria and Cameroon is reduced. The practical implication of this study is that students' actual academic potentials may not be seen if education policy makers and University administrators do not always strive to ensure that all measures, including technical support that can reduce fear associated with use of computer for assessment, are introduced.

Keywords: E-Learning · E-Assessment · Anxiety · Computer anxiety

1 Introduction

The application of Information technology in educational context and environment has dramatically changed the pattern at which people teach and learn. These effects have been extended to areas of assessment most especially towards reducing the cost and examination misconduct associated with traditional paper based assessment methods. Nevertheless learning is a continuous process which begins at an early age and one of

Published by Springer Nature Switzerland AG 2019
Y. Dwivedi et al. (Eds.): TDIT 2019, IFIP AICT 558, pp. 48–72, 2019.
https://doi.org/10.1007/978-3-030-20671-0_5

the major importance of learning is assessment [1]. It is a measure used to evaluate the rate at which individuals are progressing [2, 3]. E-assessment; also known as electronic testing or computer based test, has become an important tool for learning and teaching and it is a form of assessment which is conducted electronically [4]. Nevertheless the potential benefits of the classification of this assessment, it is unclear if prospective learners are willing to accept it. One of the factors mentioned to be affecting its exploit is anxiety related to the use of technology on the prospective learners; which in other words can be termed as computer anxiety. In the field of e-assessment acceptance, a number of studies have been done on computer anxiety [5–7], only few of such studies have mentioned the role of provision of technical support most especially if the examinees cannot find their way around using some of the inherent features of the technology efficiently during assessment. The purpose of this study therefore is to examine the role of technical support towards mitigating effects of computer anxiety on electronic assessment amongst University students in Nigeria and Cameroon.

1.1 Problem Background

In students' academic assessment, institutions of higher learning globally are increasingly adopting e-Assessment as a replacement for traditional pen on paper examination [8, 9]; and in comparison with paper based assessment, e- assessment has advantages of cost effectiveness, improved reliability due to machine marking, unbiased assessment, greater storage capability, quick submission and grade report retrieval, effective record keeping, accurate and timely assessment [10]. In addition to the benefits inherent in e-assessment, researchers are still finding ways to ensure that prospective learners utilize its potential benefits. One of the factors affecting its exploit is anxiety related to the use of technology on the prospective learners. Naturally, fear or anxiety is an emotional and psychological phenomenon which is correlated with any form of assessments. It is an intuition caused by identified fear or instability which changes the entire biochemical processes that occur within living organism and ultimately lead to a change in behavior such as sudden movement away from the point of danger. Fear in humans can manifest as a result of sharp response to a certain stimuli occurring presently or in anticipation of a life threatening future occurrence. According to the Diagnostic and Statistical Manual of Mental Disorders, 4th Edition (DSM IV) of the American Psychiatric Association and cited by Beckers, Wicherts [11] defined "*anxiety as a mood state in which a subject experiences fear, apprehension, nervousness, worry, tension*".

Naturally, anxiety's task is to warn ahead of an impending danger and consequently build an adequate coping mechanism against it. However, when this fear becomes extreme; there is an element of frustration which often makes this anxiety difficult to manage [11]. This apprehension can also be extended to traditional classroom assessment most especially when the learners are lacking adequate preparation towards the assessment and if such test were to be examined using electronic means, this level of anxiety increases particularly if the users have low computer self-efficacy. Notwithstanding, preliminary investigation has revealed that most test takers would prefer to have a handy technical assistance that can provide timely solutions to any technical issues that might come up during assessment. In view of this, it becomes important to conduct more studies on ways to reduce the level of anxiety on test takers so that their academic mastery and emotional intelligence are not measured by their inability to manipulate the technology driving the assessment. Nevertheless, a number of studies have been conducted to establish links between computer anxiety and related factors; using suitable theoretical model such as Technology Acceptance Model (TAM), extended TAM, Unified Theory of Acceptance and Use of Technology (UTAUT), Computer based assessment acceptance model (CBAAM); only few of this study have mentioned impact of technical support [12] on prospective test takers during assessment most especially when there are reported low level of computer self-efficacy on the prospective test takers. In addition, it is unclear whether presence of technical support variable actually has the potentials to reduce computer anxiety on prospective University students in Nigeria and Cameroon context; besides, the researchers seek to address the research question: *Does technical support has capability to reduce computer anxiety amongst University students in Nigeria and Cameroon?* Hence, it becomes necessary to investigate this and proffer a suitable theoretical model to address this gap.

2 Literature Review

2.1 Learning and Assessment

Lachman [13] stressed that, most textbook definitions defined learning as behavioural transformation brought about by change in experience. This definition is fundamental; as in the contemporary world, learning is perceived as an instrument that delineates experience into behavior. In other words, it is considered as an outcome of a circumstance or behavior [14]. Over 50 years ago, Ausubel, Novak [15] suggested that *"the most important factor influencing learning is what the learner already knows. Ascertain this and teach him accordingly"*. Assessment is an important element that measures how a learner is progressing and it can be employed to provide feedback (formative assessment) or applied for grading purposes (Summative assessment). Whatever the reason behind assessment, learning cannot be said to be complete without assessments. Naturally, fear is a phenomenon which is correlated with any form of assessments most especially when the learners are afraid of their performance due to the perceived threat of failure. There is an ongoing feeling of worry and apprehension, and this constant fear can hinder learners' attempts to understand the information that is required for academic success. According to an online article entitled *Strategies for Addressing Student Fear in the Classroom* written by Scott Bledsoe Psy.D. and Janice Baskin stressed that "*…Fear can cause students to experience adverse responses which can be physiologically (e.g., shortness of breath), cognitively (inability to focus or concentrate, obsessive thinking, replaying in their minds problematic incidents that occurred in previous classes), and emotionally (easily agitated, overcome by excessive nervousness, frustration), and other negative feelings…*". However, due to many obvious benefits inherent in the use of technology in assessing learners, there is an increase in the level of apprehension most especially when the learners cannot find their way around using the technology. The objective of this study therefore is to minimize the effects of computer anxiety using technical support on University students in Nigeria and Cameroon.

2.2 E-Learning and E-Assessment

In comparison with traditional classroom learning system, E-learning has obvious advantages including real time availability, elimination of barrier of distance to learning, and personalized learning pace. Often, e-learning and e-assessment are considered to be one and the same thing, but it is not so. E-Assessment can be simply defined as the use of ICT for the purpose of carrying out assessment for measuring a student's learning [16]. E-Assessment can be categorized according to different measuring guidelines. It can be classified as formative and summative in context of examination. Formative assessment helps to examine how learners are progressing towards their learning goals and it is also used to provide feedback to the students, e.g. in class quiz, assignment; whereas summative assessment is for grading purpose, e.g. end of session or semester exams [17]. This assessment classification can come in form of multiple choice questions, adaptive tests, and open-ended questions. In adaptive tests, the difficulty level of questions is adapted as per the response of the user. In case of wrong response, the difficulty level of the next questions is usually dropped. The most complex of these three types are essay type questions, as evaluating them using computers is still a major obstacle and an important area of research that has received little academic attention in the field of e-assessment [18–21].

E-Assessment can also be classified according to the type of technology used to conduct the examination. One of such technologies is Optical Mark Recognition (OMR) sheets which have become very popular over the last ten years. However, the use of dedicated scanners to read OMR sheets is an added financial and technical burden. The other popular types include E-Portfolios, standalone systems and network/web based systems. E-Portfolios provides assessment of the student as all the student's activities during the course lifetime are recorded in it. Standalone systems on the other hand usually apply some external devices to record the test output while networked systems' output are usually saved on a server [17, 19, 22]. Other advantages of e-assessment are quick appraisal of examinations, developing pragmatic questions by using audio-visual mediums, simulation etc. This type of examination can also be administered for children with special needs. Nevertheless, both e-learning and e-assessment or computer based test are not without their limitations. Researchers have stressed that high level of self-discipline and motivation are required greatly on the part of learners using e-learning mode of instruction while e-assessment shortfalls include high cost, security risks and technological hitch [17, 23].

2.3 E-Learning and E-Assessment Acceptance in Sub-Saharan African Countries

Universal interest in the use of information and communication technologies (ICT) is evident in Africa and tertiary education institutions are increasingly shifting focus towards distance education and the establishment of virtual communities [24]. E-learning in not new in Africa, a survey conducted by Unwin [25] on the status of e-learning in Africa from 46 countries, revealed that e-learning has been adopted by many countries in Africa, including Nigeria and Cameroon. Countries all around Africa are willing to tap the benefits of using technology to aid learning and assessment.

In Nigeria, for instance, not many institutions have fully adopted electronic examination as an assessment method due to many factors which may be related to issues with infrastructural challenges [26, 27]. However, some institutions have come to terms with e-assessment as an option due to its inherent benefits which are not available in traditional pen on paper type of assessment.

For instance, National Open University of Nigeria (NOUN) is an institution of higher learning operating on open and distance learning mode. As at 2010, NOUN had 90,767 registered students and conducting assessment for this number without a corresponding human and infrastructural resources posed a great challenge for the university; hence the need to adopt electronic examination as an alternative to pen-on-paper examination [28]. Although previous study conducted by [28] focused on reactions of academic staff to e-examination, there is little known if anxiety plays a significant role towards academic staff adoption of electronic examination as a form of assessment.

Similarly, there had been a growing concern about the conduct, authenticity and reliability of qualifying examinations into Nigerian tertiary institutions. It is in this regard that the Joint Admission and Matriculation Board (JAMB) introduced the computer-based testing (CBT) with the objective of eliminating all forms of examination malpractices and promote the use of electronic testing in Nigeria [29]. In their study, many challenges such as economic, social, technological factors were mentioned [30]; though there were sensitization campaign going on to ensure students were well informed on the modalities surrounding CBT exams, but a study on whether failure of some students to pass Unified Tertiary Matriculation Examination (UTME) can be attributed to fear of using computer for assessment is yet to be seen.

2.4 Related Studies on Computer Anxiety and E-Assessment

A number of studies have been conducted in the field of computer anxiety role on e-assessment adoption. Beckers, Wicherts [11] defined computer anxiety as one of the most common anxiety disorders, it is a feeling of fear and apprehension experienced by prospective learners when they have the thought of using computer for assessment [31]. In this study, computer anxiety was classified into temporary or state anxiety which is experienced as a result of the state of the learner most especially when technology is introduced in assessment [31–33] while the other is trait-like which may be difficult to treat since the source of this anxiety is profound. The purpose of their study was to confirm if computer anxiety is a permanent attribute of humans or an anxiety that is subject to the introduction of a particular situational stressor such as computer use. Their study examined relationship between computer anxiety, trait and state anxiety and to measure the effect of this anxiety when a stressor like computer technology is introduced to assessment. The findings of their study highlighted that computer anxiety is more strongly correlated to trait anxiety than state anxiety. They further suggested that computer anxiety is deep-rooted in trait anxiety and therefore remains a composite occurrence which requires multi-dimensional approach.

Jimoh, Yussuff [8] extended Perceived Usefulness (PU) and Perceived Ease of Use (PEOU) in TAM with additional variable; perceived fairness (PF) towards acceptability of CBT for undergraduate courses in computer science. The findings of their study highlighted that PEOU of CBT positively influences its PU and PEOU, PU and PF of CBT systems have statistical significant effect on Behavioral Intention of students to accept the CBT systems. The important finding here is that students will use the CBT when they have the feeling that the system is fair to them; since those students who did well have a feeling that CBT was fair to them while those who did not do well perceived it as being unfair. This outcome is similar to a study conducted by Daly and Waldron [34] who suggested that students who performed better during assessment preferred CBT more. Despite this productive outcome, there was no indication that those who performed poorly did so as a result of fear associated with computer usage or low level of computer self-efficacy; since they have the perception that CBT platform might not have been fair to them after all.

In a related study conducted by Babo, Azevedo [35], this study ascertains the students' perceptions about the use of Multiple Choice Question (MCQ) e-assessment using Moodle quizzes features. From the analysis, it was observed that students have positive perceptions about the MCQ test type. Although, technical issues such as servers' instability and lack of sufficient time for the test were reported. Despite the effect a new type of test has on levels of anxiety, higher levels of fear and nervousness were not observed compared to traditional tests. In other words, students agreed that there are no differences in the complexity level of the two tests classifications, therefore suggesting that when the reported technical challenges are resolved, computer anxiety may not really have an effect on the subjects under investigation.

Alruwais, Wills [3] developed a conceptual model where Decomposed Theory of Planned Behavior (DTPB) [36, 37] (which has all important constructs of TAM and TPB) was extended with IT support (Conceptual Model of Acceptance and Usage of E-assessment (MAUE)) towards finding impacts of E-assessment used by lecturers in Saudi universities. However, this extension did not explain the role of computer self-efficacy and IT support in minimizing the effect of e-assessment on prospective learners. Similarly, Farzin and Dahlan [12] proposed a model to explore students' perception of e-assessment. Their study extended UTAUT with two constructs which include Habit and Computer anxiety towards Behavioral Intention (BI) and Usage intention. Lack of technical support [38–40], a component of facilitating condition was also considered as a factor affecting e-assessment. However their proposed model did not provide an empirical evidence to highlight the effect of computer anxiety on prospective e-assessment users. Therefore, in view of the outcomes of the related studies, it becomes necessary to find ways to reduce the effect of computer anxiety on the examinee most especially if the inherent benefits of using this technology for assessment are necessary to be harnessed.

2.5 Theoretical Model of Adoption

Technology Acceptance Models (TAM) have been applied in many fields to understand factors that encourage prospective users to use a particular technology. For instance, TAM by Davis mentioned that users will rather use a technology if it is perceived to be beneficial and easy to use [41]. TAM shown in Fig. 1, represents an important theoretical contribution towards understanding Information Systems (IS) utilization and IS acceptance behaviors [42, 43, 96, 97] and the adoption and usage of new IS [44]. However in the context of e-assessment, a number of studies have applied TAM and extended versions of TAM to establish relationships between computer anxiety and related factors [8, 41, 45].

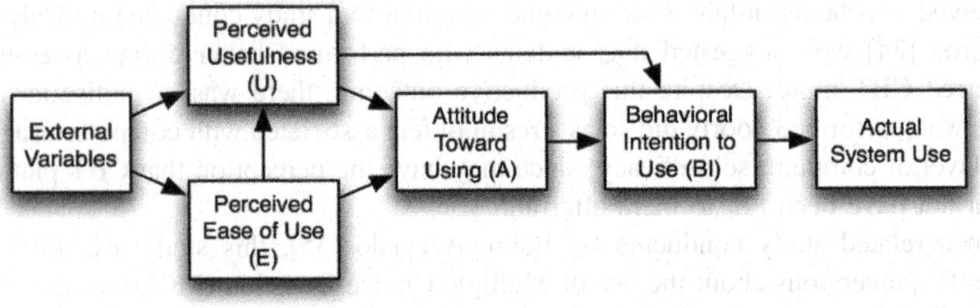

Fig. 1. The technology acceptance model [42]

In TAM, Perceived Ease of Use (PEOU) is defined as the extent to which a system or innovation is easy to use [41] and Perceived Usefulness, which is the extent to which a person believes that using a particular system will enhance his/her job performance, are important predictors of BI of technology use. PEOU predicts PU while PEOU and PU are predictors of Attitude (A) towards using a technology. In addition, Attitude predicts BI and BI consequently predicts actual use of a technology. TAM explains the relationship that existed among perceived ease of use, perceived usefulness, user attitudes, behavioral intention and actual system use constructs [46]. According to TAM, behavioral intention determines if prospective users make decision to use the system or not. In this study, TAM was considered for extension since it is regarded as one of the mostly applied technology adoption models in e-learning context that measures user's intention towards the use of technology in learning [6, 47, 48].

2.6 Conceptual Model Development and Research Hypotheses

Over the years, tremendous work has been published in the area of e-assessment most especially in the developed countries where e-assessment has recorded a huge success [17, 49–52]. Relatively little has been handled in the developing countries [8, 53] most especially in Nigeria and Cameroon context which forms the scope of this study. In addition, a number of studies have been conducted to establish links between computer anxiety and related factors, using suitable theoretical model such as TAM [41, 45], extended TAM [8], UTAUT [12, 54, 55, 94, 95], Social Cognitive Theory [93], Computer based assessment acceptance model [17] (CBAAM) only few of them have used TAM without extending it in the field of e-learning and e-assessment. This research therefore aims to investigate the role of technical support towards mitigating the effect of computer anxiety of prospective test takers. This study focuses on students in sub Saharan African countries where there are reported low level of computer self-efficacy. The effect of this technical support variable and other variables will be tested randomly across Universities in Nigeria and Cameroon.

However, the researchers of this study seek to maximize the strength of this model and adapt it within the context of e-assessment adoption towards reducing the effects of computer anxiety on prospective test takers most especially when the latter are perceived to have low computer self-efficacy. In this study, this extension did not include attitude and actual use variables of TAM since Venkatesh, Morris [45] mentioned that researchers are often faced with huge number of related constructs provided by many theories and discovered that they "pick and choose" variables from these models or simply go for a preferred model. In view of this, the researchers hypothesized based on the conceptual model in Fig. 2.

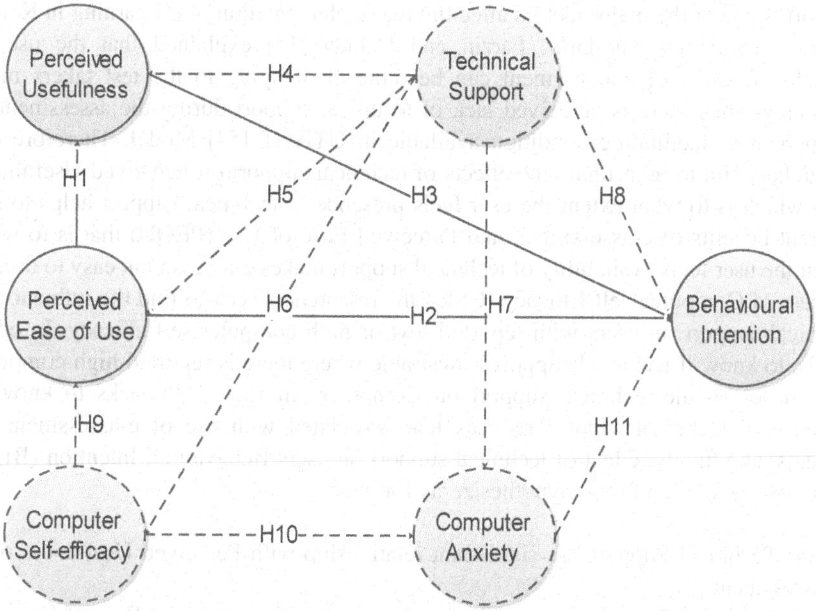

Fig. 2. Proposed model for e-Assessment acceptance

Perceived Ease of Use

In technology acceptance model (TAM), Perceived Ease of Use (PEOU) is defined as the extent to which a system or innovation is easy to use [41]. PU and BI are found to be influenced by PEOU [45, 56].

Therefore the researchers hypothesize as follows:

H1: Perceived Ease of Use has significant relationship with Perceived Usefulness of E-Assessment.

H2: Perceived Ease of Use has significant relationship with Behavioural Intention Use of E assessment.

Perceived Usefulness
Perceived Usefulness (PU) is defined as the extent to which a person believes that using a particular system will enhance his/her job performance [41, 96]. A strong relationship PU on BI were reported by many studies [17, 48, 57] and it is considered as one of the most important predictors of technology acceptance and actual use.

H3: Perceived Usefulness has significant relationship with Behavioural Intention use of E assessment.

Technical Support
Tarus, Gichoya [58] as cited by Saidu, Clarkson [59] mentioned that lack of technical support is one of the major factors affecting the implementation of e-Learning in Kenya public Universities. Similarly, Farzin and Dahlan [12] explained that the use of available features of e-assessment can be quite challenging to the test takers most especially when there is perceived lack of technical support during the assessment, a component of facilitating condition available in UTAUT [54] Model. Therefore the researchers aim to investigate the effects of technical support on Perceived Usefulness (PU) which is to what extent the user feels presence of technical support helps to see inherent benefits of e-assessment, and Perceived Ease of Use (PEOU) that is to what extent the user feels availability of technical support makes e-assessment easy to use. In the case of Computer Self-Efficacy (CSE), the researchers seek to find the influence of technical support on users with reported low or high computer self-efficacy. In other words, to know if technical support is desirable where there is reported high computer self-efficacy, while technical support on Computer Anxiety (CA) seeks to know if presence of technical support reduces fear associated with use of e-assessment on students, and finally, effect of technical support on users Behavioural Intention (BI) to use e-assessment, and thus hypothesize as follows:

H4: Technical Support has significant relationship with Perceived Usefulness of E assessment.
H5: Technical Support has significant relationship with Perceived Ease of Use of E assessment.
H6: Technical Support has significant relationship with Computer Self-efficacy use of E assessment.
H7: Technical Support has significant relationship with Computer Anxiety use of E assessment.
H8: Technical Support has significant relationship with Behavioural Intention to use E assessment.

Computer Self-Efficacy
Computer Self-Efficacy (CSE) is determined as the individual's beliefs on his/her ability to use computers [60]. In Computer Based Assessment, computer self-efficacy is an important factor which influences students' performance during assessment.

Students with higher CSE were reported to gain significant time only by clicking, typing or reading through the PC quicker. Previous studies reported relationships between Computer Self-Efficacy and Perceived Ease of Use [17, 61, 62], and thus the researchers hypothesized that:

H9: Computer Self-Efficacy has significant relationship with Perceived Ease of Use of E assessment.
H10: Computer Self-Efficacy has significant relationship with Computer Anxiety use of E assessment.

Computer Anxiety
Computer anxiety is defined as the extent to which an individual expresses uneasiness or fear when he/she is faced with the possibility of using computers for assessment. Anxiety can be classified into three: trait anxiety (permanent since the source is fundamental), state anxiety (temporary or induced by the present circumstance), and dependent anxiety (a mixture of both trait and state anxiety) [63]. Farzin and Dahlan [12] suggested that the construct, computer anxiety, can be classified under the second type of anxiety (state anxiety) since the feeling will emerge before or during an engagement with an information system. The researchers of this study therefore support this notion by focusing on state anxiety since they are of the opinion that the anxiety associated with computer usage may be temporary since it might have been induced by the presence of computer technology for assessment. [64] in their study of citizen adoption of e-government systems also stressed that Anxiety will have significant relationship with behavioral intention and therefore the researchers hypothesized that:

H11: Computer Anxiety has significant relationship with behavioural Intention to use E assessment.

3 Research Method

3.1 Data Collection

This study followed a positivist research paradigm and in order to investigate e-assessment acceptance for this study, survey methodology was applied. The final questionnaire consisted of 24 questions (see Appendix I). All the questions were multiple choice close ended, five point likert scales (1–5), from strongly disagree to strongly agree. A random probability sampling technique was adopted and in order to ensure the adequacy of the sample size in this study, G* power software concept derived from [65, 66] was applied and total sample size was given at seventy-four 74. (See Appendix II). This was necessary to obtain a representative sample [67] that is generalizable to a larger population [68]. The study applied online survey methodology (see Appendix III) to distribute questionnaire across Universities in Cameroon and Nigeria. A total of one hundred and five (105) questionnaires were retrieved out of which 3 were excluded due to incomplete responses; thereby giving one hundred and two (102) responses as highlighted in Table 1. The final sample consisted of 64 (62.75%) male and 38 (37.25%) female. 44 participants (43.14%) were above average in ability to use computer, 52 respondents (50.98%) were average while only 6 students (5.88%) were below average. According to level of study, Undergraduate Year 1 respondents were 55 (53.92%), Year 2 were 18 (17.65%), Year 3 were 13 (12.74%) while Year 4 were 14 (13.72%) of the sample respectively.

Table 1. Data distribution table

Measure	Items	Frequency	Percentage
		N=102	100%
Gender	Male	64	62.75%
	Female	38	37.25%
Computer *Proficiency* Level	Above Average	44	43.14%
	Average	52	50.98%
	Below Average	6	5.88%
University Study Level	Year 1	55	53.92%
	Year 2	18	17.65%
	Year 3	13	12.75%
	Year 4	16	15.68%

3.2 Data Analysis

This study applied structural equation modeling (SEM) for data analysis. SEM is a causal modeling procedure with sole objective of maximizing the explained variation of the dependent latent variables to examine the quality of data with reference to the attributes of the measurement model [69]. Our applying SEM for data analysis in this study is necessary to ascertain if the measurement and structural model meet the quality criteria for evidence-based research. Empirical studies that applied structural equation modeling (SEM) are very common lately in the field of information systems [70] and it can be considered as having another distinctive and very functional approach called partial least square (PLS).

3.3 Measurement Model

To examine measurement model assessment, the PLS algorithm method was applied by examining the construct validity and reliability. This involved measuring the convergent, discriminant validity and loadings of all items with respect to the individual variables [70].

The first consideration for this study is the reliability of internal consistency. Reliability of a measurement has been defined as the consistency of a particular research instrument, and also regarded as the level to which a test consistently measures whatever it measures, as it is primarily concerned with the extent of stability between multiple measurements of constructs [71]. A construct is considered reliable when the value of a composite reliability for a construct is greater than 0.7 and according to Hair, Sarstedt [72], composite reliability (CR) measure of 0.7 and over is acceptable. Cronbach's alpha (CA), (coefficient alpha), a type of reliability coefficient reported most often in the literature, is known to provide the conventional measure for this internal consistency reliability. Cronbach's alpha measures internal consistency reliability, or the degree to which responses are consistent across the items of a measure. If internal consistency is low, then the content of the items may be so heterogeneous that the total score is not the best possible unit of analysis. A conceptual equation is

$$\alpha_C = \frac{n_i \overline{r_{ij}}}{1 + (n_i - 1)\overline{r_{ij}}} \tag{1}$$

where n_i is the number of items, not cases, and r_{ij} is the average Pearson correlation between all pairs of items [73]. Although, CA presumes that all items of a construct are equally dependable and therefore, sometimes perceived as having characteristics of measuring internal consistency conservatively. In view of these limitations, therefore, composite reliability was considered a good substitute for CA. [74] mentioned that generally accepted threshold for CA is 0.7. In social science, it may go down to 0.6 and still be considered valid [75, 76]. [77] maintained that in theoretical studies, even modest reliabilities of 0.60 or 0.50 may be acceptable for Cronbach's alpha [78, 79]. Therefore the result suggested that construct reliability for this study may be accepted as shown in Table 2.

Table 2. Composite reliability and internal consistency reliability

Construct	Composite Reliability	Cronbach's Alpha	AVE
Perceived Usefulness	0.937	0.900	0.833
Perceived ease of Use	0.852	0.736	0.658
Computer Self efficacy	0.792	0.610	0.559
Computer Anxiety	0.867	0.774	0.686
Technical Support	0.866	0.809	0.564
Behavioural Intention	0.913	0.857	0.778

Convergent validity in this study was established with three criteria: item factor loading, composite reliability, and average variance extracted [80]. Firstly, the convergent validity was evaluated from the measurement model by evaluating the factor loading greater than or equal to 0.7 which is preferred as mentioned by [81] and cited in [82]. Therefore, factor loading lower than 0.7 were removed from the study as shown in Table 3. This is also mentioned by Hair, Sarstedt [72], that ordinarily composite reliability should be above 0.70. Consequently, AVE denotes the average variance from a set of items that were inspected. The indicators removed as highlighted in Table 3. (PEOU_1, PEOU_4, CSE_2 and CA_2) from the initial measure increased the AVE value of Computer self-efficacy from **0.412** to **0.559**. Therefore, value of AVE greater than 0.5 indicates that the set of items has sufficient convergence in measuring the constructs, as reported by [83].

Table 3. Convergent validity for research constructs

Constructs	Indicators	Loadings	Composite Reliability	AVE
Perceived Usefulness	PU_1	0.915	0.937	0.833
	PU_2	0.924		
	PU_3	0.898		
Perceived ease of Use	PEOU_1	0.668	0.852	0.658
	PEOU_2	0.807		
	PEOU_3	0.729		
	PEOU_4	0.666		
	PEOU_5	0.890		
Computer Self-Efficacy	CSE_1	0.750	0.792	0.559
	CSE_2	0.251		
	CSE_3	0.769		
	CSE_4	0.724		
Computer Anxiety	CA_1	0.761	0.867	0.686
	CA_2	0.260		
	CA_3	0.845		
	CA_4	0.874		
Technical Support	TS_1	0.712	0.866	0.564
	TS_2	0.774		
	TS_3	0.785		
	TS_4	0.732		
	TS_5	0.751		
Behavioural Intention	BI1	0.885	0.913	0.778
	BI2	0.873		
	BI3	0.888		

Discriminant validity is often considered as the extent to which a construct empirically varies from other constructs. Thus, discriminant validity is confirmed when a construct exhibits a different characteristic not captured by another construct in the same model. In this study, discriminant validity was measured using Fornell-Larcker criterion which is measured by substituting the square root of AVE for the correlation coefficient matrix diagonals, with values greater than the correlation coefficients in the other dimension as highlighted in Table 4. The AVE of this study ranged between **0.559 and 0.833**. In view of these, this study however shows the square root of AVE is well above the correlation coefficients in other dimensions, which indicates that the model in this study has discriminant validity.

Table 4. Discriminant validity for research constructs

Constructs	BI	CA	CSE	PEOU	PU	TS
Behavioural Intention	**0.882**	0	0	0	0	0
Computer Anxiety	-0.218	**0.828**	0	0	0	0
Computer Self-Efficacy	0.386	-0.281	**0.748**	0	0	0
Perceived Ease of use	0.407	0.122	0.135	**0.811**	0	0
Perceived Usefulness	0.547	-0.051	0.266	0.549	**0.913**	0
Technical Support	0.360	0.206	0.185	0.359	0.525	**0.751**

3.4 Structural Model

The Coefficient of Determinant (R^2)

The first important measure in examining the structural model is the assessment of the coefficient of determinant (R^2) for dependent constructs. The R-square measures the proportion of the variance of a dependent variable that is explained by the independent constructs [72]. It signifies model's capability to interpret the dependent variable [84]. Following recommendation by [85], measures of approximately 0.670 is substantial, measure around 0.333 is considered moderate, and values less than or equal to 0.190 is weak. In this study, the predictive power of constructs for the model is 38% of the variance in students' intention to use e-assessment thereby implying the descriptive strength of the whole model as well as the evaluation of the predictive power of the independent variables highlighted in Fig. 3.

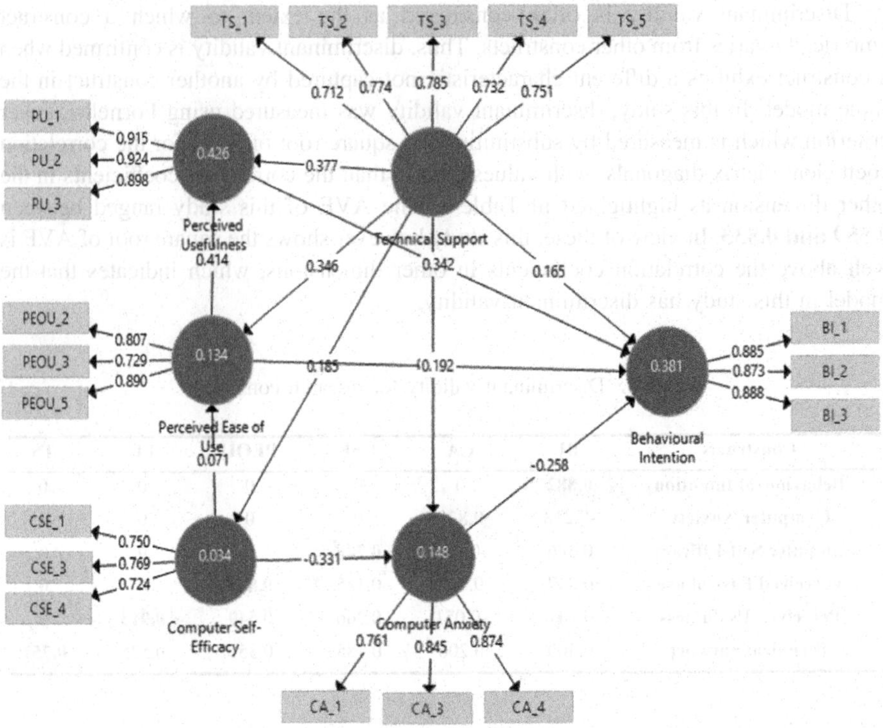

Fig. 3. Outcome of PLS algorithm analysis

4 Discussion and Implication

The hypotheses for this study were verified by evaluating the statistical importance of the path coefficients using t-statistics computed by means of the bootstrap resampling approach utilizing 5000 samples as highlighted below, and Non-parametric bootstrapping [86] was then applied with 5000 replications as recommended by [87]. The two tailed t-tests used as the hypotheses were directional and unidirectional [88]. The t-value and the Degree of Freedom (DF) were used to calculate the p-value for each hypothesis. Eleven hypotheses were evaluated for this study. The p-value results are shown in Table 5 and Fig. 4 along with the degree of significance for each p-value.

The purpose of this study is to examine the role of technical support in mitigating the effect of computer anxiety on acceptance of electronic assessment. Technology acceptance model (TAM) was extended to include Technical Support (TS), Computer Anxiety and Computer Self-Efficacy (CSE) and hypotheses formed based on the proposed model. The findings from the analysis reveal that Perceived Ease of Use has significant positive relationship with Perceived Usefulness. This indicates that students are able to see the potential benefits inherent in the use of e-assessment and thus can be considered useful. The outcome is consistent with findings from previous studies on computer-based assessment acceptance [8, 89].

Table 5. Hypothesis testing

Hypothesis	Path	Path Coefficient	t-Value	Results
H1	PEOU→PU	0.414	4.128***	Supported
H2	PEOU→BI	0.192	1.826*	Supported
H3	PU→BI	0.342	3.680***	Supported
H4	TS→PU	0.377	3.897***	Supported
H5	TS→PEOU	0.346	2.386**	Supported
H5	TS→CSE	0.185	0.745	Not Supported
H7	TS→CA	0.267	2.574**	Supported
H8	TS→BI	0.165	1.479	Not Supported
H9	CSE→PEOU	0.071	0.624	Not Supported
H10	CSE→CA	-0.331	2.294**	Supported
H11	CA→BI	-0.258	3.031***	Supported

*t0.1 = 1.65, **t0.05=1.960, ***t0.01=2.576

Perceived Ease of Use was found to have positive significant relationship with behavioural intention. This outcome supports previous studies on acceptance of learning management system [48, 90]. This further suggested that when students see potential benefits of e-assessment, their will to use the technology increases. Similarly, Perceived Usefulness was found to have a very strong positive relationship with behavioural intention. This means that when students are convinced on the usefulness of e-assessment, it will enhance their decisions to use it. This is supported by Padilla-Meléndez, Garrido-Moreno [91] on acceptance of learning management systems and related study on students attitude to use blended learning systems by Padilla-Meléndez, del Aguila-Obra [92].

On the role of Technical Support, there were no empirical studies found prior to conducting this study. Although, Tarus, Gichoya [58] as cited by Saidu, Clarkson [59] did mention that lack of technical support is one of the major factors affecting the implementation of e-Learning in Kenya, and Farzin and Dahlan [12] stressed that e-assessment can be quite challenging to the test takers most especially when there is lack of technical support during assessment. The findings of the analysis show that Technical Support has strong relationship with Perceived Usefulness of e-Assessment system. This indicates that students are able to see the usefulness of e-Assessment when technical assistance is provided. On the other hand, Technical Support correlates with Perceived Ease of Use. This outcome indicates that availability of prompt technical assistance during assessment would help the students see the relative advantage hence the validity of this hypothesis. Nevertheless, outcome of the analysis did not show any significant relationship between Technical Support and Computer Self-Efficacy; therefore not supporting the hypothesis.

Technical Support has strong positive relationship with Computer Anxiety. This outcome indicates that presence of Technical Support has the capability to reduce fear associated with the use of computer for assessment by University students in Nigeria and Cameroon. This confirms the objective of this study which is to confirm if Technical Support has the capability to reduce computer anxiety on Undergraduate students during electronic assessment. Although, the outcome of the analysis did not support the hypothesis that Technical Support has relationship with students' behavioural intention to use e-Assessment, the researchers believed that with larger sample size, the relationship between these two constructs might be significant since there is significant relationships between Technical Support and Perceived Usefulness and Perceived Ease of Use as reflected in Fig. 4.

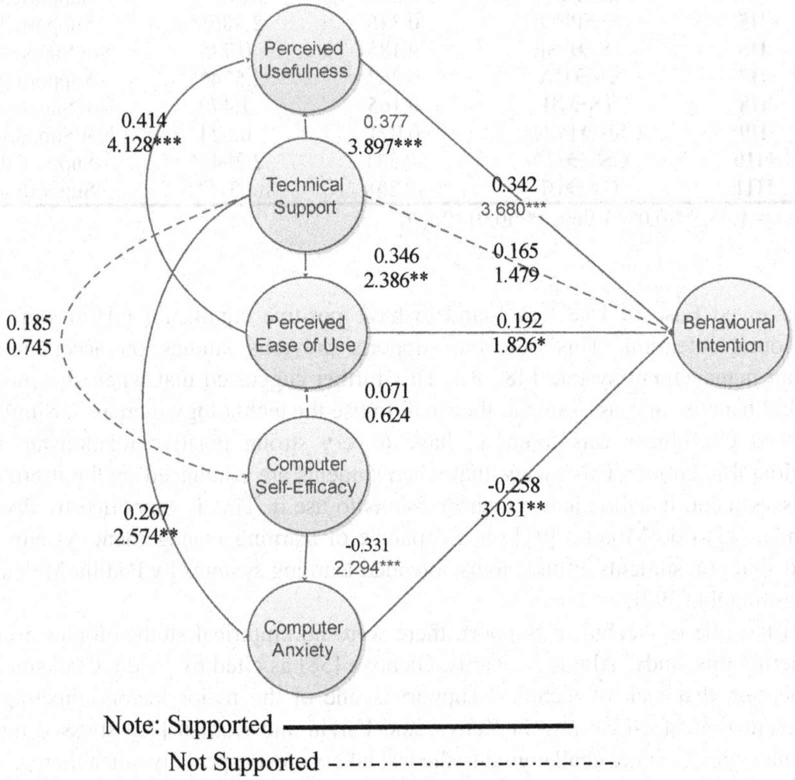

Fig. 4. Outcome of structural model analysis

Computer Self-Efficacy did not report any significant relationship with Perceived Ease of Use. The researchers believed CSE may not be an important factor for them since they are comfortable using computer and therefore using e-Assessment by this group of students would not be an issue after all. This is contrary to previous studies where there are reported relationships between Computer Self Efficacy and Perceived Ease of Use [17, 61, 62]. Notwithstanding, there is a strong relationship but negative path between Computer Self-efficacy and Computer Anxiety. This indicates that Computer Anxiety is likely to affect the students' performance during assessment regardless of their level of proficiency in the use of Computer. This outcome is evident from the survey as most of the respondents claimed to have average and above average skills in the use of computer. Finally, there is a negative significant relationship

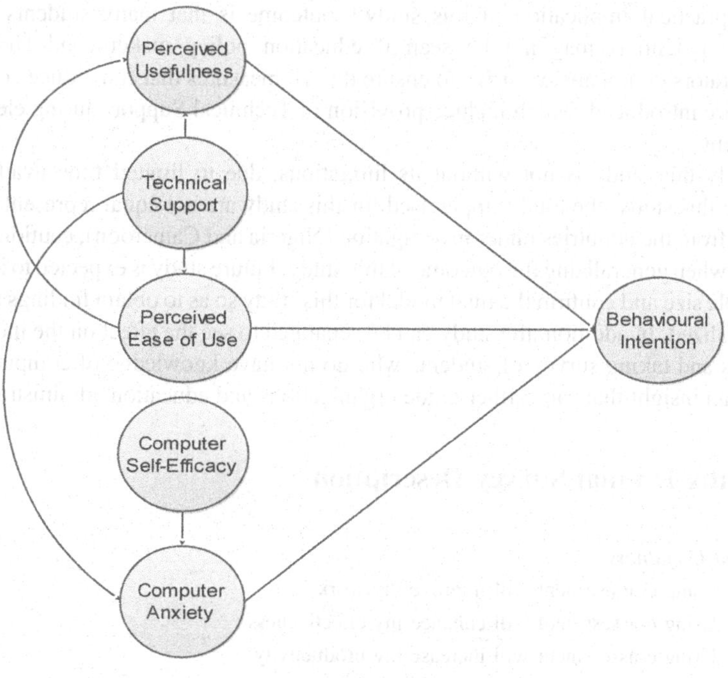

Fig. 5. e-Assessment Acceptance Model (e-AAM)

between Computer Anxiety and students' behavioural intention to use e-Assessment. This confirms the objective of this study which is to find ways to reduce fear that arises when students are faced with using computer for assessment.

5 Conclusion

The purpose of this study is to examine the role of technical support in mitigating effect of computer anxiety on students taking e-assessment in sub Saharan African countries, Cameroon and Nigeria in particular. This study extended Technology Acceptance Model (TAM) with additional variables such as Computer Self-Efficacy, Computer Anxiety and Technical Support. The model hypothesized eleven relationships and eight of them were found to be significant. The theoretical contribution of this study filled the research gaps where empirical validation of role of Technical Support construct towards mitigating effect of computer anxiety on University students during e-Assessment had not been carried out by any other researcher in the field of e-assessment acceptance. The conceptual model was found to be reliable having subjected it to measurement and structural analysis giving birth to the final model for this study (e-Assessment Acceptance Model, shown in Fig. 5). In addition, this study supports the body of knowledge by establishing that Computer Anxiety is an important factor which can affect University students regardless of their level of computer proficiency. It also revealed that when technical assistance is available, computer anxiety during e-Assessment on majority of University students in Nigeria and Cameroon is reduced.

The practical implication of this study's outcome is that many students' actual academic potentials may not be seen if education policy makers and University administrators do not always strive to ensure that all measures that can reduce computer anxiety are introduced, which include provision of Technical Support during electronic assessment.

Finally this study is not without its limitations, due to limited time available to complete this study, the total sample used for this study are not equal representation of students from the countries under investigation (Nigeria and Cameroon); caution should be taken when generalizing the outcome of this study. Future study is expected to increase the sample size and confirm the final model for this study so as to obtain findings that can be generalized. In addition, the study can be separated to see the effect on the individual countries and taking survey of students who do not have knowledge of computer may provide an insight that can further guide organizations and education administrators.

Appendix I: Final Survey Description

Perceived Usefulness	
PU1	Using e-assessment will improve my work
PU2	Using e-assessment will enhance my effectiveness
PU3	Using e-assessment will increase my productivity
Perceived Ease of Use	
PEOU1	My interaction with e-assessment is clear and understandable
PEOU2	It is easy for me to become skilful in using the e-assessment
PEOU3	E-assessment system enabled me to take exams easily
PEOU4	I find the e-assessment easy to use
PEOU5	Using e-assessment to take exams was a good idea
Computer Self-Efficacy	
CSE1	I could complete a job or task using the computer
CSE2	I could complete a task using the computer if someone showed me how to do it first
CSE3	I can navigate easily through the web to find any information I need
CSE4	I believe I have the basic skills required to use internet and computer before I begin to use e-assessment
Computer Anxiety	
CA1	The e-assessment system is somewhat intimidating to me (Reverse)
CA2	I hesitated to use the e- assessment system for fear of making mistakes that I couldn't correct (Reverse)
CA3	I am afraid about using the e-assessment system (Reverse)
CA4	Working with the e-assessment system made me nervous (Reverse)
Technical Support	
TS1	It will be easy to use e-assessment if there is technical staff around me
TS2	It will be easy to use e-assessment if I'm shown its inherent benefits
TS3	I will use e-assessment if I'm guided on how to use some of its features during assessment

(continued)

(*continued*)

TS4	Fear of e-assessment is reduced if I have a feeling that technical support staff is around
TS5	Technical support is important for me to use e-assessment
Behavioural Intention	
BI1	I intend to use e-assessment in the future
BI2	I predict I would use e-assessment in the future
BI3	I plan to use e-assessment in the future

Appendix II: G* Power Analysis

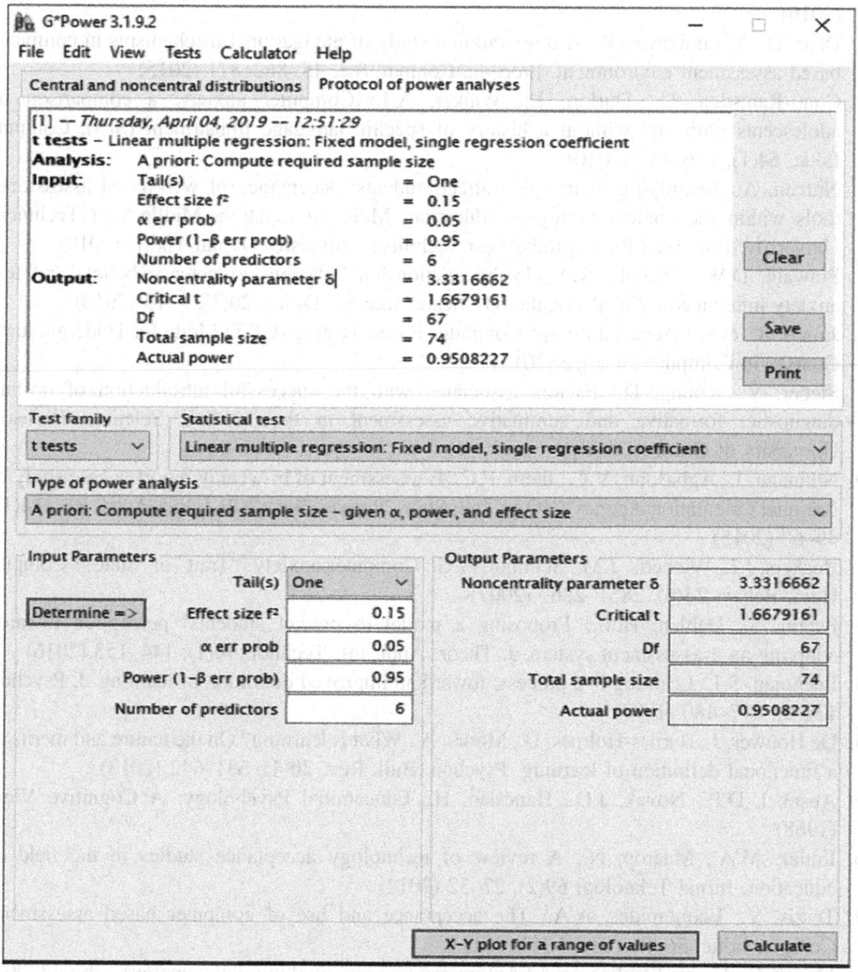

Appendix III: Data Source Link

https://www.surveymonkey.com/analyze/CHYvAqnK1Bpo9mahSbtI6INn5leHha2UuA3sFPNd3bN95RZ3ZIEN5b_2Bk5COgaH5.

References

1. Gilbert, L., Whitelock, D., Gale, V.: Synthesis report on assessment and feedback with technology enhancement (2011)
2. Llamas-Nistal, M., et al.: Blended e-assessment: migrating classical exams to the digital world. Comput. Educ. **62**, 72–87 (2013)
3. Alruwais, N., Wills, G., Wald, M.: Identifying factors that affect the acceptance and use of E-assessment by academics in Saudi Universities. IJAEDU-Int. E-J. Adv. Educ. **2**(4), 132–140 (2016)
4. Dhar, D., Yammiyavar, P.: A cross-cultural study of navigational mechanisms in computer based assessment environment. Procedia Comput. Sci. **45**, 862–871 (2015)
5. Conti-Ramsden, G., Durkin, K., Walker, A.J.: Computer anxiety: a comparison of adolescents with and without a history of specific language impairment (SLI). Comput. Educ. **54**(1), 136–145 (2010)
6. Nurcan, A.: Identifying factors that affect students' acceptance of web-based assessment tools within the context of higher education. M.Sc. dissertation. Midlle East Technical University. Retrieved from Middle East Technical University Digital Thesis (2010)
7. Putwain, D.W., Daniels, R.A.: Is the relationship between competence beliefs and test anxiety influenced by goal orientation? Learn. Individ. Differ. **20**(1), 8–13 (2010)
8. Jimoh, R., et al.: Acceptability of Computer Based Testing (CBT) Mode for Undergraduate Courses in Computer Science (2013)
9. Sieber, V., Young, D.: Factors associated with the successful introduction of on-line diagnostic, formative and summative assessment in the Medical Sciences Division University of Oxford (2008)
10. Ndunagu, J., Agbasonu, V.C., Ihem, F.C.: E-assessment of bi-weekly report: a case study of National Orientation Agency (NOA), Imo State, Nigeria. West Afr. J. Ind. Acad. Res. **14**(1), 49–60 (2015)
11. Beckers, J.J., Wicherts, J.M., Schmidt, H.G.: Computer anxiety: "Trait" or "state"? Comput. Hum. Behav. **23**(6), 2851–2862 (2007)
12. Farzin, S., Dahlan, H.M.: Proposing a model to predict students' perception towards adopting an e-assessment system. J. Theor. Appl. Inf. Technol. **90**(1), 144–153 (2016)
13. Lachman, S.J.: Learning is a process: toward an improved definition of learning. J. Psychol. **131**(5), 477–480 (1997)
14. De Houwer, J., Barnes-Holmes, D., Moors, A.: What is learning? On the nature and merits of a functional definition of learning. Psychon. Bull. Rev. **20**(4), 631–642 (2013)
15. Ausubel, D.P., Novak, J.D., Hanesian, H.: Educational Psychology: A Cognitive View (1968)
16. Imtiaz, M.A., Maarop, N.: A review of technology acceptance studies in the field of education. Jurnal Teknologi **69**(2), 27–32 (2014)
17. Terzis, V., Economides, A.A.: The acceptance and use of computer based assessment. Comput. Educ. **56**(4), 1032–1044 (2011)
18. Mason, O., Grove-Stephensen, I.: Automated free text marking with paperless school (2002)

19. Bennett, R.E.: Inexorable and inevitable: the continuing story of technology and assessment. Comput.-Based Test. Internet: Issues Adv. **1**, 201–217 (2006)
20. Siozos, P., et al.: Computer based testing using "digital ink": participatory design of a tablet PC based assessment application for secondary education. Comput. Educ. **52**(4), 811–819 (2009)
21. Mohamadi, Z.: Comparative effect of online summative and formative assessment on EFL student writing ability. Stud. Educ. Eval. **59**, 29–40 (2018)
22. Deutsch, T., et al.: Implementing computer-based assessment–a web-based mock examination changes attitudes. Comput. Educ. **58**(4), 1068–1075 (2012)
23. Singleton, C.: Computer-based assessment in education. Educ. Child Psychol. **18**(3), 58–74 (2001)
24. Darkwa, O., Mazibuko, F.: Virtual learning communities in Africa: challenges and prospects. FirstMonday (2002)
25. Unwin, T.: Survey of e-Learning in Africa. E-Learn. UNESCO Chair in ICT for Development, Royal Holloway, University of London, UK, pp. 1–10 (2008)
26. Nwana, S.: Challenges in the applications of e-learning by secondary school teachers in Anambra State, Nigeria. Afr. J. Teach. Educ. **2**(1), 1–9 (2012)
27. Ajadi, T.O., Salawu, I.O., Adeoye, F.A.: E-learning and distance education in Nigeria. Online Submission **7**(4), 1–10 (2008)
28. Osang, F.: Electronic examination in Nigeria, academic staff perspective—case study: National Open University of Nigeria (NOUN). Int. J. Inf. Educ. Technol. **2**(4), 304–307 (2012)
29. Abubakar, A.S., Adebayo, F.O.: Using computer based test method for the conduct of examination in Nigeria: prospects, challenges and strategies. Mediterr. J. Soc. Sci. **5**(2), 47 (2014)
30. Adomi, E.E., Kpangban, E.: Application of ICTs in Nigerian secondary schools. Library Philosophy and Practice (2010)
31. Simonson, M.R., et al.: Development of a standardized test of computer literacy and a computer anxiety index. J. Educ. Comput. Res. **3**(2), 231–247 (1987)
32. Laguna, K., Babcock, R.L.: Computer anxiety in young and older adults: implications for human-computer interactions in older populations. Comput. Hum. Behav. **13**(3), 317–326 (1997)
33. Rosen, L.D., Maguire, P.: Myths and realities of computerphobia: a meta-analysis. Anxiety Res. **3**(3), 175–191 (1990)
34. Daly, C., Waldron, J.: Introductory programming, problem solving and computer assisted assessment (2002)
35. Babo, R.B., Azevedo, A.I., Suhonen, J.: Students' perceptions about assessment using an e-learning platform. In: 2015 IEEE 15th International Conference on Advanced Learning Technologies. IEEE (2015)
36. Chien, S.-P., Wu, H.-K., Hsu, Y.-S.: An investigation of teachers' beliefs and their use of technology-based assessments. Comput. Hum. Behav. **31**, 198–210 (2014)
37. Taylor, S., Todd, P.: Decomposition and crossover effects in the theory of planned behavior: a study of consumer adoption intentions. Int. J. Res. Mark. **12**(2), 137–155 (1995)
38. Fluck, A.: State wide adoption of e-assessments. In: Ensuring Quality and Standards for e-Assessments in Tertiary Education: Redefining Innovative Assessment in the Digital Age (2012)
39. Fluck, A.E., Mogey, N.: Comparison of institutional innovation: two universities' nurturing of computer-based examinations. In: 10th IFIP World Conference on Computers in Education (2013)

40. Al-Qeisi, K., et al.: Website design quality and usage behavior: unified theory of acceptance and use of technology. J. Bus. Res. **67**(11), 2282–2290 (2014)
41. Davis, F.D.: Perceived usefulness, perceived ease of use, and user acceptance of information technology. MIS Q. **13**(3), 319–340 (1989)
42. Davis, F.D., Bagozzi, R.P., Warshaw, P.R.: User acceptance of computer technology: a comparison of two theoretical models. Manag. Sci. **35**(8), 982–1003 (1989)
43. Robey, D.: Research commentary: diversity in information systems research: threat, promise, and responsibility. Inf. Syst. Res. **7**(4), 400–408 (1996)
44. Malhotra, Y., Galletta, D.F.: Extending the technology acceptance model to account for social influence: theoretical bases and empirical validation. In: Proceedings of the 32nd Annual Hawaii International Conference on Systems Sciences, HICSS-32. IEEE (1999)
45. Venkatesh, V., et al.: User acceptance of information technology: toward a unified view. MIS Q. **27**(3), 425–478 (2003)
46. Szajna, B.: Empirical evaluation of the revised technology acceptance model. Manag. Sci. **42**(1), 85–92 (1996)
47. Park, S.Y.: An analysis of the technology acceptance model in understanding university students' behavioral intention to use e-learning. Educ. Technol. Soc. **12**(3), 150–162 (2009)
48. Van Raaij, E.M., Schepers, J.J.: The acceptance and use of a virtual learning environment in China. Comput. Educ. **50**(3), 838–852 (2008)
49. Sun, P.-C., et al.: What drives a successful e-Learning? An empirical investigation of the critical factors influencing learner satisfaction. Comput. Educ. **50**(4), 1183–1202 (2008)
50. Terzis, V., Moridis, C.N., Economides, A.A.: The effect of emotional feedback on behavioral intention to use computer based assessment. Comput. Educ. **59**(2), 710–721 (2012)
51. Terzis, V., Moridis, C.N., Economides, A.A.: Continuance acceptance of computer based assessment through the integration of user's expectations and perceptions. Comput. Educ. **62**, 50–61 (2013)
52. Kalogeropoulos, N., et al.: Computer-based assessment of student performance in programing courses. Comput. Appl. Eng. Educ. **21**(4), 671–683 (2013)
53. Bhuasiri, W., et al.: Critical success factors for e-learning in developing countries: a comparative analysis between ICT experts and faculty. Comput. Educ. **58**(2), 843–855 (2012)
54. Venkatesh, V., et al.: Individual reactions to new technologies in the workplace: the role of gender as a psychological construct. J. Appl. Soc. Psychol. **34**(3), 445–467 (2004)
55. Venkatesh, V., Brown, S.A., Bala, H.: Bridging the qualitative-quantitative divide: Guidelines for conducting mixed methods research in information systems. MIS Q. **37**(1), 21–54 (2013)
56. Agarwal, R., Karahanna, E.: Time flies when you're having fun: cognitive absorption and beliefs about information technology usage. MIS Q. **24**(4), 665–694 (2000)
57. Ong, C.-S., Lai, J.-Y.: Gender differences in perceptions and relationships among dominants of e-learning acceptance. Comput. Hum. Behav. **22**(5), 816–829 (2006)
58. Tarus, J.K., Gichoya, D., Muumbo, A.: Challenges of implementing e-learning in Kenya: a case of Kenyan public universities. Int. Rev. Res. Open Distrib. Learn. **16**(1), 120–141 (2015)
59. Saidu, A., Clarkson, M.A., Mohammed, M.: E-Learning Security Challenges, Implementation and Improvement in Developing Countries: A Review (2016)
60. Compeau, D.R., Higgins, C.A.: Computer self-efficacy: development of a measure and initial test. MIS Q. **19**(2), 189–211 (1995)

61. Agarwal, R., Sambamurthy, V., Stair, R.M.: The evolving relationship between general and specific computer self-efficacy—an empirical assessment. Inf. Syst. Res. **11**(4), 418–430 (2000)
62. Venkatesh, V., Davis, F.D.: A model of the antecedents of perceived ease of use: development and test. Decis. Sci. **27**(3), 451–481 (1996)
63. Oye, N., Iahad, A., Rabin, A.: Behavioral intention to accept and use ICT in public universities: integrating quantitative and qualitative data. J. Emerg. Trends Comput. Inf. Sci. **3**(6), 957–969 (2012)
64. Rana, N.P., Dwivedi, Y.K.: Citizen's adoption of an e-government system: validating extended social cognitive theory (SCT). Gov. Inf. Q. **32**(2), 172–181 (2015)
65. Mayr, S., et al.: A short tutorial of GPower. Tutorials Quant. Methods Psychol. **3**(2), 51–59 (2007)
66. Erdfelder, E., Faul, F., Buchner, A.: GPOWER: a general power analysis program. Behav. Res. Methods Instrum. Comput. **28**(1), 1–11 (1996)
67. Schreuder, H.T., Gregoire, T.G., Weyer, J.P.: For what applications can probability and non-probability sampling be used? Environ. Monit. Assess. **66**(3), 281–291 (2001)
68. Kasunic, M.: Designing an effective survey. Carnegie-Mellon Univ Pittsburgh PA Software Engineering Inst (2005)
69. Ahmad, S., Afthanorhan, W.M.A.B.W.: The importance-performance matrix analysis in partial least square structural equation modeling (PLS-SEM) with smartpls 2.0 M3. Int. J. Math. Res. **3**(1), 1–14 (2014)
70. Urbach, N., Ahlemann, F.: Structural equation modeling in information systems research using partial least squares. JITTA: J. Inf. Technol. Appl. **11**(2), 5–40 (2010)
71. Sitzia, J.: How valid and reliable are patient satisfaction data? An analysis of 195 studies. Int. J. Qual. Health Care **11**(4), 319–328 (1999)
72. Hair, J.F., et al.: An assessment of the use of partial least squares structural equation modeling in marketing research. J. Acad. Mark. Sci. **40**(3), 414–433 (2012)
73. Kline, R.B.: Principles and Practice of Structural Equation Modeling. Guilford Publications, New York (2015)
74. Hair, J.F., Ringle, C.M., Sarstedt, M.: PLS-SEM: indeed a silver bullet. J. Mark. Theory Pract. **19**(2), 139–152 (2011)
75. Santos, J.R.A.: Cronbach's alpha: a tool for assessing the reliability of scales. J. Extension **37**(2), 1–5 (1999)
76. Peterson, R.A.: A meta-analysis of Cronbach's coefficient alpha. J. Consum. Res. **21**(2), 381–391 (1994)
77. Nunnally, J.C., Bernstein, I.H., Berge, J.M.F.: Psychometric Theory, vol. 226. McGraw-Hill, New York (1967)
78. Ozturk, M.A.: Confirmatory factor analysis of the educators' attitudes toward educational research scale. Educ. Sci.: Theory Pract. **11**(2), 737–748 (2011)
79. Nazari, J.A., et al.: Organizational culture, climate and IC: an interaction analysis. J. Intellect. Capital **12**(2), 224–248 (2011)
80. Fornell, C., Larcker, D.F.: Evaluating structural equation models with unobservable variables and measurement error. J. Mark. Res. **18**(1), 39–50 (1981)
81. Hulland, J.: Use of partial least squares (PLS) in strategic management research: a review of four recent studies. Strateg. Manag. J. **20**(2), 195–204 (1999)
82. Wong, K.K.-K.: Partial least squares structural equation modeling (PLS-SEM) techniques using SmartPLS. Mark. Bull. **24**(1), 1–32 (2013)
83. Barclay, D., Higgins, C., Thompson, R.: The partial least squares (PLS) approach to casual modeling: personal computer adoption and use as an Illustration (1995)

84. Ringle, C.M., Sarstedt, M., Straub, D.: A critical look at the use of PLS-SEM in MIS Quarterly. MIS Q. (MISQ) **36**(1), 3–14 (2012)
85. Chin, W.W.: The partial least squares approach to structural equation modeling. Mod. Methods Bus. Res. **295**(2), 295–336 (1998)
86. Efron, B., Tibshirani, R.J.: An Introduction to the Bootstrap. CRC Press, Boca Raton (1994)
87. Hair Jr., J.F., et al.: A Primer on Partial Least Squares Structural Equation Modeling (PLS-SEM). Sage Publications, Thousand Oaks (2016)
88. Gudergan, S.P., et al.: Confirmatory tetrad analysis in PLS path modeling. J. Bus. Res. **61** (12), 1238–1249 (2008)
89. Terzis, V., Economides, A.A.: Computer based assessment: gender differences in perceptions and acceptance. Comput. Hum. Behav. **27**(6), 2108–2122 (2011)
90. Teo, T.: A path analysis of pre-service teachers' attitudes to computer use: applying and extending the technology acceptance model in an educational context. Interact. Learn. Environ. **18**(1), 65–79 (2010)
91. Padilla-Meléndez, A., Garrido-Moreno, A., Del Aguila-Obra, A.R.: Factors affecting e-collaboration technology use among management students. Comput. Educ. **51**(2), 609–623 (2008)
92. Padilla-Meléndez, A., del Aguila-Obra, A.R., Garrido-Moreno, A.: Perceived playfulness, gender differences and technology acceptance model in a blended learning scenario. Comput. Educ. **63**, 306–317 (2013)
93. Rana, N.P., Dwivedi, Y.K.: Citizen's adoption of an e-government system: validating extended social cognitive theory (SCT). Govern. Inf. Q. **32**(2), 172–181 (2015)
94. Rana, N.P., Dwivedi, Y.K., Williams, M.D., Weerakkody, V.: Adoption of online public grievance redressal system in India: Toward developing a unified view. Comput. Hum. Behav. **59**, 265–282 (2016)
95. Rana, N.P., Dwivedi, Y.K., Lal, B., Williams, M.D., Clement, M.: Citizens' adoption of an electronic government system: towards a unified view. Inf. Syst. Front. **19**(3), 549–568 (2017)
96. Dwivedi, Y.K., Wade, M.R., Schneberger, S.L. (eds.): Information Systems Theory: Explaining and Predicting Our Digital Society, vol. 1. Springer, Heidelberg (2011). https://doi.org/10.1007/978-1-4419-6108-2
97. Dwivedi, Y.K., Mustafee, N., Carter, L.D., Williams, M.D.: A bibliometric comparision of the usage of two theories of IS/IT acceptance (TAM and UTAUT). In: AMCIS 2010 Proceedings, Paper #183 (2010). http://aisel.aisnet.org/amcis2010/183

ICT Laws, Uncertainty Avoidance, and ICT Diffusion: Insights from Cross-Country Data

Anupriya Khan and Satish Krishnan(✉)

Indian Institute of Management Kozhikode, Kozhikode, India
{anupriyak09fpm, satishk}@iimk.ac.in

Abstract. The economic future of a country depends on the degree to which information and communication technologies (ICTs) diffuse among its key stakeholders—citizens, businesses, and government. Yet, there is a dearth of cross-country analysis of ICT diffusion jointly examining technology diffusion among these key stakeholders in a single research model. Further, while environmental factors are significant for ICT diffusion, there is limited understanding on the impact of ICT laws on ICT diffusion among these three stakeholders across countries. Drawing on the literature on ICT diffusion and Hofstede's typology of national culture, this study contends that ICT laws in a country can positively influence the ICT diffusion among its citizens, businesses, and the government, and these relationships can be contingent on the national cultural dimension of uncertainty avoidance. The proposed research model is examined using publicly available archival data from 90 countries. The findings suggest that sound ICT laws are necessary for achieving a greater diffusion of ICTs among citizens, businesses, and the government in a country. Further, the study provides important implications that would encourage future research on the phenomenon.

Keywords: ICT laws · Uncertainty avoidance · ICT diffusion · Citizens · Businesses · Government

1 Introduction

The increasing use of information and communication technologies (ICTs) in the recent decade has led to produce considerable research on ICT diffusion, conceptualized as the extent to which ICTs spread to general use within and across economies [1]. ICT refers to "a diverse set of technological tools and resources used to communicate, create, disseminate, store, and manage information" [2, p. 63], and is widely realized as an important element for driving economic growth, productivity, and overall competitiveness of a country [3–5]. Specifically, ICTs are noted to deliver numerous benefits to all the stakeholders in a country. For instance, ICTs can enhance the well-being of citizens by enabling access to basic services including health, education, and financial services [4]. For businesses, ICTs can increase choice in the marketplace, widen the geographic scope of potential markets, and reduce transaction costs [4]. For the government, ICTs can increase the transparency of policy making, enhance the quality of public services, and improve the government dealings [6].

Published by Springer Nature Switzerland AG 2019
Y. Dwivedi et al. (Eds.): TDIT 2019, IFIP AICT 558, pp. 73–89, 2019.
https://doi.org/10.1007/978-3-030-20671-0_6

It is long believed that the economic future depends on the extent to which ICTs are embraced by citizens, businesses, and the government [7], indicating the importance of these three ICT users in a country. Further, it requires a society-wide effort for fully leveraging ICTs in which the government, the business sector, and the citizenry each have an important and vital role to play [8]. Stakeholders involved in prior research examining ICT use is largely seen to involve citizens, businesses, or governments [7], albeit distinctly most of the time. Accordingly, we identify citizens, businesses, and the government as the key stakeholders in this study, and contend that it is crucial to provide insights into the driving factors of the diffusion of ICTs among these three stakeholders. It is likely that the influence of a potential factor on ICT diffusion would vary depending on the stakeholder [9] as in the extent to which a factor influences the Internet use by citizens would be different from the extent to which that same factor influences ICT use by businesses. Therefore, studying them together may offer interesting insights into the phenomenon of ICT diffusion. Nevertheless, prior studies on technology diffusion have hardly analyzed these three stakeholders jointly in a single research model. To address this void, this study investigates ICT diffusion among citizens, businesses, and government organizations.

Although the diffusion of ICTs is considered as a major factor driving a country's pace of economic growth [11, 12], the ICT-driven growth and productivity has varied significantly across countries, largely due to the difference in the degree of diffusion of ICTs among countries [5]. While some countries appear to be more receptive to the technological changes, other countries are less receptive [13]. Thus, a cross-country analysis becomes important to enhance the understanding of the phenomenon of ICT diffusion. Given that only a few studies have considered cross-country analysis of the diffusion of ICTs [5, 14, 15], this study aims to account for the variation in the level of ICT diffusion across countries, and focuses on ICT diffusion among citizens, businesses, and government organizations across countries.

Acknowledging the myriad benefits of ICTs, efforts have been put to investigate the potential determinants of the diffusion of ICTs, which can broadly be classified into (1) socio-related factors, such as user behavior and organizational characteristics [16]; (2) technology-related factors, such as ICT infrastructure and information technology (IT) knowledge [5]; and (3) environmental factors, such as economic environment and regulatory environment [17]. Nevertheless, little is known about the impact of technology-related regulatory environment on ICT diffusion across countries. Despite the relevance of technology-related regulatory environment, only a handful of studies [14, 18] examined its role in determining ICT diffusion. A well-developed technology-related regulatory framework may not only help countries to formulate legal structure and standards for collecting, storing, and sharing electronic data, but also address various ICT-related legal and regulatory issues. This study, therefore, strives to explore the role of technology-related regulatory environment in influencing ICT diffusion among citizens, businesses, and the government across countries, and contributes to the literature on technology diffusion by investigating an under-explored but important environmental aspect in the context of cross-country ICT diffusion.

We characterize technology-related regulatory environment by ICT laws, described as the regulations designed to address variety of ICT-related legal and regulatory issues [19]. It can be conceived as a significant environmental factor considering ICT to be a double-edged sword [20]. To elaborate, though ICTs have enormous potential to improve human, organizational, and governmental performance, ICTs have brought various legal and regulatory challenges, ranging from the validity of electronic ways of contracting and the associated security risks, to concerns over protecting intellectual property rights online and over cybercrime [19, 20]. Given that ICT laws would be able to address such legal and regulatory issues [21], it becomes imperative to understand the extent to which ICT laws can affect the diffusion of ICTs among different stakeholders (i.e., citizens, businesses, and the government) in a country. Accordingly, this study focuses on the impact of ICT laws on cross-country ICT diffusion.

A country's culture is often found to have profound influence on the way the country conducts [22]. Consistent with this, prior research has argued that national cultural values account for the significant variation in ICT diffusion among countries [23–25]. Therefore, it can be expected that though technology diffusion would be influenced by a country's ICT-related legal framework, the degree of such influence would vary depending on the cultural values embedded in that country. This study draws on Hofstede's typology of national culture [26, 27], and focus on the cultural dimension of uncertainty avoidance, in particular. Uncertainty avoidance describes the degree to which members of a society feel comfortable with uncertainty [27]. Considering that uncertainty avoidance could have the most direct influence on the use of an electronic medium [22], we believe that it will be interesting to know how the relation of ICT laws in a country with the ICT diffusion is contingent on the uncertainty avoidance culture. In essence, the key research questions that the current study addresses are:

RQ1: *What is the relationship between ICT laws in a country and the diffusion of ICTs among its citizens, businesses, and government organizations?*

RQ2: *How does the national cultural dimension of uncertainty avoidance affect the relation of ICT laws in a country with the diffusion of ICTs among its citizens, businesses, and government organizations?*

In an effort to address the above research questions, the current research uses the publicly available archival data of 90 countries, and analyses (1) the direct effects of ICT laws on ICT diffusion among citizens, businesses, and the government; and (2) the moderating effect of uncertainty avoidance on the relationships of ICT laws with ICT diffusion among citizens, businesses, and the government. The study makes several crucial contributions to research and practice. First, this research is one among the very few empirical studies that understand the diffusion of ICTs from a macro-level perspective. Second, this study explores the importance of an under-explored environmental factor, ICT-oriented regulatory environment, in facilitating the diffusion of ICTs, and understands whether ICT laws can influence the diffusion of ICTs among three key stakeholders—citizens, businesses, and the government. Third, drawing on Hofstede's typology of national culture, this study investigates how the relationship between ICT laws in a country and the ICT diffusion is contingent on the cultural dimension of uncertainty avoidance. From a practical viewpoint, this study underscores the need for developing ICT laws in order to harness the benefits of ICTs for citizens, businesses, and the government in a country. Second, the interaction effects would help practitioners to have insights into the significance of the national cultural dimension of uncertainty avoidance in explaining the differences in ICT laws and ICT diffusion relationships across countries.

2 Theory and Hypotheses

This section describes the related literature and theories in the context of ICT diffusion, and develops the research hypotheses by relating ICT laws, the culture of uncertainty avoidance, and ICT diffusion. Figure 1 shows the proposed research model.

2.1 ICT Diffusion and ICT Laws

In general, technology diffusion research is characterized by two metaphors [28]. The dominant representation suggests that diffusion is a process whereby potential users are communicated about the availability of new technologies and are persuaded to adopt by prior users [10]. The other metaphor takes an economic standpoint to perceive diffusion in terms of cost and benefit; the higher the cost, the slower diffusion will take place [28]. We define ICT diffusion as the degree to which ICTs spread to general use within and across economies [1]. The extant literature has investigated ICT diffusion from several theoretical lenses. Some of the predominant theories and models are Technology Acceptance Model (TAM) [29], Theory of Planned Behavior (TPB) [30], the Diffusion of Innovation (DoI) theory [11, 59, 60], Unified Theory of Acceptance and Use of Technology (UTAUT) [31, 61–63], the Technology-Organization-Environment (TOE) framework [32, 64], and Institutional theory [33, 65]. As argued by Xiao and associates [7], the potential determinants of the diffusion of ICTs can broadly be classified into (1) socio-related factors [34]; (2) technology-related factors [14]; and (3) environmental factors [17]. Table 1 shows the classification and describes some of the primary factors determining ICT diffusion.

Table 1. Classification of determinants of ICT diffusion

Classification	Potential determinants	Exemplary research
Socio-related factors	User behavior, management behavior, organizational characteristics	[16, 34, 35]
Technology-related factors	ICT infrastructure, IT resources, IT knowledge, IT skills	[5, 14, 36]
Environmental factors	Policy and standards, regulation, economic and cultural environment, competitive pressure	[13, 17, 37]

In this study, we take interest in considering external environmental elements, specifically technology-oriented environmental factors that can impact ICT diffusion across different countries. While a number of socio-centric, technology-centric, and environment-centric factors are investigated as shown in Table 1, little is known about the role of technology-oriented environmental factors such as technology-related legal frameworks in determining ICT diffusion. We believe that with the rapid advancement of technology, technology-oriented environmental factors would have a more relevant role to play, which is worth investigating.

Environmental factors refer to the conditions and settings of the environment within which organizations or businesses operate [32], and are regarded to play a significant role in the technology diffusion [14]. Prior research has explored several environmental conditions in diverse domains. For instance, environmental turbulences and mimetic pressure were found as the main drivers of ICT innovation for the financial services companies [38]. At the country level, the quality of the environment (government support and the presence of a sound institutional environment) appeared to be the key enabler for the development of e-business, but not for e-government [9].

In this study, environmental conditions refer to the development of ICT-oriented legal frameworks or ICT laws in a country. In generic, ICT laws refer to the regulations designed to address variety of ICT-related legal and regulatory issues [19]. These laws enable a legal framework for gathering, storing and sharing electronic information. Specifically, ICT laws provide legal acknowledgment of transactions carried out through electronic data interchange and electronic communication, also referred to as "electronic commerce", facilitate electronic filling of documents, and provide secure environment to carry out electronic transactions through information technology standards, cryptography, digital signatures, and digital certificates [19, 21]. Prior research has shown the relevance of ICT laws to the adoption of ICTs in different contexts. In their study, Boyer-Wright and Kottemann found the ICT legal environment to be a significant factor for the adoption of online government services [39]. In another study, Qu and Pinsonneault demonstrated that when companies were facilitated by established laws, it influenced the adoption of IT outsourcing [18]. Further, Larosiliere and associates argued that people would be more likely to adopt social networking systems in the presence of a sound ICT-related legal environment [14].

Consistent with these arguments, we posit three mechanisms explaining how ICT laws can influence the diffusion of ICTs in a country. First, as mentioned before, ICT laws enable a secure mode of online transaction. These laws ensure protection of individuals with regard to the ownership, processing and transfer of personal data [19]. Citizens may not participate in online financial transactions and electronic banking unless they are assured of the confidentiality and security of electronic communications. ICT laws can address these issues by facilitating the adoption of security measures, reducing the risks associated with information security and ensuring appropriate protection against harmful conduct over Internet, which would lead citizens to have more confidence in ICT and eventually boost their ICT use. This is also in line with Larosiliere and associates [14] who posited that individuals in countries with well-developed ICT laws would experience less concerns about privacy, data protection, or similar other issues, and thus would be motivated to use social network systems. Hence, when ICT laws are developed in a country, the stakeholders, especially citizens and businesses would have minimal concerns about information security issues, and they would be more likely to use various ICTs to access different services, leading to a greater diffusion of ICTs among citizens and businesses in a country. Second, when

ICT laws are developed and efficient enforcement mechanisms are in place in a country, organizations would experience less uncertainty over the validity, enforceability and treatment of electronic contracts, and would be more willing to use ICTs for business transactions and enter into exchanges with each other [19, 39]. To elaborate, many regulatory provisions specify requirements for documents to be produced in writing and for a contract to be signed manually without having certainty as to the validity and enforceability of electronic documents, messages or signatures, thereby placing legal obstacles to electronic communications. ICT laws have the potential to address such issues regarding legal recognition of electronic messages and formation and validation of electronic contracts, and create a more encouraging environment for electronic commerce [19]. Third, businesses and the government would be able to acquire trust of their end-users and partners by providing secure online platforms (e.g., electronic commerce and electronic government) for communication and transaction, which would again lead to a greater diffusion of ICTs among citizens, businesses, and government organizations. Taken together, we propose:

> ***H1****: ICT laws in a country is positively associated with the diffusion of ICTs among its citizens (****H1a****), among businesses (****H1b****), and among government organizations (****H1c****).*

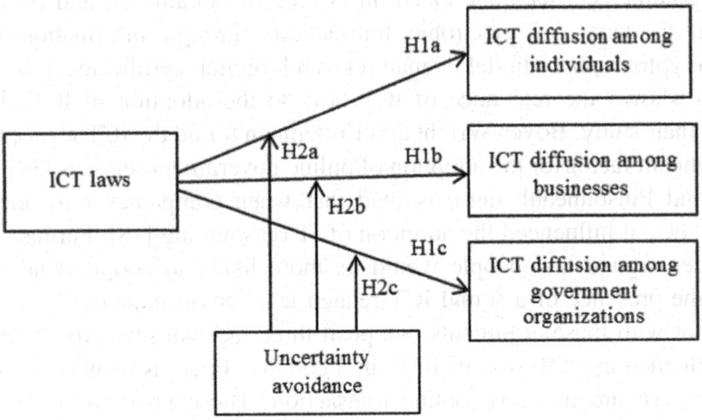

Fig. 1. Research model

2.2 Moderating Influence of the Cultural Dimension of Uncertainty Avoidance

The concept of culture is defined in various ways in the literature [40], yet a commonly held view is that the cultural environment shapes the values shared by the members of the society. In this study, we rely on Hofstede's definition of culture, and draw on Hofstede's cultural dimensions theory, which is arguably the most widely used theory of national culture in the literature [41]. According to Hofstede, national culture is "the collective programming of the mind which distinguishes the members of one human group from another" [26, p. 260]. Hofstede identified four dimensions of national culture namely, (1) power distance (large vs. small); (2) individualism vs. collectivism; (3) masculinity vs. femininity; and (4) uncertainty avoidance (strong vs. weak) [26, 27].

The concept of national culture has been used to study different cross-country phenomena across disciplines. In Information Systems (IS) literature, prior research attributed the significant variation in ICT adoption, diffusion, and implementation between countries to national culture [23–25]. Specifically, the research linking IS and culture has broadly been classified into six themes: (1) culture and IS development; (2) culture, ICT adoption and diffusion; (3) culture, ICT use and outcomes; (4) culture, ICT management and strategy; (5) the influence of ICT on culture; and (6) information technology (IT) culture [15]. While it is important to build understanding on all the above themes, only a few studies have focused on the influence of culture on ICT adoption and diffusion [42], with many studies considering a particular region or a group of countries [22, 43]. For instance, Straub compared the effect of the cultural dimension of uncertainty avoidance on the firm-level ICT diffusion in Japan and the U.S. [22]. In another study, Dotan and Zaphiris performed a cross-cultural analysis of Flickr users of 5 countries—Iran, Israel, Peru, Taiwan, and the United Kingdom [43]. Further, little research is done to have a combined understanding of the cross-cultural ICT diffusion among three stakeholders—citizens, businesses, and government organizations in a country. Hence, motivated by the lack and the need of macro-level studies, this research analyses the moderating effect of uncertainty avoidance on the relationship of ICT laws in a country with its ICT diffusion.

Uncertainty avoidance is defined as "the degree to which members of a society feel uncomfortable with uncertainty and ambiguity" [27, p. 83]. To elaborate, while strong uncertainty avoidance cultures are less comfortable in unstructured situations characterized by ambiguity and uncertainty, weak uncertainty avoidance cultures are more comfortable with ambiguity, chaos, and novelty [45]. Furthermore, individuals in strong uncertainty avoidance cultures would tend to take familiar risks and avoid the risk induced by the unknown, i.e. unstructured situation, whereas individuals in weak uncertainty avoidance cultures would tend to take unknown risks [44, 45]. The current research focuses on uncertainty avoidance for two reasons. First, ICTs may lead to an uncertain situation by causing concerns over electronic contracting, electronic transactions, and privacy, to name a few. As uncertainty avoidance is more related to such uncertain situations, this cultural dimension can be conceived to be more relevant in this study. Second, among four of Hofstede's cultural dimensions—power distance, individualism, masculinity, and uncertainty avoidance [26, 27], uncertainty avoidance may have the most direct influence on the preference for and use of an electronic medium [22]. This is further supported by Leidner and Kayworth who argued uncertainty avoidance to have a lasting influence on the ICT diffusion in a country [15]. Therefore, it is the cultural dimension that is related to environmental factor, in this study, to analyze their joint influence on ICT diffusion.

Researchers argue that the inclination of members of a culture to avoid uncertainty and ambiguity profoundly affects the diffusion of ICTs [22, 46]. Countries with strong uncertainty avoidance would experience a slow rate of ICT diffusion. Consistent with this logic, we argue that ICTs attributed by numerous mobile applications, multimedia, transactional online media, and continuously evolving technological features would create inherent risks including privacy and security issues for citizens to use ICTs for the communication and exchange of information. As a result, despite the presence of sound ICT laws, citizens in strong uncertainty avoidance cultures will be more hesitant towards using ICTs than those in weak uncertainty avoidance cultures, leading to a lower diffusion of ICTs among citizens in strong uncertainty avoidance cultures. Similarly, with respect to organizational communication behavior, uncertainty and ambiguity are conceived as principal factors in predicting media use [22]. For instance, electronic mode of contracting for businesses and governments may raise uncertainties whether a contract formed by the interaction of an automated electronic message and a natural person can be accepted as valid, or whether electronic message or records can be submitted as evidence in courts. Although well-developed ICT laws attempt to answer these uncertainties, in a strong uncertainty avoidance culture, stakeholders' natural tendency to avoid uncertainties (ICT-induced uncertainties in this context) may prevent them to use ICT at its full potential. Hence, despite that the sound ICT laws may decrease the legal and regulatory concerns associated with ICT use, it can be expected that businesses and the government in strong uncertainty avoidance cultures would be more sluggish in the usage of ICTs than those in weak uncertainty avoidance cultures. Taken together, we propose:

*H2: Uncertainty avoidance moderates the relationship of ICT laws in a country with ICT diffusion among its citizens (**H2a**), businesses (**H2b**), and government organizations (**H2c**), such that the effect of ICT laws on ICT diffusion among citizens (**H2a**), businesses (**H2b**), and government organizations (**H2c**) would be less in a strong uncertainty avoidance culture than that in a weak uncertainty avoidance culture.*

3 Research Design

To test the hypotheses, we collected archival data from multiple publicly available sources, in line with Jarvenpaa [47], and Srivastava and Teo [9]. Further, as many studies suggest that the effects of an independent variable may not be instantaneous [36], we maintain 1-year lag between the independent and dependent variables. Hence, we collected data for the dependent variable for year 2016, which was 1-year ahead of the 2015 data for independent variables.

Hypotheses were tested through a cross-sectional analysis of 90 countries (after omitting missing values). The dependent variables in this study are (1) ICT diffusion among citizens; (2) ICT diffusion among businesses; and (3) ICT diffusion among government organizations. ICT diffusion among citizens refers to the extent to which ICTs spread to general use by citizens in a country, and it was measured using a composite of three indicators: (i) percentage of individuals using the Internet; (ii) fixed (wired)-broadband Internet subscriptions per 100 inhabitants; and (iii) active mobile-broadband subscriptions per 100 inhabitants. The indicators were sourced from the International Telecommunication Union report [48]. The second dependent variable, ICT diffusion among businesses refers to the extent to which ICT use spreads through businesses in a country, and it was measured using a composite formed by computing the statistical mean of four indicators, obtained from the Global Information Technology report [8]. The four indicators represent (i) the extent to which businesses in a country adopt new technology; (ii) the extent to which companies in a country have the capacity to innovate; (iii) the extent to which businesses in a country use ICTs for transactions with other businesses; and (iv) the extent to which businesses in a country use ICTs for selling goods and services to consumers. All four indicators were anchored on 1-to-7 scale with "1" representing "not at all", and 7 representing "to a great extent". The third dependent variable, ICT diffusion among government organizations, refers to the extent to which ICTs spread to general use by government organizations in a country, and it was measured using the Online Service Index, which indicates the extent to which the government in a country has an online presence. The values for this index were within 0 and 1, with the higher values indicating the higher level of online presence characterized by the higher level of ICT use by the government, and the scores were obtained from the United Nations (UN) e-government survey report [49].

The independent variable is a technology-oriented environment factor and measures the overall sophistication of laws relating to ICTs in a country [50]. This variable was measured by a single indicator evaluating whether ICT-related laws that govern the understanding and use of IT (i.e., electronic commerce, digital signatures, consumer protection, etc.) were either non-existent or well-developed and enforced. It was measured asking the respondents, "How developed are your country's laws relating to the use of ICTs (e.g., e-commerce, digital signatures, consumer protection)?", and anchored on a 1-to-7 scale with "1" representing "not developed at all", and 7 representing "extremely well developed". The cultural dimension of uncertainty avoidance was used as the moderating variable. Uncertainty avoidance refers to the extent to which members of a society feel comfortable with ambiguity and uncertainty, and its measure was obtained from Hofstede's multinational study of cultural values [46].

Most prior macro-level studies demonstrated the direct influence of financial indicators on ICT use [14]. Accordingly, we controlled for a country's financial stability that was measured by the macroeconomic environment index obtained from the Global Competitiveness report [51]. This index was composed of five financial sub-indices: government budget balance, gross national savings, inflation, government debt, and country credit rating. Apart from this financial indicator, three Hofstede's cultural dimensions, namely, power distance, individualism, and masculinity were also opted as control variables in this study for their potential influence on ICT diffusion. Measures for these national cultural dimensions were taken from Hofstede's multinational research on cultural values [46].

4 Analysis and Results

4.1 Descriptive Statistics and Correlations

Table 2 presents the descriptive statistics and correlations for all variables. As shown, most of the correlations were significant at $p < 0.05$. Further, correlations between the explanatory variables were below the threshold value of 0.8, indicating minimal concern for multicollinearity [52]. This is also supported by the results of the collinearity tests measuring variance inflation factor (VIF), in which VIFs were found to range from 1.07 to 2.15 with all tolerance levels above 0.47. Having VIFs < 4.0 and tolerance levels > 0.25 [53], we can confirm that our research model is not largely affected by the multicollinearity concern.

Table 2. Descriptive statistics and correlations

Variables	M	SD	MEC	PDI	IDV	MAS	UAI	ITL	IDC	IDB
MEC	4.83	1.05	–							
PDI	63.13	21.55	−0.25*	–						
IDV	40.96	22.23	0.27*	−0.68**	–					
MAS	47.63	18.94	−0.13	0.11	0.05	–				
UAI	65.01	21.95	−0.14	0.17	−0.19	0.01	–			
ITL	4.21	0.86	0.59**	−0.45**	0.49**	−0.12	−0.06	–		
IDC	46.32	24.85	0.48**	−0.52**	0.65**	−0.03	0.08	0.73**	–	
IDB	4.76	0.68	0.59**	−0.51**	0.56**	−0.09	−0.12	0.89**	0.77**	–
IDG	0.65	0.20	0.39**	−0.42**	0.50**	−0.02	0.14	0.65**	0.73**	0.62**

Note. N = 90; M: Mean; SD: Standard deviation; MEC: Macroeconomic conditions; PDI: Power distance; IDV: Individualism; MAS: Masculinity; UAI: Uncertainty avoidance; ITL: ICT laws; IDC: ICT diffusion among citizens; IDB: ICT diffusion among businesses; IDG: ICT diffusion among government organizations; *$p < 0.05$ **$p < 0.001$ (2-tailed).

4.2 Hypotheses Testing

The research hypotheses were tested by jointly estimating a system of equations through the seemingly unrelated regression (SUR) approach [54]. We preferred SUR approach over ordinary least squares (OLS) regression to account for contemporaneous correlations. To elaborate, our research model had a system of multiple dependent variables. As they were correlated (see, Table 2), the error terms were likely to be correlated, which could lead to biased estimates if OLS regression were used. SUR models are able to accommodate such autocorrelation in the unobserved error terms, and tend to generate more efficient estimates than OLS [21].

Three SUR equations were formed with three dependent variables—ICT diffusion among citizens, ICT diffusion among businesses, and ICT diffusion among government organizations. These equations were jointly estimated in three steps: in Step 1, control variables were entered; in Step 2, main effects as described in hypotheses H1a–H1c were tested; and in Step 3, the interaction term was included to test the moderation effects as stated in hypotheses H2a–H2c.

Table 3. Seemingly unrelated regression results

Variables and statistics	B								
	Dependent variable: IDC			Dependent variable: IDB			Dependent variable: IDG		
Step 1: Controls									
MEC	7.623***	2.926	2.992	0.295***	0.059	0.060	0.053**	0.013	0.013
PDI	−0.128	−0.072	−0.064	−0.005	−0.002	−0.002	−0.001	−0.001	0.000
IDV	0.543***	0.436***	0.429***	0.010**	0.003	0.003	0.003**	0.002*	0.002*
MAS	−0.006	0.025	0.040	−0.001	0.001	0.001	0.001	0.000	0.001
Step 2: Main effects									
ITL		13.040***	25.385***		0.594***	0.643***		0.113***	0.260***
UAI		0.240**	1.116**		−0.001	0.003		0.002**	0.013***
Step 3: Interaction effects									
ITL* UAI			−0.204**			−0.001			−0.002**
R^2	0.528	0.693	0.714	0.542	0.833	0.834	0.333	0.525	0.569
R^2 Change	–	0.165	0.021	–	0.291	0.001	–	0.192	0.044

Note. N = 90; B: Unstandardized regression coefficients; MEC: Macroeconomic conditions; PDI: Power distance; IDV: Individualism; MAS: Masculinity; ITL: ICT laws; UAI: Uncertainty avoidance; IDC: ICT diffusion among citizens; IDB: ICT diffusion among businesses; IDG: ICT diffusion among government organizations; All models are significant at $p < 0.001$ (2-tailed); $^{*}p < 0.05$ $^{**}p < 0.01$ $^{***}p < 0.001$ (2-tailed).

Table 3 summarizes the results of the seemingly unrelated regression. The models were effective in explaining the variance in ICT diffusion among citizens (with $R^2 = 0.714$), among businesses (with $R^2 = 0.834$), and among government organizations (with $R^2 = 0.569$). As shown in Table 3 (Step 3), ICT laws were positively and significantly ($p < 0.001$) related to all three dependent variables, and hence, hypotheses H1a, H1b, and H1c were supported. It thus can be expected that sound ICT laws in a country will lead to a greater diffusion of ICTs among citizens, businesses, and the government within that country. Further, the interaction effects were negative and statistically significant ($p < 0.01$) for ICT diffusion among citizens and the government. Nevertheless, the joint influence was statistically insignificant for ICT diffusion among businesses ($p > 0.05$), implying that hypothesis H2b is not supported. In order to further understand the role of the moderator for hypotheses H2a and H2c for which the interaction effects were found significant, we plotted the interaction effects (see, Fig. 2), as suggested by Cohen and Cohen [55]. In addition, slope analysis was performed as recommended by Aiken and West [56]. The analysis showed that the strength of the relation "ICT laws—ICT diffusion among citizens" was less (slope = 7.67, t = 2.48, $p < 0.05$) in a strong uncertainty avoidance culture than that in a weak uncertainty avoidance culture (slope = 16.61, t = 208.78, $p < 0.001$), which is also apparent in Fig. 2(a). This implies that when uncertainty avoidance is strong, the effect of ICT laws on ICT diffusion among citizens is less than that in a weak uncertainty avoidance culture. Hence, hypothesis H2a is supported. For government organizations, the slope analysis revealed that in a strong uncertainty avoidance culture, the relation "ICT laws—ICT diffusion" was insignificant, and its slope value was less (slope = 0.05, t = 1.56, n.s.) than that (slope = 0.16, t = 195.18, $p < 0.001$) in a weak uncertainty avoidance culture.

This is also in line with Fig. 2(b), which implies that ICT laws may not necessarily lead to a greater diffusion of ICTs among government organizations in a strong uncertainty avoidance culture, whereas ICT laws could be more effective in a weak uncertainty avoidance culture. Hence, hypothesis H2c is supported. Amongst the control variables, only the cultural dimension of individualism was found to be significantly related to ICT diffusion among citizens ($p < 0.001$) and ICT diffusion among government organizations ($p < 0.05$), indicating that a country scoring high on individualism may experience a higher level of ICT diffusion. Other control variables such as macroeconomic environment, power distance, and masculinity were not significantly related to the dependent variables.

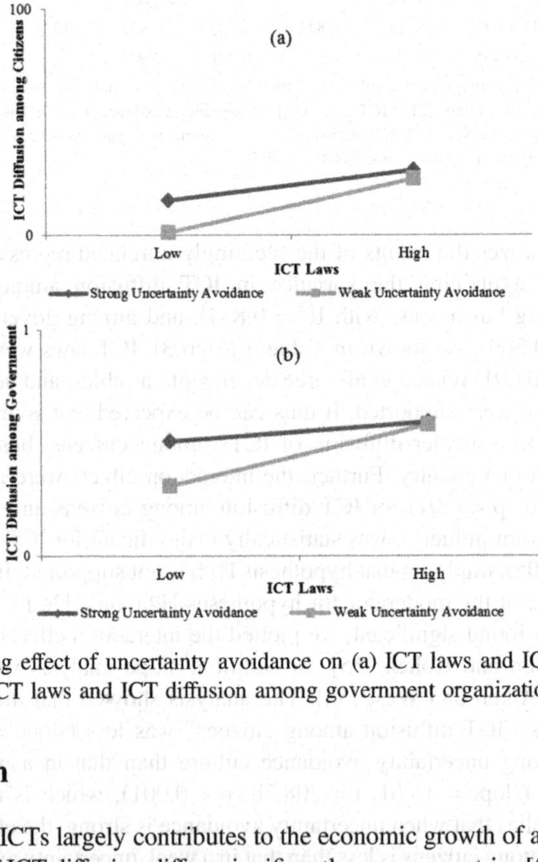

Fig. 2. Moderating effect of uncertainty avoidance on (a) ICT laws and ICT diffusion among citizens; and (b) ICT laws and ICT diffusion among government organizations.

5 Discussion

The diffusion of ICTs largely contributes to the economic growth of a country [11, 12], yet the degree of ICT diffusion differs significantly across countries [5, 13]. In an effort to understand the phenomenon of the cross-country variation in ICT diffusion, this study investigates the role of ICT laws and uncertainty avoidance in influencing ICT diffusion among three key stakeholders—citizens, businesses, and the government across countries. Analyzing archival data from 90 countries, we contend that ICT laws, if developed well in a country, may lead to a greater diffusion of ICTs among the stakeholders. Further, our findings suggest that the effect of ICT laws in a country on the ICT diffusion might be contingent on the cultural dimension of uncertainty avoidance. In a strong uncertainty avoidance culture, the effect of ICT laws on ICT diffusion among citizens and government organizations would be less than that in a weak uncertainty avoidance culture. However, for businesses, our analysis did not find statistically significant support for such influence of uncertainty avoidance culture, which could be due to the limitation in our cross-sectional dataset. Interestingly, the joint effect was in the desired direction (i.e., negative), thereby partly supporting our line of argument that the influence of ICT laws on ICT diffusion among businesses could be less in strong uncertainty avoidance culture than that in a weak uncertainty avoidance culture.

Our study offers several implications for research and practice. First, given the dearth of macro-level studies simultaneously examining technology diffusion among different stakeholders, this study is one of the first few studies that capture and jointly estimate ICT diffusion among three key stakeholders (i.e., citizens, businesses, and government) in a single model. Second, drawing on the literature on ICT diffusion, this study underscores the importance of an under-explored environmental factor, namely, technology-oriented legal framework characterized by ICT laws. The study thus extends the literature on technology diffusion by investigating the linkage between ICT laws and ICT diffusion across countries. Third, the current study also acknowledges the significance of national cultural values embedded in a country. Hence, this study examines the joint influence of ICT laws and uncertainty avoidance, and shows that the relation of ICT laws in a country with the technology diffusion becomes weaker for its citizens and the government in a strong uncertainty avoidance culture. Taken together, this study explores a potential relationship among technology-related legal framework, national culture, and technology diffusion across three stakeholders in a country, and we believe that our theoretically driven empirical research would be instrumental in encouraging future research on this phenomenon.

From a practical standpoint, the study indicates that ICT laws are useful for ICT diffusion among all three users. ICT laws may help define the legal structure and standards for gathering, sharing, and storing digital information [21], and could enable citizens, businesses, and the government to electronically communicate and transact with other parties by minimizing legal and regulatory issues [19]. For instance, Information Technology Act 2000 of India states that “Where any law provides that information or any other matter shall be in writing or in the typewritten or printed form, then, notwithstanding anything contained in such law, such requirement shall be deemed to have been satisfied if such information or matter is—(a) rendered or made available in an electronic form; and (b) accessible so as to be usable for a subsequent reference” [58]. It essentially provides legal recognition of electronic records that would encourage businesses to make contracts through electronic means, which would not only help electronic commerce in a country to thrive but also lead to a greater level of ICT diffusion in the country. Henceforth, it becomes crucial that a country invests in building sound ICT laws and regulations to facilitate its law enforcement that would further enable increased diffusion of ICTs among citizens, businesses, and governmental organizations. Second, the moderating effect of uncertainty avoidance culture would help practitioners understand its significance in explaining the differences in “ICT laws—ICT diffusion” relationship across countries. We suggest that policymakers in a country have to be mindful about the potential effect of the cultural value of uncertainty avoidance. A country not only needs to develop and reform ICT laws but also has to ensure that the laws benefit the users without creating further problems. Sometimes piecemeal law reform may lead to more problems than it solves [19]. Hence, it becomes important to decide upon the approach of developing ICT laws within the broader context of a country's ICT development and diffusion. Further, as sophisticated laws could be intricate, countries may consider educating and making ICT users aware of the effectiveness and application of ICT laws for creating an encouraging environment for ICT use.

The study has two key limitations. First, this study uses secondary data compiled from multiple third-party sources to undertake a large scale cross-country analysis. The use of secondary data was mainly motivated by the infeasibility of collecting primary data at the country-level. Nevertheless, as these reputable agencies use stringent guidelines for their data collection, the choice of secondary sources can be perceived as productive for conducting a large scale study. Second, data is used from countries that are common to all the primary sources, and countries such as, Algeria, North Korea, Oman and others became excluded from the sample. As a result, data from 90 countries were examined, which appears to be adequate considering that 50 is the minimum number necessary to avert the concerns over degrees of freedom and efficiency [57]. Future studies can focus on various directions. First, our findings can be limited by the cross-sectional nature of the study. Thus, future research may consider analyzing a panel data set to build more rigorous understanding of the phenomenon. Second, this study employs the cultural dimension of uncertainty avoidance to empirically examine its moderating effects on the relation of ICT laws with technology diffusion. Future study may investigate the moderating effects of other Hofstede's [27] cultural dimensions to have a holistic understanding of ICT diffusion based on the influence of environmental determinants and cultural values. Third, ICT laws may affect the ICT diffusion of countries differently depending on the basic economic conditions of the countries. Future research may categorize countries into developing and developed countries, and compare the effect of ICT laws on ICT diffusion.

6 Concluding Remarks

Despite the increased use of ICTs within and across countries, limited research is carried out to understand the role of the technology-related environmental factor in shaping the ICT diffusion across countries. This study, as an initial step towards building such understanding, underlines the importance of ICT laws in a country, and proposes a conceptual model, by drawing on the literature on ICT diffusion and Hofstede's national culture dimensions, to (1) investigate the impact of ICT laws in a country on ICT diffusion among the key stakeholders (citizens, business, and the government) within that country, and (2) examine the moderating effect of uncertainty avoidance on the relationships of ICT laws in a country with its ICT diffusion. The research model is empirically validated using publicly accessible archival data. The findings suggest that ICT laws in a country can increase the level of ICT diffusion among the stakeholders. Nevertheless, such relationship is dependent on the cultural value of uncertainty avoidance, specifically for citizens and the government in a country. We believe that the study brings a different perspective to the phenomenon of ICT diffusion by emphasizing ICT-related regulatory frameworks and would encourage future research in that direction.

References

1. Keller, W.: International technology diffusion. J. Econ. Literature **XLII**, 752–782 (2004)
2. Charoensukmongkol, P., Moqbel, M.: Does investment in ICT curb or create more corruption? A cross-country analysis. Public Organ. Rev. **14**(1), 51–63 (2012)
3. Bollou, F., Ngwenyama, O.: Are ICT investments paying off in Africa? An analysis of total factor productivity in six West African countries from 1995 to 2002. Inf. Technol. Dev. **14** (4), 294–307 (2008)
4. Kramer, W., Jenkins, B., Katz, R.: The Role of the Information and Communications Technology Sector in Expanding Economic Opportunity. Harvard University, Cambridge (2007)
5. Lee, S., Nam, Y., Lee, S., Son, H.: Determinants of ICT innovations: a cross-country empirical study. Technol. Forecast. Soc. Change **110**, 71–77 (2016)
6. Khan, A., Krishnan, S.: Conceptualizing the impact of corruption in national institutions and national stakeholder service systems on e-government maturity. Int. J. Inf. Manag. **46**, 23–36 (2019)
7. Xiao, X., Califf, C.B., Sarker, S., Sarker, S.: ICT innovation in emerging economies: a review of the existing literature and a framework for future research. J. Inf. Technol. **28**, 264–278 (2013)
8. GITR: The Global Information Technology Report. World Economic Forum (2016)
9. Srivastava, S., Teo, T.: E-government, e-business, and national economic performance. Commun. Assoc. Inf. Syst. **26**, 267–286 (2010)
10. Rogers, E.: Diffusion of Innovations, 3rd edn. Free Press, New York (1983)
11. Rogers, E.: Diffusion of Innovations, 4th edn. Free Press, New York (1995)
12. Rosenberg, N.: Factors affecting diffusion of technology. Explor. Econ. History **10**(1), 3–33 (1972)
13. Erumban, A.A., Jong, S.B.: Cross-country differences in ICT adoption: a consequence of culture? J. World Bus. **41**(4), 302–314 (2006)
14. Larosiliere, G.D., Carter, L.D., Meske, C.: How does the world connect? Exploring the global diffusion of social network sites. J. Assoc. Inf. Sci. Technol. **68**(8), 1875–1885 (2017)
15. Leidner, D., Kayworth, T.: A review of culture in information systems research: towards a theory of information technology culture conflict. MIS Q. **30**(2), 357–399 (2006)
16. Abukhzam, M., Lee, A.: Factors affecting bank staff attitude towards E-banking adoption in Libya. Electron. J. Inf. Syst. Dev. Countries **42**(2), 1–15 (2010)
17. Brown, D.H., Thompson, S.: Priorities, policies and practice of E-government in a developing country context: ICT infrastructure and diffusion in Jamaica. Eur. J. Inf. Syst. **20** (3), 329–342 (2011)
18. Qu, W., Pinsonneault, A.: Country environments and the adoption of IT outsourcing. J. Glob. Inf. Manag. **19**, 30–50 (2011)
19. UN-Report: Information and communication technology policy and legal issues for Central Asia. United Nations, New York and Geneva (2007)
20. Liang, H., Xue, Y.: Avoidance of information technology threats: a theoretical perspective. MIS Q. **33**(1), 71–90 (2009)

21. Bhattacherjee, A., Shrivastava, U.: The effects of ICT use and ICT Laws on corruption: a general deterrence theory perspective. Gov. Inf. Q. **35**(4), 703–712 (2018)
22. Straub, D.W.: The effect of culture on IT diffusion: E-mail and FAX in Japan and the U.S. Inf. Syst. Res. **5**(1), 23–47 (1994)
23. Maitland, C., Bauer, J.: National level culture and global diffusion: the case of the Internet. In: Ess, C. (ed.) Culture, Technology, Communication: Towards an Intercultural Global Village, pp. 87–128. State University of New York Press, Albany (2001)
24. Veiga, J.F., Floyd, S., Dechant, K.: Towards modeling the effects of national culture on IT implementation. J. Inf. Technol. **16**(3), 145–158 (2001)
25. Zhao, F.: Impact of national culture on e-government development: a global study. Internet Res. **21**(3), 362–380 (2011)
26. Hofstede, G.: Cultural Consequences: International Differences in Work-Related Values. Sage Publications, Beverly Hills (1980)
27. Hofstede, G.: Cultural dimensions in management and planning. Asia Pac. J. Manag. **1**, 81–99 (1984)
28. Attewell, P.: Technology diffusion and organizational learning: the case of business computing. Organ. Sci. **3**(1), 1–19 (1992)
29. Davis, F.: Perceived usefulness, perceived ease of use, and user acceptance of information technology. MIS Q. **13**, 319–340 (1989)
30. Ajzen, I.: The theory of planned behavior. Organ. Behav. Hum. Decis. Process. **50**(2), 179–211 (1991)
31. Venkatesh, V., Morris, M., Davis, G., Davis, F.: User acceptance of information technology: toward a unified view. MIS Q. **27**, 425–478 (2003)
32. Tornatzky, L., Fleischer, M.: The Process of Technology Innovation. Lexington Books, Lexington (1990)
33. DiMaggio, P.J., Powell, W.W.: The iron cage revisited: Institutional isomorphism and collective rationality in organizational fields. Am. Sociol. Rev. **48**, 147–160 (1983)
34. Teo, T.S., Ranganathan, C., Dhaliwal, J.: Key dimensions of inhibitors for the deployment of web-based business-to-business electronic commerce. IEEE Trans. Eng. Manag. **53**(3), 395–411 (2006)
35. Zhu, K., Kraemer, K.: Post-adoption variations in usage and value of e-business by organizations: cross-country evidence from the retail industry. Inf. Syst. Res. **16**, 61–84 (2005)
36. Krishnan, S., Lymm, J.: Determinants of virtual social networks diffusion: insights from cross-country data. Comput. Hum. Behav. **54**, 691–700 (2016)
37. Kuan, K., Chau, P.: A perception based model for EDI adoption in small business using a technology-organization-environment framework. Inf. Manag. **38**, 507–512 (2001)
38. Wolf, M., Beck, R., König, K.: Environmental dynamics as driver of on-demand computing infrastructures—empirical insights from the financial services industry in UK. In: Proceedings of the European Conference on Information Systems (ECIS), article 242, Barcelona, Spain (2012)
39. Boyer-Wright, K., Kottemann, J.: High-level factors affecting global availability of online government services. In: Proceedings of the 41st Hawaii International Conference on System Sciences, pp. 199–205. IEEE, Waikoloa (2008)
40. Sørnes, J.-O., Stephens, K.K., Sætre, A.S., Browning, L.D.: The reflexivity between ICTs and business culture: applying Hofstede's theory to compare Norway and the United States. Informing Sci. J. **7**, 1–30 (2004)
41. Myers, M., Tan, F.: Beyond models of national culture in information systems research. J. Glob. Inf. Manag. **10**(1), 24–32 (2002)

42. Srite, M., Karahanna, E.: The role of espoused national cultural values in technology acceptance. MIS Q. **30**(3), 679–704 (2006)
43. Dotan, A., Zaphiris, P.: A cross-cultural analysis of Flickr users from Peru, Israel, Iran, Taiwan and the United Kingdom. Int. J. Web Based Communities **6**(3), 284–302 (2010)
44. Hofstede, G.: Cultures and Organizations: Software of the Mind. McGraw-Hill, New York (1991)
45. Hofstede, G.: Culture's Consequences: Comparing Values, Behaviors, Institutions, and Organizations Across Nations. Sage Publications, Thousand Oaks (2001)
46. Hofstede, G., Hofstede, G., Minkov, M.: Cultures and Organizations: Software of the Mind. McGraw-Hill, New York (2010)
47. Jarvenpaa, S.: Panning for gold in information systems research: 'Second-hand' data. In: Nissen, H.E., Klein, H.K., Hirschheim, R. (eds.) Information Systems Research: Contemporary Approaches and Emergent Traditions, IFIP TC/WG 8.2, pp. 63–80. Alfred Waller Ltd., North Holland (1991)
48. ITU: Measuring the Information Society. International Telecommunication Union (2016)
49. UN-Report: United Nations E-Government Survey Report 2016. United Nations, New York (2016)
50. GITR: The Global Information Technology Report. World Economic Forum (2015)
51. GCR: The Global Competitiveness Report. World Economic Forum (2015)
52. Gujarati, D., Porter, D.: Basic Econometrics. McGraw-Hill, New York (2009)
53. Fox, J.: Regression Diagnostics. Sage Publications, Newbury Park (1991)
54. Greene, W.: Econometric Analysis, 7th edn. Pearson, Boston (2012)
55. Cohen, J., Cohen, P.: Applied Multiple Regression/Correlation Analysis for the Behavioral Sciences. Lawrence Erlbaum, Hillsdale (1983)
56. Aiken, L., West, S.: Multiple Regression: Testing and Interpreting Interactions. Sage Publications, Thousand Oaks (1991)
57. Hair, J.F., Anderson, R.E., Tatham, R.L., Black, W.C.: Multivariate Data Analysis with Readings. Prentice Hall, Englewood Cliffs (2006)
58. Ministry of Electronics and Information Technology, Government of India. https://meity.gov.in/content/information-technology-act-2000-0. Accessed 26 Mar 2019
59. Kapoor, K.K., Dwivedi, Y.K., Williams, M.D.: Rogers' innovation adoption attributes: a systematic review and synthesis of existing research. Inf. Syst. Manag. **31**(1), 74–91 (2014)
60. Kapoor, K.K., Dwivedi, Y.K., Williams, M.D.: Innovation adoption attributes: a review and synthesis of research findings. Eur. J. Innov. Manag. **17**(3), 327–348 (2014)
61. Dwivedi, Y.K., Rana, N.P., Janssen, M., Lal, B., Williams, M.D., Clement, M.: An empirical validation of a unified model of electronic government adoption (UMEGA). Gov. Inf. Q. **34** (2), 211–230 (2017)
62. Dwivedi, Y.K., Rana, N.P., Jeyaraj, A., Clement, M., Williams, M.D.: Re-examining the unified theory of acceptance and use of technology (UTAUT): towards a revised theoretical model. Inf. Syst. Front. 1–16 (2017). https://doi.org/10.1007/s10796-017-9774-y
63. Williams, M.D., Rana, N.P., Dwivedi, Y.K.: The unified theory of acceptance and use of technology (UTAUT): a literature review. J. Enterprise Inf. Manag. **28**(3), 443–488 (2015)
64. Dwivedi, Y.K., Wade, M.R., Schneberger, S.L. (eds.): Information Systems Theory: Explaining and Predicting Our Digital Society, vol. 1. Springer, Heidelberg (2011). https://doi.org/10.1007/978-1-4419-6108-2
65. Weerakkody, V., Dwivedi, Y.K., Irani, Z.: The diffusion and use of institutional theory: a cross-disciplinary longitudinal literature survey. J. Inf. Technol. **24**(4), 354–368 (2009)

Internet-Based Channel Orientation for Domesticated Services Firm: Some Drivers and Consequences

Michael Adu Kwarteng[1(✉)], Abdul Bashiru Jibril[1], Fortune Nwaiwu[1], Michal Pilik[1], and Maged Ali[2]

[1] Faculty of Management and Economics, Tomas Bata University in Zlin, Mostni 5139, 760 01 Zlin, Czech Republic
{kwarteng,jibril,nwaiwu,pilik}@utb.cz

[2] Essex Business School, EBS.3.84 Colchester Campus, Colchester, UK
maaali@essex.ac.uk

Abstract. Undeniably, several studies have reported on both antecedents and the consequents of infusing internet-based channel orientation into the operations of small or micro domesticated firms. However, in the developing and to be precise the African context, such studies are somewhat scant. To address this yearlong theoretical and practical gap, this study takes inspirations from the theoretical underpinnings of both micro-institutional view of the firm as well as resource strategic action. Henceforth, this study supplements the existing internet orientation literature and adds to the on-going debate why internet channel orientation stands as the focal point and engine of survival in small and midsized enterprises. In light of this, this study proposes that entrepreneurial capability of the firm and industry competition predict Internet-based channel orientation (IORIENT) of the firm. Furthermore, the study tests the assumption that the utilisation IORIENT not only potentially contributes to greater market-sensing capability but that it can also indirectly lead to firm competitiveness. Survey data from 198 firms offer initial support for the research propositions. Overall, the research study encourages firms not to only invest in Internet marketing tools but also to effectively use these tools as this is critical to their long-term competitiveness.

Keywords: Internet orientation · Firm's competitiveness · Domesticated service firms · Drivers · Consequences

1 Introduction

Since the late 1990s, there has been extensive research on the implications of Internet technologies to the firm [6, 10, 12, 18, 20, 30, 36]. While most of this research has improved our collective understanding of the criticality of the Internet to organizational well-being, there is still a lot that we do not know about how the use of the Internet as a strategic resource can effectively translate into competitive gains for the domesticated small and midsized services firm. For example, many academics and practitioners alike are still grappling with the big question on how firm orientation toward the Internet, or

Published by Springer Nature Switzerland AG 2019
Y. Dwivedi et al. (Eds.): TDIT 2019, IFIP AICT 558, pp. 90–103, 2019.
https://doi.org/10.1007/978-3-030-20671-0_7

more technically Internet-based channel orientation (IORIENT hereafter), intersects with competitiveness of the firm. It is frequently mentioned in the journalistic, as well as academic, press that the mere adoption of (and/or investments in) Internet technologies can lead to greater firm competitiveness, this invitation paper, however, takes a sophisticated view of the relationship between IORIENT and firm competitiveness by arguing that it is (absolutely) not straightforward. The thinking behind the argument is that since IORIENT is a lower-order strategic resource, its effect on firm outcomes particularly the construct competitiveness will be most likely mediated by a higher-order strategic resource of the firm which we refer here to as 'market sensing capability' [10, 16, 52]. Besides, some studies have revealed that orientations such as IORIENT and/or digital technologies use are incapable of directly improving firm competitiveness) [5, 13, 23, 26]. While the above argument makes sense, it remains to be explicitly investigated.

Besides, empirical information on the influential predictors of IORIENT in the firm particularly in the domesticated small to midsize services firm is barely available in the literature. Although scant but growing body of work argues that the construct entrepreneurial capability (ENCAP) plays an important role for Internet capabilities, with a particular focus on marketing functions particularly relating to marketing functions [8, 16, 34]; past research studies, such as the research of Mostafa et al. [34], have called upon investigators to explicitly investigate the commonly overlooked link between ENCAP and commitment toward the use of Internet for performing marketing related tasks (i.e., ORIENT). This invitation paper heeds to the call. At the same time, a growing body of research [2] writes that micro-institutional factors (including the degree of industry competition) dictate that firms leverage IORIENT as a means for them to remain relevant in this era of increasing digitalisation. As such, it is important to understand whether extraneous factors, such as the degree of industry competition (hereafter: INDCOM), incentivize the small to midsize services firm to develop greater IORIENT.

Indeed, a new analysis presented a detailed analysis of the contribution of competitive pressures on the Mexican firm's ability to take advantage of Internet-based tools [24] whether the finding extends to the domesticated small and midsized services firm as well as countries outside Mexico is not known yet. As such, it is important to understand whether extraneous factors, such as the degree of industry competition (hereafter: INDCOM), incentivize the small to midsize services firm to develop greater IORIENT It is against the background that this study is cast in the resource - strategic action - competitive advantage framework [29] combined with the micro-institutional view of the firm to identify the process through which IORIENT potentially leads to greater firm competitiveness. Similarly, this framework is relied upon to explicitly assess the relationship between the themes of IORIENT, INDCOMP, and ENCAP; arguing that the latter two are strong predictors of the former (i.e. IORIENT). In integrating these two lenses, we believe this study shines a bright light on the antecedent and consequent factors of IORIENT. As such, our contributions to knowledge in this area should be seen in this light. Overall, the intended purpose has been to stimulate new academic thinking in this area. To recap, while there are no shortages of ideas on how the domesticated small to midsize service firms can gain competitiveness in today's extremely challenging business environment, our focus here is majorly understanding the process through which IORIENT potentially influences firm competitiveness. The initial findings of this research could also be interesting to owner-managers of the domesticated (small to midsize) organization who are deeply concerned about finding more practical and/or sustainable paths to their organizational competitiveness.

The rest of the paper is outlined as follows; theoretical underpinnings (background) of the study is elaborated, conceptual development and subsequent hypotheses are provided, Data collection procedure and sample overview follows suit, finally discussions and recommendations as well as limitations of the study are given.

2 Theoretical Background

This study is cast in the resource- strategic action- competitive advantage framework combined with the micro-institutional view of the firm [29]. To understand competitiveness inherent in the domesticated services firms under the perspective of Internet-based channel orientation (Herein refer as ORIENT), as earlier stipulated we review two streams of research. The resource- strategic action- competitive advantage framework attest to the fact that most decisions of the firms are embedded in the internal strategies geared towards practical and prolific attributes initiated by the firm. Again, this theory is seen as one of the most influential theories used by researchers to model continuance existence of micro enterprises [43]. Whiles micro-institutional view of the domesticated firm pinpoints on the radical innovations bedeviling the implementation of innovations that will broaden and compete in sustenance within the business front [38, 49]. Hence the presence study lay it grounds on combined theory of resource- strategic action- competitive advantage and micro-institutional view of firm to obtain a deeper insight for the aforementioned theme. Again, these attributes intend enhance the enactment of smooth operations of the firm in question [4]. Hence, the multiple actions taken by organisations surfaces a positive outcome at the longer run in terms of competition, sustainability among others for the small-midsized firms. As earlier on mentioned, this study is poached and serves as one of the fundamental basis for this study.

The basic argument of the strategic action theory is that micro enterprises in their bid to sustain in the business front does not entirely Centre on their internal activities, but also of competitive and the environmental factors. Reflecting on the works of Aragón-Correae et al. [3] the underlying premise for the survival of midsized or micro enterprises are regulated by the quantum of the competitive nature of the business, and by the environment through external forces. Tilley [48] opines that for efficiency and effectiveness of the micro enterprises, there should be an innate collaboration of both internal resources and the skills. With this in mind, Russo and Fouts [44] went ahead to cite the example of Michael Porter's analysis of industry organogram and the competitive nature in terms of positioning. Alternatively, the rational of the micro institutional perspective of the firm here elaborates on the cohesion of different strategic thought to curb these so crises at the shorter to longer run of domesticated firms.

3 Conceptual Development and Hypotheses

Figure 1 depicts the constructs Entrepreneurial capability (ENCAP) and industry competitiveness (INDCOMP) as independent variable predicting internet based channel orientation (ORIENT) as dependent whiles Marketing sensing capability (MKTSENSE) is dependent on internet based channel orientation yet predicting competitive advantage. This competitive advantage is however controlled by training and investments. Even though marketing sensing capability mediates competitive advantage and internet based channel orientation.

3.1 Entrepreneurial Capability (ENCAP) and Internet-Based Channel Orientation IORIENT

In relations to the entrepreneurial capability of the firm, Muthee and Ngugi [35] in their study on the influence of entrepreneurial marketing on growth of SMEs in Kenya, they make a case to link the competitiveness of SMEs and their continued survival to entrepreneurial marketing strategies. They find that a lack of entrepreneurial marketing strategies anchored on innovation and technologies such as e-CRM and internet based technologies could significantly constrain the competitiveness of SMEs. Their findings are supported by a similar study that investigated the impact of e-CRM in SMEs conducted by Harrigan et al. [19] in Northern Ireland, they find that the use of internet technologies can significantly improve customer relationships with SMEs and also help them in expanding into new markets by reducing barriers to entry, this is significant because they do not have sufficient financial resources to enter new markets through traditional marketing means. Hence, it is evident that the effective deployment of internet-based channels has become an effective equaliser for SMEs. Zeng and Glaister [51] adopt a "firm specific advantages" (FSAs) perspective in entrepreneurial capabilities of the firm and the benefits derivable from internet based channels. They argue that for companies that adopt an internet only channel such as internet platform companies (IPCs), they are able to achieve sustainable competitive advantage because they are able to achieve levels of flexibility and experimentation that are uncommon with other companies who go through the traditional route in engaging clients. Based on evidence above; there is sufficient ground to propose the hypothesis that:

***H1a**: Holding other factors constant, ENCAP positively predicts IORIENT.*

3.2 Industry Competitiveness (INDCOMP) and Internet-Based Channel Orientation (IORIENT)

While in terms of industry competitiveness, Chaston and Mangles [11] argue that technology especially when deployed strategically through internet marketing especially internet based channels, offer an effective pathway for both small and large firms to enhance their existing, and transactional marketing strategies. This can also be viewed from the perspective of transactional marketing orientation which is linked to the firm's operating expenses (OPEX). This view is supported by Anandarajan et al. [1], in their study, they observed that firms exhibited a transactional marketing orientation through their commitment to using technology in achieving cost reduction across all aspects of their firm's transaction processes, from initial inquiry through to post-purchase product usage and support. Their study identified a number of opportunities for achieving operational cost reductions when using the internet to manage business-to-business (B2B) supply chains. For impact on customer relationships, it is important to understand how internet based channel orientation can be beneficial to a domesticated small business operator in its quest to create new customers or retain already existing customers. Communication is the primary utility provided by the internet and other information and communications technologies (ICTs), while communication is at the very heart of marketing for big business organisations and SMEs [11, 32]. Harrigan et al. [20] agree with the important role of communication in improving SME competitiveness, they argue that SMEs relationships with customers offers them a major competitive advantage over larger competitors, especially technologies such as e-CRM offer significant opportunities to improve such relationships. Based on evidence above, there is sufficient ground to propose the hypothesis that:

***H1b**: Holding other factors constant, managerial perceptions regarding INDCOMP positively predict IORIENT.*

3.3 Internet-Based Channel Orientation (IORIENT) and Market Sensing Capabilities (MKTSENSE)

To understand how internet based channel orientation impacts the entrepreneurial capabilities of SMEs especially from the perspective of industry competitiveness and market sensing capabilities, it is imperative to adopt an approach that investigates internet marketing by examining its impacts through considerations of impact assessment viewed from a multidimensional approach that covers areas of SME performance in terms of impact on customer relationships, financial performance (profit and loss, balance sheet), impact on operating expenditures (OPEX), and brand equity. Hence, competitive advantage is very important for every SME because it is a guarantor of sustainable growth. The entrepreneurial capability of the firm is anchored on its competitive advantage, which emanates from innate SME communication activities such as interacting and participating in social, business and trade activities which altogether form a veritable source of market intelligence upon which SME business strategy can be anchored [37, 45, 50].

Hence, the customer relationship management (CRM) component of its internet marketing activities should have as its primary objective, to shape the customers' perceptions of the firm through a process that identifies its customer segment, create customer knowledge, and build committed customer relationships [42]. Also, they acknowledge the importance of CRM as an integral component of a firm's business strategy because of its usefulness in managing and optimising all customer interactions across the firm's traditional and internet based channels. Hence, the following hypothesis is proposed:

H2: Holding other factors constant, IORIENT positively predicts MKSENSE.

3.4 Internet-Based Channel Orientation (IORIENT), Market Sensing Capabilities (MKTSENSE) and Competitive Advantage (COMPADV)

Porter [39] argued that "many of the companies that succeed will be ones that use the Internet as a complement to traditional ways of competing, not those that set their Internet initiatives apart from their established operations." Several authors have acknowledged in general that "internet technology provides better opportunities for companies to establish distinctive strategic positioning than did previous generations of information technology" [39]. Leeflang et al. [28, 32, 33] agree with this view, they argue that as usage of the Internet continues to explode across the world, digital based channels are becoming an increasingly important source of competitive advantage in both Business 2 Consumer (B2C) and Business 2 Business (B2B), they cite different examples of companies that have recorded significant successes by effectively deploying internet based channels as a means of boosting their competitive positions in the market.

Nevertheless, they also point out some of the challenges faced by companies in effectively harnessing internet based channels with regards to their market sensing capabilities, some of these challenges are: the inability to generate and leverage deep customer insights, managing brand reputation in a marketing environment prone to excessive influence of social media, and how to measure the effectiveness of digital marketing efforts [32]. As Porter [39] argues, internet technology is an enabling technology—a powerful set of tools that can be used, wisely or unwisely, in almost any industry and as part of almost any strategy. Hence, this makes it imperative to investigate further by proposing the hypothesis below as it would further illuminate the relationship between internet based channel orientation and competitive advantage by controlling for factors such as investments in training and market sensing capabilities of the firm.

H3 Controlling for investments in training, MKTSENSE positively mediates the relationship between IORIENT and COMPADV.

This explorative study is guided by the conceptual framework seen in Fig. 1 below:

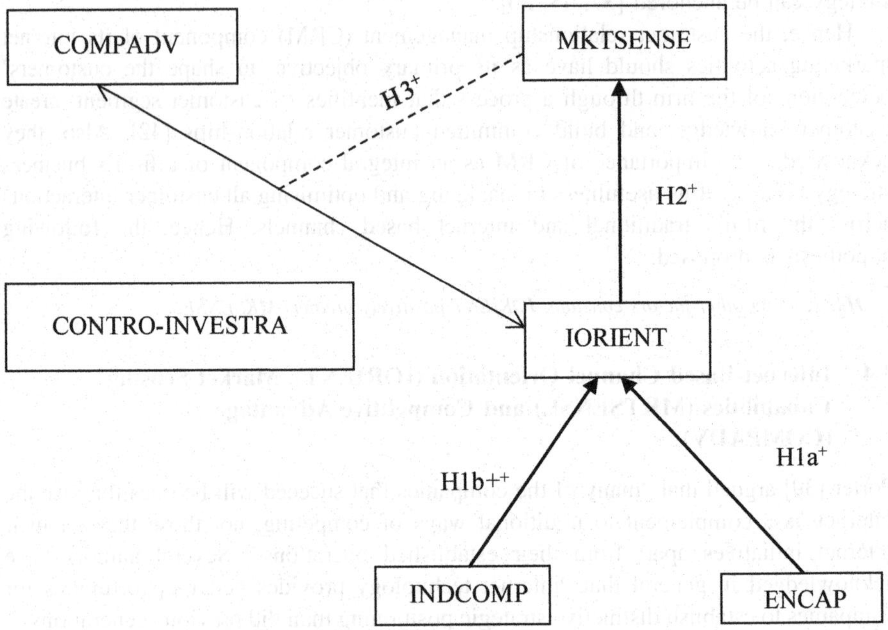

Fig. 1. The conceptual model and hypotheses

4 Data Collection Procedure and Sample Overview

This study uses self-reported surveys. Survey method was adhered to because it is suitably relied upon as one of the approaches used in the social sciences to empirically study variables or units under investigations [52]. We should note that the instrument and sample data used in the current analysis came from a recent faculty-sponsored research project that mainly targeted the domesticated firms in Nigeria, typically micro, small and medium-sized firms. However, in this study, the focus is on boutique financial services firms, mainly insurance brokers (micro finance banks). In the end, out of 221 completed responses, 198 were found to be eligible and then used in the analysis. Demographically, all the firms employ between 10 and 49 employees. Most (i.e., about 83%) of the respondents were male executives. Geographically, all the participating firms are located in southern Nigeria. Finally, about 51% of the firms reported that they invest, at least on a yearly basis, in the human capital development of their people assets.

4.1 Statistical Technique

In terms of the statistical method, this study relied exclusively on PLS-SEM (for an overview of the benefits of this technique in performing organisation study [17]. All the statistical computations have been (effortlessly) aided by ADANCO 2.0 [21] and the IBM SPSS Statistics software.

4.2 Measures

Apart from the new scale on IORIENT, this study makes use of existing scales. Specifically, COMPADV is operationalized using a two-item scale borrowed from the initial work of Hinson et al. [41]. The scale for managerial perceptions of INDCOMP is well-established in the literature [26, 46], INDCOMP was measured using a three-item scale adapted from Jaworski and Kohli [26]. Similarly, the five-item measure for ENCAP was extensively borrowed from the work of Laukkanen et al. [31]. Finally, the two-items measuring MKSENSE were from a recent study Fang et al. [14]. All the scales were measured on a five-point scale, ranging from strongly disagree to strongly agree.

4.3 Hypotheses Testing

With a quick preview of the path coefficients on the constructs Industry competitiveness linked with Internet –based channel orientation seems to have the strongest (direct) effect to enhance smooth operations of small and midsized firms ($\beta = 0.529$, $p \leq 0.001$), followed by Market- sensing capabilities ($\beta = 0.512$, $p \leq 0.001$) and with Entrepreneurial capability recording a weak but significant effect of ORIENT ($\beta = 0.201$, $p \leq 0.001$). In our case of showing the significant relationships of our constructs, we test the indirect effect of our construct indicating that ORIENT and COMPADV are mediated to and contends that is insufficient to achieve strong gains in firm competitiveness but rather this effect is indirectly anchored via MKTSENSE ($\beta = 0.326$, $p \leq 0.001$). Based on the analysis retrieved from Table 2, we can affirm that all our hypothetical relationships are statistically significant. Hence, all our four (4) hypothesis are supported.

Again, TRAINIV correlated significantly with COMPADV ($\beta = 0.322$, $t = 5.100$, $p \leq 0.001$) which offers support for H3. Whiles IORIENT and COMPADV are indirectly mediated with MKTSENSE ($\beta = 0.162$, $t = 3.517$, $p \leq 0.001$) even though the relationship is moderately weak.

4.4 Construct Reliability and Validity

In line with recent recommendations in the PLS-SEM literature, the constructs' reliabilities were checked using Dijkstra-Henseler's rho along with Cronbach's alpha coefficients. As shown in Table 1, all the values exceeded the cut-off values of 0.7. At the same time, the loadings of the reflective constructs were all ≥0.89. Concerning convergent validity, as shown in Table 1, AVEs exceeded the minimum threshold of 0.5. Regarding discriminant validity, apart from using the well-known Fornell-Lacker's (1981) criterion; this study also uses the recently introduced Heterotrait-monotrait (HTMT) criterion by Henseler et al. [22]. Results from the two criteria indicated that constructs satisfy both basic and stringent assumptions of discriminant validity. More specifically, using the HTMT inferential statistics it produced 0.89 for MSENSE and INDCOMP (output not presented here but it is available on request). Taken together, our constructs not only display good internal consistency, but they also have higher reliabilities; convergent and discriminant validity are equally supported (see Table 1).

Table 1. Construct reliability and convergent validity

Construct		Indicator reliability	Dijkstra-Henseler's rho (ρA)	Cronbach's alpha(α)	AVE
ENCAP			0.97	0.97	0.89
	Encap1	0.87[68.99]			
	Encap2	0.93[134.63]			
	Encap3	0.87[46.77]			
	Encap4	0.90[86.24]			
	Encap5	0.89[83.90]			
IORIENT			0.94	0.93	0.88
	Iorient1	0.81[37.11]			
	Iorient2	0.94[188.69]			
	Iorient3	0.87[62.96]			
MKSENSE			0.97	0.97	0.95
	Mksense1	0.96[71.35]			
	Mksense2	0.93[55.81]			
COMPADV			0.90	0.90	0.91
	Compadv1				
	Compadv2				
INDCOMP					
	Indcomp1	0.82[70.33]	0.89	0.88	0.81
	Indcomp2	0.79[38.47]			
	Indcomp3	0.80[43.69]			

Note: [] indicates t-values of loadings; n = 198 with 1000 bootstrap attempts
indicator reliability is loadings2
sources: Authors computation from ADANCO

Table 2. Correlation among constructs

Construct	MKSENSE	IORIENT	COMPADV	INDCOMP	ENCAP	TRAININ
MKSENSE	*0.95*					
IORIENT	0.26	*0.88*				
COMPADV	0.17	0.45	*0.91*			
INDCOMP	0.59	0.40	0.28	*0.81*		
ENCAP	0.27	0.22	0.15	0.27	*0.89*	
TRAININ	0.01	0.12	0.18	0.13	0.23	1.00

Note: Squared correlations; AVE in the diagonal [in bold and italicized font]
TRAININ (Investment in training is operationalized here as a binary response)
sources: Authors' computation from ADANCO

5 General Discussions

In this study, we have demonstrated and empirically tested a model of Internet-based channel orientation (IORIENT hereafter) as a touchstone of proffering a strategically position of small and midsized firms. This study was spearheaded by knowledge acquisition attributed to market sensing capabilities, competitive advantage of the firm, entrepreneurial capabilities as well as the industry competitive phenomenon. We argued that both entrepreneurial capability of the firm and industry competition envisage Internet-based channel orientation (IORENT) of the firm, yet the effect of IORIENT in the long run do not only enhance a greater market-sensing capability but can ultimately aid in a firms' competitiveness.

As a matter of fact, recent research works corroborates the assertion of IORIENT in creating an enabling environment for competitive advantages, given the current technological and digital world firms find themselves nowadays [40, 47]. In this circumstances, the onus of the matter lies in the ability of the firms to position itself with the ever changing technological dispensation. Our findings however show the more or the magnitude of in which SMEs integrates IORIENT, the greater the propensity to lure more customers into their fold and hence surpasses the enormous competition to sustain in the wider business front. This assertion is consistent with the works of [7, 10, 18, 34] which concluded that the milieu of effective competition is hinged on implementation of internet based orientation.

This study harnesses the entrepreneurial capability with the internet based circumstances governing small and midsized companies, in the wake of taking off from downstream businesses like the earlier instigated, it becomes prudent for such companies to adopt and blend these two scenarios into their fold. On this note, our findings uphold this affirmation with statistically significant measures or hypothesis. Moreover, as the core mandate of every business, thus being micro or small size company to survive in this competitive business front, it is expedient to take a careful look at how this situation could be achieved since it becomes the engine of survival in the business front. Hence, our finding indicates that there is a positive relationships emanating from these two streams, thus from both industry competitiveness and the internet based channel orientation. This finding affirms that of Jones et al. [27] who argued from that same angle, as well as Foley and Fahy [15] who opined that the interrelationships between the business and its counterparts coexist and fused together to ensure sustainability. Hence, the for businesses like small and midsized to adopt internet based orientation at the initial stages of its operations, it should consider the environment in which they are bent on operating, that is to say the kind of customers they are in to deal with.

In all these significant contributions, our findings initiates and proposes that, the managerial suggestion of the small and midsized governing the competitivity and sustainability hinges on the tendency to realize and measure the training and development of the firm. This in effect will serve as a cornerstone for blending both internet based channel orientation to outwit the competitive nature that awaits the firm in the shorter to longer run. In this scenario, our findings confirmed that indeed there is a significant relationship between those two earlier on mentioned constructs with the focus of training and development being the interception.

6 Conclusion

This research drew inferences from both resource- strategic action-competitive advantage and micro-institutional theory with the aim of testing the antecedence of how entrepreneurial capability of the firm and industry competition predict Internet-based channel orientation (IORIENT of the firm. Our research constructs elucidate how internet based channel orientation and entrepreneurial capability mediate the influence of competitiveness of the domesticated small sized firms. Analyses grounded on 198 SMEs from a domesticated enterprise in Africa's' biggest economy (Nigeria) corroborated with constructs relationships elicited for the research.

This study attempts to fill the yearlong theoretical and empirical gap governing small and midsized firms in the developing economies. As the internet has come to stay, and companies are incorporating it into their businesses with the aim of multiple reasons, such as creating customer loyalty, reaching out to customers etc. This study thus provides an empirical insight on firms (financial firms), specifically small and midsized firms on how best they can sustain in the business. Unlike any other research and consistent with the fact that this is one of the first study in the African sub region and in particular the Nigerian context, this study is not immune to limitations. While there are multiple reasons that can be outlined in the limitations. It is expedient and reasonable to outline some of the set-back and limitations of the research that stands out.

First, the findings of the study cannot be generalised around the length and breadth of the entire African sub region. As we can appreciate, the study was centred on a particular segment even within the Nigerian context. We therefore encourage researchers stimulate a wake-up call for researchers in the academia and the industry to look at other part or segment of the African sub regions or the developing countries as a whole. Secondly, the data used for our study was entirely cross-sectional and hence looked at the relationships between the enumerated variables. This in its simplest understanding calls for future research on embarking on longitudinal research so as to test for the causality of the variables.

Acknowledgement. This work was supported by the Internal Grant Agency of FaME through TBU in Zlín No. IGA/FaME/2019/008; Project title: *Country-of-origin effect on domestic product (brand) purchasing intention and SME's sustainability in developing countries.* Also by the financial support of research project NPU I no. MSMT-7778/2018 RVO - Digital Transformation and its Impact on Customer Behaviour and Business Processes in Traditional and Online markets.

References

1. Anandarajan, M., Anandarajan, A., Wen, H.J.: Extranets: a tool for cost control in a value chain framework. Ind. Manag. Data Syst. **98**(3), 120–128 (1998)
2. Aragon-Correa, J., Cordón-Pozo, E.: The influence of strategic dimensions and the environment on the introduction of internet as innovation into small and medium-sized enterprises. Technol. Anal. Strategic Manag. **17**(2), 205–218 (2005)
3. Aragón-Correa, J.A., Hurtado-Torres, N., Sharma, S., García-Morales, V.J.: Environmental strategy and performance in small firms: a resource-based perspective. J. Environ. Manag. **86** (1), 88–103 (2008)
4. Armstrong, G., Adam, S., Denize, S., Kotler, P.: Principles of Marketing. Pearson Australia (2014)
5. Auger, P., BarNir, A., Gallaugher, J.M.: Strategic orientation, competition, and internet-based electronic commerce. Inf. Technol. Manag. **4**(2–3), 139–164 (2003)
6. Avlonitis, G.J., Karayanni, D.A.: The impact of internet use on business-to-business marketing: examples from American and European companies. Ind. Market. Manag. **29**(5), 441–459 (2000)
7. Becherer, R.C., Halstead, D., Haynes, P.J.: Marketing orientation in SMEs: effects of the internet environment. N. Engl. J. Entrepreneurship **6**(1), 13 (2003)
8. Bengtsson, M., Boter, H., Vanyushyn, V.: Integrating the internet and marketing operations a study of antecedents in firms of different size. Int. Small Bus. J. **25**(1), 27–48 (2007)
9. Glavas, C., Mathews, S.: How international entrepreneurship characteristics influence Internet capabilities for the international business processes of the firm. Int. Bus. Rev. **23**(1), 228–245 (2014)
10. Celuch, K., Murphy, G.: SME Internet use and strategic flexibility: the moderating effect of IT market orientation. J. Market. Manag. **26**(1–2), 131–145 (2010)
11. Chaston, I., Mangles, T.: Relationship marketing in online business-to-business markets: a pilot investigation of small UK manufacturing firms. Eur. J. Market. **37**(56), 753–773 (2003)
12. Sigalas, C., Pekka Economou, V., Georgopoulos, N.B.: Developing a measure of competitive advantage. J. Strategy Manag. **6**(4), 320–342 (2013)
13. Doherty, E., Ramsey, E., Harrigan, P., Ibbotson, P.: Impact of broadband internet technologies on business performance of Irish SMEs. Strategic Change **25**(6), 693–716 (2016)
14. Fang, S.-R., Chang, E., Ou, C.-C., Chou, C.-H.: Internal market orientation, market capabilities and learning orientation. Eur. J. Market. **48**(1/2), 170–192 (2014)
15. Foley, A., Fahy, J.: Towards a further understanding of the development of market orientation in the firm: a conceptual framework based on the market-sensing capability. J. Strateg. Market. **12**(4), 219–230 (2004)
16. Ghasemaghaei, M., Hassanein, K., Turel, O.: Increasing firm agility through the use of data analytics: the role of fit. Decis. Support Syst. **101**, 95–105 (2017)

17. Hair, F.J., Sarstedt, M., Hopkins, L., Kuppelwieser, V.G.: Partial least squares structural equation modeling (PLS-SEM) an emerging tool in business research. Eur. Bus. Rev. **26**(2), 106–121 (2014)
18. Hamill, J., Gregory, K.: Internet marketing in the internationalisation of UK SMEs. J. Market. Manag. **13**(1–3), 9–28 (1997)
19. Harrigan, P., Ramsey, E., Ibbotson, P.: e-CRM in SMEs: an exploratory study in Northern Ireland. Market. Intell. Plan. **26**(4), 385–404 (2008). https://doi.org/10.1108/02634500810879296
20. Harrigan, P., Ramsey, E., Ibbotson, P.: Entrepreneurial marketing in SMEs: the key capabilities of e-CRM. J. Res. Market. Entrepreneurship **14**(1), 40–64 (2012). https://doi.org/10.1108/14715201211246760
21. Henseler, J., Dijkstra, T.K.: ADANCO 2.0. Kleve: Composite Modeling (2015)
22. Henseler, J., Ringle, C.M., Sarstedt, M.: A new criterion for assessing discriminant validity in variance-based structural equation modelling. J. Acad. Market. Sci. **43**(1), 115–135 (2015)
23. http://www.compositemodeling.com
24. Iacovone, L., Pereira-Lopez, M.D.L.P., Schiffbauer, M.P.: ICT use, competitive pressures and firm performance in Mexico. In: Policy Research Working Paper; no. WPS 7629. Washington, D.C.: World Bank Group (2016). http://documents.worldbank.org/curated/en/129511467999689857/ICT-use-competitive-pressures-and-firm-performance-in-Mexico
25. Hamill, J., Gregory, K.: Internet marketing in the internationalisation of U.K. SME's. J. Market. Manag. **13**(1/3), 9–28 (1997)
26. Jaworski, B.J., Kohli, A.K.: Market orientation: antecedents and consequences (1993)
27. Jones, C., Hecker, R., Holland, P.: Small firm Internet adoption: opportunities forgone, a journey not begun. J. Small Bus. Enterprise Dev. **10**(3), 287–297 (2003)
28. Han, J.K., Kim, N., Srivastava, R.K.: Market orientation and organizational performance: is innovation a missing link? J. Market. **62**(4), 30–45 (1998)
29. Ketchen Jr., D.J., Hult, G.T.M., Slater, S.F.: Toward greater understanding of market orientation and the resource-based view. Strateg. Manag. J. **28**(9), 961–964 (2007)
30. Lagrosen, S.: Effects of the internet on the marketing communication of service companies. J. Serv. Market. **19**(2), 63–69 (2005)
31. Laukkanen, T., Nagy, G., Hirvonen, S., Reijonen, H., Pasanen, M.: The effect of strategic orientations on business performance in SMEs: a multigroup analysis comparing Hungary and Finland. Int. Market. Rev. **30**(6), 510–535 (2013)
32. Leeflang, P.S.H., Verhoef, P.C., Dahlström, P., Freundt, T.: Challenges and solutions for marketing in a digital era. Eur. Manag. J. **32**(1), 1–12 (2014). https://doi.org/10.1016/j.emj.2013.12.001
33. Mostafa, R.H., Wheeler, C., Jones, M.V.: Entrepreneurial orientation, commitment to the Internet and export performance in small and medium sized exporting firms. J. Int. Entrepreneurship **3**(4), 291–302 (2005)
34. Mostafa, R.H., Wheeler, C., Jones, M.V.: Entrepreneurial orientation, commitment to the Internet and export performance in small and medium sized exporting firms. J. Int. Entrepreneurship **3**(4), 291–302 (2006)
35. Muthee, J., Ngugi, K.: Influence of entrepreneurial marketing on the growth of SMEs in Kiambu Town-CBD, Kenya. Eur. J. Bus. Manag. **11**(11), 361–377 (2014)
36. del Aguila Obra, A.R., Cámara, S.B., Meléndez, A.P.: Internet usage and competitive advantage: the impact of the Internet on an old economy industry in Spain. Internet Res. **12** (5), 391–401 (2002)
37. O'Dwyer, M., Gilmore, A., Carson, D.: Innovative marketing in SMEs. Eur. J. Market. **43** (1/2), 46–61 (2009)

38. Peng, M.W., Sun, S.L., Pinkham, B., Chen, H.: The institution-based view as a third leg for a strategy tripod. Acad. Manag. Perspect. **23**(3), 63–81 (2009)
39. Porter, M.E.: Strategy and the Internet. Harvard Bus. Rev. **79**(3), 62–78, 164 (2001). https://doi.org/10.1108/eb025570
40. Powell, T.C., Dent-Micallef, A.: Information technology as competitive advantage: the role of human, business, and technology resources. Strateg. Manag. J. **18**(5), 375–405 (1997)
41. Hinson, R., Adjasi, C.: The Internet and export: some cross-country evidence from selected African countries. J. Internet Commerce **8**(3), 309–324 (2009)
42. Ragins, E.J., Greco, A.J.: Customer relationship management and E-business: more than a software solution. Rev. Bus. Winter **24**(1), 25–30 (2003)
43. Rumelt, R.P.: Towards a strategic theory of the firm. Resources, firms, and strategies: a reader in the resource-based perspective, pp. 131–145 (1997)
44. Russo, M.V., Fouts, P.A.: A resource-based perspective on corporate environmental performance and profitability. Acad. Manag. J. **40**(3), 534–559 (1997)
45. Quinton, S., Canhoto, A., Molinillo, S., Pera, R., Budhathoki, T.: Conceptualising a digital orientation: antecedents of supporting SME performance in the digital economy. J. Strateg. Market. (2017). Advanced online publication. https://doi.org/10.1080/0965254x.2016.1258004
46. Sørensen, H.E.: Why competitors matter for market orientation. Eur. J. Market. **43**(5/6), 735–761 (2009)
47. Teo, T.S., Pian, Y.: A contingency perspective on Internet adoption and competitive advantage. Eur. J. Inf. Syst. **12**(2), 78–92 (2003)
48. Tilley, F.: The gap between the environmental attitudes and the environmental behaviour of small firms. Bus. Strategy Environ. **8**(4), 238–248 (1999)
49. Van Dijk, S., Berends, H., Jelinek, M., Romme, A.G.L., Weggeman, M.: Micro-institutional affordances and strategies of radical innovation. Organ. Stud. **32**(11), 1485–1513 (2011)
50. Zeng, J., Glaister, K.W.: Competitive dynamics between multinational enterprises and local internet platform companies in the virtual market in China. Br. J. Manag. **27**(3), 479–496 (2016)
51. Zhou, K.Z., Li, C.B.: How strategic orientations influence the building of dynamic capability in emerging economies. J. Bus. Res. **63**, 224–231 (2010)
52. Roberts, E.S.: In defence of the survey method: an illustration from a study of user information satisfaction. Account. Finance **39**(1), 53–77 (1999)

Understanding the Factors Influencing Mobile Commerce Adoption by Traders in Developing Countries: Evidence from Ghana

Mercy Kwofie and Joseph Kwame Adjei(✉)

School of Technology, Ghana Institute of Management and Public Administration, Accra, Ghana
Mercy.kwofie@st.gimpa.edu.gh, jadjei@gimpa.edu.gh

Abstract. The proliferation of wireless communication networks and relative reduction in cost of mobile devices have contributed to exponential growth in mobile device usage, and mobile commerce (m-commerce). Increasingly, mobile devices are being used in various ways by traders. This study analysed the factors that influence m-commerce adoption by traders and the role of Gender in mobile device adoption. The work extends the User Acceptance and Use of Information Technology (UTAUT2) model by highlighting the role of Trust. This study took place in one of the biggest markets in Ghana which is a hub for sale and distribution of agricultural and farm produce. The study analysed responses to a survey of two hundred and fifteen (215) traders using regression analysis. It was discovered that gender has moderating effect on Performance Expectancy, Facilitating Conditions, Habit, Price Value, and Trust and therefore, confirming the need for extension of the UTAUT2 model in relation to the study of adoption and use of m-commerce.

Keywords: UTAUT2 · Micro trading · m-commerce · Adoption · Gender

1 Introduction

The proliferation of wireless communication technology coupled with the increasing number of mobile devices, are contributing to the increasing use of mobile devices for many human endeavor and emergence of mobile mediated commercial activities. A recent study revealed a worldwide mobile penetration rate of 68% with 5.135 billion unique mobile users (Kemp 2018). The same study showed that, unique mobile user penetration rate in Ghana is about 67% (Kemp 2018). The popularity of smart mobile devices, and mobile operating systems like android and Apple IOS are major factors accounting for growth in m-commerce (Chang et al. 2014). Such demand for mobile applications for business transactions and other social interactions are projected to grow (Chang et al. 2014).

It has been observed that the inherent characteristics of mobile technology, including; personalization, flexibility, mobility offers greater potential for businesses harness emerging market opportunities efficiently (Alfahl et al. 2012; Boateng et al. 2014). M-commerce has therefore, emerged as a major enabler of many commercial

Published by Springer Nature Switzerland AG 2019
Y. Dwivedi et al. (Eds.): TDIT 2019, IFIP AICT 558, pp. 104–127, 2019.
https://doi.org/10.1007/978-3-030-20671-0_8

transactions (Laudon and Traver 2016). Yoo (2010) observed that mobile technologies and wireless connectivity are unavoidable and irresistible in many commercial transactions. Notwithstanding the enormous potentials that m-commerce brings, developing countries like Ghana have not been able to fully realise such potentials (Chimaobi 2014; Sey 2011). According to Laudon and Traver (2016), m-commerce adoption is an evolving issue hence, needs constant updates to the knowledge and the needed skills of the researchers to study and assist businesses or organizations and individuals to take advantage of the potentials it brings to them.

It is however important to investigate the factors that influence adoption of m-commerce from a developing country perspective. We adopt the UTAUT2 model by combining the effects of trust as an additional construct and the effects of Gender serving as a moderating variable. The use of a quantitative techniques to identify the key factors that influences intention to adopt m-commerce for trading activities is a major methodological contribution. The study also contributes theoretically by providing a model that extends the existing technology acceptance models with new construct. Finally, the study will also help m-commerce service providers to clearly appreciate the key factors that influence the m-commerce adoption.

2 Overview of Mobile Commerce Adoption

Many researchers have observed an increasing number of micro trading enterprises in many developing giving the limited options of income generation in the formal sector ((Abor and Quartey 2010), Dzogbede (2014)). Micro trading activities are witnessed as engine of growth and poverty reduction (Anwar 2015; Boateng et al. 2014). Previous studies have shown that adoption of Information Technology (IT) by micro enterprises usually contribute to faster growth (Good and Qureshi 2009; Packalén 2010; Anwar 2015). M-commerce adoption has the potential to lower transaction cost in terms of communication challenges among parties involved in trading activities (Laudon and Traver 2016). M-commerce involves the use of mobile devices including mobile phones, mobile computers and tablets (Dwivedi et al. 2014; Yang 2005). Högler and Stucky (2006) observed that the concept of mobility makes m-commerce a medium for reaching and serving the needs of many potential customers. For the purpose of this study, m-commerce is seen as the adoption of mobile devices connected through telecommunication network for trading activities.

A research work conducted by Donner (2008) depicted an increase in profit in the usage of mobile phones for trading activities by micro traders. Boateng et al. (2014) researched into the impact of using mobile phones by farmers and fishermen on the trading activities and discovered that m-commerce assisted in cost reduction for fishermen and farmers and has improved the relationship between the business partners. The usage of mobile devices for micro trading activities was discovered to have increased contact between customers and clients better than any other type of communication which was clearly shown in a research survey conducted by (Esselaar et al. 2007). Mobile phones are being transformed from a single voice communication device to robust communication device which can provide text messages, voice and video messaging, entertainment functions, financial instrument for trading and others, as a result of m-commerce. Its usage in the banking sector enables users to transfer money between Bank accounts and payment of bills (Tobbin 2012). Even in our electoral politics, mobile technologies can be used to monitor and capture incidences before, during and after election. Mobile devices together with the advancement of telecommunication are new technologies which would create new opportunities for businesses. And this would help create more jobs and this computerisation would proceed to bring down the cost of goods and service in production and to cut down cost while increase revenue. Technological advancement is improving which make businesses to strive with no due time to market for products and services which can bring about keen competition with its accompanying advantages. Many argue that advances in communication technology play a vital role in promoting transparency, liquidity, and efficiency in capital markets (Boadi et al. 2007). With the increasing use of mobile devices, a lot of businesses in Ghana today are using mobile phones to transact businesses. This has given them a new way of thinking by embracing technology in the world of business.

As users globally accept mobile technology in its varied states, m-commerce transactions are estimated to flourish based on mobile devices which serve as the best medium for customers to receive immediate feedback in the form of short messages tailored to user's needs (Bigne et al. 2005). The penetration of these technologies in the developed countries has affected every sphere of their daily lives positively (Boateng et al. 2014). This rapid growth in m-commerce application is significant for both enterprises and consumers (Wu and Wang 2005). Based on theoretical framework used, a lot of researchers have recommended to include individual characteristics into a research model either as dependent variable or independent variable to the study of the affective, cognitive or Behavioural Intensions of individuals to adopt a technology. Emerging literature from developing countries provide several examples of innovative application of ICTs to support micro trading enterprises. For instance, farmers in Bangladesh have been using mobile phones to monitor market prices of vegetables, rice and other farm produce (Kshetri and Dholakia 2002). The authors also reported that farmers in remote areas of Cote d'lvoire use mobile phones to track the hourly fluctuations in cocoa and coffee prices. These examples and many others provide the opportunity to assess the extent of mobile commerce adoption in Ghana. M-commerce is seen as a means of conducting business transactions through mobile telecommunication network by using a communication, information and mobile devices such as Personal Digital Assistant (PDA), mobile phones, android phones to mention by a few (Chong et al. 2014). Kalakota and Marcia (2001) posit that the success of m-commerce depends on mobile infrastructure and devices, applications and experiences, and relationships and supply chain which run in a wireless environment. Because of the ubiquitous features of the various mobile devices, m-commerce offers consumers the opportunity to access information 24/7 and this is as the result of the continuous growth of mobile devices. Boateng et al. (2014) view m-commerce as the combination of time, location and personalization. However, other researchers group the above features as currency, immediacy, instant connectivity and identification but all could be equated into time, location and personalization (Boateng et al. 2014).

In other words, commerce is not only a transaction, but also involves the provision of services and information. Mobile devices possess varied characteristics through which different applications, purposes and services are secured as m-commerce is seen as an evolving arena which deals with applications, portable devices, and other functionalities. While most of the initial e-commerce applications could be adapted to run in wireless environment, m-commerce also deals with a lot of current applications which is enabled by wireless infrastructure (Laudon and Traver 2016). It is seen as an effective tool for rendering e-commerce to end-users irrespective of the time and location. In striving for competitive advantage, most companies offer m-commerce alongside e-commerce (Alfahl et al. 2012).

3 Theoretical Background

There has been numerous Technology acceptance and use research (Dwivedi et al. 2011; Williams et al. 2009) and so, Goodhue (2007) opine that these research have reached the maturity stage hence must be moved outside its confines and should pay attention to current growing need of businesses. Consequently, by increasing the explanatory power of UTAUT model, a lot of researchers have amended the model based on the research work in question (Dwivedi et al. 2017a, b; Goodhue 2007; Rana et al. 2016; 2017; Williams et al. 2015). Venkatesh et al. (2012) proposed UTAUT2 by modifying UTAUT to a consumer context. The authors added three new constructs to the UTAUT model and they are: Hedonic Motivation, Price Value and Habit. UTAUT2 maintain the constructs and definition of Performance Expectancy, Effort Expectancy, Social Influence and Facilitating Condition in UTAUT in a consumer use context and so Performance Expectancy, Effort Expectancy, Social Influence, Facilitating Condition, Hedonic Motivation, Price Value, Habit influence the Behavioural Intent to adopt a technology (Venkatesh et al. 2012). In other words, the Behavioural Intent to adopt a technology to ascertain individuals' actual usage of a technology. Age, gender, and experience are moderating factors that influence these constructs on Behavioural Intent and the use of a technology (Venkatesh et al. 2012).

Venkatesh et al. (2012) defined Hedonic Motivation as an enjoyment or fun resultant from using a technology which is key in the determination of technology acceptance and use behaviour. Hedonic motivation captured as Perceived Playfulness (Tamilmani et al. 2019) as an additional construct to UTAUT of the study conducted by Alwahaishi and Snášel (2013), it came out that Facilitating Conditions, Perceived Value, Performance Expectancy, Effort Expectancy, Social Influence among other variables are the factors affecting end-users adoption of Information and Communication Technology (ICT).

Habit is defined by Limayem et al. (2007) as the degree to which people tend to perform behaviour spontaneously through learning and Kim and Malhotra, (2005) explain Habit as initial behaviour. The above explanations differentiate habits in two distinct ways: that is, an initial behaviour and as an automatic behaviour. Celik (2016) integrated Habit into UTAUT to increase the explanatory power of the model and it was noticed that Habit affects Behavioural Intention to use a technology. However,

Ajzen and Fishbein (2005), posit that response from earlier experiences will affect numerous beliefs and also affect forthcoming behavioural performance. A detailed discussion on use of habit construct has been provided by Tamilmani et al. (2018a).

Price Value according to Venkatesh et al. (2012) is a distinction between the organizational use context and consumer use context because the users normally incur the cost of a technology. Unlike in an organization, employees do not have to bear the cost of a technology. The authors also opine that the commitment of using a technology coupled with financial commitment have significant impact on ones' technology use. Price Value in this research work means traders' perception of the gains to be derived in adopting m-commerce and financial commitment born by the trader (Dodds and Monroe, 1991; Tamilmani et al. 2018b; Venkatesh et al. 2012). When a trader anticipates that the gains are more than the financial commitments of using a technology, the Price Value is positive or else it is negative. The results of research work of Alkhunaizan and Love (2012) stated that Cost, Trust and Performance Expectancy significantly predict users' intention to use a technology.

Besides the addition of three constructs to UTAUT, there is a change of the Facilitating Condition direct relationship with technology use to Behavioural Intention because in a consumer context, facilitations available to each consumer depend on applications, mobile devices and others of which the difference can be very significant among the individual consumers while in the organizational context, the Facilitating Conditions such as training, are made available by the organization but not the individual employees (Venkatesh et al. 2012). Facilitating Condition is moderated by age, gender and experience. Moreover, voluntariness is not included into the UTAUT2 based on the fact that individual consumers are not under any institutional directive to adopt a technology (Venkatesh et al. 2012). Based on the above discourse, UTAUT2 is qualified as a technology acceptance model needed to investigate the factors that affect the traders' intention to adopt m-commerce and to analyse whether Gender moderates those factors. Hence, this study adopted it as a base of the conceptual framework of the study.

In order to make the UTAUT2 more appropriate for this study, an external factor (Trust) was introduced to the constructs of the UTAUT2 model. Previous researchers had acknowledged the importance of Trust in m-commerce adoption (Chong et al. 2014; Slade and Williams 2013; Slade et al. 2015a, b; Wei et al. 2009. For example, Trust was among other variables to influence consumers in Malaysia and China to adopt m-commerce. Venkatesh et al. (2012) suggested that future work should examine other major factors vital to different research context. A number of constructs used within the context of m-commerce can be corresponded with UTAUT2's constructs. Since m-commerce is in the infancy stage in development countries like Ghana, Trust would play a key role to affect consumers' Behavioural Intention to adopt m-commerce (Chong et al. 2014).

Table 1. Definition of constructs of this study

Factors	Type	Factor measurement definitions for this study	Items	References
Performance Expectancy (PE)	Independent, 5 point-Likert scale	The extent to which a trader perceives that adopting m-commerce will improve his or her performance	3	Venkatesh et al. (2012) Venkatesh et al. (2003)
Effort Expectancy (EE)	Independent, 5 point-Likert scale	The extent to which a trader perceives that adopting m-commerce is easy	3	Venkatesh et al. (2012) Venkatesh et al. (2003)
Social Influence (SI)	Independent, 5 point-Likert scale	The degree to which a trader believes that people who matter to him or her believes he or she should adopt m-commerce	3	Venkatesh et al. (2012) Venkatesh et al. (2003)
Facilitating Condition (FC)	Independent, 5 point-Likert scale	The degree to which a trader believes that the necessary help and facilities are available to him or her to adopt m-commerce	3	Venkatesh et al. (2012) Venkatesh et al. (2003)
Hedonic Motivation (HM)	Independent, 5 point-Likert scale	The extent to which a trader experiences enjoyment and pleasure from adopting m-commerce	3	Venkatesh et al. (2012)
Price Value (PV)	Independent, 5 point-Likert scale	The degree of a traders' perception of the benefits to be derived in adopting m-commerce and the financial commitment to be borne by him or her	3	Venkatesh et al. (2012) Dodds et al. (1991)
Habit (HT)	Independent, 5 point-Likert scale	The extent to which a trader believes that adopting m-commerce is automatic	3	Venkatesh et al. (2012) (Limayem et al. 2007)
Trust (T)	Independent, 5 point-Likert scale	The extent to which the traders are confident and willing to adopt m-commerce	3	Venkatesh et al. (2012) (Chong et al. 2014)
Behavioural Intentions (BI)	Dependent, 5 point-Likert scale	The extent of a trader's willingness to use and continue to adopt m-commerce	3	Venkatesh et al. (2012)

Source: Author's construct

It is very vital to emphasise the definition of constructs which depict how they are measured through empirical studies. This is because the constructs from the conceptual framework were adopted from initial studies to suit the context of this study (m-commerce adoption). Table 1 above exhibits the definition of the constructs as used in this research with its related references to the reviewed literature.

3.1 Performance Expectancy

Effort Expectancy is one of the important factors proven in initial studies on the technology adoption, Perceived usefulness of a technology such as mobile credit card was found to have a positive effect on Behavioural Intentions to use mobile credit card (Tan et al. 2014). Also, Performance Expectancy was proven to have considerable effect on the consumers' intent in the use of m-commerce (Chong et al. 2014; Wei et al. 2009), mobile internet (Venkatesh et al. 2012), mobile payment system (Slade et al. 2013) to mention but a few. Therefore, it is believed that PE will impact users' intent to adopt m-commerce. Thus, the ensuing hypothesis is proposed:

H1: Performance Expectancy significantly influence Behavioural Intention to adopt mobile commerce in Ghana.

3.2 Effort Expectancy

Earlier research supports that latent variables linked to EE was significant in determining a person's desire to adopt a new technology (Venkatesh et al. 2012; Wei et al. 2009). M-commerce presents users with various opportunities such as not being limited to a particular physical locations. Mobile devices are portable and easy to use when compared to handling a notebook for the various micro trading activities. Effort Expectancy is one of the vital factors in prior studies on the technology adoption, where Perceived Ease of Use in adopting a technology influence significantly the Behavioural Intention of several technologies such as: mobile credit card (Tan et al. 2014); mobile commerce (Chong et al. 2014; mobile payment (Slade et al. 2013; Slade et al. 2015a, b) and others. Thus, the ensuing hypothesis is proposed:

H2: Effort Expectancy has significant influence on Behavioural Intention to adopt m-commerce in Ghana.

3.3 Social Influence

M-commerce is a technology which is not compulsory, because the users have the free option to adopt it or not. SI was significant in affecting the Behavioural Intention to adopt m-commerce in the study of (Chong et al. 2014). The authors also found out that SI was among the salient factors that affect users' intent to use m-commerce in Malaysia. In the research work of Jaradat and Rababaa (2013), the results showed that users adoption of mobile commerce services could be anticipated from the individuals' desire in its usage which were propelled by Performance Expectancy, Effort Expectancy and Social Influence. The research further depicted that among fore-mentioned factors, Social Influence was the highest predictor that directly influenced the users' decision to adopt m-commerce services. Thus, the ensuing hypothesis is proposed:

H3: Social Influence has significant influence on Behavioural Intention to adopt m-commerce in Ghana.

3.4 Facilitating Conditions

Shao and Siponen (2011) posit that, Facilitating Condition in Information System studies principally refers to education, direction, structures, and practical support needed to operate a system, and when these facilities are not considered, it can either improve or impede IT use. The submission is well supported by (Seppo et al. 2011; Venkatesh et al. 2003) that, Facilitating Conditions have direct influence on Behavioural Intention to use a technology. Practical verification showed that when individuals who adopt a technology are given assistance in varied ways, they would be motivated to use a system (Alwahaishi and Snášel 2013). Thus, the ensuing hypothesis is proposed:

H4: Facilitating Condition significantly affect Behavioural Intention to adopt m-commerce in Ghana.

3.5 Hedonic Motivation

Venkatesh et al. (2012) explained in the context of their study that Hedonic Motivation has direct effect against Behavioural Intention. Furthermore, if the users are entertained through the adoption of a technology, they adore it, which affect their Behavioural Intention to continue to adopt an information system (Venkatesh et al. 2012). A lot of studies have confirmed that in a consumer perspective, Hedonic Motivation is a good predictor in technology acceptance and use (Raman and Don 2013; Harsono and Suryana 2014). Thus, the ensuing hypothesis is proposed:

H6: Hedonic Motivation significantly affect Behavioural Intention to adopt m-commerce in Ghana.

3.6 Price Value

According to Wei et al. (2009), cost could be a basis for users to accept or reject the adoption of a technology. The authors opine that cost of the device, internet, and other applications constitute the costs normally born by individuals who adopt m-commerce. Venkatesh et al. (2012) also posit that the financial commitment and other charges associated with the usage of a technology can affect users' technology adoption decisions. Therefore, if the gains in adopting a technology is more than the financial commitment, then consumers are likely to use that particular technology else it may hinder them to successfully adopt it. Thus, the ensuing hypothesis is proposed:

H6: Price Value significantly affect Behavioural Intention to adopt m-commerce in Ghana.

3.7 Habit

According to Venkatesh et al. (2012) when experience gained in adopting a particular technology increases, the individuals begin to yearn to use the technology automatically. When actions n carried out in the past frequently, the subsequent behaviour becomes habitual which helps to forecast future behaviour of an individual. For example, the results of the research done by Venkatesh et al. (2012) and Pahnila et al. (2011) depicted that Habit had considerable effect on Behavioural Intention to use a technology. Therefore, once the users adopt m-commerce, it becomes a habitual which influences their adoption decisions. Thus, the ensuing hypothesis is proposed:

H7: Habit significantly affect Behavioural Intention to adopt m-commerce in Ghana.

3.8 Trust

Trust has to do with one's decision to agree on those who provide m-commerce services, vendours' condition or services. However, an option is normally considered after adopting the varied features of providers which include security confidence in the service delivery (Chong et al. 2014). Chong et al. (2012) modified the TAM model to study about m-commerce adoption in China. Among the other factors, Trust was the highest predictor of m-commerce adoption behaviour. When risk is considered as a major factor in taking a decision, Trust is seen as an important indicator of users' adoption behaviour.

Telecommunication networks have its own challenges such as limitation in bandwidth, inconsistent networks assurance functionality and vulnerability in data transmission over the network (Laudon and Traver 2016). It should be noted that, Trust is a vital issue in m-commerce adoption during the elementary stages of technology acceptance and use. When there is disappointing performances of the wireless communication system, users doubt the ability to deliver on promises. Personalized handling of goods, services and money, face-to-face interactions are missing in m-commerce.

In the context of m-commerce, because it is still in its infancy stage in most of the developing countries like Ghana, there are numerous means of payment systems, formalities in regulating policies, rules and procedures and global acceptable standards that are supposed to be streamlined because Trust is one of the principal factors for user acceptance and vital to achieve success in m-commerce adoption. Siau and Shen (2003) posit that Trust should be one of the cardinal variables to be considered during m-commerce studies especially in m-commerce service delivery. Therefore, the researcher proposed that:

H8: Trust significantly affect Behavioural Intention to adopt m-commerce in Ghana.

One moderating variable (Gender) was introduced to the eight factors of the conceptual framework to answer the second research question (Are the effects of these adoption factors on the intention of traders to adopt m-commerce moderated by Gender?). This moderating factor contributed in assessing the strength of the relationships between the independent and the dependent variables according to the inherent features of the users (Baron and Kenny 1986). Venkatesh et al. (2012) hypothesised that when Gender is considered as a moderating variable, it plays a vital part to establish the relationship between the inner factors of the UTAUT2 framework. Thus, Gender has a moderating effect on the relationship between the constructs of the UTAUT2 model. Furtherance to the numerous researches which echoed that Gender has significant impact where a technology is used and implemented in the business perspective. Especially it was revealed in the study of Boateng et al. (2014) that, there was increasing influx of women into the field of micro trading activities in developing countries and it was clear that women were dominating in the field of micro trading activities despite the numerous challenges hindering their growth. Wei et al. (2009) established that demographic features of users should be considered in forecasting users' adoption behaviour.

The effect of Performance Expectancy was skewed in favour of men (Venkatesh et al. 2000), whilst Effort Expectancy and Social Influence were also skewed in favour of women in technology acceptance and use (Cheng et al. 2006). It could be envisaged that performance is a major concern to males when it comes to technology acceptance and use. On the other hand, females consider ease of use and recommendations made by peers and other people they perceive to be important to them. It was seen in the research of He and Freeman (2010) that men show more enthusiasm in exploring technology features and feel more comfortable with technology. In other words, different Gender gives a different impact on the use of any information system either being compelled by policies or having chosen the technology willingly. It was further explained that Gender difference in computer anxiety will be reduced as time goes on because of ubiquitous computing of our daily life. Following the assertion made by Tan and Teo (2000) that most of the studies also revealed inconclusive results in using Gender as a moderator and so the moderating effect of Gender requires further investigation.

The hypotheses associated to the mediating effects of Gender are as follows:

H9: Performance Expectancy significantly affect Behavioural Intention to adopt m-commerce is moderated by Gender.

H10: Effort Expectancy significantly affect Behavioural Intention to adopt m-commerce is moderated by Gender.

H11: Social Influence significantly affect Behavioural Intention to adopt m-commerce is moderated by Gender.

H12: Facilitating Condition significantly affect Behavioural Intention to adopt m-commerce is moderated by Gender.

H13: Hedonic Motivation significantly affect Behavioural Intention to adopt m-commerce is moderated by Gender

H14: Price Value significantly affect Behavioural Intention to adopt m-commerce is moderated by Gender.

H15: Habit significantly affect Behavioural Intention to adopt m-commerce is moderated by Gender.

H16: Trust significantly affect Behavioural Intention to adopt m-commerce is moderated by Gender.

The model adopted for the study is exhibited in Fig. 1 below.

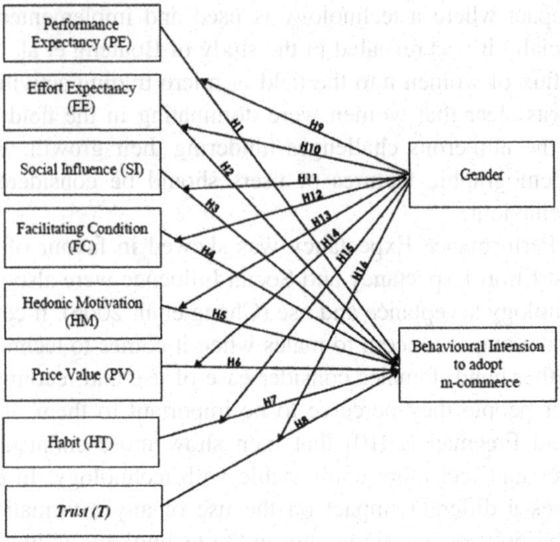

Fig. 1. Proposed research model (adapted from Venkatesh et al. 2012)

4 Methodology

The significance of this section to the entire study is to describe the methodology used in conducting the study by critically looking at the objectives set. This stage is very important because it is the pivot of the study and if not carried out assiduously, else the whole study might not be justifiable (Klein and Myers 1999). The approach adopted is highly dependent on the objectives set. That is, there is no single approach to the entire work. This study was handled by bringing all the main components of the study together in a comprehensive manner to address the issues under investigation.

This research population is limited to traders in the Techiman market in the Bono East Region of Ghana. This market is amongst the largest markets in Ghana. The market is not only serving as a converging point for interest groups from other countries like Burkina Faso, Togo, Mali, Ivory Coast or Niger but also attract farm produce from most nearby farming jurisdictions in the country. The market activities in Ghana tend to resonate to other nearby countries connected to Ghana through trade. Taken a closer look at other countries, the researchers envisaged the effect of m-commerce adoption on the small scale enterprises in Ghana would have likely larger influence.

According to a book written by Alreck and Settle (1985), it was indicated that sample size of about 200 to 1000 respondents is appropriate for a population of 10,000 or more. This informed this study by selecting a sample size of 215 which the above submission strongly supports based on the fact that the sample frame as already indicated could not be ascertained. The researchers went to the area of interest which was the Techiman Market.

Data collection method adopted was based on the exiting literature to ensure validity of research instrument. The development of the instrument was also based on the guidelines suggested by Information Systems literature (e.g. Gao and Deng 2012). Most measurement issues were picked from existing measures and modified to fit the current circumstances of the study.

A questionnaire was structured to reflect the framework presented in Fig. 1. It was designed to be clear and simple to complete. The interviewees of this research were asked to specify their observations of the modified UTAUT2 framework which involved the following constructs: Effort Expectancy, Effort Expectancy, Facilitating condition, Social Influence, Price Value, Hedonic Motivation, Habit and Trust to adopt mobile commerce for their micro trading activities which were obtained by adapting a five point likert scale from 1 to 5 continuum with its associated weights as: 1 = Strongly Disagree, 2 = Disagree, 3 = Neutral, 4 = Agree and 5 = Strongly agree. The researchers seek results that can strengthen the validity of the theoretical framework (Fig. 1). The questionnaire was used to solicit the survey participants' opinions on the focal constructs of the research to help meet the purpose and objectives of the research, and also to come out with the research issues in the study.

The data gathered were coded and analysed by the use of Statistical Package for Social Science (SPSS). In line with other studies, related items were grouped together to ensure reliability and validity of the model (Tan et al. 2014; Venkatesh et al. 2012). Descriptive analysis used frequency and percentage to examine the profile of the respondents. Also, any discrepancies of assumptions underlying the chosen statistical technique were addressed.

Multiple regressions was then done in order to validate the hypotheses that were established in the previous section (Foon and Fah 2011). This was done to answer the two research questions. Firstly, the regression was done to identify factors that influenced the intention to adopt m-commerce. Secondly, regression was done on the factors and the moderating factor (Gender) to determine their significance. The margin of error for this study was 0.05. Thus, the confidence level was 95%.

The traders were assured by the researchers of the confidentiality of the information they gave because the study was for academic purpose.

5 Findings

5.1 Respondents' Profile and Characteristics

Two hundred and fifteen (215) valid questionnaires were completed by the traders. Twenty three (23%) of respondents were males while the remaining (77%) constitute females. (18.50%) of the respondents were within the ages of 18–26. The sample quota allocation made room for various age category however, most were skewed towards 38–48 years. Majority (48%) of the respondents interviewed were Junior High School graduates, Tertiary graduates constitute (14%) and (14%) of the respondents never attended school.

Table 2. Average income of respondents per day

Average income (GhȻ)	Frequency	Percentages
Less than 50	157	73.0
50–100	45	20.9
Above 100	13	6.1
Total	215	100

The Table 2 above shows that, out of the (215) respondents that were included in the sample, (73.0%) of them made an average income less than GhȻ50.00, (20.9%) were within GhȻ50.00- GhȻ100.00 and the remaining (6.1%) made above GhȻ100.00 daily.

Table 3. Adoption experience of respondents

Duration	Frequency	Percentages
3–6 months	68	31.6
7–12 months	74	34.4
2–3 years	44	20.5
Above 3 years	29	13.5
Total	215	100

The Table 3 above shows that, out of the of the (215) respondents that were included in the sample, (31.6%) of respondents indicated that they had adopted m-commerce within 3–6 months, (34.4%) indicated 7–12 months, (20.5%) indicated 2–3 years and the remaining (13.5%) indicated above 3 years. Majority of the respondents in the survey had adopted m-commerce within one year, which shows that m-commerce adoption is relatively a new trend in Ghana.

Table 4. Residence of respondents

Country	Frequency	Percentages
Ghana	200	93.02
Burkina Faso	8	3.72
Togo	4	1.86
Ivory Coast	2	0.86
Niger	1	0.47
Total	215	100

The Table 4 above shows that, out of the of the (215) respondents that were included in the sample, (93.02%) of respondents indicated that they were residence in

Ghana, (3.72%) indicated Burkina Faso, (1.86%) indicated Togo, (0.86%) indicated Ivory Coast and the remaining (0.47%) indicated Niger.

6 Inferential Analysis

According to Cresswel (2009), reliability refers to as the consistency and stability of results. In order to achieve a solid reliability, this study is based on a well-discussed theory (modified UTAUT2). Cronbach's alpha was used in this study to evaluate the internal consistency of the scale measurement and the research variables. The results presented in Table 5 suggested that all the measures in this study ranged from 0.602 to 0.845 were reliable as recommended by (Hair et al. 2003).

Table 5. Regression coefficients

Variable	S. E	Beta	T	P-value
Performance Expectancy (PE)	0.114	0.432	0.316	<0.05
Effort Expectancy (EE)	0.102	0.204	1.221	<0.05
Social Influence (SI)	0.036	0.036	1.421	>0.05
Facilitating Condition (FC)	0.011	0.256	0.421	<0.05
Hedonic Motivation (HM)	0.064	0.016	0.336	>0.05
Price Value (PV)	0.031	0.167	0.256	<0.05
Habit (HT)	0.204	0.138	1.042	<0.05
Trust (T)	0.108	0.034	0.368	<0.05
PExGender	0.106	0.135	0.223	<0.05
EExGender	0.143	0.302	1.431	>0.05
SIxGender	0.109	0.112	3.056	>0.05
FCxGender	0.511	−0.240	−0.169	<0.05
HMxGender	0.065	0.072	0.046	>0.05
PVxGender	0.131	−0.261	−0.122	<0.05
HTxGender	0.104	0.156	1.001	<0.05
TxGender	0.204	−0.333	−0.442	<0.05

Dependent variable: Use Behaviour; Sig: 0.05; S.E: Standard Error; B: Beta Coefficient; T: Test Statistic

The results as shown below reveals a relatively high Cronbach alpha which indicate that the selected factors are consistent in explaining the adoption of mobile commerce for micro trading activities by traders in Ghana. The individual variables showed a Cronbach alpha greater than 0.6 with an overall Cronbach alpha of 0.887.

The coefficient table indicates that the independent variables and their influence to the model fitting. Their coefficients and significance are seen in Standard Beta column and Sig respectively in the table discussed.

Table 6. Reliability test

Factors	Cronbach's alpha	Items
Performance Expectancy (PE)	0.794	3
Effort Expectancy (EE)	0.683	3
Social Influence (SI)	0.774	3
Facilitating Condition (FC)	0.845	3
Behavioral Intentions (BI)	0.740	3
Hedonic Motivation (HM)	0.765	3
Price Value (PV)	0.791	3
Habit (HT)	0.602	3
Trust (T)	0.641	3
Overall	0.887	27

Source: Field Survey, 2018

6.1 Pearson Correlation Analysis

Convergent validity and discriminant validity are assessed by Pearson correlation analysis.

Multicollinearity has to do with highly correlated independent variables in a multiple framework and it emerges where the coefficients between the independent variables are moderate or too high (Pallant and Tennant 2007). By subjecting this study into multicollinearity, it is evident that it does not suffer from Multicollinearity because the independent variables were less than 0.7 (Pallant and Tennant 2007). Pearson Correlation Analysis was performed to check for the presence of linear relationship between the independent and the dependent variable. It is a measure of the association between two variables, where one indicates direct positive association, zero (0) indicates no association, and −1 exhibits negative association between the variables under consideration.

The results as presented in the Table 7 below revealed that the Pearson Correlation Coefficient Analysis for all of the independent variables have a relationship with the

Table 7. Pearson correlation coefficients analysis results

Variable	PE	EE	SI	FC	HM	PV	HT	T	BI
PE	**1.000**								
EE	.534	**1.000**							
SI	.432	.433	**1.000**						
FC	.602	.699	.266	**1.000**					
HM	.467	.370	.357	.426	**1.000**				
PV	.107	.456	.107	.566	.458	**1.000**			
HT	.623	.521	.023	.354	.391	.543	**1.000**		
T	.489	.466	.435	.598	.663	.621	.543	**1.000**	
BI	.678	.438	.378	.625	.566	.542	.647	.578	**1.000**

Source: Field Survey, 2018

dependent variable, as the value of the correlation is greater than 0. The results therefore reveal the existence of linear relationship between the dependent and the independent variables and permits the use of multiple linear regression analysis. Again, the positive coefficient in all the cases depict a positive relationship between the independent variables and the dependent variable (Table 5).

Table 8. Summary of results of hypotheses testing

Hypothesis	Result
H1: *Performance expectancy significantly affect the Behavioural Intention to adopt m-commerce in Ghana*	**Accepted**
H2: *Effort expectancy significantly affect the Behavioural Intention to adopt m-commerce in Ghana*	**Accepted**
H3: *Social influence significantly affect the Behavioural Intention to adopt m-commerce in Ghana*	**Rejected**
H4: *Facilitating condition significantly affect the behavioural Intention to adopt m-commerce in Ghana*	**Accepted**
H5: *Hedonic motivation significantly affect the Behavioural Intention to adopt m-commerce in Ghana*	**Rejected**
H6: *Price value significantly affect the Behavioural Intention to adopt m-commerce in Ghana*	**Accepted**
H7: *Habit significantly affect the Behavioural Intention to adopt m-commerce in Ghana*	**Accepted**
H8: *Trust significantly affect the Behavioural Intention to adopt m-commerce in Ghana*	**Accepted**
H9: *Performance Expectancy significantly affect Behavioural Intention to adopt m-commerce is moderated by Gender*	***Accepted***
H10: *Effort Expectancy significantly affect Behavioural Intention to adopt m-commerce is moderated by Gender*	***Rejected***
H11: *Social Influence significantly affect Behavioural Intention to adopt m-commerce is moderated by Gender*	***Rejected***
H12: *Facilitating Condition significantly affect Behavioural Intention to adopt m-commerce is moderated by Gender*	***Accepted***
H13: *Hedonic Motivation significantly affect Behavioural Intention to adopt m-commerce is moderated by Gender*	***Rejected***
H14: *Price Value significantly affect Behavioural Intention to adopt m-commerce is moderated by Gender*	***Accepted***
H15: *Habit significantly affect Behavioural Intention to adopt m-commerce is moderated by Gender*	***Accepted***
H16: *Trust significantly affect Behavioural Intention to adopt m-commerce is moderated by Gender*	***Accepted***

7 Discussions

7.1 Effort Expectancy

Effort Expectancy was found to be statistically significant to Intention to Use, implying that the traders' decision to accept m-commerce is affected by EE. This finding is consistent with previous technology adoption studies (Chong 2013; Venkatesh et al. 2012; Davis et al. 1989). It should however be noted that the analysis of this study revealed a contrary disposition of the work done by Wei et al. (2009), which discovered that there is no significant relationship between the Perceived Ease of Use of m-commerce and consumer intention to use m-commerce. Also, Effort Expectancy was not found to have a significant influence on undergraduate students' intention to use mobile learning through the discovery of the research work of (Yang 2013). Based on the results of this study, the features and the functions of the various mobile devices should be easier to use by the traders so as to encourage them to adopt m-commerce for their micro trading activities.

7.2 Social Influence

The analysis of this research revealed that Social Influence does not affect the Behavioural Intention of the traders to adopt m-commerce. Surprisingly, Social Influence has been discovered in prior research as vital and influential indicator of technology adoption. The findings from the study indicates that social ties might not influence BI of the traders either to use or not to use m-commerce. Also, m-commerce adoption is not well embraced in developing countries and so, most people the traders perceive important, might not be using m-commerce hence, the users would not be able to be influenced significantly by them. The above assertion is not in supportive of the study conducted by Chong et al. (2014) which depicted that SI plays an important role in predicting m-commerce adoption in China and Malaysia. The authors further suggested that consumers are more likely to be influenced by trends, social media, and peers when it comes to adopting m-commerce.

7.3 Facilitating Condition

A growing number of studies suggest that FC plays an essential role in the actual usage behaviour of technology (Venkatesh et al. (2003) and the discovery of this study confirms the aforementioned analysis in the context of m-commerce adoption. Facilitating condition has largely affected the behavioural intention of the traders to accept m-commerce. This follows that the traders' see FC as vital to have the reasonable support whilst adopting m-commerce. This means that the more they get the support, the more they will be willing and able to adopt m-commerce.

7.4 Hedonic Motivation

The analysis of this research reveals that Hedonic Motivation does not influence the Behavioural Intention of the traders to adopt m-commerce. This is consistent with the study done by (Harsono and Suryana 2014). This revelation is not in line with prior research work conducted by (Xu 2014; Venkatesh et al. 2012). However from the analysis of this research, it could be deduced that the traders do not depend on how entertaining and enjoyable the features and the functions of m-commerce are before they adopt m-commerce.

7.5 Price Value

Price Value has been indicated to have a stronger effect on Behavioural Intention to adopt m-commerce. This is in conformity with the work done by Venkatesh et al. (2012) and Alkhunaizan and Love (2012). Wei et al. (2009) also posit that cost is one of the cardinal challenges that influence m-commerce adoption in Malaysia which is the situation in Ghana as well according to the findings of this study. This juxtapose that exorbitant prices would negatively influence one's intention to accept m-commerce services. Majority of the people in the study indicated that they would accept m-commerce if they envisage the price is relatively low and that they could afford it.

7.6 Habit

Habit is also seen as a significant factor affecting traders' Behavioural Intention to adopt m-commerce in this study. The analysis of this study revealed that there is direct relationship to the work done by (Venkatesh et al. 2012). Similar result was ascertained when Hew et al. (2015) conducted a study in technology acceptance in the area of mobile applications, and indicated that Habit is one of the most vital variables that influence the intention to adopt mobile services. Also, currently in Ghana, almost everyone uses a mobile device. And it has become important means of communication that can not be done away with. This would make it easy to adopt m-commerce in everyday activities especially in micro trading. It could be suggested that due to the individual's prior adoption of m-commerce because of its importance, one would continue to use the service. When adoption of m-commerce becomes inelastic, it would increase one's interest to continue adopting the technology (Venkatesh et al. 2012). In lieu to mobile commerce acceptance, Habit influences Behavioural Intentions to adopt m-commerce.

7.7 Trust

This research found out that Trust is a major function in m-commerce acceptance by Ghanaians. The analysis of data exhibit that when the people want high level of security and privacy, Trust is the option to consider. It is observed that the traders in the Techiman market rarely follow an option where physical contact is elusive. The findings are in line with the work conducted by Alkhunaizan and Love (2012) which also views Trust as a salient factor in technology adoption. According to Chong et al. (2012) who further contributed to the TAM framework in their work in m-commerce acceptance in China, Trust was a major factor that affected the intention to adopt m-commerce with a path coefficient of 0.315 and a p-value of <0.001. This is consistent with suggestions made by Laudon and Traver (2016) whereby most developing countries hardly take the risk than those in developed countries. M-commerce is not a well-developed technology among the traders in the Techiman market which means more attention is needed to develop their interest in order to adopt the technology. Qingfei et al. (2008) opine that user acceptance include both acceptance of technology and the acceptance of m-commerce service providers. In view of the above assertion, Trust is seen by Siau and Shen (2003) as: Trust of a technology and Trust of m-commerce service providers. Moreover, m-commerce is not well embraced by the people in developing countries, so systems should be put in place to solidify the Trust of the traders to adopt m-commerce.

7.8 Adoption Factors with Moderating Variables

Gender moderated the following adoption factors: Performance Expectancy, Facilitating Condition, Price Value, Habit and Trust. However, it did not have moderating effect on the following adoption factors: Effort Expectancy, Social Influence and Hedonic Motivation. The disparity in the findings could be explained by the environment in which the studies were carried out. Indeed, the study of Venkatesh et al. (2012) was carried out in the area of Mobile Internet Technology which adopted online internet survey but in the market environment, the situation may be different in terms of the traders' experience with the technology, and the attention that they pay to the opinions of their peers.

7.9 Implication for Research

In terms of research, this study contributes to the body of knowledge in m-commerce adoption by applying the UTAUT2 model in an African perspective. Thus, this study is one of the forefront studies extending the applicability of UTAUT2 by examining new technologies (m-commerce) in a new context (micro trading activities) in a developing country (Ghana).

7.10 Implication for Practice

The study contributes to practice by drawing to the attention of interested parties and other stakeholders to specific factors that either enable or hinder traders' adoption of m-commerce. They can use these findings to develop strategies to align traders' expectations with technology used for their trading activities.

7.11 Implication for Policy

In terms of policy, it is understood that creating a conducive ICT environment will positively influence the adoption of m-commerce.

7.12 Limitations and Future Research Directions

In addition, this study was limited to only the Techiman market, so future studies should be carried out using more than a single market to provide for comparison and testing of findings. This was to allow for easy access to respondents and data that the researcher needed to gather for the study. Moreover, m-commerce is not a well-developed technology among the traders in the Techiman market (Table 3) which means more attention to develop their interest in order to adopt the technology by making the features of the mobile devices very simple to use.

8 Conclusion

The purpose of this research was to assess the factors that affect traders to adopt m-commerce in Ghana. The study has shown that PE, EE, FC, PV, HT and T influence the traders' BI to adopt m-commerce for their micro trading activities in Ghana. However, SI and HM did not influence the traders' intention to adopt m-commerce. Interestingly, Gender moderated PE, FC, PV, HT and T but SI, EE and HM did not have a moderating impact on the traders' BI to adopt m-commerce. In all, Performance Expectancy was the strongest determinant among the adoption factors in this study. Trust as an external construct introduced by the researcher to the UTAUT2 model, has been justified to have an impact in determining the traders' Behavioural Intention to adopt m-commerce. Based on the above development, the objectives for this study have been duly achieved.

References

Abor, J., Quartey, P.: Issues in SME development in Ghana and South Africa. Int. Res. J. Finance Econ. **39**(39), 215–228 (2010). ISSN 1450-2887

Ajzen, I., Fishbein, M.: The Influence of Attitudes on Behavior, January 2005

Alfahl, H., Sanzogni, L., Houghton, L.: Mobile commerce adoption in organizations: a literature review and future research directions. J. Electron. Commer. Organ. **10**(2), 61–78 (2012). https://doi.org/10.4018/jeco.2012040104

Alkhunaizan, A., Love, S.: What drives mobile commerce? An empirical evaluation of the revised UTAUT model. Int. J. Manag. Market. Acad. **2**(1), 82–99 (2012)

Alreck, P.L., Settle, R.B.: The survey research handbook (Ill) (1985)

Alwahaishi, S., Snášel, V.: Consumers' acceptance and use of information and communications technology: a UTAUT and flow based theoretical model. J. Technol. Manag. Innov. © **8**(2), 61–73 (2013)

Anwar, M.: Mobile phones and the livelihoods of indonesian micro-entrepreneurs: evidence of capability expansion. In: Pacific Asia Conference on Information Systems (2015). http://aisel.aisnet.org/pacis2015/61

Baron, R.M., Kenny, D.A.: The moderator-mediator variable distinction in social the moderator-mediator variable distinction in social psychological research: conceptual, strategic, and statistical considerations. J. Pers. Soc. Psychol. **51**(6), 1173–1182 (1986)

Bigne, E., Ruiz, C., Sanz, S.: The impact of internet user shopping patterns and demographics on consumer mobile buying behaviour. J. Electron. Commer. Res. **6**(3), 193–209. http://www.csulb.edu/journals/jecr/issues/20053/paper3.pdf

Boadi, R.A., Boateng, R., Hinson, R., Opoku, R.A.: Preliminary insights into M-commerce adoption in Ghana. Inf. Dev. **23**(4), 253–265 (2007). https://doi.org/10.1177/02666669 07084761

Boateng, R., Hinson, R., Galadima, R., Olumide, L.: Preliminary insights into the influence of mobile phones in micro-trading activities of market women in Nigeria. Inf. Dev. **30**(1), 32–50 (2014). https://doi.org/10.1177/0266666912473765

Celik H.: Customer online shopping anxiety within the Unified Theory of Acceptance and Use Technology (UTAUT) framework. APJML 28,2 278 Received 9 May 2015 Revised 14 August 2015 9 September 2015 Accepted 15 September 2015 Customer Online Shopping Anxiety within the Unified Theory of Acceptance and Use Technology (UTAUT) Framework Hakan Celik Department of Marketing, Bileci, 28 No. 2, 278–307 (2016). https://doi.org/10.1108/APJML-05-2015-0077

Chang, J.M., Williams, J., Hurburg, G.: Mobile Commerce. IEEE, 14–15 June 2014 (2014). http://searchmobilecomputing.techtarget.com/definition/m-commerce

Cheng, T.C.E., Lam, D.Y.C., Yeung, A.C.L.: Adoption of internet banking: an empirical study in Hong Kong. Decis. Support Syst. **42**(3), 1558–1572 (2006). https://doi.org/10.1016/j.dss.2006.01.002

Chong, A.Y.-L., Ooi, K.-B., Bao, H.: Computers in human behavior: an empirical analysis of the determinants of 3G adoption in China. Comput. Hum. Behav. **28**(2), 360–369 (2012)

Chong, A.Y., Chan, F.T.S., Ooi, K.: Predicting consumer decisions to adopt mobile commerce: cross country empirical examination between China and Malaysia. Decis. Support Syst. **53**(1), 34–43 (2014). https://doi.org/10.1016/j.dss.2011.12.001

Donner, J.: Research approaches to mobile use in the developing world: a review of the literature. Inf. Soc. **24**(3) (2008). https://doi.org/10.1080/01972240802019970

Dwivedi, Y.K., Wade, M.R., Schneberger, S.L. (eds.): Information systems theory: explaining and predicting our digital society, vol. 1. Springer, Heidelberg (2011). https://doi.org/10.1007/978-1-4419-6108-2

Dwivedi, Y.K., Tamilmani, K., Williams, M.D., Lal, B.: Adoption of M-commerce: examining factors affecting intention and behaviour of Indian consumers. Int. J. Indian Cul. Bus. Manag. **8**(3), 345–360 (2014)

Dwivedi, Y.K., Rana, N.P., Janssen, M., Lal, B., Williams, M.D., Clement, M.: An empirical validation of a unified model of electronic government adoption (UMEGA). Gov. Inf. Q. **34**(2), 211–230 (2017)

Dwivedi, Y.K., Rana, N.P., Jeyaraj, A., Clement, M., Williams, M.D.: Re-examining the unified theory of acceptance and use of technology (UTAUT): towards a revised theoretical model. Inf. Syst. Front. 1–16 (2017b). https://doi.org/10.1007/s10796-017-9774-y

Esselaar, S., Stork, C., Ndiwalana, A., Deen-Swarray, M.: ICT usage and its impact on profitability of SMEs in 13 African countries. In: 14 African Universities and Research Institutions Working on ICT Policy and Regulation. ©, vol. 4, no. 1, pp. 87–100 (2007)

Foon, S., Fah, B.C.Y.: Internet banking adoption in Kuala Lumpur: an application of UTAUT model. Int. J. Bus. Manag. **6**(4), 161 (2011)

Gao, T., Deng, Y.: A study on users' acceptance behavior to mobile e-books application based on UTAUT model, pp. 376–379. IEEE (2012)

Good, T., Qureshi, S.: Investigating the effects of micro-enterprise access and use of ICTs through a capability lens: implications for global development. In: Second Annual SIG GlobDev Workshop, pp. 1–28 (2009)

Goodhue, D.L.: Consumer acceptance and use of information technology: adding consumption theory to UTAUT2. J. Assoc. Inf. Syst. **8**(4), 219–222 (2007)

Hair, J., Babin, B., Money, A., Samouel, P.: Essentials of Business Research Methods (2003)

He, J., Freeman, L.: Are men more technology-oriented than women? The role of gender on the development of general computer self-efficacy of college students. J. Inf. Syst. Educ. **21**(2), 203–213 (2010)

Klein, H.K., Myers, M.D.: A set of principles for conducting and evaluating interpretive field studies in information systems. MIS Q. **23**(1), 67–94 (1999)

Hew, J.-J., Lee, V.-H., Ooi, K.-B., Wei, J.: What catalyses mobile apps usage intention: an empirical analysis. Emeraldinsight **115**(7), 1269–1291 (2015)

Högler, T., Stucky, W.: Exploring the critical success factors for mobile commerce. In: 2006 International Conference on Mobile Business, November 2015, p. 40 (2006). https://doi.org/10.1109/ICMB.2006.15

Harsono, I.L.D., Suryana, L.A.: Factors affecting the use behavior of social media using UTAUT 2 model. In: Proceedings of the First Asia-Pacific Conference on Global Business, Economics, Finance and Social Sciences, 1–3 August (2014)

Jaradat, M.R.M., Al Rababaa, M.S.: Assessing key factor that influence on the acceptance of mobile commerce based on modified UTAUT. Int. J. Bus. Manag. **8**(23), 102–112 (2013). https://doi.org/10.5539/ijbm.v8n23p102

Kalakota, R., Robinson, M.: M-Business: The Race to Mobility (2001)

Khan, A., Woosley, J.M.: Comparison of contemporary technology acceptance models and evaluation of the best fit for health industry organizations. Int. J. Comput. Sci. Eng. Technol. **1**(11), 709–717 (2011)

Kim, S.S., Malhotra, N.K.: A longitudinal model of continued IS use: an integrative view of four mechanisms underlying postadoption phenomena. Manag. Sci. **51**(5), 741–755 (2005). https://doi.org/10.1287/mnsc.1040.0326

Kshetri, N., Dholakia, N.: Determinants of the global diffusion of B2B e-commerce. Electron. Markets **12**(2), 1–10 (2002). https://doi.org/10.1080/10196780252844562

Laudon, K.C., Traver, G.C.: E-Commerce: Business. Technology. Society, 12 edn (2016)

Limayem, M., Hirt, S.G., Cheung, C.M.K.: How habit limits the predictive power of intention: the case study of information systems continuance. MIS Q. **31**, 705–737 (2007)

Pahnila, S., Sipeon, M., Zheng, X.: Integrating habit into UTAUT: the Chinese eBay case. Pac. Asia J. Assoc. Inf. Syst. **3**(2), 1–30 (2011)

Pallant, J.F., Tennant, A.: An introduction to the Rasch measurement model: an example using the Hospital Anxiety and Depression Scale (HADS). Br. J. Clin. Psychol. **46**(1), 1–18 (2007). https://doi.org/10.1348/014466506X96931

Raman, A., Don, Y.: Preservice teachers' acceptance of learning management software: an application of the UTAUT2 model. Int. Educ. Stud. **6**(7), 157–164 (2013). https://doi.org/10.5539/ies.v6n7p157

Rana, N.P., Dwivedi, Y.K., Lal, B., Williams, M.D., Clement, M.: Citizens' adoption of an electronic government system: towards a unified view. Inf. Syst. Front. **19**(3), 549–568 (2017)

Rana, N.P., Dwivedi, Y.K., Williams, M.D., Weerakkody, V.: Adoption of online public grievance redressal system in India: toward developing a unified view. Comput. Hum. Behav. **59**, 265–282 (2016)

Saunders, M., Lewis, P., Thornhill, A.: Research Methods for Business Students. Business, vol. 5 (2009). https://doi.org/10.1017/CBO9781107415324.004

Sey, A.: "We use it different, different": making sense of trends in mobile phone use in Ghana. New Media Soc. **13**, 375–390 (2011). https://doi.org/10.1177/1461444810393907

Shao, X., Siponen, M.: Consumer acceptance and use of information technology: Adding consumption theory to UTAUT2. In: Proceedings of SIGSVC Workshop. Sprouts: Working Papers on Information Systems, vol. 11, no. 157, pp. 11–157 (2011)

Siau, K., Shen, Z.: Building customer trust in mobile commerce. Commun. ACM **46**(4), 91–94 (2003). https://doi.org/10.1145/641205.641211

Slade, E., Williams, M., Dwivedi, Y.: Extending UTAUT2 to explore consumer adoption of mobile payments. In: UK Academy for Information Systems Conference Proceedings, p. 36 (2013)

Slade, E.L., Dwivedi, Y.K., Piercy, N.C., Williams, M.D.: Modeling consumers' adoption intentions of remote mobile payments in the United Kingdom: extending UTAUT with innovativeness, risk, and trust. Psychol. Market. **32**(8), 860–873 (2015a)

Slade, E., Williams, M., Dwivedi, Y., Piercy, N.: Exploring consumer adoption of proximity mobile payments. J. Strateg. Market. **23**(3), 209–223 (2015b)

Tan, G.W.H., Ooi, K.B., Chong, S.C., Hew, T.S.: NFC mobile credit card: the next frontier of mobile payment? Telematics Inform. **31**(2), 292–307 (2014). https://doi.org/10.1016/j.tele.2013.06.002

Tan, M., Teo, T.S.H.: Factors influencing the adoption of internet banking. J. Assoc. Inf. Syst. **1** (1), 1–44 (2000). https://doi.org/10.1016/j.elerap.2008.11.006

Tamilmani, K., Rana, N.P., Prakasam, N., Dwivedi, Y.K.: The battle of Brain vs. Heart: a literature review and meta-analysis of "hedonic motivation" use in UTAUT2. Int. J. Inf. Manag. **46**, 222–235 (2019)

Tamilmani, K., Rana, N.P., Dwivedi, Y.K.: Use of 'Habit' is not a habit in understanding individual technology adoption: a review of UTAUT2 based empirical studies. In: Elbanna, A., Dwivedi, Y., Bunker, D., Wastell, D. (eds.) TDIT 2018, vol. 533, pp. 277–294. Springer, Cham (2018a). https://doi.org/10.1007/978-3-030-04315-5_19

Tamilmani, K., Rana, N.P., Dwivedi, Y.K., Sahu, G.P., Roderick, S.: Exploring the role of 'Price Value'for understanding consumer adoption of technology: a review and metaanalysis of UTAUT2 based empirical studies. In: Twenty-Second Pacific Asia Conference on Information Systems, Japan (2018b)

Tobbin, P.: Towards a model of adoption in mobile banking by the unbanked: a qualitative study. Emeraldinsight **14**(5), 74–88 (2012). https://doi.org/10.1108/14636691211256313

Venkatesh, V., Thong, J.Y.L., Xu, X.: Consumer acceptance and use of information technology: extending the unified theory of acceptance and use of technology. MIS Q. **36**(1), 157–178 (2012). https://doi.org/10.1111/j.1540-4560.1981.tb02627.x

Venkatesh, V., Davis, F.D.: A theoretical extension of the technology acceptance model: four longitudinal field studies. JSTOR **46**(2), 186–204 (2000a)

Venkatesh, V., Morris, M.G.D., Davis, G.B., Davis, F.D.: User acceptance of information technology: toward a unified view. MIS Q. **27**(3), 425–478 (2003). https://doi.org/10.2307/30036540

Wei, T.T., Marthandan, G., Chong, A.Y.-L., Ooi, K.-B., Arumugam, S.: What drives Malaysian m-commerce adoption? An empirical analysis. Ind. Manag. Data Syst. **109**(3), 370–388 (2009). https://doi.org/10.1108/02635570910939399

Dodds, W.B., Monroe, K.B., Grewal, D.: Effects of price, brand, and store information on buyers' product evaluations. J. Market. Res. **18**(307–319) (1991)

Williams, M.D., Rana, N.P., Dwivedi, Y.K.: The unified theory of acceptance and use of technology (UTAUT): a literature review. J. Enterprise Inf. Manag. **28**(3), 443–488 (2015)

Williams, M.D., Dwivedi, Y.K., Lal, B., Schwarz, A.: Contemporary trends and issues in IT adoption and diffusion research. J. Inf. Technol. **24**(1), 1–10 (2009)

Wu, J.H., Wang, S.C.: What drives mobile commerce? An empirical evaluation of the revised technology acceptance model. Inf. Manag. **42**(5), 719–729 (2005). https://doi.org/10.1016/j.im.2004.07.001

Xu, X.: Understanding users' continued use of online games : an application of UTAUT2 in social network games. In: The Sixth International Conferences on Advances in Multimedia, pp. 58–65 (2014)

Yang, C.K.: Exploring factors affecting the adoption of mobile commerce in Singapore. Telematics Inform. **22**(3), 257–277 (2005). https://doi.org/10.1016/j.tele.2004.11.003

Yang, S.: Understanding undergraduate students' adoption of mobile learning model: a perspective of the extended UTAUT2. J. Convergence Inf. Technol. (JCIT) **8**(10), 969–979 (2013). https://doi.org/10.4156/jcit.vol8.issue10.118

Yoo, Y.: Computing in everyday life: a call for research on experiential computing. MIS Q. **34** (2), 213–231 (2010)

A Literature Review of Mobile Payments in Sub-Saharan Africa

Richard Boateng and Maame Yaa Prempeh Sarpong(✉)

OMIS Department, University of Ghana Business School, Accra, Ghana
richard.boateng@gmail.com, sarpstess@yahoo.com

Abstract. The influx of mobile technologies during 1990's saw to the purchase of mobile phones and subsequently mobile terminals in the form of tablets, PDAs among others. The trend in adoption has seen increasing hikes and drastic impact on business transactions also recorded. Mobile payments have emerged as one of the electronic payment platforms that are creating convenience for many consumers. In order to strengthen the field and to examine the knowledge gap over a decade (2007–2017), a review of literature was opportune. Hence 37 studies conducted in Sub-Saharan Africa were retrieved, classified based on TOE framework and Porter's five competitive forces. The thematic areas identified based on the framework were reviewed. In addition, geographical cover, methodological issues, conceptual frameworks and gaps identified for further studies were also studied. The analysis showed that, similar to earlier findings; Changes in technology, merchant adoption and consumer adoption have been well researched into with grey areas like traditional payment systems, socio-cultural factors that affect implementation of mobile payment system. The research gaps and direction of future research were discussed.

Keywords: Mobile phone · Sub-Saharan Africa · Mobile payment services market · M-commerce · Mobile money · Ghana

1 Introduction

The influx of mobile technologies during 1990's saw to the purchase of mobile phones and subsequently mobile terminals in the form of tablets, PDAs among others. Evidently, users of mobile phones worldwide reached 3.74 million in 2009 [28]; 4.01 billion users in 2013 to 4.77 billion users in 2017 and marginal increase recorded for 2018 at 4.93 billion users. Future projections for 2019 stands at 5.07 billion users as reported by Statistica ("Mobile Phone Users Worldwide 2013–2019").

Sub-Saharan Africa has not been left in the coverage as it has been found that, a large part of coverage is taking place in developing countries [76]. It has been realized that, in the Sub Region, more than 60% of the population is connected to mobile coverage with more than 367 million new phone subscribers by mid-2015 [29]. As the first transaction of payment made using mobile phones was carried out in 1997, researchers have developed keen interest in Mobile payments. Hitherto, practitioners have not been left out as emerging technologies are refocusing on mobile computing,

Published by Springer Nature Switzerland AG 2019
Y. Dwivedi et al. (Eds.): TDIT 2019, IFIP AICT 558, pp. 128–146, 2019.
https://doi.org/10.1007/978-3-030-20671-0_9

wireless web and m-commerce providing increasing value for customers and banking transactions [1, 2].

In the early 2000s, mobile payments became part of the already established list of electronic payments; internet banking and electronic cards (debit and credit cards). However, m-payments used to be seen as a new technological innovation to handle, for instance, small cash transactions (micro-payments) though there were reports of tried and failed solutions. Nevertheless, prospects and numerous benefits have been identified [14, 65, 75]. Mobile payments are of benefit to consumers, business entities or merchants and service providers. It enables users to perform their transaction independent of location and complements the wide range of existing e-payment systems, such as digital credit cards, digital wallets systems, micro-payment systems [75]. On the other hand, M-payments could be developed into a "well-functioning e-payment system which have much relevance on financial stability, monetary policy and overall economic activity" creating the enabling environment to move towards cashless economy [11, 36].

Notably, mobile payments being almost non-existent in 2007 are currently having 277 million subscribers registered out of which 100 million are active users [30]. This trend looks promising noting that mobile telephony is regarded as 'single most transformative technology for development' as stated by Jeffrey Sachs, an economist ("Bloomberg Business Week [40]"). Contributing to the growing literature, extant reviews on m-commerce in different context and geographical cover have been conducted; a review involving developing and developed countries, found the disparity in the research areas conducted on mobile payments; Consumer adoption and technological factors being well researched whilst merchant adoption, social and cultural factors, ecosystem of mobile payments were under-researched [14, 15].

The global interest in the role of mobile phone technologies in developing countries from donors, governments, regulators and the banking and commerce had been growing since 2007, being the beginning of coverage specifically Africa [16, 22]. In sync with the assertion by Webster and Watson [86] of a need to strengthen the field through reviews, researchers have acted such so far. One of such reviews centered on mobile payment for local adoption identifying methodological, geographical and conceptual gaps [16, 18] similar to findings iterated in the review conducted by Duncombe and Boateng [22] though the later focused on M-finance whilst the former was centered on Mobile money and Mobile payments. Boadi et al. [8] also looked into the impact of Mobile money and M-commerce on SMEs. As found by Wanjala [85] and Minischetti [61], women across countries in Sub-Saharan Africa have less access to banking than men, increasing the likelihood of women to be excluded from all financial services. This goes to suggest a need for enhancement to the design features of Mobile money services in order to reach the financially excluded and those beyond reach [30, 73].

More than half a decade on after the reviews by Diniz et al. [18] and Albuquerque et al. [16], with more studies having been published thereafter, it is well-timed to assess the spread and depth of research conducted on Mobile payments. This intends to set the agenda for future studies hitherto evaluate whether there is a sustained interest in Mobile payment research in Sub-Saharan Africa. The overall aim of this paper is to provide a literature review and synthesis of research concerning mobile payments in sub-Saharan Africa, classify and analyze conceptual approaches, evaluate methodologies used to carry out the studies, discuss evidences from those studies, identify gaps and outline the future research directions.

Subsequently Sect. 2 covers framing and methodology for review. Sections 3 and 4 entails the presentation and discussion of facts. Research gaps and future of research is covered in Sect. 5 and finally conclusion is drawn in Sect. 6.

2 Framing and Methodology for Review

2.1 Conceptualization of Mobile Payments

The context of mobile payments can be defined as follows: Any payment where a mobile device is used in order to initiate, activate, and/or confirm this payment where the mobile device has mobile phone capabilities (e.g. smartphones) and not general wireless capabilities like tablet PC [42]. It may refer to bill payments, acquisition payments, or a transfer of funds or money between financial agents, as well as being employed in the banking sector [16]. It is also considered as mobile proximity payments which could be conducted online as well as offline [25]. In this study, Mobile payments can therefore be generically viewed as leveraging digital mobility technologies to conduct payments or perform mobile form of transactions with or without the use of mobile telecommunications networks. Electronic money which is characterized by mobility and portability is termed as mobile-money or mobile-cash [16]. Mobile payments system is viewed as multi-sided platforms thus, are the set of stable components like high technology component while the other components are the merchants and consumers who are connected by a buyer-seller linkage. On the supply side, what is regarded as the chicken-egg dilemma is observed, when more actors are present to share resources and provide mobile payments platforms to consumers, the more consumers would like to adopt and use their mobile phone to pay and vice versa [14, 25]. Most of the key actors in Mobile Payment services market includes but not limited to consumers, merchants, Mobile Network Operators (MNO) and financial institutions. Additionally, vendors of handsets, software, networks also participate in significant numbers in order to realize positive externalities [14, 74]. In developing countries, which subscribe to the business model; the user centric models, primary actors of mobile money ecosystems have evolved from consumers, distribution agents and operators to include Technology partners, banks, merchants and regulatory bodies [81].

2.2 Classification of Literature

There are different types of literature review; systematic, which raise a defined question and seek answers to questions narrowing the quality of studies accessed [4]; 'A meta-analysis which uses statistical procedures to incorporate research findings from varying studies' (cf: [16]). The overall aim of the study as mentioned earlier is best featured as scoping or mapping study [45, 52]. As such, it aims at summarizing evidences from studies, examine the scope and nature of research activities, identifying gaps and set the agenda for future research.

In order to produce a good review, Webster and Watson [86] recommended that such reviews should be conceptually structured and based on a guiding theory. This enables past research to be classified, findings of such studies analyzed and aid in setting the agenda for future research. Therefore in scoping of this study, TOE framework and Porters 5 competitive factors strategy model were adopted as was done by Dahlberg et al. [14].

Porter's Competitive 5 Forces

This model is considered as one of the most influential management tools used by quite a number of practitioners and academics [41]. It is used to analyze the competitive environment on the level of business units [7]. The basic intention is that, industry structure dictates organizational performance. One of the strengths identified for the model is that, it provides one simple approach to analyze industry structure [38, 69].

Primarily, mobile payment market services actors are made up of mobile payment service providers and customers. The parties that assume these functions are merchants, consumers, telecoms among others. Additionally, software vendors, network as well as handset vendors could form part of the parties that interact in the market. Porter's model therefore describes and analyze key role of the mobile payment service providers and other market factors. The above arguments propose the suitability of the model to guide the classification of mobile payments services markets. The representation of the five forces within the literature framework is as follows; Traditional payment services, new e-payment systems, consumer power, merchant power and rivalry among the mobile payment service providers (Fig. 1).

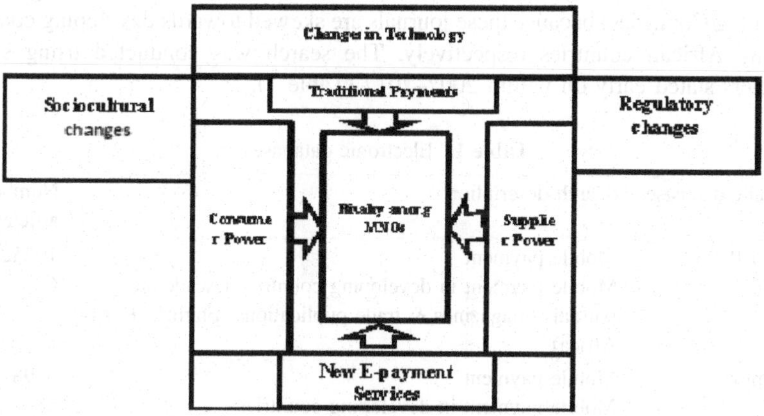

Fig. 1. Framework for literature review

TOE Framework

Apart from the competitive forces existing within the mobile payment's services markets, there are yet, other factors that impact like technology, regulatory activities, habits, national economy. Therefore, with the assumption that mobile payment services markets serve as unit of analysis (organization), these other factors serve as external forces that influence performance of the unit. The TOE framework purposefully developed to study organizational adoption of technological innovation by Tornatzky and Fleisher [84] consist of 3 elements; technological context, the organizational context, and the environmental context. Technological and environmental facts are external influences on the 'organization'. The 'organization' component of TOE framework is likened to the Mobile payment ecosystem. Therefore, the TOE framework is appropriate to classify mobile payments research and other external factors which are characteristic of mobile payment services markets.

2.3 Methodology for Review

Papers retrieved were from both academic source (peer-reviewed, working papers, conference papers) and practitioner sources (non-peer reviewed consultant report, technical reports). Google scholar does harness articles of these varied sources aforementioned. The search parameters were "Mobile Payments"; "Mobile Payments in developing countries" or "Mobile Payments in Africa" with time frame (2007–2017). Thereafter Elsevier's Scopus which is one of the largest abstracts and citation databases of peer-reviewed literature was chosen. Out of about 36,377 titles, 34,346 are peer-reviewed journals in top-level subject fields are represented in Scopus serving as great academic source. IEEE which is a database with engineering or technology inclination was also searched into with the same parameters. Upon critical examination of the papers, abstracts or citation that was spooled as search results, few represented studies conducted in sub Saharan Africa on Mobile payments. In this regard, the next searches were purposefully made in INFORMS- information systems, Africa Journals online and Wiley Online Library (specifically Electronic Journal of Information Systems in Developing Countries) because these journals are skewed towards developing countries including African countries respectively. The search was conducted using similar parameters stated early on within 2007–2017 (Table 1).

Table 1. Electronic databases

Electronic database	Search description	Number of articles
EBSCO ISTA	Mobile payment Mobile payment in developing countries (Academic journals, magazines & trade publications, English, Kenya, Africa)	10352 6
IEEExplore	Mobile payment Mobile payment in developing countries	3198 28
INFORMS - Information systems	Mobile payment Mobile payment in developing countries	113 43
Scopus	Mobile payment in developing countries	27
African journals online (AJOL)	Mobile payment	1
Wiley online library (EJISDC)	Mobile payment	159
Google scholar	Mobile payment Mobile payment in developing country	7

51 articles drawn from the search were critically examined with a few eliminated. The criteria for elimination were studies conducted in developing countries but not within Sub-Saharan Africa, studies conducted in no stated location though tagged as developing country, books and periodicals. Books were exempted as they are good for understanding concepts, theories and conceptual frameworks and periodicals has some level of uncertain accuracy [9]. 37 articles were left for the intended review (List shown in Appendix A) (Table 2).

Table 2. Electronic database with corresponding articles retrieved

Electronic database	Number of articles
EBSCO ISTA	3
IEEExplore	3
Scopus	12
African journals online (AJOL)	1
Google scholar	7
Wiley online library (EJISDC)	11

3 Presentation of Findings

The findings attained after reviewing the 31 articles were classified and represented subsequently (Fig. 2).

3.1 Publication Year and Outlets

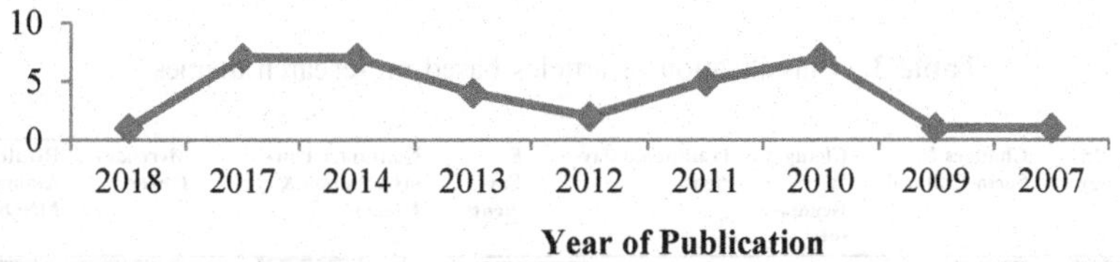

Fig. 2. Articles distribution (2007–2018)

About 31% of the articles were from the journal, Electronic Journal of Information Systems for Developing Countries (EJISDC) with 6% each retrieved from The Journal of Language, Technology & Entrepreneurship in Africa and IEEE.

3.2 Geographical Concentration and Authorship

The geographical location category tagged Africa is representative of studies conducted with holistic view of all countries on the continent or comparative analysis of two African countries; 26% of such studies were found. This was the highest followed by Kenya of about 17% with Ghana, Nigeria, Tanzania and Malawi pooling 9% each.

Other countries like Zimbabwe, Mauritius and Egypt were represented though marginally. In terms of authorship, all with the exception of Irwin Brown of South Africa, whose name appeared in two publications, the rest appeared once.

Nature of the Studies

Most of the studies reviewed on a yearly basis showed the nature of conceptual study which basically took the form of narrative or case study analysis and document analysis, others showed evidence of field data thus empirical in nature then there were a few which had traits of both conceptual and empirical in the study hence tagged as "Mixed" in this study (Fig. 3).

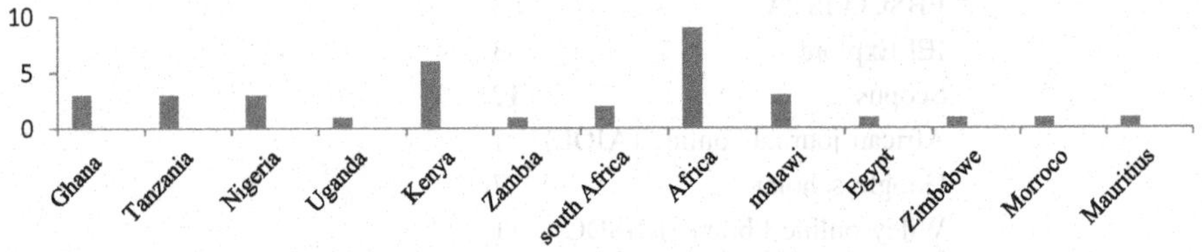

Fig. 3. Geographical concentration

3.3 Research Themes

Using the Tag Numbers of the articles shown in Appendix A, the respective classification of literature earmarked showed that most of the studies were oriented towards the technological platforms that aid in mobile payment services or mobile banking services followed by Consumer adoption, the Socio-cultural changes or contextual changes. Studies on Traditional payments were the least represented (Table 3).

Table 3. Classification of articles based on research themes

Changes In Technology	Changes In Socio-Cultural	Changes In Regulatory	Traditional Payments	E-Payments	Consumer Power(Adoption & Usage)	Merchant Power	Rivalry Among MNOs
3, 8 14, 15 17, 18, 19, 32 27, 13	13 34 35	7 22 28		20, 21 23, 27 13	1, 5 9, 16 25,0	6, 24 26,11 31,2	2, 4 10,1 2

Using the Tag Numbers of the articles shown in Appendix A, the respective classification of literature earmarked showed that most of the studies were oriented towards the technological platforms that aid in mobile payment services or mobile banking services followed by Consumer adoption, the Socio-cultural changes or contextual changes. Studies on Traditional payments were the least represented (Table 4).

3.4 Research Frameworks

Table 4. Research themes with respective dominant theories used

Changes in Technology	System Development process framework Most were of narrative or case study nature with no specific theory
Sociocultural Changes	Review of related work 3Cs used by Kalakota and Whinston (2002); The New Institutional Economics approach (NIE)
Regulatory Changes	Activity Theory
Traditional Payments	None
Repayment	TAM,DOI, Revised UTAUT TAM, Extended TAM with environmental variables
Consumer power	
Merchant Power	multilevel perspective of sociotechnical transformation (MLP),Actor Network Theory
Rivalry among MNOs	

3.5 Research Methodology

Most of the studies were exploratory in nature followed by few others that used empirical data to validate models and ascertaining relationships among determinants. The least representation was the approach of using both quantitative and qualitative methods.

3.6 Level of Analysis

In the analysis of the studies, there were those whose focus where on individuals or consumers (Micro level), then those that looked within the industry or business sector (Meso level), nationwide (Macro) and inter country or regional analysis (Meta) (Table 5).

Table 5. Level of analysis

Micro	Meso	Macro	Meta
1, 5, 6, 9, 24, 25,26,34,37,	10 11 12 30	3,4,7,8,16,17,18,19,20,21, 22,23,29,31,35,	2,14, 15,27,28,32, 33,36

Most of the analyses were based on the national level moving on to Meta level of studies.

4 Discussion of Findings

4.1 Publication Year and Outlets

The publications over the period, which were exclusively centered on Sub-Saharan Africa, were scanty in nature though quite a sizeable number that were retrieved focused on developing countries. This scanty representation is a confirmation of Boadi et al. [8] observation. Thus, the lack of contributions to global m-commerce debate from African perspective is rather parsimonious. The outlets from which these publications were found seemed narrowed as majority were from EJISDC whilst the rest were sparsely distributed in other outlets.

4.2 Geographical Concentration and Authorship

Though there were countries almost from East, West, Central, South and North of the African continent, the concentration was mainly in Kenya. Most of the studies grounded their argument on the fact that the success story of M-Pesa in Kenya has sparked a lot of interest amongst researchers on the continent hence most of the studies if wasn't conducted in Kenya, had direct references to M-Pesa as case study.

4.3 Research Themes and Sub-themes

Changes in Technology
Most of the studies were more into technological framework of mobile payment platform, drawbacks or challenges pertaining to the adoption of mobile technology among others. The drawbacks identified were cybercrime, resistance to change, and compatibility of mobile gadgets. On the other hand, few of the studies found that of group meetings. Mobile-banking applications have the potential to encourage financial discipline in even more effective ways. Further to, some of the studies developed mobile payment solutions e.g. The web API developed for Orange Money shows how secure access can aid in the development of mobile applications using Orange Money as mobile payment per articles reviewed represented in Appendix with tag [14, 17].

Changes in Socio-Cultural factors
The political environments as well as quality of existing retail infrastructure, regulatory contribute to the impact of mobile technology but the study did not restrict itself to only socio-cultural factors. Nevertheless, values appealing to rural dwellers are cost, convenience and communication due to the nature of social interaction among especially rural dwellers [8].

Changes in Regulatory factors
Regulatory factors like authorization of payment institutions, surveillance of money transfers, and ownership of foreign currency accounts were identified as key factors that influence the quality of the Mobile payment system. One of the studies tagged [22] as

shown in Appendix explored the framework that best fit the Nigerian context and regulatory factors happen to be an area which needed further investigation.

Consumer Power
Similar to the findings of the reviews conducted by Dahlberg et al. [14] and Dahlberg et al. [15], consumer adoption issues have been well researched into [89]. Mostly, factors determining adoption were found to be ease of use and risk perception; serving as most influential factors in mobile banking adoption; cultural values influencing factor in adoption; using early adopters as ambassadors; membership of an association (social influence) serve as factor for adoption were picked up from the reviewed articles [1, 16, 26, 30].

Merchant Power
Most of the merchant adoption studies reviewed was narrowed to the Agriculture sector. It dwelt basically on microbusinesses or micro entrepreneurs in the markets, fishing communities. It was found in one of the studies represented that Mobile money facilitate growth in business [6]; Use of mobile phones enabled fishermen to improve their incomes, expand their markets, feel more secure at sea, and remain in closer touch with both families and other fishermen [24].

Traditional payments
Similar to what was found in earlier reviews [14, 15], virtually none of the studies dwelt on the traditional form of payments. There is always a need to review earlier forms of payments, examine the flaws and setbacks in order to strengthen the numerous electronic payments products being introduced into the market.

Electronic Payments
The studies under this classification took a look specifically at mobile banking and mobile payments as a form of electronic payments and the institutional set up required to implement them. There was also a comparative analysis done between mobile payment systems and the traditional systems with no reference to the other forms of electronic products like electronic cards [21].

Rivalry Among MNOs
As Mobile payment system was conceived as multi-sided platform, the studies in this category looked at the various constituents of such platform and proposed different business levels; bank independent, collaborative nature, MNO led or Bank dependent. Each of the business proposal obviously comes with various forms of 'rivalry' [4].

4.4 Research Frameworks

Technology Acceptance Model (TAM) was highly used in relation to Consumer and Merchant adoption and usage. This was followed by Diffusion of Innovations (DOI) theory then Unified theory of Acceptance and Use of Technology (UTAUT). However, the TAM was extended with other environmental factors in some cases when was used as theoretical basis in Merchant adoption. The same occurred for UTAUT. This is similar to an earlier study which found that, the conceptual model mostly used in mobile technology adoption has been found to be Technology Acceptance Model (TAM) then UTAUT the third widely used.

4.5 Research Methodology

Qualitative research seeks to understand situations in their uniqueness as part of a particular context and the interactions there whilst Quantitative research determines the extent of a problem or existence of a relationship [9]. Usually as qualitative research seeks to explore phenomenon which should be tested using quantitative methodology, the studies under review did not show this trend. There are 11 studies using qualitative methodology and only 6 using quantitative. There are bound to be knowledge gap between phenomenon explored and the confirmation of hypothesis about the phenomenon. Mixed form of methodology is highly commendable both approaches are carried out in one study bringing some level of finality to nature of the study. Notably, the dominant methods used for qualitative approach were observations, interviews, focus groups; case studies whilst survey characterized most of the studies conducted using quantitative study.

4.6 Level of Analysis

The national outlook of analysis took the form of analyzing contextual, regulatory, technological framework that either ensures successful implementation of mobile technology or also ensures sustenance. Meta, the inter-national or regional level of analysis was the next predominant level along with micro. For the latter, most of the studies had Kenya M-Pesa case as the reference point of analysis. The studies that entailed the comparative analysis of two African countries was either between Kenya and another African country.

5 Research Gaps and Future Research

This study identified Contextual, Theoretical and Methodological gaps as was found in earlier studies [16, 22].

5.1 Contextual Gaps

As was earlier mentioned, due to the M-peas success story in Kenya, it was expected that most of the countries on the continent should record same. However, this has not been the case hence further investigations need to be conducted to understand the factors determining the disparities in adoption even in Kenya.

5.2 Theoretical Gaps

Although earlier studies used TAM to explain the adoption of m-payment services, to the authors′ best knowledge, few studies have focused on the impact of user-centric, security factors, system characteristics and gender differences on m-payment adoption by the general public in Tanzania.

5.3 Methodological

Fewer studies have undertaken exploratory form of research to have a deeper understanding of the interactions and relationships that are created amongst stakeholders of a national mobile payment system and by so doing build on theories thus using interpretive approach.

Additional to the three forms of gaps identified is undeniably the unfortunate dearth of studies that examine the limitations of mobile money implementations and provide recommendations for improving this important tool for financial inclusion and a lack of African perspective in the debate surrounding global m-commerce debate.

5.4 Direction of Future Research

Studies likely to be conducted in the future on the basis of the eight classifications of literature are as follows

i. Changes in Technology

The mobile solution requirements needed by merchants would have to be looked at and examine how they could participate in the development of these solutions. In addition, studies should look at how fruitful and profitable collaboration could be carried out between developers of innovative solutions and telecom operators.

ii. Changes in Socio-cultural factors

A few of the studies on adoption looked into the rural setting which is characterized by several unique socio-cultural factors hence further studies could look at different settings either urban or even national or Regional. This will aid in determining the unique factors that distinguish between different contexts.

iii. Changes in Regulatory system

The business model opted for by a country determines the nature of regulation to be conducted. Therefore, investigations into the different proposed business models and how regulatory systems are to be changed to reflect this choice would be required.

iv. Consumer adoption

Thoroughly researched but further studies could be conducted to extend the theories used for adoption to include the outcome or impact of adoption and post adoption behaviors (continual use or addiction).

v. Merchant adoption

Factors that facilitate adoption by Merchants or micro-entrepreneurs of various business sectors should be determined. Though studies focused more on Agriculture sector, other sectors could be look at.

vi. E-payment systems

Further studies could be conducted to have a comparative study of all electronic payment systems and to understand the nature of usage at the macro level to find out which of the e-payment systems could drive the cashless economy agenda of most developing countries.

vii. Traditional payments

Studies would have to examine the characteristics of the various scenarios for which traditional payment is applicable and also the flaws plaguing it and how knowledge of this could be used to enhance the mobile payment platform.

viii. Rivalry among MNOs

Looking forward to providing a business model that would suit the context within which mobile payment systems are to be introduced. A thorough investigations into which type of model suit a particular defined context.

6 Conclusion

The influx of mobile phones worldwide has given way to mobility digital systems aiding varying businesses. The Sub Saharan Africa has enjoyed a large part of the coverage. In order to strengthen the field, there was a need to review literature and to be informed of the knowledge gaps setting agenda for researchers and practitioners. This study focused on studies conducted in the sub region and drew from TOE framework and Porter's five competitive forces to classify the literature. There weren't many articles found in the limited outlets available. Merchant adoption, Consumer adoption and Changes in Technology were found to be well researched similar to earlier reviews by Dahlberg et al. [14] and Dahlberg et al. [15]. Most of the analysis were based on Micro and Macro levels thus consumer and nationwide levels as well as inter-national or regional analysis. These findings led to the identification of contextual, theoretical and methodological gaps and hitherto chart the path for the nature of studies to be undertaken by researchers.

Appendix A

List of Articles

Tag	Year	Author names	Title
1	2018	Gichuki, C.N., Mulu-Mutuku, M.	Determinants of awareness and adoption of mobile money technologies: evidence from women micro entrepreneurs in Kenya
2	2017	Jan Lepoutre, Augustina Oguntoye	The (Non-)emergence of mobile money systems in sub-saharan africa: a comparative multilevel perspective of Kenya and Nigeria

(*continued*)

(*continued*)

Tag	Year	Author names	Title
3	2017	Kanjo, C., Phiri, Y., Mtumbuka, F., Manda, T.	ICT solutions for financial inclusion: reaching out to the unbanked in low resource settings
4	2017	Goher, M., Rizka, M.A. - abstract	An extension for the mobile payment collaborative model proposed for developing countries—Egypt case study
5	2017	Lwoga, E.T., Lwoga, N.B.	User acceptance of mobile payment: the effects of user-centric security, system characteristics and gender
6	2017	Amegbe, H., Hanu, C., Nuwasiima, A.	Small-scale individual entrepreneurs (Sies) and the usage of mobile money (M-Money) and mobile commerce (M-Commerce) in facilitating business growth in Ghana
7	2017	Frederick Kanobe, Patricia M Alexander, Kelvin J Bwalya	Policies, regulations and procedures and their effects on mobile money systems in Uganda
8	2017	Paul Mupfiga and Tafadzwa Padare	The rise of mobile technology on the financial sector in Zimbabwe
9	2014	Nyirenda, M., Chikumba, P.A.	Consumer adoption of mobile payment systems in Malawi: case of airtel Malawi ZAP in Blantyre city
10	2014	Harry, R., Sewchurran, K., Brown, I.	Introducing a mobile payment system to an emerging economy's mobile phone subscriber market. an actor network perspective
11	2014	Dismas Anthony2 and Darlene K. Mutalemwa	Factors influencing the use of mobile payments in Tanzania: insights from Zantel's Z-Pesa1 services
12	2014	Ricardo Harry Kosheek Sewchurran Irwin Brown	Introducing a mobile payment system to an emerging economy's mobile phone subscriber market. An actor network perspective
13	2014	Patrick K. Wamuyu	The role of contextual factors in the uptake and continuance of mobile money usage in Kenya
14	2014	Jake Kendall and Rodger Voorhies	The mobile-finance revolution: how cell phones can spur development
15	2014	Dibia Victor	On the user-centric evolution of mobile money technologies in developing nations: successes and lessons
16	2013	Berrado, A., Elfahli, S., El Garah, W.	Using data mining techniques to investigate the factors influencing mobile payment adoption in Morocco

(*continued*)

(*continued*)

Tag	Year	Author names	Title
17	2013	Doolhur, N., Suddul, G., Foogooa, R., Richomme, M.	An open API to monetize mobile micro-services for emerging countries
18	2013	Nana Mbinkeu, R.C	Analysis and design of mobile payment platform in African context
19	2013	Zilole Simate	Evaluation of mobile network security a case of mobile transactions in Zambia
20	2012	Suri, Tavneet; Jack, William; Stoker, Thomas M.	Documenting the birth of a financial economy
21	2012	Kabanda, S.K., Downes, A., Baltazar Dos Ramos, S.	Mobile banking services in South Africa: the case of M-Pesa
22	2011	Ayo, C.K., Adewoye, J.O., Oni, A.A.	Development of a framework for mobile money implementation in Nigeria
23	2011	Austin Briggs/Laurence Brooks	Electronic payment systems development in a developing country: the role of institutional arrangements
24	2011	Mahamadu Salia, Nicholas N.N. Nsowah-Nuamah, William F. Steel	Effects of mobile phone use on artisanal fishing market efficiency and livelihoods in Ghana1
25	2011	Felix O. Bankole, Omolola O. Bankole, Irwin Brown	Mobile banking adoption in Nigeria
26	2011	Bjorn Furuholt, Edmund Matotay	The developmental contribution from mobile phones across the agricultural value chain in rural Africa
27	2010	Goodman, Seymour; Harris, Andrew	The coming African tsunami of information insecurity
28	2010	Brown, Bethany	Mobile phones: reshaping the flow of Urban-To-Rural remittances
30	2010	Benjamin Ngugi, Matthew Pelowski, Javier Gordon Ogembo	M-Pesa: a case study of the critical early adopters' role in the rapid adoption of mobile money banking in Kenya
31	2010	Marion Mbogo	The impact of mobile payments on the success and growth of micro-business: the case of m-pesa in Kenya
32	2010	Sebastiana Etzo and Guy Collender	Briefing: the mobile phone 'revolution' in Africa: rhetoric or reality?
33	2010	Jenny C. Aker and Isaac M. Mbiti	Mobile phones and economic development in Africa
34	2010	Alfred Said Sife, Elizabeth Kiondo and Joyce G. Lyimo-Macha	Contribution of mobile phones to rural livelihoods and poverty reduction inmorogoro region, Tanzania
35	2011	Austin Briggs and Laurence Brooks	Electronic payment systems development in a developing country: the role of institutional arrangements

(*continued*)

(*continued*)

Tag	Year	Author names	Title
36	2009	Amrik Heyer and Ignacio Mas1	Seeking fertile grounds for mobile money
37	2007	Raymond A. Boadi, Richard Boateng, Robert Hinson and Robert A. Opoku	Preliminary insights into m-commerce adoption in Ghana

References

1. Afshan, S., Arshian, S.: Acceptance of mobile banking framework in Pakistan. Telematics Inform. **33**(2), 370–387 (2016)
2. Aker, J.C., Boumnijel, R., McClelland, A., Tierney, N.: Payment mechanisms and antipoverty programs: evidence from a mobile money cash transfer experiment in Niger. Econ. Dev. Cult. Change **65**(1), 1–37 (2016)
3. Al-Jabiri, M.I., Sohail, M.S.: Mobile banking adoption: application of diffusion of innovative theory. J. Electron. Commer. Res. **13**(4), 379–391 (2012)
4. Arksey, H., O'Malley, L.: Scoping studies: towards a methodological framework. Int. J. Soc. Res. Methodol. **8**(1), 19–32 (2005)
5. Ashoka, M.L., Rakesh, T.S., Madhushree, S.: Consumer perception and satisfaction towards internet banking and mobile banking with reference to nationalized banks in rural India. Int. J. Asian Bus. Inf. Manag. (IJABIM) **8**(4), 29–40 (2017)
6. Au, Y.A., Kauffman, R.J.: The economics of mobile payments: understanding stakeholder issues for an emerging financial technology application. Electron. Commer. Res. Appl. **7**(2), 141–164 (2008)
7. Breedveld, E., Meijboom, B., De Roo, A.: Labour supply in the home care industry: a case study in a Dutch region. Health Policy **76**(2), 144–155 (2006)
8. Boadi, R.A., Boateng, R., Hinson, R., Opoku, R.A.: Preliminary insights into m-commerce adoption in Ghana. Inf. Dev. **23**(4), 253–265 (2007)
9. Boateng, R.: Research Made Easy (2016)
10. Cao, X., Yu, L., Liu, Z., Gong, M., Adeel, L.: Understanding mobile payment users' continuance intention: a trust transfer perspective. Internet Res. **28**(2), 456–476 (2018)
11. Central Bank of Nigeria. The Cashless Nigeria Project (2011)
12. Chaffey, D.: E-Business And E-Commerce Management: Strategy, Implementation and Practice. Pearson Education, London (2009)
13. Chou, C.H., Chiu, C.H., Ho, C.Y., Lee, J.C.: Understanding mobile apps continuance usage behavior and habit: an expectance-confirmation theory. In: PACIS, p. 132 (2013)
14. Dahlberg, T., Mallat, N., Ondrus, J., Zmijewska, A.: Past, present and future of mobile payments research: a literature review. Electron. Commer. Res. Appl. **7**(2), 165–181 (2008)
15. Dahlberg, T., Guo, J., Ondrus, J.: A critical review of mobile payment research. Electron. Commer. Res. Appl. **14**, 265–284 (2015)
16. de Albuquerque, J.P., Diniz, E.H., Cernev, A.K.: Mobile payments: a scoping study of the literature and issues for future research. Inf. Dev. **32**(3), 527–553 (2014)
17. Dennehy, D., Sammon, D.: Trends in mobile payments research: a literature review. J. Innov. Manag. **3**(1), 49 (2015)

18. Diniz, E.H., Porto de Albuquerque, J., Cernev, A.K.: Mobile money and payment: a literature review based on academic and practitioner-oriented publications (2001–2011) (2011)
19. Donovan, K.: Mobile money for financial inclusion. Inf. Commun. Dev. **61**(1), 61–73 (2012)
20. Donner, J., Escobari, M.X.: A review of evidence on mobile use by micro and small enterprises in developing countries. J. Int. Dev. **22**(5), 641–658 (2010)
21. Duncombe, R., Boateng, R.: Mobile phones and financial services in developing countries: a review of concepts, methods, issues, evidence and future research directions. Third World Q. **30**(7), 1237–1258 (2009)
22. Effah, J.: Institutional effects on e-payment entrepreneurship in a developing country: enablers and constraints. Inf. Technol. Dev. **22**(2), 205–219 (2016)
23. Flood, D., West, T., Wheadon, D.: Trends in mobile payments in developing and advanced economies. RBA Bull. 71–80 (2013)
24. Gannamaneni, A., Ondrus, J., Lyytinen, K.: A post-failure analysis of mobile payment platforms. In: 2015 48th Hawaii International System Sciences Conference (HICSS), pp. 1159–1168, January 2015
25. Gaur, A., Ondrus, J.: The role of banks in the mobile payment ecosystem: a strategic asset perspective. In: Proceedings of the 14th Annual International Conference on Electronic Commerce, pp. 171–177). ACM, August 2012
26. Giovanis, A.N., Binioris, S., Polychronopoulos, G.: An extension of TAM model with IDT and security/privacy risk in the adoption of internet banking services in Greece. EuroMed J. Bus. **7**(1), 24–53 (2012)
27. GSM Intelligence (2009). www.gsmworld.com. Accessed 9 Apr 2007
28. G.S.M.A.: Global Data. GSMA Intelligence (2015)
29. GSMA: State of the Industry Report on Mobile Money: Decade Edition 2006–2016. GSMA, London, UK (2017)
30. Groupe Spéciale Mobile Association (GSMA). State of the Industry Report on (2017)
31. Mobile Money, Decade Edition: 2006 – 2016 (Tech.). London
32. Heyer, A., Mas, I.: Fertile grounds for mobile money: towards a framework for analysing enabling environments. Enterp. Dev. Microfinance **22**(1), 30–44 (2011)
33. Hsu, C.S., Chou, S.W., Min, H.T.: Understanding post-adoption of online shopping continuance usage through the social exchange theory. In: PACIS, p. 75, June 2014
34. Ikpefan, O.A., Omankhanle, O.A.: Fast tracking business transactions through cashless economy. Niger. Banker, 17–26 (2012)
35. Ismail, R., Jeffery, R., Van Belle, J.P.: Using ICT as a value adding tool in South African SMEs. J. African Res. Bus. Technol. **2011**, 1–12 (2011)
36. Johnson, G., Scholes, K.: Exploring Corporate Strategy, 6th edn. Financial Times/Prentice Hall, Harlow (2002)
37. Juniper Research 2009. Mobile payment on the rise. http://www.mobiletechnews.com/info/2006/05/09/112000.html. Accessed 09 Apr 2007
38. 'Upwardly mobile in Africa', Bloomberg Business Week. businessweek.com/magazine/content/07_39/b4051054. Accessed 24 Sept 2007
39. Karagiannopoulos, G., Georgopoulos, N., Nikolopoulos, K.: Fathoming Porter's five forces model in the Internet era. J. Policy Regul. Strategy Telecommun. **7**(6), 66–76 (2005)
40. Karnouskos, S., Fokus, F.: Mobile payment: a journey through existing procedures and standardization initiatives. IEEE Commun. Surv. **6**(4), 44–66 (2004). The Electronic Magazine of Original Peer-Reviewed Survey Articles, Fourth Quarter
41. Kemal, A.A.: Mobile banking in the government-to-person payment sector for financial inclusion in Pakistan. Inf. Technol. Dev. 1–28 (2018)

42. Khan, J., Craig-Lees, M.: "Cashless" transactions: perceptions of money in mobile payments (2009)
43. Kitchenham, B.A., Budgen, D., Brereton, O.P.: Using mapping studies as the basis for further research – a participant-observer case study. Inf. Softw. Technol. **53**(6), 638–651 (2011)
44. Kim, H.W., Chan, H.C., Gupta, S.: Value-based adoption of mobile internet: an empirical investigation. Decis. Support Syst. **43**(1), 111–126 (2007)
45. Kshetri, N., Acharya, S.: Mobile payments in emerging markets. IT Professional **14**(4), 9–13 (2012)
46. Laary, D.: Ghana: mobile phone penetration soars to 128% (2016)
47. Isaac Owusu-Dankwa, Emmanuel Eris Appiah, Godfred Mawutor
48. Lai, P.M., Chuah, K.B.: Developing an analytical framework for mobile payments adoption in retailing: a supply-side perspective. In: 2010 Fourth International Conference on Management of e-Commerce and e-Government (ICMeCG), pp. 356–361, October 2010
49. Waverman, L., Meschi, M., Fuss, M.: The impact of télécoms on economic growth in developing countries. In: Vodafone, p. 2. * Africa: the impact of mobile phones'
50. Levac, D., Colquhoun, H., O'Brien, K.K.: Scoping studies: advancing the methodology. Implementation Sci.: IS **5**, 69 (2010)
51. Lippincott, J.K.: A mobile future for academic libraries. Ref. Serv. Rev. **38**(2), 205–213 (2010)
52. Linck, K., Pousttchi, K., Wiedemann, D.G.: Security issues in mobile payment from the customer viewpoint (2006)
53. Martens, M., Roll, O., Elliott, R.: Testing the technology readiness and acceptance model for mobile payments across Germany and South Africa. Int. J. Innov. Technol. Manag. **14**(06), 1750033 (2017)
54. Mas, I., Radcliffe, D.: Mobile payments go viral: M-PESA in Kenya (2010)
55. Mathew, M., Magnier-Watanabe, R., Pratheeba, S., Balakrishnan, N.: Assessing technology differences in electronic and mobile payment systems among developed and developing countries. Int. J. Innov. Technol. Manag. **11**(02), 1450005 (2014)
56. Mallat, N., Rossi, M., Tuunainen, V.K.: Mobile banking services. Commun. ACM **47**(5), 42–46 (2004)
57. Merritt, C.: Mobile money transfer services: the next phase in the evolution of person-to-person payments. J. Payments Strategy Syst. **5**(2), 143–160 (2011)
58. Miao, M., Jayakar, K.: Mobile payments in Japan, South Korea and China: cross-border convergence or divergence of business models? Telecommun. Policy **40**(2–3), 182–196 (2016)
59. Minischetti, E.: Mapping the mobile money gender gap: Insights from Côte d'Ivoire and Mali (2017)
60. Mubarik, A.: Bog Advocates For Cashless Economy: The Move Is in Collaboration With the Ghana Interbank Payment and Settlement Systems Limited (Ghipps) (2016)
61. Nyavor, G.: Five major crimes increase by 45% in Accra'- Dr Aning highlights troubling figures (2018)
62. Ondrus, J., Pigneur, Y.: Towards a holistic analysis of mobile payments: a multiple perspectives approach. Electron. Commer. Res. Appl. **5**(3), 246–257 (2006)
63. Ondrus, J., Lyytinen, K., Pigneur, Y.: Why mobile payments fail? Towards a dynamic and multi-perspective explanation. In: 42nd Hawaii International Conference on System Sciences, HICSS 2009, pp. 1–10. IEEE, January 2009
64. Owusu-Dankwa, I., Appiah, E.E., Mawutor, G.: Customers perception and usage of E-Payments in Ghana. J. Contemp. Integr. Ideas **2**(2) (2014)

65. Ozcan, P., Santos, F.M.: The market that never was: Turf wars and failed alliances in mobile payments. Strateg. Manag. J. **36**(10), 1486–1512 (2015)
66. Ondrus, J., Pigneur, Y.: A multi-stakeholder multi-criteria assessment framework of mobile payments: an illustration with the Swiss public transportation industry. In: Proceedings of the 39th Annual Hawaii International Conference on System Sciences, HICSS 2006, vol. 2, p. 42a. IEEE, January 2006
67. Pearce, J., Robinson, R.: Strategic Management, 9th edn. McGraw-Hill, New York (2005)
68. Pope, M., et al.: Mobile payments: The reality on the ground in selected Asian countries and the United States. Int. J. Mobile Market. **6**(2) (2011)
69. Porter, M.E.: Competitive Strategy, p. 1998. Free Press, New York (1998)
70. Reynolds et al. CICOs
71. Rochet, J.C., Tirole, J.: Platform competition in two-sided markets. J. Eur. Econ. Assoc. **1** (4), 990–1029 (2003)
72. Rouibah, K.: The failure of mobile payment: evidence from quasi-experimentations. In: Proceedings of the 2009 Euro American Conference on Telematics and Information Systems: New Opportunities to increase Digital Citizenship, p. 29. ACM, June 2009
73. Russell, C., Cieslik, N.: Mobile phone access reaches three quarters of planet's population. The World Bank (2012)
74. San Martín, S., López-Catalán, B., Ramón-Jerónimo, M.A.: Factors determining firms' perceived performance of mobile commerce. Ind. Manag. Data Syst. **112**(6), 946–963 (2012)
75. Shankar, A., Datta, B.: Factors affecting mobile payment adoption intention: an Indian perspective. Global Bus. Rev. **19**(3_suppl), S72–S89 (2018)
76. Slade, E.L., Dwivedi, Y.K., Piercy, N.C., Williams, M.D.: Modeling consumers' adoption intentions of remote mobile payments in the United Kingdom: extending UTAUT with innovativeness, risk, and trust. Psychol. Market. **32**(8), 860–873 (2015)
77. Sulaiman, A.: The status of e-commerce applications in Malaysia. Inf. Technol. Dev. **9**(3–4), 153–161 (2000)
78. Tobin, P.: Understanding the mobile money ecosystem: Roles, Structure and Strategies. In: 10th International Conference on Mobile Business, Aalborg (2011)
79. Tobbin, P., Kuwornu, J.K.: Adoption of mobile money transfer technology: structural equation modeling approach. Eur. J. Bus. Manag. **3**(7), 59–77 (2011)
80. Tornatzky, L.G., Fleisher, M.: The context of technological innovation (1990)
81. Wanjala, B.M.: Gendered asset inequalities in Africa. Development **57**(3–4), 472–480 (2014)
82. Webster, S., Watson, R.: Analyzing the past to prepare for the future: writing a literature review. MIS Q. **26**(2), pixie–xxiii (2002)
83. Zhou, T., Lu, Y., Wang, B.: Integrating TTF and UTAUT to explain mobile banking user adoption. Comput. Hum. Behav. **26**(4), 760–767 (2010)
84. Zwass, V.: Electronic commerce: structure and issues. Int. J. Electron. Commer. **1**(1), 3–23 (1996)
85. Slade, E.L., Williams, M.D., Dwivedi, Y.K.: Mobile payment adoption: classification and review of the extant literature. Market. Rev. **13**(2), 167–190 (2013)
86. Slade, E.L., Williams, M.D., Dwivedi, Y.K.: Devising a research model to examine adoption of mobile payments: an extension of UTAUT2. Market. Rev. **14**(3), 310–335 (2014)
87. Slade, E., Williams, M., Dwivedi, Y., Piercy, N.: Exploring consumer adoption of proximity mobile payments. J. Strat. Market. **23**(3), 209–223 (2015)
88. Kapoor, K.K., Dwivedi, Y.K., Williams, M.D.: Examining the role of three sets of innovation attributes for determining adoption of the interbank mobile payment service. Inf. Syst. Frontiers **17**(5), 1039–1056 (2015)

Explaining Technology Adoption with Financial Motivation

Joseph Budu[1(✉)], Jefferson Seneadza[2], Edward Entee[3], Michael Fosu[4], Bismark Tei Asare[5], and Charles Mensah[6]

[1] Ghana Institute of Management and Public Administration, Accra, Ghana
josbudu@gimpa.edu.gh
[2] Tech Nation Ghana, Accra, Ghana
js@technationgh.com
[3] University of Ghana Business School, Accra, Ghana
eddy.entee@gmail.com
[4] University of Cape Coast, Cape Coast, Ghana
mikifosu@gmail.com
[5] Ghana Technology University College, Accra, Ghana
bismarkson@gmail.com
[6] Withrow University College, Kumasi, Ghana
rfcsmw@yahoo.com

Abstract. Several theories and their variant extensions have been posited to explain or to suggest factors that influence technology adoption. However, these theories seem inadequate in certain scenarios. For instance, none of such technology adoption theories identify or account for the possible influence of external non-personal and non-technology incentives or rewards or compensation on persons faced with the choice to accept or use a technology. However, existing psychology research posits a positive correlation between the offer of financial motivation and the performance of tasks. Therefore, this paper purposes to explain the relationship between financial motivation and individuals' technology adoption.

Keywords: Technology adoption · Financial motivation · Developing country

1 Introduction

The acceptance and use of new technology is not an exhausted issue in information systems research. This observation is evidenced by the many theories and their variant extensions that attempt either to explain or to suggest factors that influence technology adoption (Dwivedi et al. 2011; Williams et al. 2009). Despite their utility, these theories still harbour some inadequacies which yearn for fixing. Specifically, these theories have the understood assumption that people will accept and use technology because of factors pertaining to the technology in question, social conditions, and some personal considerations. For instance, Technology Acceptance Model holds that perceived usefulness and perceived ease of use drive people's intention to use a technology (Davis 1989). The Unified Theory of Acceptance and Use of Technology (UTAUT) also holds that

Published by Springer Nature Switzerland AG 2019
Y. Dwivedi et al. (Eds.): TDIT 2019, IFIP AICT 558, pp. 147–153, 2019.
https://doi.org/10.1007/978-3-030-20671-0_10

individuals within an organisation adopt technology because of performance expectancy, effort expectancy, social influence, and facilitating conditions (Dwivedi et al. 2017a, b; Rana et al. 2016; 2017; Venkatesh et al. 2003; Williams et al. 2015). UTAUT2 also posits that private individuals adopt technology because of UTAUT's factors plus hedonic motivation, price value, and habit (Venkatesh et al. 2012). The foregoing theories and their variables do not account for the potential for financial motivation to influence a private individual to adopt technology. Venkatesh et al. (2012) for instance, speaks of only hedonic motivation, thus overlooking non-hedonic extrinsic material motivation or rewards such as recognition programs, profit-sharing programs, pay increase, benefits and incentives (see Govindarajulu and Daily 2004).

Consequently, these theories fail to explain technology adoption in contexts in which technology adoption could be considered a task. For instance, an advertising company contracts with individuals to install a digital advertising screen in their vehicles. In such a scenario, the factors posited by extant technology adoption theories become inadequate because these individuals may consider financial compensation before accepting such a technology in their cars. Further, existing psychology research posits a positive correlation between the offer of financial incentives and task performance (Becker et al. 2010). Therefore, this paper argues that financial motivation can influence technology adoption. This study thus purposes to explain how financial motivation leads to individuals' adoption of technology.

Addressing consumers' economic motivations for accepting technology is not a minor issue because of the glaring evidence which points to positive correlations they have with task performance (see Becker et al. 2010). This study makes two main contributions to technology acceptance research. First, the study provides alternate explanations for the acceptance and use of new technology. Given Fishbein and Ajzen's (1975) observation that many variables affect the choice of how and when users will use a new technology, focusing on only the extant factors is a way of blinding ourselves to other working factors like financial motivation. Therefore, this paper in responding to calls for alternative theoretical mechanisms in information technology adoption research (see Bagozzi 2007; Venkatesh et al. 2007; Venkatesh et al. 2016), argues that there is a propensity for people to accept technology not just because it is useful or easy to use, or other people are using it, but because of expected financial incentive. Second, using interpretive epistemology and critical realism ontology, the study presents a case study of a very unique situation in which financial motivation influences the uptake of a new technology. Further, an accompanying in vivo analytical technique is used to extend the frontiers of a traditional technology acceptance theory, the UTAUT. Given the theorising nature of the case study method and in vivo analytical technique, it is plausible to consider the ensuing explanations as improvements in existing explanations for technology acceptance.

2 Preliminary Literature Review

Several predictive and explanatory theories of technology adoption and/use have been advanced (see Rondan-Cataluna et al. 2015 for a comprehensive review of technology acceptance theories). Despite their usefulness, the myriad of extension and revision attempts suggest their seeming insufficiency to explain either the adoption of certain technologies, or of technologies in certain contexts and situations. For instance, Ozkan et al. (2010) advance perceived advantage—the perception of a system's potential to reduce paperwork and be cost-effective—as an important factor in individual's adoption of electronic payment systems (see Venkatesh et al. 2012; Wang and Lin 2012; Alotaibi 2013; Slade et al. 2014; Slade et al. 2015a, b; Sheng and Zolfagharian 2014; Kapoor et al. 2015; Liu et al. 2015 for more examples of such extensions). Beneath such extensions lie the assumption of a separate human entity deciding to adopt and/use a certain technology. The context of this assumption is pertinent, hence, Venkatesh et al. (2012) distinguishes between an individual's adoption of technology within an organisation, and the other outside an organisation i.e. a private consumer, in advancing the UTAUT2 model. Private consumers face peculiar situations like financial risk, price value and motivation (Sheng and Zolfagharian 2014; Venkatesh et al. 2012).

We may be tempted to forcibly classify such peculiar factors under UTAUT's facilitating conditions – individual's perceptions of the resources and support available to adopt technology (Venkatesh et al. 2003). The implausibility of such attempt, however, is evidenced by the advancement of hedonic motivation and price value as factors for private consumer adoption of technology (Venkatesh et al. 2012). Whilst there has been an attempt to extend technology adoption theories with motivation, the focus of such attempts have been insufficient with regards to all its possible forms. Venkatesh et al. (2012) for instance, speaks of only hedonic motivation, thus overlooking non-hedonic extrinsic material motivation or rewards. In fact, such forms manifest in several forms as recognition programs, profit-sharing programs, pay increase, benefits and incentives (Govindarajulu and Daily 2004). The argument here then is that these material forms of motivation can influence private consumers who consider financial risk, and are looking for tangible benefits, to adopt some technology or vice versa.

Such an argument is not far-fetched if we further consider the private consumer in two forms; on one the one hand, the private consumer who is buying/adopting a technology for personal use and to achieve hedonic or even work-related satisfaction, and on the other hand, the private consumer who is acquiring/adopting a technology for financial gain. As Venkatesh et al. (2012) as already demonstrated the existence of hedonic motivation, let us consider its opposite. We know that a person will voluntarily act because of gaining a selfish reason after identifying a higher pay-off in a cost-benefit analysis of acting; and a financial pay-off guarantees more action (Darrington and Howell 2011, p. 43). We also know that financial incentives shape individual's preferences, and can even destroy her intrinsic motivation (Bowles 2008). Therefore, direct financial rewards attracting individuals to share their internet service and act as hotspots is not at all trivial (see Becker et al. 2010). Based on this argument, and attempting to move away from existing theories' limited explanatory or predictive possibilities, triviality and lack of practical value (Garača 2011), this study aims at explaining that when private individuals perceive the adoption of a technology as a task, they need to be financially motivated.

3 Proposed Methodology and the Way Forward

The empirical study will be approached with interpretive epistemology (Walsham 2006) which suggests the gathering of qualitative data. Interpretivism is important because private consumers may have different conditions that motivate them to adopt technology, and different conceptions concerning such conditions. Thus, the aim to understand how individuals view financial motivation, and why it influences them to adopt technology makes it important to capture subjects' interpretative meanings.

3.1 Research Approach

A case study approach (Cresswell 2007) will be used to examine the influence of financial motivation in individual's adoption of technology. We observed this issue observation of the In-Taxi Ad Project (iTAP) executed by Tech Nation, an Australian/Ghanaian owned technology-based company operating in Ghana (Tech Nation 2015). iTAP involves the installation of interactive headrest screens showing paid advertisement and free video clips to passengers who board commercial vehicles. Drivers who agree to the installation in their vehicles sign an agreement which guarantees monthly financial rewards for ensuring daily operation, and indemnity if the device is broken or lost. To this end this study explore how Tech Nation recruits commercial drivers, and what drivers consider before allowing Tech Nation to install the digital headrests in their cars. In operationalising this approach, purposive sampling will be used to select drivers who will be respondents; these drivers are those who have the screen installed in their cars.

3.2 Data Collection Methods

Data will be collected from meetings with Tech Nation management and staff, the company's website, and members of driver unions that Tech Nation has approached and installed their digital headrests. Documents like contracts, terms and conditions, and product descriptions and manuals will also be examined to ensure credibility of the interpretive epistemology to be adopted, and the veracity and dependability of the data.

Meetings. Face-to-face meetings will be held with the management and implementation or technical staff of Tech Nation to understand the rationale for giving financial rewards to taxi drivers who subscribe to iTAP, and the impact of such rewards on subscription.

Interviews. 30 taxi drivers who have joined iTAP, and 30 drivers in the same taxi terminals but have not joined iTAP will be interviewed to solicit their reasons for subscribing or otherwise, respectively. The interview data will be coded to reveal the perspectives of the interviewees concerning what influences their adoption decisions.

Website Content Analysis. Videos, audios, images, and text on Tech Nation's website will be analysed for information concerning iTAP. Such data will serve as triangulation and corroborative data for information gathered from interviews and meetings.

Document Analysis. Subscription contracts and service level agreements will be reviewed to verify payment amounts and risk management arrangements between the subscribing drivers and Tech Nation, as corroborative data.

3.3 Data Analysis

Analysis of this study's data will be approached with deductive reasoning (Ven de Ven 2007). Deduction will be adopted to explain how material rewards influence the uptake of technologies by private individuals outside an organisational setting. The other reasons for technology adoption as proposed by version 2 of the Unified Theory of Acceptance and Use of Technology (see Venkatesh et al. 2012) will also be identified from the data and coded using NVivo qualitative analysis software, and their inherent and contextual explanatory inadequacies discussed.

4 Conclusion and Directions for Future Work

This study proposes to explain how financial motivation contributes to the individuals' adoption of technology. This is an explanation which is largely missing in the technology adoption literature. Due to the peculiar contextual differences between individuals in an organisation, and those outside, future research needs to be interested in what factors could lead to individuals' adoption of technology. This paper in pursuit of explanations to fill this observed knowledge gap seeks to explain how financial motivation contributes to individuals' adoption of technology. Going forward, this study would execute the proposed methodology to collect empirical data. The data would be analysed to identify the extent to which financial motivation motivated individuals to allow digital headrests in their taxis to display advertisements and free videos to passengers. For theory, we hope this endeavour would contribute to a better explanation of factors that contribute to individuals' adoption of information technology. For practice, we hope that this study would illuminate how certain individuals consider technology adoption a task, and hence their expectation of financial motivation.

References

Alotaibi, M.B.: Determinants of mobile service acceptance in Saudi Arabia: a revised UTAUT model. Int. J. E-Serv. Mobile Appl. **5**(3), 43–61 (2013)

Bagozzi, R.P.: The legacy of the technology acceptance model and a proposal for a paradigm shift. J. AIS **8**(4), 244–254 (2007)

Becker, J.U., Clement, M., Schaedel, U.: The impact of network size and financial incentives on adoption and participation in new online communities. J. Media Econ. **23**, 165–179 (2010)

Bowles, S.: Policies designed for self-interested citizens may undermine 'the moral sentiments': evidence from economic experiments. Science **320**(5883), 1605–1609 (2008)

Cresswell, J.W.: Qualitative Inquiry and Research Design. Sage, Thousand Oaks (2007)

Darrington, J.W., Howell, G.A.: Motivation and incentives in relational contracts. J. Financ. Manag. Property Constr. **16**(1), 42–51 (2011)

Davis, F.: Perceived usefulness, perceived ease of use, and user acceptance of information technology. MIS Q. **13**(3), 319–340 (1989)

Dwivedi, Y.K., Wade, M.R., Schneberger, S.L. (eds.): Information Systems Theory: Explaining and Predicting our Digital Society, vol. 1. Springer, Heidelberg (2011)

Dwivedi, Y.K., Rana, N.P., Janssen, M., Lal, B., Williams, M.D., Clement, M.: An empirical validation of a unified model of electronic government adoption (UMEGA). Gov. Inf. Q. **34**(2), 211–230 (2017a)

Dwivedi, Y.K., Rana, N.P., Jeyaraj, A., Clement, M., Williams, M.D. Re-examining the unified theory of acceptance and use of technology (UTAUT): towards a revised theoretical model. Inf. Syst. Frontiers, 1–16 (2017b). https://doi.org/10.1007/s10796-017-9774-y

Fishbein, M., Ajzen, I.: Belief, Attitude, Intention, and Behaviour: An Introduction to Theory and Research. Addison-Wesley, Reading, MA (1975)

Garača, Z.: Factors related to the intended vuse of ERP systems. Management **16**(2), 23–42 (2011)

Govindarajulu, N., Daily, B.F.: Motivating employees for environmental improvement. Ind. Manag. Data Syst. **104**(4), 364–372 (2004)

Kapoor, K.K., Dwivedi, Y.K., Williams, M.D.: Examining the role of three sets of innovation attributes for determining adoption of the interbank mobile payment service. Inf. Syst. Frontiers **17**(5), 1039–1056 (2015)

Liu, F., Zhao, X., Chau, P.Y., Tang, Q.: Roles of perceived value and individual differences in the acceptance of mobile coupon applications. Internet Res. **25**(3), 471–495 (2015)

Ozkan, S., Bindusara, G., Hackney, R.: Facilitating the adoption of e-payment systems: theoretical constructs and empirical analysis. J. Enterp. Inf. Manag. **23**(3), 305–325 (2010)

Rana, N.P., Dwivedi, Y.K., Lal, B., Williams, M.D., Clement, M.: Citizens' adoption of an electronic government system: towards a unified view. Inf. Syst. Frontiers **19**(3), 549–568 (2017)

Rana, N.P., Dwivedi, Y.K., Williams, M.D., Weerakkody, V.: Adoption of online public grievance redressal system in India: toward developing a unified view. Comput. Hum. Behav. **59**, 265–282 (2016)

Rondan-Cataluna, F.J., Arenas-Gaintan, J., Ramirez-Correa, P.E.: A comparison of the different versions of popular technology acceptance models. Kybernetes **44**(5), 788–805 (2015)

Sheng, X., Zolfagharian, M.: Consumer participation in online product recommendation services: augmenting the technology acceptance model. J. Serv. Mark. **28**(6), 460–470 (2014)

Slade, E.L., Dwivedi, Y.K., Piercy, N.C., Williams, M.D.: Modeling consumers' adoption intentions of remote mobile payments in the United Kingdom: extending UTAUT with innovativeness, risk, and trust. Psychol. Market. **32**(8), 860–873 (2015a)

Slade, E., Williams, M., Dwivedi, Y., Piercy, N.: Exploring consumer adoption of proximity mobile payments. J. Strat. Market. **23**(3), 209–223 (2015b)

Slade, E.L., Williams, M.D., Dwivedi, Y.K.: Devising a research model to examine adoption of mobile payments: an extension of UTAUT2. Market. Rev. **14**(3), 310–335 (2014)

Tech Nation: About Tech Nation Ghana (2015). http://technationgh.com/about-tech-nation-ghana/. Accessed 2 Sept 2015

Van de Ven, A.H.: Engaged Scholarship: A Guide for Organisational and Social Research. New York, Oxford (2007)

Venkatesh, V., Davis, F.D., Morris, M.G.: Dead or alive? The development, trajectory and future of technology adoption research. J. AIS **8**(4), 268–286 (2007)

Venkatesh, V., Morris, M.G., Davis, G.B., Davis, F.D.: User acceptance of information technology: toward a unified view. MIS Q. **27**(3), 425–478 (2003)

Venkatesh, V., Thong, J.Y., Xu, X.: Consumer acceptance and use of information technology: extending the unified theory of acceptance and use of technology. MIS Q. **36**(1), 157–178 (2012)

Venkatesh, V., Thong, J.Y., Xu, X.: Unified theory of acceptance and use of technology: a synthesis and the road. J. Assoc. Inf. Syst. **17**(5), 328–376 (2016)

Walsham, G.: Doing interpretive research. Eur. J. Inf. Syst. **15**(3), 320–330 (2006)

Wang, K., Lin, C.-L.: The adoption of mobile value-added services. Investigating the influence of IS quality and perceived playfulness. Managing Serv. Qual. **22**(2), 184–208 (2012)

Williams, M.D., Rana, N.P., Dwivedi, Y.K.: The unified theory of acceptance and use of technology (UTAUT): a literature review. J. Enterp. Inf. Manag. **28**(3), 443–488 (2015)

Williams, M.D., Dwivedi, Y.K., Lal, B., Schwarz, A.: Contemporary trends and issues in IT adoption and diffusion research. J. Inf. Technol. **24**(1), 1–10 (2009)

A Comparative Study of Business-to-Government Information Sharing Arrangements for Tax Reporting

Rizky Amalia Kurnia, Dhata Praditya(✉), and Marijn Janssen

Faculty of Technology, Policy, and Management,
Delft University of Technology, Jaffalaan 5, 2628 BX Delft, The Netherlands
rizkyamaliakurnia@student.tudelft.nl,
{D.Praditya,m.f.w.h.a.janssen}@tudelft.nl

Abstract. Having tax transparency is getting more important and enforced by more and more countries around the world. To deal with tax evasion, OECD has developed an Automatic Exchange of Information (AEOI) standard. The implementation of this standard differs among countries. In this study, we explore factors explaining the differences between two information sharing arrangements in implementing the AEOI standard. In both cases, the information sharing architecture and the accompanying governance arrangement are investigated. The findings of the exploratory study show that the differences are influenced by available IT capabilities, interoperability, trust among information sharing partners, power difference, inter-organizational relationship, and perceived benefits of implementing such arrangements. Ten propositions are derived explaining the differences which can be tested in further research.

Keywords: Information sharing · Inter-organizational information sharing · Standardization · AEOI · Tax report · Business-to-government · E-government

1 Introduction

Access to private sector data for public interest purposes can provide benefits to companies, governments, as well as to society[1]. Most governments have legislation requiring businesses to report their data to government agencies. These data can be used as evidence of regulatory compliance or inputs for policymaking. Governments can use information originating from businesses to fight against tax evasion, drug trafficking, or terrorisms [1].

In the tax domain, recent initiatives have been established by the Organization for Economic Co-operation and Development or OECD[2] to promote international tax transparency and fighting tax evasion. The Automatic Exchange of Information (AEOI)

[1] https://ec.europa.eu/digital-single-market/en/guidance-private-sector-data-sharing, accessed on 06/02/2019.

[2] http://www.oecd.org/tax/transparency/automaticexchangeofinformation.htm, accessed on 06/02/2019.

Published by Springer Nature Switzerland AG 2019
Y. Dwivedi et al. (Eds.): TDIT 2019, IFIP AICT 558, pp. 154–169, 2019.
https://doi.org/10.1007/978-3-030-20671-0_11

is a standard for facilitating the exchange of tax data among countries [2]. The main driver of this standard is a tax revenue loss of around USD$500 billion from tax evasion [3]. Figure 1 provides an overview of the information sharing process for foreign account holder data residing in one country to exchange information with the accounts' in the home country. To implement the standard, a country should meet the following four core requirements: (1) translate the reporting and due diligence procedure into domestic law; (2) select a legal basis for the automatic information exchange; (3) putting in place IT infrastructure and administrative resource; (4) protect confidentiality and data safeguard [4].

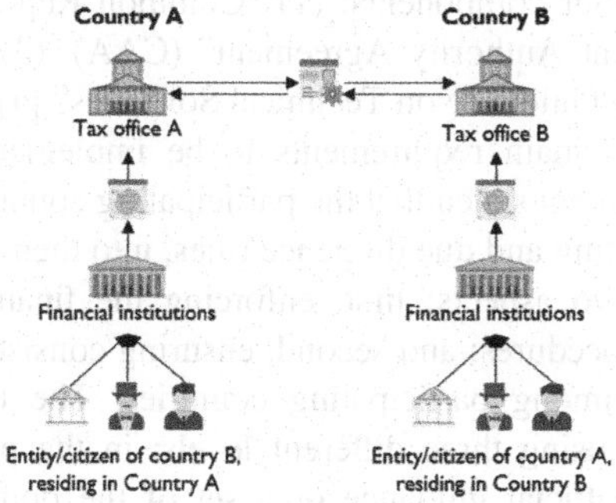

Fig. 1. AEOI sharing process

Developing such an information sharing infrastructure enabling AEOI can be challenging especially for the developing countries [5]. First, all countries involved in the exchange must ensure high quality of information. This requires readiness in the IT systems, for financial institutions and especially, the tax office. Within internal jurisdiction, the different organizations may have their own information systems which are unique to their specific needs. Integration of those various systems can bring technological challenges [6, 7]. Second, the complexity of inter-organizational information sharing can become an obstacle to the implementation of such systems [8] and often it might require changes in the business processes of the organizations [9]. In addition, the governance structure would affect the effectiveness of the collaboration within the inter-organizational context [10].

Based on the previous explanation, the aim of this explorative study is to identify factors that result in differences in the AEOI implementation. For this, types of architecture and governance that enable the AEOI are compared. Thereafter factors influencing the selection of the information sharing infrastructure and governance to enable AEOI are identified. Two different information sharing infrastructure and governance structure are used in enabling AEOI. These factors are formulated as propositions which can be tested in further research. The scope is limited to the exchange of information between financial institutions and tax administration (business-to-government).

The rest of the paper is structured as follows: Sect.2 provides the literature background. Section 3 explains the research approach taken. Section 4 describes the results of the case studies. Section 5 contains the cross-case comparison and resulting propositions, and finally, Sect. 6 provides the research conclusion.

2 Theoretical Foundation

2.1 AEOI Standard

The AEOI standard is intended to be a "tool" in eradicating international tax evasion. The standard itself has four components: (1) "Common Reporting Standard" (CRS), (2) The Model Competent Authority Agreement" (CAA), (3) the "Commentaries of CRS and CAA", and (4) "Guidance on Technical Solutions" [4]. These components are then translated into four main requirements to be implemented by a participating country. The first requirement stated that the participating country needs to translate the standard, including reporting and due diligence rules, into their domestic law [11]. This requirement addresses two aspects: first, enforcing the financial institutions implementing the reporting procedures; and second, ensuring consistencies of the scope and quality of information among participating countries. The OECD suggests implementing this translation using three different levels: in the primary legislation, secondary legislation, and official guidance or a set of the domestic FAQ (Frequency Asked Questions)[3].

For the second requirement, a participating country must select the international framework that enables the information exchange with other countries. The second requirement consists of several legal instruments that permit the automatic exchange under the standard and other separate agreements between the participating countries. This agreement defines the information sharing mechanism, including what information will be exchanged, how it is going to be exchanged, and when the exchange will take place [11]. Then, the participating country must allocate the required IT infrastructure and administrative resources. According to AEOI standard, this third requirement is divided into three parts: (1) from the financial institutions to the tax office, including collecting and reporting the required information; (2) internal tax office, including receiving, processing and sending the information to other jurisdictions; (3) inter-jurisdictions, including transmitting and receiving information between two jurisdictions [11]. In this research, we focus on the first part.

The fourth requirement is about protecting confidentiality and safeguarding data. For this purpose, the Global Forum, part of the OECD, carried out preliminary confidentiality and data exchange assessments[4].

[3] http://www.oecd.org/ctp/exchange-of-tax-information/automaticexchangeofinformationreport.htm, accessed on 06/02/2018.

[4] http://www.oecd.org/tax/transparency/global-forum-launches-a-plan-of-action-for-developing-countries-participation-in-automatic-exchanges-of-financial-account-information.htm, accessed on 06/02/2018.

A literature review was conducted in several leading journal databases such as the SCOPUS, JSTOR, Springer, and Elsevier using keyword: ("Automatic Exchange of Information" OR "Common Reporting Standard") AND ("implementation" OR "adoption"). Table 1 presents the summary of topics related to AEOI from prior research. Most of the researches have been focusing on reinforcing the argument on why it is necessary to exchange tax information inter-jurisdictions by implementing AEOI, as well as potential challenges faced in the adoption of AEOI. Some studies have provided empirical data from the AEOI implementation, see [12–16]. However, few studies discussing how to implement AEOI from the information sharing perspective.

Table 1. The topic addressed regarding AEOI standard in the literature

Topic addressed	Source
Prior assessment of the important needs for AEOI standard	[17–19]
Challenges and benefits of AEOI standard	[20–24]
Evaluation of the Common Reporting Standard (CRS)	[5, 25–30]
Evaluation of the AEOI standard and its implications	[31–34]
Implementation of AEOI standard within National Laws	[12–16]
AEOI standard and privacy issues	[5, 35, 36]

From the technological point of view, the CRS from AEOI standard can be seen as a standardization effort taking place on the data level, including the use of XML schema and the use of generic data definition [11, 26, 37]. Developing the information sharing infrastructure that enabling the CRS reporting is still challenging [5] due to, for example, different IT maturity, inexperience dealing with the standard, unawareness about required reporting processes as well as the ambiguity of risks, costs, and benefits. Since the focus of this research is on the reporting of financial institutions to the tax office, the AEOI implementation under study is in the field of business-to-government information sharing.

2.2 Inter-organizational Information Sharing System

Inter-organizational information sharing system (ISS) is a system that includes the sharing of resources between organizations [38]. ISS aims to facilitate inter-organizational information sharing and collaboration which could enable the flow of information between an organization beyond the organizational boundaries [39]. Klievink et al. [40] argued that governance mechanism and information technology infrastructure are interrelated, and they are considered as an information sharing arrangement in the form of a public-private platform. Governance structure and information sharing infrastructure interconnect two or more different actors from both the public and private sectors [40, 41]. Governance structure deals with decision making, control mechanism, and data ownership, while information sharing infrastructure including systems, interfaces, ontologies, and data standards.

Regarding the infrastructure that enables the information sharing, Yang et al. [42] proposed a different category of how information can be shared among the boundaries of the government agencies, namely the (1) Centralized type; (2) Semi-Centralized type; (3) Decentralized type. Each of the infrastructures has their typical determinants that influence the decision making for their adoption [42]. Moreover, de Corbière and Rowe [43] proposed configurations for the ISSs from a structural linkage perspective. The structural linkage refers to the interconnection of the sending partner and the receiving partners in the inter-organizational information sharing context. There are three forms of ISSs along the continuum, which the two on the extreme continuum are previously proposed by Choudhury [44] namely the dyadic ISSs and the multilateral ISSs. The intermediary between the two forms is called the hybrid forms of ISSs. Furthermore, Bekkers [45] provided four types of back-office data integration model: the centralized database, the interface type, information broker type, and shared database type.

The success of inter-organizational information sharing also depends on the system governance [10] which provides the structure that allows the relationship of stakeholders to align their objective in the implementation and monitoring to control whether the objectives has achieved [46]. In this research, we use the definition from Cumming [47] in identifying the governance structure which complemented the already founded hierarchical (top-down or bottom-up) and network (peer-to-peer) approach with the heterarchical structure. The heterarchical structure bridging the ideas of hierarchical institutional and organizational power theories with the interaction and connectivity of the actors in the network and thus provide a conceptual tool for the analysts to have a more fruitful and contextualized perspective regarding governance structure [47].

2.3 Factors Influencing the Inter-organizational Information Sharing

Previous studies have found factors influencing inter-organizational information sharing. For example, information sharing in the public sector is influenced by three categories of factors, namely (1) Organizational and managerial perspective (2) Political and Policy Perspective, and (3) Technological perspective [7]. The factors in each category can either hinder or have positive impacts on inter-organizational information sharing. Gil-Garcia and Sayogo [48] proposed a framework to assess the success of the inter-organizational information sharing project. The model they used composed of four categories of influencing factors: (1) managerial and organizational; (2) political and institutional; (3) information and technology, and (4) contextual.

In addition, Praditya and Janssen [49] identified the influencing factors of information sharing arrangements classified into organizational, inter-organizational and technological factors. The organizational category includes factors such as resource, perceived benefits, perceived costs, perceived risks, organizational compatibilities, and experience. Organizational compatibilities are including firm size, firm structure, firm governance, and firm strategy [49]. Similarly, Singerling et al. [50] found that firm size and availability of the resource is indeed influencing the information sharing arrangements specifically regarding the decision to choose the information sharing system configuration.

Moreover, in the inter-organizational category, the factors of the model by Praditya and Janssen [49] include power, trust, investment methods, inter-organizational relationship, diversity of users, pressure, and shared strategies. Power and trust in the inter-organizational context especially influence the willingness to participate in the inter-organizational information sharing initiatives and are determining information sharing infrastructure and infrastructure governance [8, 50, 51].

Lastly, in the technological category, the factors included are types of shared data, IT capabilities, and compatibility and interoperability. The IT capabilities comprise the standardization of data, the volume of data and transaction of data, and the types of data used. In the same vein, several studies also found that the success of inter-organizational information sharing is determined through the choice of technical infrastructure [48, 50, 52].

Taken together, the previously described concepts will be used in our analytical framework to identify factors explaining different implementations. The next section explains the research approach and methods employed in this study.

3 Research Approach

A case study is an empirical inquiry that investigates a contemporary phenomenon in depth and within its real-life context, especially when the boundaries between phenomenon and context are not evident [53, 64]. Case study copes with the technically distinctive situation in which there will be many more variables of interest than data points, as one result relies on multiple sources of evidence, with data needing to converge in a triangulating fashion, and thus provide benefits in guiding the data collection and analysis [53]. Furthermore, a case study is an appropriate approach for this research since the current implementation of AEOI is a contemporary phenomenon that applies to a particular country within a specific time [53]. Different contributing stakeholders in the implementation process and the strive for depth in the analysis in this research makes case study preferable than other research methods such as survey and experiments. In addition, case studies are particularly well-suited for extensive and in-depth descriptions of complex social phenomena [53]. In selecting the case we were considering two main criteria, the case should reveal different arrangements used in implementing AEOI and provide access to data, both primary and secondary.

This research began with a literature review which conducted to gain the theoretical framework for the research. Then, semi-structured interviews were conducted due to its flexible characteristic and thus allow the researcher to gain a deeper understanding of the interviewee's perspective [54]. In guiding the interview, we developed an interview protocol which is derived from the concepts in the previous section. As for the respondents, we interviewed respondents from different roles in the implementation of AEOI to different perspectives and thus yields to an extensive view of the implementation process. In addition, we also consider their experience in the AEOI implementation, For the Netherlands case, we interviewed the AEOI program manager and IT architect from *Belastingdienst*. For the Indonesian case, we interviewed four respondents from the business department and IT department of Indonesian FSA, and one respondent from the Department of International Tax Exchange of Indonesian Tax Administration. Each interview lasted for about 90–120 min.

Interviews for the Netherlands case were conducted in English, while for Indonesia case were conducted in Bahasa. All interviews were transcribed in accordance with the chosen language during the interview. During the transcription, irrelevant information that does not contribute to answering questions such as off-topic information, personal details, or repetition were excluded. These transcripts were sent back to each respondent to ensure correct interpretations and validity of the findings. For data analysis, all interview transcripts were then translated to English and coded using *Atlas.ti* version 7. The 2 cases are presented in the next section.

4 Comparative Case Studies

4.1 Netherlands Case

The implementation of AEOI started in the year of 2014, marked by the signing of the Convention on the Mutual Administrative Assistance in tax matters by the Ministry of Finance and followed by the established FATCA/CRS guidelines. In the following years in 2016, the Netherlands through its *Belastingdienst* (tax administration) prepares the system to enable the automatic exchange. Accordingly, the financial institutions in the Netherlands need to prepare themselves to provide the required data and to perform the due diligence procedures. The Netherlands successfully performed its first exchange of CRS reporting by October 1st, 2017.

There are eight stakeholders involved in the implementation of AEOI in the Netherlands and can be categorized into three levels, strategic, operational and technical. Firstly, in the strategic level, there are Ministry of Finance, OECD, and EU TAXUD which all of them is the secondary stakeholder that directly participate in the reporting process.

The interaction between *Belastingdienst* with the secondary stakeholders identified here are mostly related to the regulation or the technical interoperability matters for the inter-jurisdiction exchange. The Ministry of Finance, for example, has established the act to implement the AEOI/CRS per 2016 in the Netherlands, and thus mandate the *Belastingdienst* as the operational government body to be responsible for enforcing the law. With OECD, *Belastingdienst* is also involved in the development process of the (Common Transition System) CTS that is used to exchange the report between countries. As for the EU-TAXUD (European Taxation and Customs Union), the discussion is about the use of a network gateway to connect non-EU countries to the member states.

Secondly, at the operational level, there are the financial institutions and the auditors. The financial institutions have a role as a data provider for the reporting and the Auditors, which is considered as the secondary stakeholder, ensure that the financial institutions have the eligible capability to provide the correct required data.

Lastly, at the technical level, there are *Logius* and the service provider. *Logius* is the organization that is responsible for the *Digipoort* – the infrastructure used for the reporting purpose - and they provide helpdesk and technical support for the *Digipoort* services to the *Belastingdienst* and the Financial Institutions. The service providers refer to the IT services companies which assist either financial institutions, *Logius* or *Belastingdienst* and not constrained to one specific organization.

4.2 Indonesian Case

Indonesia is one of the late adopters of the AEOI standard. The implementation in the Information sharing infrastructure is executed in 2017, and the first exchange took place in 2018. The main stakeholders in the implementation in Indonesia are the Indonesian tax administration and the Indonesian Financial Service Authority (FSA). There is a significant difference with the Netherlands case in terms of the institutional structure because in Indonesia several types of financial institutions are supervised directly under the FSA. Therefore, the report from the financial institutions need to be sent first the FSA, and then to the tax administration.

In total there are six stakeholders involved, which can be categorized into the strategic, operational, and technical level. At the strategic level, there are the Ministry of Finance and the OECD. The Ministry of Finance is the highest hierarchy in this case that gives a mandate to both Indonesian tax administration and FSA to implement the AEOI and CRS reporting. Regarding OECD, the interaction between OECD and Indonesian tax administration is related to the reporting mechanism, that is the assistance and assessment of confidentiality and safeguarding data. As for the primary stakeholder, the tax administration and FSA, the interaction occurs during the development of *SiPINA* application and through the workshop regarding CRS and *SiPINA* application for the financial institutions.

At the operational level, the financial institutions under the FSA, need to submit their report to the system developed by the FSA, the SIPINA web application. And other financial institutions outside the supervision of FSA can directly submit their report to the system by the tax administration, called the EOI portal. The division of the financial institutions' supervision is regulated under the Ministry of Finance decree.

Lastly, the technical level is related to the development of SiPINA application. The tax administration instructs the FSA to develop the web-based system and provide the requirements to be fulfilled and the type of data format to be in place. Here, the application owner of *SiPINA* is the Business Department of the FSA. The first phase of the system development is the creation of user requirements. This is done by the business department of FSA with the tax administration, together in a coordination meeting they produce the user requirements for the *SiPINA* application. Then, the user requirements are translated by the IT Department of the FSA into the User System Specification. And during this time, they assess whether to develop it in-house or to use a service provider for the implementation. The chosen decision then to use the service provider. Regarding changes, should there be any changes required for the data formats or other functionality, the higher instruction comes from the tax administration to the business department of FSA as the application owner. The business department then communicates the changes to the IT department, and accordingly, the changes will be carried out.

4.3 Comparing the Information Sharing Infrastructure and Governance

To identify the type of arrangements used in these two cases, we are using a framework provided by [42] for the type of information sharing infrastructure and [47] for inter-organizational governance. The Netherlands is implementing a centralized – multilateral ISSs type. To accommodate the reporting from the financial institutions to the *Belastingdienst*, the Netherlands has been using a Government Service Platform (*Digipoort*) which is designed as the intermediary that enables the inter-organizational information sharing. GSP employs the star-shaped network so that any organization that wishes to exchange the information could connect to the GSP through the interface from their legacy system [42]. Moreover, the *Digipoort* infrastructure is a multilateral ISSs that could facilitate information sharing from private sectors to the many government bodies in the Netherlands, although in this case, the government is only the *Belastingdienst*. In this case, the multilateral ISSs enable the interconnection with all the partners, and that the sending partners do not need to build a direct connection to each receiving partner [44]. However, in terms of data management, *Digipoort* does not store the report being sent from the financial institutions, rather it only acted as the hub that routes the report to the *Belastingdienst* internal system. Thus, according to [45], *Digipoort* can be categorized as the information broker type of data management.

Regarding the governance structure, the identified structure is heterarchical that according to [47] is a combination of hierarchical and network structure. As previously mentioned, despite many stakeholders are involved in the implementation of AEOI in the Netherlands, there is a strong link between two players here that is the *Belastingdienst* and *Logius*.

In the Indonesian case, the identified infrastructure is the semi-centralized – hybrid ISSs. Semi-decentralized type which is illustrated through an electronic gateway is designed to realize a real-time information search and verification [42] while hybrid ISSs defined as the ISSs form that could interconnect partners with different preference on the structural linkages, meaning that there exists partner that implement the dyadic linkage and multilateral linkages [43]. In accommodating the reporting Indonesia used a web-based system that resembles a type of gateway in facilitating the reporting from financial institutions to the FSA and Indonesian tax administration. Both systems resemble a hybrid ISS type of interconnection because, though the financial institutions need to report to the FSA through *SiPINA* application, financial institutions still need to report directly also to the tax administration through the portal EOI application for some reports. In this sense, there is no single window that becomes the central ISS facilitating the many-to-many connection between the information provider and receiver. Thus, it cannot be said as a multilateral ISS. In terms of data management, both *SiPINA* and portal EOI application did store the report and thus it can be seen that the centralized database type according to the categorization proposed by [45].

For the governance structure, Indonesia implements a hierarchical governance structure, in which the Indonesian tax administration dictate the whole arrangements (Table 2).

Table 2. Comparing the AEOI requirements fulfillment

	The Netherlands	Indonesia
	• *Digipoort* (Government service platform) • CRS XML schema • Encryption and validation mechanism • Sharing mechanism: System-to-System	• *SiPINA* web-based application and EOI portal web-based application • CRS XML schema • Encryption and validation mechanism • Sharing mechanism: Human-to-System
ISSs	Centralized and multilateral	Semi-centralized and hybrid
Data management	Type C: information broker	Type A: centralized database
Governance	Heterarchical	Hierarchical

5 Propositions of Factors

In this section, we identified the factors that influence the choice of information sharing infrastructure and governance structure in the two countries. Our findings suggested that some contextual factors are found in one case and not the other, and some factors are found in both cases but in different degree. We present the influencing factors in the following propositions.

5.1 IT Capability

IT capability refers to the level of the organization's IT infrastructure, employees' IT skills and ability to leverage IT to serve the organization's goals [55, 56]. IT capability is a critical factor in participating in interorganizational information sharing [57]. An integrated ISS as a complex system requires a certain level of IT capability of actors.

From the cases, *Belastingdienst* and financial institutions in the Netherlands already sharing their financial information through a mature and integrated IT system. They prefer to utilize their existing reporting infrastructure in meeting the requirements of AEOI since all the requirements can be fulfilled using the existing capabilities. The ISS that connects the financial institutions to the tax administrations (*Digipoort*) and the processing modules in the internal system tax administration are already sufficient to enable AEOI in the Netherlands. In addition, *Belastingdienst* and most of the financial institutions are familiar with the use of a standardized reporting format of XML.

On the other hands, Indonesia had no existing system that could accommodate the requirements of AEOI reporting. They decided to develop two separate web-based applications to implement AEOI. The involved actors in Indonesia perceive this solution is easier and faster to develop, even though they are aware of further issues such as scalability or data aggregation issues could arise in the future. This is aligned with a finding in a study by [58] which claimed an organization that has less extensive IT infrastructure capabilities will tend to decide to fulfill the current needs. New technology adoption required employees with certain IT skills [59]. According to the interviewees, there is a lack of employees with XML skills (as requested in AEOI) as well as experienced in orchestrating an integrated system-to-system reporting either in Tax administration and especially in financial institutions. Because of that, the Indonesian tax office decides to build web-based systems which accommodate xls and XML. So, the financial institutions can upload the reports in both formats. However, this situation creates a burden in the internal Tax office, since they have to translate the xls document into XML and then aggregate it before sending it to the requesting countries.

Proposition 1: *Higher IT capability results in the use of an integrated system*
Proposition 2: *Lower IT capability results in the use of a less integrated system*

5.2 Interoperability

Interoperability plays an important role in establishing interorganizational information sharing [7]. According to the European Interoperability Framework[5], there are three levels of interoperability: technical, semantic and organizational level.

Based on the previous explanation, we can infer that the Netherlands has already acquired a higher degree of interoperability in the system used between the tax administration and the financial institutions. This is depicted by the fact that the systems they used has already employed a system-to-system sharing mechanism and has enabled the used of the standardized report which is in XML format.

Indonesia has a lower degree of interoperability in their existing systems. The reporting system is still using the human-to-system mechanism through the web application, and the input data used are still employing two types of data format:.xls and XML format. There are still plenty of manual works to be done in the Indonesian case. Thus, we argue that the degree of interoperability has an influence on whether the integrated or more fragmented system will be used.

Proposition 3: *Higher interoperability requirement results in the use of an integrated system*

Proposition 4: *Lower interoperability requirement results in the use of a less integrated system*

5.3 Trust and Power Difference Among Actors

Regarding trust and power difference, both factors are considered as important factors in interorganizational information sharing [49, 60]. Our findings in the Netherlands suggest that a higher level of trust among the participants in the reporting chain leads to a chosen heterarchical governance structure. This could be due to that in the Netherlands, *Belastingdienst*, *Logius*, and the financial institutions have already had lots of collaborations especially in developing the existing reporting system. Financial institutions have been actively involved in the decision making, and their trust to the government is enforced also by the "goal binding strategy" in the Netherlands regulation that stated the data can only be used for the stated purposed.

[5] https://ec.europa.eu/isa2/eif_en. Accessed on 20/03/2019.

Proposition 5: *A higher level of trust among participants results in the less hierarchical governance structure*

The first requirement of AEOI is to adopt AEOI into national laws. Regulation can be considered as a basic incentive for users to adopt the standard, however, it also gives tax office full authority to arrange the implementation. The latter results in power difference amongst involved stakeholders. In both cases, the decision making regarding the implementation relies on the tax office, with different degree. The case study findings also show both cases cannot implement network structure for the governance of the system Therefore, we argue that power difference between institutions due to regulation, can yield to a less networked governance structure.

Proposition 6: *Power difference due to regulation results in less network governance structure*

5.4 Perceived Benefits

Perceived benefits are considered as a critical factor in arranging information sharing, especially in private organizations' perspective [61]. Perceived benefits have an influence on the choice of Information sharing infrastructure in both cases. The perceived benefits that we found in the Netherlands are that by using the current IT environment, they could develop a building block, that could make the future exchange easier since they already have the general tooling. In addition, because they already have everything in place (IT capability and IT maturity) it would be more expensive to build a whole new system, rather than using the existing one. By doing so, the Netherlands perceived that by using the current integrated system they could gain efficiency, scalability and less administrative burden. An integrated ISS also can help involved actors in the Netherlands to streamline the sharing process and develop further capabilities to create societal values [62]. Indonesia on the other hand, choose the web-based system because they perceive that it is simpler, easier and faster to develop because they need to fulfill the reporting deadline as soon as possible. Therefore, based on our findings, we propose:

Proposition 7: *When the objective is to develop as simple as possible, faster to deliver, and easy to develop then the less integrated system is preferable*
Proposition 8: *If the objective is to reduce administrative burden, more efficient, and highly scalable then the integrated system is preferable*

5.5 Inter-organizational Relationship

In terms of inter-organizational relationship [63], a good inter-organizational relationship between the tax administration and financial institutions have already formed in the Netherlands. In developing the Standard Business Reporting, active participation from governments and businesses is considered as a critical success factor [41]; built from this background, the similar governance structure is also applied in enacting AEOI.

In Indonesia, the relationship between governments and businesses still considered as "client and server", which limit business participation in developing B2G ISS. Existing reporting system serves the government goals rather than the shared goals of the involved actors. This type of relationship is accommodated by the hierarchical structure.

Proposition 9: *Active participation of all actors in inter-organizational collaboration results in the use of less hierarchical governance structure.*

Proposition 10: *No or limited participation of some actors in inter-organizational collaboration results in the use of hierarchical governance structure.*

6 Conclusion

Although the standard is the same, countries implement the same standard using different information sharing arrangements. This paper identified factors explaining the differences. According to the case studies findings, the level of IT capability of actors, interoperability, and perceived benefits of certain arrangements are influencing the type of information sharing infrastructure used to enable AEOI. For the selection of governance structure, inter-organizational relationship, power difference among actors, and trust to sharing partners are found as influencing factors. The factors are formulated as propositions which can be tested in further research. The findings of this research underscore the importance of performing the technology assessment of the current environment comprising the IT capability, experiences and resource, and business case creation which might become an important thing to note for the program manager of AEOI implementation in the countries that have not yet implement the standard.

The insights gained from this study and the model we proposed may be of assistance for the program manager of AEOI implementation in their decision making regarding the type of information sharing infrastructure and governance structure of AEOI that has been employed in developed and developing countries. Furthermore, the propositions and the lessons learned can be used for benchmarking of AEOI implementation in other countries.

Future research in AEOI implementation with more cases employed would increase the generalizability of the findings. Further empirical research is also needed to identify more information sharing arrangements to implement AEOI, related to varied type of infrastructure and system governance. Moreover, perspectives from other stakeholders such as the financial institutions and secondary stakeholders would provide a rich source for the data analysis and thus could create more insights, although more efforts will be needed in the data collection. Finally, understanding the relationship between the factors influencing the information sharing arrangements would be worth to be explored as it will also add to the body knowledge of interorganizational information sharing.

References

1. Cate, F.H., Dempsey, J.X., Rubinstein, I.S.: Systematic Government Access to Private-Sector Data. Oxford University Press, Oxford (2012)
2. HJI Panayi, C.: Current trends on automatic exchange of information. Singapore Manag. Univ. School Accountancy Res. Paper **2016**, 43 (2016)
3. Cobham, A., Janský, P.: Global distribution of revenue loss from corporate tax avoidance: re-estimation and country results. J. Int. Dev. **30**(2), 206–232 (2018)
4. OECD: Standard for Automatic Exchange of Financial Account Information in Tax Matters, 2nd (edn.). OECD, Cedex (2017)
5. Knobel, A.: Findings of the 2nd TJN Survey on Automatic Exchange of Information (AEOI) (2017)
6. Fedorowicz, J., Gogan, J.L., Ray, A.W.: The ecology of interorganizational information sharing. J. Int. Inf. Manag. **13**(2), 1 (2004)
7. Yang, T.-M., Maxwell, T.A.: Information-sharing in public organizations: a literature review of interpersonal, intra-organizational and inter-organizational success factors. Gov. Inf. Q. **28**(2), 164–175 (2011)
8. Luna-Reyes, L.F., Gil-Garcia, J.R., Cruz, C.B.: Collaborative digital government in Mexico: some lessons from federal web-based interorganizational information integration initiatives. Gov. Inf. Q. **24**(4), 808–826 (2007)
9. Gil-García, J.R., Chengalur-Smith, I.N., Duchessi, P.: Collaborative e-Government: impediments and benefits of information-sharing projects in the public sector. Eur. J. Inf. Syst. **16**(2), 121–133 (2007)
10. van den Broek, T., van Veenstra, A.F.: Modes of governance in inter-organizational data collaborations. In: European Conference on Information Systems. Munster, Germany (2015)
11. OECD: Standard for Automatic Exchange of Financial Information in Tax Matters - Implementation Handbook, 2nd (edn.). OECD, Paris (2018)
12. Filipova-Slancheva, A.: Bulgarian experience in curbing tax evasion - automatic exchange of financial information: status and expectations. In: Problem of Development Modern Science: Theory and Practice, pp. 11–14 (2016)
13. Filipova-Slancheva, A.: Automatic exchange of tax information: Initiation, implementation and guidelines in Bulgarian context (2017)
14. Tavares, D.P., Santos, J.P.: Tax transparency - Portugal: report. In: European Association of Tax Law Professors, Switzerland, Zurich (2018)
15. Akhtar, J.: Exchange of Information: Indian Experience, Developing Country Implications. Tax Cooperation Policy Brief, p. 4 (2018)
16. Meyer-Nandi, S.: Swiss Policy Coherence in International Taxation: Global Trends in AEOI and BEPS in Development Assistance and a Swiss Way Forward. The University of Zurich, Zurich, Switzerland (2018)
17. Meinzer, M.: Policy paper on automatic tax information exchange between northern and southern countries. In: Tax Justice Briefing. Tax Justice Network (2010)
18. Moss, M.: Panama papers highlight the urgency: from FATCA to the OECD CRS. J. Secur. Oper. Custody **8**(3), 248–258 (2016)
19. Winkleman, T.J.: Automatic information exchange as a multilateral solution to tax havens. Indiana Int. Comp. Law Rev. **22**, 193 (2012)
20. Hakelberg, L.: The power politics of international tax co-operation: Luxembourg, Austria and the automatic exchange of information. J. Eur. Public Policy **22**(3), 409–428 (2015)
21. Highfield, R.: Adopting the New International Tax Rules and Standards. Asian Development Bank (2017)

22. Knobel, A., Meinzer, M.: Automatic exchange of information: an opportunity for developing countries to tackle tax evasion and corruption. Tax Justice Network (2014)
23. Sadiq, K., Sawyer, A.: Developing countries and the automatic exchange of information standard-a one-size-fits-all solution. Aust. Tax Forum **31**, 99 (2016)
24. Urinov, V.: Developing country perspectives on automatic exchange of tax information. Law, Soc. Justice Global Dev. J. **1**(19), 1–28 (2015)
25. Andrés-Aucejo, E.: Towards an International Code for administrative cooperation in tax matter and international tax governance. Revista Derecho del Estado **40**, 45–85 (2018)
26. Casi, E., Spengel, C., Stage, B.: Cross-border tax evasion after the common reporting standard: game over? ZEW-Centre for European Economic Research Discussion Paper No. 36 (2018)
27. Knobel, A., Cobham, A.: Country-by-Country reporting: How restricted access exacerbates global inequalities in taxing rights. Tax Justice Network (2016)
28. Knobel, A., Meinzer, M.: 'The End of Bank Secrecy'? Bridging the Gap to Effective Automatic Information Exchange. Tax Justice Network (2014)
29. Noked, N.: FATCA, CRS, and the wrong choice of who to regulate. Florida Tax Rev. **22**(1), 77–119 (2019)
30. Scarfone, J., Kerr, M.: Paved paradise: analysis of the common reporting standard to combat tax avoidance. Liberated Arts: A J. Undergraduate Res. **4**(1), 4 (2018)
31. Noked, N.: Tax evasion and incomplete tax transparency. Laws **7**(3), 31 (2018)
32. Fischer, M., Rohner, T.F.: Discretionary trusts—last exit before AEOI? Swiss View. Trusts Trustees **22**(4), 393–400 (2015)
33. Gadžo, S., Klemenčić, I.: Effective international information exchange as a key element of modern tax systems: promises and pitfalls of the OECD's common reporting standard. Public Sector Econ. **41**(2), 207–226 (2017)
34. Nicolescu, I.: The relationship between offshore evasion and 'Aggressive'Tax avoidance arrangements: the HSBC case. Financ. Regul. Int. (Informa Law) **19**(02), 1–22 (2016)
35. Cockfield, A.J.: Protecting taxpayer privacy rights under enhanced cross-border information exchange: toward a multilateral taxpayer bill of rights. UBCL Rev. **42**, 419 (2009)
36. Noseda, F.: CRS and beneficial ownership registers—what serious newspapers and tabloids have in common: the improbable story of a private client lawyer turned human rights activist. Trusts Trustees **23**(6), 601–609 (2017)
37. McGill, R.K., Haye, C.A., Lipo, S.: GATCA: A Practical Guide to Global Anti-Tax Evasion Frameworks. Springer, Heidelberg (2017)
38. Barrett, S., Konsynski, B.: Inter-organization information sharing systems. MIS Q. **06**, 93–105 (1982)
39. Johnston, H.R., Vitale, M.R.: Creating competitive advantage with interorganizational information systems. MIS Q. **12**(2), 153–165 (1988)
40. Klievink, B., Bharosa, N., Tan, Y.-H.: The collaborative realization of public values and business goals: governance and infrastructure of public–private information platforms. Gov. Inf. Q. **33**(1), 67–79 (2016)
41. Praditya, D., Janssen, M., Sulastri, R.: Determinants of business-to-government information sharing arrangements. Electron. J. E-Gov. **15**(1), 44–55 (2017)
42. Yang, T.-M., Pardo, T., Wu, Y.-J.: How is information shared across the boundaries of government agencies? An e-government case study. Gov. Inf. Q. **31**, 637–652 (2014)
43. de Corbière, F., Rowe, F.: Understanding the diversity of interconnections between IS: towards a new typology of IOS. In: European Conference on Information Systems, Pretoria, South Africa (2010)
44. Choudhury, V.: Strategic choices in the development of interorganizational information systems. Inf. Syst. Res. **8**(1), 1–24 (1997)

45. Bekkers, V.: The governance of back-office integration: organizing co-operation between information domains. Public Manag. Rev. **9**(3), 377–400 (2007)
46. Wimmer, M.A., Boneva, R., di Giacomo, D.: Interoperability governance: a definition and insights from case studies in Europe. In: Proceedings of the 19th Annual International Conference on Digital Government Research: Governance in the Data Age. ACM (2018)
47. Cumming, G.S.: Heterarchies: reconciling networks and hierarchies. Trends Ecol. Evol. **31** (8), 622–632 (2016)
48. Gil-Garcia, J.R., Sayogo, D.S.: Government inter-organizational information sharing initiatives: understanding the main determinants of success. Gov. Inf. Q. **33**, 572–582 (2016)
49. Praditya, D., Janssen, M.: Assessment of factors influencing information sharing arrangements using the best-worst method. In: Kar, A.K., et al. (eds.) I3E 2017. LNCS, vol. 10595, pp. 94–106. Springer, Cham (2017). https://doi.org/10.1007/978-3-319-68557-1_10
50. Singerling, T., et al.: Exploring factors that influence information sharing choices of organizations in networks. In: AMCIS 2015: Americas Conference on Information Systems, Puerto Rico, 13–15 August 2015 (2015)
51. Arendsen, R., et al.: Does e-government reduce the administrative burden of businesses? An assessment of business-to-government systems usage in the Netherlands. Gov. Inf. Q. **31**(1), 160–169 (2014)
52. Yang, T.-M., Wu, Y.-J.: Exploring the determinants of cross-boundary information sharing in the public sector: an e-Government case study in Taiwan. J. Inf. Sci. **40**(5), 649–668 (2014)
53. Yin, R.K.: Case Study Research: Design and Methods. Applied Social Research Methods Series, vol. 5, 4th edn. SAGE, Newbury Park (2009)
54. Daymon, C., Holloway, I.: Qualitative Research Methods in Public Relations and Marketing Communications. Routledge, London (2010)
55. Bharadwaj, A.S.: A resource-based perspective on information technology capability and firm performance: an empirical investigation. MIS Q. **24**(1), 169–196 (2000)
56. Kamal, M., Themistocleous, M.: A conceptual model for EAI adoption in an e-government environment (2006)
57. Premkumar, G., Ramamurthy, K.: The role of interorganizational and organizational factors on the decision mode for adoption of interorganizational systems. Decis. Sci. **26**(3), 303–336 (1995)
58. Broadbent, M., Weill, P., Neo, B.-S.: Strategic context and patterns of IT infrastructure capability. J. Strateg. Inf. Syst. **8**(2), 157–187 (1999)
59. Mikalef, P., et al.: Big Data analytics capability: antecedents and business value. In: PACIS (2017)
60. Hart, P., Saunders, C.: Power and trust: critical factors in the adoption and use of electronic data interchange. Organ. Sci. **8**(1), 23–42 (1997)
61. Romochkina, I., Van Baalen, P.J., Zuidwijk, R.A.: A Tug-of-War: shaping the landscape of inter-organizational information systems. Available at SSRN 2754040 (2016)
62. Pappas, I.O., et al.: Big data and business analytics ecosystems: paving the way towards digital transformation and sustainable societies. Inf. Syst. e-Bus. Manag. **16**(3), 479–491 (2018)
63. Cheng, J.-H.: Inter-organizational relationships and information sharing in supply chains. Int. J. Inf. Manag. **31**(4), 374–384 (2011)
64. Choudrie, J., Dwivedi, Y.K.: Investigating the research approaches for examining technology adoption issues. J. Res. Pract. **1**(1), 1–9 (2005). Article D1

Brightening Physical University Admission Through Digital Process Virtualization: An Action Case Study in Ghana

John Effah(✉)

Department of Operations and Management Information Systems, University of Ghana Business School, Accra, Ghana
jeffah@ug.edu.gh

Abstract. The purpose of this study is to understand how digital process virtualization can be used to address problems with physical admission in a developing country university. Bright ICT research calls for solutions to practical problems in society including education. However, related studies in education have focused more on teaching and learning. Therefore, less is known about education management and administration. This study addresses this research gap through an action case study of a digital process virtualization project to address problems with a physical admission system in the University of Ghana. The research findings show that problems such as delays, inconvenience of submitting physical documents, difficulty of accessing lecturers in their offices to serve as referees and untimely feedback can be addressed by inscribing virtual functionalities into digital platforms for affordance actualization by users. However, in situations where personal knowledge is needed for providing academic references, additional functionalities are needed to promote digital interactions between actors.

Keywords: Bright ICT · Process virtualization · Digital platform · Higher education · Virtual functionality · Inscription · Affordance · Action case study · Ghana

1 Introduction

IT enabled-capabilities for efficient and effective organisational processes are critical for organisational performance and stakeholder values [1, 2]. Conversely, organisational processes can be problematic in terms of delays, bureaucracy and inconsistencies thereby constraining satisfactory performance and value creation. Business process re-engineering with ICT is considered as an effective approach to address such problems [3, 4, 40]. Moreover, recent advancement in digital technologies such as the Internet and the Web presents opportunities to address problems with traditional, face-to-face and paper-based processes by converting to virtual processes via digital platforms [5]. Doing so however requires that organisations develop the necessary IT-enabled capabilities [1] such as digital virtual processes that enable remote actors to interact without the need for face-to-face contact in a physical location.

Published by Springer Nature Switzerland AG 2019
Y. Dwivedi et al. (Eds.): TDIT 2019, IFIP AICT 558, pp. 170–179, 2019.
https://doi.org/10.1007/978-3-030-20671-0_12

In line with this background, the purpose of this study is to understand how digital process virtualization can be used to address problems with physical, face-to-face and paper-based processes. Digital process virtualization involves the migration of offline face-to-face process in physical locations onto digital platform for online interactions among people in geographically distributed locations [6, 7]. In recent years, several interactions that used to occur in physical locations have undergone virtual digital process transformation, resulting in online innovations such as e-commerce and e-learning [8].

Bright ICT refers to an IS (information systems) research initiative that focuses on solving real problems in society [9]. Within the IS literature, calls for bright ICT research [10] have been made to help address technology-induced and general problems various areas of society including education [11]. However, bright ICT research in education has focused largely on e-learning. Therefore, not much research exists on university administrative areas such as student admission. In line with this research gap, the research question for this study is how digital process virtualization can be used as a bright ICT initiative to address problems with physical admission in a university. To address the research question, this study draws on an action case study [12, 13] and actor-network theory concept of inscription [14–16] combined with the theory of affordance [17–19] to investigate a digital virtualization of a physical graduate admission process in the University of Ghana.

The rest of this paper is organized as follows. The following section reviews relevant literature on bright ICT and digital process virtualization. The next section presents affordances and inscription as the theoretical lens. The section after describes the research setting and the action case study. The subsequent section reports on the action case study findings. The section after analyses the findings. The discussion follows while the final section serves as the conclusion.

2 Bright ICT and Digital Process Virtualization

Bright ICT: Advancement in ICT has generated benefits for IT-enabled capabilities [1, 2] and business process re-engineering [3, 4] for process efficiency and effectiveness [10]. However, ICT advancement has also induced problems, which have been referred to as dark ICT, such as cybercrime, internet privacy and security breaches [20]. Bright ICT has been proposed as a grand IS research initiative to address dark ICT issues [9] as well as societal problems in healthcare, education, and poverty. Thus education has become a research stream in bright ICT research [10]. This study therefore responds to research calls for bright ICT by focusing on how digital process virtualization can be used to address problems associated with physical admission process in a university.

Digital Process Virtualization: Digital process virtualization involves migrating processes and interactions from offline onto digital platforms [7, 21, 22]. As virtual environments, digital platforms offer functionalities for remote interactions among geographically distributed people without the need for direct and face-to-face contact in a physical location [23, 24]. Process virtualization can be physical such as in the case of distance learning and postal services or digital such as in the case of e-commerce and the internet [5]. As this study concerns digital admission, the focus is on digital process virtualization involving an online admission system rather than a physical process virtualization.

3 Theoretical Foundation: Affordances and Inscription

The theoretical foundation for this study is the combined lens of actor-network theory (ANT) concept of inscription [14, 15] and the theory of affordance [17, 18, 25]. *Inscription* is the act of embedding functionalities into technological artefacts [26, 27] such as software. The outcomes of the inscription process are functionalities that enable or constrain users. In relation to IS, inscription refers to embedded prescriptions in components such as software, hardware, manuals, standards, processes and procedures. For this study, inscription concerns the embedding of virtual functionalities digital platforms during at the development phase.

Affordance refers to action possibilities or constrains that objects present to people as actors [28, 29]. In relation to IS, objects are technologies that present possibility or inhibition to users. As a theoretical principle, an affordance is neither a property of the object nor a property of the actor [30]. Rather, an affordance is an emergent property of interactions between actors and objects [31, 32]. Affordances emerge an actor's perception and become actualized when the actor practically engages with the object [33] for intended goals [34].

Inscription was used to analyse virtual functionalities that got embedded in the digital admission platform while affordance was used to explain the enabling or constraining mechanisms of such functionalities.

4 Research Setting and Methodology

Research Setting: The research setting is the University of Ghana, the oldest and the biggest higher education institution in the country. Over the years, the university has been dealing with increasing number of graduate applications. Yet, its graduate admission system was largely paper-based and fraught with problems such as delays, document misclassification and losses as well as untimely feedback. To address the problems, the author initiated an action case study for digital process virtualization with web developers from the university's ICT unit. The project occurred over a five-year period from 2014 to 2018.

Methodology: Action case study [12, 35] is a qualitative research methodology that combines action research and interpretive case study [12, 13, 36]. It is a form of participatory approach to bring positive changes to real-life problem situation while seeking research understanding to contribute to knowledge at the same time [13].

Qualitative data was gathered from multiple sources, namely participant observation, project documents, project meetings, focus group discussions as well as interviews with applicants, students, administrators and faculty. Initial analysis of the data occurred alongside data gathering and project activities. Detailed theoretical analysis was based on concepts from ANT inscription and affordance theory. Emerging findings were evaluated through member checking [37–39] with the research participants.

5 Case Description

Up to 2009, the University of Ghana's graduate admission system was offline. In 2010, the physical application form was migrated online at the university's website. However, graduate applicants had to physically submit or post supporting documents to the university. In 2012, the action case team, led by the author, analysed the existing system and identified several problems.

Problems with the Existing System: First-year graduate students, who had used the system to apply, complained of delays in completing and submitting the online forms due to slow internet connectivity and frequent downtimes. Some of them also questioned why their supporting documents could not be uploaded alongside the online form. Others also complained about the difficulty of getting three former lecturers to complete their academic reference forms. According to them, the process required physically chasing the lecturers in their offices to get them to complete the forms.

Among the students were past students of the university who complained about why they had to pay for and submit their transcripts to the same university. They wondered why the university could not use their academic records for the admission process. The administrators also complained about limited staff and the tedious process as follows:

> *we even have to print the online forms and together with the supporting documents sort and arrange them per applicant, per programme and per department. Sometimes due to work overload, we mismatch and lose some documents.*

There were instances when documents were wrongly dispatched to various departments. Selection committee members in the departments also complained about delays in getting application documents from the admission office and the excessive paperwork. Another problem with the existing system was the need for the admission office to write, sign and post individual offer letters to successful applicants. Given the huge numbers, the office found it a daunting task and wished that the process could be automated.

Developing the Digital Platform: After the problem diagnosis, the project team developed functional requirements for the digital platform, using PHP and MYSQL. The functionalities inscribed into the virtual application include a document upload service to enable applicants to complete the online forms and upload all supporting documents. Another functionality was past student records retrieval service to avoid the need for past students of the university to submit transcripts and certificates when applying.

Online referencing service was included to automatically request references from academic referees. The e-mail request included a link to an online reference form which the referees could complete and submit electronically. The system was also designed to ensure that admission committee members in various departments could access submitted application documents and related records of applications anytime anywhere, without the need for the admission office to dispatch paper documents to them. To address the problem of manual generation and physical posting of offer letters to applicants, the team embedded a functionality to e-mail successful candidates to download their offer letters.

Subsequently, the project team demonstrated the digital platform to deans of schools, heads of department and various user groups. Comments and feedback from the demonstration sessions were used to address potential challenges. The team also organized training sessions during which users' feedback on errors and inconsistencies were used to address inherent challenges. The newly developed application was launched on the university's web platform in January 2013.

Positive and negative feedbacks have been used to improve the system. The following positive feedback came from a student:

> *It was very exciting to do everything online and I did not need to go to campus to queue and submit documents or go to the post office to post photocopies.*

However, the following negative feedback on getting academic references came from an admission officer:

> *With the previous system, we always received reference reports together with the supporting documents. However, with the new system so many referees fail to send their reference reports.*

In relation to referencing, some academics complained of not knowing the students for whom they were to write references after receiving the automatic e-mail request.

6 Case Analysis

Framework: This section presents the analysis of the action case findings based on the ANT concept of inscription for functionalities embedded in the digital platform, affordance for their actualization and the relationship between the two theoretical concepts.

Functionality Inscription: The findings reveal document upload, online referencing, online selection and online admission as the virtual functionalities that the action case team got inscribed into the platform. Table 1 shows the functionalities, their target user groups and the intended solutions.

Each of the inscribed virtual functionalities was an intended solution to problems with the existing system.

Affordance Actualization: The use phase of the virtual admission platform revealed how the inscribed functionalities were converted into actual affordances or not. The upload functionality was actualized as an affordance for electronically attaching and submitting supporting documents with the completed online application form. This affordance was consistent with the intention for inscribing the functionality to enable applicants to avoid the need for posting or submitting physical documents.

Similarly, the functionality for past student ID entry was also actualized as an affordance for past students to supply their previous IDs to avoid the need to submit

Table 1. Inscribed functionalities

Functionalities	Target users	Solutions
Document upload	• Applicants	• Enable applicants to upload supporting documents • Avoid printing and submission of physical documents
Online access to past students' records	• Past student applicants • Digital platform • Selection committee	• Enable past students to enter their previous ID numbers • Enable digital platform to use ID numbers to retrieve past student records • Enable selection committee access past student records online
Online referencing	• Applicants • Referees	• Get applicants to enter referees' e-mail addresses on the online application form • Get virtual admission platform to e-mail reference request to referees • Get referees to complete and submit online referencing form
Online selection	• Selection committee • Admissions officer	• provide electronic access to the selection committee • virtualize selection and admission of qualified applicants • enable applicants to receive SMS feedback to download admission letters
Online admission	• Admissions office • Application	• Enable admissions office to digitally review selected qualified applications • Enable admissions office to decide on admit or reject

physical copies of their certificates and transcripts as before. However, the intention behind this affordance could not be realized without the digital platform playing the role of electronically retrieving the academic records from the students' database. Thus the affordance actualization for the Student ID entry could only serve as a trigger for records retrieval.

Conversely, actualizing the online referencing functionality as an affordance for virtual referencing was not straight forward. The applicants generally perceived the affordance and supplied the e-mail addresses. However, in some cases, the use of wrong e-mail addresses rendered the affordance unsuccessful. Even in situations where the e-mail addresses were correct, some referees did not actualize the affordance for online referencing due to difficulties in remembering some of the applicants, especially those who failed to contact the referees directly to agree.

The online admission functionality was actualized between the selection committees and the admission office. The committees actualized the online selection as an affordance to review and recommend applications for acceptance or rejection by the admission office without the need for paper documents. The functionality also afforded an opportunity for committee members to do the selection without the need for physical meetings in collocated offices as before. Similarly, the admissions office actualized the online admission functionality as an affordance for vetting and admitting or rejecting applications online without the need for physical documents.

Affordance Actualisation and Re-inscription: In areas where the inscribed functionalities failed to become actualized affordances, the action case team initiated a re-inscription process to modify such functionalities to meet the needs of the various user groups. The two cases involving the re-inscription were online referencing and online admission communication. For the online referencing, it was realised that just getting applicants to enter e-mail addresses of referees for the system to send them links to complete the form was not enough. The functionality was therefore re-inscribed with a requirement for applicants to indicate that they had contacted the referees and had their consent before nominating them. In addition, additional data fields were added for applicants to provide their pictures and contact details to help referees remember the applicants and also contact them when necessary.

The second issue concerned the lack of tracking functionality for applicants to monitor the status and outcome of their applications. The virtual platform was subsequently re-inscribed with a tracking functionality for applicants to check the status of their application. Some applicants actualized the functionality as the affordance to monitor referees' responses. Following the re-inscription, applicants had the opportunity to change referees. The tracking functionality also afforded the applicants the opportunity to have feedback on the outcome of their application. Successful applicants were therefore able to know about their admission and login to download their offer letters.

7 Discussion

In line with the research question, the findings for this study are discussed based on the problems with the previous physical admission system and the solutions from the new virtual system. Based on this, the discussion is centred around the virtualization of documents and person-to-person contact, reliability of internet connectivity, and mutual relationship between virtual functionality inscription and affordance actualization.

The findings show that an admission system virtualization in a university can afford opportunities to address problems of delays and errors that result from document misclassification and losses associated with physical admission processes. From the case, the shift from physical document environment to a digital platform with digital forms and electronic document exchange helped to reduce the errors, delays and misclassification associated with the existing physical system. Within the IS literature, reported benefits of digital virtualization include the removal of space and time constraints for geographically dispersed people [26], anytime anywhere access and flexible working arrangements [21, 41, 42]. From this study, the new findings on the benefits of digital process virtualization are reduction in delays, misclassification errors and losses associated with physical document processes.

However, additional findings show that in situations where people need to know or remember others in order to perform an online action such as in the case of academic referencing, virtualization is not enough. Such situations require personal interactions to avoid mistrust, suspicion and false entity, which constitute key limitations in virtual interactions [21, 26]. Complementing virtual interaction with intermittent face to face contacts has been proposed as a solution to such situations [7, 8]. The findings from this case show that virtual interaction reduces the willingness of people to provide references for others without additional functionality to remember or interact with them. This finding shows the need for digital platform developers to inscribe functionalities for online interaction in such situations.

Another finding from this study is that where people expect to know the status of activities, online tracking becomes an essential functionality for user affordance. From the case analysis, once the direct contact between applicants, referees and admission officers was removed, applicants needed a functionality to track the status of their application and references. Before the digital virtualization, physical contact between applicants, faculty, admission officers, and paper documents served that purpose. However, with virtual submission and referencing, it became necessary to include online tracking functionalities for status monitoring.

On the relationship between virtual functionality inscription and affordance actualization, the findings reveal a mutual shaping between the two. As shown from the case, the inscribed functionalities served as the basis for affordance actualization while the affordance actualization served as the evaluation framework for feedback for the functionality re-inscription. The combined theoretical lens of inscription and affordances was found useful for explaining the emerging and changing nature of digital virtual functionalities.

8 Conclusion

This study began with the aim of understanding how digital process virtualization can be used to address problems with a physical admission system. The research findings show that the key problems applicants faced under the physical admission process were delays, frustrations in physical document submission, difficulty in getting physical access to lecturers to serve as referees and not getting feedback on time. The action case study approach used as the methodology shows that problems associated with physical processes can be addressed through an interactive process between virtual digital functionality inscription and affordance actualization. However, the findings also demonstrate the need for interpersonal communication functionalities and affordances where personal knowledge is needed such as in the case of providing references for people.

Based on the findings, the study contributes to bright ICT research in IS by focusing on how digital process virtualization can be used to address problems with physical processes in the under-researched area of higher education admission. For practice, the findings show that functionality inscription and affordance virtualization can be used as an evaluation framework for achieving intended goals of digital process virtualization. Future research can focus on the relationships between inscribed virtual functionalities, unintended affordances and socio-cultural dimensions of digital processes virtualization as bright ICT research in a developing country context.

References

1. Mikalef, P., Pateli, A.: Information technology-enabled dynamic capabilities and their indirect effect on competitive performance: findings from PLS-SEM and fsQCA. J. Bus. Res. **70**, 1–16 (2017). https://doi.org/10.1016/j.jbusres.2016.09.004
2. Mikalef, P.: Developing IT-enabled dynamic capabilities: a service science approach. In: Johansson, B., Andersson, B., Holmberg, N. (eds.) BIR 2014. LNBIP, vol. 194, pp. 87–100. Springer, Cham (2014). https://doi.org/10.1007/978-3-319-11370-8_7
3. Ahmad, H.: Business process reengineering: critical success factors in higher education. Bus. Process Manag. J. **13**, 451–469 (2007)
4. Lee, Y.-C., Chu, P.-Y., Tseng, H.-L.: Exploring the relationships between information technology adoption. J. Manag. Organ. **15**, 170–185 (2009)
5. Overby, E., Slaughter, S.A., Konsynski, B.: The design, use, and consequences of virtual processes. Inf. Syst. Res. **21**, 700–710 (2010)
6. Balci, B.: The state of the art on process virtualization: a literature review. In: Twentieth Americas Conference on Information Systems, Savanna, pp. 1–14 (2014)
7. Overby, E.: Process virtualization theory and the impact of information technology. Organ. Sci. **19**, 277–291 (2008)
8. Overby, E.: Migrating processes from physical to virtual environments: process virtualization theory. In: Dwivedi, Y.K., Wade, M., Schineberger, S. (eds.) Information Systems Theory: Explaining and Predicting Our Digital Society, vol. 1, pp. 107–124. Springer, New York (2012). https://doi.org/10.1007/978-1-4419-6108-2_6
9. Lee, J.: Invited commentary—reflections on ICT-enabled bright society research. Inf. Syst. Res. **27**, 1–5 (2016)
10. Lee, J., Fedorowicz, J.: Identifying issues for the bright ICT initiative: a worldwide delphi study of IS journal editors and scholars. Commun. Assoc. Inf. Syst. **42**, 301–333 (2018). https://doi.org/10.17705/1CAIS.04211
11. Dalal, N., Pauleen, D.J.: The wisdom nexus: guiding information systems research, practice, and education. Inf. Syst. J. **29**, 224–244 (2019)
12. Braa, K., Vidgen, R.: Interpretation, intervention, and reduction in the organizational laboratory: a framework for in-context information system research. Inf. Organ. **9**, 25–47 (1999)
13. Lee, J.S., Baskerville, R., Pries-Heje, J.: The creativity passdown effect: applying design theory in creating instance design. Inf. Technol. People. **28**, 529–543 (2015)
14. Latour, B.: Science in Action: How to Follow Scientists and Engineers Through Society. Harvard University Press, Cambridge (1987)
15. Latour, B.: Where are the missing masses? The sociology of a few mundane artifacts. In: Bijker, W.E., Law, J. (eds.) Shaping Technology/Building Society: Studies in Sociotechnical Change, pp. 225–258. MIT Press, Cambridge (1992)
16. Akrich, M.: The de-scription of technical objects. In: Bijker, W.E., Law, J. (eds.) Shaping Technology/Building Society: Studies in Sociotechnical Change, pp. 205–224. MIT Press, Cambridge (1992)
17. Gibson, J.: The Theory of Affordances: The Ecological Approach to Visual Perception. Houghton Mifflin Company, Boston (1979)
18. Norman, D.: The Design of Everyday Things. Basic Books, New York (2013)
19. Leonardi, P.: When flexible routines meet flexible technologies: affordance, constraint, and the imbrication of Human and material agencies. MIS Q. **35**, 147–167 (2011)
20. Tarafdar, M., Gupta, A., Turel, O.: Special issue on 'dark side of information technology use': an introduction and a framework for research. Inf. Syst. J. **25**, 161–170 (2015)

21. Breu, K., Hemingway, C.: Making organisations virtual: the hidden cost of distributed teams. J. Inf. Technol. **19**, 191–202 (2004)
22. Balci, B., Rosenkranz, C.: "Virtual or material, what do you prefer?" A study of process virtualization theory. In: Twenty Second European Conference on Information Systems, pp. 1–15 (2014)
23. Griffith, T., Sawyer, J., Neale, M.: Virtualness and knowledge in teams: managing the love triangle of organizations, individuals, and information technology. MIS Q. **27**, 289–323 (2003)
24. Fiol, C.M., O'connor, E.J.: Identification in face-to-face, hybrid, and pure virtual teams: untangling the contradictions. Organ. Sci. **16**, 19–32 (2005)
25. Gibson, J.: The Ecological Approach to Visual Perception. Lawrence Erlbaum Associates, Hillsdale (1986)
26. Sarker, S., Sarker, S., Sidorova, A., Taylor, P.: Understanding business process change failure: an actor-network perspective. J. Manag. Inf. Syst. **23**, 51–86 (2006)
27. Shin, D.-H., Lee, C.-W.: Disruptive innovation for social change: how technology innovation can be best managed in social context. Telemat. Inf. **28**, 86–100 (2011)
28. Zammuto, R., Griffith, T.L., Majchrzak, A., Dougherty, D., Faraj, S.: Information technology and the changing fabric of organization. Organis **18**, 749–762 (2007)
29. Jensen, T., Vatrapu, R.: Ships & roses : a revelatory case study of affordances in international trade. In: Proceedings of the European Conference on Information Systems, pp. 1–18 (2015)
30. Volkoff, O., Strong, D.M.: Critical realism and affordances: theorizing IT-associated organizational change process. MIS Q. **37**, 819–834 (2013)
31. Markus, M.L., Silver, M.S.: A foundation for the study of IT effects: a new look at DeSanctis and poole's concepts of structural features and spirit. J. Assoc. Inf. Syst. **9**, 609–632 (2008)
32. Hutchby, I.: Technologies, texts and affordances. Sociology **35**, 441–456 (2001)
33. Pozzi, G., Pigni, F., Vitari, C.: Affordance theory in the IS discipline: a review and synthesis of the literature. Twent. Am. Conf. Inf. Syst. Savannah **2014**(13), 1–12 (2014)
34. Strong, D.M., et al.: A theory of organization-EHR affordance actualization. J. Assoc. Inf. Syst. **15**, 53–85 (2014)
35. Hughes, J., Wood-Harper, T.: Systems development as a research act. In: Willcocks, L.P., Sauer, C., Lacity, M.C. (eds.) Enacting Research Methods in Information Systems, pp. 83–94 (2016)
36. Goldkuhl, G.: Pragmatic qualities of information systems – actability criteria for design and evaluation. In: 11th International Conference on Informatics and Semiotics in Organisations (ICISO), 11–12 April 2009, Beijing, China, pp. 1–14 (2009)
37. Trauth, E.M., Hall, H., Jessup, L.M.: Understanding computer-mediated discussions: positivist and interpretive analyses of group support system use. MIS Q. **24**, 43–79 (2000)
38. Creswell, J.: Qualitative, Quantitative, and Mixed Methods Approaches. SAGE Publications, London (2013)
39. Miles, M., Huberman, M., Saldana, J.: Qualitative Data Analysis: A Methods Sourcebook. Sage, London (2014)
40. Weerakkody, V., Janssen, M., Dwivedi, Y.K.: Transformational change and business process reengineering (BPR): lessons from the British and Dutch public sector. Govern. Inf. Q. **28**(3), 320–328 (2011)
41. Lal, B., Dwivedi, Y.K.: Investigating homeworkers' inclination to remain connected to work at "anytime, anywhere" via mobile phones. J. Enterp. Inf. Manage. **23**(6), 759–774 (2010)
42. Lal, B., Dwivedi, Y.K.: Investigating homeworkers' usage of mobile phones for overcoming feelings of professional isolation. Int. J. Mob. Commun. **6**(4), 481–498 (2008)

Use of Digital-Physical Security System in a Developing Country's Port: A Case Study of Ghana

Fred Amankwah-Sarfo(✉)

Department of Operations and Management Information Systems, University of Ghana Business School, Accra, Ghana
famankwah-sarfo001@st.ug.edu.gh

Abstract. The purpose of this study is to understand how the use of digital-physical security (DPS) improves port security by enabling or constraining stakeholders' goals in a developing country. Information Systems (IS) research on digital-physical security has focused more on power networks, automotive, manufacturing, and healthcare sectors. Digital-physical security (DPS) research on ports in developing countries remains limited. Therefore, port security systems as a significant IS research is yet to receive the necessary attention. To address this gap, this study employed affordance theory as the analytical lens and qualitative interpretive case study as the methodology to investigate use of digital-physical security for a port in Ghana. The research findings show that developing countries can use digital-physical security systems to improve port security. The findings have implication for research, practice, and policy. The originality of the paper lies in its focus on how a developing country can use digital-physical systems to improve port security as a significant IS research phenomenon.

Keywords: Digital-physical security system · Affordance theory · Interpretive case study · Developing country · Ghana

1 Introduction

The purpose of this study is to understand how the use of digital-physical security system improves port security by enabling or constraining stakeholders' goals in a developing country. The efficiency of digital-physical systems and the effectiveness of port facilities are observed phenomena [1]. Digital-physical systems are the basic information technologies, organizational structures, the related services and facilities necessary for an enterprise or industry to function [2]. Moreover, the process of embedding digital capabilities and standards in organizational practices enables new social behaviors and/or regulations [3] and involves a heterogeneous mix of people and technologies built on an installed base [4].

In IS, digital-physical system can be defined as "a shared, open (and unbounded), heterogeneous and evolving socio-technical system (which we call installed base) consisting of a set of IT capabilities and their users, operations, and design" [5] and the relationships between organized practices [6]. Research on digital-physical security

Published by Springer Nature Switzerland AG 2019
Y. Dwivedi et al. (Eds.): TDIT 2019, IFIP AICT 558, pp. 180–190, 2019.
https://doi.org/10.1007/978-3-030-20671-0_13

system in different countries and universities has been conducted [7] in industrial control systems [8]. In interpretive research considerable attention has been paid to the evolution of digital-physical systems in the complex interdependencies between socio-technical elements; networks of human and nonhuman actors; and the relationship between organized practices [6]. However, little empirical research exists on how digital-physical security improves organizational security by enabling or constraining of stakeholders' goals. Following this research gap, the research question motivating this study is: how do digital physical security systems improve security in a developing country's port? In addressing this question, the study employs Gibson's [9] affordance theory as the analytical lens, and an interpretive qualitative case study approach [10] to understand how the adoption of digital-physical security system improves port security in a developing country.

The Tema Port was chosen for this research as it is considered a typical developing country port which has recently deployed a digital-physical security system. Research on digital-physical security for ports is considered a significant e-government initiative for trade facilitation. Moreover, the use of digital-physical systems can help address security lapses at the port and thus require a need for research to help address inherent challenges. Results of this effort will help inform decision makers of emerging and available digital-physical technologies to enhance and improve existing capabilities, as well as to uncover potential challenges between security needs and enabling technologies. In sum, this study advances existing knowledge by offering rich insight into how and why a developing country's use of digital-physical system foster improvement of port security.

The remaining part of the paper is structured as follows: Sect. 2 reviews relevant literature on digital infrastructure and port community systems. Section 3 discusses the affordance theory as the theoretical lens for the data analysis. Section 4 presents the methodology for the data collection whilst Sect. 5 presents the case study description. Section 6 is the case analysis based on the selected theoretical foundation. Section 7 is the discussion of findings and finally, Sect. 8 concludes the paper with its contribution to knowledge and recommendation for further research.

2 Digital-Physical Security

Digital-physical security system refers to the integration of digital and physical components using modern sensors, computing and network technologies [11]. It is noted that these systems require communication, computation and control infrastructures with several separated components for the physical and IT "world" resources such as sensors, actuators, network nodes, computers and services [12].

DPS research is gaining interest in applications in electricity generation and distribution, medical and healthcare systems [13], automotive and manufacturing sectors [7]. Substantial amount of research work on DPS also referred to as cyber-physical systems and applications of dynamic infrastructures [14] exist. However, DPSs are vulnerable to potential security threats and disruption to the physical system [15]. Moreover, research has highlighted issues in the digital-physical security of WAMPAC (Wide-Area Monitoring, Protection and Control) [16].

In relation to power networks, studies show how the integration of digital technologies in smart grids enable efficient distribution of power [17]. These may however, come with security threats as a result of new data collection, communication, and information sharing capacities in the power system along with, vulnerabilities and associated cyber-physical attacks [7]. In relation to health, research on digital physical security has focused on interoperable medical devices, networking and coordination functionalities [18].

It is noted that digital physical security solutions enable plug-n-play secure communication which has been analyzed for intrusion detection of medical devices embedded in a medical cyber physical system [19]. In addition, cyber-security tools specifically designed for manufacturing allow communication among industrial machines [20] from posing threat to ensure products conformity and maintain the safety of equipment, employees, and consumers [7]. Attacks can alter a manufacturing system, resulting in impaired communication, functionality or reduced performance.

In relation to automotive [21], the digital-physical system protects against malicious design and interaction faults to guarantee correctness and reliable operation, a computer-mediated physical distributed complex systems have a significant impact [17]. Nonetheless, research specifically focusing on digital-physical security in developing countries remains limited. This study therefore seeks to extend the existing knowledge on digital physical security in developing countries.

3 Theoretical Foundation: Affordance Theory

The concept of affordance was introduced by ecological psychologist James Gibson (1977) to account for how various users may perceive or use the same object in different ways [22]. The foundational elements of affordance are (1) object; (2) observer; (3) environment; and (4) complementary relations between these elements [23]. Based upon the concepts of affordances: (1) affordances emerge in perception from the relation between these elements; they are not 'in' any of these elements per se; (2) affordances refer to action possibilities, that is, what the perceiver can do with the object; (3) affordances exist independent of the perceiver's ability to perceive it; (4) affordances exist independent of need.

'Affordance' refers to the perceived and actual properties of a thing, primarily those functional properties that determine just how the thing could possibly be used [24]. An affordances perspective represents a relational approach to understanding how people interact with technology [25]. The perceived affordances are the opportunities for action that the object enables the user to carry out and may be different depending on users context, competences, and objectives [26]. A conceptual definition of affordances broadly described as possibilities for action is the "multifaceted relational structure" [27] between an object/technology and the user that enables or constrains potential behavioral outcomes in a context [28].

In IS literature, affordance has been described as emerging from the relation between IT systems and organization systems and defined as "the possibilities for goal-oriented action afforded to specified user groups by technical objects" [27]. An affordance arises from the relation between a structure or object and a goal-directed actor or actors. [29]. When the object of study is information technology, and the question relates to how the introduction of that technology affects an organization, the more focused nature of the affordance concept is useful [29]. IS scholars have explained affordance actualization as the immediate-concrete outcome. Affordance actualization is the action taken by actors as they take advantage of one or more perceived affordances through their use of technology to achieve outcomes in support of organizational goals.

Affordance theory from ecological psychology has received insufficient attention to the ontological status of affordances [29]. While affordance-based IS research has largely focused on how different visual cues support the perception of affordances, or how perceptual cues can be learned as social conventions, there is still much more to be learned by understanding the affordances themselves. To address this gap, this study adopts the interpretive paradigm to research into port security systems in a developing country. The underlying research paradigm of this study is based on subjective ontology and epistemology. This helps to understand how digital-physical security can be used to improve port security systems. The use of affordance theory for digital-physical port security systems research is important as it allows the understanding of how various actors perceive and use of digital infrastructure as an important aspect to improve port security systems.

4 Research Setting and Methodology

Generally, qualitative research seeks an in-depth understanding of a research phenomenon This study's methodology was qualitative, interpretive case study [10, 30–32, 40]. Generally, the qualitative research seeks an in-depth understanding of a research phenomenon [33] involving human and social interpretations, experiences and action. Based on a qualitative research approach, the interpretive case study in information systems seeks to understand interactions between information technologies and their social contexts.

As a result, the underlying research paradigm of this study is based on subjective ontology and epistemology on the assumption that the research phenomenon under study and the knowledge output are both socially constructed rather than objectively given [34, 35]. In line with this philosophy, this study considers interpretive case study as suitable to understand how the use of digital-physical security system improves port security by enabling or constraining stakeholders' goals in a developing country. Data collection occurred over a period f six months, from September 2017 to March 2018. In line with the interpretive case study tradition [10], we gathered qualitative data from multiple sources, including interviews, observations and websites, field notes, and documentary materials. Interviews are one of the most important sources of case study information and are an efficient method to gather rich insights.

In line with this philosophy, this study considers interpretive case study as suitable for making sense of the digital infrastructure for port security systems. The data collection occurred in two main stages. The first was a stage of familiarization to develop an understanding of the context of the study, the technology employed, and the actors involved. This was achieved by observing meetings, demonstration sessions, tests and training sessions to build an understanding of the digital infrastructure for the port security systems.

The interview guide was semi-structured [36] and lasted between 30 min and 1 h. Some of the interview sessions were audio recorded, subject to the informed consent of the interviewee. Interviews were subsequently transcribed for more detailed analysis. Initial data analysis occurred alongside data collection [10] and based on Hermeneutics cycle. In line with interpretive tradition, data analysis took place concurrently with the data collection [10]. The data analysis was aided by affordance theory concepts of enabling affordance and constraining affordance to analyze the case findings.

5 Case Description

This study was conducted in Tema Port. The port is located in the southeastern part of Ghana, along the Gulf of Guinea. The port serves both as a loading and unloading port for goods and a major transit point for land-locked countries to the north of Ghana. The port receives an average of 1,650 vessel calls per year. Stretching over 3.9 million square meters of land area, a high level of security is a major priority. This means that certain areas of the port can be inaccessible all the time as far as patrolling is concerned and therefore could lead to stealing of cargo from the cargo containers. It could also be prone to smuggling of weapons and arsenal into the country and issues of stowage and illegal immigration. The digital port security system which was put in place helps to provide multiple solutions.

5.1 Port Security

As a major entry point to countries, seaports are targets for unauthorized activities such as sabotage, terrorist threats, piracy, cargo theft, and smuggling. It is vital that ports are given security infrastructure and surveillance strategies and technologies that limit illegal activities and minimize threats and facilitate trade as well as enhance the ability to assess cargo for risk, examine high-risk shipments at the earliest possible point, and increase the security of the supply chain.

Port security is the defense, laws and treaty enforcement, and counterterrorism activities that fall within the port and maritime domain. It includes the protection of the seaports themselves, the protection and inspection of the cargo moving through the ports, and maritime security. The port security manager observed:

> *Our security is made of systems that work together to combat unlawful activities. The systems comprise an interrelated part to achieve a goal. For security to thrive, various systems must work to complement each other. These are electronic, personnel, procedures and physical barriers.*

These systems are mutually re-enforcing and interdependent meaning where one falls short, the other should complement. Whenever a breach of security occurs, the electronic system gives the earliest possible warning, the human being gives the quickest possible response, procedures give the fairest possible control and the physical barriers give the longest possible delay for a security breach to occur.

The deputy port security manager stated:

The possible threat of terrorist attacks and the increasingly sophisticated activities of organized criminal gangs have heightened the focus on electronic security. The result is increasing requirements for these high security and mission critical systems to be continuously available with no downtime.

The electronic security system at the Tema Port has an underlying technology infrastructure with following capabilities: virtualization-ready with a wide range of support for different applications; continuous availability of technologies is critical and consolidated to a shared set of server resources, unplanned downtime is not an option. There are many ways to mitigate the risk of unplanned downtime, with a high available or fault-tolerant solution which is easy to deploy and easy to service in the event of a failure.

One of the most difficult challenges in operating a digital physical security system is understanding and resolving operational issues. Digital technology greatly reduces the complexity of systems. This means that an end-to-end view of the entire security system (devices, applications, and hardware) decrease the challenges of identifying and even preventing issues before occurring. The deputy port security manager explained that:

Port security is a part of the maritime security which comes under International Maritime Organization (IMO) and the International Ship and Port Facility Security Code introduced in the year 2002 as a part of the Safety of Life at Sea (SOLAS) convention. Apart from these two organizations, a lot of port security measures are incorporated from the United Nation's own marine security enforcement agenda.

In line with the international ship and port security (ISPS) code, Tema Port has high security measures to prevent acts of terrorism and other security threats. An electronic gating system and security surveillance optical character recognition cameras, as well as CCTV's, have been installed. The head of port security explained:

All these have created a haven in our navigational waters and port operational areas giving shippers a great sense of security. Major Security Initiatives by the Ghana Ports and Harbours Authority, Electronic Gate Systems, ISPS, and Maritime Security (MARSEC) level 1 compliance in both commercial ports.

The new Meridian Port Services terminal is designed to run automated and semi-automated processes, enabled by digital technologies at the various stages of the terminal operations, to facilitate and save valuable time, a secure online portal enables initial registration of customers. The online portal is used to make appointments through the "Truck Appointment System" (TAS) for visit to the MPS Terminal at their convenience. Each customer has access to a dashboard containing personal information and available containers.

The Truck Appointment System and online portal are opened 24 h a day, 7 days a week and avoid waiting times compared to a manual process. The TAS communicate in real-time with a centralized and high-available Digital Terminal Operating System (DTOS) to retrieve and validate all data. An importer reiterated:

Once an appointment is confirmed your registered truck driver is welcomed at our MPS Terminal and allowed to enter based upon biometric fingerprint validation. Using this advanced technology in the early stage of your visit allows MPS Terminal and Tema Port to grant access only to those truck drivers who are registered and authorized.

This ensures that visitors, staff, facility, and cargo is kept safe and is fully compliant with The International Ship and Port Facility Security (ISPS) code. Besides performing identity checks, this biometric validation is used in parallel to confirm the validity of appointment through the Digital Truck Appointment System (DTAS). This will avoid traffic congestion and waiting times. When trucks enter the port premises an automated workflow is initiated. Automated access portals read the truck license plate using the License Plate Recognition (LPR). In addition to the LPR, each truck is identified through a unique and tamper proof identification sticker based upon RFID technology.

A terminal operator stated:

The automated portals are equipped Digital Optical Recognition Cameras to recognize: Container Number; IMO Hazard Codes; Number of Containers loaded; Presence of seals; IMDG Classification.

All data is captured and verified in real time when the truck drives through the automated portals, without stopping, towards the Terminal gates. By the time the truck reached the Terminal gates, all captured data is processed, and the weight is taken through automated weighbridges. The truck is automatically identified through RFID and can proceed to its destination at the container yard. Soon as the truck driver is on its way to his destination in the yard the eRTG operator will be automatically informed through the digital terminal operating system, upon arrival the visiting truck will be served by the operator. An officer at the CCTV central control room stated that:

The electronic gate is used to control access to the restricted areas of the port. All vehicles (personal and truck) entering the restricted area must be screened before access is granted. Using cameras, proximity readers, magnetic-stripe readers, biometrics, OCR readers, cameras, and microphones all vehicles and persons are screened, and equipment information are captured and stored.

All port users must have an identification card, a valid visitor card, or a valid driver's license to enter the restricted area. The visitor will present a form of ID to one of the devices and then authentication of said ID is done; providing all requirements to allow entry is complete access is granted. If access is granted, a gate pass is issued for the individual(s) inside the vehicle. A gate pass for trucks is a paper printout of the time, date, name of the driver, and list of equipment brought into the restricted area. For cars, an electronic gate pass is created capturing similar information. This system also allows trucking companies to review their gate transaction logs and balances via the internet.

6 Case Analysis

In this section, the concepts of affordance theory are used for the case analysis. Digitalization denotes a complex transformation, where the physical and the digital are entwined and configured in new ways. From the case description, the port security system is the digital infrastructure that enables truckers, terminal operators and security personnel to use a digital port security system from the relationship between these goal-oriented actors.

The concepts of affordance were used to explain digital port security processes. The key principles of affordance theory are enabling and constraining affordances. The concepts of affordance are a technical object (digital technology), actor groups, and their goals were used to analyze the case findings.

6.1 Enabling Affordance of Digital Port Security System

From the case description, the digital infrastructure for the port security system enables port stakeholders to achieve intended goals. Table 1 shows a summary of the enabling affordance of the digital port security system. The next section detail how digital port security system enables truckers, security personnel and terminal operators achieve the goals. The electronic gate system enables control access to the restricted areas of the port by ensuring that visitors to the port have pre-authorized clearance from the port security office. Truck drivers use the digital truck appointment system to book appointment to specific parts of the port to load/off load cargo.

Table 1. Enabling affordance of digital infrastructure for port security system

Affordance	Digital technology	Actors
Access control	Electronic gate systems	Port users *goal: authorized access*
Booking	Digital truck appointment system	Truck operators *goal: schedule appointment*
Identification	Digital optical recognition cameras	Security personnel *goal: authorization*
Surveillance	CCTV	Port authority *goal: real time recording*

Port security personnel use the digital optical recognition cameras to identify authorized users of the port and CCTVs allow port authorities to monitor in real time critical positions within the port. The footages of the CCTV are transmitted via the intranet to a central monitoring room for monitoring and analysis. The e-gate and CCTV are embedded with digital transmission chips and together with the network connectivity, hardware and storage devices constitute the digital-physical security system.

6.2 Constraining Affordance of Digital Infrastructure for Port Security System

The constraining affordances are an unauthorized access smuggling. Table 2 is a summary of the constrains of the digital port security system.

Table 2. Constraints of digital infrastructure for port security system

Constraints	Digital technology	Actors
Unauthorized access	Electronic gate systems	Unauthorized persons *goal: pilfering*
Smuggling	3D scanners	Security personnel *goal: prevent smuggling*

The electronic gate prevents unauthorized persons from accessing the port facility. This is achieved by authorized card holder slotting digital card at the point of entry. The 3 D scanners constrain smuggling of illegal items by importers who may want to outwit port authorities from detecting such goods. The goal of pilfers is to have unauthorized access into the electronic gating (E-Gate) system that allows only biometrically verified persons into the port space. The e-gate, therefore, serves as a constrain against pilfering.

7 Discussion

The section discusses how the research question is answered using affordance as the theoretical lens. It is important to state that the digital port security system is a technical object with component parts [37]. In line with the research question of how the use of digital-physical security system for the port security enabled or constrained stakeholders' goals as shown in Tables 1 and 2 above. The study sought to achieve this by examining the literature on digital-physical security systems and conducting empirical research at Ghana's Tema port.

From the case study, the port security system is conceptualized as a digital-physical security system which enables interactions between stakeholders to achieve goals [38] whilst restricting unauthorized activities [39]. The interactions between these actors and the digital-physical security system identified in the case study raise interesting issues for discussion, however, based on the research question and the affordance theory, the affordance, and constraints for the port security system in a developing country are discussed.

This study has sought to achieve this by explaining affordance and constrains resulting from the digital port security system and its stakeholders. The research findings show that developing countries can use port security to enable (1) access control (2) booking (3) identification and (4) surveillance. Whilst the port security system also prevents unauthorized access and smuggling. To obtain authorized access to the port, temper-proof biometric identity card at the office of the port security is issued to authorized users. Hence on arrival at the gate, the truck driver showed the card to the electronic gate sensor for the gates to be automatically open.

8 Conclusion

The purpose of this study was to understand how the use of digital-physical system improves port security by enabling or constraining stakeholders' goals in a developing country. The paper's originality lies in its affordance theory-based explanation of how digital-physical security improves to port security. The improved outcomes are a result of digital-physical security enabling or constraining stakeholders' goals. The findings have implications for research, practice, and policy. For research, affordance theory is considered useful for studying digital infrastructure phenomena involving heterogeneous actor groups. For practice, digital infrastructure can significantly help streamline port security systems. For policy, port digital infrastructure can help improve the efficiency of port security. The study is limited as a single case study in one developing country. However, from an interpretive perspective, the findings are applicable to other countries with similar settings. Future research can focus on digital infrastructure for export.

References

1. Di Vaio, A., Varriale, L.: AIS and reporting in the port community systems: an Italian case study in the landlord port model. In: Reshaping Accounting and Management Control Systems, pp 153–165 (2017)
2. Tilson, D., Lyytinen, K., Sørensen, C.: Digital infrastructures: the missing IS research agenda. Inf. Syst. Res. **21**, 748–759 (2010)
3. Edwards, P.N., Jackson, S.J., Bowker, G.C., Knobel, C.P.: Understanding infrastructure: dynamics, tensions, and design (2007)
4. Bygstad, B., Hanseth, O., Siebenherz, A., Ovrelid, E.: Process innovation meets digital infrastructure in a high-tech hospital. In: Proceedings of European Conference on Information Systems 2017, pp. 1–14 (2017)
5. Hanseth, O., Lyytinen, K.: Design theory for dynamic complexity in information infrastructures: the case of building internet. J. Inf. Technol. **25**, 1–19 (2010)
6. Star, S.L., Ruhleder, K.: Steps toward an ecology of infrastructure: design and access for large information spaces. Inf. Syst. Res. **7**(1), 111–134 (1996)
7. Lu, T., Zhao, J., Zhao, L., Li, Y., Zhang, X.: Towards a framework for assuring cyber physical system security. Int. J. Secur. its Appl. **9**, 25–40 (2015)
8. Syed, D., Chang, T.-H., Svetinovic, D., Rahwan, T., Aung, Z.: Security for complex cyber-physical and industrial control systems: current trends, limitations, and challenges. In: Pacific Asia Conference on Information Systems (2017)
9. Burrell, M.: Burrell and Morgan's. Sociol. J. Br. Sociol. Assoc. **3**, 380–381 (1979)
10. Walsham, G.: Doing interpretive research. Eur. J. Inf. Syst. **15**, 320–330 (2006)
11. Zeadally, S., Jabeur, N.: Cyber-Physical System Design with Sensor Networking Technologies. Institution of Engineering and Technology (2016)
12. Teslya, N., Smirnov, A., Levashova, T., Shilov, N.: Ontology for resource self-organisation in cyber-physical-social systems. In: Klinov, P., Mouromtsev, D. (eds.) KESW 2014. CCIS, vol. 468, pp. 184–195. Springer, Cham (2014). https://doi.org/10.1007/978-3-319-11716-4_16
13. Kim, K.-D., Kumar, P.R.: An overview and some challenges in cyber-physical systems. J. Indian Inst. Sci. **93**, 341–352 (2013)
14. Sandkuhl, K.: Feature models as support for business model implementation of cyber-physical systems. Int. Conf. Inf. Syst, Dev (2018)
15. Mahmoud, M.S., Hamdan, M.M., Baroudi, U.A.: Modeling and control of cyber-physical systems subject to cyber attacks: a survey of recent advances and challenges. Neurocomputing **338**, 101–115 (2019)
16. Alguliyev, R., Imamverdiyev, Y., Sukhostat, L.: Cyber-physical systems and their security issues. Comput. Ind. **100**, 212–223 (2018). https://doi.org/10.1016/j.compind.2018.04.017

17. El, Z., Kaabouch, N., El, H., El, H.: Cyber-security in smart grid: Survey and challenges. Comput. Electr. Eng. **67**, 469–482 (2018)
18. Venkatasubramanian, K.K., Vasserman, E.Y., Sokolsky, O., Lee, I.: Security and interoperable-medical-device systems, part 1. IEEE Secur. Priv. **10**, 61–63 (2012)
19. Mitchell, R., Chen, R.: Behavior rule specification-based intrusion detection for safety critical medical cyber physical systems. IEEE Trans. Dependable Secur. Comput. **12**, 16–30 (2015)
20. Wells, L.J., Camelio, J.A., Williams, C.B., White, J.: Cyber-physical security challenges in manufacturing systems. Manuf. Lett. **2**, 74–77 (2014)
21. Wasicek, A., Derler, P., Lee, E.A.: Aspect-oriented modeling of attacks in automotive cyber-physical systems. In: 2014 51st ACM/EDAC/IEEE Design Automation Conference (DAC), pp 1–6. IEEE (2014)
22. Fayard, A.-L., Weeks, J.: Affordances for practice. Inf. Organ. **24**, 236–249 (2014)
23. Burlamaqui, L., Dong, A.: The use and misuse of the concept of affordance. Des. Comput. Cogn. DCC 7–12 (2014). https://doi.org/10.1007/978-3-319-14956-1_17
24. Salomon, G.: Distributed Cognitions: Psychological and Educational Considerations. Cambridge University Press, Cambridge (1997)
25. Treem, J.W., Leonardi, P.M.: Social media use in organizations: exploring the affordances of visibility, editability, persistence, and association, p. 8985 (2016)
26. Vaast, E.: Social media affordances and governance in the workplace: an examination of organizational. J. Comput. Commun. **19**, 78–101 (2013). https://doi.org/10.1111/jcc4.12032
27. Faraj, S., Azad, B.: The materiality of technology: an affordance perspective. Mater. Organ. Soc. Interact. Technol. World **237**, 258 (2012)
28. Evans, S.K., Pearce, K.E., Vitak, J., Treem, J.W.: Explicating affordances: a conceptual framework for understanding affordances in communication research. J. Comput. Commun. **22**, 35–52 (2017). https://doi.org/10.1111/jcc4.12180
29. Volkoff, O., Strong, D.M.: Critical realism and affordances: theorizing it-associated organizational change processes. MIS Q. **37**, 819–834 (2013)
30. Iivari, J., Hirscheim, R., Klein, K.H.: Beyond methodologies: keeping up with information systems development approaches through dynamic classification. In: Proceedings of the 32nd Hawaii International Conference on System Sciences. IEEE (1999)
31. Walsham, G.: Interpretive case studies in IS research: nature and method. Eur. J. Inf. Syst. **4**, 74–81 (1995)
32. Myers, M., Klein, H.K.: A set of principles for conducting critical research in information systems. MIS Q. **35**, 17–36 (2011). https://doi.org/10.2307/249410
33. Miles, M.B., Huberman, A.M., Saldana, J.: Qualitative Data Analysis. A Methods Sourcebook. Sage Publications Inc., Thousand Oaks (2016)
34. Myers, M.: Qualitative Research in Business and Management. Sage, Thousand Oaks (2013)
35. Orlikowski, W.J., Baroudi, J.J.: Studying information technology in organizations: research approaches and assumptions. Inf. Syst. Res. **2**, 1–28 (1991)
36. Myers, M., Newman, M.: The qualitative interview in IS research: examining the craft. Inf. Organ. **17**, 2–26 (2007)
37. Glowalla, P., Rosenkranz, C., Sunyaev, A.: Evolution of IT use: a case of business intelligence system transition. In: ICIS, pp. 1–19 (2014)
38. Leonardi, P.M.: When does technology use enable network change in organizations? A comparative study of feature use and shared affordances. MIS Q. **37**, 749–775 (2013)
39. Dini, A.A., Wahid, F., Sæbo, Ø.: Affordances and constraints of social media use in eParticipation: perspectives from Indonesian politicians (2016)
40. Choudrie, J., Dwivedi, Y.K.: Investigating the research approaches for examining technology adoption issues. J. Res. Pract. **1**(1), 1 (2005). http://jrp.icaap.org/index.php/jrp/article/viewFile/4/7

Understanding the Adoption and Use of E-tail Websites: An Empirical Analysis Based on the Revised UTAUT2 Model Using Risk and Trust Factors

Kayode Odusanya[1(✉)], Olu Aluko[1], and Banita Lal[2]

[1] Nottingham Business School, Nottingham Trent University, Nottingham, UK
kayode.odusanya@ntu.ac.uk

[2] Department of Management and Business Systems, University of Bedfordshire, Bedford, UK

Abstract. Although electronic retail platforms offer a more efficient means for providing goods and services, its adoption by users in developing countries remains encumbered with deep skepticism. Despite substantial investments, many users are reluctant to use electronic retail websites due to trust and risk issues. The objective of this study therefore is to develop and empirically test a model for predicting the factors affecting users' acceptance of electronic retail websites. We adapted the revised United Theory of Acceptance and Use of Technology (UTAUT) model to evaluate the importance of risk and trust factors on the behavioral intentions and use of e-tail websites within a sub-Saharan African context. For this purpose, we employed the variance-based Structural Equation Model (SEM) to analyze survey data collected from 207 e-tail users in Nigeria. The proposed model explained 67.5% of the variance in behavioral intention and 43.5% in use behavior. While our empirical results show that behavioral intention and use of electronic retail websites are mainly influenced by habit, the risk-trust inter-relationships to behavioral intention portray mixed findings.

Keywords: E-tail websites · UTAUT2 · Technology adoption · Sub-Saharan Africa · E-commerce

1 Introduction

Consumer-use platforms such as electronic retail websites (hereafter, e-tail) provide a medium for various transactions to take place between businesses and consumers. These platforms have long been adopted in developed countries where the necessary institutional conditions underlying its delivery is widely available. However, the increasing internet user penetration around the world in the last decade (GSMA 2018) has meant that the use of e-tail platforms is also beginning to gain traction in developing countries such as those in sub-Saharan Africa. For instance, KPMG predicts that e-commerce activities are expected to make up to 10% of total retail sales in key African markets by 2025 (KPMG 2018). Yet, while there is an extensive body of

Published by Springer Nature Switzerland AG 2019
Y. Dwivedi et al. (Eds.): TDIT 2019, IFIP AICT 558, pp. 191–211, 2019.
https://doi.org/10.1007/978-3-030-20671-0_14

literature that has investigated factors that influence the intention and usage of e-tail platforms within the Information Systems (IS) literature, these studies have predominantly been conducted in developed country contexts (Williams et al. 2015). This study therefore aims to fill a gap in the literature by exploring factors that predict the acceptance and use of e-tail websites in a developing country, Nigeria. To fulfil this objective, we use the revised UTAUT model (Venkatesh et al. 2012). Revised by Venkatesh et al. (2012), the UTAUT2 allows for a structured analysis of constructs affecting the decision to use a technology within a consumer-use context. Particularly, we considered that the revised UTAUT model affords a significant explanation of behavioral intention (74%) and technology usage (52%) (Venkatesh et al. 2012). We also considered that the UTAUT2 model provides a better explanation of variance in usage intention and the fact that it has been specifically developed for application in the consumer-use technology contexts.

Nigeria provides a suitable case country to situate our study because it fulfils the requirements of the context, we aim to shed insight on. Located in sub-Saharan Africa, Nigeria is regarded as Africa's most populous country, while its population is projected to become the third largest in the world by 2050 (UN 2017). Along with the high proportion of potential online consumers, that is, 50% of the entire population, Nigeria has been regarded as the largest e-commerce hub in Africa (Paypal 2016). Institutionally, Nigeria is faced with weak institutions, poor consumer rights, online fraud etc. These environmental conditions can impede e-tail adoption. Incorporating the UTAUT2 model in the Nigerian context allows us to expand the conversation around the use of UTAUT2 in sub-Saharan Africa where infrastructures that facilitate the adoption of online retail platforms are not widespread. Hence, we are interested in answering the research question: Drawing on the UTAUT model, what factors influence the behavioral intention and use of e-tail websites?

It is expected that this study will offer useful insights by contributing to the advancement of knowledge for researchers and practitioners in two main ways. First, we evaluate the antecedents of e-tail website adoption and use by using the UTAUT2 model – thereby responding to Venkatesh et al.'s (2012) call for future studies to test the UTUAT2 in different countries and different technologies, particularly developing countries. Secondly, we integrated risk and trust factors in the model to investigate their impact on e-tail website use. In other words, our study follows the suggestion of Venkatesh et al. (2012) to "examine other key constructs that are salient to different research contexts…" (p. 171). The structure of the paper is as follows. The proceeding section presents a review of the literature and background covering the theoretical framework employed in this study. In addition, an overview of the relevant theoretical literature pertaining to technology acceptance leading to the development of hypotheses is presented. Subsequently, the methodology is described, and the results are presented. The paper concludes with a discussion of the research findings and the theoretical and practical implications of this study, as well as limitations and suggestions for future research.

2 Literature Review and Background

2.1 E-tail Use and Adoption in Developing Countries

A growing number of studies have explored electronic commerce adoption in developing countries. Kurnia et al. (2015) argues that developing countries lack adequate technological, social, cultural, legal infrastructures to allow for the effective adoption of e-tail technologies. For example, recent studies have emphasized to the cruciality of institutional factors in facilitating e-commerce adoption at firm and user-level. Using the resource-based view perspective, Boateng (2016) highlights the weakness of institutional underpinnings as significant constraints to the realization of e-commerce benefits for small enterprises in Ghana. Similarly, Okoli et al. (2010) echoes this position using a sample of SMEs in Latin America and sub-Saharan Africa. Overall, these studies suggest that institutions matter in e-tail adoption, and that the characteristically weak institutional environments in developing countries represent significant impediments mitigating e-commerce adoption. We find these characteristics also represented in the context of this study. For instance, while Nigeria is one of the developing countries at the forefront of investments in e-commerce (McKinsey 2014), its institutional infrastructure is weak and highly fragmented. The country is saddled with weak legal environment, poor enabling facilities (such as power), poor consumer rights and weak policies protecting the rights of e-tail customers. As a result, many still treat e-commerce activities with deep skepticism (Ayo et al. 2011). As such, there is still a reluctance to adopt and utilize e-commerce platforms when engaging in online transactions due to associated perceived risk such as internet fraud and advanced fee fraud (Oghenerukevbe 2008). It is therefore crucial to analyze how perceptions of risk and trust relationships influence consumers' behavioral intentions and subsequent use of e-tail websites – the goal of this study.

2.2 Theoretical Approaches Concerning the Adoption and Use of Technology

Since the evolution of e-services in the 1980's, a number of theories have been proposed that attempt to explain their acceptance and use. Two important theoretical positions are worth noting. The first pertains to studies investigating adoption and usage from an innovation standpoint with the view to evaluate the adoption or diffusion among a group of users (e.g. Dwivedi et al. 2011; Lin 2011; Xu et al. 2017). Theoretically, these studies have majorly relied on the Diffusion of Innovation (DOI) perspective (Kapoor et al. 2014a, b; Rogers 1995) which suggests that the adoption of a technology depends on the attributes of the innovation (as measured by its relative advantage, compatibility, complexity, observability, and trialability). The second theoretical position worth noting is with regards to the use of intention-based models to investigate the adoption and use of technology. These models mainly include the Theory of Planned Behavior (TPB) (Ajzen 1991), the Theory of Reasoned Action (TRA) (Ajzen and Fishbein 1977) and the Technology Acceptance Model (TAM) (Davis 1989). The TRA explains the inter-relationships between individuals' attitudes, behaviors and subsequent actions across a variety of domains (Fishbein and

Ajzen 1975). It links individuals' beliefs, attitudes and norms to their ultimate intention and behavior towards a technology. However, one of the key assumptions of TRA is that every individual has free control over their behaviors; however, this may not always be the case (Ajzen 1991). The TPB (Taylor and Todd 1995) is a cognitive framework that seeks to understand and explain human behavior. From a TPB viewpoint, individual actions and behaviors manifest from an underlying intention to perform that behavior. The TAM coalesces both TRA and TPB to propose the use of a technology as determined by two major beliefs: perceived ease of use and perceived usefulness (Davis 1989). Yet, TAM has been criticized for being too simple as it excludes important contextual and process-based variables that might influence the acceptance of a technology (Bagozzi 2007).

By integrating different technology acceptance models, Venkatesh et al. (2003) developed the UTAUT model to provide a broader evaluation of individual adoption and use behaviors within organizational settings. In addition, the model encapsulates the moderating effects of gender, experience, age and voluntariness in the adoption process. However, this model could not be used outside of the organizational environment because it does not account for two critical factors (that is, hedonic motivation and price value) of adoption and use in a consumer use environment (Venkatesh et al. 2012). As a result, the UTAUT model (Venkatesh et al. 2003) was revised to integrate additional constructs related to the consumer environment such as hedonic motivation; price value; and habit. The present study adopts UTAUT2 for a few reasons: first, the context of the study is in a consumer acceptance and use context for which the UTAUT2 was ideally proposed. Second, compared to previous models, UTAUT2 yields a higher variance explained in behavioral intention and actual use compared to other models (Venkatesh et al. 2012). While there is a growing strand of literature that has adopted this model in various technological and research contexts, to our knowledge, no study has attempted to investigate antecedent factors of behavioral intention and usage in Nigeria using the UTAUT2 model. In the next section, we present the set of hypotheses portraying how the risk-trust relationship is incorporated to the UTAUT model.

2.3 Research Model Development

Performance Expectancy. Performance expectancy is conceptualized as "the degree to which using a technology will provide benefits to consumers in performing certain activities" (Venkatesh et al. 2012, p. 159). It represents the perceived value that users attach to a technology and how that perception affects their decision to adopt and use the technology. This construct was found to be the strongest predictor of intention in a study by Venkatesh et al. (2003). In the revised UTAUT2 model, it was also found to be one of the highest predictors of behavior intention (Venkatesh et al. 2012). The role this construct has also been examined by subsequent studies (Dwivedi et al. 2016, 2017a, b; Rana et al. 2016, 2017; Slade et al. 2015a, b). Using this construct within our study, we aim to capture the degree to which using e-tail websites provides benefits (e.g. convenience and ease of accessing retail products) to consumers. Thus, we hypothesize that performance expectancy in relation to the use of e-tail websites plays a significant role in influencing behavioral intention.

H1: Performance expectancy has a positive impact on the behavior intention to use e-tail websites.

Effort Expectancy. Effort expectancy is "the degree of ease associated with consumers' use of technology" (Venkatesh et al. 2012, p. 159). This construct allows us to explore the difficulty faced by users, associated with using a technology. Thus, effort expectancy in this context reflects the extent to which individuals find online shopping easy to engage in. It also examines the extent to which a technology is easy to understand and use without any skillset (Venkatesh et al. 2003). In the Nigerian context, for example, institutional infrastructures such as access to fast and reliable internet connection are limited to urban cities. This invariably may impede on consumers' access to e-tail goods and services. Logically, if a product or service is easy to use, users are more likely to possess a positive attitude towards its use. In Nigeria, while e-tail websites are a growing phenomenon and a large segment of the youth population have readily adopted these websites, several external factors such as access to reliable internet connections mentioned earlier still pose significant adoption challenges.

Therefore, in this study, the following hypothesis is proposed:

H2: Effort expectancy will have a positive impact on the behavioral intention to use e-tail websites.

Social Influence. Social influence is defined as "the extent to which consumers perceive that important others (e.g., family and friends) believe they should use a particular technology" (Venkatesh et al. 2012, p. 159). It refers to the role that socially-acceptable norms and practices play in influencing the decisions that individuals make. Previous studies have shown that social influence (such as those of friends and family), play a dominant role in explaining the use of IT in the African context (Anandarajan et al. 2002). Positive adoption and use behavior is more likely when more friends and family members use a particular technology (Brown et al. 2010). Dulle and Minishi-Majanja (2011) confirmed this relationship between social influence and behavioral intention to use open access publishing among academics in Tanzania. Therefore, within the African consumer environmental context, we posit that individuals' adoption decisions are likely to be influenced by the opinions of referent others within their social circles. Hence, we hypothesize that:

H3: Social influence will have a positive impact on the behavioral intention to use e-tail websites.

Facilitating Conditions. Facilitating conditions represent the degree to which individuals consider that the technical and organizational infrastructure exists to support the use of a technology (Venkatesh et al. 2003). In the Nigerian context, there are several challenges which impact on the availability and access to internet services needed for online shopping. Challenges such as shortages of energy supply and access to the internet across the country impact on consumers' online behavioral intentions. These challenges limit the extent to which the average Nigerian consumer can access the internet which, in turn, restricts the use of e-commerce sites. Hence, the user's belief about the availability of all the support that is necessary to use e-tail websites positively influences behavioral intention and their use behavior. Thus, for this study we hypothesize that:

H4a: Facilitating conditions have a positive impact on the behavioral intention to use e-tail websites.

H4b: Facilitating conditions have a positive impact on the use behavior of e-tail websites.

Hedonic Motivation. Hedonic motivation is defined as "the fun or pleasure derived from using a technology" (Venkatesh et al. 2012, p. 161). It represents the extent to which users of IS systems find it entertaining (Baptista and Oliveira 2015). Extant research has established the positive relationship between hedonic motivation and behavioral intention (Martins et al. 2014), with Venkatesh et al. (2012) finding that it represents one of the second strongest predictors of behavioral intention in the UTAUT2 model. More recent work by Alalwan et al. (2018) has confirmed hedonic motivation to be the most dominant predictor of behavioral intention to adopt internet banking amongst Jordanian customers. These studies chime with Tamilmani et al. (2019) who have emphasized the importance of ensuring consumer technologies are designed to fulfil the hedonic needs of users in order to facilitate increase adoption. Therefore, the more e-tail websites meet consumers' hedonic needs, the more likely consumers are to adopt and use them. Therefore, it is hypothesized that:

H5: Hedonic motivation has a positive impact on the behavioral intention to use e-tail websites

Price Value. Defined as "consumers' cognitive trade-off between perceived benefits of the applications and monetary cost for using them" (Tamilmani et al. 2018a; Venkatesh et al. 2012, p. 191), price value is positive when the returns of using a technology are perceived greater than the monetary cost for using them. If the perception of price value to use e-tail websites is that it provides greater returns compared to its monetary cost (e.g. internet connectivity charges, cost of mobile phones), consumers will be more willing to adopt e-tail websites. Using responses from 375 respondents, Dwivedi et al. (2016) have demonstrated that price value is a crucial factor that influences behavioral intention to use mobile health among individuals in Bangladesh. Therefore, the subsequent hypothesis is suggested:

H6: Price value has a positive impact on the behavioral intention to use e-tail websites.

Habit. Another factor that was also added to the revised UTAUT2 model is habit. Habit was added to the UTAUT model to account for the extent to which individuals perform a behavior automatically as a result of learning (Tamilmani et al. 2018b; Venkatesh et al. 2012). Consistent with several previous studies, habit has been found to be a significant predictor of behavioral intention across a range of technologies. For example, Dhir et al. (2018) demonstrated that habit is the most dominant predictor of behavioral intention to use social network sites among users in India. When users use e-tail websites to access a range of goods and services routinely, repeatedly and frequently, their habit may influence the behavioral intention to adopt and use e-tail websites. Therefore, it is hypothesized that:

H7a: Habit has a positive impact on the behavioral intention to use e-tail websites.
H7b: Habit has a positive impact on the use behavior of e-tail websites.

Behavioral Intention and Use Behavior. Behavioral intention is defined as the subjective probability that a behavior will be performed (Fishbein and Ajzen 1975), while use behavior represents the actual use of the technology. Behavioral intention assesses the degree to which a technology will be utilized by its intended users. In line with the Venkatesh et al. (2012), use behavior is significantly influenced by behavioral intention. In other words, users that exhibit a strong behavioral intention have a higher propensity of acceptance and use for that technology. Therefore, it is hypothesized that:

H8: Behavioral intention has a positive impact on the use behavior of e-tail websites.

Augmenting the UTAUT2 with Risk and Trust Factors. Trust is defined as the degree to which consumers are willing to believe that their expectations will be met during online transaction (McKnight et al. 2002), while risk represents the consumer's subjective belief about the potential for something to go wrong when undertaking online transactions (Garbarino and Strahilevitz 2004). Within the e-commerce literature, there is a long-standing debate on how the risk-trust relationship influences the uptake of electronic services (Gefen et al. 2008). On the one hand, risk is viewed as an antecedent to trust; studies adopting this view (e.g. Chandra et al. 2010) suggest that risk concerns hinder the trust in online services and that the need for consumers to develop trust is predicated on their perceptions of risk. On the other hand, trust is viewed as an antecedent to risk (Pavlou and Gefen 2005). This perspective recognizes the need to facilitate trusting beliefs that reduce the risk concerns among consumers (Mou et al. 2017). Despite the well-established positions concerning the risk-trust relationships, there are still limited studies that have focused on how the risk-trust relationships might be integrated into the UTAUT model (Schaupp et al. 2009). Moreover, to the best of our knowledge, no study has investigated how the risk-trust relationships might influence behavioral intention to use e-tail websites in a sub-Saharan context.

In this study, trust is investigated with reference to the technology, that is e-tail websites; while risk refers to the consumer's perceived risk of using e-tail websites. Together, these risk and trust factors particularly inhibit the adoption of e-services within several African countries (Ayo et al. 2011). For instance, a recent study carried by Ipsos (2015) in Nigeria has shown that users exhibit high suspicions of online transactions (such through e-tail websites) due to the high levels of cybercrimes reported within the country. Furthermore, spamming has been recognized as one of the most prevalent activities on the Nigerian Internet landscape, with many Nigerians believing they are susceptible to identity theft when they engage in online transactions (Osei and Gbadamosi 2011). The perceived risk of e-tail websites may thus keep potential consumers from engaging with such online platforms. In other words, it can be argued that the lack of consumer trust in e-tail websites has translated to an increase in the perceived risk of engaging in online shopping transactions. In support, Kim et al. (2008) has portrayed how risk and trust factors influence consumers' e-commerce purchasing decisions such that their disposition to trust e-commerce platforms had the strongest influence on their purchase intention. Hence, in the context of e-tail websites, we hypothesize that:

H9a: Consumer trust in e-tail websites has a positive impact on their behavioral intention to use e-tail websites.
H9b: Consumer trust in e-tail websites has a negative impact on consumers' perceived risk of using e-tail websites.

In addition, risk perceptions have been found to have a negative impact on intentions (Slade et al. 2015a). The higher levels of risk perceptions are likely to negatively affect a consumer's intention to use e-tail websites. Empirical findings have confirmed this relationship in different technological contexts (Pavlou 2003). Hence, it is hypothesized that:

H10: Perceived risk of using e-tail websites has a negative impact on the behavioral intention to use e-tail websites.

Based on the stated hypotheses, Fig. 1 presents the theoretical research model for this study.

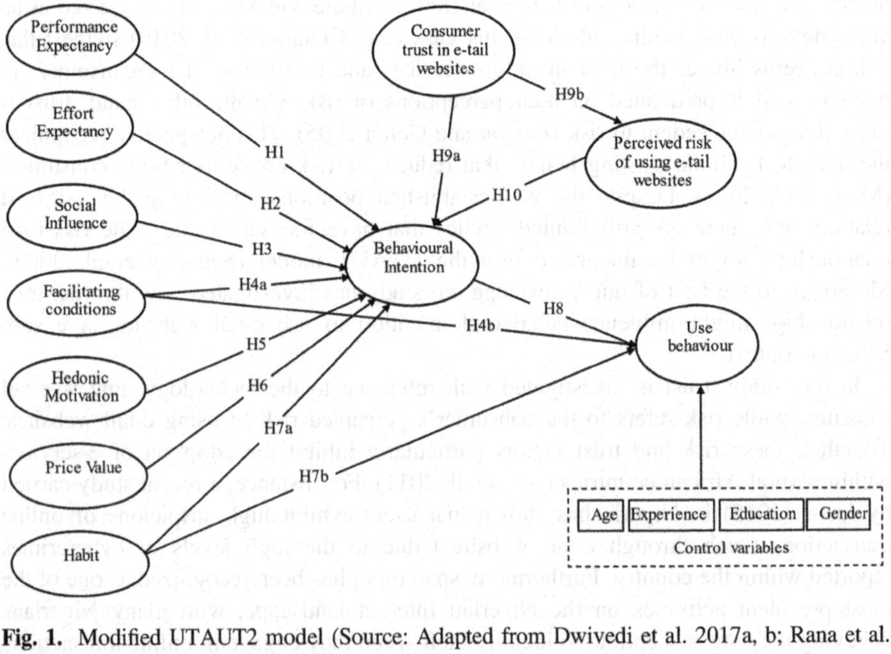

Fig. 1. Modified UTAUT2 model (Source: Adapted from Dwivedi et al. 2017a, b; Rana et al. 2016, 2017; Venkatesh et al. 2012)

3 Methodology

To empirically test the proposed research model (Fig. 1), the study used an online survey. A non-probability convenience sampling technique was used to collect data, first by circulating the URL to the questionnaire setup on Qualtrics to a population of students from a university located in south-west Nigeria. An introduction to the survey, its aims and objectives were provided on first page of the online survey questionnaire. In addition, we asked them to spread the URL to their friends and family members who have used e-tail websites. They were informed that participation was voluntarily and that their answers were confidential, to be used for research purposes only. We also assured respondents of anonymity to ensure that we minimized common method bias (Podsakoff et al. 2003). All constructs were measured using previously validated and well-documented multi-item scales. The scale for the UTAUT2 constructs were adapted from Venkatesh et al. (2012). All UTAUT2 measures as well as risk and trust measures were reflective except use behavior which is a formative measure. Perceived risk of using e-tail websites and consumer trust in e-tail websites were measured using items adapted from Rana et al. (2015) and Chandra et al. (2010) respectively; while demographic data such as age, gender, education, as well as how long respondents had been using e-tail websites was also collected. The items for all constructs are included in Table 1. The reflective constructs were measured using seven-point Likert scales ranging from totally disagree (1) to totally agree (7). Following the example of Venkatesh et al. (2012) to measure use behavior, a list of five popular e-tail websites (that is, Jumia, Konga, SMEMarketHub, Yudala and Gloo) in Nigeria was provided, and respondents were asked to indicate their usage frequency for each. The anchors used for these questions was a seven-point scale that ranged from "less than once a month" to "several times a day".

Harman's single-factor test was computed based on principal component analysis (PCA) and revealed the largest variance explained by one factor was 30%. Since the one factor did not account for more than 50% variance, common method bias was deemed unlikely (Podsakoff et al. 2003). This approach provides easy access to respondents in a practical and quick manner (Neuman 2011). Overall, the survey questionnaire was sent to 404 users of e-tail websites. Among these, a total of 197 responses were disregarded for the following reasons. (1) the responses were completed within 5 min, whereas the researchers had estimated in a pre-test that the questionnaire would take at least 10 min to complete. Such rapid responses therefore suggest that respondents had not completed in a haste; (2) responses were incomplete and could not be used for the data analysis because questions indicating relevant variables were left unanswered; (3) responses collected from participants outside Nigeria were removed using the reported IP address of each participant. This ensured only those based on Nigeria remained for the final sample. In total, we obtained a sample of 207 valid responses, indicating a 51% sample response rate.

This sample size satisfies three different criteria for the lower bounds of sample size for PLS-SEM: (1) ten times the largest number of structural paths directed at a particular construct in the inner path model (therefore for the model tested here the sample size threshold for the model in this study would be 90 cases) (Chin 1998) and (2) according to Anderson and Gerbing (1988), a threshold for any type of SEM is approximately 150 respondents for models where constructs comprise of three or four indicators. (3) Moreover, the sample size also satisfies stricter criteria relevant for variance-based SEM: that is, the recommended ratio of five cases per observed variable (Bentler and Chou 1987). In this case, the sample size threshold would be 175 cases. Most respondents in our sample were males (63.8%) compared to females (36.2%). Participants varied with respect to their level of education as 66.2% reported having attended and obtained a bachelor's degree, while 16.4% had completed a postgraduate qualification (e.g. master's and PhD program). In addition, most of respondents in the sample were aged between 18–35 years and reported to have been using e-tail websites for at least 2 years or more (67.6%).

4 Analysis and Results

The data collected was analysed using SmartPLS 3.2.7 to perform the Partial Least Square (PLS) (Ringle and Wende 2015). PLS allows the modelling of formative and reflective measures in the same model. It also makes fewer assumptions about how the data are distributed compared to more widespread covariance-based SEM techniques (Hair et al. 2016). Using PLS, our research model was analysed in two stages guided by Hair et al. (2016): (1) the assessment of the measurement model: which includes calculating the reliability and validity of the various constructs in the model; and (2) the assessment of the structural model. These two stages represent the process through which conclusions can be drawn concerning the hypothesized paths among the constructs (Ringle and Wende 2015).

Table 1. Measurement model

	Construct/Dimension/Item	Loadings	CA[a]	CR[b]	AVE[c]
	Performance Expectancy (PE)		0.832	0.888	0.665
1	I find online shopping useful in my daily life	0.802			
2	Using online shopping increases my chances of achieving things that are important to me	0.826			
3	Using online shopping helps me accomplish things more quickly	0.804			
4	Using online shopping increases my productivity	0.830			
	Effort Expectancy (EE)		0.769	0.852	0.592
1	Learning how to use online shopping websites is easy for me	0.764			
2	My interaction with online shopping websites is clear and understandable	0.788			
3	I find online shopping websites easy to use	0.852			
4	It is easy for me to become skillful at using online shopping websites	0.662			
	Hedonic Motivation (HM)		0.718	0.840	0.637
1	Using online shopping website is fun	0.814			
2	Using online shopping website is enjoyable	0.817			
3	Using online shopping website is very entertaining	0.763			
	Habit		0.893	0.933	0.824
1	The use of online shopping websites has become a habit for me	0.891			
2	I am addicted to using online shopping websites	0.933			

(continued)

Table 1. (*continued*)

	Construct/Dimension/Item	Loadings	CA[a]	CR[b]	AVE[c]
3	I must use online shopping websites	0.898			
	Price Value (PV)		0.820	0.893	0.737
1	Online shopping is reasonably priced	0.884			
2	Online shopping is good value for money	0.898			
3	At the current price, online shopping provides a good value	0.789			
	Social Influence (SI)		0.864	0.917	0.786
1	People who are important to me think that I should use online shopping websites	0.864			
2	People who influence my behavior think that I should use online shopping websites	0.902			
3	People whose opinions that I value prefer that I use online shopping websites	0.893			
	Consumer trust in e-tail websites (CT)		0.912	0.938	0.792
1	I trust online shopping websites are reliable	0.873			
2	I trust online shopping websites are secure	0.917			
3	I trust online shopping websites are trustworthy	0.909			
4	I trust the quality of products displayed on online shopping websites	0.859			
	Perceived risk of using e-tail websites (PR)		0.747	0.836	0.561
1	Use of online shopping websites may cause my personal information to be stolen	0.682			
2	I will feel uneasy psychologically when I use online shopping websites	0.787			
3	I think it would be unsafe to use online shopping websites because of privacy and security concerns	0.761			
4	I believe that there could be negative consequences by using online shopping websites	0.760			
	Facilitating conditions (FC)		0.723	0.828	0.547
1	I have the resources necessary to use online shopping websites	0.746			
2	I have the knowledge necessary to use online shopping	0.774			
3	Online shopping is compatible with other technologies I use	0.776			
4	I can get help from others when I have difficulties using online shopping	0.656			
	Behavioral Intention (BI)		0.770	0.866	0.684
1	I intend to continue using online shopping websites in the future	0.776			
2	I will always try to use online shopping websites in my daily life	0.815			
3	I plan to continue to use online shopping websites frequently	0.887			

Note: [a] *Cronbach alpha;* [b] *Composite reliability;* [c] *Average variance extracted*

4.1 Measurement Model

The measurement model for the reflective constructs in our model is examined in terms of construct validity of the measurement scales, indicator reliability, convergent and discriminant validity (Bagozzi and Yi 1988). The internal consistency of each construct was also well above the recommended threshold of 0.7 (Hair et al. 2016). According to Chin and Newsted (1999), all indicator loadings should be greater than 0.7. As can be seen in Table 1, all loadings except two (that is, EE4 and PR1) were above this recommended threshold. We kept both indicators because their loadings were close to the threshold. Besides, Chin (1998) has suggested that indicator loadings of 0.6 is still adequate for inclusion in the measurement model. To establish convergent validity, we examined the average variance extracted (AVE). The average variance extracted (AVE) measures the amount of variance captured by the focal construct from its indicators relative to the measurement error (Chin 1998). MacKenzie et al. (2011) point out that AVE should be greater than 0.5 to ensure constructs account for more than 50% of the variance in its indicators. As can be inferred from Table 2, the reported AVE values of the constructs met this criterion. Finally, we examined the discriminant validity of our measurement model. It represents the extent to which each of the constructs in our model differ from each other (Fornell and Larcker 1981). To assess whether discriminant validity between the constructs in our model had been established, we used two approaches: the Fornell–Larcker criterion (Fornell and Larcker 1981) and the Heterotrait–Monotrait (HTMT) ratio of correlations (Henseler et al. 2015).

Concerning the Fornell-Larcker criterion, the square root of the AVE was computed for each construct. For adequate discriminant, validity, the diagonal elements should be significantly greater than the off-diagonal elements in the corresponding rows and columns (Fornell and Larcker 1981). As can be seen in Table 2, all reflective constructs satisfy this condition; therefore, the Fornell-Larcker criterion was met. With respect to the second criterion, this study applies the HTMT ratio – which computes the ratio between the average correlations across constructs measuring different phenomena relative to the average correlations of indicators measuring the same construct. In the guidance provided on how to handle discriminant validity issues in covariance-based SEM, Henseler et al. (2015) have suggested that an HTMT threshold value of 0.9 is adequate for the UTAUT model. As can be observed in Table 3, all values were lower than Henseler et al.'s recommended threshold value. Therefore, we can conclude that discriminant validity was established for our study based on the Fornell-Larcker and HTMT criteria.

Table 2. Discriminant validity – Fornell-Larcker criterion.

	BI	EE	FC	Habit	HM	Risk	PE	PV	SI	Trust
BI	**0.827**									
EE	0.539	**0.770**								
FC	0.482	0.640	**0.740**							
Habit	0.644	0.292	0.275	**0.908**						
HM	0.558	0.427	0.430	0.389	**0.908**					
Risk	−0.032	−0.065	−0.022	−0.039	−0.089	**0.749**				
PE	0.654	0.443	0.391	0.576	0.440	−0.064	**0.816**			
PV	0.547	0.266	0.173	0.515	0.451	−0.074	0.539	**0.858**		
SI	0.585	0.296	0.246	0.516	0.362	−0.007	0.548	0.467	**0.886**	
Trust	0.477	0.357	0.319	0.350	0.443	−0.347	0.416	0.443	0.313	**0.890**
Use	0.467	0.315	0.214	0.608	0.301	−0.116	0.462	0.407	0.410	0.407

Note: BI: Behavioral intention; EE: Effort expectancy; FC: Facilitating conditions; HM: Hedonic motivation; PE: Performance expectancy; PV: Price value; SI: Social influence; Square root of AVE is shown in bold at diagonal, while off-diagonal values are the estimates of inter-correlation between the latent constructs.

Table 3. Discriminant validity – Heterotrait-Monotrait ratio (HTMT)

	BI	EE	FC	Habit	HM	Risk	PE	PV	SI	Trust
BI										
EE	0.692									
FC	0.645	0.858								
Habit	0.765	0.346	0.342							
HM	0.730	0.552	0.577	0.480						
Risk	0.137	0.171	0.160	0.082	0.193					
PE	0.800	0.555	0.502	0.663	0.544	0.120				
PV	0.677	0.332	0.221	0.602	0.584	0.132	0.649			
SI	0.707	0.374	0.303	0.585	0.456	0.057	0.646	0.551		
Trust	0.558	0.420	0.381	0.386	0.535	0.394	0.475	0.517	0.351	

Note: BI: Behavioral intention; EE: Effort expectancy; FC: Facilitating conditions; HM: Hedonic motivation; PE: Performance expectancy; PV: Price value; SI: Social influence

4.2 Structural Model

To assess the structural model, we used two main criteria: the level of significance of the path coefficients and the variance explained (R^2) (Hair et al. 2016). T-values were computed based on a bootstrapping procedure using 5000 resamples and the statistical significance of the path coefficients were determined using a two-tailed distribution (Ringle and Wende 2015). In total, the results indicate that nine out of thirteen hypotheses in the model were supported. Performance expectancy ($\beta = 0.152$, $\rho = 0.012$), effort expectancy ($\beta = 0.171$, $\rho = 0.011$), social influence ($\beta = 0.172$, $\rho = 0.000$), hedonic motivation ($\beta = 0.135$, $\rho = 0.031$), consumer trust in e-tail websites ($\beta = 0.097$, $\rho = 0.033$) and habit ($\beta = 0.262$, $\rho = 0.000$) all had a positive impact on the behavioral intention to use e-tail websites. However, contrary to initial predictions, we found no empirical evidence for the direct effect of price value ($\beta = 0.087$, $\rho = 0.074$), facilitating conditions ($\beta = 0.096$, $\rho = 0.062$) and perceived risk of using e-tail websites ($\beta = 0.055$, $\rho = 0.118$) on the behavioral intention to use e-tail websites. In addition, behavioral intention ($\beta = 0.137$, $\rho = 0.022$) and habit ($\beta = 0.493$, $\rho = 0.000$) were found to have a positive impact on use, while the influence of facilitating conditions on use as hypothesized was not supported ($\beta = -0.024$, $\rho = 0.349$). A summary of hypothesized relationships is found in Table 4.

This study went further and included four control variables, namely experience with using e-tail websites, level of education, gender and age. All control variables except gender variables were found to significantly impact on the behavioral intention to use e-tail websites. To assess the quality of the model, the coefficient of determination (R^2), which represents the amount of variance explained of each endogenous latent variable computed (Hair et al. 2016). The literature prescribes R^2 of 0.67, 0.33 and 0.19 as large, moderate and weak, respectively (Chin 1998). Overall, the model was found to explain 67.5% of variance ($\rho < 0.001$) in behavioral intention and 43.5% in use behavior. Therefore, we believe that the research model substantially explains variations in the behavioral intention to use e-tail websites. Finally, we used the standardized Root Mean Square Residual (SRMR) to assess the approximate fit for the research model. Defined as the difference between the observed correlation and the model implied correlation matrix, Hu and Bentler (1999) have suggested a cut-off value of 0.08. The model presented in this study shows an acceptable fit (SRMR = 0.067).

Table 4. Results of structural model assessments

Direct relationships	β	t-value	Hypothesis validation
Performance expectancy → Behavioral intention	0.152*	2.274	Supported
Effort expectancy → Behavioral intention	0.171*	2.282	Supported
Social Influence → Behavioral intention	0.172***	3.475	Supported
Facilitating conditions → Behavioral intention	0.096	1.539	Not supported
Hedonic motivation → Behavioral intention	0.135*	1.869	Supported
Price value → Behavioral intention	0.087	1.135	Not supported
Habit → Behavioral intention	0.262***	4.687	Supported
Risk → Behavioral intention	0.055	1.183	Not supported
Trust → Behavioral intention	0.097*	1.833	Supported
Trust → Risk	−0.347***	4.399	Supported
Facilitating conditions → Use	−0.024	0.387	Not supported
Habit → Use	0.493***	7.643	Supported
Behavioral intention → Use	0.137*	2.006	Supported
Control variables	β	t-value	Hypothesis validation
Age → Use	−0.110*	1.808	Supported
Gender → Use	0.007	0.133	Not supported
Education → Use	0.156*	2.420	Supported
Experience → Use	0.170*	2.808	Supported

Note. Bootstrap is based on 5000 resamples; [$^{*}p < 0.05$; $^{**}p < 0.01$; $^{***}p < 0.001$]

5 Discussion

The purpose of this study was to investigate the factors that influence users' behavioral intention and usage of e-tail websites. Specifically, we employed an integrated model which combines the UTAUT2 with risk and trust factors to explore the adoption and use of e-tail websites in Nigeria. The model explained 67.5% variance of behavioral intention and 43.5% variance of the e-tail use behavior. In predicting behavioral intention, performance expectancy, effort expectancy, social influence, hedonic motivation, trust and habit were all significant. On the other hand, risk, price value, facilitating conditions did not exert any influence on behavioral intention. With regards to the direct predictors of e-tail use behavior, the results of the structural model analysis showed that habit and facilitating conditions were significant and non-significant predictors respectively.

With respect to the significant predictors, Habit had the greatest impact on users' behavioral intention to use e-tail websites with a coefficient value of 0.262 (p < 0.001). This suggests that users' behavioral intention regarding the use of e-tail websites is highly influenced by the extent to which it has become a habit in their day-to-day lives. This finding is consistent with recent studies that has been conducted in developing countries in Africa (Baptista and Oliveira 2015). The second most important predictor of behavioral intention was social influence with a coefficient value of 0.172 ($p < 0.001$), suggesting that for Nigerian users, the behavioral intention to use e-tail websites is reinforced by the opinions of close social referents. This can be explained by the fact that African countries such as Nigeria tend to score low along the dimensions of individualism-collectivism as it pertains to the influence of national culture. On this dimension, Nigeria scores 30 on a scale of 100, which means it is a collectivist-oriented environment (Hofstede Insights 2018). In other words, the adoption of e-tail websites is likely to be influenced by the recommendations of people with whom close social ties are shared. This result is consistent with the revised UTAUT2 model (Venkatesh et al. 2012) that have also portrayed the significant influence of social influence on behavioral intention in other similar country contexts.

Consistent with previous UTAUT assumptions, the results also show that effort expectancy, with a coefficient value of 0.171 had a significant influence ($p < 0.05$) on behavioral intention to adopt e-tail websites. This suggests that the intention to use e-tail websites is also reinforced when they are easy to use. In other words, e-tail websites which are easy to use should likely lead to more consumers using them. Also, performance expectancy had a significant effect on the behavioral intention to use e-tail websites. This result reflects the importance of the perceived usefulness of e-tail websites by consumers as a means to encourage adoption behavior. Similar results have been obtained in Kaba and Touré (2014) and Baptista and Oliveira (2015) whose studies focused on the use of Social Network Sites and mobile banking respectively. Finally, hedonic motivation was found to positively influence behavioral intention to use e-tail websites, indicating that making use of e-tail websites fun and enjoyable makes it more likely that the adoption of e-tail websites will be successful. This positive relationship between hedonic motivation and behavioral intention is also in line with recent studies (Alalwan et al. 2018; Dhir et al. 2018).

With respect to the risk-trust inter-relationships to the adoption and use of e-tail websites, the results are mixed. Empirical results showed that while consumer trust in e-tail websites significantly influenced their behavioral intention ($\beta = 0.097$, $p < 0.05$), the hypothesized relationship between the perceived risk of using e-tail websites and behavioral intention yielded an insignificant result. As a result, the expected relationship between trust and risk as hypothesized was confirmed. In other words, consumer trust in e-tail websites has a negative influence on the perceived risk to use e-tail websites ($\beta = -0.347$, $p < 0.001$). This shows that trust plays an important role in motivating consumers' adoption of e-tail websites by reducing perceived risk concerns and increasing behavioral intention to use e-tail websites. This finding is in line with previous IS literature regarding the influence of perceived trust and risk on behavioral intention (Kim et al. 2008).

However, contrary to our expectation, perceived risk in e-tail websites had no significant influence on behavioral intention. Given the high levels of skepticism that follows online transactions in Nigeria, we had expected that consumers' perceived risk of using e-tail websites will have a significantly negative influence on their behavioral intention. One plausible explanation for this result may be that most respondents in our sample are majorly younger adults who are often well-acquainted with technologies. Studies have shown that this user demographic exhibit high risk-tolerant behaviors with regards to technology adoption (Martin et al. 2014). This result is consistent with some extant studies that have been conducted in African countries using similar age-groups (see Kaba and Touré 2014), and contradicts some (such as Martins et al. 2014; Slade et al. 2015a, b), conducted in non-African contexts. Furthermore, contrary to our expectation, the results showed that facilitating conditions and price value all had no significant influence on behavioral intention. With respect to price value, the results show that consumers do not consider it to be a fair trade-off been the associated costs and benefits.

5.1 Theoretical Implications

With the rapid rise in internet penetration experienced in Africa, the use of e-tail websites and the online retail industry is set to gain rapid prominence (McKinsey 2014). Hence, there is a need to evaluate the factors that predict adoption and usage of e-tail websites. To date, the majority of studies investigating these factors have been mainly focused on developed countries. Less attention has been paid to developing countries, such as those in sub-Saharan Africa. Besides, there is limited research that has employed robust theoretical frameworks such as UTAUT to comprehensively explain adoption and use of technology in a sub-Saharan context (Kaba and Touré 2014). This study thus makes a significant contribution by broadening our understanding of factors that predict the adoption of e-tail websites in Nigeria. In this study, it was found that habit was the most important factor influencing e-tail website behavioral intention, as well as use behavior. In other words, this study contributes to expanding the geographical scope of adoption research by focusing on an emerging consumer-use phenomenon.

Second, in addition to evaluating the predictive relevance of the UTAUT2 model in the Nigerian context, this study also assesses risk and trust factors as additional predictors of behavior intention to use e-tail websites. The integrated model provides a more holistic view of a consumer's purchase decision-making process as it pertains to the use of e-tail websites, incorporating the effects of consumer's trust and risk factors alongside the UTAUT2. The support of trust's influence on behavioral intention to use e-tail websites is concurrent with several previous studies in the e-commerce literature (e.g. Bélanger and Carter 2008). Interestingly, while higher levels of trust in e-tail websites decreased consumers' perceived risk of using e-tail websites as expected, perceived risk of using e-tail websites did not decrease their behavioral intention. The perceived risk result in relation to behavior intention contradicts earlier research (Schaupp and Carter 2010; Martins et al. 2014).

Third, our study demonstrates the application of the UTAUT2 model as a valuable theoretical toolkit to explore the adoption of consumer-use technologies in different contexts. It examines the predictive value of the revised UTAUT2 model (Venkatesh et al. 2012). While Venkatesh et al. (2012) found that the UTAUT2 explains 74% of the variance in behavioral intention and 52% of technology use, the authors have highlighted the need for future research to test the model among different age groups, technologies and countries. On account of the partial least squares structural equation modelling undertaken in this research, this research responds to this call by evaluating predictive relevance of the revised UTAUT2 model on a sample of e-tail users from a relatively under-researched country context – Nigeria. It provides empirical support for most of the hypothesized relationships, thereby validating the revised UTAUT2 model using robust analytical techniques.

5.2 Practical Implications

From a practical perspective, based on our set of empirical results, we suggest e-tail providers in Nigeria to build the trust of e-tail users. In business in general, trust is viewed as one of the most important antecedents of a stable long-term relationship in Business to Consumer (B2C) business models. To build trust, e-tail providers can take necessary actions to ensure security on their platforms and provide clear information about what they are doing on their platforms to consumers. Our results also suggest that e-tail providers could improve packages that appeal to social groups such as family and friends to bolster consumer-use of their e-tail platforms. Also, strategies aimed at improving the adoption of e-tail websites are more likely to be successful if they emphasize the benefits of e-tail usage amongst family and friends within their campaigns. To this end, e-tail service providers could promote their online platforms through social media, for instance. Such marketing activities could utilize social networks when targeting marketing campaigns to different consumers.

6 Conclusion, Limitations and Future Research

This aim of this study was to understand factors that influence the adoption and use of e-tail websites in a sub-Saharan country context. We tested the factors using the revised UTAUT model augmented with risk and trust factors. By understanding the factors that influence adoption and use of e-tail websites, investments into the e-commerce industry can evolve, aligning online service provisions with important consumers' needs. The findings reveal that performance expectancy, effort expectancy, social influence, consumer trust in e-tail websites, hedonic motivation and habit were important to form consumers' behavioral intentions. In other words, we provide researchers and policy makers with insights on how to encourage the adoption and usage of e-tail websites in Nigeria. Given the expected rise in the use of e-tail websites, we recommend that more research is needed to explore the adoption and use of e-tail websites attention in future studies.

However, this study suffers from some limitations which should be considered when interpreting its findings. First, the survey used in the study was conducted using online-based forms and employed non-random convenience sample, because obtaining a larger sample using random sampling method would be costly. As a result, the resulting sample for the study was limited to only respondents with internet access. Thus, to enhance generalizability in a context like Nigeria, future research could utilize the use of paper-based questionnaires to augment online versions. Second, the relationships were assessed using cross-sectional data, resulting in findings that apply to a single point in time. However, perceptions change over time as individuals gain experience (Venkatesh et al. 2012), and it is likely that perceived risk and trust factors may also be influenced over time. As a result, further studies may enhance our understanding of the interrelationships between the key variables predicting the adoption and use of e-tail websites by utilizing longitudinal research. In addition, future studies can extend this work by investigating how the relationships used in this study might vary among different samples such as older users. Another study may compare results among users in urban and rural contexts to draw attention to the digital divide that often exists in developing country contexts. This empirical study thus provides insights upon which future research can build upon.

References

Ajzen, I.: The theory of planned behavior. Organ. Behav. Hum. Decis. Process. **50**(2), 179–211 (1991)

Ajzen, I., Fishbein, M.: Attitude-behavior relations: a theoretical analysis and review of empirical research. Psychol. Bull. **84**(5), 888 (1977)

Alalwan, A.A., Dwivedi, Y.K., Rana, N.P., Algharabat, R.: Examining factors influencing Jordanian customers' intentions and adoption of internet banking: extending UTAUT2 with risk. J. Retail. Consum. Serv. **40**, 125–138 (2018)

Anandarajan, M., Igbaria, M., Anakwe, U.P.: IT acceptance in a less-developed country: a motivational factor perspective. Int. J. Inf. Manag. **22**(1), 47–65 (2002)

Anderson, J.C., Gerbing, D.W.: Structural equation modeling in practice: a review and recommended two-step approach. Psychol. Bull. **103**(3), 411 (1988)

Ayo, C.K., Adewoye, J.O., Oni, A.A.: Business-to-consumer e-commerce in Nigeria: prospects and challenges. Afr. J. Bus. Manag. **5**(13), 5109–5117 (2011)

Bagozzi, R.P.: The legacy of the technology acceptance model and a proposal for a paradigm shift. J. Assoc. Inf. Syst. **8**(4), 3 (2007)

Bagozzi, R.P., Yi, Y.: Testing hypotheses about methods, traits, and communalities in the direct-product model. Appl. Psychol. Meas. **16**(4), 373–380 (1992)

Baptista, G., Oliveira, T.: Understanding mobile banking: the unified theory of acceptance and use of technology combined with cultural moderators. Comput. Hum. Behav. **50**, 418–430 (2015)

Bélanger, F., Carter, L.: Trust and risk in e-government adoption. J. Strateg. Inf. Syst. **17**(2), 165–176 (2008)

Bentler, P.M., Chou, C.P.: Practical issues in structural modeling. Sociol. Methods Res. **16**(1), 78–117 (1987)

Boateng, R.: Resources, electronic-commerce capabilities and electronic-commerce benefits: conceptualizing the links. Inf. Technol. Dev. **22**(2), 242–264 (2016)

Brown, S.A., Dennis, A.R., Venkatesh, V.: Predicting collaboration technology use: integrating technology adoption and collaboration research. J. Manag. Inf. Syst. **27**(2), 9–54 (2010)

Chandra, S., Srivastava, S.C., Theng, Y.L.: Evaluating the role of trust in consumer adoption of mobile payment systems: an empirical analysis. Commun. Assoc. Inf. Syst. **27**(29), 27 (2010)

Chin, W.W.: The partial least squares approach to structural equation modeling. Mod. Methods Bus. Res. **295**(2), 295–336 (1998)

Chin, W.W., Newsted, P.R.: Structural equation modeling analysis with small samples using partial least squares. Stat. Strateg. Small Sample Res. **1**(1), 307–341 (1999)

Davis, F.D.: Perceived usefulness, perceived ease of use, and user acceptance of information technology. MIS Q. 319–340 (1989)

Dhir, A., Kaur, P., Rajala, R.: Why do young people tag photos on social networking sites? Explaining user intentions. Int. J. Inf. Manag. **38**(1), 117–127 (2018)

Dulle, F.W., Minishi-Majanja, M.K.: The suitability of the unified theory of acceptance and use of technology (UTAUT) model in open access adoption studies. Inf. Dev. **27**(1), 32–45 (2011)

Dwivedi, Y.K., Rana, N.P., Jeyaraj, A., Clement, M., Williams, M.D.: Re-examining the unified theory of acceptance and use of technology (UTAUT): towards a revised theoretical model. Inf. Syst. Front. (2017a). https://doi.org/10.1007/s10796-017-9774-y

Dwivedi, Y.K., Rana, N.P., Janssen, M., Lal, B., Williams, M.D., Clement, R.M.: An empirical validation of a unified model of electronic government adoption (UMEGA). Gov. Inf. Q. **34** (2), 211–230 (2017b)

Dwivedi, Y.K., Shareef, M.A., Simintiras, A.C., Lal, B., Weerakkody, V.: A generalised adoption model for services: a cross-country comparison of mobile health (m-health). Gov. Inf. Q. **33**(1), 174–187 (2016)

Dwivedi, Y.K., Wade, M.R., Schneberger, S.L. (eds.): Information Systems Theory: Explaining and Predicting Our Digital Society, vol. 1. Springer, New York (2011). https://doi.org/10.1007/978-1-4419-6108-2

Fishbein, M., Ajzen, I.: Belief, Attitude, Intention, and Behavior: An Introduction to Theory and Research. Addison-Wesley Publication Company, Reading (1975)

Fornell, C., Larcker, D.F.: Structural equation models with unobservable variables and measurement error: algebra and statistics. J. Mark. Res. 382–388 (1981)

Garbarino, E., Strahilevitz, M.: Gender differences in the perceived risk of buying online and the effects of receiving a site recommendation. J. Bus. Res. **57**(7), 768–775 (2004)

Gefen, D., Benbasat, I., Pavlou, P.: A research agenda for trust in online environments. J. Manag. Inf. Syst. **24**(4), 275–286 (2008)

GSMA: The Mobile Money (2018). https://www.gsma.com/mobileeconomy/wp-content/uploads/2018/02/The-Mobile-Economy-Global-2018.pdf. Accessed 16 July 2018

Hair Jr., J.F., Hult, G.T.M., Ringle, C., Sarstedt, M.: A Primer on Partial Least Squares Structural Equation Modeling (PLS-SEM). Sage Publications, Thousand Oaks (2016)

Henseler, J., Ringle, C.M., Sarstedt, M.: A new criterion for assessing discriminant validity in variance-based structural equation modeling. J. Acad. Mark. Sci. **43**(1), 115–135 (2015)

Hofstede Insights: What about Nigeria? (2018). https://www.hofstede-insights.com/country-comparison/nigeria. Accessed 13 July 2018

Hu, L.T., Bentler, P.M.: Cutoff criteria for fit indexes in covariance structure analysis: conventional criteria versus new alternatives. Struct. Equ. Model. Multidisc. J. **6**(1), 1–55 (1999)

Ipsos: PayPal cross-border consumer research (2015). https://www.paypalobjects.com/digitalassets/c/website/marketing/global/pages/jobs/paypal-insights-2015-global-report-appendix-added.pdf). Accessed 08 May 2018

Kaba, B., Touré, B.: Understanding information and communication technology behavioral intention to use: applying the UTAUT model to social networking site adoption by young people in a least developed country. J. Assoc. Inf. Sci. Technol. **65**(8), 1662–1674 (2014)

Kapoor, K.K., Dwivedi, Y.K., Williams, M.D.: Rogers' innovation adoption attributes: a systematic review and synthesis of existing research. Inf. Syst. Manag. **31**(1), 74–91 (2014a)

Kapoor, K.K., Dwivedi, Y.K., Williams, M.D.: Innovation adoption attributes: a review and synthesis of research findings. Eur. J. Innov. Manag. **17**(3), 327–348 (2014b)

Kim, D.J., Ferrin, D.L., Rao, H.R.: A trust-based consumer decision-making model in electronic commerce: the role of trust, perceived risk, and their antecedents. Decis. Support Syst. **44**(2), 544–564 (2008)

KPMG: Africa's Consumer Story (2018). http://www.blog.kpmgafrica.com/africas-consumer-story-demographics/
Kurnia, S., Choudrie, J., Mahbubur, R.M., Alzougool, B.: E-commerce technology adoption: a Malaysian grocery SME retail sector study. J. Bus. Res. **68**(9), 1906–1918 (2015)
Lin, H.F.: An empirical investigation of mobile banking adoption: the effect of innovation attributes and knowledge-based trust. Int. J. Inf. Manag. **31**(3), 252–260 (2011)
MacKenzie, S.B., Podsakoff, P.M., Podsakoff, N.P.: Construct measurement and validation procedures in MIS and behavioral research: Integrating new and existing techniques. MIS Q. **35**(2), 293–334 (2011)
Martins, C., Oliveira, T., Popovič, A.: Understanding the Internet banking adoption: a unified theory of acceptance and use of technology and perceived risk application. Int. J. Inf. Manag. **34**(1), 1–13 (2014)
McKinsey: Nigeria's renewal: delivering inclusive growth in Africa's largest economy (2014). https://www.mckinsey.com/~/media/McKinsey/Global%20Themes/Middle%20East%20and%20Africa/Nigerias%20renewal%20Delivering%20inclusive%20growth/MGI_Nigerias_renewal_Full_report.ashx. Accessed 30 Apr 2018
McKnight, D.H., Choudhury, V., Kacmar, C.: Developing and validating trust measures for e-commerce: an integrative typology. Inf. Syst. Res. **13**(3), 334–359 (2002)
Mou, J., Shin, D.H., Cohen, J.F.: Trust and risk in consumer acceptance of e-services. Electron. Commer. Res. **17**(2), 255–288 (2017)
Neuman, W.L.: Social Research Methods, Qualitative and Quantitative Approaches, 7th edn. Pearson Education Inc., Boston (2011)
Oghenerukevbe, E.A.: Perception of security indicators in online banking sites in Nigeria (2008)
Okoli, C., Mbarika, V.W., McCoy, S.: The effects of infrastructure and policy on e-business in Latin America and sub-Saharan Africa. Eur. J. Inf. Syst. **19**(1), 5–20 (2010)
Osei, C., Gbadamosi, A.: Re-branding Africa. Mark. Intell. Plan. **29**(3), 284–304 (2011)
Pavlou, P.A.: Consumer acceptance of electronic commerce: integrating trust and risk with the technology acceptance model. Int. J. Electron. Commer. **7**(3), 101–134 (2003)
Pavlou, P.A., Gefen, D.: Psychological contract violation in online marketplaces: antecedents, consequences, and moderating role. Inf. Syst. Res. **16**(4), 372–399 (2005)
PayPal: PayPal Ranks Nigeria 3rd in Mobile Shopping (2016). http://investorsking.com/paypal-ranks-nigeria-3rd-in-mobile-shopping/. Accessed 30 Aug 2017
Rana, N.P., Dwivedi, Y.K., Williams, M.D., Weerakkody, V.: Investigating success of an e-government initiative: validation of an integrated IS success model. Inf. Syst. Front. **17**(1), 127–142 (2015)
Rana, N.P., Dwivedi, Y.K., Lal, B., Williams, M.D., Clement, M.: Citizens' adoption of an electronic government system: towards a unified view. Inf. Syst. Front. **19**(3), 549–568 (2017)
Rana, N.P., Dwivedi, Y.K., Williams, M.D., Weerakkody, V.: Adoption of online public grievance redressal system in India: toward developing a unified view. Comput. Hum. Behav. **59**, 265–282 (2016)
Ringle, C.M., Wende, S., Becker, J.M.: SmartPLS 3. Boenningstedt: SmartPLS GmbH (2015). http://www.smartpls.com
Rogers, E.M.: Diffusion of Innovations, 4th edn. The Free Press, New York (1995)
Schaupp, L.C., Bélanger, F., Fan, W.: Examining the success of websites beyond e-commerce: an extension of the IS success model. J. Comput. Inf. Syst. **49**(4), 42–52 (2009)
Schaupp, L.C., Carter, L.: The impact of trust, risk and optimism bias on E-file adoption. Inf. Syst. Front. **12**(3), 299–309 (2010)
Slade, E.L., Dwivedi, Y.K., Piercy, N.C., Williams, M.D.: Modeling consumers' adoption intentions of remote mobile payments in the United Kingdom: extending UTAUT with innovativeness, risk, and trust. Psychol. Mark. **32**(8), 860–873 (2015a)

Slade, E., Williams, M., Dwivedi, Y., Piercy, N.: Exploring consumer adoption of proximity mobile payments. J. Strateg. Mark. **23**(3), 209–223 (2015b)

Tamilmani, K., Rana, N.P., Dwivedi, Y.K., Sahu, G.P., Roderick, S.: Exploring the role of 'Price Value' for understanding consumer adoption of technology: a review and metaanalysis of UTAUT2 based empirical studies. In: Twenty-Second Pacific Asia Conference on Information Systems, Japan (2018a)

Tamilmani, K., Rana, N.P., Dwivedi, Y.K.: Use of 'habit' is not a habit in understanding individual technology adoption: a review of UTAUT2 based empirical studies. In: Elbanna, A., Dwivedi, Y.K., Bunker, D., Wastell, D. (eds.) TDIT 2018. IAICT, vol. 533, pp. 277–294. Springer, Cham (2019a). https://doi.org/10.1007/978-3-030-04315-5_19

Tamilmani, K., Rana, N.P., Prakasam, N., Dwivedi, Y.K.: The battle of brain vs. heart: a literature review and meta-analysis of "hedonic motivation" use in UTAUT2. Int. J. Inf. Manag. **46**, 222–235 (2019b)

Taylor, S., Todd, P.A.: Understanding information technology usage: a test of competing models. Inf. Syst. Res. **6**(2), 144–176 (1995)

UN: World population prospects: key findings and advance tables (2017). https://esa.un.org/unpd/wpp/Publications/Files/WPP2017_KeyFindings.pdf. Accessed 06 Sept 2018

Venkatesh, V., Morris, M.G., Davis, G.B., Davis, F.D.: User acceptance of information technology: toward a unified view. MIS Q. 425–478 (2003)

Venkatesh, V., Thong, J.Y., Xu, X.: Consumer acceptance and use of information technology: extending the unified theory of acceptance and use of technology. MIS Q. **36**, 157–178 (2012)

Williams, M.D., Rana, N.P., Dwivedi, Y.K.: The unified theory of acceptance and use of technology (UTAUT): a literature review. J. Enterp. Inf. Manag. **28**(3), 443–488 (2015)

Xu, X., Thong, J.Y., Tam, K.Y.: Winning back technology disadopters: testing a technology readoption model in the context of mobile internet services. J. Manag. Inf. Syst. **34**(1), 102–140 (2017)

Theoretical Framework for Digital Payments in Rural India: Integrating UTAUT and Empowerment Theory

Manisha Sharma[1] and Sujeet K. Sharma[2](✉)

[1] School of Management, Gautam Buddha University, Greater Noida, India
manisha@gbu.ac.in

[2] MIS Area, Indian Institute of Management Tiruchirappalli, Tiruchirappalli, India
sujeet@iimtrichy.ac.in

Abstract. Indian economy is considered as one of the most promising and fast growing among all developing countries in the world. In the current global scenario, India has a number of strengths namely younger population, greater access to mobile phones, increasing technical competence and digital literacy among others. Indian government initiated a number of steps to incorporate information technology (IT) tools in public institutions to increase transparency, remove middlemen, and minimize digital divide. Digital payment is one of the prominent applications of the ICT in the past couple of years due to some of the initiatives of government of India like demonetization, and digital India. However, around 67% of Indian Population still lives in rural areas and thereby it is imperative to understand the behavioral intention to use and its continuous usage of digital payments in rural population of India. This research attempts to develop a theoretical research framework by integrating psychological empowerment theory and the unified theory of acceptance and use of technology (**UTAUT**) to explore and understand perception of rural population towards digital payments in Indian context. Researchers using structural equation modeling or other statistical models may test the proposed research framework. In this research framework, second order of empowerment construct is proposed, which is rarely available in the extant literature. The findings of this research will be useful to government agencies, financial institutions, mobile and telecommunications operators, and researchers. This paper is a working paper and intends to further test the theoretical model proposed as the ongoing work.

Keywords: Digital payments · UTAUT · Empowerment theory · Rural India

1 Introduction

The Information and Communication Technologies augmented with the rise of the Internet have opened new opportunities for the growth of business worldwide and one of the path breaking technological inventions till date is the technology based transactions. The developments in the field of technological innovations have boosted an inspiring shift towards digital platforms and completely transformed the dynamics of commerce

Published by Springer Nature Switzerland AG 2019
Y. Dwivedi et al. (Eds.): TDIT 2019, IFIP AICT 558, pp. 212–223, 2019.
https://doi.org/10.1007/978-3-030-20671-0_15

(Hromcová et al. 2014; Beijnen and Bolt 2009; Bolt and Humphrey 2007). The advancements of these payment methods intend to seize the customary mode of transactions as the digitized payment methods not only provide the higher level of security through secured gateways but also create a virtual terminal to its users and thereby offer a win-win situation for the user and the bank as well by enabling the direct transfer of money between the merchant bank's account and the user's bank account.

The worldwide digital payment segment amounts to the total transaction value of US $ 3402,168 million in 2018 and expected to show an annual growth rate of 13.9% by 2022 (Statista 2018). The increasing trend towards digital payments is certainly promising however it is important to note that cash transaction still leads as the most preferred mode of payment (Arango-Arango et al. 2018). Therefore, the challenge lies in not only making the users switch towards digital payments but also retain them as continuous users so that they not only accept the technology of digital payments but also continue to use the same.

The key determinants that influence the acceptance of digital payments have been developed in the extant literature (Patil et al. 2018a, b; 2017) on the basis of theoretical models such as technology acceptance model (TAM: Davis 1989), unified theory of acceptance and use of technology (UTAUT: Venkatesh et al. 2003) and some extensions of these well-established models such as TAM2 (Chauhan 2015), UTAUT2 (Slade et al. 2015a, b) among others. However, developing a theory for digital payments from electronic participation perspective is rarely available in the existing literature. Venkatesh et al. (2016) argued that it is important to integrate other theoretical models to understand better acceptance of information technology phenomenon for greater citizen participation to exploit maximum potential of the technology. Kang (2014) suggested that citizen empowerment is one of the key factors to enhance citizen participation. As a result, the amalgamation of UTAUT with citizen empowerment theory in the proposed research model may provide some useful insights for better understanding of digital payment adoption among rural population in the Indian context.

This study makes mainly three contributions to extend the extant literature of digital payments among rural population in the Indian context. Firstly, this study develops a research model on the basis of UTAUT model and the citizen empowerment theory to understand key determinants of continuous intention to use the digital payments. Secondly, we propose amalgamation of UTAUT with citizen empowerment theory to increase the predictive power of the UTAUT model. Finally, this framework is proposed in the context of Indian economy, which is the one of fastest growing economies in the world.

2 Literature Review and Development of Hypotheses

2.1 Digital Payments in India

India experienced the demonetization of all INR 500 and INR 1000 banknotes on November 8, 2016 in order to curb the shadow economy and control the use of illicit and counterfeit cash (India Today 2016; ToI 2016). Post the execution of demonetization, the country faced the challenges of prolonged cash shortages in the following weeks and the use of digital payment methods observed an impressive upward trend then onwards (The Economist 2016). According to the National Payments Corporation of India (NPCI), the value of the digital payments transactions reached to INR 115490.3 billion on February 2018 from INR 671.5 billion in November 2016 while the volume of transactions reached 1098 million from 671.5 million in the same period (NPCI statistics 2018). Despite the positive buzz around the digital payments post demonetization, Indians still rely heavily on cash transactions. The total currency put in circulation has more than doubled to over INR 19.3 lakh crore from about INR 8.9 lakh crore post demonetization (ToI Business 2018). There are costs associated with digital alternatives, particularly due to the reason that an average user lacks the technical knowledge to use an app and hesitate to adopt new alternatives (Creehan 2018). This indicates that India offers a huge growth potential for digital payments if the users are sensitized towards the technology adaption to increase the level of acceptance towards the same which leads to the specific direction of this work. However, it is equally important to realize that the growth of digital transactions in India is hugely dominated by urban population and rural India is heavily untapped till date in terms of digitization particularly digital payments. The urban population of India constitutes 33.2% with digital payment customers as 44% but the 66.8% rural population of India has only 16% digital payment customers (IMAI 2018). This paper therefore attempts to explore the opportunities of digital payments in Rural India and offer a specific model that fits the rural surroundings of India in order to enhance the usage of digital payments in rural India.

2.2 Gaps in the Existing Body of Knowledge and the Consequent Theoretical Development

The UTAUT model developed by Venkatesh et al. (2003) has been considered as a theoretical lens in several technology adoptions studies under various settings. The UTAUT model was developed through a rigorous review and empirical validations of eight prominent adoption theories. The UTAUT is the most suitable theoretical model to understand intention of rural population in India as it is developed on the basis of technological and social determinants (Zuiderwijk et al. 2015). However, over the years, a need however a need has constantly been felt over the applicability and generalizability of these models (Gregor 2006; Weber 2003; Lee and Baskerville 2003). Hong et al. (2014) further examined the role of context-specific theory development and further provided directions so as to contextualize theories in IS research. Therefore, it necessitated to provide a theoretical model to build constructs of digital payments adoption and continuous usage specific for Indian rural perspective.

In this context, the current work has two specific distinctions in order to seek the applicability and suitability for the fit of any model. Firstly, research is based in Rural India and the rural people being ignorant of the benefits of the digital payments, need to be oriented and motivated towards going digital before actually placing the advantages of digital payments in front of them. Through the interactions with rural inhabitants, it was noticed that the rural people carry a certain perception that only those who are literate and have knowledge of computers use things like digital payments, or only those who have enough money can use digital payments. The rural India has its own sets of constraints which are context and geography specific. They being ignorant and uneducated to a large extent show a very slow rate of adoption of the Kisan Credit Card (KCC) system (IndiaStat 2018; Bista et al. 2012) which was developed for them only and are also not aware of Aadhaar enabled payment system, introduced by government of India as part of digital drive as realized during the interaction with them. Moreover, the role of local shops and traders offer a very strong hindrance in achieving a cashless rural India.

Therefore, it was felt that apart from the conceptualization and implementation of UTAUT theory in order to enhance the functional usage of digital payments in rural India, there is a need to sensitize the rural inhabitants towards the digital payments by associating them with the idea of empowerment with the usage of digital payments so that they not only feel the need to go digital but also necessitates its usage with a sense of being digitally empowered.

This led the researchers to explore the possibilities of developing a construct in the form of Citizen empowerment theory as suggested by Kang (2014), resulted in second order construct, in order to enhance the usage of digital payments in rural India. Moreover, the IS literature lacks studies on IT empowerment which also substantiates the exploration of Citizen empowerment theory in the context of digital payments in rural India.

Secondly, the research attempts to seek the continuous use of the digital payment which is not addressed in the UTAUT and thereby the integration of the citizen empowerment constructs with UTAUT model helps to grasp the continuous use of the digital payment.

2.3 Unified Theory of Acceptance and Use of Technology (UTAUT)

The UTAUT model has been used to understand the user behavior in various information technology domains such as mobile Internet (Alalwan et al. 2018), mobile banking (Alalwan et al. 2017), mobile health (Dwivedi et al. 2016), mobile payments (Slade et al. 2015a, b; Kapoor et al. 2015), online information services (Oh and Yoon 2014). Researchers (William et al. 2011; Dwivedi et al. 2017a, b) re-examined the UTAUT model and provided some useful insights to researchers and practitioners. In case of the applications of the UTAUT model, the aforementioned researchers have adapted hypotheses from the original UTAUT model developed by Venkatesh et al. (2003). In this study also, we have adapted four hypotheses from the UTAUT model in the context of digital payments from Indian perspective.

2.3.1 Performance Expectancy

Performance expectancy has been one of the key determinants which influences intention to use a new technology without any effect of settings. We have adapted performance expectancy from Venkatesh et al. (2003) and defined in this study as the degree to which rural population considers that using digital payments is beneficiary or helpful in increasing productivity. Pikkarainen et al. (2004) believed that consumers easily accept a system if they find it easy to use and learn. Performance expectancy has been identified as a significant indicator in the decision making towards the acceptance of a new information system (Thakur and Srivastava 2014; Alalwan et al. 2017; Tamilmani et al. 2019). Moreover, performance expectancy has been taken a strong predictor of behavioral intention towards the mobile apps and m-commerce (Luo et al. 2010; Venkatesh et al. 2012; Chong 2013). The rural population of India has been customized of doing cash transactions and due to lack of education not aware with the benefits of making digital payments and it is perceived that if they are educated towards the benefits of digital transactions, it might shift their preference towards digital payments. Therefore, we hypothesize that

H1: Performance expectancy positively influences intention to use digital payments.

2.3.2 Effort Expectancy

Effort expectancy is defined by Venkatesh et al. (2003) as "the degree of ease associated with the use of a given technology, which influences the use of that technology". Effort expectancy is similar to perceived ease of use in another advanced TAM Model. Leong et al. (2013) identified the ease of technology use increases the adoption rate among individuals. In fact, it has consistently been identified as a very significant predictor of behavioral intention towards technology adoption (Venkatesh et al. 2012; Thakur 2013; Slade et al. 2015a, b). Slade et al. (2015a, b) later found that effort expectancy influences the decision to adopt mobile payments. It is believed that rural population would expect the use of digital payment with minimal efforts. In the case of rural India, people who are still in the initial stage of technology acceptance, the comfort of using it might influence their inclination towards the acceptance of new technology and eventually impact their decision of switching towards digital payments and if they have some difficulty in the use of digital payments, they might not accept the technology. Hence, we hypothesize that

H2: Effort expectancy positively influences intention to use digital payments.

2.3.3 Social Influence

Social influence is another important factor of UTAUT model which influences decision of users towards intention to use a new information technology. Venkatesh et al. (2003) defined social influence as "the extent to which an individual perceives that other who are important to him/her, consider that he or she should use the system". Wei et al. (2009) categorized social influence as mass media influence and personal influence. Social influence has been identified as a strong predictor of behavioral intention (Crabbe et al. 2009; Venkatesh et al. 2012). Further, Slade et al. (2015a, b) observed that individuals have a tendency to seek opinions from their social network before embarking upon a new technology. Alalwan et al. (2018) found that social influence is one of the key predictors of the intent to use a new technology. We believe that in the rural settings, social influence would play a significant role in the decision to accept digital payments as rural people in India have very strong social culture and work in small social units and thereby, their chances of getting influenced from social surroundings are invariably high and in the case of accepting new technology of payments, the chances of getting influenced by the surroundings increase as it will ease out their pressure of not being accepted by others while embarking upon a new system of digital payments and give them a sense of acceptance amongst their peers. Therefore, we hypothesize that

H3: Social influence positively influences intention to use digital payments.

2.3.4 Facilitating Conditions

Facilitating conditions are defined by Venkatesh et al. (2003) as "the degree to which the individual perceives the existence of resources and support to use certain technology whenever necessary". Digital payments are supported by digital infrastructure such as desktop, smartphones, electricity in the context of rural India, and Internet service providers among others. Lewis et al. (2013) opined that individuals seek for assistance while adopting any new technology and might not adopt the same due to insufficient facilitating conditions. Zuiderwijk et al. (2015) found that facilitating conditions are important predictor of intention to use a new information technology or system. Facilitating conditions has been proven to be a very strong predictor in the case of m-commerce and mobile apps adoption (Crabbe et al. 2009; Venkatesh et al. 2012; Chong 2013; Hew et al. 2015; Tamilmani et al. 2018). In the case of Indian rural settings, the rural habitants may seek facilitating conditions in the form of internet connection, low cost wi-fi facility as the resources and quick online assistance through customer care as the support. It is very critical to have good facilitating conditions to promote digital payments in the rural settings as rural people are used to making payments through traditional system and the facilitation of required assistance and resources might influence their inclination towards digital payments and bring out the hesitation of using new technology. Therefore, we hypothesize that

H4: Facilitating conditions positively influences intention to use digital payments.

2.4 Citizen Empowerment Theory

Researchers (Zimmerman and Rappaport 1988; Zimmerman 1995) proposed psychological citizen empowerment theory and defined as "the connection between a sense of personal competence, a desire for, and a willingness to take action in the public domain". This theory attempts to comprehend the motivation in the work settings. However, Kang (2014) observed that psychological empowerment is crucial in motivating large population to engage in an activity with positive outcomes. Naranjo-Zolotov and Oliveira (2018) studied the citizens' intention to use and recommend for electronic participation in e-government services. The empowerment theory is context specific and constructs impact, meaning, competence and self- determination as motivational aspect of empowerment. In this study, we define empowerment as the second order construct developed on the first order four constructs however we felt that motivational empowerment at workplace cannot be generalized when it comes to motivating the rural people towards the use of digital payments. Spreitzer (1996), way back believed that it is important to assess the empowerment through perception. This extended our work in the form of exploratory discussion with the rural people in general in the surrounding areas so as to understand the meaning of rural empowerment towards digitization. With 20 such in depth discussions, it turned out that the rural population, especially the middle age group and old age group are apprehensive towards the use of digital payments however the younger rural population showed their eagerness towards digital payments. The rural youth is highly inclined to bridge this social gap between the rural people and urban ones and believe that if given the orientation, they are willing to learn and adopt the new technologies and also showed their inclination towards learning the benefits of digital payments. On exploring further, they acknowledged that the use and understanding of digital payments give them a sense of self-esteem and equality vis-à-vis their urban counterparts. Thereby, it is recommended to reframe the citizen empowerment theory constructs in the context of Indian rural population towards digital payments. Thereby, we propose the empowerment constructs as sense of self-esteem, sense of equality, competence and self-determination. Thus, we propose to replace the two constructs as impact and meaning by self-esteem and sense of equality in the case of acceptance of digital payments in rural India. The existing literature however suggests that empowerment theory may contribute significantly in the adoption of a new system. Therefore, we hypothesize that

H6: Citizen empowerment positively mediates intention to use digital payments to enhance continuous intention to use.

2.5 Intention to Use and Continuous Intention to Use

As observed by Tam and Oliveira (2016), retention of the customers is as important as attracting them for the potential purchase. If the users feel satisfied from the services offered by merchant, they are more likely to repeat the use of the services, which will lead to their intention of continuous usage (Kuo et al. 2009; Moon and Kim 2001). It has been also observed that users will be involved in the continuous usage if they intend to use services at all, as users want to have an enjoyable experience while using a service (Kim, Ferrin and Rao 2009; Kim, Chan and Gupta 2007). Sharma and Sharma (2019) also observed that intention to use leads to actual usage particularly in the case of m-banking. It is believed that if rural people get positive inclination towards digital payments, the associated benefits, the use of ease, the supporting facilities and also the sense of empowerment might influence their decision of continuously using it. Thereby, the intention to use tends to positively and significantly impact the continuous intention of usage which leads to the development of the following hypotheses:

H7: Intention to use positively influences continuous intention to use digital payments.

3 Proposed Research Model

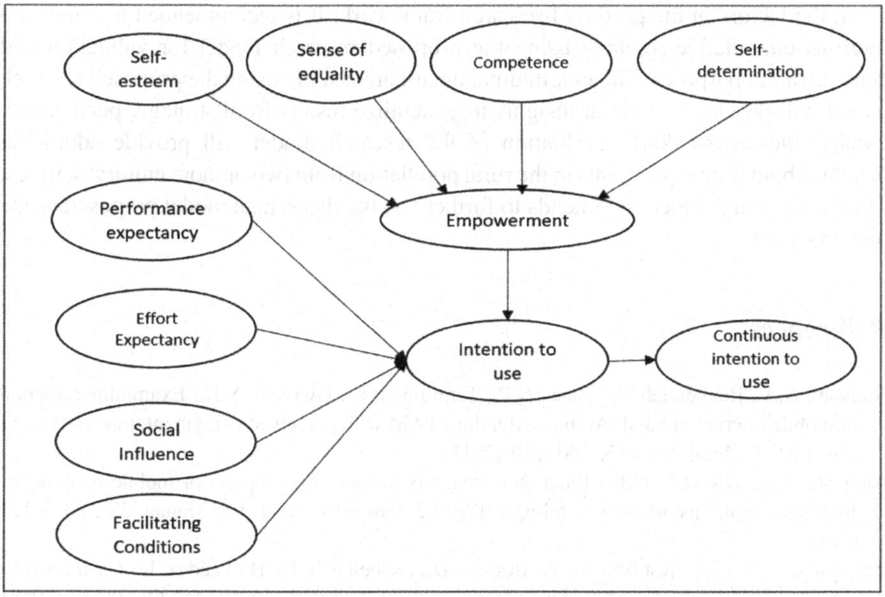

Fig. 1. Research model (Adapted from Venkatesh et al. 2003)

4 Concluding Remarks

In the era of digital world, the use of ICT applications for rural development is increasing day by day. Digital payments under ICT applications are one of the prominent applications with far reaching objectives and have potential to minimize the gap of financial inclusion. Furthermore, digital payments applications among rural population provide a sense of true empowerment that enables them to perform financial transactions during odd hours. The success of digital payments in the rural population primarily depends upon the acceptance of this financial technology by rural inhabitants. Consequently, objective of this study was to develop a research framework on the basis of the amalgamation of UTAUT with citizen empowerment theory, which will help in identifying key determinants influencing the decision to accept digital payments in the rural population in the context of India. The another main objective of the paper was to build a theoretical model that can promote continuous usage of the digital payments in rural India. Digital payment is vital for rural India but it was comprehended from the extant literature there is no complete existing framework to understand the intention to adopt and the continuous use of the digital payment. Thereby, this research attempts to overcome this research gap through integrating UTAUT model and citizen empowerment theory.

The proposed framework can be used for empirical investigations by researchers and practitioners. The empirical validation of the research model will help in understanding the effect of independent variables on the dependent variables. In addition, qualitative research such as structured interviews, case studies may provide some deeper insights about the factors in the proposed research framework. It is recommended to conduct a rigorous quantitative research using the proposed research model for validation and generalization purposes. The longitudinal quantitative study using the proposed research model will provide consistent insights to generalize results from strategic perspective. Finally, the cross-cultural evaluation of the research model will provide additional insights about digital payments in the rural population from two or more cultural settings. This is a working paper and intends to further test the theoretical model proposed as the ongoing work.

References

Alalwan, A.A., Baabdullah, A., Rana, N.P., Tamilmani, K., Dwivedi, Y.K.: Examining adoption of mobile internet in Saudi Arabia: extending TAM with perceived enjoyment, innovativeness and trust. Technol. Soc. **55**, 100–110 (2018)

Alalwan, A.A., Dwivedi, Y.K., Rana, N.P.: Factors influencing adoption of mobile banking by Jordanian bank customers: extending UTAUT2 with trust. Int. J. Inf. Manag. **37**(3), 99–110 (2017)

Arango-Arango, C.A., Bouhdaoui, Y., Bounie, D., Eschelbach, E., Hernandez, L.: Cash remains top-of-wallet! International evidence from payment diaries. Econ. Model. **69**, 38–48 (2018)

Beijnen, C., Bolt, W.: Size matters: economies of scale in European payments processing. J. Bank. Financ. **33**(2), 203–210 (2009)

Bista, D.R., Kumar, P., Mathur, V.C.: Progress and performance of Kisan Credit Card Scheme with a case study of Bihar. Agric. Econ. Res. Rev. **25**(1), 125–135 (2012)

Bolt, W., Humphrey, D.: Payment network scale economies, SEPA, and cash replacement. Rev. Netw. Econ. **6**(4), 1–21 (2007)

Crabbe, M., Standing, C., Standing, S., Karjaluoto, H.: An adoption model for mobile banking in Ghana. Int. J. Mob. Commun. **7**(5), 515–543 (2009)

Chauhan, S.: Acceptance of mobile money by poor citizens of India: integrating trust into the technology acceptance model. Info **17**(3), 58–68 (2015)

Chong, A.Y.L.: Predicting m-commerce adoption determinants: a neural network approach. Expert Syst. Appl. **40**(2), 523–530 (2013)

Creehan, S.: India's Digital Payments: growing consumer trust, but merchants needed (2018). https://www.frbsf.org/banking/asia-program/pacific-exchange-blog/indias-digital-payments-growing-consumer-trust-but-merchants-needed

Davis, F.: Perceived usefulness, perceived ease of use, and user acceptance of information technology. MIS Q. **13**(3), 319–340 (1989)

Dwivedi, Y.K., Rana, N.P., Janssen, M., Lal, B., Williams, M.D., Clement, M.: An empirical validation of a unified model of electronic government adoption (UMEGA). Gov. Inf. Q. **34** (2), 211–230 (2017a)

Dwivedi, Y.K., Rana, N.P., Jeyaraj, A., Clement, M., Williams, M.D.: Re-examining the unified theory of acceptance and use of technology (UTAUT): towards a revised theoretical model. Inf. Syst. Front. 1–16 (2017b). https://doi.org/10.1007/s10796-017-9774-y

Dwivedi, Y.K., Shareef, M.A., Simintiras, A.C., Lal, B., Weerakkody, V.: A generalised adoption model for services: a cross-country comparison of mobile health (m-health). Gov. Inf. Q. **33**(1), 174–187 (2016)

Gregor, S.: The nature of theory in information systems. MIS Q. **30**(3), 611–642 (2006)

Hew, J.J., Lee, V.-H., Ooi, K.-B., Wei, J.: What catalyses mobile apps usage intention: an empirical analysis. Ind. Manag. Data Syst. **115**(7), 1269–1291 (2015)

Hong, W., Chan, F.K.Y., Thong, J.Y.L., Chasalow, L.C., Dhillon, G.: A framework and guidelines for context-specific theorizing in information systems research. Inf. Syst. Res. **25** (1), 111–136 (2014)

Hromcová, J., Callado-Muñoz, F.J., Utrero-González, N.: Effects of direct pricing of retail payment methods in Norway. Econ. Model. **37**, 428–438 (2014)

Indiastat: Quarterly Performance of Kisan Credit Card Scheme (2012–2018) (2018). https://www.indiastat.com/agriculture-data/2/kisan-credit-card/206866/quarterly-performance-of-kisan-credit-card-scheme-2012-2018/1129252/stats.aspx

India Today: Here is what PM Modi said about the new Rs. 500, Rs. 2000 notes and black money (2016). Accessed 9 Nov 2016

Internet and mobile association of India (IMAI) (2018)

Kang, M.: Understanding public engagement: conceptualizing and measuring its influence on supportive behavioral intentions. J. Pub. Relat. Res. **26**(5), 399–416 (2014)

Kapoor, K.K., Dwivedi, Y.K., Williams, M.D.: Examining the role of three sets of innovation attributes for determining adoption of the interbank mobile payment service. Inf. Syst. Front. **17**(5), 1039–1056 (2015)

Kim, H.W., Chan, H.C., Gupta, S.: Value-based adoption of mobile internet: an empirical investigation. Dec. Supp. Syst. **43**(1), 111–126 (2007)

Kim, D.J., Ferrin, D.L., Rao, H.R.: Trust and satisfaction, two stepping stones for successful e-commerce relationships: a longitudinal exploration. Inf. Syst. Res. **20**(2), 237–257 (2009)

Kuo, Y.-F., Wu, C.-M., Deng, W.-J.: The relationships among service quality, perceived value, customer satisfaction and post-purchase intention in mobile value-added services. Comput. Hum. Behav. **25**, 887–896 (2009)

Lee, A.S., Baskerville, R.L.: Generalizing generalizability in information systems research. Inf. Syst. Res. **14**(3), 221–243 (2003)

Leong, L.-Y., Hew, T.-S., Tan, G.W.-H., Ooi, K.-B.: Predicting the determinants of the NFC-enabled mobile credit card acceptance: a neural networks approach. Expert Syst. Appl. **40** (14), 5604–5620 (2013)

Lewis, C.C., Fretwell, C.E., Ryan, J., Parham, J.B.: Faculty use of established and emerging technologies in higher education: a unified theory of acceptance and use of technology perspective. Int. J. High. Educ. **2**(2), 22–34 (2013)

Luo, X., Li, H., Zhang, J., Shim, J.P.: Examining multi-dimensional trust and multifaceted risk in initial acceptance of emerging technologies: an empirical study of mobile banking services. Dec. Supp. Syst. **49**(2), 222–234 (2010)

Moon, J.W., Kim, Y.G.: Extending the TAM for a world-wide-web context. Inf. Manag. **38**(4), 217–230 (2001)

Naranjo-Zolotov, M., Oliveira, T., Casteleyn, S.: Citizens' intention to use and recommend e-participation: drawing upon UTAUT and citizen empowerment. Inf. Technol. People **32**(2), 364–386 (2018)

NPCI Statistics: Electronic Payment System-representative data by RBI (2018). https://www.npci.org.in/statistics

Oh, J.-C., Yoon, S.-J.: Predicting the use of online information services based on a modified UTAUT model. Behav. Inf. Technol. **33**(7), 716–729 (2014)

Patil, P.P., Rana, N.P., Dwivedi, Y.K.: Digital payments adoption research: a review of factors influencing consumer's attitude, intention and usage. In: Al-Sharhan, S., et al. (eds.) Challenges and Opportunities in the Digital Era. LNCS, vol. 11195, pp. 45–52. Springer, Cham (2018a). https://doi.org/10.1007/978-3-030-02131-3_6

Patil, P.P., Rana, N.P., Dwivedi, Y.K.: Digital payments adoption research: a meta-analysis for generalising the effects of attitude, cost, innovativeness, mobility and price value on behavioural intention. In: Elbanna, A., Dwivedi, Y., Bunker, D., Wastell, D. (eds.) Smart Working, Living and Organising. IFIPAICT, vol. 533, pp. 194–206. Springer, Cham (2018b). https://doi.org/10.1007/978-3-030-04315-5_14

Patil, P.P., Dwivedi, Y.K., Rana, N.P.: Digital payments adoption: an analysis of literature. In: Kar, A., et al. (eds.) Digital Nations – Smart Cities, Innovation, and Sustainability. LNCS, vol. 10595, pp. 61–70. Springer, Cham (2017). https://doi.org/10.1007/978-3-319-68557-1_7

Pikkarainen, T., Pikkarainen, K., Karjaluoto, H., Pahnila, S.: Consumer acceptance of online banking: an extension of the technology acceptance model. Internet Res. **14**(3), 224–235 (2004)

Sharma, S.K., Sharma, M.: Examining the role of trust and quality dimensions in the actual usage of mobile banking services: an empirical investigation. Int. J. Inf. Manag. **44**, 65–75 (2019)

Slade, E.L., Dwivedi, Y.K., Piercy, N.C., Williams, M.D.: Modeling consumers' adoption intentions of remote mobile payments in the United Kingdom: extending UTAUT with innovativeness, risk, and trust. Psychol. Mark. **32**(8), 860–873 (2015a)

Slade, E., Williams, M., Dwivedi, Y., Piercy, N.: Exploring consumer adoption of proximity mobile payments. J. Strat. Mark. **23**(3), 209–223 (2015b)

Spreitzer, G.M.: Social structural characteristics of psychological empowerment. Acad. Manag. J. **39**(2), 483–505 (1996)

Statista: Digital Payments (2018). https://www.statista.com/outlook/296/100/digital-payments/worldwide#market-revenue

Tamilmani, K., Rana, N.P., Dwivedi, Y.K.: Use of 'habit' is not a habit in understanding individual technology adoption: a review of UTAUT2 based empirical studies. In: Elbanna, A., Dwivedi, Y., Bunker, D., Wastell, D. (eds.) Smart Working, Living and Organising. IFIPAICT, vol. 533, pp. 277–294. Springer, Cham (2018). https://doi.org/10.1007/978-3-030-04315-5_19

Tamilmani, K., Rana, N.P., Prakasam, N., Dwivedi, Y.K.: The battle of brain vs. heart: a literature review and meta-analysis of "hedonic motivation" use in UTAUT2. Int. J. Inf. Manag. **46**, 222–235 (2019)

Tam, C., Oliveira, T.: Understanding the impact of m-banking on individual performance: DeLone & McLean and TTF perspective. Comput. Hum. Behav. **61**, 233–244 (2016)

Thakur, R.: Customer adoption of mobile payment services by professionals across two cities in India: An empirical study using modified technology acceptance model. Bus. Perspect. Res. **1**, 17–29 (2013)

Thakur, R., Srivastava, M.: Adoption readiness, personal innovativeness, perceived risk and usage intention across customer groups for mobile payment services in India. Internet Res. **24**, 369–392 (2014)

The Economist: the dire consequences of india's demonetisation initiative. The Economist 3 December 2016. Accessed 5 Jan 2017

ToI Business: At Rs. 18.5 lakh crore, cash with public at record high (2018). https://timesofindia.indiatimes.com/business/india-business/at-rs-18-5-lakh-crore-cash-with-public-at-record-high/articleshow/64534468.cms

ToI: Notes out of circulation (2016). Accessed 8 Nov 2016

Venkatesh, V., Morris, M.G., Davis, G.B., Davis, F.D.: User acceptance of information technology: toward a unified view. MIS Q. **27**(3), 425–478 (2003)

Venkatesh, V., Thong, J.Y., Chan, F.K., Hu, P.J.: Managing citizens' uncertainty in e-government services: the mediating and moderating roles of transparency and trust. Inf. Syst. Res. **27**(1), 87–111 (2016)

Venkatesh, V., Thong, J.Y.L., Xu, X.: Consumer acceptance and use of information technology: extending the unified theory of acceptance and use of technology. MIS Q. **36**(1), 157–178 (2012)

Weber, R.: Editor's comments. MIS Q. **27**(2), iii–xii (2003)

Wei, T.T., Marthandan, G., Chong, A.Y.L., Ooi, K.B., Arumugam, S.: What drives Malaysian m-commerce adoption? An empirical analysis. Ind. Manag. Data Syst. **109**(3), 370–388 (2009)

Williams, M.D., Rana, N.P., Dwivedi, Y.K., Lal, B.: Is UTAUT really used or just cited for the sake of it? A systematic review of citations of UTAUT's originating article. In: ECIS, p. 231, June 2011

Zimmerman, M.A.: Psychological empowerment: issues and illustrations. Am. J. Community Psychol. **23**(5), 581–599 (1995)

Zimmerman, M.A., Rappaport, J.: Citizen participation, perceived control, and psychological empowerment. Am. J. Community Psychol. **16**(5), 725–750 (1988)

Zuiderwijk, A., Janssen, M., Dwivedi, Y.K.: Acceptance and use predictors of open data technologies: drawing upon the unified theory of acceptance and use of technology. Gov. Inf. Q. **32**(4), 429–440 (2015)

Big Data and Business Intelligence

Impact of Business Intelligence on Firm's Performance in Cameroon

Varelle Fossi Maffock[1(✉)], Samuel Fosso Wamba[2(✉)], and Jean Robert Kala Kamdjoug[1(✉)]

[1] Catholic University of Central Africa, Yaounde, Cameroon
fossivarelle@gmail.com, jrkala@gmail.com
[2] Toulouse Business School, Toulouse, France
s.fosso-wamba@tbs-education.fr

Abstract. Globally, virtually all companies pursue the same goals, which range from increasing revenues and attracting new customers to nurturing a good image, while using the least possible resources. To achieve those goals, many available IT (information technologies) tools and systems have to be used to make the process easier. "Information systems and IT become the metaphors that provide different tools and techniques to the businesses that intend to overcome the challenge of these environments". One of those systems or tools is Business Intelligence (BI). What are the prerequisites to the adoption of BI tools by a given company? What are the significant values that prove that BI leads better performance? To answer to these questions, we have decided to investigate the impact of BI on firm's performance in the Cameroonian context. Our research model is built on the TAM (Technology Acceptance Model), the Extended TAM and the IS Success Model. To test and analyze our proposed model, we used a mixed research method.

Keywords: Business Intelligence · Enterprise performance · TAM · IS Success Model

1 Introduction

The term Business Intelligence (BI) refers to technologies, applications and practices for the collection, integration, analysis and presentation of business information. BI includes a variety of tools, applications and methodologies that enable organizations to collect data from internal and external sources; prepare it for analysis; develop and run queries against such data; and create visual supports to make the analytical results available to corporate decision-makers and operational workers. BI is defined as "a combination of processes, policies, culture and technologies for gathering, manipulating, storing and analyzing data collected, in order to communicate information, create knowledge, and inform decision making" [3].

As Golfareli and Rizzi (2009) put it, "The potential benefits of business intelligence are accelerating and improving decision-making, optimizing internal business processes, increasing operational efficiency, driving new revenues and gaining competitive advantage over business rivals." Thanks to BI systems, companies can easily identify

Published by Springer Nature Switzerland AG 2019
Y. Dwivedi et al. (Eds.): TDIT 2019, IFIP AICT 558, pp. 227–233, 2019.
https://doi.org/10.1007/978-3-030-20671-0_16

market trends and spot various business challenges, they said. For [3], "BI helps report business performance, uncover new business decisions regarding competitors, suppliers, customers, financial issues, strategic issues, products and services". And Regarding the adoption of this technology, these authors estimate that BI is implemented by 80% of U.S. companies in the U.S.A. and by 50% of European firms. Out of these BI adopters, 89% of them believe that they might lose their market if they don't adopt BI [4]. Cameroonian companies have been following this global trend as an increasing number of them are adopting BI tools for improved performance; they include mobile service providers MTN Cameroon and Orange Cameroun, as well as Jumia or AfikMarket for e-commerce.

Generally, the BI is marginally used by organizations in Cameroon economic context. But, we can notice that there is effective used of BI by Cameroonian branches of Foreign Companies like Orange, MTN, Jumia or AfrikMarket.

Yet, a number of impediments to adopting BI tools exist, including their heavy cost and the ambiguity about how the adoption of BI impacts firm performance [5–9]. Under such circumstances, a company planning to adopt BI should fully grasp the advantages and significant value added of BI adoption. There is a wide range of studies on BI's impact on enterprise's performance worldwide [7, 8]. However, the Cameroonian context is still under investigation and there remains a long way to go; and this explains the significance this study on the "Impact of business intelligence on company's performance" in Cameroun. The purposes of this study is to show how BI adoption in an enterprise could lead it to a better performance and also to serve as example to others in this economic context. As a reminder, the following research questions will be answered herein:

- How does BI impact on enterprise performance?
- What are the key drivers of BI leading to increased enterprise performance?

2 Conceptual Model and Hypotheses

For this study, the hypothesized variables and their relationships in the model are being derived from the available literature, and the model is being drawn on TAM, Extended TAM and IS success Model. We combine these models to catch entirely BI success in both individual and organisational level. And variables, from these models, will helps use to have a better measure of firm's performances. Our different constructs and hypotheses are as follows:

2.1 Core Constructs

Subjectives Norms: A person's perception that most people who are important to him/her think he/she should or should not perform the behavior in question [10].

H1: Subjective Norms will impact on image.
H2: Subjective Norms will impact on Perceived Usefulness.

Image: The degree to which the use of BI is perceived as being able to enhance one's status in one's social system [11].

H3: Image will have positive effects on Perceived Usefulness.

Output Quality: Is about how BI will impact one's ability to well perform a job [11].

H4: Output Quality has a positive impact on Perceived Usefulness.

Result Demonstration: is about how easy is to show the benefits of accepting BI [10].

H5: Result Demonstration will have positive effects on Perceived Usefulness.

Job Relevance: the adequate application of BI in the job to do [11].

H6: Job Relevance will have positive effects on Perceived Usefulness.

Perceived Usefulness of BI: is "the degree to which a person believes that using a BI system would enhance his or her job performance" [12].

H11: Perceived Usefulness will significantly impact the Attitude Toward Using BI.
H14: Perceived Usefulness will significantly impact the Intension to Use BI.

Perceived Ease of Use: is defined as "the degree to which a person believes that using a particular system would be free of effort" [12].

H12: Perceived ease of use will positively impact Perceived Usefulness of BI.
H10: Perceived ease of use will positively impact the Attitude Toward Using BI.

Service Quality: Service quality refers to through the following attributes: tangible, reliability, responsiveness, assurance, functionality, interactivity, and empathy [13–15].

H20: Service quality will impact the Intension to Use BI.
H21: Service quality will impact the Satisfaction.

System Quality: it is "concerned with whether or not there are bugs in the systems, the consistency of the user interface, ease of use, response rate in interactive systems, documentation, and, sometimes quality and maintainability of the of the program code" [16].

H17: System Quality will impact the Intension to Use.
H19: System Quality will impact the Satisfaction.

Information Quality: it is "concerned with such issue as timeliness, accuracy, relevance, and format of information generated by BI" [16].

H16: Information Quality will impact the Intension to Use.
H18: Information Quality will impact the Satisfaction.

Attitude Toward Using BI: evaluation of an attitudinal object either representing a positive or negative valence [10, 17, 18, 28–31].

H15: The Attitude Toward Using BI will have a direct positive impact on the Intention to Use.

Intention to Use BI: It is "the degree and manner in which employees utilize the capabilities of an e-government system" [19].

H23: Intention to Use will have direct positive effect on Use.

Satisfaction: it is defined as the "system user's satisfaction with regard to system speed, number of functions, quality and format" [20].

H22: Satisfaction will impact positively Job Satisfaction and Intension to Use.

Use of BI: it examines the actual use of BI, the extent of use of BI in the users' work, and the number of system applications used in the users' work [21].

H24: The Use of BI will impact the Satisfaction.
H30: The Use of BI will impact the Job Satisfaction.

Job Satisfaction: it is concerned with examining the successful interaction between BI and its users [22].

H26: Job Satisfaction will positively impact the Satisfaction.
H27: Job Satisfaction will positively impact the Job Performance.

Job Performance: it examines the impact of IS on the users' performance [21].

H28: Job Performance will have a positive direct impact on Financial Performance.
H29: Job Performance will have a positive direct impact on Market Performance.

Financial Performance: it is concerned with Customer retention, Sales growth, Profitability, and Return on investment [5].

Market Performance: it refers to the entering of new markets, the introduction of new products or services more quickly than competitors, and to the implementation of the best success rate for new products or services and market shares [5].

2.2 Moderating Constructs

Experience: is define as previous contact or easy use of IS technologies [11].

H7, H8: "The direct effect of Subjective norm on intentions may subside over time increased system experience" [11].

Voluntariness: "extend to which potential adopters perceive the adoption decision to be non-mandatory" [11].

H9: Voluntariness will significantly impact the relationship between Subjective Norms and the Intention to Use.

Our proposed research model for this study adapted from IS Success Model [23], TAM model [24, 25] and extended TAM [11] is being designed as follows (Fig. 1):

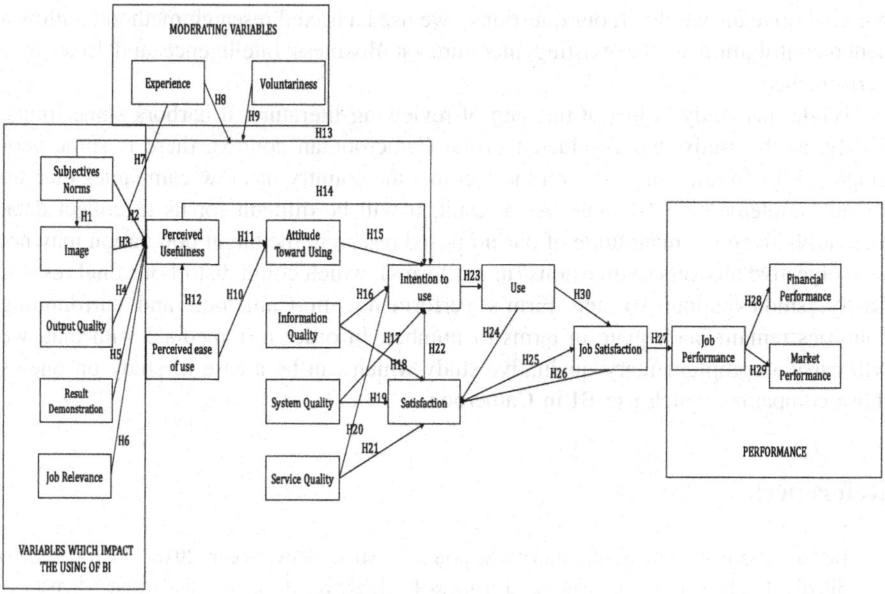

Fig. 1. Research model

3 Methodology

A mixed methods research is used in this paper to test and analyze the adopted model research. [11, 26] defined the mixed methods research as a method combining quantitative and qualitative conceptions in the same research study, and which is developed in response to the observed limitations of such conceptions. For our model, we started with a quantitative study, which was followed by a qualitative study in order to better understand and justify result of the quantitative research. This study was carried out in an enterprise that used BI tools like MTN Orange Jumia AfrikMarket. The first step of the study will consist on conducting multiples interviews to obtain viewpoints about BI and Cameroonian Enterprise performance; this will be follow by a pre-test phase, and after with a pilot study and will proceed with collect of data in those enterprise by using Google forms. This approach is recommended by Frippiat and Marquis [27]. Its main advantages are twofold: (1) the possible to surpass the geographical constraints and (2) the wider follow-up of BI development. Our structural research model will be tested with SmartPLS 3.2.7 software.

4 Expected Contribution

This research is expected to help understand the impact of Business Intelligence on Companies performance in the Cameroonian environment. The purposes of this study is to show how BI adoption in Cameroon economic context could lead firms to a better performance and serve as example for others in the same economic context. To achieve our goal (give answer to all our questions), we used a mixed research method to allow a better contribution to the existing literature on Business Intelligence and Enterprise Performance.

While this study is just at the step of reviewing literature, it harbors some limits. Firstly, as the study was conducted in the Cameroonian context, there is some geographical limitation, coupled with the fact that the country has few companies that are already implementing BI tools. As a result, it will be difficult for us to collect data. Secondly, given the magnitude of our proposed research, the target population may not give objective answers to questions (in our forms), which could distort our final results. Lastly, studies about BI and Firm's performance in Cameroon and surrounding countries remain inadequate in terms of number. In order to remediate with that, we will carry a complementary qualitative study which can be a case of study on one of those companies which use BI in Cameroon.

References

1. Bedell-Pearce, J.: Safe digital transformation for SMEs. Netw. Secur. **2018**(11), 6–7 (2018)
2. Sharda, R., Delen, D., Turban, E.: Business Intelligence, Analytics, and Data Science: A Managerial Perspective. Pearson-Prentice Hall, Saddle River (2016)
3. Foley, E., Guillemette, M.G.: What is Business Intelligence? Int. J. Bus. Intell. Res. **1**(4), 1–28 (2010)
4. Columbus, L.: 84% of enterprises see big data analytics changing their industries competitive landscapes in the next year. Forbes (2014)
5. Akter, S., et al.: How to improve firm performance using big data analytics capability and business strategy alignment? Int. J. Prod. Econ. **182**, 113–131 (2016)
6. Ramanathan, R., et al.: Adoption of business analytics and impact on performance: a qualitative study in retail. Prod. Plann. Control **28**(11–12), 985–998 (2017)
7. Sharma, R., Mithas, S., Kankanhalli, A.: Transforming decision-making processes: a research agenda for understanding the impact of business analytics on organizations. Eur. J. Inf. Syst. **23**(4), 433–441 (2014)
8. Trailor, M., et al.: Perception, reality, and the adoption of business analytics: evidence from North American professional sport organizations. Omega **59**, 72–83 (2016)
9. Yeoh, W., Popovic, A.: Extending the understanding of critical success factors for implementing business intelligence systems. International Funders for Indigenous Peoples (2018)
10. Ajzen, I., Fishbein, M.: Understanding Attitudes and Predicting Social Behavior. Prentice Hall, Englewood Cliffs (1980)
11. Venkatesh, V., Davis, F.D.: A theoretical extension of the technology acceptance model: four longitudinal field studies. Manag. Sci. **46**(2), 186–204 (2000)

12. Davis, F.D., Bagozzi, R.P., Warshaw, P.R.: Extrinsic and intrinsic motivation to use computers in the workplace. J. Appl. Soc. Psychol. **22**(14), 1111–1132 (1992)
13. DeLone, W.H., Mclean, E.R.: The DeLone and McLean model of information systems success: a ten year update. J. Manag. Inf. Syst. Spring **19**(4), 9–30 (2003)
14. Lin, F., Fofanah, S.S., Liang, D.: Assessing citizen adoption of e-Government initiatives in Gambia: a validation of the technology acceptance model in information systems success. Gov. Inf. Q. **28**(2), 271–279 (2011)
15. Pituch, K.A., Lee, Y.: The influence of system characteristics on e-learning use. Comput. Educ. **47**(1), 222–244 (2006)
16. Seddon, P.B., Kiew, K.Y.: A partial test and development of the DeLone and McLean's model of IS success. In: 1994 Proceeding of the 15th International Conference on Information Systems, Vancouver, Canada (1994)
17. Berger, I.E., Mitchell, A.A.: The effect of advertising on attitude accessibility, attitude confidence, and the attitude-behavior relationship. J. Consum. Res. **16**(3), 269–279 (1989)
18. Fazio, R.H.: How do attitudes guide behavior? In: The Handbook of Motivation and Cognition Foundations of Social Behavior, pp. 204–243 (1986)
19. Petter, S., DeLone, W., McLean, E.R.: Information systems success: the quest for the independent variables. J. Manag. Inf. Syst. **29**(4), 7–62 (2013)
20. Lin, W.-S., Wang, C.-H.: Antecedences to continued intentions of adopting e-learning system in blended learning instruction: a contingency framework based on models of information system success and task technology fit. Comput. Educ. **58**(1), 88–99 (2012)
21. Doll, W.J., Torkzadeh, G.: The measurement of end-user computing satisfaction. MIS Q. **12** (2), 259–274 (1988)
22. Seddon, P., Yip, K.: An empirical evaluation of user information satisfaction (UIS) measures for use with general ledger account software. J. Inf. Syst. **6**, 75–92 (1992)
23. Delone, W.H., Mclean, E.R.: Information systems success: the quest for the dependent variable. Inf. Syst. Res. **3**(1), 60–95 (1992)
24. Davis, F.D.: Perceived usefulness, perceived ease of use, and user acceptance of information technology. MIS Q. **13**(3), 319–339 (1989)
25. Davis, F.D., Bagozzi, R.P., Warshaw, P.: User acceptance of computer technology: a comparison of two theoretical models. Manag. Sci. **35**, 982–1003 (1989)
26. Caruth, G.D.: Demystifying mixed methods research design: a review of the literature (2013)
27. Frippiat, D., Marquis, N.: Web surveys in the social sciences: an overview. Population **65**(2), 309–338 (2010)
28. Dwivedi, Y.K., Rana, N.P., Janssen, M., Lal, B., Williams, M.D., Clement, M.: An empirical validation of a unified model of electronic government adoption (UMEGA). Gov. Inf. Q. **34** (2), 211–230 (2017)
29. Dwivedi, Y.K., Rana, N.P., Jeyaraj, A., Clement, M., Williams, M.D.: Re-examining the unified theory of acceptance and use of technology (UTAUT): towards a revised theoretical model. Inf. Syst. Front. 1–16 (2017). https://doi.org/10.1007/s10796-017-9774-y
30. Rana, N.P., Dwivedi, Y.K., Lal, B., Williams, M.D., Clement, M.: Citizens' adoption of an electronic government system: towards a unified view. Inf. Syst. Front. **19**(3), 549–568 (2017)
31. Rana, N.P., Dwivedi, Y.K., Williams, M.D., Weerakkody, V.: Adoption of online public grievance redressal system in India: toward developing a unified view. Comput. Hum. Behav. **59**, 265–282 (2016)

Challenges of Identifying and Utilizing Big Data Analytics in a Resource-Constrained Environment: In the Case of Ethiopia

Tigabu Dagne Akal[1(✉)], Tibebe Beshah[2], Stefan Sackmann[3], and Solomon Negash[4]

[1] Addis Ababa University, Addis Ababa, Ethiopia
tigabu.dagne@aau.edu.et
[2] School of Information Science, Addis Ababa University, Addis Ababa, Ethiopia
tibebe.beshah@aau.edu.et
[3] Institute of Information Science, Martin Luther University of Halle-Wittenberg, Halle, Germany
Stefan.sackmann@wiwi.uni-halle.de
[4] Kennesaw State University, Kennesaw, USA
snegash@kennesaw.edu

Abstract. Big data analytics (BDA) is the process of capturing and storing huge volume of data which has different formats and generated in high Velocity. It also refers to the process of analyzing big data for the purpose of decision making, strategic planning and policy formulation. Some of the applications of BDA include market segmentation, sales forecasting, weather forecasting, payment fraud detection, crop diseases detection, e-commerce analysis and users purchasing recommendation and others. The application of BDA is not only left for economically developed regions. It is also important for resource-constrained environments. In this study, challenges of identifying and utilizing big data analytics in the resource-constrained environment in the case of Ethiopia have been explored using some case. The case studies considered potential industries that can generate big data in Ethiopia. Ethiopian Telecommunication Corporation, Agricultural Transformation Agency, Payment systems like Hello Cash and Ethiopian Educational Networks (EthERNet) were considered as a case study. In the study, a qualitative grounded approach has been applied. Data was collected using a semi-structured interview approach. As data analysis result and discussion indicated that even if the selected potential industries have been generated big data they are not using it fully for the purpose of decision making. Potential challenges were identified in the identifying and utilizing of BDA in a resource-constrained environment. Some of these areas: lack of BDA awareness, data integration challenge, lack of skilled experts in the area, lack of data correctness and completeness, lack of standardized data registry, lack of leadership and management skill, issue of data privacy and infrastructure challenges including a huge volume of storage device constraint. Based on the identified challenges of BDA implementations in this study and possible application areas of BDA in those industries, a conceptual framework of the study were formulated.

Published by Springer Nature Switzerland AG 2019
Y. Dwivedi et al. (Eds.): TDIT 2019, IFIP AICT 558, pp. 234–254, 2019.
https://doi.org/10.1007/978-3-030-20671-0_17

1 Introduction

Big Data Analytics (BDA) is using large, diverse, and dynamic sets of user and machine-generated data as well as applying new methods of analytics to generate some interesting and prevailing knowledge [5, 20]. Data Analytics (DA) is the application of Business intelligence & analytics technologies that are based on data mining and statistical analysis [5, 38].

The application of big data (BD) and BDA in making an organizational data-driven decision has created a centre of attention over the past a few years. Some of the major areas of BD and analytics application areas are identified. Service providing divisions such as banking and finance, e-government and politics, smart health and wellbeing, telecommunication, information technology companies, security and public safety, science, technology and electronic-commerce are quickly adopted BD [5].

The application of BDA is not left only for high-income countries. It can be also highly applicable in low-income countries. But in low-income countries like Ethiopia, there is an issue of infrastructure development and know-how (understanding) of organizations on the application of BD, which are both low and hindering BDA availabilities in the organizations. The main motivation of this research is to identify and utilize the opportunities of BD and BDA application in the context of low-income countries like Ethiopia where there are different challenges like infrastructure. Through the research, the following research question were addressed: what are the challenges of identifying and utilizing BDAs in a resource-constrained environment? In this research, potential industries like Ethio-telecom, Agricultural transformation agency, payment systems (like hello cash) and education institutions were considered as a case study. The researcher has selected these cases studies due to their hugeness in producing data with different varieties and at a high-speed rate. In the meantime, these organizations are leading in the country on having a huge number of customers. The other reason behind considering these organizations is due to BDA analytics is flourishing or applying a lot in high-income countries in those industries which are addressed in the related work section.

Although big data has lots of benefits, there are some challenges related to storage and scalability issue of which "storage systems are not capable enough to store data" [1, 7, 12, 17]. Some scholars were addressed challenges related to lack of expert in the domain area, privacy and security challenge [12, 29, 39], data error [10] and challenge on representation of heterogeneous data [5, 17]. Other challenges are lie in data collection, storing, searching, analysis, sharing and visualization [1].

2 Related Works

As addressed by some scholars BD and BDA have been used to address huge volume of datasets (from terabytes to exabytes) and complex datasets (captured from large-scale enterprise systems, online social graphs, mobile devices, internet-of-things and open data/public data) that they need highly developed storage management and apply systematic use of analytical applications and data representation technologies [3, 5].

BDA is magnificently being used in different industries, such as telecom, environmental studies banking, education, insurance, social media user behavior identification [8, 26]. As addressed by [16] government industries use BDA to improve their capability to give services for the citizens by addressing different national challenges related to healthcare, job creation, economy, terrorism and natural disasters. For example, telecom companies have long had access to extensive bits of data with a large base of their subscribers connecting daily to their network and services [28]. As addressed by [4] telecommunication industries are now capturing more and more data volume that is consumers are making more calls and connecting more and more to connect to the internet that is benefitting from a larger variety of sources as well as from higher velocity in data generation. Having these huge volumes of data helps companies to classify their customers' behaviors and usage patterns. Countries like China use big data to conduct predictive analytics and enhance their businesses in the banking industry by analyzing customers' behaviours through analytical modelling methodologies and techniques [25].

The other BDA application area is the agricultural sector. For the sake of addressing the current agricultural production challenges, there is a need for applying modern information technologies that help to monitor the physical environment continuously [13]. As addressed by Kamilaris and his colleagues applying modern agricultural digital technologies can produce huge quantities of data. Big data analytics technologies are applicable to the agricultural sector. For example, Hadoop and cloud-based analytics were applied in the crop identification with comparisons to prices in different seasons [22]. Hence, "big data analysis" is the term used to describe a new generation of practices [14, 24] designed so that farmers and related organizations can extract economic value from very large volumes of a wide variety of data by enabling high-velocity capture, discovery, and/or analysis [18, 27]. The application of BDA enable farmers, agricultural transformation agencies, and researchers companies to extract value-driven information form the huge collection that will enable agricultural productivity and environmental sustainability [13]. Data generated from the agricultural sector "big data" demands large investments in resource utilization including resources like a skilled expert, infrastructures for data capture, store and process [21]. The big data analysis needs to "*operate almost in real-time for some applications (e.g. weather forecasting, monitoring for crops' pests and animals' diseases*)" [11].

BDA application lies in the banking industries. The Intelligent Customer Analytics for Recognition and Exploration (iCARE) model coming with IBM software platforms has been addressed to analyze banking. As addressed by [25] the applications of the iCARE framework have been confirmed in a real case study of a bank in Southeast China. As indicated in the case study, iCARE helps generate insights for active customers based on their transaction behaviour, using close to 20 terabytes of data. Payment systems are generating huge datasets from customers in different services. But there are challenges in the application of BDA in the banking and payment systems. The challenge is related to the organizational level of handling BD for the application of BDAs. For example, smartphone users in the United Kingdom (UK) tend to do 220 tasks in every day and use their phone 1500 times per week versus only a few calls and short messages in the recent past [4]. There are also web-based applications which are encountering BD regularly, like "*recent hot spots social computing (including social network analysis, online communities, recommender systems, reputation systems, and prediction markets), Internet text and documents, Internet search indexing*" [5].

Higher education institutions need to capture and record students' academic record (tutorial data, registration data, courses data, assessment data, social activities, reading behaves, internet access inside in the university…), students behaving activities in the universities portal and social media [19]. But most of the higher education is facing challenges in the application of BDA such as lack appropriate information infrastructure, data collection tools, automated software systems, skilled experts for effective and efficient data collection, data preparation tools for data cleansing, analysis and visualization of data [12]. As addressed by [19] some sources of higher education data are learning management systems, social media communication data, registration data, assessment data, student information data, employees' data, graduate data and others. "*Big Data can influence higher education practice, from enhancing students experience to improved academic programming, to more effective evidence-based decision making, and to strategic response to changing global trends*" [9]. But there are many implementation challenges of BDA in higher education. Some of these are data integration challenge, challenge associated with the quality of data collection and reporting and users' acceptance on the development of new processes and changing the management approach [9].

In the implementation of BDA, there are issues related to the uneven distribution of resources between the urban and rural regions that impact the development of BDA in different countries [30]. As discussed by [30], two major issues related to difficulty in the expansion of information infrastructure for the healthcare industry have been mentioned for low-income countries. There are also challenges related to data quality development of BDAs. Researches for data quality have been in the 1990s, and numerous researchers have been diverse explanations of the quality of data and distribution approaches of quality measurements [31]. The total Data Quality Management group of the Massachusetts Institute of Technology University directed by Professor Wang has done deep research in the data quality area [30]. As addressed by Wang and Strong "data quality" means "fitness of use" and argued the quality of data highly related to data from customers. As addressed by [30, 31] for uniformity data use in the healthcare industry, data should be of high quality and available so that different stakeholders are confidence to provide data-driven informed decisions making.

In addition to data quality and infrastructure challenges, organizational readiness and understanding what BD is recognized as one of the most steps prior to implementation and an important prerequisite to the achievement of BDA in relations of acceptance rate. Readiness assessment, as a comprehensive measure in order to provide a proper image of existing conditions and the preparedness of healthcare organization to change, is also a way to identify the potential cause of failure in innovation such as organizational resistance [32].

The remaining section of this paper addressed Research design in section three, data analysis in section four, discussion of the analysis result in section five and the concluding remark of the study in section six.

3 Research Design

3.1 Research Methodology

Qualitative research approach is employed to investigate the problem mentioned above. As a result preliminary inputs (concepts) to a potential theory has been developed from collected data and analyzed from different management and other employees of the company using the semi-structured interview approach. The grounded theory was undertaken in this research. Because the nature of the research seeks to understand and explains social phenomenon or process within the context of a given application and it demands to approve the validity of the theory from the point of those employees of the company who participated within the context during the study [14]. A summary of guidelines for information system researchers applied in the research of BDA, which includes research question, data collection, data analysis and result interpretation [20]. As discussed by Muller and his colleagues BDA researches are comfortable with data instead of theory and position either predictive or explanatory research methodology. In this research project, explanatory research methodology is selected because the researchers require the development of BDA concepts or generalizable properties associated with the challenges of identifying and utilizing BDA in a resource-constrained environment.

3.2 Research Paradigm

The interpretive research paradigm applied in terms of data collection and data analysis in this study. Because interpretive research paradigm can help Information system (IS) researchers to recognize human thinking and action in social and organizational contexts; it has the potential to construct thoughtful insights into information systems happenings [33]. A new conceptual framework derived from data that collected and analyzed from different stakeholders using the semi-structured interview approach. The grounded theory undertaken in this research. Because the nature of the research sought to understand and explains social phenomenon or process within the context of a given applications and it demanded to approve the validity of the justifications from the point of those stakeholders who participated within the context during the study [15].

3.3 Data Collection and Analysis Approach

The research instrument consisted of different sets of semi-structured interview guides and codes for thematic analysis. For data collection, semi-structured interviews which area open-ended and process oriented applied [34]. Primary data comprised of semi-structured interviews obtained from respondents of Ethiopian Telecommunication Corporation (ETC), Agricultural Transformation Agency (ATA), Payment Systems (Hello Cash), Ethiopian Educational Networks (EthERNet) and Independent Researcher.

During data collection, a method of purposive sampling was used to identify the sample group that have been participated in the interview. It is purpose because the interview participants were identified based on their knowledge, relationship and expertise on BDA. Table 1 below shows the different categories who were sampled, including the number of interviewees.

Table 1. Interview sample per category

Stakeholder category	Semi-structured interviews
Independent researcher	1
ETC customer operation manager	1
Hello cash data analyst	1
ATA data analyst	1
EthERNet big data researcher	1

There were different types of interview guides depending on the participant's role. The face to face interview range between 12 min to 19 min. The collected data was analyzed thematically following from [35, 37].

4 Analysis Result and Findings

This section presented the process and results of data analysis in order to identify patterns to come up with conceptual framework. The seven principles of interpretive research method suggest by [33], selected principles applied in this research with evidence. Since the type of data that collected is context-rich qualitative data and analysis also was qualitative (e.g., coding or content analysis). The following steps are adapted from [35, 37].

4.1 Developing the Code Manual

The coding manual a data management approach that helps to organize portions of similar or related text and to come with a new understanding from the evolving patterns [37]. This was designed prior to analysis and was based on the research question. As demonstrated in Table 2, the code manual is a data management tool that assists in organizing portions of similar or related text and deriving new insights from the emerging patterns [37]. It consists of the name, definition of what the theme concerns, and description of how to know when the theme exists. Researchers know to code in the qualitative analysis of interview data is also focus on something which is repeated in several phases, something that the interviewee explicitly states that it is important, something which is similar in the previously published reports and something which reminds a theory or concept [36, 37].

Table 2. Code manual

No.	Code	Definition	Description
1	Big data	Data in different formats including text, audio, video, log files: both structured and unstructured. Its volume is huge and increasing with high velocity and different varieties	Availability of big data in the organizations
2	Big data analytics	Process of data collection, storing and analyzing huge datasets (big data) in order to discover patterns and important information for researching and decision making	Availability of big data analytics tools
3	Big data analytics and telecommunication	This indicates that the impact of big data analytics in the telecommunication industry for customer relationship management, sales forecasting, marketing, fraud detection, security, intrusion detection and others	Decision makers, policy makers and researchers applying big data analytics for the telecommunication sectors
4	Big data analytics and agriculture	This indicates that the impact of big data analytics in the agricultural industry for weather forecasting, crop diseases detection, productivity forecasting, accurate crop predictions and policy making	Decision makers, policy makers and researchers applying big data analytics for the Agricultural sectors
5	Big data analytics and payment systems	This indicates that the impact of big data analytics in the payment systems for customers segmentation and identifying customers product buying behaviors	Decision makers, policy makers and researchers applying big data analytics for the Payment sectors
6	Big data analytics and education	This indicates that the impact of big data analytics in the education sector for forecasting students behaviors, security of institutions prediction	Decision makers, policy makers and researchers applying big data analytics for the Education sectors
7	Big data analytics and lack of awareness	This is indicates that lack of awareness is one of the challenge on the application of big data analytics in organizations	Policy makers, decision makers, top managements, data collectors and users have lack of awareness on the application of big data analytics
8	Big data analytics and leadership	This indicates that lack of leadership skill is one of the challenges on the application of big data analytics in the organizations	Existence of Lack of leadership skill in the organization can hinder in the big data analytics development
9	Big data and Lack of cheaper data collection tools	This indicates that lack of cheaper data collections tools for collecting different data: images, text, senor data, logs and many other	Availability of cheaper data collection tools
10	Big data analytics and lack of qualified experts in the domain	This indicates lack of skilled expert has a negative impact on big data analytics application	Availability of big data analytics experts

(*continued*)

Table 2. (*continued*)

No.	Code	Definition	Description
11	Big data analytics and infrastructure challenge	This indicates that lack of stabled infrastructure hinders the application of big data analytics in an organizations	Availability of information communication technology infrastructure
12	Big data analytics and lack of modern data management	This indicates that modern management is required for successful application of big data analytics	Availability of modern management approaches'. Interviewees were asked whether modern management approach has been implied or not
13	Completeness and Correctness of data	This indicates that attributes of data	Participants perception about capturing and storing data by focusing on correctness of data they used
14	Data privacy Concern	Data privacy is one of the major concerns in big data when users are generating data and shared it	Data privacy need an attention for the implementation of big data analytics as addressed by the interviewees
15	Audio, video, texts, CSV files, image and others	This indicates data formats in the big data	Interviewees were dealt the different data formats that are generating by the users and machines in the organization
16	Big data analytics and Lack of standard in data registry	This indicates that compatibility/consistence of data formats	No standard in the data production

Testing the Reliability of Codes

In this phase the applicability of the codes were tested as showed in Table 3. Using **Atlas.ti**, how the codes was applied to the selected transcripts interview were checked.

Table 3. Reliability of codes

Code	Data from transcripts
Big data analytics and lack of awareness	The most important or first rank challenge from my experience is having awareness on the usage of big data There is no awareness about the value of big data in our organizations. But there huge datasets already existed. In every day more than a Tera bytes of data are captured and recorded. When I look other countries' telecom sector they are using big data for different applications/business innovations in the industry I think the fundamental challenge is related to existence awareness. I am considering awareness as the first challenge
Big data analytics and leadership	There is also lack of leadership and management capabilities of people. Leaders and managers of organizations' used to think that there is no enough data for decision-making. So our country should work on knowledge capabilities of mangers and leaders of organizations

(*continued*)

Table 3. (*continued*)

Code	Data from transcripts
	It is possible to bring traditional management approach in to the big data management but management of compartments, access policy management, data management and other issues management need skilled person so that the design need lots of time
Big data analytics and Lack of standard in data registry	The big issue is due to lack of standard in data registry. There is no standard in the data production. For example, in our organization regions, zones and woredas are producing data. But there is huge problem in compatibility/consistence and data formats. There are many missing values or incomplete data when they are capturing Every organization should have its own standard in data handling and collection. Data with its own time stamps and temporal data must be enforced. The other thing the data collection approach should digital/online mechanism
Big data analytics and lack of qualified experts in the domain	Resources availability like skilled professionals in the area will be faced as a challenge in the modern data management or big data analytics implementation The 2nd challenge is related to knowledge gap. There are huge skill gap on the knowhow of big data applications and tools As we discussed previously, currently our organization is processing data through Excel. It is challenging to process big data using Excel. This indicates that shortage of skilled manpower is challenging for big data analytics application in our organization. I think this is the same challenge in other organizations in our country. So lack of skilled manpower and big data production standardization are the main challenge in our organization might be the same throughout the country Our country should work on knowledge capabilities of mangers and leaders of organizations. In the meantime, the philosophy of big data analytics should come to our country. Because big data analytics can be applied a lot in the area of agriculture, traffic management, health sectors, payment systems and other organizations that can generate huge volume datasets from sensors and social media
Completeness and correctness of data	The second challenge is having very low quality datasets. For example when customers are purchasing products or applying for some services, they should be registered in a given from with correct data sets. Some lefts empty, some fills with unrelated issues with answer to be filled for a specific questions, some filled text data for answer that required to be filled with numeric data. The form includes information related to customer information and other issues. The second challenge also raised because of lack of awareness on the value of data. That means the huge datasets that captured from some customers might be a garbage. If awareness is coming in to the board the data quality issue will be solved The image quality that used to capture by data collectors is very low and challenging to identify potential information of customers. Do to image quality too much information of customers' are not registering properly. Therefore, there is information inconsistence

(*continued*)

Table 3. (*continued*)

Code	Data from transcripts
Big data analytics and infrastructure challenge	The third challenge is related to infrastructure especially storage capabilities. Our organization used to store maximum of 6 months for most of the users is due lack of having huge storage devices Well, big data starts with cheaper data collection mechanisms. When you look at these things, they are currently in their infancy in our country. Although it getting better, low data collection will always hinder us from using big data analytic system Even if we can collect data, storage is another bigger issue. Building a reliable, ever increasing, secured data center is not an easy task Infrastructure is challenging. The government should work on the designing of central infrastructure that can be used by many institutions at the same time. Building the infrastructure is very expensive. Imagine every company is working to have its own sophisticated data center how much it costs Big data requires huge storage infrastructure. The volume in the 3 V's shows that the volume of the data is immensely large when compared to the traditional database systems. It's often in exabytes because you store the raw uncompressed and unprocessed data
Audio, video, texts, CSV files, image and others.	Audio, text, SMS, data log files and others. All data from customers are used to capture and store for some durations. Usually from 3 to 6 months. The limit of 3 to 6 months for most users is due to lack of storage devices They are audio, video, texts, CSV files, image and others Well the core part of big data is that the 3 Vs (volume, variety and Velocity) and the Variety term implies that big data often doesn't have a single format. It can be composition of images, text, sensor data, logs and many other
Big data analytics and organization	In our organization big data analytics can be used for marketing, network intrusion detection analysis, fraud detection and analysis, operation and maintenance, sales forecasting. For example in our organization there are more than 10, 000 telecom sites and usually it is difficult to trace which site has a problem and what kinds of problem will be happen at each site. Our organization has more than 65 million mobile customers, more than 17 million internet and data customers, over 1.2 million fixed line customers Currently our organization has working on a big data warehouse project which is not yet completed

Summarizing Data and Identifying Initial Themes

In this phase the interview transcripts were summarized. The researcher went through all the process of reading notes taken during interview, listening the recorded file and summarizing dataset as showed in Table 4.

Table 4. Code summary

Research Questions	Summary of Responses
Challenges of identifying and utilizing BDAs in a resource constrained Environment:	Lack of awareness on the usage of big data
	Lack of leadership and management capabilities of people in the big data analytics
	Lack of modern data management approach
	Lack of standard in data registry by the organizations
	Resources availability like skilled professionals in the area of big data analytics
	Lack cheaper data collection tools both hardware and automated software availability
	Data quality is very low to run big data analytics
	Infrastructure challenge especially the network infrastructure and storage capabilities
	Big data is available in some organizations like telecom industry, payment systems and agricultural industry
	Big data analytics can be applicable for marketing, network intrusion detection analysis, fraud detection and analysis, operation and maintenance, sales forecasting, weather forecasting, strategy planning and policy analysis, project monitoring and evaluation, customer behavior analysis

Applying Template of Codes and Additional Coding

Using the illustration methods [37], the researcher used the codes from the code manual to the interview transcripts with the sake of identifying meaningful portions of the text as showed in Table 5.

Table 5. Sample codes from the initial code manual

Code	Description of code	Matching text
Big data analytics and lack of awareness	Policy makers, decision makers, top managements, data collectors and users have lack of awareness on the application of big data analytics	"There is no awareness about the value of big data in our organizations. But there huge datasets already existed. In every day more than a Tera bytes of data are captured and recorded. When I look other countries' telecom sector they are using big data for different applications/business innovations in the industry"

(continued)

Table 5. (*continued*)

Code	Description of code	Matching text
Big data analytics and infrastructure challenge	Availability of information communication technology infrastructure	"Infrastructure is challenging. The government should work on the designing of central infrastructure that can be used by many institutions at the same time. Building the infrastructure is very expensive. Imagine every company is working to have its own sophisticated data center how much it costs"
Completeness and correctness of data	Participants perception about capturing and storing data by focusing on correctness of data they used	"The image quality that used to capture by data collectors is very low and challenging to identify potential information of customers. Do to image quality too much information of customers' are not registering properly. Therefore, there is information inconsistence"

Based on Tables 2, 3, 4 and 5, the Groundedness and density of each considered using Atals-ti qualitative analysis tool. Table 6 below shows the Groundedness and density. Groundedness refers to total number of quotations linked to a given code. Density is the proportion of documents that link to a given code.

Table 6. Code groundedness and density

No.	Code	Groundedness	Density
1	Big data	15	15
2	Big data analytics	12	11
3	Big data analytics and telecommunication	5	4
4	Big data analytics and agriculture	5	4
5	Big data analytics and payment systems	6	5
6	Big data analytics and education	7	3
7	Big data analytics and lack of awareness	15	5
8	Big data analytics and leadership	5	1
9	Big data and Lack of cheaper data collection tools	7	1
10	Big data analytics and lack of qualified experts in the domain	15	6
11	Big data analytics and infrastructure challenge	17	13
12	Big data analytics and lack of modern data management	3	1
13	Completeness and correctness of data	17	12
14	Data privacy concern	1	1
15	Audio, video, texts, CSV files, image and others.	12	5
16	Big data analytics and lack of standard in data registry	3	1

4.2 Connecting the Codes and Identifying Themes

Connecting codes is the process of discovering themes and patterns in the data [37]. Based on the research question, the main task of this phase is connecting the codes and identifying themes which is shown in below Table 7, 8 and 9.

Definition of Big Data

Table 7 shows that the definition of big data from different viewpoints.

Table 7. Definition of big data by different organizations and researcher

Group	Definition of big data
Education policy makers	It is a huge datasets in different formats. It is different from data which generated from traditional databases
Telecom customer operation manger	Huge datasets generated by the customers, machines with high speed and different formats
Independent researcher	The core part of big data is that the 3 Vs (volume, variety and Velocity) and the Variety term implies that big data often doesn't have a single format. It can be composition of images, text, sensor data, logs and many other
Data analyst from agricultural transformation agency	Data in the form of audio, video, texts, CSV files, image and others and can be collected from different sources frequently. It can be also generated by people from projects
Data analyst from payment system	Data that that is generated by many users frequently with huge volume and can be generated repeatedly by the same customer

Benefits of Big Data Analytics

Table 8. Big data application in different organizations

Group	Benefits of big data analytics
Education institution	It is important for decision making in the educational transformation. The data generated every day from higher educational institutions can help for decision making in the area of intrusion detection, students behavior on social network access, students performance and teachers performance. The data generated by the students from the web portal of each higher education can enable decision maker to give fast and reliable decision at any time
Telecommunication industry	It is important for marketing, sales forecasting, customer behavior identification or customer segmentation, improve customer experiences, forecast network capacity and demand faster, fraud detection, for real time customer insight and

(*continued*)

Table 8. (*continued*)

Group	Benefits of big data analytics
Researchers	It is important for theoretical contributions in different disciplines
Agricultural transformation agency	For weather forecasting, for crop diseases identification, environmental prediction, for project monitoring and evaluation, for country level strategic planning and policy design. It is based on the organization accumulated and daily generated big data
Payment systems	It is important to classify or cluster customers based on their purchasing behaviors on different application or services. It is also important for payment fraud detection and managing risks and for customer transaction activity tasks

Challenges of Big Data Analytics Implementation by Different Organizations

Table 9. Challenges of big data implementation by different organizations

Group	Challenges of big data analytics implementation
Education institution	- Some students provide incomplete data - There is a challenge on awareness - Lack of skilled manpower
Telecommunication industry	- There is a challenge on awareness - Lack of integrated systems that handle all rounded information for a given customer - Infrastructure including storage device challenge - Data privacy challenge - Security is a sensitive issue to innovate the field in the organizations - Lack of Modern Management on big data analytics
Researchers	- Lack of cheaper hardware devices for data collection - There is huge gap in software system automation. And difficult to think about big data before software automation - Difficult to access data from organizations to make researches in the field. - Lack of qualified experts in the field - Infrastructure challenge
Agricultural transformation agency	- Lack of standardized data registry - Low image quality generated by agricultural extension workers which is difficult for analysis and decision making - Lack of qualified experts in the field
Payment systems	- Customer provide incomplete data that is issue of data quality - Having poor infrastructure - Lack of modern management on the big data analytics

4.3 Corroborating and Legitimating Coded Themes

This is the final stage for the further identification of themes to be clustered from the coded text in to 5 clustered themes as showed in Table 10.

Table 10. Corroborating and legitimating coded themes

First ordered theme	Clustered theme	Second order theme
Big data analytics for decision making in the educational transformation Big data analytics for marketing, sales forecasting and customer behavior identification Big data analytics for payment fraud detection Big data analytics for weather forecasting and environmental prediction Big data analytics to manage risks and for customer transaction activity tasks Data incompleteness is challenge for big data analytics Low image quality is challenge for big data analytics implementation Lack of qualified experts is challenge for big data analytics implementation Lack of cheaper data collection tool is challenge for big data analytics implementation Lack of awareness on the application of big data analytics is challenge for big data analytics implementation Lack of leadership and management skill is challenge for big data analytics implementation	Theme 1: Lack of Resources availability is a challenge for big data analytics implementation Theme 2: Data correctness and completeness is a challenge for big data analytics implementation Theme 3: Lack of awareness on the application of big data analytics is a challenge for big data analytics implementation Theme 4: Lack of leadership and management skill is challenge for big data analytics implementation Theme 5: Big data analytics is important for decision making, marketing, sales forecasting and weather forecasting Theme 6: Big data analytics for customer behavior identification, customer transaction activity tasks and payment fraud detection	Accessibility of big data Positive impacts of big data analytics Challenges of identifying and utilizing big data analytics

4.4 Challenges of Identifying and Utilizing BDAs Interrelationship

The following figure shows that the interrelationship of challenges of identifying and utilizing big data analytics in a resource constrained environment. It indicates the challenges of implementation and application of big data analytics interrelationship.

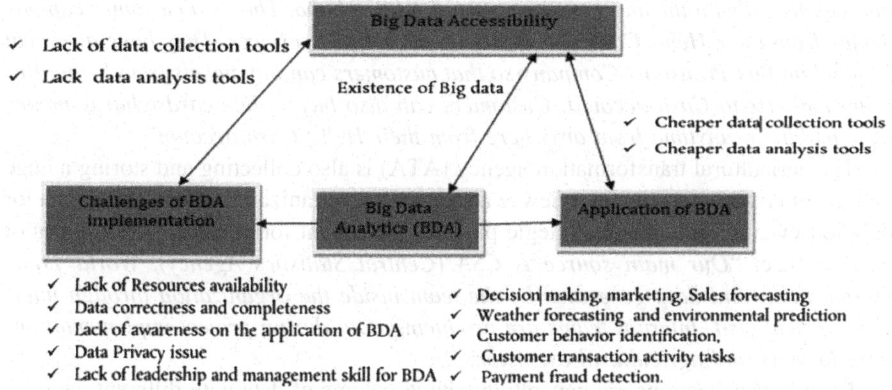

Fig. 1. Utilizing BDAs interrelationship on a resource constrained environment

As shown in Fig. 1 above shows an illustration of the dependencies and feedback loop that exists between the application of big data analytics and challenges of big data analytics implementation in the resources constrained environments in case of Ethiopia.

5 Discussions

The analysis of the semi-structured interview result indicated that all the four participated organizations are producing a huge volume of data, at alarming velocity and different varieties. The independent researcher who is participated in the interviewing process indicated that there are many industries in Ethiopia which are producing big data. However, all the organizations which are participated in the study do not have proper data capturing and handling procedures.

For example in the telecom industry, the interviewee addressed the following issue: "All data from customers are used to capture and store for some duration. Usually from 3 to 6 months. After that, it can be deleted automatically. For some selected users it can be captured and stored for an unlimited period of time. The limit of 3 to 6 months for most users is due to lack of storage devices and not using the datasets for other purposes in most scenarios. Even we look only 994 (call support to help all customers) and 980 (call support to help VIP customers- enterprise companies). For example, 994 customer support service has more than 4,000 employees. One employee can give support for 250 to 260 customers. Averagely more than 1 million customers used to call for asking help in every day. Different kinds of request". This indicated that even if they are generated a huge volume of data from customers they are not storing and applying BDA due to lack of infrastructure.

If we look at the payment system which is participated in this interview, its customers are requested many services. The organization has approximately one million customers. As the interviewee indicated that "*Customers can pay their electricity and water bill. By the way hello cash includes other major businesses services like hello sera, hello doctor and other customer support packages are available. Hello Cash also interconnected with the metro-taxi systems of Addis Ababa. That is a customer can pay money from their Hello Cash account and can get taxi services. They have also deal with Selam Bus Transport Company so that customers can buy tickets from Selam Bus using their Hello Cash account. Customers can also buy mobile cards/charge money their mobile at anytime from anywhere from their Hello Cash account*".

The agricultural transformation agency (ATA) is also collecting and storing a huge volume of datasets. As the interviewee addressed the organization is collecting data for decision making, policy and strategic planning document formulation. The sources of data sets are: "*Our main source is CSA (Central Statistics Agency), World Trade Organization and data generated by the team inside the organization through interview or field visit. Internal teams are producing data during project implementations from farmers and agricultural extensions*".

Even if organizations are generating a huge volume of data with different varieties they are not applying big data analytics. The following are the challenges that were addressed by the interviewees. Most of the challenges are related to lack of awareness, lack of skilled experts, data incompleteness, lack of stabled infrastructure, lack of leadership and management. For example, the interviewee from telecom industry addressed that "The most important or first rank challenge from my experience is having awareness on the usage of big data. There is no awareness of the value of big data in our organizations. But their huge datasets already existed. In every day more than a Terabytes of data are captured and recorded. When I look at other countries' telecom sector they are using big data for different applications/business innovations in the industry. The second challenge is having very low-quality datasets. For example, when customers are purchasing products or applying for some services, they should be registered in a given form with correct data sets. Some lefts empty, some fills with unrelated issues with an answer to be filled for specific questions, some filled text data for an answer that required to be filled with numeric data. The form includes information related to customer information and other issues. The second challenge also raised because of lack of awareness on the value of data. That means the huge datasets that captured from some customers might be garbage. If awareness is coming into the board the data quality issue will be solved. The third challenge is related to infrastructure especially storage capabilities. Our organization used to store a maximum of 6 months for most of the users is due to the lack of having huge storage devices. There is also a lack of leadership and management capabilities of people. Leaders and managers of organizations' used to think that there is not enough data for decision-making. So our country should work on the knowledge capabilities of managers and leaders of organizations".

The interview result from the educational institution addressed the challenges: "I think the fundamental challenge is related to existence awareness. I am considering awareness as the first challenge. The 2nd challenge is related to the knowledge gap. There is a huge skill gap in the know-how of big data applications and tools. The 3rd challenge is related to the preference of commercial big data tools which are too expensive, not focusing on open source technologies. Another challenge is Infrastructure is challenging".

The other challenge addressed by the agricultural transformation agency is related to lack of qualified expert and lack of data processing tool. The interviewee addressed that: “Currently our organization is processing data through Excel. It is challenging to process big data using Excel. This indicates that the shortage of skilled manpower is challenging for big data analytics application in our organization. I think this is the same challenge in other organizations in our country. So lack of skilled manpower and big data production standardization are the main challenge in our organization might be the same throughout the country. The other big issue is due to the lack of standard in data registry. There is no standard in data production. For example, in our organization regions, zones and woredas are producing data. But there is a huge problem in compatibility/consistency and data formats. There are many missing values or incomplete data when they are capturing”.

Interviewees from the different organization have provided different recommendations that have to put for the big data analytics implementation in their organization and in the country level. For example, the interviewee from the telecom industry addressed that: “our country should work on knowledge capabilities of managers and leaders of organizations. In the meantime, the philosophy of big data analytics should come to our country. Because big data analytics can be applied a lot in the area of agriculture, traffic management, health sectors, payment systems and other organizations that can generate huge volume datasets from sensors and social media”.

The interviewee from the educational institution was addressed what their organization or the country should work on the big data analytics in the future: “The government should work on the designing of central infrastructure that can be used by many institutions at the same time. Building infrastructure is very expensive. Imagine every company is working to have its own sophisticated data centre how much it costs”. Some of the challenges were identified in this study were also addressed as a challenge by other scholars in the field. Challenges related to data correctness and data privacy [1, 2, 12]. Some of challenges like having lack of awareness of the application of BDA, lack of resource availability, lack of leadership and management skill were identified as major challenge in this research.

6 Conclusion

In conclusion, big data analytics has numerous application areas in the telecom industry, payment systems, agricultural transformation agency and educational provider companies. The study indicated that all these organizations are generating a huge volume of data with different varieties and speed velocity. However, none of the organizations is applied not big data analytics for decision making, policy formulation and for future strategic planning. Rather they are using manual data analysis and simple office package software for data filtering in some situations. The challenges behind not applying big data analytics by these organizations were identified in the study. The major challenges were identified in the study. These are:

- Organizations have not their own standard in data handling and collection,
- Lack of awareness in the application of big data analytics,
- Lack of management and leadership in the area of big data analytics,
- Lack of qualified experts in the area of big data analytics,

- Lack of data correctness and completeness,
- Lack of stable infrastructure availability: there are no cheap data collection tools and software automation is still behind the current digitalization era.

Even if there are many existing challenges organizations should have come with their own integrated data storage system, cheap data collection tools. In the meantime, the government should give strong emphasis on the application of big data analytics at each organization which are generating a huge volume of data, with different varieties and speedy velocity. The government should also give emphasis on the skilled experts' development for big data analytics. Higher education should give emphasis to the hottest and highly applicable field, big data analytics. New curriculums and should be enforced in the area of big data analytics. Future research should give emphasis on the design and development of cheaper data collection and analysis tools which are more customer services oriented model.

References

1. Assunção, D., Calheiros, N., Bianchi, S., Netto, S., Buyya, R.: Big data computing and clouds. trends and future directions. J. Parallel Distrib. Comput. **79**(80), 3–15 (2015)
2. Ahrens, J., Hendrickson, B., Long, G., Miller, S., Ross, R., Williams, D.: Data-intensive science in the US DOE: case studies and future challenges. Comput. Sci. Eng. **13**(6), 14–23 (2011)
3. Baesens, B., Bapna, R., Marsden, J.R., Vanthienen, J., Zhao, J.L.: Transformational issues of big data and analytics in networked business. MIS Q. **40**(4), 807–818 (2016)
4. Bughin, J.: Reaping the benefits of big data in telecom. J. Big Data **3**(16), 1–17 (2016)
5. Chen, H., Chiang, R., Storey, V.: Business intelligence and analytics: from big data to big impact. MIS Q. **36**(4), 1165–1188 (2012)
6. Chen, M., Mao, S., Liu, Y.: Big data: a survey. Mob. Netw. Appl. **19**(2), 171–209 (2014)
7. Chen, P., Zhang, C.: Data-intensive applications, challenges, techniques and technologies: a survey on big data. J. Inf. Sci. **275**, 314–347 (2014)
8. Cooper, J., Jones, C., Kahn, E., Arbuckle, P.: Big data in life cycle assessment. J. Ind. Ecol. **17**, 796–799 (2013)
9. Daniel, B.: Big data and analytics in higher education: opportunities and challenges. Br. J. Educ. Tech. (2014)
10. Fisher, D., DeLine, R., Czerwinski, M., Drucker, S.: Interactions with big data analytics. Interactions **19**(3), 50–59 (2012)
11. Hashem, I.A.T., Yagoob, I., Anuar, N.B., Mokhtar, S., Gani, A.: The rise of "big data" on cloud computing: review and open research issues. Inf. Syst. **47**, 98–115 (2015)
12. Kaisler, S., Armour, F., Espinosa, J. A., Money, W.: Big data: issues and challenges moving forward (2013)
13. Kamilaris, A., Kartakoullis, A., Prenafeta-Boldú, F.: A review on the practice of big data analysis in agriculture. Comput. Electron. Agric. **143**, 23–37 (2017)
14. Kempenaar, C., et al.: Big Data analysis for smart farming. Wageningen University & Research **655** (2016)
15. Kempster, S., Parry, K.: Critical realism and grounded theory. In: Edwards, P., O'Mahoney, J., Vincent, S. (eds.) Studying Organizations Using Critical Realism: A Practical Guide, pp. 86–108. Oxford University Press, Oxford (2014)

16. Kim, H., Trimi, S., Chung, J.: Big-data applications in the government sector. Commun. ACM **57**(3), 78–85 (2014)
17. Li, H., Lu, X.: Challenges and trends of big data analytics. In: Ninth International Conference on P2P, Parallel, Grid, Cloud and Internet Computing (3PGCIC), Guangzhou China, pp. 566–567 (2014)
18. Lokers, R., Knapen, R., Janssen, S., Randen, Y., Jansen, J.: Analysis of big data technologies for use in agro-environmental science. Environ. Model Softw. **84**, 494–504 (2016)
19. Minimol, A.: An efficient way of applying big data analytics in higher education sector for performance evaluation. Int. J. Comput. Appl. 180(23) (2018)
20. Müller, O., Junglas, I., Brocke, J., Debortoli, S.: Big data analytics for information systems research: challenges, promises and guidelines. Eur. J. Inf. Syst. **25**(4), 1–14 (2016)
21. Nandyala, C., Kim, K.: Big and meta data management for U-agriculture mobile services. Int. J. Softw. Eng. Appl. (IJSEIA) **10**, 257–270 (2016)
22. Ravisankar, K., Sidhardha, K., Prabadevi, B.: Analysis of agricultural data using big data analytics. J. Chem. Pharm. Sci. **10**, 1132–1135 (2017)
23. Seddon, J., Currie, W.: A model for unpacking big data analytics in high-frequency trading. J. Bus. Res. **70**, 300–307 (2017)
24. Sonka, S.: Big data: fueling the next evolution of agricultural innovation. J. Innov. Manag. **4** (1), 114–136 (2016)
25. Sun, N., Morris, J.G., Xu, J., Zhu, X., Xiek, M.: iCARE: A framework for big data-based banking customer analytics. IBM **58**, 4:1–4:9 (2014)
26. Bates, D.W., Saria, S., Ohno-Machado, L., Shah, A., Escobar, G.: Big data in health care: using analytics to identify and manage high-risk and high-cost patients. Health Aff. **33**(7), 1123–1131 (2014)
27. Waga, D., Rabah, K.: Environmental conditions' big data management and cloud computing analytics for sustainable agriculture. World J. Comput. Appl. Technol. **2**(3), 73–81 (2014)
28. Yongjun, H., Ming, F., Shengyong, D., Yongbing, F.: Big data development strategy for telecom operators. Telecommun. Sci. 3(2) (2013)
29. Youssef, G., Mouhcine, G., Hussein, T.: Big Data Analytics: Security and Privacy Challenges. In: IEEE Symposium on Computers and Communication (ISCC) (2016)
30. Brra, J., Hanseth, O., Heywood, A.: Developing health information systems in developing countries: the flexible standards strategy. MIS Q. **31**(2), 381–402 (2007)
31. Wang, R., Strong, D.: What data quality means to data consumers. J. Manag. Inf. Syst. **12**(4), 5–33 (1996)
32. Ghazisaeidi, M., Safdari, R., Torabi, M., Mahboobeh, M., Jebraeil, F., Azadeh, G.: Development of performance dashboards in healthcare sector: key practical issues. J. Acad. Med. Sci. Bosnia Herzegovina **23**(5), 317–321 (2015)
33. Klein, H., Myers, M.: Set of principles for conducting and evaluating interpretive field studies in Information systems. MIS Q. **23**, 67–94 (1999)
34. Walsham, G.: Interpretive case studies in IS research: nature and method. Eur. J. Inf. Syst. **4** (2), 74–81 (1995)
35. Boyatzis, R.: Transforming Qualitative Information: Thematic Analysis and Code Development. Sage Publications, Inc., Thousand Oaks (1998)
36. Fereday, J., Muir-Cochrane, E.C.: Demonstrating rigor using thematic analysis: a hybrid approach of inductive and deductive coding and theme development. Int. J. Q. Methods **5**(1), 1–11 (2006)

37. Crabtree, B., Miller, W.: A template approach to text analysis: developing and using codebooks. In: Doing qualitative research, pp. 163–177. Sage, Newbury Park (1999)
38. Duan, Y., Edwards, J.S., Dwivedi, Y.K.: Artificial intelligence for decision making in the era of big data–evolution, challenges and research agenda. Int. J. Inf. Manag. **48**, 63–71 (2019)
39. Dwivedi, Y.K., et al.: Driving innovation through big open linked data (BOLD): exploring antecedents using interpretive structural modelling. Inf. Syst. Front. **19**(2), 197–212 (2017)

Understanding Public Sector Enterprise Resource Planning System Implementation in Developing Countries: A Literature Review

David Mpanga(✉)

Bugema University, P. O. Box 6529, Kampala, Uganda
d.mpanga@bugemauniv.ac.ug

Abstract. This paper is a literature review of articles on implementation of Enterprise Resource Planning (ERP) in public sector with a focus on developing countries. The aim of the paper is to present an in depth understanding of the implementation of ERP systems in developing countries public sector. It intends to help researchers interested in the topic to have a single source of reference, and to understand the state of ERP implementation in developing countries public sector. A systematic literature review methodology was adopted for an in-depth review of journals, conference proceedings and reviews. The review covered a range from 1998 to 2018; 72 were related to public sector. Developing countries contribute only 5% to the ERP research in public sector. The major themes identified include genesis of ERP, implementing ERP, CSF for implementing ERP, ERP implementing frameworks/methodologies, impact of ERP on Business Processes, ERP market, ERP cost and failure, and ERP trends. Findings on each theme are discussed. Areas are recommended that need to be understood in context of developing countries public sector; external and internal opposing factors, specific CSF/CFF, ERP implementing framework/methodologies, Total Cost of Ownership, ERP integration and ERP framework/architecture to ensure successful implementation of ERP and reduce cost.

Keywords: ERP · Public sector · Developing countries · Enterprise systems · CSF · CFF

1 Introduction

Many organizations have implemented information systems in order to improve efficiency in service delivery. However, information systems specific to given function area create distributed silos of heterogeneous data, inaccessible across the organization. This affects decision making at organizational level due to lack of access to organization wide real time information. Consequently the agility of the organization to promptly respond to business needs is constrained. Large organization in developed economies initiated implementation of enterprise information systems to overcome challenges caused by function-oriented information systems (Rajapakse and Seddon 2005). Among the different types of enterprise information systems, Enterprise Resource Planning (ERP) system is the most popular. ERP design is based on widely accepted best practices in a given industry be it private or public sector. Implementation of ERP system in an organization is intended to integrate business processes across

Published by Springer Nature Switzerland AG 2019
Y. Dwivedi et al. (Eds.): TDIT 2019, IFIP AICT 558, pp. 255–273, 2019.
https://doi.org/10.1007/978-3-030-20671-0_18

functional areas to enhance efficiency and effectiveness in service or product delivery in a manner universally accepted in a particular industry (Rajapakse and Seddon 2005).

Liu et al. (2011) argue that ERP implementations are the most difficult projects to undertake because of their complexity, high cost and adaptation risks. The complexity of ERP system originate from inherent business processes to ERP system. Often the recipient organization is required to redesign the organization business processes to fit ERP system. On the other hand customization of the ERP system could be carried out to fit the ERP system in the recipient organization business processes. Though numerous researchers have contributed to the field of ERP systems in regard to Critical Success Factors (CSF), Critical Failure Factors (CFF), and implementing methodologies, most of the research is private sector oriented, and from developed economies. Meaningful interaction with the citizenry and business requires integration of ERP system with other applications. Hence, there is a need to build capabilities to manage and improve relationships with business and citizenry in a seamless Government-to-Business (G2B) and Government-to-Citizenry (G2C) environment. Governments in developing countries promote Public-Private-Partnership (PPP) as strategy to increase efficiency in service delivery. The success of the public sector in developing countries to deliver quality services efficiently, will depend on the ability to integrate the diverse network of stakeholders' relationships.

ERP systems are independent solutions that cannot integrate all interaction processes in public sector environment. An effective service delivery model in public sector organizations require leveraging the functionalities of the ERP system with another enterprise application (Baran 2012).

Hence, an inevitable need arise to improve the interactions with suppliers of services and goods by integrating ERP with applications that provide interface with e-commerce solutions.

ERP systems in public sectors have to be extended to create links with other application like Customer Services Management (CSM) to manage service agreements, Supplier Relationship Management (SRM) to manage suppliers' relationships, and Citizenry Relationship Management (CRM) to manage citizens' interactions. These solutions are stand-alone systems with the aim to support different functions (Beal 2017). Integration of ERP systems with another application that manage front-end processes eliminate duplication of information and reduce IT costs and expenses related to training (Kolisnyk 2018).

ERP systems vendors are penetrating developing countries public sector, in anticipation to provide solutions that deliver efficiency similar to developed countries public sector. However, public sectors in developing countries are characterized by specific laws and government regulations, as well as specific ways of doing business that are different from those in the West (Bitsini 2015). These unique characteristics are likely to cause technology, information and roles misalignments or misfits between the best practices of a Western-designed ERP system and the organizational context in developing countries (Bitsini 2015).

Prior to this article, there is no literature review on implementing ERP systems in developing country public sector is identified. Hence, the article contributions to the knowledge of ERP systems implementation with a focus on public sector in developing countries. First, it is the first single source of reference for ERP systems implementation in developing country public sector. Secondary, the article provides a background for identifying areas that need to be understood to successfully implement ERP systems in developing countries public sector domain.

Objective
The objective of the research was to collect and analyse literature on the implementation of ERP systems in developing countries public sectors. The question the article attempts to answer is; how successful is the implementation of ERP systems in developing countries public administration? It is important to understand ERP systems in context of public sectors in developing countries; ERP systems have transformed private sector organizations and now are gaining acceptance in the public sectors (Kelemen 2014). Secondary, ERP systems were primarily targeted at private companies, though public organizations in developed economies have invested considerable resources in the implementation of these systems Alves and Matos (2011). Still the continued high failure rates with enterprise resource planning (ERP) systems remain a great concern (Ram et al. 2013). Also many ERP systems' failures in developing countries are associated with the misalignment of requirements between ERP systems and implementing organizations (Morton and Hu 2008; Roseann and Weber 2004; Strong and Volkoff 2010).

Overview of the Paper
In this article implementing ERP systems in developing countries public sector is analysed to identify the major themes researched. Secondly, the concept of cloud ERP systems is investigated in context of developing countries. A discussion of the finding is provided, and the article conclude with areas that need to be understood further.

2 Methodology

A systematic literature review (SLR) methodology for conducting a high quality standalone literature review in Information Systems field was adopted as the author of the article didn't collect or analyze any primary data (Okoli 2015). SLR methodology was considered the most appropriate for a rigorous review intended to summarize existing evidence, identify gaps in current research, and provide a basis for research endeavors in ERP systems in developing countries public sectors.

2.1 Sources of Reviewed Papers

Papers reviewed were accessed from 25 International journals indicated in Table 1, four conference/conventional proceedings, and five international reviews listed in Table 2. The research covered articles in the range from 1998 to 2018. A list of search words including Enterprise systems, public sector ERP, Enterprise Resource Planning, developing countries public were used to search the literature using Google scholar.

Selection of papers was based on three key terms; ERP implementation, public sector ERP and ERP in developing countries/economies. Paper were categorized as relevant when the author talked about ERP systems and referred to public sector globally in the text, and. papers selected in this category were 65. A second category

Table 1. Journal sources

Journal title
Journal of Enterprise Information Management
Journal of Business Administration and Management Sciences Research
Journal of the Association for Information Systems
European Journal of Information Systems
International Journal of Human–Computer Interaction
Business Process Management Journal
Information Systems Management
Journal of Enterprise Information Systems
Journal of Public Administration Research and Theory
Journal of Enterprise Resource Planning Studies
Journal of Business Administration and Management Sciences Research
Communications Of The ACM
Journal of Information Technology
Communications of the Association for Information Systems
Journal of Operations Management
Journal of Management Information Systems
The Journal of Systems and Software
Business & Information Systems Engineering
ACM Computing Surveys
International Journal of Human Computer Interaction
Communications of the IBIMA
OECD Journal on Budgeting
Journal of the Faculty of Economic & Administrative Sciences
Interdisciplinary Journal of Information, Knowledge, and Management
Journal of Enterprise Resource Planning Studies

Table 2. Reviews and Conferences

Reviews	Conventions/Conferences
Public Administration Review	International Conference on Information Systems (ICIS)
Harvard Business Review	2004 Proceedings
American review of public administration	Electronics and Microelectronics (MIPRO), 2014 37th International Convention
Government Information Quarterly	European Conference on Information Systems (2000)
MIS Quarterly	International Conference on System Sciences (2001)

was the contextual category; the article was about ERP systems in the context of a developing country, and the themes discussed are specifically focused on ERP in developing country. This category has 7 papers. A third category was the specific category; article fully dedicated to ERP systems in developing country public sector, and no paper identified in this category.

2.2 Themes Identified

This section provides a critical review of the common themes discussed in various articles on ERP. Common themes identified in articles reviewed include the genesis of ERP systems, critical success factors for implementing ERP, ERP implementation cost and failure, ERP implementing frameworks/methodologies, ERP market and Trends in ERP systems. ERP themes that have no article related to developing countries are identified in Table 3.

Table 3. Themes published about ERP by category

Theme	Author
ERP generally (one article related to public sector, but not in developing country context)	Sprecher (1999), Kumar and Van Hillegersberg (2000), Periseraset and Tarabanis (2000), Allen et al. (2002), Sally and Arnold (2002), Huang et al. (2004), Wagner and Antonucci (2004), Alshawi et al. (2004), Robert and Weston (2007), Tregear and Jenkins (2007), Liu et al. (2011), Nazami et al. (2012) and Bailey et al. (2015)
Implementing ERP (three articles related to public sector and two of which refer to developing countries)	Klaus et al. (2000), Ahituv et al. (2002), Addo-Tenkorang and Helo (2011), Abdelghaffar (2012), Sommer (2011), Abdelghaffar (2012), Ziemba and Oblak (2013), Columbus (2014) and Kelemen (2014)
ERP implementation Critical Success Factors (two article related to public sector in developing country context)	Esteves and Bohorques (2007), Frimpon (2012), Njihia and Mwirigi (2014), Kalema et al. (2014) and Simone et al. (2018)
ERP cost and failure rate (Three article related to developing country public sector context)	Bancroft et al. (1998), Govindaraju (2012), Kamhawi (2008), Soja and Paliwoda-Pekosz (2009), Seddon et al. (2010), Hawari and Heeks (2010), Lutovac and Manojlov (2012), Rouhania and Ravasan (2012), Ram et al. (2013), Harb and Twak (2015) and Bitsini (2015)
ERP Market (one article which mention developing country but not specifically public sector)	Dezdar and Ainin (2011), Shaul and Tauber (2013)

(*continued*)

Table 3. (*continued*)

Theme	Author
ERP implementing frameworks/methodology (One article related to public sector, but not in developing country context)	DiMaggio and Powell (1983), Levinson (1988), Govindaraju (2012), Parr and Shanks (2000), Shanks et al. (2000), Markus and Tanis (2000), Ross and Vitale's Model (2000), Somers and Nelson (2004), Benders et al. (2006), Bjørn-Andersen and Johansson (2007), Baxter (2010), Dantes and Hasibuan (2011), Sommer (2011), Govindaraju (2012) and Ziemba and Oblak (2013)
ERP trends (One article mentioning developing countries, but not specifically public sector domain)	Bailey et al. (2010), Bernd and Arne (2012), Saini (2011) and Tripti (2013)

3 Literature Review

3.1 Genesis of ERP Systems

Enterprise Resource Planning (ERP) was coined in the early 1990 by Gartner Group (Robert and Weston 2007). In private sectors both ERP software vendors and users understand technical, human resource, and financial resources requirements for ERP systems implementation. According to Columbus (2014) a successful ERP systems implementation requires strategic, innovative implementation and deployment approaches that incorporate business process management. ERP systems provide real-time access to information from various business processes integrating different functions (Nah et al. 2001; Al-Mashari 2003; Alsene 2007). Introduction of ERP systems in developing countries can be traced way back in 1990s. Since mid-1990's, many public sector organizations have followed the private sector to implement pre-packaged commercial ERP solutions in favor of a proprietary systems (Sommer 2011).

3.2 Implementing ERP System

Literature reveals an increasing demand for quality services in both public and private sectors. Periseras et al. (2000) and Liu and Lai (2004) observed that citizens in many countries expect public administration to provide quality services at the lowest cost. The need exists to implement technology that can increase efficiency, enhance process transparency and communication within public administration. Thus, in developing countries, enterprise systems are increasingly gaining popularity in public administration. However, according to Seddon et al. (2010) traditional implementation of ERP systems often cost millions or even hundreds of millions of dollars. Ziemba and Oblak (2013) state that information system implementation is a complex exercise in technology innovation. Organizational change management is also difficult in enterprises (Kumar et al. 2002; Markus and Tanis 2000).

Successful implementation of enterprise system may not easily be completed in short term. Hence, it requires top-level political will as any change in the existing public sector practices requires a review of legal framework. Most government agencies utilize experiences from private sectors to implement enterprise systems (Watson et al. 2003). As a result, public sectors often adopt generalized private sector ERP implementation approaches. In developed countries, the public sector administration and business processes are reformed to reflect those in the private sectors; hence, it is appropriate to adopt private sector ERP implementing approaches developing country environment. The public sector environment in developing countries is characterized by unique cultural, structural, political, and economic complexities.

Management of information systems in public sector organizations vary significantly from those of the private organizations (Bozeman and Bretschneider 1986; Bretschneider 1990). According to Bretschneider (1990) and Cats-Baril et al. (1995) variations of public sectors from private sectors can be attributed to a number of characteristics. These include interdependencies across the organizational boundaries, higher levels of red-tape, different evaluation criteria for purchasing software, extra organizational linkages, and top-level implementation management officials. In many developing countries, public sector management activities experience strong external forces. The significant forces that influence public administration functions include legislations and regulations, international funding agencies and political interference. Hence, the public sector environment in many developing countries is different from the public and private sectors in developed countries.

Bozeman and Bretschneider (1986) suggested four "models of publicness" that distinguish between public and private sector information systems. In the functioning of public administration, economic authority model play a secondary role. In private sector the emphasis is on productivity, bureaucratic regulations in public sector and political authority model, the emphasis is on political influence and monitoring mechanisms.

Bingi et al. (1999) and Davenport (1998) state that ERP system implementations generally involve massive organizational changes. The changes are a result of the shift from existing business processes to best practices inherent in ERP systems. Organizational changes required to implement ERP system include strategic areas to eliminate data silos, technology infrastructure, organization culture, management systems, human resources skills and structures (Al-Mashari 2003). These changes have widespread impacts on various departments or agencies of the organization. The strong interdependence of government entities pose a high risk failure to ERP system implementation. Successful ERP system implementations require top management commitment. (Huang et al. 2004; Somers et al. 2001; Grossman and Walsh 2004; Umble et al. 2002).

Documented models of ERP systems implementation comprise of different stages. Some researchers suggest a three-stage model (Parr and Shanks 2000; Ahituv et al. 2002). Markus and Tanis (2000) proposed a four-stage model. Most of the proposed models categorize activities into: before the project, the project stage and post-project undertakings. ERP implementation studies are commonly conducted in two approaches. The variance approach is focused on critical success factors for successful implementation of an ERP system. The process approach focuses on the change management process by identifying the dialectic forces that cause change during the ERP implementation process (Robey et al. 2002). The process approach highlights the difficulties in business process mapping, infrastructure problems, lack of technical knowledge of the key-users, difficulties in procurement of hardware, codification of master data, difficulties in collection of data, and change of implementation partners (Madhavi 2008).

According to Akkermans and Helden (2002) ERP implementations are usually large and complex projects. Faced with many unforeseen developments and resources, and involve big groups of people work under considerable time pressure. Not surprisingly, many of these implementations turn out to be less successful than originally intended (Davenport 1998; Avnet 1999; Buckhout et al. 1999).

Integrated information flows can support government processes in numerous ways to improve service delivery, accountability, and managing for results. Unfortunately, most of the literature on ERP implementation is limited to the private sector, and as such neglects a substantial uniqueness of the public sector constraint. Gulledge and Sommer (2003) argue that there is nothing special about public sector business processes that insulate them from modern private sector management methods. However, it should be noted that this argument is made in context of developed economies, where the public sector undertook the initiative to adopt private sector management structure. This is not the same experience in developing economies where skills, financing, political influences, and entrenched bureaucracy, are critical constraints in public administration.

The hierarchical organizational structure in the public sector is quite different from organizational structure in private sector. Majchrzak and Wang (1996) state that it is extremely difficult to implement process management in hierarchically managed organizations. Sommer (2011) argue that public administration has characteristics including; cultural, political, and organizational factors that negatively influence successful ERP implementation in local government administration. Tregear and Jenkins (2007) presents a list of nine key differences between the public sector and private sector. The differences include public interest, accountability, political sensitivity, whole-of-government ecosystem, budget cycle complexity, information exchange, regulating society, machinery of government changes, and culture. These differences should be considered when developing approaches to process-based management and ERP implementation in a developing country public sector organization.

One of the major changes at different levels of government is the attempt to implement best practices modeled after those of the private sector (Caudle 1996). The private or public sectors' best practices from developed countries imbedded in the ERP systems are far different from developing countries environment. Raymond et al. (2005) argue that each sector is confronted with specific environmental constraints, the transfer of IT practices from the private to the public sector would not occur automatically. Ziemba and Oblak (2013) indicated that processes in public administration have completely different characteristics compared to private organizations. Contrary to public sector, private sector processes can be improved almost anytime as organization's need emerge (Schäfermeyer et al. 2012). ERP systems are generally designed for private sector and do not meet specific public administration requirements (Ziemba and Oblak 2013).

3.3 ERP Implementing Framework/Methodologies

Govindaraju (2012) suggested an organizational perspective framework for implementing ES; focusing on two stages in ES implementation process including project stage and post project stage. Further recommend that enterprise system implementation effectiveness need to be analyzed at two levels: short term implementation effectiveness, related to the outcome of the project stage, and the long-term implementation effectiveness, related to the outcome of the post-project stage.

Dantes and Hasibuan (2011) proposed an ERP implementing conceptual framework considering two dimensions. The ERP implementation process that have five stages: project preparation, technology selection, project formulation, implementation and post-implementation. Somers and Nelson (2004) identified six stages of ERP implementation process: initiation, adoption, adaptation, acceptance, routinization, and infusion.

Ahituv et al. (2002) developed a generic hybrid ERP implementation methodology combining three structured approaches: Structured Development Life Cycle (SDLC), Prototyping and application package model. He contend that the uniqueness of ERP system renders any of the three models inadequate to be adopted solely in implementation of ERP system.

Most ERP vendors propose frameworks specific to their ERP solution to simplify the implementation process. Some of the major vendor specific frameworks include: Accelerated SAP (ASAP) by SAP, Application Implementation Method (AIM) by Oracle, Direct Path by PeopleSoft and Dynamic Enterprise Modeler by BAAN (Benders et al. 2006). Vendor specific frameworks coerce client organizations to compromise their core business processes for the sake of conforming to the vendor's prescribed implementing framework; a concept of isomorphism, DiMaggio and Powell (1983).

3.4 ERP Market

Despite the wide adoption of ERP systems, the biggest share is in developed economies, and the adoption rate in developing countries is very low more so in Africa. Shaul and Tauber (2013) indicated that ERP market was occupied 66% by North America; Europe had 22%, whereas the whole of Asia was at 9%, Africa share an estimate of only 3%.

3.5 Impact of ERP on Business Processes

Literature cite Bozeman (1993) arguing that one of the main characteristics of the public sector is the large number of formal processes that appear to be essential to ensure that the public sector functions. Successful Information System implementation requires sufficient attention to policy, processes, structure, laws, and regulations (Rose and Grant 2010). ERP systems provide an environment for business process alignment and management, and seamless flow of data and information across silo function areas. Gulledge and Sommer (2003) noted that process management is a prerequisite for successful implementation of business process-oriented enterprise systems. Localized implementations of process management have been prevalent for years (Grass 1956).

Technology adaptation in public or private sector, should be considered only to provide capabilities to support business processes deliver efficiency and effectiveness to service delivery, and deliver value to the customer (Davenport and Short 1990). Hence, the public sector should consider the primary benefits of process management to ensure alignment of cross-functional processes prior to implementation of a technology solution to support enterprise functions (Gulledge and Sommer 2002). Columbus (2014) observed that successful ERP systems implementation requires strategic, innovative implementation and deployment approaches that incorporate business process management.

According to Gulledge and Sommer (2002) business process management has received much attention in the private sector management literature, and its benefits are well known; much less has been written in the public sector management literature, and what has been written has been very general.

3.6 Trends in ERP System

Hawari and Heeks (2010) argued that the designer of the ERP software package assumed the existence of a strong local area network, servers, personal computers and broadband internet connections. Many developing countries, more so the public sectors are not yet at the level of developed countries when it comes to technology and related infrastructure. According to Saini et al. (2011) cloud computing is a new paradigm in which computing resources such as processing, memory, and storage are not physically present at the user's location. Instead, a service provider owns and manages these resources, and users access them via the Internet. The greatest challenge of ERPs is the costs related to these systems implementation which includes investing to acquire software, hardware, consultant fees, in-house staff (in charge of the installation process), staff operating on the system and the user training (Trimi et al. 2005). Armbrust et al. (2010) stated that these ERP systems can be provided in an easier and more attractive way by their provision over the cloud. Lechesa et al. (2012) stated that ERP systems are also delivered as SaaS (Software as a Service), and is increasingly adopted in the global market.

Baxter (2010) indicated that there does not appear to be one best model for the implementation of ERP system, and suggest that applying traditional methods to an ERP development project does not work. Navaneethakrishnan (2013) suggest that cloud computing gives organization all the services of computing, networking and data storage from a distinct location. Public authorities or government could benefit from these advantages by adopting cloud computing (Bernd and Arne 2012). The analysis of Alford (2009) as cited by Bernd and Arne (2012) implies that over a 13-years lifecycle the implementation costs for cloud computing would be more than 60% lower than setting up a traditional data center. Bernd and Arne (2012) argued that these advantages make cloud computing also very interesting to be adopted in the public sector and e-Government.

One of the benefits of Cloud technology to public administration is to eliminate the necessity of setting up an own IT infrastructure, hence, decreasing investment and administrative expenditures (Bernd and Arne 2012). More benefits of cloud computing for government are listed by Bhisikar (2011) including increased flexibility, access everywhere, elastic scalability and pay-as-you-go, easy implementation, service quality, sharing documents and group collaboration, data recovery, distributed data centers and availability of software updates. Maliza et al. (2012) cites Mozammel-Bin-Motalab and Shohag (2011) who argued that cloud enterprise systems is simple to deploy, and it represents the latest, greatest, and most influential IT change in years.

Vendors of Cloud ERP Systems manage, maintain and deploy IT infrastructure. Consequently, reduce the IT complexity that users face when implementing an enterprise system (Maliza et al. 2012). In the same line, Beaubouef (2011) argued that no further IT investment is required in terms of infrastructure, software and support resources upgrading. According to Bailey et al. (2010) local government administration should move aggressively to cloud computing in order to achieve service improvements and cost efficiencies.

3.7 CSF for Implementing ES

Enterprise systems CSFs in the public sector domain are grouped into: procurement procedure, government processes management, project team competence, and project management process (Ziemba and Oblak 2013; Hasibuan and Dantes 2012). Wang et al. (2008) further considered the importance of: top management support, vender's support, consultant's competence, users' support, IT capability, and project management leadership; to mitigate the costly failure of ERP system implementation. Ustasüleyman and Percin (2010) considers project management, consultant planning activities and internal audit to be significant in predicting the ERP implementation success. Many developing countries still experience severe constraints in these dimensions.

During the implementation of enterprise systems, often the business must be modified to fit the system (Davenport 1998). This means the organizations' business processes need to be reengineered to fit the best practices that comprise the system. This considerably add to the expense and risk of introducing enterprise systems (Kumar and Van Hillegersberg 2000; Markus and Tanis 2000). Moreover, vendors try to structure the systems to reflect best practices, but it is the vendor, not the costumer who define what "best" means (Davenport 1998). Hence, the adopting organization is dependent on the vendor for updates of the package (Markus and Tanis 2000).

Abdelghaffar (2012) identified ten factors which had impact on ERP implementation in Egypt. Authors identified different CSFs, and also categorized them differently: Kelemen (2014) proposed 37; Frimpon (2012) identified 28, all obtained from literature review, and Frimpon (2012) identified 5 from SMEs in Kenya. However, ERP system design assumes a set of organizational processes that match the best practice in the industry (Strong and Volkoff 2010). Hence, the importance of a factor may differ from one context to another (Momoh and Shehab 2010).

3.8 ERP Implementation Cost and Failure

Implementation of ERP systems in the public sector is considered to be challenging and require enormous investment and still with risk of failure (Kelemen 2014). According to Bjørn-Andersen and Johansson (2007) the implementation of ERP project itself is far more expensive than the costs of the software licenses. Organizations leaders usually were unsatisfied with ERP implementation timelines, regularly exceeding two years (Bozaa et al. 2015). Exceeding timelines is caused by: inadequate preparation, lack of knowledge and experience, inability to predict and find an appropriate solution. According to Rouhania and Ravasan (2012) these projects are on average 178% over budget, take 2.5 times longer than intended, and deliver only 30% of the promised benefit. Harb and Twak (2015) further cite Lutovac and Manojlov (2012) that more than 80% of companies in Indonesia failed to implement ERP and 50% of companies in the world failed to obtain the optimal return value. Wu et al. (2008) and Kwahk and Ahn (2010) and Salmeron and Lopez (2010) list a number of failed ERP systems implementations with magnitude of financial losses; resulted from not properly implementing ERP systems. Most developing countries public sector administration often rely on borrowed or donor funds. Hence, ERP systems implementation projects require extra caution to mitigate ES implementation failure.

Nazemi et al. (2012) found out that the total cost including: hardware, software, professional services, training, and internal staff costs could range between \$300 and \$400 million with an average of \$15 million. This average cost is close to the US \$ 30 to US\$70 stated by (Rodin-Brown 2008). As a consequence some developing countries continue to run enterprise systems not successfully implemented that constrain the ES efficiency (Rodin-Brown 2008).

The continued high failure rates with enterprise resource planning (ERP) systems remain a great concern (Ram et al. 2013). Most of ERP systems' failures in developing countries are attributed to misalignment of requirements between ERP systems and implementing organizations (Morton and Hu 2008; Rosemann et al. 2004; Strong and Volkoff 2010). Misalignment originate from mismatches in different contexts where ERP system is developed. Dezdar and Ainin (2011) argued that when organizations implement an ERP system that was developed in a different social context, they are more likely to experience misalignment or misfit embedded within software packages with business models designers believe represent the best practice in certain contexts (Rosemann et al. 2004). Software packages are subjected to institutional procedures, processes and forces that set rules of rationality (Gosain 2004). The standard practice in many ERP implementations force a match between client business processes and ERP system design through business process reengineering (BPR) resulting into massive changes and ultimately lead to failure (Hawari and Heeks 2010).

Nevertheless, Information Technology (IT) governance and Total Cost of Ownership (TCO) could be another source of ERP system implementation failure. IT governance has two aspects, information technology resource management and performance measurement, that impact the alignment of the organization and the IT solutions. These IT governance components have significant positive impact on alignment of IT with business strategies (Mohammad 2012). IT governance provides a description of the deployment of information technology in an organization. The IT governance also provides the leadership, organizational structure and processes to ensure that the implemented IT sustain and support organization's strategy (Broadbent et al. 2002). During the implementation of ERP system, IT governance team assess the IT infrastructure, and implement a framework to calculate the ERP system TCO. TCO is a comprehensive system approach that enable management make better decisions in regard to direct and indirect costs associated with IT resources. Any organization attempting to implement ERP system need a TCO framework to enable better decision making in regard to ERP implementation project. Though in many cases the TCO is consider under the purchasing cost, underestimating hidden costs of technology solutions can result into implementation failure. A comprehensive TCO framework captures ERP implementation cost from the onset to post implementation of the project. Literature on ERP system TCO is sparse, hence, lack of clear understanding of ERP TCO is likely to be one of the major causes of budget overrun.

4 Findings and Discussion

Research on ERP in public sector is still low more so in developing countries. Out of 112 article relevant to ERP that were reviewed, 72 were related to public sector. Developing countries contribute only 5% to the ERP research in public sector. Though there is an increase in ERP adoption in the public sector, in many aspects developing countries are far less than developed countries; caused by differences in technological advancements and supporting infrastructure. The growth of ERP implementation in developing countries is not supported by literature indicating reduction in failure rate. Factors associated with lack of skills and technology, absence of good quality data, lack of money, user resistance and cultural issues identified by Hawari and Heeks (2010), Kamhawi (2008), Soja and Paliwoda-Pekosz (2009) and are still prevailing. The ERP design – reality gap identified by Hawari and Heeks (2010) is still one of the key causes of ERP implementation failures in developing countries due to adoption of developed country perspective solutions. The challenges are even more pronounced in developing countries public domain, where business processes are highly hieratical; culture and business practices reinforced by poor motivation. The practice of reengineering business process to fit the recipient organization into ERP best practice framework reinforce the challenge. Hawari and Heeks (2010) argue that Standard practice in many ERP implementations has been to force a match between client business processes and ERP system design through business process reengineering (BPR) which results in too much change and ultimately leads to failure. Understanding the critical success factors or rather critical failure factors for implementing ERP systems in developing countries public sector in critical to reduce the design- reality gap. Understanding ERP system has to be contextualized because of the conflicting ideas that emanate from the fact that there are no universal best practices that fit different industries and environments, and particularly developing countries (Bitsini 2015).

Though the impact of ERP system on business processes and job environments are not among the identified themes discussed in the context of public sector, they prominently future in private sector. ERP fundamentally impact on the business processes and the work practices. In public sector environment more so in developing countries where political, legislative, and financial constraint are high, a successful implementation of ERP in such environment require an attention on public sector business processes. Columbus (2014) observed that successful ERP systems implementation requires strategic, innovative implementation and deployment approaches that incorporate business process management. Bailey et al. (2017) found that ERP systems affect the quality of work life, in a study from African countries. This is likely to be caused by business process improvement, which result into the demand of new set of skills and different work practices.

Implementation of ERP system touches the core process of the business. Hence, adoption of a hybrid methodology universally is likely to result into unexpected failure due to cultural, organizational and political influences experienced in environments that are characteristically different. Existing frameworks/methodologies are private sector based and focus on what should be done at a particular stage with no consideration of variations in different domains. Characteristic variations between private sector and public sector significantly impact on the way activities are carried out in a given environment. ERP implementation in developing countries should also take into account the fact that developing countries have limited resources unlike the developed countries. Hence, ERP systems implementation process should be administered differently as suggested by Addo-Tenkorang and Helo (2011). Sommer (2011) state that public administration has characteristics including: cultural, political, and organizational factors that negatively influence successful ERP implementation in local government administration.

Research Implication

Shaul and Tauber (2013) findings indicated that ERP market was occupied 66% by North America; Europe had 22%, whereas the whole of Asia was at 9%, Africa share an estimate of only 3%; this gives an indication on why ERP issues in developing countries are not well researched, hence, not well understood. Dwivedi et al. (2014) envisaged the need to extend ERP research focus to include further public sector ERP systems implementation. The market percentage also don't separate the private from public sectors. However, from a business perspective this gives an indication on the ERP market trend being focused towards developing countries as they provide unsaturated market. Hence, developing countries have become a major target for ERP vendors (Dezdar and Ainin 2011). The academic perspective, a percentage of only 5.04 research work done on ERP subject in developing countries, is an indicator of inadequate understanding of the subject in various aspects. Developing countries are still highly constrained with Information Technology infrastructure required to implement ERP systems. However, the proliferation of cloud computing technology promise ERP systems provisioning opportunities. It is important to understanding how cloud facility with "pay-as-use" and SaaS provisioning present opportunities of implementing ERP in developing countries public sector at far lower infrastructure costs and skills requirements despite other underlying issues. Though literature promote cloud computing benefits to be adopted in the public sector and e-Government (Bernd and Arne 2012).

5 Conclusion

In this paper reviewed 112 articles and identified 74 articles with relevance to public sector. Out of which only 5% of these articles were related to ERP in developing countries. However, the major themes identified include; genesis of ERP, CSF/CFF, ERP implementation cost and failure, ERP implementation frameworks/ Methodologies, ERP market and trends. A critical analysis of these themes is carried out to highlight the available knowledge and gaps on ERP in public sectors in developing countries.

Limitations and Feature Research

The search didn't reveal substantial literature on developing country public sector issues. Identified literature does not also clearly distinguish public sector organisations, like agencies or authorities, from public sector administrations like local governments. Policies, regulations, business processes and mandates of public sector institutions differ from those of public administration. Most of the identified research on developing country public sectors focus on non-administrative public sectors (Simone et al. 2018). Successful implementation of ERP systems in developing countries public sectors requires understanding of: the policy and regulatory frameworks relevant to developing country unique challenges; impacts caused by external influences like donor funding and vendor's highly inscribed designs; comprehensive CSF/CFF specific to developing country public sectors, Total Cost of Ownership framework, ERP integration with other application, and contextualized ERP implementation frameworks. An ERP architecture grounded on local business processes rather that considering universal best practices is critical to successful implementation of ERP system. A study on an alternative architecture that can harness capabilities of other technologies like Multi-Agent Systems and SOA could help to develop ERP systems that minimize on business process improvement, which is highly disruptive in developing countries public sectors. This could reduce the ERP system implementation cost and failure rate. The listed research dimensions contribute to the fact that despite the wide adoption of ERP systems, the biggest share is in developed economies; the adoption rate in developing countries is still very low more so in Africa. Hence, the studies are recommended to create knowledge on implementation of ERP systems in developing country public sectors.

References

Abdelghaffar, H.: Success factors for ERP implementation in large organizations: the case of Egypt. Electron. J. Inf. Syst. Dev. Ctries. **52**(1), 1–13 (2012)

Addo-Tenkorang, R., Helo, P.: Enterprise resource planning (ERP): a review literature report. In: Proceedings of the World Congress on Engineering and Computer Science, vol. II (2011)

Ahituv, N., Neumann, S., Zviran, M.: A system development methodology for ERP systems. J. Comput. Inf. Syst. **42**(3), 56–67 (2002)

Akkermans, H., Helden, K.: Vicious and virtuous cycles in ERP implementation: a case study of interrelations between critical success factors. Eur. J. Inf. Syst. **11**, 35–46 (2002)

Allen, D., Kern, T., Havenhand, M.: ERP Critical Success Factors: an exploration of the contextual factors in public sector institutions. In: Proceeding of the 35th Hawaii International Conference on Systems Sciences Hawaii, USA (2002)

Alford, T.: The Economics of cloud computing. Booz Allen Hamilton (2009)

Al-Mashari, M.: A process change-oriented model for ERP application. Int. J. Hum.-Comput. Interact. **16**(1), 39–55 (2003)

Alshawi, S., Themistocleous, M., Almadani, R.: Integrating diverse ERP systems: a case study. J. Enterp. Inf. Manag. **17**(6), 454–462 (2004)

Armbrust, M., et al.: A View of Cloud Computing. Commun. ACM **53**(4), 50–58 (2010)

Alsene, E.: ERP systems and the coordination of the enterprise. Bus. Process Manag. J. **13**(3), 417–432 (2007)

Alves, M.C., Matos, S.I.: An investigation into the use of ERP systems in the public sector. J. Enterp. Resour. Plann. Stud. **2011**, Article ID 950191 (2011). https://doi.org/10.5171/2011.950191

Avnet: ERP not living up to promise. Global Supply Chain 2, 7 (1999)

Bailey, L., Seymour, L.F., Belle, J.V.: Impact of ERP implementation on the quality of work life of users: a sub-Saharan African study. Afr. J. Inf. Syst. **9**(3), 3 (2017)

Bailey, M., Katz, B., West, D.: Building a Long-Term Strategy for Growth Through Innovation. The Brookings Institution, Washington, D.C. (2010)

Bancroft, N., Seip, H., Sprengel, A.: Implementing SAP R/3: How to Introduce a Large System into a Large Organisation, 2nd edn. Manning Publications, Greenwich (1998)

Baran, R.: ERP vs. CRM software – What is the difference? (2012). http://www.positivevision.biz/blog/bid/132694/erp-vs-crm-software-what-s-the-difference. Accessed 03 Apr 2019

Baxter, G.: White paper: Key issues in ERP system implementation, the UK national research and training initiative (2010)

Beal, V.: The Difference between CRM and ERP (2017). https://www.webopedia.com/DidYouKnow/Hardware_Software/the-difference-between-crm-and-erp.html. Accessed 03 Apr 2019

Beaubouef, B.: Cloud Can Bring Out the Best of ERP (2011). http://gbeaubouef.wordpress.com/2011/11/23/cloud-erp-advantage

Benders, J., Batenburg, R., Van der Blonk, H.: Sticking to standards: technical and other isomorphic pressures in deploying ERP-systems. Inf. Manag. **43**, 194–203 (2006)

Bernd, Z., Arne, T.: The public cloud for e-government. In: IADIS International Conferences Web Based Communities and Social Media and Collaborative Technologies, pp, 129–136 (2012)

Bingi, P., Sharma, M., Godla, J.: Critical issues affecting an ERP implementation. Inf. Syst. Manag. **16**(3), 7–14 (1999)

Bitsini, N.: Investigating ERP misalignment between, ERP systems and implementing, organizations in developing countries. J. Enterp. Resour. Plann. Stud. (2015). https://doi.org/10.5171/2015.570821

Bhisikar, A.: GCloud: new paradigm shift for online public services. Int. J. Comput. Appl. **22**(8), 24–29 (2011)

Bjørn-Andersen, N., Johansson, B.: Identifying requirements for future ERP systems (2007). www.3gerp.org

Bozaa, A., Cuenca, L., Polera, R., Michaelides, Z.: The interoperability force in the ERP field. Enterp. Inf. Syst. **9**(3), 257–278 (2015). Research Centre on Production Management and Engineering (CIGIP), pp. 257–278. Published online: Liverpool, UK (2015)

Bozeman, B.: A theory of government red tape. J. Public Adm. Res. Theory **3**(3), 273–303 (1993)

Bozeman, B., Bretschneider, S.: Public management information systems: theory and prescription. Public Adm. Rev. **46**(6), 475–487 (1986)

Bretschneider, S.: Management information systems in public and private organizations: an empirical test. Public Adm. Rev. **50**(5), 536–545 (1990)

Broadbent, M.: Creating effective IT governance. In: Gartner Symposium IT EXPO, Orlando Florida (2002)

Buckhout, S.E., Frey, J., Nemec, J.R.: Making ERP succeed; turning fear into promise. In: Strategy and Business, 2nd quarter. Booz-Allen and Hamilton (1999). http://www.strategybusiness.com

Cats-Baril, W., Thompson, R.: Managing information technology projects in the public sector. Public Adm. Rev. **55**(6), 559–566 (1995)

Caudle, S.L.: Strategic information resources management: fundamental practices. Gov. Inf. Q. **13**(1), 83–97 (1996)

Columbus: Seven ways that business process management can improve your ERP implementation, special report series, ERP in 2014 and beyond (2014). http://www.columbusnsc.dk/daDK/DynamicsNAV/~/media/90634D9A7EE4D3FBB360D6330189D7.pdf

Dantes, G.R., Hasibuan, Z.A: Enterprise resource planning implementation framework based on key success factors (KSFs). In: UK Academy for Information Systems Conference Proceedings (2011). http://aisel.aisnet.org/ukais2011/13

Davenport, T.H.: Putting the enterprise into the enterprise system. Harvard Bus. Rev. **76**(4), 121–131 (1998)

Davenport, T.H., Short, J.E.: The new industrial engineering: information technology and business process redesign. Sloan Manag. Rev. **31**(4), 11–27 (1990)

Dezdar, S., Ainin, S.: The influence of organizational factors on successful ERP implementation. Manag. Decis. **49**(6), 911–926 (2011)

DiMaggio, P.J., Powell, W.W.: The iron cage revisited; institutional isomorphism and collective rationality in organizational fields. Am. Sociol. Rev. **48**(1), 147–160 (1983)

Dwivedi, Y.K., Wastell, D., Laumer, S., Henriksen, H.Z., Myers, M., Bunker, D., Srivastava, S. C.: Research on information systems failures and successes: status update and future directions. Inf. Syst. Front. **17**(1), 143–157 (2014)

Esteves, J., Bohorquez, V.: An updated ERP systems annotated bibliography: 2001–2005. Instituto de Empresa Business School Working Paper No. WP 07-04, 19(1) (2007)

Frimpon, M.F.: A Project Approach to Enterprise Resource Planning Implementation. Int. J. Bus. Manage. **7**(10) (2012)

Gosain, S.: Enterprise information systems as objects and carriers of institutional forces: the new iron cage? J. Assoc. Inf. Syst. **5**(4), 6 (2004)

Grass, I.: Processing and operation planning. In: Maynard, H. (ed.) Industrial Engineering Handbook. McGraw-Hill, New York (1956)

Grossman, T., Walsh, J.: Avoiding the pitfalls of ERP system implementation. Inf. Syst. Manag. **20**(2), 38–42 (2004)

Govindaraju, R.: Enterprise Systems Implementation Framework: an organizational perspective. Proc. - Soc. Behav. Sci. **65**, 473–478 (2012). International Congress on Interdisciplinary Business and Social Sciences

Gulledge, T.R., Sommer, R.A.: Business process management: public sector implications. Bus. Process Manag. J. **8**(4), 364–376 (2002)

Gulledge, T.R., Sommer, R.A.: Public sector enterprise resource planning. Ind. Manag. Data Syst. **103**(7), 471–483 (2003). https://doi.org/10.1108/02635570310489179

Harb, A., Tawk, R.: A comprehensive compilation of critical success factors for the implementation of enterprise resources planning (ERP) information system. Int. J. Res. Soc. Sci. **4**(9) (2015)

Hawari, A., Heeks, R.: Explaining ERP failure in a developing country: a Jordanian case study. J. Enterp. Inf. Manag. **23**(2), 135–160 (2010)

Hasibuan, Z., Dantes, G.: Priority of key success factors (KSFS) on enterprise resource planning (ERP) system implementation life cycle. J. Enterp. Resour. Plann. Stud. **2012**, 1–15 (2012)

Huang, S.M., Chang, I.C., Li, S.H., Lin, M.T.: Accessing risk in ERP projects: identify and prioritize the factors. Ind. Manag. Data Syst. **104**(8), 681–688 (2004)

Kalema, B.M., Oludayo, O., Ray, M.: Identifying critical success factors: the case of ERP systems in higher education. Afr. J. Inf. Syst. **6**(3), 65–84 (2014)

Kamhawi, E.M.: Enterprise resource-planning systems adoption in Bahrain: motives, benefits, and barriers. J. Enterp. Inf. Manag. **21**(3), 310–334 (2008)

Kelemen, R.: ERP systems in public sector. In: 37th International Convention on Microelectronics, Information and Communication Technology, Electronics and Microelectronics (MIPRO), pp. 1537–1543 (2014)

Klaus, H., Michael, R., Gable, G.: What is ERP? Inf. Syst. Front. **2**(2), 141–162 (2000)

Kolinsky, M.: The relationship between ERP and CRM (2018). https://diceus.com/a-relationship-between-erp-and-crm/. Accessed 03 Apr 2019

Kumar, V., Maheshwari, B., Kumar, U.: Enterprise resource planning systems adoption process: a survey of Canadian organizations Enterprise resource planning systems adoption process. Int. J. Prod. Res. **40**(3), 509–523 (2002)

Kumar, K., Van Hillegersberg, J.: ERP experiences and evolution. Commun. ACM **43**(4), 22–26 (2000)

Kwahk, K., Ahn, H.: Moderating effects of localization differences on ERP use: a socio technical systems perspective. Comput. Hum. Behav. **26**, 186–198 (2010)

Lechesa, M., Seymour, L., Schuler, J.: ERP Software as Service (SaaS): factors affecting adoption in South Africa. In: Møller, C., Chaudhry, S. (eds.) CONFENIS 2011. LNBIP, vol. 105, pp. 152–167. Springer, Heidelberg (2012). https://doi.org/10.1007/978-3-642-28827-2_11

Levinson, E.: The line manager and system-induced organizational change. In: Bloche, K. (ed.) Success Factors for Change from Manufacturing Viewpoint, Dearborn, Michigan (1988)

Liu, L., Feng, Y., Hu, Q., Huang, X.: From transactional user to VIP: how organizational and cognitive factors affect ERP assimilation at individual level. Eur. J. Inf. Syst. **20**(2), 186–200 (2011)

Liu, H., Lai, P.: Managing process centred e-government in Taiwan: a customer relationship management approach. Electron. Gov. **1**(4), 398–419 (2004)

Lutovac, M., Manojlov, D.: Impact of ERP consulting companies in surveillance of personal and business data in e-commerce. In: 19th International Conference on Technology, Culture, and Development, Tivat, Montenegro (2012)

Madhavi, L.: ERP Implementation in Public Sector Organisation: A dialectic perspective (2008). https://www.researchgate.net/publication/306378265_ERP_Implementation_in_a_Public_Sector_Organization_A_dialectic_perspective

Majchrzak, A., Wang, Q.: Breaking the functional mind-set in process organizations. Harvard Bus. Rev. **74**(5), 93–9 (1996)

Maliza, S., Teoh, S.Y., Chan, C.: Cloud enterprise systems: a review of literature and its adoption. In: PACIS 2012 Proceedings. Paper 76 (2012)

Markus, M.L., Tanis, C.: The enterprise systems experience – from adoption success. In: Zmud, R.W. (ed.) Framing the Domains of IT Research: Glimpsing the Future Through the Past, pp. 173–207. Pinna ex Educational Resources, Cincinnati (2000)
Mohammad, J.: The role and relevance of IT governance and IT capability in Business–IT alignment in medium and large companies. Acad. Taiwan Bus. Manag. Rev. **2**(6), 16–23 (2012)
Momoh, A., Shehab, E.: Challenges in enterprise resource planning implementation: state-of-the-art. Bus. Process Manag. J. **16**(4), 537–565 (2010)
Morton, N.A., Hu, Q.: Implications of the fit between organizational structure and ERP: a structural contingency theory perspective. Int. J. Inf. Manag. **28**(5), 391–402 (2008)
Mozammel-Bin-Motalab, Shohag, S.A.M.: Cloud computing and the business consequences of ERP use. Int. J. Comput. Appl. **28**(8), 31–37 (2011)
Nah, F.F.-H., Lau, J.L.-S., Kuang, J.: Critical factors for successful implementation of enterprise systems. Bus. Process Manag. J. **7**(3), 285–298 (2001)
Navaneethakrishnan, C.M.: A comparative study of cloud based ERP systems with traditional ERP and analysis of cloud ERP implementation. Int. J. Eng. Comput. Sci. **2**(9), 2866–2869 (2013). ISSN 2319-7242
Nazemi, E., Tarokh, M., Djavanshir, G.: ERP: a literature survey. Int. J. Adv. Manuf. Technol. **61**, 999–1018 (2012)
Njihia, E., Mwirigi, F.: The effects of enterprise resource planning systems on firm's performance: a survey of commercial banks in Kenya. Int. J. Bus. Commer. **3**(8), 120–129 (2014)
Okoli, C.: A guide to conducting a standalone systematic literature review. Commun. Assoc. Inf. Syst. **37**(43) (2015)
Parr, A., Shanks, G.: A model of ERP implementation. J. Inf. Technol. **15**, 289–303 (2000)
Periseraset, V., Tarabanis, K.: Towards enterprise architecture for public administration using a top-down approach. Eur. J. Inf. Syst. **9**(4), 252–260 (2000)
Rajapakse, J., Seddon, P.: Why ERP may not be suitable for organisations in developing countries in Asia. Working Paper, Department of Information Systems. The University of Melbourne, Australia (2005)
Ram, J., Corkindale, D., Wu, M.L.: Implementation critical success factors (CSFs) for ERP: do they contribute to implementation success and post-implementation performance? Int. J. Prod. Econ. **144**, 157–174 (2013)
Raymond, L., et al.: ERP adoption for E-Government: an analysis of motivations. In: Paper Presented at the Proceedings eGovernment Workshop. Brunel University, West London, UK (2005)
Robert, J., Weston, T.: Enterprise resource planning (ERP) - a brief history. J. Oper. Manag. **25**, 357–363 (2007)
Robey, D., Ross, J.W., Boudreau, M.C.: Learning to implement enterprise systems: an exploratory study of the dialectics of change. J. Manag. Inf. Syst. **19**(1), 17–46 (2002)
Rodin-Brown, E.: Integrated Financial Management Information Systems: A practical guide (2008). http://pdf.usaid.gov/pdf_docs/PNADK595.pdf
Rose, W.R., Grant, G.: Critical issues pertaining to the planning and implementation of e-government initiatives. Gov. Inf. Q. **27**, 26–33 (2010)
Rosemann, M., Vessey, I., Weber, R.: Alignment in enterprise systems implementations: the role of ontological distance. In: International Conference on Information Systems (ICIS) Proceedings (2004)
Ross, J.W., Vitale, M.R.: The ERP revolution: surviving vs. thriving. Inf. Syst. Front. **2**(2), 233–241 (2000)
Rouhani, S., Ravasan, B.: ERP success prediction: an artificial neural network approach. Scienti Iranica **20**(3), 992–1001 (2012)
Saini, et al.: Cloud computing and enterprise resource planning systems. In: Proceedings of the World Congress on Engineering, WCE 2011, London, UK, vol. I (2011)
Salmeron, J., Lopez, C.: Multicriteria approach for risks assessment in ERP maintenance. J. Syst. Softw. **83**, 1941–1953 (2010)

Sally, W., Arnold, M.W.: Information system assurance for enterprise resource planning systems: unique risk considerations. J. Inf. Sci. **16**, 99–113 (2002)

Schäfermeyer, M., Rosenkranz, Ch., Holten, R.: The impact of business process complexity on business process standardization. Bus. Inf. Syst. Eng. **4**(5), 261–270 (2012). https://doi.org/10.1007/s12599-012-0224-6

Seddon, P., et al.: A multi-project model of key factors affecting organizational benefits from enterprise systems. MIS Q. **34**, 305 (2010)

Shanks, G., Parr, A., Hu, B., Corbitt, B., Thanasankit, T., Seddon, P.: Differences in critical success factors in ERP systems implementation in Australia and China: a cultural analysis. In: Conference: Proceedings of the 8th European Conference on Information Systems, Trends in Information and Communication Systems for the 21st Century, ECIS 2000 (2000)

Shaul, L., Tauber, D.: Critical success factors in enterprise resource planning systems. ACM Comput. Surv. **45**(4), 55 (2013)

Simone, S., Célio, S., Julliane, E.: Critical success factors for ERP implementation in sector public: an analysis based on literature and a real case. In: Twenty-Sixth European Conference on Information Systems (ECIS 2018), Portsmouth, UK (2018)

Soja, P., Paliwoda-Pekosz, G.: What are real problems in enterprise system adoption? Ind. Manag. Data Syst. **109**(5), 610–627 (2009)

Somers, T.M., Nelson, K.: The impact of critical success factors across the stages of enterprise resource planning implementations. In: Proceedings of the 34th Hawaii International Conference on System Sciences, Maui, Hawaii (2001)

Sommer, R.: Public sector ERP implementation: successfully engaging middle management! Commun. IBIMA **2011**, Article ID 162439 (2011). https://doi.org/10.5171/2011.162439

Somers, T.M., Nelson, K.G.: A taxonomy of players and activities across the ERP project life cycle. Inf. Manag. **41**, 257–278 (2004)

Sprecher, M.: The future of ERP in the public sector. Gov. Finance Rev. **15**(4), 49–50 (1999)

Strong, D.M., Volkoff, O.: Understanding organization-enterprise system fit: a path to theorizing the information technology artifact. MIS Q. **34**(4), 731–756 (2010)

Tregear, R., Jenkins, T.: Government Process Management: a review of key differences between the public and private sectors and their influence on the achievement of public sector process management. BPTrends, 10-07-ART. Govt. process Mgt. (2007)

Tripti, M.N.: Indian SMEs perspective for election of ERP in cloud. J. Int. Technol. Inf. Manag. 22(1), Article ID 5 (2013). http://scholarworks.lib.csusb.edu/jitim/vol22/iss1/5

Trimi, S., Lee, S.M., Olson, D.L., Erickson, J.: Alternative means to implement ERP: internal and ASP. Ind. Manag. Data Syst. **105**(2), 184–192 (2005)

Umble, E.J., Umble, M.M.: Avoiding ERP implementation failure. Ind. Manag. **44**(1), 25–33 (2002)

Ustasüleyman, T., Percin, S.A.: Structural model suggestion about the effect of critical control (success) factors on enterprise resource planning (ERP) implementation success. J. Fac. Econ. Adm. Sci. Marmara Univ. **28**(1), 293–312 (2010)

Wagner, W., Antonucci, L.: An analysis of the imagine PA public sector ERP project. In: Proceedings of the 37th Hawaii International Conference on System Sciences (2004)

Wang, E., Shih, S., Jiang, J., Klein, G.: The consistency among facilitating factors and ERP implementation success: a holistic view of fit. J. Syst. Softw. **81**(2008), 1609–1621 (2008)

Watson, E., Vaught, S., Dan Gutierrez, D., Rinks, D.: ERP Implementation in State Government. Annals of IT Case Studies. Idea Group Inc., Calgary (2003)

Wu, L., Ong, C., Hsu, Y.: Active ERP implementation management: a real options perspective. J. Syst. Softw. **81**, 1039–1050 (2008)

Ziemba, E., Oblak, I.: Critical success factors for ERP systems implementation. Interdisc. J. Inf. Knowl. Manag. **8** (2013)

A Framework for Cloud ERP System Implementation in Developing Countries: Learning from Lower Local Governments in Uganda

David Mpanga[1(✉)] and Amany Elbanna[2]

[1] Bugema University, P. O. Box 6529, Kampala, Uganda
d.mpanga@bugemauniv.ac.ug
[2] Royal Holloway University of London, Egham, Surrey TW20 0EX, UK

Abstract. Local government entities like municipalities are also challenged to provide services efficiently and effectively and hence increasingly consider ERP systems to support their operations. Successful implementation of an ERP system depends on several factors including having a viable framework to guide the organizational effort. This research aim to examine the nature and content of a possible framework to implement ERP system that could be useful for developing countries. To this end, it adopts an exploratory methodology involving focus groups to understand the activities essential to successful municipality ERP system implementation in a developing country, Uganda. Our finding shows that even when adopting cloud computing model, implementing ERP system in local governments in developing countries should take into account the fact developing countries should take into account the specificity of the developing countries' context. This research offers a unique framework integrating monitoring and evaluation with contextualization, implementation, transition and realization categories of activities to successfully implement a cloud ERP system in a developing country local government. The findings support decision makers and vendors to reduce the total or partial failure rate of ERP implementation in developing country local governments.

Keywords: ERP · Implementation framework · Public sector · Cloud computing · Local government

1 Introduction

ICT holds potentials for transformation and change. In this paper, we attempt to develop a framework for Cloud ERP implementation from a developing country's perspective. Enterprise Resource Planning (ERP) is a software solution that assimilates business functions and data into a single system that is shared within the business (Rajeshwar 2015). According to Matos and Alves (2011) enterprise systems are typically off-the-shelf software solutions that have become popular in private sectors where organizations are aligning information systems with business strategy through elimination of fragmented information sources; replacing legacy information systems

Published by Springer Nature Switzerland AG 2019
Y. Dwivedi et al. (Eds.): TDIT 2019, IFIP AICT 558, pp. 274–292, 2019.
https://doi.org/10.1007/978-3-030-20671-0_19

with ERP software that cut across functional areas. Enterprise systems originated from manufacturing industry and later extended to private sector broadly. According to Carutasu and Carutasu (2016) ERP is multifunctional software package and extends to the entire enterprise with the same database for the entire company. ERP systems are, generally, characterized by their complexity and wide footprint in the enterprise with regards to scope (Ramburn et al. 2016). Shaul and Tauber (2013) stated that ERP use is widely accepted in developed countries, however, Hawari and Heeks (2010) had observed that the market for ERP systems in developing countries was still in early stages. ERP systems were developed by software houses in developed countries, and initially adopted by large organizations; lately adopted by small and medium enterprises in the West (Rajapakse and Seddon 2005).

ERP systems were initiated by large organizations in the developed countries (Rajapakse and Seddon 2005). Nevertheless, implementation of ERP systems in public sectors was ongoing, despite the enormous investments and the risk of failure (Kelemen 2014). High failure rates in ERP systems still remained a great concern Ram, Corkindale and Wu (2013), and public sector is characterized by a high rate of failures in ERP projects (Bitsini 2015). However, developing countries have also embarked on implementing ERP systems in public sectors, so as to attain efficiency and transparency by adopting the best practices from public sectors in developed countries. Few studies have targeted public sector implementations of ERP systems (Chang et al. 2000; Dwivedi et al. 2014). However, inadequate work has been performed on implementing ERP in public sectors (Narçyz and Renata 2017; Ziemba and Oblak 2013). According to Kaunda and Kennedy (2013) developing countries are still far less than developed countries in many areas of ERP systems implementation. Guided by western and developed countries perspectives, current ERP frameworks lack understanding of developing countries contextual conditions. Indeed, implementing ERP systems in lower public sector organizations without a contextualized ERP implementation framework will result in more failures (Hawari and Heeks 2010). There is a need for in-depth understanding and bottom-up approach to guide the development of ERP implementation framework that seriously take the contextual conditions of developing countries into consideration as the contextual differences between developing and developed countries cannot be overlooked (Soja 2012). Dwivedi et al. (2014) envisaged the need to extend ERP research focus to include further public sector ERP systems implementation. Huang et al. (2004) listed the top ten risks for ERP system's framework implementation failures. ERP system implementation involves more than changing an organization's software; it involves repositioning the organization and transforming its business operations, processes and practices (Rajeshwar 2015).

While ERP implementation has been considered important to enhance efficiency, reduce corruption, and improve services, it has been an expensive solution to many developing countries. The rise of the cloud computing has been argued to provide an opportunity for developing countries to catch up technologically and obtain ERP capability is a fast and less expensive manner. Cloud computing technology is a network based service model that enables on demand network access to a shared pool of configurable resources. It is a model that provides special services over the Internet; this service could be a server, storage, or software (Bahssas et al. 2015). Many ERP vendors have moved to cloud computing platforms that house ERP solutions. Cloud computing technology is capable of hosting an ERP system through the models of Infrastructure as a service (IaaS) and Software as a Service (SaaS) (Lenart 2011). According to Bahssas et al. (2015) cloud ERP has many advantages that include less staff, mobility, easy expandability and cost reduction.

Traditional ERP systems implementations are on premise using local servers on an organisation's network. In cloud-based ERP environments, a service provider practically provide the resources for hosting and running the application. The benefits that come with cloud computing has made Cloud-based solutions one of the fastest growing segments of IT industry (Popovic 2010). Enhancement of service delivery, and cutting of operational costs by 25%–50% are achievable at all level of government by adopting cloud computing solutions (Bailey et al. 2011). Hence, cloud computing has become a strategic direction for many government agencies and that it has the capability to be employed in critical areas of the government's IT-infrastructures (Sædberg and Haddara 2015).

Cloud technology under SaaS model is gaining popularity in private sectors, promising low deployment costs, low price with pay-as-use and considerably reduced time-to-deployment (Carutasu and Carutasu 2016; Weng and Hung 2014). Local governments in developing countries could benefit from SaaS; however, a successful deployment requires a comprehensive contextual implementation framework to ensure compliance with local government regulations and unique constraints. Cloud ERP SaaS module will enable multiple local governments to access and share a pool of ERP software services via the Internet.

This paper consists of seven sections. Following the introduction, section two provides research background discussing the context of Uganda as a developing country. Section three presents implementation frameworks/methodologies and their limitation. The following section explains the methodology used to collect data for the research. Findings and a framework of major activities for implementing cloud ERP system at local governments are presented and discussed in subsequent sections.

2 Research Background

Uganda is a landlocked country with 21% of the 34.6 million population living in urban centers, and GDP per capita of US$ 642 (Uganda bureau of statistics abstracts [UBOS] 2017). Urban administrative centers include 1 City, 41 Municipalities, 122 Municipal councils and 357 Town councils. Adoption of cloud computing at local governments is still very low due to high costs, lack of experts and access problems (National IT report, 2017/18, p. 104). The most popular Cloud computing service is email, followed by storage and Software as a Service. The lack of investment and budgetary constraints are the key internal barrier to wider implementation of e-government services. On average 0.9% of public sector total institutional expenditure is the budget for Information Technology. The Internet bandwidth average market cost of 1 Mbs/per month is US$ 237, which is very high for local government. However, the penetration of computing devices in public sectors is high, and fixed broadband fiber cable is the most popular internet connectivity followed by 3G and 4G mobile broadband. In 2016, Uganda was estimated to be 36% e-Government ready, which is lower than the World's average of 49.2%. The United Nations e-Government Development Index (EGDI) ranked Uganda at 128, comparing with neighboring Kenya at 119, South Africa at 76, and Ghana at 120 (National IT report 2018, p. 38). Municipalities are lower local government public sectors that provide services to local communities and businesses. Their structure consist of cells, the lowest unit, wards and divisions. Municipalities are designated to provide broadly three services: planning, garbage management and provision of social services. Increased demand for effectiveness in service delivery has made the implementation of information systems and access to real time information no longer a requirement unique to private and public sectors; it is also a critical requirement for local governments like municipalities. However, there are many substantial challenges faced by local governments and information systems developers. For instance, some municipal governments in developing countries are: scattered geographically, lack sufficient technological infrastructure, highly constrained by requirements to comply with government regulations, and deficient in funds and technical IT skills. Software vendors and managers have to address these issues to successfully deploy information systems that meet the requirements of local governments.

Since 2003, Uganda government embarked on implementing an Enterprise Information System (EIS) to improve efficiency in budget preparation, execution and financial reporting at ministry, agencies and local governments. The EIS is based on a centralised architecture, managed at ministry level, and provide a web browser interface for users' access (Semakula and Muwanga 2012). In Uganda, adoption of Cloud solutions and services in public sector organizations is still low, though indicators show a positive trend. (National Information Technology Authority [NITA] 2018).

A clearly defined framework to guide the implementation process is required to successfully implement an enterprise information system for municipalities. Failures in information system implementation are not necessarily the product of software design. The failures could be caused by solution-organization misfits that are contextually unique to a particular organization (Hawari and Heeks 2010).

The paper provides a framework for implementing a cloud-based ERP systems at local governments in a developing country from the local experience. It asks what is: a suitable framework for cloud ERP implementation in developing countries, and in particular government and public sectors? It answers this question through focusing on municipalities in Uganda as a typical example of public sector in a developing country.

3 ERP Implementation Frameworks and Their Limitations

3.1 Existing ERP Implementation Frameworks

This section provides a discussion of the most popular ERP systems implementation frameworks, covering articles from 1983 to 2015. The discussion is focused on ERP systems implementation approaches, frameworks, and methodologies adopted in various organizations. Literature on this subject is sparse; they predominantly focus on Critical Success Factors (CSFs) and developed country private sectors. Furthermore, research from developing countries on ERP implementation in public sectors is very scarce (Matos and Alves 2011). There is a need to understand the maturity level of business processes in public sectors in developing countries. Hasibuan and Dantes (2012), suggested an impact of 42.20% weight of business process reengineering on the priority key success factor of ERP implementation cycle.

Govindaraju (2012) suggested an organization perspective framework for implementing Enterprise Systems (ES). It consists of two stages: the project and post project stages. It has been recommended that the analysis of ES implementation effectiveness should be performed in short and long terms (Govindaraju 2012). The short-term implementation effectiveness is related to the outcome of the project stage. The long-term implementation effectiveness is related to the outcome of the post-project stage. This framework is generic and does not specifically highlight the critical factors for consideration at each stage.

Dantes and Hasibuan (2011) proposed an ERP implementing conceptual framework considering two dimensions; ERP implementation process having five stages: project preparation, technology selection, project formulation, implementation and post-implementation. Somers and Nelson (2004) identified six stages of ERP implementation process: initiation, adoption, adaptation, acceptance, routinization, and infusion.

Ahituv et al. (2002) developed a generic hybrid ERP implementation methodology combining three structured approaches: Structured Development Life Cycle (SDLC), Prototyping and application package model. He contend that the uniqueness of ERP system renders any of the three models inadequate to be adopted solely in implementation of ERP system. Implementation of ERP system touches the core process of the business. Hence, adoption of a hybrid methodology universally is likely to result into unexpected failure due to cultural, organizational and political influences experienced in environments that are characteristically different.

Helo et al. (2008) stated that the major impediments to successful ERP implementations are not technologically related issues such as compatibility, technological complexity, and standardization, but most are organization and human related issues including as resistance to change, organizational culture and business processes. These challenges could be dealt with by using a well contextualized framework appropriate. Universality adoption of implementing frameworks overlook organizational culture, behavior, and change management impact on ERP implementation failure.

Huang et al. (2004) listed the top ten risks that cause ERP implementation failures, which are related to implementing framework. ERP implementation involves more than changing an organization's software; it involves repositioning the organization and transforming its business operations, processes and practices (Rajeshwar 2015).

Markus and Tannis (2000) prescribed a four phased framework for implementing ERP system. The phase include; chartering phase, which comprises decisions leading up to the funding of an enterprise system; the project phase, which comprises activities intended to get the system up and running in one or more organizational units; shakedown phase, when the organization comes to grips with the enterprise system. The phase, which is said to end when "normal operations" have been achieved or the organization gives up, and dis-installing the system. The onward and upward phase, which continues from normal operation until the system is replaced with an upgrade or a different system, a stage during which the organization is finally able to ascertain the benefits (if any) of its investment.

3.2 Limitations of Existing Frameworks

ERP system implementation frameworks identified were generated from private sector organisations. In private sectors, top management make decisions independently unlike in public sectors; decisions are highly influenced politically and constrained by government legislations. Hence, the critical success factors identified in the private sectors do not translate directly into the public sectors. Some existing ERP system implementation frameworks suggest what should be done at a particular stage, however the unique variations in different domains are not considered. Characteristic variations between private sector and public sector significantly influence the way ERP systems implementation is carried out. Sommer (2011) argued that public administration has unique cultural, political, and organizational factors that negatively influence successful ERP system implementation in public administration. Implementation of ERP systems in developing countries public sectors should also take into account the fact that developing countries have limited resources. Hence, ERP systems implementation process in developing country public sectors should be administered differently as suggested by Addo-Tenkorang and Helo (2011).

Implementation of ERP systems is based on assumption of best practices, which is likely to be the major source of misfit between ERP systems and recipient organization's business processes. Universality of best practices masks the need to recognize the variation in business processes among organizations, be it private or public, and developed or developing countries. Klaus et al. (2000) stated that the transferability of ERP best practices on a global scale might be limited due to every country's specific requirements relating to fundamental processes. Maditinos et al. (2011) argued that most of ERP failures are not caused by ERP software. The complexity and massive changes caused by ERP systems in an organization cause the failures. The major impediments to successful ERP systems implementation are not technologically related issues such as compatibility, technological complexity, and standardization; most of them are organization and human related issues including resistance to change, organizational culture and business processes (Helo et al. 2008). Hence, adopting an ERP system implementation framework based on universal best practices overlooks the impact of organizational culture, behavior, and change management.

Most ERP system vendors propose frameworks specific to their ERP solutions to simplify the implementation process. Some of the popular vendor specific frameworks include: Accelerated SAP (ASAP) by SAP, Application Implementation Method (AIM) by Oracle, Direct Path by PeopleSoft and Dynamic Enterprise Modeler by BAAN ((Benders, Batenburg and Van der Blonk 2006). These ERP implementation frameworks require conformity to prescribed approach, which compromise recipient organisation core business processes. This confirm the isomorphism concept promoted by DiMaggio and Powell (1983).

4 Research Methodology

Data for the research was obtained from different sources following the Design Science Research Methodology (DSRM) (Peffers et al. 2008). The research used a qualitative approach that involved three focus groups discussion, review of reports and other relevant documents. The nature of developing country local government complexities are reflected mostly from: business processes, organizational structure, IT acquisition and maintenance process, data storage and security regulations, staffing levels and funding and resources mobilisation mechanisms. These public sector contextual complexities were also observed by Sædberg and Haddara (2016). Further to this, entrenched practices, requirements to learn new skills and the fear of layoffs among staff, reinforce public sector complexity (Semakula and Muwanga 2012). Nevertheless, little is known about the implementation of cloud-based ERP systems in developing country local government's contextual complexity. On the ground of this research gap, this study attempted to understand the activities essential to successful implementation of cloud-based ERP system at developing country local government. The study reviewed literature to explore previous research on the implementation of ERP systems at public sectors in developing countries.

The focus group method suggested by (Krueger and Casey 2000) was adopted, to obtain quality data from multiple participants. The study engaged three focus groups, two of them each consisted of five municipality employees, who were department heads, and one focus group of IT experts. This number of five participants in each focus group is appropriate based on the recommendation by Morgan (1997); Baumgartner et al. (2002).

The focus group method in the Design Science Research Methodology was considered the appropriate method to collect data required to build the artifact in a complex local government environment. Participants also had varying experiences acquired from different local governments from where they were transferred. In-depth understanding of the context required a group discussion to generate a consensus rather than considering individual participant views. Three focus groups, exploratory (EFG), verification (VFG), and Technical (TFG) were used to collect data required to develop the framework artifact iteratively rather than linear approach (Kuechler and Vaishnavi 2008; Tremblay et al. 2010). Data collection started with EFG, VFG was need to verify data collected from EFG. EFG and VFG consisted five participants each, who were all head of departments. All participants had experience of more than 3 years, and were conversant with regulations, information systems and business processes at local government. The IT experts Focus Group (TFG) was used to verify the essential activities from a technical perspective. Participants in VFG were information Technology professions from different government department who were familiar with implementation of hosted enterprise information system in government. Though the size of TFG is lower than the recommended lower boundary of four (Morgan, 1997), it was considered appropriate due to the difficulty of identifying experts who understand the technical complexity of Organisation – Technology – Fit in developing country public sector.

Emergent-systematic focus group design was adopted for exploratory and verification investigations. Participants were purposefully selected to tap the opinions of information system experts. Each focus group discussion session lasted approximately 1 h 20 min. The objective was to gain an in-depth understanding of information systems and business processes in municipalities, which impacted by implementation of ERP system rather than the behaviors, opinions and attitudes of employees towards municipality information systems. Hence, interactions among focus group participants were not measured as recommended by Myers (2006) and Onwuegbuzie et al. (2009).

The key questioning route below was used to guide the exploratory focus group discussion coordinated by the moderator and assistant moderator, while the assistant moderator typed the notes.

What type of information systems implemented in your organisation? What should be done to ensure a successful implementation of a computer based information system that cut across all departments in the organisation? To ensure a successful implementation of an enterprise information system, how should the enterprise information system implementing process be managed? What where the noticeable phases of the implementation process? What activities would be considered crucial at each stage? How do you compare the benefits and challenges of a computer solution implemented on a computer within the organization and the one hosted by a third party? How can the stakeholders ascertain a successful implementation of an enterprise information system?

Classical content analysis method was used to code and count the responses from the focus group discussions. Two elements from Morgan (1997) three-element coding framework were adopted to identify the codes used by each participant and each group. The response codes were analyzed to generate the consensus statements for the participants. Specifically, the percentage of agreement for each statement was computed to explore the reliability of the data. This data analysis is in agreement with the degree of consensus and dissent proposition of argumentative-interactions (Kitzinger 1994; Onwuegbuzie et al. 2009; Sim 1998). Reducing and transforming data in qualitative research can be achieved in different ways including; *"...through selection, through summary or paraphrase, through being subsumed in larger pattern"* (Miles and Huberman 1994). The municipalities involved in the research had implemented a hosted enterprise system with human resource and financial management modules 2 years prior to this study.

5 Findings: Implementation Phases

This section present the findings from the three focus. The framework of essential activities for successful implementation of cloud ERP system in a lower local government in a developing country is presented. The activities have been grouped according to categories created from the interpretation of focus group discussion. Activities were formulated from the codes generated from individual participant and re-echoed in another focus groups.

5.1 Contextualization Phase

In this study, Contextualization is the stage where key stakeholders study the case to understand its unique characteristics. Findings show that in a municipality case, activities indicated in Fig. 1 should be carried out prior to the implementation of the cloud-based ERP system.

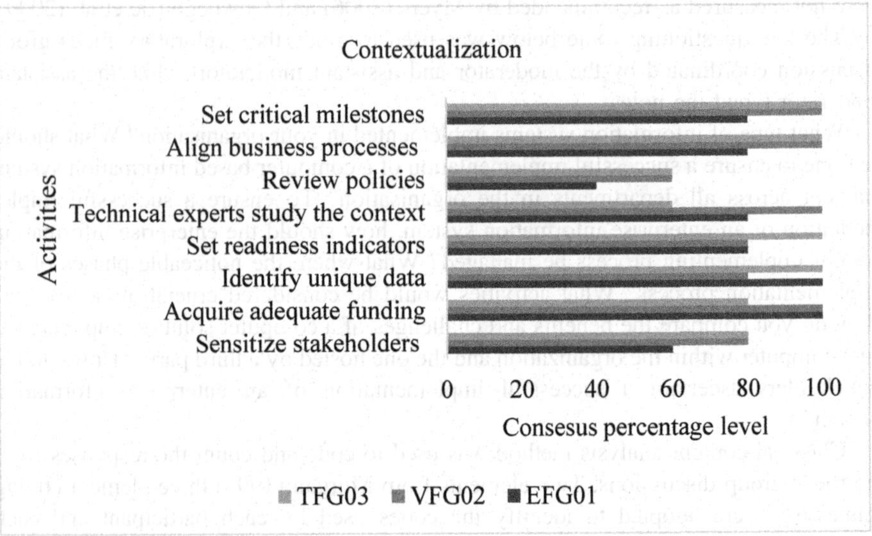

TFG = Technical Focus Group; VFG = Verification Focus Group; EFG = Exploratory Focus Group

Fig. 1. Essential contextualization activities

In regard to contextualization phase, setting critical mile stones and alignment of business processes received 100% consensus levels from both technical and verification groups (TFG and VFG). These activities were considered crucial to the understanding of how the local government organizations function. Operations of municipality could be challenging to understand due to political and technical competing powers. This was reflected in statements such as:

> *"in most cases what we do and how we do it is highly influenced by political gains" (VFG)*
> *"unless milestones are clearly defined, political influences will surely shape the project direction and objective" (TFG)*

Though business process alignment was considered essential in local government as it is in private sectors, however, unique complexities in public sector business processes were highlighted as also observed by Sædberg and Haddara (2016).

> *"though alignment of processes is required, changing processes in local government environment is extremely difficult, ... we operate within stringent compliance requirement stipulated from various ACTS" (EFG, VFG)*

Unlike the private sector where the executive decide on business processes within the confines of internal policies, public sector operations are externally regulated by different Acts of government. This explains why the review of policies attained low consensus percentage levels from all focus groups. Review of policies was considered to be a tedious long process that may involve change in legislation as a participant in the verification focus group discussion echoed:

"public sector policy formulation and reviews are initiated from top authorities,... they have to have interest in a policy to be reviewed"

The activity to study the context of the local government by experts received a 100% consensus from the VFG. This was attributed to the complexities caused by frictions between the two arms that govern the functions of a municipality, the technical staff and elected political teams. These two teams are expected to work hand in hand, however, they often exhibit competing interests. This explains the low consensus percentage level from the TFG as reflected in the following statement.

"experts involved in implementation of computer systems will always find it very difficult to understand operations in a context where political gains override technical principles"

Identification of readiness indicators seems to be a unique activity to local governments. Understanding of the readiness of an organization to implement ERP system, specifically Cloud-based ERP is not mentioned in private sector ERP systems implementation framework. Semakula and Muwanga (2012) affirm that readiness to address emerging challenges is essential to ensure success in implementing enterprise information systems. Due to its complex nature, challenges will emerge throughout the implementation process (Semakula and Muwanga 2012). This is supported by a statement from the TFG:

"most of these administrative units lack basic IT infrastructures and resources, required computer skills and highly constrained by meager conditional remittances from central government.... IT solutions implementation will always face readiness consequences"

Local governments are expected to raise funds from local tax revenues. However, in most cases local tax revenue stream does not bring in adequate funds. Consequently, central government funds almost over 80% of the local government budget. Most of local government large ERP system implementation projects are funded by donations. Unfortunately, such project usually overrun initial budgets (Helo et al. 2008). This highlights the advantage of implementing Cloud ERP systems that requires low initial investment. Nevertheless, it is essential to ensure availability of adequate funds to sustain the ERP system implementation life cycle. The donor funding mechanism could result in a project failure. This activity seems to be characteristic to the public sector in developing countries.

Surprisingly, sensitization of stakeholders was strongly emphasized by all groups, though it received a low consensus percentage level. This is attributed to the existence of a wide range of stakeholders with limited influence on local government functions. The following statement from the VFG is in support of the sensitization consensus.

"we interact with many stakeholders....sensitization is majorly required for political correctness......when staff know what to do, and resources are available, internal projects will be successful"

5.2 Implementation Phase

In this paper, implementation means the deployment process of the ERP system, rather than the construction of the system as it is understood in software engineering field. A set of essential activities constituting the implementation phase is shown in Fig. 2.

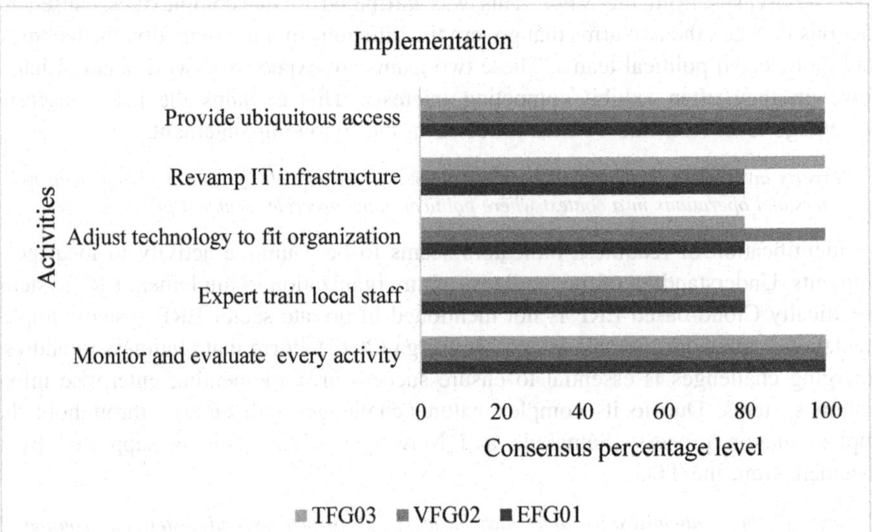

TFG = Technical Focus Group; VFG = Verification Focus Group; EFG = Exploratory Focus Group

Fig. 2. Essential implementation activities

Providing ubiquitous access to local government data received 100% consensus from all groups. Local government staff are often engaged in activities out of office. Hence, access to information resources anywhere any time is crucial to the utility of any local government information system. This confirms the need to implement a Cloud ERP systems in local government domain.

Participants had 2 to 3 years' experience using a hosted ERP system, hence they were aware of the challenges faced during enterprise information systems implementation. That experience was the basis for the high consensus levels of the activities in the implementation phase. Successful Could ERP systems implementation in lower local can be achieved when a monitoring and evaluation Action-Research model is adopted, focusing on continuous planning, action and reflection. Markus et al. (2000) also argued that success of ERP systems implementation depends on when it is measured, and success at one point in time may only be loosely related to success at another point in time. Monitoring and evaluation should be activity based throughout the project life. Larsen and Myers (1997) affirm that an ERP experience could be an early success and a later failure. Monitoring and evaluation is not only necessary to ensure compliance to regulations, also to assess activities progress, and timely identification of success or failure indicators. Other aspects of monitoring and evaluation should include identifying factors that account for the progress or constrain to the progress of activities, and measure of responses and reactions to implementation activities. These measures help to plan an effective change management program. The high consensus percentage on revamping IT infrastructure, reflect the state of IT infrastructure in the cases where the study was conducted; characterised by lack IT infrastructure. Implementation of Cloud ERP system enables local governments to overcome IT infrastructure challenges. The TFG stated that:

> *"it is not feasible to install IT infrastructure and also recruit IT experts required to implement and maintain complex systems like ERP in each and very local government unit across the country.....new units will always be created, resource will never be available"*

> *" ..... there has to be another approach to e-government deployment in local governments"*

However, public sector organisations' functions and operations differ depending on the sector, and the regulations that guide the business processes in a given sector also vary. Hence, it is not suitable for all public sector organisations to deploy the same cloud computing services model (Metha and Panda 2018). Software as a Service (SaaS) model promise better benefits to local governments. The functions and business processes of a given local government category are similar. SaaS model supports Cloud ERP multi-tenancy architecture, where multiple local governments in the same cluster share a single ERP system instance (AlJahdali et al. 2014; Saraswathi and Bhuvaneswari 2013). The SaaS cloud model will alleviate most constrains related to IT infrastructural and human resources capabilities reflected in implementation phase activities. Further to this, local government budgets preferably support operating expenditure rather than capital expenditure. Hence, the SaaS Cloud ERP model is a suitable solution in this regard.

5.3 Transition Phase

Findings revealed five major activities that need to be carried out after deployment of enterprise information systems to include schedule appraisal period, establish a central support service, upgrade skills, and assess regulatory compliance, which are shown in Fig. 3. An action "Cancel when failure indicators increase" was raised as a measure to avoid consequential huge failure costs after deployment of enterprise information system.

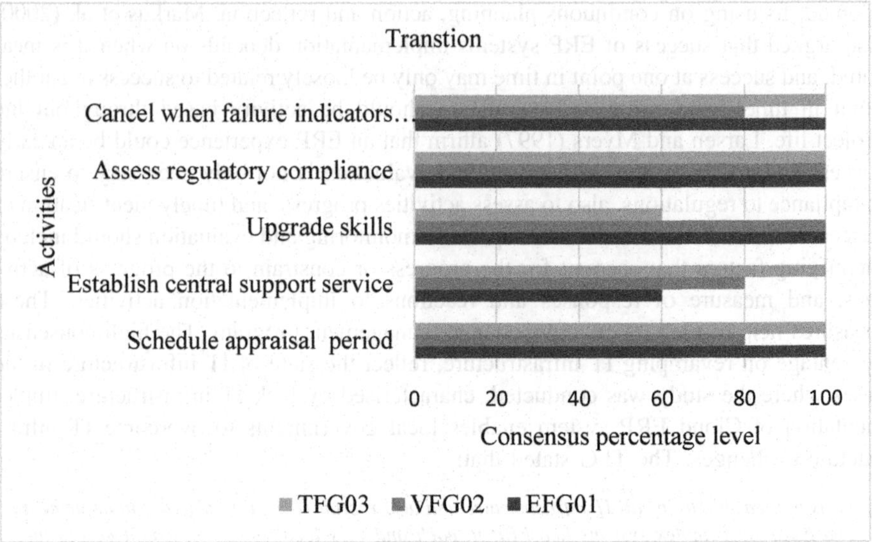

TFG = Technical Focus Group; VFG = Verification Focus Group; EFG = Exploratory Focus Group

Fig. 3. Essential transition activities

In this study, the transition phase start before the closure of implementation phase, and ends when key stakeholders confirm that the ERP system stabilized or failed to stabilize. In local governments the success of Cloud ERP system implementation shouldn't be considered as a deployment activity only; should be measured also against the degree of compliance to existing policies, procedure and regulations. This phase does not future in existing ERP systems implementation frameworks. Developing advanced computer skills at lower local government level raised mixed reactions. Apart from being costly, retention of skilled staff is a big challenge. This is not only in regard to remuneration issues, also the transfers of public sector employees and recruitment in rural areas continuously create skills gaps. The following statement explains the low consensus level from the TFG to develop advanced IT skills at local government.

"it is not cost effective to employee IT skilled personnel at every local government unit, they can be deployed from a central government center to work on specific tasks"

Establishing a central support service center that provide technical services to all local governments received 100% consensus. Local governments operate under common regulations and characterized similar challenges including lack of advanced IT skills, and inadequate budgets to fund IT activities. Hence, it is appropriate to establish a central support center for the Cloud ERP systems implementation. However, deployment of an appropriate cloud computing service model could eliminate the need for establishing IT support centers.

Scheduling appraisals is considered as a mechanism to mitigate transmission of failure from one activity to another. The high consensus received to this activity depict the need to ensure that the implementation project achieve the intended objectives. Implementation of Cloud E RP system require a conscious approach, given the local government complexity, the various perceptions surrounding cloud computing technology, and other constraints due to limited resources.

5.4 Realization Phase

Three activities were found to be essential in realization phase indicated in Fig. 4.

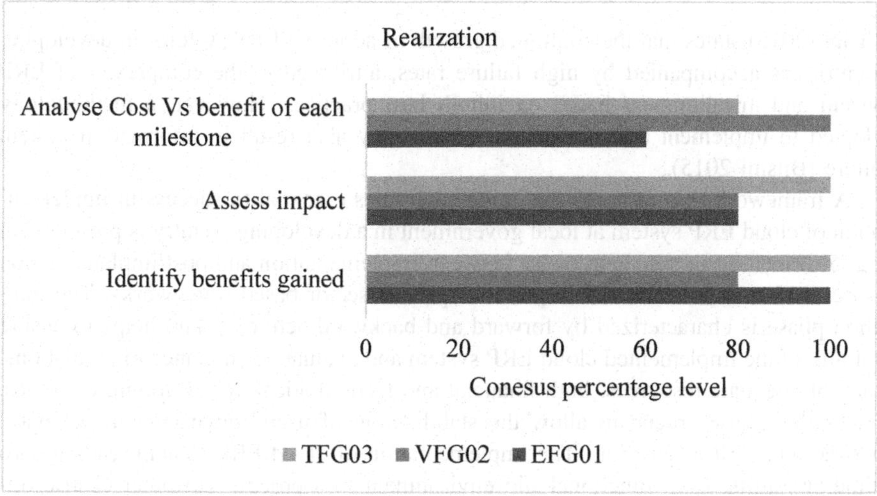

TFG = Technical Focus Group; VFG = Verification Focus Group; EFG = Exploratory Focus Group

Fig. 4. Essential realization activities

In this study, *Realization phase* is a stage where the local government is certain of achievement of intended objective. Local governments provide public service for public good rather than return on investment, however, administrators are concern with value for money for every intended objectives. This explain the high consensus percentage from administrators in regard to cost – benefit analysis. Though from local government perspective, funding the implementation of ERP system is an investment where return on investment is considered not important, understanding the value acquired out of the expenditure, provide insight on justification for the expenditure. What matters in local governments is improvement in performance, though political gain could be another motivation for implementation of such systems. The consensus levels obtained from "*assess impact*" and "*identify benefits gained*" activities are confirmed by Markus et al. (2000). It was found important to analyse the gained benefits in relation to cost, and assess the overall impacts on the local government functions. Impacts of ERP on public sector organization show mixed findings

(Fernandez et al. 2016; NITA 2018). The following statement from the verification group highlight another importance of impact assessment; to help in the development of policies that will guide future information systems implementation, and the management of knowledge in regard to implementation of Cloud solutions.

> *"understanding the impacts and gains support policy formulation and knowledge creation in regard to IT implementation in local governments"*

6 Discussion: Proposed Framework

Bitsini (2015) states that the continued growth of adopting ERP systems in developing countries is accompanied by high failure rates, attributed to the complexity of ERP system and misalignment based on inbuilt best practices. However, a methodology adopted to implement an information system may also result in information system failure (Bitsini 2015).

A framework that captures the unique activities essential to successful implementation of cloud ERP system at local government in a developing country is presented in Fig. 5. It includes a transition phase between implementation and post implementation phases which is not included in previous private sector based frameworks. The transition phase is characterized by forward and backward activities, and helps to ensure stability of the implemented cloud ERP system and evaluate compliance to regulations. Lack of adequate resources, both financial and technological in developing countries, makes this phase crucial to allow the stabilization of users' environment; behavior, cultural and skill acquisition. The implementation of cloud ERP system leads to two paradigm shifts; from functional-silo environment to a process–customer centric orientation; and from on-premise to remote access to information resources. Hence, the transition phase is critical for stabilization of organization and individuals' cultures. External forces that result from interfaces of various stakeholders also need to be stabilized. At this stage the local government organization and various stakeholders struggle to strike an equilibrium of change caused by process change, policy reviews, new skills demands, budget reallocations, new roles and responsibilities.

This newly-developed framework provides new features including activities unique to local governments in developing countries, activity based monitoring and evaluation, and a transition phase, which do not exist in the most popular framework from Markus et al. (2000). Differences in this framework and the existing frameworks, could be a result of differences in study context and domain. This study was conducted in a developing country local government. Markus et al. (2000) framework was generated from private sector companies in a developed country. Existing frameworks also do not consider what activities should be done within the organization to understand the organization before the project phase of ERP life cycle.

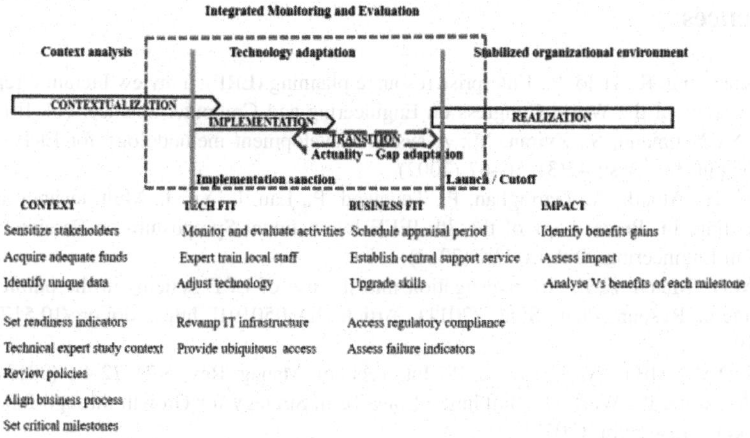

Fig. 5. Framework for cloud ERP system implementation

7 Conclusion

This paper presents focus group findings from a developing country municipality context in relation to implementation of a Cloud ERP system. The paper briefly presented existing frameworks adopted to implement ERP systems. Limitation of existing frameworks unveiled include: vendor specificity, private sector focus, universality of best practices, and lack of consideration of developing countries uniqueness. On the basis of the research findings, a new framework for cloud ERP system implementation in lower local government in a developing country was developed. The framework prescribes identified essential activities required in contextualization, implementation, transition, and realization phases to guide the implementation of Cloud ERP system. The continuous activity-based monitoring and evaluation mechanism is prescribed. The paper contributes to ERP systems implementation literature. ERP system vendors, academicians and practitioners with interest in developing countries public sector will benefit from the paper. The paper is beneficial also to local government decision makers and ERP system implementers. It provides a comprehensive contextualized framework that can help to mitigate partial or total failure of ERP system implementations in developing countries local governments. In terms of future research, understanding the suitable cloud ERP architecture; appropriate policies, regulation and theory related to cloud solutions implementation; usage, security and privacy of cloud-based solutions, and effective IT governance framework in context of developing country public sector is required.

Regarding the limitations of the study, the implementation of Cloud ERP system in developing country local government is still in infancy stage. Rigorous verification of the framework would be achieved using a Delphi techniques (Giannarou and Zervas 2014; Okoli and Pawlowski 2004). However, experts were difficult to find as expressed by Tremblay et al. (2010). Hence, a confirmatory field test is required to confirm the utility and efficacy of the framework a developing country local government environment.

References

Addo-Tenkorang, R., Helo, P.: Enterprise resource planning (ERP): a review literature report. In: Proceedings of the World Congress on Engineering and Computer Science, vol. II (2011)

Ahituv, N., Neumann, S., Zviran, M.: A system development methodology for ERP systems. J. Comput. Inf. Syst. **42**(3), 56–67 (2002)

AlJahdali, H., Albatli, A., Garraghan, P., Townend, P., Lau, L, Xu, J.: Multi-tenancy in cloud computing. In: Proceedings of the 8th IEEE International Symposium on Service-Oriented System Engineering. Oxford, UK (2014)

Alves, M.G., Matos, A.S.: An investigation into the use of ERP systems in the public sector. J. Enterp. Resour. Plan. Stud. (2011). Article ID 950191, https://doi.org/10.5171/2011.950191

Bahssas, D.M., AlBar, A.M., Hoque, R.: Int. Technol. Manag. Rev. **5**(2), 72–81 (2015)

Bailey, M., Katz, B., West, D.: Building a Long-Term Strategy for Growth through Innovation: Brookings Institution (2011)

Baumgartner, T.A., Strong, C.H., Hensley, L.D.: Conducting and Reading Research in Health and Human Performance, 3rd edn. McGraw-Hill, New York (2002)

Benders, J., Batenburg, R., Van der Blonk, H.: Sticking to standards: technical and other isomorphic pressures in deploying ERP-systems. Inf. Manag. **43**, 194–203 (2006)

Bitsini, N.: Investigating ERP misalignment between ERP systems and implementing organizations in developing countries. J. Enterp. Resour. Plan. Stud. (2015). Article ID 570821. http://www.ibimapublishing.com/journals/JERPS/jerps.html, https://doi.org/10.5171/2015.570821

Carutasu, N., Carutasu, G.: Cloud ERP implementation. Bus. Manag. J. Q. Rev. **4**(1) (2016)

Chandiwana, T., Pather, S.: A citizen benefit perspective of municipal enterprise resource planning systems. Electron. J. Inf. Syst. Eval. **19**(2), 85–98 (2016). http://www.ejise.com/main.html

Chang, S.I., Gable, G., Smythe, E., Timbrell, G.: A Delphi examination of public sector ERP implementation issues. In: Proceedings of the Twenty First International Conferences on Information Systems, Brisbane, Queensland, Australia, pp. 494–500 (2000)

Dantes, G.R., Hasibuan, Z.A.: Enterprise resource planning implementation framework based on key success factors (KSFs). In: UK Academy for Information Systems Conference Proceedings (2011). http://aisel.aisnet.org/ukais2011/13

DiMaggio, P.J., Powell, W.W.: The iron cage revisited; institutional isomorphism and collective rationality in organizational fields. Am. Sociol. Rev. **48**(1), 147–160 (1983)

Dwivedi, Y.K., Wastell, D., Laumer, S., Henriksen, H.Z., Myers, M., Bunker, D., Srivastava, S. C.: Research on information systems failures and successes: status update and future directions. Inf. Syst. Front. **17**(1), 143–157 (2014)

Fernandez, D., Zainol, Z., Ahmad, H.: The impacts of ERP systems on public sector organizations.In: 8th International Conference on Advances in Information Technology, IAIT, pp. 19–22 (2016)

Giannarou, L., Zervas. E.: Using Delphi technique to build consensus in practice. Int J. Bus. Sci. Appl. Manag. **9**(2), 65–82 (2014)

Govindaraju, R.: Enterprise systems implementation framework: an organizational perspective. Int. Congr. Interdiscip. Bus. Soc. Sci. Procedia - Soc. Behav. Sci. **65**, 473–478 (2012)

Hawari, A., Heeks, R.: Explaining ERP failure in a developing country: a jordanian case study. J. Enterp. Inf. Manag. **23**(2), 135–160 (2010)

Helo, P., Anussornnitisarn, P., Phusavat, K.: Expectation and reality in ERP implementation: consultant and solution provider perspective. Ind. Manag. Data Syst. **108**(8), 1045–1059 (2008)

Huang, S.M., Chang, I.C., Li, S.H., Lin, M.T.: Assessing risk in ERP projects: identify and prioritize the factors. Ind. Manag. Data Syst. **104**(8), 681–688 (2004)

Kaunda, M.J., Kennedy, O.: Factors influencing adoption and use of information and communication technology at the ethics and anticorruption commission of Kenya. J. Bus. Adm. Manag. Sci. Res. **2**(11), 224–309 (2013)

Kelemen, R.: ERP systems in public sector (2014). https://www.researchgate.net/publication/269291638_ERP_systems_in_public_sector, https://doi.org/10.1109/mipro.2014.6859810

Kitzinger, J.: The methodology of focus groups: the importance of interaction between research participants. Sociol. Health Illn. **16**(1), 103–121 (1994)

Klaus, H., Michael, R., Gable, G.: What is ERP? Inf. Syst. Front. **2**(2), 141–162 (2000)

Krueger, R.A., Casey, M.A.: Focus Groups: A Practical Guide for Applied Researchers, 3rd edn. Sage, Thousand Oaks (2000)

Kuechler, W., Vaishnavi, V.: The emergence of design research in information systems in North America. J. Des. Res. **7**(1), 1–16 (2008)

Larsen, M.A., Myers, M.D.: BPR success or failure? A business process reengineering model in the financial services industry. In: Proceedings of the International Conference on Information Systems, pp. 367–82 (1997)

Lenart, A.: ERP in the cloud – benefits and challenges. In: Wrycza, S. (ed.) SIGSAND/PLAIS 2011. LNBIP, vol. 93, pp. 39–50. Springer, Heidelberg (2011). https://doi.org/10.1007/978-3-642-25676-9_4

Maditinos, D., Chatzoudes, D., Tsairidis, C.: Factors affecting ERP system implementation effectiveness. J. Enterp. Inf. Manag. **25**(1), 60–78 (2011)

Markus, M.L., Tanis, C.: The enterprise systems experience – from adoption success. In: Zmud, R.W. (ed.) Framing the Domains of IT Research: Glimpsing the Future Through the Past (Pinna ex Educational Resources, Cincinnati, OH), pp. 173–207 (2000)

Markus, M.L., Axline, S., Petrie, D., Tanis, C.: Learning from adopters' experiences with ERP: problems encountered and success achieved. J. Inf. Technol. **15**(4), 245–265 (2000)

Mehta, A., Panda, S.N.: Design of infrastructure as a service (IAAS) framework with report generation mechanism. Int. J. Appl. Eng. Res. **13**(2), 942–946 (2018)

Miles, M.B., Huberman, A.M.: Qualitative Data Analysis: an Expanded Sourcebook. Sage Publications, Thousand Oaks (1994)

Morgan, D.L.: Focus Groups as Qualitative Research, 2nd edn. Sage, Thousand Oaks (1997)

Myers, G.: Where are you from? Identifying place. J. Socioling. **10**, 320–343 (2006)

National Information Technology Authority. NATIONAL IT SURVEY REPORT, pp. 75–78 (2018)

National Information technology Survey. NITA Report (2017/18). https://www.nita.go.ug/sites/default/files/publications/National%20IT%20Survey%20April%2010th.pdf

Okoli, C., Pawlowski, S.D.: The Delphi method as a research tool: an example, design considerations and applications. Inf. Manag. **42**(1), 15–29 (2004)

Onwuegbuzie, A.J., Dickinson, W.B., Leech, N.L., Zoran, A.G.: A qualitative framework for collecting and analyzing data in focus group research. Int. J. Qual. Methods **8**(3), 1–21 (2009)

Peffers, K., Tuunanen, T., Rothenberger, M.A., Samir Chatterjee, S.: A design science research methodology for information systems research. J. Manag. Inf. Syst. **24**(3), 45–78 (2008)

Rajapakse, J., Seddon, P.: Why ERP may not be suitable for organisations in developing countries in Asia. Working paper, Department of Information Systems. The University of Melbourne, Australia (2005)

Rajeshwar, V.: ERP implementation challenges & critical organizational success factors. Int. J. Curr. Eng. Technol. **5**(4), 2759 (2015)
Ram, J. Corkindale, D., Wu, M.L.: Implementation critical success factors (CSFs) for ERP: do they contribute to implementation success and post-implementation performance? Int. J. Prod. Econ. **144**, 157–174 (2013)
Ramburn, G., Mwalemba, A., Gwamaka, M., Lisa, S.: Organizational & knowledge challenges faced during an ERP implementation: the case of a large public sector organization. In: CONF-IRM Proceedings, p. 29 (2016). http://aisel.aisnet.org/confirm2016/29
Renata, G., Narcyz, R.: Effects of BPM on ERP adoption in the public sector. BPM and ERP adoption in the public sector. In: Twenty-third Americas Conference on Information Systems, (AMCIS), Boston (2017)
Saraswathi, M., Bhuvaneswari, T.: Multitenancy in cloud software as a service application. Int. J. Adv. Res. Comput. Sci. Softw. Eng. 3(11) (2013)
Sædberg, A., Haddara, M.: An exploration of adoption factors for cloud- based ERP systems. The Public Sector Paper presented at NOKOBIT 2016, Bergen, 28–30 November, vol. 24, no. 1, p. 1 (2016). Bibsys Open Journal Systems
Semakula, L., Muwanga, R.: Uganda: Implementing an Integrated Financial Management System and the Automation of the Budget Process. Country Learning Note, Odi (2012)
Shaul, L., Tauber, D.: Critical success factors in enterprise resource planning systems: review of the last decade. ACM Comput. Surv. **45**(4), 1–39 (2013)
Sim, J.: Collecting and analyzing qualitative data: issues raised by focus group. J. Adv. Nurs. **28** (2), 345–352 (1998)
Soja, P.: Determinants of Enterprise system adoption across the system lifecycle: insights from a transition economy. In: AMCIS 2012 Proceedings. Paper 4 (2012). http://aisel.aisnet.org/amcis2012/proceedings/ICTinGlobalDev/4
Sommer, R.: Public sector ERP implementation: successfully engaging middle management. Commun. IBIMA (2011). Article ID 162439, https://doi.org/10.5171/2011.162439
Tremblay, M.C., Hevner, A.R., Berndt, D.J.: Focus groups for Artifact refinement and evaluation in design research. CAIS **26**(27), 599–618 (2010)
Uganda Bureau of Statistics: Statistical Abstract (2017). https://www.ubos.org/wpcontent/uploads/publications/03_20182017_Statistical_Abstract.pdf
Weng, F., Hung, M.: Competition and challenge on adopting cloud ERP. Int. J. Innov. Manag. Technol. **5**(4), 309 (2014)
Ziemba, E., Oblak, I.: Critical success factors for ERP systems implementation. Interdiscip. J. Inf. Knowl. Manag. **8** (2013)

Effect of Inter-Organizational Systems Use on Supply Chain Capabilities and Performance

David Asamoah[1], Benjamin Agyei-Owusu[1(✉)], Francis Kofi Andoh-Baidoo[2], and Emmanuel Ayaburi[2]

[1] Kwame Nkrumah University of Science and Technology, Kumasi, Ghana
bagyei-owusu.ksb@knust.edu.gh
[2] University of Texas Rio Grande Valley, Brownsville, TX, USA

Abstract. Inter-Organizational Systems (IOS), which are information systems that extend beyond organizational borders, have seen growing use in linking companies to their supply chain partners. This paper empirically explores the relationship between IOS use, Supply Chain Capabilities, and Supply Chain Performance. The research model proposes that IOS use directly enhances Supply Chain Performance, and indirectly enhances Supply Chain Performance through Supply Chain Capabilities. To test the model, a survey of 200 firms operating in Ghana that use IOS was conducted. Analysis of the model was conducted using Partial Least Squares Structural Equation Modeling techniques. The results of the study confirmed that IOS use positively impacted Supply Chain Capabilities and Supply Chain Performance. Supply Chain Capabilities also positively impacted Supply Chain Performance. Additionally, Supply Chain Capabilities was found to partially mediate the effect of IOS use on Supply Chain Performance. Implications of the study for research and practice are discussed.

Keywords: Inter-Organizational Systems · Supply chain capabilities · Supply chain performance

1 Introduction

Inter-Organizational Systems (IOS) generally refer to information systems that extend beyond organizational borders. IOS is believed to have been coined by Kaufman (1966) who encouraged business executives to view their companies beyond their organizational boundaries and consider linking their companies to their supply chain partners and enterprises undertaking related functions. These systems are essential to augment the effectiveness of business activities and promote coordination among partners through timely exchange of information. IOS facilitate the electronic integration of business dealings and processes undertaken by more than one business entity (Chatterjee and Ravichandran 2004). IOS have been important in the rise of Supply Chain Management, a concept which deals with the design of seamless value-added processes across organizational boundaries to meet the real needs of the end customer (Fawcett et al. 2013). Supply chain management seeks to help organizations create a systemic and holistic view of their organization, having the consumer as the focus in

Published by Springer Nature Switzerland AG 2019
Y. Dwivedi et al. (Eds.): TDIT 2019, IFIP AICT 558, pp. 293–308, 2019.
https://doi.org/10.1007/978-3-030-20671-0_20

the value chain, with the focal firm looking at improving interactions within and without in order to enhance the lot of the consumer. Thus, IOS can be seen as information systems that facilitate effective management of the supply chain (Agbenyo et al. 2018). In supply chain management, IOS use is seen in the use of electronic data interchange (EDI) systems, vendor managed inventory (VMI) systems, and collaborative planning, forecasting and replenishment (CPFR) systems, all of which enable firms to communicate in real time with supply chain partners (Steinfield 2014). Various IOS are also used to support just-in-time inventory practices in supply chains.

IOS have significantly transformed the way business is carried out in many industries. In today's information age, large volumes of data are created by and exchanged between supply chain partners, and IOS have been widely adopted to help manage this information exchange (Premkumar et al. 1994). IOS use is perceived to be more prevalent in developed countries than in developing countries (Agbenyo et al. 2018). Research into the effects of IOS use in developed countries is also more matured, relative to those studies in the developing countries context (Agbenyo et al. 2018; Bakunzibake et al. 2016; Ali and Kurnia 2011). The literature on IOS in Sub-Saharan Africa is particularly underdeveloped with very few studies exploring how IOS use enhances performance. Given that environmental and contextual influences are perceived to influence outcomes of information systems use (Asamoah et al. 2015; Agbenyo et al. 2018; Agyei-Owusu et al. 2018), it is important to explore the effects of IOS use in Sub-Saharan Africa. Thus, this study seeks to answer the following research question: *how does IOS use influence supply chain capabilities and performance?* Our study proposes that IOS use enhances supply chain performance directly and indirectly through supply chain capabilities.

This study has some practical and theoretical contributions. First, the study explains how IOS may enhance supply chain performance. The study presents insights into the effects of IOS use in Sub-Saharan Africa, a context which has not been properly explored previously. The study also helps to bridge the IOS research gap between developed and developing countries. The rest of the paper is structured as follows. The theoretical background and conceptual framework is presented next, followed by a discussion of the methodology. The results of the study are then presented. The paper concludes with a discussion of the implications, recommendations and limitations of the study.

2 Theoretical Background

Chatterjee and Ravichandran (2004) note that despite the increasing interest and volume of research into IOS, not much theoretical generalization has emerged. The study of the outcomes of IOS have been explored from different perspectives such as, the transactions cost (Malone et al. 1994; Gurbaxani and Whang 1991; Choudhury et al. 1998), agency cost (Gurbaxani and Whang 1991), power and interest (Boonstra and de Vries 2005), incomplete contracts (Bakos and Brynjolfsson 1993; Banker et al. 2000), diffusion of innovation (Gurbaxani and Whang 1991; Premkumar et al. 1994; Mukhopadhay et al. 1995; Chwelos et al. 2001), theory of constraints (Geri and Ahituv

2008), resource-based view (McClaren et al. 2004), and coordination theory (Saeed et al. 2011).

This study is grounded on the resource-based view (McClaren et al. 2004). The resource-based view suggests that the resources and capabilities that firms possess are the basis of superior performance. The focus is on the resources and capabilities controlled by a firm, which is seen as the basis for persistent differences in performance among competing firms (Barney 1991; Peteraf and Barney 2003). The resource-based view of the firm conceptualizes firms as a bundle of resources and suggests that the type and quality of resources a firm controls is the basis for competitive advantage. Firms achieve competitive advantage by possessing resources which are valuable, rare, imperfectly imitable, and unique, and these enable companies to pursue opportunities and avoid threats (Barney 1991). McClaren et al. (2004) explored IOS from the resource-based view perspective and argued that supply chain management information systems resulted in the creation of supply chain management information systems capabilities.

Information systems and IT infrastructure are critical organizational resources that can generate capabilities, which can be leveraged to enhance enterprise wide performance (Kayworth and Sambamurthy 2000; Kumar 2001). IOS serve a similar purpose, but instead are used between two firms rather than departments or business units within a firm. This study thus views IOS as an important inter-organizational resource that can serve as the basis for gaining supply chain capabilities and achieving superior supply chain performance.

3 Theoretical Framework and Hypotheses

The study proposes that using IOS results in superior supply chain capabilities and higher supply chain performance. We argue IOS Use can directly enhance the supply chain performance of firms, and indirectly enhance supply chain performance through enhanced supply chain capabilities.

IOS Use in this study refers to the extent to which firms have adopted and are using IOS in their operations. Extant literature identifies three broad uses of IOS, namely for communication, integration, and intelligence (Agbenyo et al. 2018; Zhang and Cao 2018). These are explored as dimensions of IOS Use. *Supply Chain Capabilities* refer to the ability of an organization to identify, utilize, and assimilate both internal and external resources/information to facilitate the entire supply chain activities (Wu et al. 2006). Four primary Supply Chain Capabilities are identified in the literature – Integration, Coordination, Information Exchange, and Responsiveness (Wu et al. 2006). We explore these dimensions of Supply Chain Capabilities in this study. Finally, *Supply Chain Performance* is a measure of how well the supply chain can meet its functional objectives (Agbenyo et al. 2018; Sezen 2008). Three dimensions of Supply Chain Performance which have been identified in the literature – Reliability, Efficiency (cost containment) and Flexibility (Lee et al. 2007; Sezen 2008) – are explored in this study. The theoretical framework for the study is presented in Fig. 1.

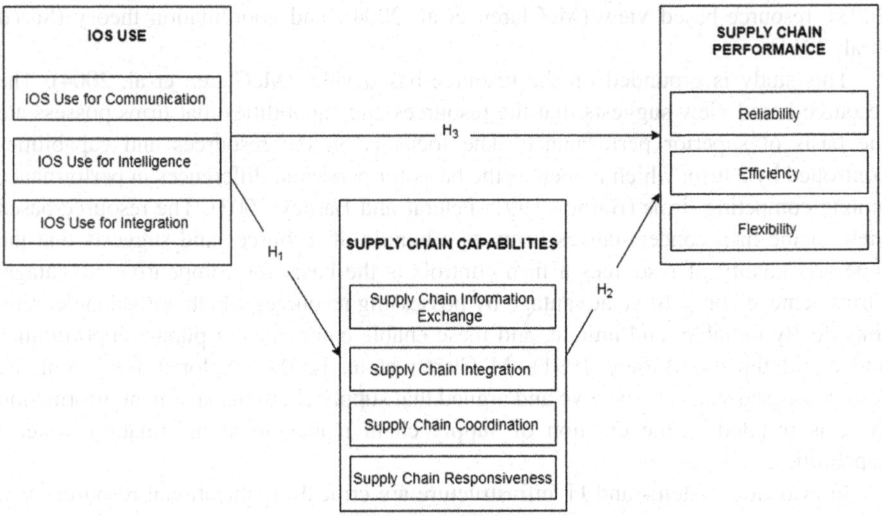

Fig. 1. Conceptual model

Several studies have noted that the benefits achievable from an information system are often dependent on the extent to which they are implemented and utilized (Dwivedi et al. 2011; 2015; Karimi et al. 2007; Asamoah et al. 2015; Agbenyo et al. 2018). Some researchers have argued that IOS can directly enhance the performance of the firms in the supply chain in terms of higher efficiency and service levels (Bakos and Tracey 1986; Charterjee and Ravichandran 2004). McClaren et al. (2004) observed that the broad use of IOS in supply chains creates important capabilities for firms. The study of Wang et al. (2006) further lends credence to this view, by showing that using IOS leads to higher supply chain collaboration and integration. Previous studies show that the supply chain capabilities developed from IOS are important in driving performance of firms in the supply chain. Wang et al. (2006) survey study of Taiwanese manufacturing firms found that IOS, by integrating a set of suppliers for tighter supply chain collaboration, enables manufacturers to achieve greater manufacturing flexibility in addition to comparative cost advantages in supply-chain operations (Wang et al. 2006). Premkumar et al. (2005) study also revealed that IOS, by increasing information-processing capabilities, reduces supply-chain uncertainties, and that designing IOS to fit the information-processing needs for coping with supply chain uncertainties has a large positive impact on firm performance. Knowledge sharing and shared decision making which arises from IOS use leads to collaborative advantages in terms of productivity, agility, innovation and reputation (Chi and Holsapple 2005). Again, Hartono et al. (2010) noted that using IOS enabled higher quality data sharing, which positively impacted firms' operational supply chain performance. Based on these arguments, it is hypothesized that:

H_1: The broader use of IOS lead to higher levels of Supply Chain Capabilities
H_2: Higher levels of Supply Chain Capabilities lead to higher levels of Supply Chain Performance
H_3: The broader use of IOS lead to higher levels of Supply Chain Performance

4 Methodology

Measurement instruments for the constructs were obtained from previous studies and adapted to suit the context of this study. IOS Use was adopted from Zhang and Cao (2018), Supply Chain Capabilities was adopted from Wu et al. (2006), and Supply Chain Performance was adopted from Kocoglu et al. (2011) and Lee et al. (2007). The research items were positively framed using five-point Likert scales. The selected research items were then critically reviewed by three experts in the subject area whose input helped refine the measures. Finally, a pilot test involving 30 organizations that use IOS was performed to help further refine the research items. We conducted exploratory factor analysis on the pilot data, which confirmed the good factor loadings and multi-dimensionality of the research items. This helped to ensure valid measurement items were used in our survey. The measurement items used in this study are presented in Appendix I.

A survey of 200 randomly selected firms in Ghana that use IOS systems in their operations was conducted to obtain data to test the proposed model. Our data collection targeted manufacturers and key distributors of fast moving consumer goods. In Ghana, the big manufacturers of fast moving consumer goods and their key distributors typically use IOS to share inventory and sales information, as well as to plan and execute restocking decisions. Questionnaires were delivered to each selected firm with a cover letter detailing the purpose of the study. In all, eighty-six (86) responses were successfully retrieved, representing a reasonably high response rate of 43%. Power tests revealed that given a total of ten predictors of the dependent variable, a medium effect size of 0.15, and observed R^2 of 0.410, a sample size of 86 gives a statistical power of 0.99, which sufficiently exceeds the recommended threshold of 0.80 (Cohen 1998).

5 Results

5.1 Demographic Results

Analysis of the demographic data collected revealed that 15.1% of the respondents were manufacturers of fast moving consumer goods, with the remaining 84.9% being distributors. There was a fairly even distribution in terms of maturity of the organizations surveyed, with about 36% of the firms being in existence for up to 10 years, 32.5% of firms operating for 11 to 20 years, and about 31.4% of the firms operating for more than 20 years. Finally, majority of firms (57%) had revenue levels of one million Ghana Cedis or less (approximately US$186, 219). The full demographic results are presented in Table 1.

Table 1. Demographic data

Firm type	Frequency	Percent	Cumulative percent
Manufacturers	13	15.1	15.1
Distributors	73	84.9	100.0
Total	86	100.0	
Years of operation	Frequency	Percent	Cumulative percent
Up to 10 years	31	36.0	17.4
11 to 20years	28	32.5	68.5
More than 20 years	27	31.4	100.0
Total	86	100.0	
Annual revenue (in US$)	Frequency	Percent	Cumulative percent
Less than 9,310	11	12.8	12.8
9,310 to 18,621	8	9.3	22.1
18,622 to 93,109	20	23.3	45.3
93,110 to 186,219	10	11.6	57.0
186,220 to 931,098	4	4.7	61.6
931,098 to 1,862,197	11	12.8	74.4
1,862,198 to 9,310,986	14	16.3	90.7
9,310,987 and above	8	9.3	100.0
Total	86	100.0	

5.2 Measurement Model Results

The measurement model was analysed by assessing the convergent validity and discriminant validity of the model. Convergent validity can be assessed by measuring the reliability of survey items, that is, assessing the composite reliability of constructs, average variance extracted (AVE), Cronbach's Alpha, and factor analysis (Hair et al.

Table 2. Attributes of constructs

Constructs	Cronbach's alpha	rho_A	Composite reliability	AVE
IOS use for communication	0.905	0.907	0.933	0.777
Efficiency	0.917	0.920	0.942	0.801
Flexibility	0.918	0.921	0.938	0.753
Supply chain information exchange	0.895	0.897	0.927	0.761
IOS use for intelligence	0.722	0.724	0.844	0.644
IOS use for integration	0.772	0.781	0.853	0.594
Reliability	0.867	0.872	0.904	0.654
Supply chain coordination	0.881	0.885	0.913	0.678
Supply chain integration	0.871	0.894	0.911	0.720
Supply chain responsiveness	0.849	0.855	0.892	0.624

2014). We tested the attributes of the constructs by measuring the psychometric properties of the constructs and comparing them against recommended benchmarks. The AVEs of all the constructs were higher than 0.5 as required (Barclay et al. 1995). Composite Reliabilities values were high (least value was 0.825) and comfortably exceeded the suggested threshold of 0.7 (Chin 1998). Cronbach Alpha values also exceeded the 0.7 threshold as recommended (Hair et al. 2014). The summary of the psychometric properties of the constructs are presented in Table 2.

We examined item loadings to ensure that all items loaded highly on their constructs (0.7 or higher) (Hair et al. 2014). Items with poor loadings were dropped as recommended (Hair et al. 2014). The loadings of the remaining items were adequate as can be seen in appendix II.

The items were tested for sufficient discriminant validity. Discriminant validity examines the extent to which a measure correlates with measures of constructs that are different from the construct they are intended to assess (Barclay et al. 1995). The factor loadings and cross loadings table indicates good discriminant validity because the loading of each measurement item on its latent variable is larger than its loading on any other construct (see appendix II). Further, discriminant validity can be assessed by comparing the square root of the AVE for each factor against the correlation of constructs against each other, with the former required to be higher than the latter (Fornell and Larcker 1981). In Table 3, the bold diagonal figures represent square roots of AVEs whilst the off-diagonal figures represent correlation among constructs. It can be seen that the bold diagonal values are all greater than the off-diagonal ones, confirming adequate discriminant validity.

Table 3. Intercorrelation among constructs

	COMM	EFF	FLEX	INFEX	INTEL	INTG	REL	SCCOR	SCINT	SCRES
COMM	**0.882**									
EFF	0.611	**0.895**								
FLEX	0.411	0.571	**0.868**							
INFEX	0.497	0.536	0.486	**0.872**						
INTEL	0.490	0.343	0.295	0.443	**0.802**					
INTG	0.440	0.384	0.182	0.526	0.636	**0.771**				
REL	0.420	0.567	0.412	0.479	0.515	0.612	**0.809**			
SCCOR	0.559	0.449	0.378	0.620	0.303	0.452	0.328	**0.823**		
SCINT	0.470	0.308	0.250	0.462	0.565	0.475	0.541	0.557	**0.848**	
SCRES	0.488	0.433	0.467	0.757	0.528	0.625	0.615	0.592	0.625	**0.790**

Finally, discriminant validity was tested using the HTMT test. HTMT is the average of the heterotrait-heteromethod correlations (i.e., the correlations of indicators across constructs measuring different phenomena), relative to the average of the monotrait-heteromethod correlations (i.e., the correlations of indicators within the same construct) (Henseler et al. 2015). HTMT test approach indicates that HTMT values

Table 4. HTMT results

	COMM	EFF	FLEX	INFEX	INTEL	INTG	REL	SCCOR	SCINT	SCRES
COM										
EFF	0.665									
FLEX	0.443	0.617								
INFX	0.546	0.586	0.526							
INTEL	0.598	0.420	0.382	0.552						
INTG	0.505	0.451	0.225	0.625	0.858					
REL	0.466	0.627	0.456	0.539	0.646	0.744				
SCCOR	0.621	0.496	0.415	0.687	0.380	0.533	0.368			
SCINT	0.515	0.342	0.282	0.502	0.723	0.586	0.607	0.607		
SCRES	0.544	0.484	0.519	0.860	0.678	0.774	0.712	0.667	0.724	

must be significantly less than 1, with a value of less than 0.85 ideal (Henseler et al. 2015). Table 4 indicates that the highest HTMT value is 0.791, confirming the model possesses adequate discriminant validity.

5.3 Structural Model Results

After confirming that the measurement model was sound, we proceeded to analyze the structural model and hypothesized relationships. PLS-SEM provides the magnitude and significance of the hypothesized causal relationships as standardized path coefficients. The parameter estimate of the hypothesized structural path should be statistically significant in the hypothesized direction of the effect. A path is considered to be statistically significant if its *p* value is less than the 0.05 significance level. The R^2 values represent the variance explained by the latent variables. The results of the structural model analysis are presented in Fig. 2 and Table 5 below.

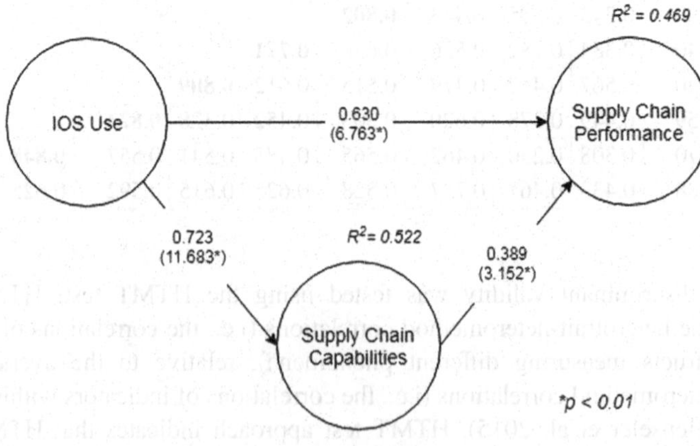

Fig. 2. Research model

Table 5. Hypotheses results

Hs	Hypothesis	Path co-efficient	T statistics	P values	Decision
H1	IOS use → Supply chain capabilities	0.723	11.683	0.000	Supported
H2	Supply chain capabilities → Supply chain performance	0.389	3.152	0.002	Supported
H3	IOS use → Supply chain performance	0.630	6.763	0.000	Supported

The co-efficient of determination (R^2) values of Supply Chain Capabilities and Supply Chain Performance were 0.522 and 0.469 respectively. This means that about 52.2% of the variation in Supply Chain Capabilities was predicted by IOS Use, and about 46.9% of the changes in Supply Chain Performance were predicted by IOS Use and Supply Chain Capabilities. These represent moderate levels of explanatory power (Hair et al. 2017). The results of the structural model analysis revealed that all three hypothesized paths were supported. The effect of IOS use on supply chain capabilities was positive and significant, supporting hypothesis 1. This confirms that firms that use IOS to a high level are better able to achieve higher levels of supply chain information exchange, supply chain integration, supply chain coordination, and supply chain responsiveness. The results further indicated that firms with higher supply chain capabilities are able to achieve higher levels of supply chain performance. This indicates that the supply chain capabilities developed through IOS use are useful building blocks that aid firms achieve greater reliability, efficiency and flexibility in their supply chains. Finally, the findings of the study indicated that IOS use can directly enhance the supply chain performance of firms, supporting hypothesis 3. Thus, it can be said that IOS use both directly and indirectly enhances the supply chain performance of firms.

6 Conclusion

The study explored the effects of IOS use in a developing country and observed that IOS use directly enhances supply chain performance and supply chain capabilities. The study also observed that supply chain capabilities directly enhance supply chain performance. There are a number of implications of the study for research and practice.

By way of implication for research, the study conceptualizes and empirically confirms that IOS use enables the development of supply chain capabilities for firms and as well enhances the performance of the supply chain. The relationship between IOS Use, Supply Chain Capabilities, and Supply Chain Performance has not been explored in this way in previous research and as such the findings of the study provide new insights on the outcomes of IOS use. Previous studies that explore IOS have largely done so from an information systems perspective, where the focus is on the characteristics of the IOS, or from a supply chain management perspective, where the focus is on how the IOS enhances collaboration. The study provides an integrative look at IOS and their outcomes from the resource-based view perspective, enriching both IOS use and supply chain management theories and providing new insights.

The study also provides context-specific insights into the outcomes of IOS use in Sub-Saharan Africa, a context which has not been empirically explored previously (Andoh-Baidoo 2017). Research suggests that environmental and contextual influences are perceived to influence outcomes of information systems use and supply chain management initiatives (Asamoah et al. 2015; Asamoah et al. 2016), providing the need to properly explore information systems and supply chain management initiatives within the Sub-Saharan African context. The results of the study also point to a mediating effect of supply chain capabilities in the effect of IOS use on supply chain performance. Thus, using IOS enhances the ability of firms to manage their supply chains, which subsequently enhances the performance of their supply chains. By way of implications for practice, the study provides insights that can guide IOS use in Sub-Saharan Africa.

There were some limitations to the work. Even though IOS Use, Supply Chain Capabilities, and Supply Chain Performance were conceptualized as second-order constructs having first order dimensions, structural model analysis was conducted at the second-order level to prevent the model becoming overly complex. This however means the relationship between dimensions of these constructs could not be explored into greater detail. Also, as the study focused on the Sub-Saharan African context, the findings of the study may not be supported in other developing regions of the world. We call for more empirical studies to explore effects of IOS use in other developing countries. Future research should also be directed at exploring the mediating role of supply chain capabilities into more detail.

Appendix I: Measurement Scales of Constructs

IOS Use for Communication

Our firm and supply chain partners use IOS for workflow coordination
Our firm and supply chain partners use IOS for conferencing
Our firm and supply chain partners use IOS for message services
Our firm and supply chain partners use IOS for frequent contacts
Our firm and supply chain partners use IOS for multiple channel communication

IOS Use for Integration

Our firm and supply chain partners use IOS for integrating business functions across firms
Our firm and supply chain partners use IOS for joint forecasting, planning, and execution
Our firm and supply chain partners use IOS for order processing, invoicing and settling accounts
Our firm and supply chain partners use IOS for exchange of shipment and delivery information

Our firm and supply chain partners use IOS for managing warehouse stock and inventories

IOS Use for Intelligence

Our firm and supply chain partners use IOS for understanding trends in sales and customer preferences
Our firm and supply chain partners use IOS for storing, searching, and retrieving business information
Our firm and supply chain partners use IOS for deriving inferences from past events (e.g., process exceptions, patterns of demand shifts, what worked and what did not work)
Our firm and supply chain partners use IOS for combining information from different sources to uncover trends and patterns
Our firm and supply chain partners use IOS for interpreting information from different sources in multiple ways depending upon various requirements

Supply Chain Information Exchange

Our firm exchanges more information with our supply chain partners
Our firm benefits more from information exchange with our supply chain partners
Information flows more freely between our firm and supply chain partners
Information exchange with our supply chain partners is accurate and timely

Supply Chain Coordination

Our firm is more efficient in coordination activities with our supply chain partners
Our firm conducts transaction follow-up activities more efficiently with our supply chain partners
Our firm spends less time coordinating transactions with our supply chain partners than our competitors
Our firm has reduced coordinating costs more than our competitors
Our firm can conduct the coordination activities at less cost than our competitors

Supply Chain Integration

Our firm develops strategic plans in collaboration with our supply chain partners
Our firm collaborates actively in forecasting and planning with our supply chain partners
Our firm projects and plans future demand collaboratively with our supply chain partners
Our firm always forecasts and plans activities collaboratively with our supply chain partners

Supply Chain Responsiveness

Our firm and supply chain partners understand trends in sales and customer preferences
Our firm and supply chain partners promote storing, searching, and retrieving business information (share common database)
Our firm and supply chain partners derive inferences from past events (e.g., process expectations, patterns of demand shifts, what worked and what did not work)

Our firm and supply chain partners use information from different partners in multiple ways depending upon various requirements

Reliability

Our firm with supply chain partners offers products that are highly reliable
Our firm with supply chain partners offers high quality products to our customers
Our firm and supply chain partners have helped each other to improve product quality
Our firm with supply chain partners increases the rate at which we fulfill customer orders
Our firm with supply chain partners increases our inventory turns

Efficiency

Our firm with supply chain partners reduces inbound and outbound cost of transport
Our firm with supply chain partners reduces warehousing and inventory holding costs
Our firm with supply chain partners meets on-time delivery requirements for all product
Our firm with supply chain partners reach agreed costs per unit as compared with industry

Flexibility

Our firm with supply chain partners offers a variety of products and services efficiently
Our firm with supply chain partners offers customized products and services with different features
Our firm with supply chain partners meets different customer volume requirements efficiently
Our firm with supply chain partners has short customer response time as comparison to industry
Our firm with supply chain partners responds to and accommodate demand variations

Appendix II: Item Loadings

	COMM	EFF	FLEX	INFEX	INTEL	INTG	REL	SCCOR	SCINT	SCRES
APCOM2	**0.865**	0.452	0.348	0.335	0.370	0.357	0.299	0.509	0.388	0.383
APCOM3	**0.887**	0.403	0.279	0.362	0.440	0.338	0.287	0.405	0.393	0.296
APCOM4	**0.897**	0.625	0.340	0.479	0.362	0.400	0.459	0.529	0.455	0.551
APCOM5	**0.877**	0.657	0.471	0.558	0.543	0.447	0.427	0.525	0.422	0.480
APINTG1	0.119	0.211	0.027	0.272	0.517	**0.735**	0.492	0.202	0.395	0.418
APINTG2	0.377	0.359	0.185	0.443	0.444	**0.701**	0.452	0.357	0.315	0.422
APINTG3	0.360	0.314	0.097	0.439	0.531	**0.830**	0.511	0.373	0.375	0.542
APINTG4	0.452	0.289	0.228	0.443	0.478	**0.809**	0.440	0.429	0.383	0.527
APINTL1	0.398	0.273	0.132	0.235	**0.750**	0.543	0.393	0.180	0.551	0.351

(*continued*)

(continued)

	COMM	EFF	FLEX	INFEX	INTEL	INTG	REL	SCCOR	SCINT	SCRES
APINTL2	0.469	0.292	0.223	0.398	**0.838**	0.465	0.434	0.271	0.421	0.395
APINTL3	0.305	0.258	0.360	0.434	**0.817**	0.526	0.410	0.279	0.387	0.530
SCCOD1	0.464	0.376	0.431	0.581	0.244	0.396	0.322	**0.763**	0.423	0.478
SCCOD2	0.404	0.297	0.262	0.523	0.276	0.434	0.171	**0.836**	0.475	0.494
SCCOD3	0.581	0.459	0.353	0.536	0.169	0.409	0.303	**0.891**	0.475	0.512
SCCOD4	0.383	0.321	0.216	0.344	0.237	0.306	0.175	**0.804**	0.348	0.369
SCCOD5	0.452	0.384	0.282	0.537	0.321	0.306	0.357	**0.818**	0.547	0.558
SCINFX1	0.560	0.621	0.367	**0.867**	0.349	0.560	0.512	0.521	0.413	0.591
SCINFX2	0.311	0.282	0.300	**0.863**	0.394	0.406	0.300	0.461	0.350	0.642
SCINFX3	0.380	0.452	0.427	**0.908**	0.421	0.447	0.449	0.574	0.369	0.719
SCINFX4	0.478	0.507	0.585	**0.850**	0.381	0.426	0.405	0.596	0.476	0.683
SCINTG1	0.483	0.267	0.193	0.447	0.482	0.416	0.487	0.583	**0.890**	0.578
SCINTG2	0.478	0.287	0.248	0.523	0.436	0.385	0.532	0.575	**0.896**	0.584
SCINTG3	0.271	0.280	0.209	0.296	0.560	0.458	0.435	0.389	**0.851**	0.454
SCINTG4	0.324	0.205	0.198	0.244	0.469	0.364	0.353	0.276	**0.749**	0.487
SCRESP1	0.174	0.194	0.319	0.463	0.444	0.475	0.463	0.339	0.604	**0.756**
SCRESP2	0.453	0.350	0.414	0.649	0.444	0.463	0.459	0.563	0.515	**0.790**
SCRESP3	0.507	0.378	0.471	0.671	0.413	0.455	0.412	0.601	0.480	**0.830**
SCRESP4	0.475	0.366	0.355	0.642	0.423	0.512	0.577	0.429	0.462	**0.843**
SCRESP5	0.269	0.418	0.261	0.541	0.360	0.585	0.537	0.368	0.414	**0.725**
SPEFF1	0.512	**0.849**	0.460	0.412	0.329	0.313	0.449	0.403	0.262	0.303
SPEFF2	0.548	**0.913**	0.511	0.480	0.304	0.377	0.481	0.426	0.266	0.347
SPEFF3	0.570	**0.920**	0.531	0.446	0.243	0.280	0.463	0.332	0.260	0.329
SPEFF4	0.556	**0.897**	0.537	0.570	0.351	0.399	0.625	0.445	0.312	0.553
SPFLX1	0.231	0.544	**0.823**	0.388	0.078	0.141	0.366	0.209	0.084	0.398
SPFLX2	0.269	0.376	**0.838**	0.315	0.319	0.168	0.257	0.280	0.219	0.335
SPFLX3	0.401	0.471	**0.884**	0.438	0.356	0.220	0.389	0.427	0.276	0.387
SPFLX4	0.425	0.535	**0.910**	0.402	0.231	0.089	0.367	0.317	0.239	0.415
SPFLX5	0.439	0.535	**0.882**	0.548	0.304	0.174	0.392	0.400	0.264	0.480
SPREL1	0.436	0.550	0.393	0.448	0.470	0.568	**0.846**	0.306	0.570	0.667
SPREL2	0.380	0.506	0.336	0.429	0.475	0.600	**0.849**	0.268	0.423	0.580
SPREL3	0.270	0.363	0.344	0.349	0.474	0.537	**0.824**	0.275	0.442	0.439
SPREL4	0.263	0.326	0.325	0.375	0.411	0.373	**0.793**	0.219	0.429	0.428
SPREL5	0.327	0.525	0.258	0.321	0.237	0.366	**0.725**	0.249	0.302	0.32

References

Agbenyo, L., Asamoah, D., Agyei-Owusu, B.: Drivers and Effects of inter-organizational systems (IOS) use in a developing country. In: Twenty-Fourth Americas Conference on Information Systems, New Orleans (2018)

Agyei-Owusu, B., Asamoah, D., Agbenyo, L.: Examining the effects of information technology outsourcing on competitive advantage. In: Twenty-Fourth Americas Conference on Information Systems, New Orleans (2018)

Ali, M., Kurnia, S.: Inter-organizational systems (IOS) adoption in the Arabian Gulf region: the case of the Bahraini grocery industry. Inf. Technol. Dev. **17**(4), 253–267 (2011)

Andoh-Baidoo, F.K.: Context-specific theorizing in ICT4D research. Inf. Technol. Dev. **23**(2), 195–211 (2017)

Asamoah, D., Andoh-Baidoo, F.K., Agyei-Owusu, B.: Impact of ERP implementation on business process outcomes: a replication of a United States study in a Sub-Saharan African Nation. AIS Trans. Replication Res. **1**(1), 1–19 (2015)

Asamoah, D., Andoh-Baidoo, F., Agyei-Owusu, B.: Examining the relationships between supply chain integration, information sharing, and supply chain performance: a replication study. In: Proceedings of the 22nd Americas Conference on Information Systems, San Diego, California, no. 4, pp. 2749–2758 (2016)

Bakos, J.Y., Treacy, M.E.: Information technology and corporate strategy a research perspective. MIS Q. **10**(2), 107–119 (1986)

Bakos, J.Y., Brynjolfsson, E.: Infroamtion technology, incentives and the optimal number of suppliers. J. Manag. Inf. Syst. **10**(2), 37 (1993)

Bakunzibake, P., Grönlund, Å., Klein, G.O.: E-government implementation in developing countries: enterprise content management in Rwanda. In: 15th IFIP Electronic Government (EGOV)/8th Electronic Participation (ePart) Conference, Univ Minho, Guimaraes, Portugal, 5–8 September 2016, pp. 251–259, September 2016

Banker, R., Kalvenes, J., Patterson, R.: Information technology, contract completeness and buyer-supplier relationships. In: The 21st Annual International Conference on Information Systems, Brisbane, Australia (2000)

Barclay, D., Higgins, C., Thompson, R.: The partial least squares (PLS) approach to causal modeling: personal computer adoption and use as an illustration. Technol. Stud. **2**, 285–309 (1995)

Barney, J.: Firm resources and sustained competitive advantage. J. Knowl. Manag. **17**, 99–120 (1991)

Boonstra, A., De Vries, J.: Analyzing inter-organizational systems from a power and interest perspective. Int. J. Inf. Manag. **25**(6), 485–501 (2005)

Chatterjee, D., Ravichandran, T.: Inter-organizational information systems research: a critical review and an integrative framework. In: Proceedings of the 37th Hawaii International Conference on System Sciences (2004)

Chi, L., Holsapple, C.W.: Understanding computer-mediated interorganizational collaboration: a model and framework. J. Knowl. Manag. **9**(1), 53–75 (2005)

Chin, W.W.: Commentary: issues and opinion on structural equation modeling. MIS Q. **22**(1), vii–xvi (1998)

Choudhury, V., Hartzel, K.S., Konsynski, B.R.: Uses and consequences of electronic markets: an empirical investigation in the aircraft parts industry. MIS Q. **22**, 471–507 (1998)

Chwelos, P., Benbasat, I., Dexter, A.S.: Research report: empirical test of an EDI adoption model. Inf. Syst. Res. **12**, 304–321 (2001)

Cohen, J.: Statistical Power Analysis for the Behavioral Sciences, 2nd edn. Lawrence Erlbaum Associates, Publishers, Hillsdale (1988)

Dwivedi, Y.K., Wade, M.R., Schneberger, S.L. (eds.): Information Systems Theory: Explaining and Predicting Our Digital Society, vol. 1. Springer, Heidelberg (2011). https://doi.org/10.1007/978-1-4419-6108-2

Dwivedi, Y.K., et al.: Research on information systems failures and successes: status update and future directions. Inf. Syst. Front. **17**(1), 143–157 (2015)

Fawcett, S.E., Ellram, L.M., Ogden, J.A.: SCM: Pearson New International Edition: From Vision to Implementation. Pearson Higher Education (2013)

Fornell, C., Larcker, D.F.: Structural equation models with unobservable variables and measurement error: algebra and statistics. J. Mark. Res. **18**(3), 328–388 (1981)

Geri, N., Ahituv, N.: A theory of constraints approach to interorganizational systems implementation. Inf. Syst. e-Bus. Manag. **6**(4), 341–360 (2008)

Gurbaxani, V., Whang, S.: The impact of information systems on organizations and markets. Commun. ACM **34**(1), 59–73 (1991)

Hair Jr, F., Sarstedt, J.M., Hopkins, L., Kuppelwieser, G.V.: Partial least squares structural equation modeling (PLS-SEM) an emerging tool in business research. European Business (2014)

Hair, J.F., Hult, G.T.M., Ringle, C.M., Sarstedt, M.: A Primer on Partial Least Squares Structural Equation Modeling (PLS-SEM). SAGE, Los Angeles (2017)

Hartono, E., Li, X., Na, K.S., Simpson, J.T.: The role of the quality of shared information in interorganizational systems use. Int. J. Inf. Manag. **30**(5), 399–407 (2010)

Henseler, J., Ringle, C.M., Sarstedt, M.: A new criterion for assessing discriminant validity in variance-based structural equation modeling. J. Acad. Mark. Sci. **43**(1), 115–135 (2015)

Karimi, J., Somers, T.M., Bhattacherjee, A.: The impact of ERP implementation on business process outcomes: a factor-based study. J. Manag. Inf. Syst. **24**(1), 101–134 (2007)

Kaufman, F.: Data Systems that Cross Company Boundaries, pp. 141–155. Harvard Business Review (1966)

Kayworth, T.R., Sambamurthy, V.: Facilitating localized exploitation and enterprise wide integration in the use of IT infrastructures: the role of PC/LAN infrastructure standards. DATABASE Adv. Inf. Syst. **31**(4), 54–77 (2000)

Kocoglu, I., Imamoglu, S.Z., Ince, H., Keskin, H.: The effect of supply chain integration on information sharing: enhancing the supply chain performance. Procedia – Social and Behavioral Sciences **24**, 1630–1649 (2011)

Kumar, K.: Technology for supporting supply chain management. Commun. ACM **44**(6), 57–61 (2001)

Lee, C.W., Kwon, I.-W.G., Severance, D.: Relationship between supply chain performance and degree of linkage among supplier, internal integration and customer's. Supply Chain. Manag.: Int. J. **12**(6), 444–452 (2007)

Malone, T.W., Yates, J., Benjamin, R.I.: Electronic Markets and Electronic Hierarchies, pp. 61–83. Oxford University Press, New York (1994)

McLaren, T.S., Head, M.M., Yuan, Y.: Supply chain management information systems capabilities. An exploratory study of electronics manufacturers. Inf. Syst. e-Bus. Manag. **2**(2–3), 207–222 (2004)

Mukhopadhay, T., Kekre, S., Kalathur, S.: Business value of information technology: a study of electronic data interchange. MIS Q. **19**(2), 137–156 (1995)

Peteraf, M.A., Barney, J.B.: Unraveling the resource-based tangle. Manag. Decis. Econ. **24**(4), 309–323 (2003)

Premkumar, G., Ramamurthy, K., Nilakanta, S.: Implementation of electronic data interchange: an innovation diffusion perpective. J. Manag. Inf. Syst. **11**(2), 157–816 (1994)

Premkumar, G., Ramamurthy, K., Saunders, C.S.: Information processing view of organizations: an exploratory examination of fit in the context of interorganizational relationships. J. Manag. Inf. Syst. **22**(1), 257–294 (2005)
Saeed, K.A., Malhotra, M.K., Grover, V.: Interorganizational system characteristics and supply chain integration: an empirical assessment. Decis. Sci. **42**(1), 7–42 (2011)
Sezen, B.: Relative effects of design, integration and information sharing on supply chain performance. Supply Chain. Manag.: Int. J. **13**, 233–240 (2008)
Steinfield, C.: Inter-organizational information systems. In: Tucker, A., Gonzalez, T., Topi, H. and Diaz-Herrera, J. (eds.) Computing Handbook, Third Edition, Volume 2: Information Systems and Information Technology (Chapter 69). CRC Press, Boca Raton, pp. 69-1–69-15 (2014)
Wang, E.T., Tai, J.C., Wei, H.L.: A virtual integration theory of improved supply-chain performance. J. Manag. Inf. Syst. **23**(2), 41–64 (2006)
Wu, F., Yeniyurt, S., Kim, D., Cavusgil, S.T.: The impact of information technology on supply chain capabilities and firm performance: a resource-based view. Ind. Mark. Manag. **35**, 493–504 (2006)
Zhang, Q., Cao, M.: Exploring antecedents of supply chain collaboration: effects of culture and interorganizational system appropriation. Int. J. Prod. Econ. **195**, 146–157 (2018)

Smart Cities

Role of Smart Cities in Creating Sustainable Cities and Communities: A Systematic Literature Review

Elvira Ismagiloiva[1(✉)], Laurie Hughes[2], Nripendra Rana[2], and Yogesh Dwivedi[2]

[1] Faculty of Management, Law and Social Sciences, University of Bradford, Bradford, UK
e.ismagilova@bradford.ac.uk

[2] Emerging Markets Research Centre, School of Management, Swansea University, Swansea, UK
{d.l.hughes,n.p.rana,y.k.dwivedi}@swansea.ac.uk

Abstract. Seventeen United Nations Development Goals (UN SDG) focus on peace and prosperity for people and the planet. Smart cities can help in achieving UN SDG. This research carries out a comprehensive analysis of the role of smart cities on creating sustainable cities and communities, which is one of 17 UN sustainable goals. Current research focuses on number of aspect of sustainable environment such as renewable and green energy, energy efficiency, environmental monitoring, air quality, and water quality. This study provides a valuable synthesis of the relevant literature on smart cities by analysing and discussing the key findings from existing research on issues of smart cities in creating sustainable cities and communities. The findings of this study can provide an informative framework for research on smart cities for academics and practitioners.

Keywords: Smart cities · Literature review · Sustainable development goals

1 Introduction

The United Nation developed Sustainability Development Goals in 2015, which aim to achieve peace and prosperity for people and the planet, focusing on the present and the future. As a result 17 goals were established aiming to act as an urgent call for action for countries all over the world [1]. The SDG emphasise that ending poverty and other deprivations must go hand-in-hand with strategies to improve health and education, reduce inequality, and engender economic growth whilst tackling climate change and preserving our forests and oceans [1]. Some researchers proposed that smart cities have the potential to deliver many of the UN Sustainability Development goals [2–5].

A city is defined as smart if it "balances economic, social, and environmental development, and if it links up to democratic processes through a participatory government. A smart city involves the implementation and deployment of information and communication technology (ICT) infrastructures to support social and urban growth through improving the economy, citizens' involvement and government efficiency" [6].

Published by Springer Nature Switzerland AG 2019
Y. Dwivedi et al. (Eds.): TDIT 2019, IFIP AICT 558, pp. 311–324, 2019.
https://doi.org/10.1007/978-3-030-20671-0_21

Examples of smart cities include Busan (South Korea), London (United Kingdom), Santander (Spain) to name a few. Technology spending on smart cities initiatives worldwide is currently $81 billion and predicted to reach $158 billion in 2022 [7]. The smart cities topic attracted significant attention from both academics and practitioners. This is evidenced by the growing number of research outputs within academic journals, books and conference proceedings. Some studies provided comprehensive literature review on smart cities [8–11] and barriers affecting its development [12]. Even though these existing reviews provided a timely overview of the overall subject area, there is a lack of studies focusing on the connection of the concept of smart cities and UN SDG goals. Thus this study aims to bridge this gap in the literature by conducting a comprehensive analysis of the role of smart cities on creating sustainable cities and communities, which is one of the 17 UN sustainable goals. The findings of this study can provide an informative framework for research on smart cities for academics and practitioners.

The remaining sections of this study are organised as follows. Section 2 provides a brief overview of the methods used to identify relevant studies to be included in this review. Section 3 synthesises the studies identified in the previous section and provides their detailed overview and analysis. Finally the study is concluded in Sect. 4 by discussing the key aspect of the research, challenges faced by smart cities in creating sustainable cities and communities, and outlining limitations of the current research and proposing further directions.

2 Literature Search Method

This research used a keyword search based approach in order to identify relevant studies on smart cities [4]. The following keywords were used: "Smart City" OR "Smart Cities" OR "Digital City" OR "Information City" OR "Intelligent City" OR "Knowledge-based City" OR "Ubiquitous City" OR "Wired City" in Scopus database. As a result 1473 articles were identified. By going through each of the articles manually 40 articles were selected which focused on sustainable cities and communities. The selected studies appeared in 33 separate journals, including Management Journals, Engineering Journals, and Urban studies journals. It demonstrates that smart cities attracted attention of researchers from multiple disciplines.

3 Literature Synthesis

The studies on smart cities focusing on SDG sustainable cities and communities goal were divided into the following themes: renewable and green energy, energy efficiency, air quality, environment monitoring and water quality monitoring (see Table 1). The following subsections provide overview of each theme.

Table 1. Themes in smart cities research

Theme	Studies
Renewable and green energy	[13–19]
Energy efficiency	[20–41]
Environment monitoring	[42, 43]
Air quality	[44–48]
Water quality monitoring	[2, 49, 50]

3.1 Renewable Energy

The concept of smart cities involves specifically modified infrastructure of energy, which is mainly distributed in the form of electricity. Power system provides the core functionality to many important entities of the cities such as telecom networks, wireless sensor network, water distribution, waste management, mobility, route guidance, public healthcare, information amenities and others. The power system operation has to be optimised by being intelligent and environmental friendly [13]. It can be reached by including renewable resources and green ICT systems which help to achieve greater energy efficiency. The use of renewable and efficient energy will lead to climate improvement. Number of studies focused on renewable and smart energy for smart cities [13–19].

A study by Aamir et al. [13] focused on implementation of smart grids. Smart grid places ICN into electricity generation, distribution, and consumption. As a result, the system becomes more clean, secure, reliable, and efficient. The proposed framework can provide a simulation platform for detailed study of power system. It will help to deal with issues such as susceptibility of failure, critical situations and restoration scheme by adding renewable energy resources. Thus, the framework can be used in a simulation platform for analysing power system operation in smart cities. It can also be used to develop operational algorithms to optimize the generation, transmission and distribution schemes and taking advantage of smart infrastructure in a more effective manner. The calculation of Locational Marginal Prices is mandatory as prices vary by location in case of congestion. It will be resulted in more economic dispatch of electricity as most of the contingent conditions will be resolved in proactive manner. A study by Sanchez-Miralles et al. [18] discusses the use of renewable energy systems for distributed generation for households or districts. The authors reviewed the main renewable energies and companion technologies and investigated their current economic feasibility. As a result a simplified architecture is presented, which consists of three interconnected layers, the intelligence layer, the communication layer and the infrastructure layer.

Smart energy is one of the most important components of smart cities, which includes electricity generation, transmission and distribution [15, 51]. Main goals of smart cities are to reduce energy consumption, provide renewable energy and reduce carbon footprints. The study by Ahuja and Khosla [15] proposes a hierarchical architecture to solve the problem of lacking of necessary interoperability and integration of communication standards, which affect successful deployment of communication networks. The proposed system aims to support smart energy system infrastructure and help smart cities to provide ubiquitous communication. The system consists of two computing zones. First is fog computing which will help to reduce latency response to anomalous and hazardous events in real time. Second is cloud computing which will provide access to data from anywhere for deep analysis.

Studies on green energy focused on two types of energy: solar and wind. A study by Abdullah et al. [14] focuses on wind energy as one of the renewable sources, which has advantage such as sustainability and being environmentally friendly. The authors proposed an improved one-power-point solution maximum power point tracking algorithm for wind energy conversion system in order to overcome problems such as difficulty in getting a precise value of the optimum coefficient, requiring pre-knowledge of system parameters, and non-uniqueness of the optimum curve. The proposed solution is based on the combination of two algorithms: the particle swarm optimisation and optimum-relation based MPPT algorithms. By using MATLAB/Simulink simulation and experiments the study proved that the proposed algorithm demonstrates the improved performance in terms of tracking efficiency and energy extracted.

Wang et al. [19] focus on solar energy and wind energy, by presenting the approach of maximising their use in the cities, as there is a problem of utilization of wind turbine generators in the cities due to their large volumes and safety issues. The authors designed a hybridized nanogenerator, which includes collar cell and a triboelectic nanogenerator. It allows to scavenge solar and wind energies by installing these nanogenerators on the roofs of the city buildings. The hybridized nanogenerator has better performance than the individual solar and wind generators.

Barresi [16] also focused on solar energy. The study proposed the solutions for urban planners how to ensure that unobstructed flow of solar energy through adjacent lots when designing a particular urban area. The study also defined ordinances specifying the standards for the exact size and location of the easement and indicating limitations on buildings or structures that could prevent the passage of light through it. These solutions will increase flexibility for the integration of solar and local energy sources.

Hung and Peng [17] proposed green-energy water-autonomous greenhouse system, which is more responsive and efficient as an alternative-technology approach towards sustainable, smart-green vertical greening in smart cities. Future studies should establish a real model of prototype for conducting experimental studies.

3.2 Energy Efficiency

Some of the studies focused on improving energy efficiency in smart cities [20–41]. For example, study by Peña et al. [37] proposed a new method to solve the problem of energy efficiency anomalies in smart buildings. The proposed solution is based on a rule-based system, which is developed by using data mining techniques and applying knowledge of energy efficiency experts. The result of this work provided a set of rules which can be used a part of a decision support system for the improving energy consumption and the detection of anomalies in smart buildings by controlling the activation of devices and minimising power taking into consideration different requirements of users. Battista et al. [21] aimed to define the approach for assessment of building energy savings. The study used a single building located in Rio de Janeiro. They calculated the annual energy demands through dynamic software. Additionally, different energy efficiency interventions were simulated. After this, a graph was created to summarize the energy demand percentage variations as a function of the selected parameter variation, such as solar absorbance coefficient, vertical and horizontal surface thermal transmittance and window g-value. Based on the results of this study, it will be possible to choose the most effective building intervention.

Jung et al. [30] also focus on energy efficiency of buildings in the city. However, they argue that not just energy efficient devices to equip buildings are important but also an efficient management. The study measures the energy consumption and environmental data through establishing a Building Energy Management System. The proposed technologies will integrate real-time energy consumption monitoring with Building Energy Information Modeling. By using Genetic Algorithms an optimal energy-saving method was found. The study plans to apply the proposed energy optimization tool to the micro-energy grid system in the future. A study by Sanseverino et al. [39] is focusing on sustainable territorial planning, by investigating the possibility to draft a basic structure on Municipal Building Regulations. It will help to guide local administrators and technicians and limit discretionary power of bureaucracy. Brundu et al. [23] proposed and tested an IoT software infrastructure enabling energy management and simulation of new control policies in a city district. The platforms allow the interoperability and the correlation of real-time building energy profiles with environmental data from sensors, buildings and grid models. This will simulate novel energy policies at district level and provide optimization of the energy usage. After the testing platform in real world it was found that this platform is suitable to run energy distribution policies simulations from the district level down to the building room level, with a special focus on both district energy savings and end-user comfort level.

Calvillo et al. [24] also focused on buildings, as one of the bigger energy users of the city. The paper proposed a linear programming model which finds optimal operation and planning of distributed energy sources in a residential district. The proposed model was successfully tested using data from Madrid. Another study by Caponio et al. [25] is focusing on buildings for improving their energy efficiency. The study proposed a simulation model based on System Dynamic applied to a medium-sized Italian city. The proposed model enables the testing of "what-if" scenarios and analysing the result of implementing energy efficiency policies. Obtained results demonstrate the importance of a holistic view of urban energy process. The simulation trends can be used as essential information for the city's future energy and carbon emission profiles. It will help policymakers to accomplish their goals. Carli et al. [26] proposed decision process which will help the city energy manager and local policy makers use decision from one urban sector on another.

Zhang [40] proposed a novel routing algorithm named as power controlled and stability-based routing protocol (PCSR). The proposed protocol aims to improve the energy efficiency and route stability. The power for transmitting both control packers and datagrams is reduced in PCSR. By using expensive simulations the findings show that proposed PCSR consumes less energy and extends network lifetime with guaranteed packet delivery. Alzahrani and Ejaz [20] propose a resource management scheme for cognitive IoT network with radio frequency energy harvesting in 5G networks, which can improve spectral efficiency and accommodate a large number of IoT devices. The study applies mixed linear programming and greedy approaches in order to solve the optimization problem. The proposed scheme is tested by using simulation and shows the significant positive impact on the performance of the IoT network.

Bhati et al. [22] focused on the ways how Singapore household perceive smart technology and their usage to reduce energy consumption. By suing interviews and case studies the research found that the behavioural patterns of consumers may not change in order to save energy. Some individuals will still prefer comfort and security over their concerns about environment and energy saving. As a result the study demonstrated the gap in the designing technology, which does not take into consideration people's behaviours and perceptions when designing smart home design functionality.

Kai et al. [31] studied device-to-device (D2D) communication which helps to improve data rate and reduce power consumption, D2D allows two physically nearby located user equipment to communicate directly with each other. Authors aim to achieve green communications by using D2D. Thus, they investigated the joint optimization of uplink subcarrier assignment (SA) and power allocation (PA) in D2D underlying cellular networks. Orsino et al. [35] also focused on D2D communications. The study adapted the Modulation and Coding Scheme on the communication links in order to maximise the radio resource utilization as a function of the total amount of data to be sent. As a result, the transmission power will be reduced when a robust modulation and coding scheme is applied.

Lu et al. [32] investigated the joint optimization of subcarrier grouping, subcarrier pairing, and power allocation such that the transmission rate performance is maximized with the energy harvesting constraint. The joint optimization problem is solved via dual decomposition after transforming it into an equivalent convex optimization problem. Simulation results tested with the real wireless sensor networks system data indicate.

Maier [33] provides a comprehensive methodology for planning and assessing the development of 'smart' energy systems leading to complex energy provision technology networks using different on-site as well as off-site resources. The results of the study can be used to form smart energy supply solutions as an integral part for the discussion of the stakeholders (investors, city department) to guide the forming of their action plan through the development of the city quarter.

Mohapatra et al. [34] proposed dynamic cluster-head scheme and modified LEACH protocol. By using simulation it was found that the proposed system ensures minimal energy waste and consolidated a green model for smart cities. The study proposes that future research should focus on existing fault diagnosis protocols for incorporating dynamic faults in the network.

The study by Pardo-García et al. [36] presents the design and development of the innovative SuperCity Platform which makes cities sustainable. The platform is transparent and user friendly which can be used by non-technical staff, such as politicians. Also, it enables the assessment of urban policies and measures by using holistic optimisation of the whole energy system towards low carbon energy system. As the proposed model is generic it can be applied to any cities. Pardo-García et al. [36] claim that it is important to create a platform for users with different level of expertise, which can improve communication between city actors.

Pirisi et al. [38] presented the optimization of a Tubular Permanent Magnetic-Linear Generator for energy harvesting from vehicles. The optimization process is developed by means of hybrid evolutionary algorithms to reach the best overall system efficiency and the impact on the environment and transportation systems. The proposed system is experimentally validated. Zhu et al. [41] presented energy savings algorithms (network-wide energy-saving algorithms and customer-side energy-saving algorithm), which can be used by cable operators in order to enhance the energy efficiency of cable access networking using channel bonding. The numerical results of this study suggest that effective energy saving can be achieved in wideband cable access networks with the proposed algorithms, and the packet delay and protocol overhead can be reduced if the key parameters are chosen properly.

Causone et al. [27] discusses the importance of establishing appropriate key performance indicators for different aspects of the cities, such as economy, education, environment etc. The study focuses on creating KPI to assess the energy performance of cities and to determine if energy is used with appropriate and smart approaches. The study proposed exergy as an indicator of the energy quality, which offers a quantitative basis to measure the degradation of energy (the decrease of its capacity to generate useful work) in conversion process. Causone et al. [27] used data collected from European cities to access the possibilities and limitations of the proposed KPI.

Chui et al. [28] focus on artificial intelligence and by investigating ways it can provide support in providing sustainable energy in smart cities. By conducting pilot study and creating prototypes this paper examined smart metering and non-intrusive load monitoring (NILM) to propose NILM value added in context of profiling electric appliances' electricity consumption.

Colmenar-Santos et al. [29] focused on energy storage system with high power density. The authors designed an electrical and control adaptation circuit for storing energy, which consisted of three blocks (passive filter, converter system, chopper). By using simulations the study found the possibility of controlling the energy supply as well as storage. These findings enable to adapt to different contingencies which may include the wiring of the charge in the new and different types of charges. However, the disadvantages of this system can be high cost of manufacturing and maintenance in comparison with other cheaper systems.

3.3 Environmental Monitoring

Some studies focus on the importance of environment monitoring in smart cities [43]. For example Dwevedi et al. [43] identified six environmental factors, such as landscape and geography, climate, atmospheric pollution, water resources, energy resources, and urban green spaces for Smart City Mission in India. These factors should be integrated in the development of smart cities and to be included in the monitoring system, which will be available through online platform to public to ensure that the society can participate in identifying the problems and offering help with the solutions.

Bacco et al. [42] also focused on monitoring environment of cities. They proposed and successfully tested environment monitoring system in Pisa, Italy. The system was based on a cost-effective, distributed and efficient sensor network for collecting, processing and distributed data about the air quality. The system has fixed and mobile sensor nodes. To support objective information from sensor nodes the system allows the citizens to provide additional subjective information, such as comments, pictures and videos. The information from citizens is then stored on the central host of the proposed architecture and can be correlated with the data collected by nodes. The system calculates Air Quality Index, Thermal Comfort Index and Traffic Index. After, this information is available to all stakeholders interested in receiving timely updates on the air quality in the city (e.g. city governors, local authorities, citizens).

3.4 Air Quality

Air pollution is one of the main threats for developed societies [45]. Based on the data from World Health organisation, pollution is considered as the main cause of deaths for under five years old children [45]. Number of studies investigated how to monitor and improve air quality in cities using smart technologies [44–48]. Marek et al. [44] conducted a case study of monitoring air quality in post-earthquake Chirstchurch, New Zealand. The project focused on near real-time monitoring of air pollution in fine scale and its association with respiratory diseases. The intention of the project was to create the continuous air pollution surface of the city in real time and provide the data as an interactive dynamic map and the raw data stream. The data was collected using a grid of four dustmote devices and low cost IoT air quality sensors. The air quality data is designed to be provided to all citizens and interested stakeholders in primary forms and in the form of maps and tables. It aims to engage citizens to check information about air quality in the way which is easy to understand. Also, citizens can check and understand their individual exposure.

Data collection in smart cities is possible by employing sensors. However, data obtaining through sensors can have errors. As a result, it is important to develop a model which can predict values of interest in order to control air quality. Martínez-España et al. [45] analysed different machine learning techniques to predict ozone levels (Random Forest, Random Committee, Bagging and KNN) and obtained the best model which can predict ozone levels (Random Forest). As a result, if the sensors fail to record the data correctly, the model can predict with the least possible error the amount of ozone in the air to create a warning in case of the recommended thresholds levels are exceeded. The test of the proposed model was conducted in four cities at the Region of Murcia (Spain) by using real data from 4 stations for air quality measurement. This model can help to predict pollution levels and to establish thresholds and action plans for local authorities and industries. The future work can focus on automatic generation of recommendation to local authorities, drivers and other stakeholders about the impact of air-quality factors according to the alerts raised by the system.

Smart cities infrastructure provides information about air quality using data from low-cost sensors, which can report information in a timely and accurate manner. This information can be used to propose solutions to mitigation strategies to reduce pollution. Miles et al. [46] proposed a decision support system which can monitor air quality, forecast atmospheric pollution, as well as suggest and implement pollution reducing strategies in real time using IoT. This decision support system can help and improve decisions of policy makers and engineers on planning of urban landscapes. The proposed decision making system is using traffic model as the input to an atmospheric model to create predictors of traffic-related atmospheric pollution levels. Also, this system can evaluate of different scenarios of how pollution levels would change when mitigation strategies that change existing conditions are implemented. The strength of this proposed system is that all required information could be gathered for different locations and the system will not be limited to a single location. As a result, it can be generalised and used in other cities. Future research can focus of simulation of more complex areas such as street canyons. Another study by Ramos et al. [47] aims to improve citizens' awareness about air pollution by offering pollution-free routes. The study applied a technology-agnostic method using air quality sensor networks, which allows creating pollution-free routes in real time across cities depending on the level of air pollution in each zone of the city. In order to develop and validate the proposed framework the study used Madrid's air quality sensor network. The system can propose the routes for pedestrians, cyclists or any vehicle. Future studies could extend a routing application into a mobile application and try to render the interpolation layer as 3D surfaces.

In smart cities data is generated and collected by sensors, which represent what is happening in the city in real time [48]. Correct and timely analysis and use of these data is important. Zaree and Honarvar [48] argue that big data mining is the most effective method for analysing this data. The study uses a K-means clustering algorithm employing the Mahout library as a big data mining tool. By using this tool Zaree and Honarvar [48] aim to increase speed and accuracy in predicting real levels of air pollution, its location, and effects of weather conditions on density of air pollution. The results indicate that temperature, low air pressure, relative increase in moisture and wind spend are causes of low pollution density at the cleanest point of the city. In order to obtain more reliable results the study aims to employ the fuzzy clustering algorithm of the Mahout library in the future research.

Finding the most polluted and cleanest areas of the city can improve environment and citizen's quality of life [48]. To be able to control air pollution is one of the main advantages of smart cities. By identifying polluted areas in real time will help manage the city. By decreasing air pollution, cities can reduce diseases like brain stroke, cardiac diseases, lung cancer, and asthma [48].

3.5 Water Quality Monitoring

Safe drinking water is a life-enabling resource, but it is a difficult task to manage its quality in crowded cities [52, 53]. Nowadays cities are faced with challenges such as old water infrastructure, expensive maintenance costs, new contaminants, and increasing water demand due to rising population level [53, 54]. As a result, cities need an effective water management system. Some researchers investigated how advanced ICT based systems can improve the quality of drinking water around the word [2, 50]. For instance, a study by Corbett and Mellouli [2] developed conceptual model, which expands the role of IS in building smart sustainable cities. The model was developed based on the data from interviews. The model explains the interactions between three interrelated spheres such as administrative, political and sustainability. After, to demonstrate the applicability of this model the study used two real-word scenarios. Also, this study focused on public green spaces, which are an essential part of sustainable cities as they provide different types of benefits, including aesthetic, environmental and health to name a few. Sun et al. [50] introduced a Bayesian network model for water controlling system. The model was successfully tested by using experiments. Another study by Chen and Han [49] proposed the quality monitoring system for Bristol is Open using wireless communication and data processing, storage and redistribution. The system includes data acquisition, data transmission, data storage and data visualisation with the help of cloud computing.

4 Conclusion and Limitations

The aim of this research was to provide a systematic review of the literature on the role smart cities play in achieving the UN SDG sustainable cities and communities goal. From the growing literature on smart cities it can be seen that the development and growth of smart cities can help to achieve many UN development goals. Based on the reviewed literature it is suggested that sustainability within smart cities is covered within the smart environmental theme. Current research reviewed the number of studies which focused on these issues. The studies focused on energy for smart cities, particularly on renewable and green energy [13–15], and energy efficiency [20–22]. Also, the reviewed studies paid attention to the environment monitoring [42, 43], air quality [44–46], and water quality [2, 49, 50]. For the city environment to be sustainable it is important to monitor the quality of water and air and also use energy resources efficiently. Thus monitoring, management, evaluation and use of the smart environment are important and can be achieved by using information and communication technologies, such as IoT and cloud computing. The following are a summary of the key observations emerging from this literature review:

- Most of the studies on sustainability of smart cities are focusing on energy efficiency, particularly on energy efficiency of buildings.
- In systematically reviewing 40 publications on smart cities it was observed that many do not rely on case related empirical data. Studies generally base they results on simulations.
- IoT and cloud computing are the technologies discussed in relation to sustainability of smart cities.
- The concept of smart cities has the full potential to deliver the UN SDG sustainable cities and communities goal.

Cities are facing multiple challenges while trying to become sustainable. Most of the proposed systems to monitor the environment are not publicly available and require expert knowledge to use and understand them. Future research should develop more user friendly systems so citizens can be informed about the environment in the places they live and be able to participate in the decision making process about future actions connected to the planning, development and improvement of smart cities infrastructure. Also, policymakers should be able to use this information for policy formulation and making the decision about the environment of the city.

Some of frameworks for improving environment in the cities as proposed by a number of studies, can be limited to their application in particular cities and/or regions [22, 42]. Future studies should try to propose solutions which can be generalised and used by a large number of cities. Additionally, there can be some technological challenges for all cities to implement and adopt the proposed solutions for sustainable environment. The level of technology development, technological skills and readiness to adopt new technologies and solutions can impact the implementation of sustainable technologies especially in case of emerging market countries. Thus, it is important to propose solutions for these countries.

Also, current studies focused mostly on parameters that can influence air quality such as temperature, humidity, and wind [42, 45–48]. Future studies should focus on other parameters such as sulphur dioxide, PM10 Particles, and Nitrogen Dioxide. Finally, with the increasing number of natural hazards and climate-related challenges [43], it is important to find a way of using resources and provisioning for the future generations.

This study has a number of limitations. Only publications from the Scopus database were included in literature analysis and synthesis. Additionally, this research focused on 1 UN sustainable goal. It is recommended that future research will conduct systematic literature review (adapting approach from [4, 55–61]) around the remaining 16 UN sustainable goals, to provide a comprehensive and informative framework for research on smart cities for academics and practitioners.

References

1. United Nations: Sustainable development goals (2018). https://www.un.org/sustainabledevelopment/sustainable-development-goals
2. Corbett, J., Mellouli, S.: Winning the SDG battle in cities: how an integrated information ecosystem can contribute to the achievement of the 2030 sustainable development goals. Inf. Syst. J. **27**, 427–461 (2017)
3. Drira, K.: Toward open smart IoT Systems: an overview of recent initiatives and future directions. In: 9th IFIP International Conference on New Technologies, Mobility & Security, NTMS 2018 (2018)
4. Ismagilova, E., Hughes, L., Dwivedi, Y.K., Raman, K.R.: Smart cities: advances in research—An information systems perspective. Int. J. Inf. Manag. **47**, 88–100 (2019)
5. Kotzé, P., Coetzee, L.: Opportunities for the Internet of Things in the water, sanitation and hygiene domain. In: Strous, L., Cerf, V. (eds.) IFIPIoT 2018. IAICT, vol. 548, pp. 194–210. Springer, Cham (2019). https://doi.org/10.1007/978-3-030-15651-0_16
6. Yeh, H.: The effects of successful ICT-based smart city services: from citizens' perspectives. Gov. Inf. Q. **34**, 556–565 (2017)
7. Statista: Smart city initiatives: global spending 2022 (2019). https://www.statista.com/statistics/884092/worldwide-spending-smart-city-initiatives/
8. Albino, V., Berardi, U., Dangelico, R.M.: Smart cities: definitions, dimensions, performance, and initiatives. J. Urban Technol. **22**, 3–21 (2015)
9. Anthopoulos, L.G.: Understanding the smart city domain: a literature review. In: Rodríguez-Bolívar, M.P. (ed.) Transforming City Governments for Successful Smart Cities. PAIT, vol. 8, pp. 9–21. Springer, Cham (2015). https://doi.org/10.1007/978-3-319-03167-5_2

10. Bibri, S.E., Krogstie, J.: Smart sustainable cities of the future: an extensive interdisciplinary literature review. Sustain. Cities Soc. **31**, 183–212 (2017)
11. Chatterjee, S., Kar, A.K.: Smart Cities in developing economies: a literature review and policy insights. In: 2015 International Conference on Advances in Computing, Communications and Informatics (ICACCI), pp. 2335–2340. IEEE (2015)
12. Rana, N.P., Luthra, S., Mangla, S.K., Islam, R., Roderick, S., Dwivedi, Y.K.: Barriers to the development of smart cities in Indian context. Inf. Syst. Front. 1–23 (2018). https://doi.org/10.1007/s10796-018-9873-4
13. Aamir, M., Uqaili, M.A., Amir, S., Chowdhry, B., Rafique, F., Poncela, J.: Framework for analysis of power system operation in smart cities. Wirel. Pers. Commun. **76**, 399–408 (2014)
14. Abdullah, M.A., Al-Hadhrami, T., Tan, C.W., Yatim, A.H.: Towards green energy for smart cities: particle swarm optimization based MPPT approach. IEEE Access **6**, 58427–58438 (2018)
15. Ahuja, K., Khosla, A.: Network selection criterion for ubiquitous communication provisioning in smart cities for smart energy system. J. Netw. Comput. Appl. **127**, 82–91 (2019)
16. Barresi, A.: Urban densification and energy efficiency in smart cities-the VerGe project (Switzerland). TECHNE-J. Technol. Archit. Environ. **1**, 28–32 (2018)
17. Hung, P., Peng, K.: Green energy water-autonomous greenhouse system: an alternative technology approach toward sustainable smart–green vertical greening in a smart city. In: Shen, Z., Huang, L., Peng, K., Pai, J. (eds.) Green City Planning and Practices in Asian Cities. SS, pp. 315–335. Springer, Cham (2018). https://doi.org/10.1007/978-3-319-70025-0_16
18. Sanchez-Miralles, A., Calvillo, C., Martín, F., Villar, J.: Use of renewable energy systems in smart cities. In: Sanz-Bobi, M.A. (ed.) Use, Operation and Maintenance of Renewable Energy Systems. GET, pp. 341–370. Springer, Cham (2014). https://doi.org/10.1007/978-3-319-03224-5_10
19. Wang, S., Wang, X., Wang, Z.L., Yang, Y.: Efficient scavenging of solar and wind energies in a smart city. ACS Nano **10**, 5696–5700 (2016)
20. Alzahrani, B., Ejaz, W.: Resource Management for Cognitive IoT Systems With RF Energy Harvesting in Smart Cities. IEEE Access **6**, 62717–62727 (2018)
21. Battista, G., Evangelisti, L., Guattari, C., Basilicata, C., de Lieto Vollaro, R.: Buildings energy efficiency: interventions analysis under a smart cities approach. Sustainability **6**, 4694–4705 (2014)
22. Bhati, A., Hansen, M., Chan, C.M.: Energy conservation through smart homes in a smart city: a lesson for Singapore households. Energy Policy **104**, 230–239 (2017)
23. Brundu, F.G., et al.: IoT software infrastructure for energy management and simulation in smart cities. IEEE Trans. Ind. Inf. **13**, 832–840 (2017)
24. Calvillo, C.F., Sánchez-Miralles, Á., Villar, J.: Synergies of electric urban transport systems and distributed energy resources in smart cities. IEEE Trans. Intell. Transp. Syst. **19**, 2445–2453 (2018)
25. Caponio, G., Massaro, V., Mossa, G., Mummolo, G.: Strategic energy planning of residential buildings in a smart city: a system dynamics approach. Int. J. Eng. Bus. Manag. **7**, 20 (2015)
26. Carli, R., Dotoli, M., Pellegrino, R.: A hierarchical decision-making strategy for the energy management of smart cities. IEEE Trans. Autom. Sci. Eng. **14**, 505–523 (2017)
27. Causone, F., Sangalli, A., Pagliano, L., Carlucci, S.: Assessing energy performance of smart cities. Build. Serv. Eng. Res. Technol. **39**, 99–116 (2018)

28. Chui, K., Lytras, M., Visvizi, A.: Energy sustainability in smart cities: artificial intelligence, smart monitoring, and optimization of energy consumption. Energies **11**, 2869 (2018)
29. Colmenar-Santos, A., Molina-Ibáñez, E.-L., Rosales-Asensio, E., López-Rey, Á.: Technical approach for the inclusion of superconducting magnetic energy storage in a smart city. Energy **158**, 1080–1091 (2018)
30. Jung, D.-K., Lee, D., Park, S.: Energy operation management for Smart city using 3D building energy information modeling. Int. J. Precis. Eng. Manuf. **15**, 1717–1724 (2014)
31. Kai, C., Li, H., Xu, L., Li, Y., Jiang, T.: Energy-efficient device-to-device communications for green smart cities. IEEE Trans. Ind. Inf. **14**, 1542–1551 (2018)
32. Lu, W., Gong, Y., Liu, X., Wu, J., Peng, H.: Collaborative energy and information transfer in green wireless sensor networks for smart cities. IEEE Trans. Ind. Inf. **14**, 1585–1593 (2018)
33. Maier, S.: Smart energy systems for smart city districts: case study Reininghaus District. Energy Sustain. Soc. **6**, 23 (2016)
34. Mohapatra, A.D., Sahoo, M.N., Sangaiah, A.K.: Distributed fault diagnosis with dynamic cluster-head and energy efficient dissemination model for smart city. Sustain. Cities Soc. **43**, 624–634 (2018)
35. Orsino, A., Araniti, G., Militano, L., Alonso-Zarate, J., Molinaro, A., Iera, A.: Energy efficient IoT data collection in smart cities exploiting D2D communications. Sensors **16**, 836 (2016)
36. Pardo-García, N., Simoes, S.G., Dias, L., Sandgren, A., Suna, D., Krook-Riekkola, A.: Sustainable and resource efficient cities platform–surecity holistic simulation and optimization for smart cities. J. Cleaner Prod. **215**, 701–711 (2019)
37. Peña, M., Biscarri, F., Guerrero, J.I., Monedero, I., León, C.: Rule-based system to detect energy efficiency anomalies in smart buildings, a data mining approach. Expert Syst. Appl. **56**, 242–255 (2016)
38. Pirisi, A., Grimaccia, F., Mussetta, M., Zich, R.: Novel speed bumps design and optimization for vehicles' energy recovery in smart cities. Energies **5**, 4624–4642 (2012)
39. Sanseverino, E.R., Scaccianoce, G., Vaccaro, V., Carta, M., Sanseverino, R.R.: Smart cities and municipal building regulation for energy efficiency. Int. J. Agric. Environ. Inf. Syst. (IJAEIS) **6**, 56–82 (2015)
40. Zhang, T.: Fairness guaranteed rating decomposition in service-oriented reputation systems. J. Inf. Sci. Eng. **34**, 1079–1094 (2018)
41. Zhu, Z., Lu, P., Rodrigues, J.J., Wen, Y.: Energy-efficient wideband cable access networks in future smart cities. IEEE Commun. Mag. **51**, 94–100 (2013)
42. Bacco, M., Delmastro, F., Ferro, E., Gotta, A.: Environmental monitoring for smart cities. IEEE Sens. J. **17**, 7767–7774 (2017)
43. Dwevedi, R., Krishna, V., Kumar, A.: Environment and big data: role in smart cities of India. Resources **7**, 64 (2018)
44. Marek, L., Campbell, M., Bui, L.: Shaking for innovation: the (re) building of a (smart) city in a post disaster environment. Cities **63**, 41–50 (2017)
45. Martínez-España, R., Bueno-Crespo, A., Timon-Perez, I.M., Soto, J., Muñoz, A., Cecilia, J. M.: Air-pollution prediction in smart cities through machine learning methods: a case of study in Murcia. Spain. J. UCS **24**, 261–276 (2018)
46. Miles, A., Zaslavsky, A., Browne, C.: IoT-based decision support system for monitoring and mitigating atmospheric pollution in smart cities. J. Decis. Syst. **27**, 56–67 (2018)
47. Ramos, F., Trilles, S., Muñoz, A., Huerta, J.: Promoting pollution-free routes in smart cities using air quality sensor networks. Sensors **18**, 2507 (2018)

48. Zaree, T., Honarvar, A.R.: Improvement of air pollution prediction in a smart city and its correlation with weather conditions using metrological big data. Turkish J. Electr. Eng. Comput. Sci. **26**, 1302–1313 (2018)
49. Chen, Y., Han, D.: Water quality monitoring in smart city: a pilot project. Autom. Constr. **89**, 307–316 (2018)
50. Sun, F., Wu, C., Sheng, D.: Bayesian networks for intrusion dependency analysis in water controlling systems. J. Inf. Sci. Eng. **33**, 1069–1083 (2017)
51. Patel, S., Yaragatti, U.R., Kumar, P.: Role of smart meters in smart city development in India. In: 2016 IEEE 1st International Conference on Power Electronics, Intelligent Control and Energy Systems (ICPEICES), pp. 1–5. IEEE (2016)
52. Hrudey, S.E., et al.: Managing uncertainty in the provision of safe drinking water. Water Sci. Technol.: Water Supply **11**, 675–681 (2011)
53. Polenghi-Gross, I., Sabol, S.A., Ritchie, S.R., Norton, M.R.: Water storage and gravity for urban sustainability and climate readiness. J.-Am. Water Works Assoc. **106**, E539–E549 (2014)
54. Hou, D., Song, X., Zhang, G., Zhang, H., Loaiciga, H.: An early warning and control system for urban, drinking water quality protection: China's experience. Environ. Sci. Pollut. Res. **20**, 4496–4508 (2013)
55. Duan, Y., Edwards, J.S., Dwivedi, Y.K.: Artificial intelligence for decision making in the era of Big Data–evolution, challenges and research agenda. Int. J. Inf. Manag. **48**, 63–71 (2019)
56. Hughes, D., Dwivedi, Y., Misra, S., Rana, N., Raghvan, V., Akella, V.: Blockchain research, practice and policy: applications, benefits, limitations, emerging research themes and research agenda. Int. J. Inf. Manag. **49**, 114–129 (2019)
57. Dwivedi, Y.K., Kuljis, J.: Profile of IS research published in the European Journal of Information Systems. Eur. J. Inf. Syst. **17**(6), 678–693 (2008)
58. Irani, Z., Gunasekaran, A., Dwivedi, Y.K.: Radio frequency identification (RFID): research trends and framework. Int. J. Prod. Res. **48**(9), 2485–2511 (2010)
59. Kapoor, K.K., Tamilmani, K., Rana, N.P., Patil, P., Dwivedi, Y.K., Nerur, S.: Advances in social media research: past, present and future. Inf. Syst. Front. **20**(3), 531–558 (2018)
60. Dwivedi, Y.K., Kapoor, K.K., Chen, H.: Social media marketing and advertising. Mark. Rev. **15**(3), 289–309 (2015)
61. Dwivedi, Y.K., Lal, B., Mustafee, N., Williams, M.D.: Profiling a decade of information systems frontiers' research. Inf. Syst. Front. **11**(1), 87–102 (2009)

A Bibliometric Analysis and Research Agenda on Smart Cities

Samuel Fosso Wamba[1(✉)] and Maciel M. Queiroz[2(✉)]

[1] Toulouse Business School (TBS), 31068 Toulouse, France
s.fosso-wamba@tbs-education.fr
[2] Paulista University (UNIP), São Paulo 04026002, Brazil
maciel.m.queiroz@gmail.com

Abstract. Smart cities or intelligent cities have been gaining visibility and importance in recent years; not only in academia but also in the agendas of governments. Smart cities represent an important and disruptive interplay of cities' infrastructure, technologies, and people. Advancements in information and communication technology (ICT) have been supported by the development of cutting-edge technologies that involve the behaviors and experiences of city dwellers. In this context, smart cities have changed drastically in the last years. However, due to the rapid advancement of this multidisciplinary field, scholars and practitioners have encountered some difficulties in catalysing the latest advances as well as identifying a consistent and robust research agenda on this hot topic. In order to understand the evolution of this field, this study used bibliometric and network analysis; and identified top authors and articles. Also, we provided research directions based on cluster classification. Lastly, this study offers theoretical and managerial contributions.

Keywords: Smart cities · Intelligent cities · Research agenda

1 Introduction

Nowadays, 55% of people in the world live in urban areas [1] and according to projected estimates, approximately 68% of the world's population will live in cities (urban areas) by 2050. This increase in population growth is already bringing unprecedented consequences to the cities, its people and their quality of life; provoking climate change. Due to this landscape and the recent advances in information and communications technologies (ICT), cities need to become smarter in terms of resource consumption.

Due to the exponential growth of data [2–4], the advances of smartphone applications, smart products (e.g., smart TVs, smart-watch, smart clothes, among others), smart semaphore, especially with the advent of internet of things (IoT) and sensors applications, the experiences of city dwellers have changed drastically in the last years. In addition, with the use of GPS in activities that depend on vehicles, cities can accumulate important data on the behaviour of citizens in order to develop government policies to address resource usage and the well-being of the population.

Published by Springer Nature Switzerland AG 2019
Y. Dwivedi et al. (Eds.): TDIT 2019, IFIP AICT 558, pp. 325–335, 2019.
https://doi.org/10.1007/978-3-030-20671-0_22

In this context, a smart city can be defined as "urban areas that exploit operational data such as; that arising from traffic congestion, power consumption statistics, and public safety events, to optimize the operation of city services" [5]. In recent years, various scholars have devoted considerable efforts to provide information about the evolution of smart cities concepts [6–8]. In this vein, a smart city occurs when its traditional infrastructure is merged with ICT in an integrated and coordinated manner [9]. Recent studies have shown two cutting-edge technologies that have the potential to leverage smart cities; big data [10, 11], and the internet of things (IoT) [12, 13]. In addition, smart cities have the potential to leverage the quality of life as well as the performance of the firms that use their infrastructure [14].

Moreover, the smart cities can be visualized by six main dimensions (smart economy, smart people, smart governance, smart mobility, smart environment, and smart living) [15, 16]. Thus, recent studies have been highlighting the importance of smart cities in various contexts [17–21]. However, there are various barriers associated with their development [22].

Despite these significant and important innovations in the smart city field, there exists a gap in the literature regarding the bibliometric perspective in organizing and analysing the advances in this research stream; same as in the current trends. In order to outperform this gap, this study aims to (1) identify the literature on smart cities taking into consideration the period from 2000 to 2018; (2) Give insights on the more influential studies using a bibliometric and network analysis approach; (3) Provide research directions to scholars and insights to practitioners and managers.

By employing a bibliometric and network analysis approach, we identified 1226 articles, which were filtered and analysed in order to understand the dynamics of this field. Therefore, our study offers an essential contribution to theory and practice by identifying the most influential articles and suggesting new research. The next section of this paper presents the smart cities brief concept. In sequence, the methodology is highlighted, followed by results analysis. Next, the discussion and research agenda is provided. Finally, the main conclusions are synthesized.

2 Smart Cities: Brief Concepts

A smart city (or intelligent city) is defined [7] as "when investments in human and social capital, traditional (transport) and modern (ICT) communication infrastructure fuel sustainable economic growth and a high quality of life, with a wise management of natural resources; through participatory governance". There are several definitions of smart cities in existing literature (see [6]). However, based on majority dynamics, there is an interplay between ICT, people, government, and resource consumption.

Recent studies on smart cities have contributed significantly by integrating and expanding concepts with frameworks. For instance, [23] presented an approach in which smart cities integrate energy (sustainability and optimization), mobility (movement), community (participation and communication), environment (enhancement), and economy (dynamism and innovation). Another interesting framework was provided by [12], whereby integrating smart cities approach with the internet of things (IoT), provided an urban information system that connects intelligent transportation, video monitoring, health monitoring, and environmental monitoring, among others.

Following the frameworks' perspective, [24] proposed an engaging framework called the SMART model. The purpose of this model was to provide insights into smart cities' implementation, integrating strategy levels and strategic steps, as well as dimensions, and focus. Finally, [25] provided a good literature review on the smart city field and proposed a framework on the smart cities schools of thought.

3 Method

This study follows a bibliometric approach [26, 27] to identify, collect, organize, and analyse articles about smart cities. Firstly, in the keywords definition, we used the following combination: smart cit* OR intelligent cit* in the titles of the articles published in English between 2000 and 2018, in the Web of Science (WOS) database. WOS is one of the largest databases worldwide [28] and has been used frequently in studies reporting literature reviews [29]. The search resulted in 1,226 articles. We analyzed the articles by employing an excel spreadsheet [30] and VOSviewer to network analysis [27].

4 Results

4.1 Articles Published by Year and Top Twenty Journals

As the initial analysis, Fig. 1 highlights the number of articles published by year during the period 2000–2018. As can be seen, between 2000 and 2009, the maximum number of papers published in a year was 4. As of 2010, the number of articles has seen

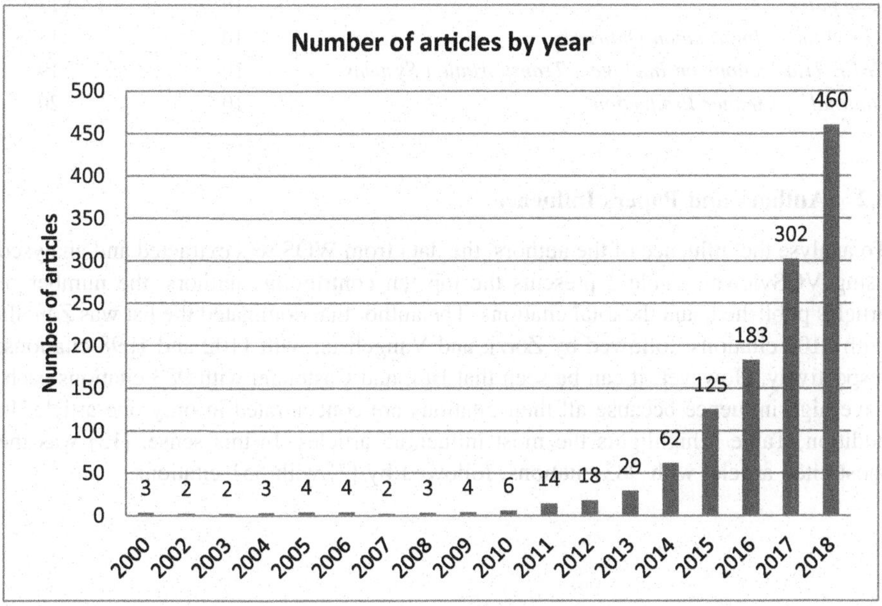

Fig. 1. Distribution of articles published between 2000–2018

exponential growth, reaching 460 articles in 2018. Moreover, Table 1 shows the top twenty journals based on the number of publications. The journal with most articles published was Sensors with 60, followed by IEEE ACCESS with 46 articles. It is important to point out that both journals are open access format.

Table 1. Top twenty journals.

Journal	Number of articles	Rank
Sensors	60	1
IEEE Access	46	2
IEEE Communications Magazine	45	3
Sustainability	36	4
Future Generation Computer Systems the International Journal of eScience	35	5
Sustainable Cities and Society	29	6
Cities	25	7
IEEE Internet of Things Journal	22	8
Journal of Urban Technology	19	9
International Journal of Distributed Sensor Networks	15	10
IEEE Transactions on Industrial Informatics	14	11
Wireless Communications Mobile Computing	12	12
Wireless Personal Communications	12	13
IEEE Internet Computing	11	14
Personal and Ubiquitous Computing	11	15
Techne Journal of Technology for Architecture and Environment	11	16
Computer	10	17
Government Information Quarterly	10	18
IEEE Transactions on Intelligent Transportation Systems	10	19
Journal of Cleaner Production	10	20

4.2 Authors and Papers Influence

To analyse the influence of the authors, the data from WOS was extracted and analysed using VOSviewer. Table 2 presents the top ten contributing authors, the number of articles published, and the total citations. The author that dominated the list was Zanella with 1104 citations, followed by Zorzi, and Vangelista, with 1102 and 1098 citations, respectively. However, it can be seen that Bui, and Castellani with 983 citations each, have high influence because all their citations are concentrated in only one article. In addition, Table 3 highlights the most influential articles. In this sense, [13] was the most cited article, with 983 citations, followed by [7] with 551 citations.

Table 2. Top ten authors based on the number of citations.

Authors	Articles	Citations	Rank
Zanella, A.	4	1104	1
Zorzi, M.	3	1102	2
Vangelista, L.	2	1098	3
Bui, N.	1	983	4
Castellani, A.	1	983	5
Nijkamp, P.	6	642	6
Caragliu, A.	3	557	7
Del bo, C.	2	551	8
De Marco, A.	3	374	9
Scorrano, F.	1	369	10

Note: Co-authored papers were counted. For example, Bui and Castellani are authors of the same article. The number of citations considered up to February 25, 2019.

Table 3. Top ten articles based on citation.

Article	Citations	Rank
[13]	983	1
[7]	551	2
[8]	369	3
[9]	356	4
[31]	332	5
[12]	308	6
[32]	265	7
[6]	237	8
[33]	193	9
[5]	192	10

4.3 Publication by Country and Research Areas

Table 4 shows the top twenty countries contributing papers. China is on the top of the list with 195 publications, followed by Italy, USA, and Spain, with 169, 164, and 144 articles, respectively. It is clear that the countries from Europe and Asia dominate the list. North America, represented by USA and Canada reached meaningful participation. In addition, Brazil was the only Latin American country represented. Moreover, Table 5 presents the most influential areas of research interested in smart cities.

Table 4. Top twenty countries contributing papers.

Countries/Regions	Number of papers	Rank	Countries/Regions	Number of papers	Rank
Peoples R. of China	195	1	Netherlands	43	11
Italy	169	2	France	42	12
USA	164	3	Germany	42	13
Spain	144	4	Saudi Arabia	38	14
England	127	5	Brazil	32	15
South Korea	71	6	Pakistan	29	16
India	55	7	Japan	28	17
Australia	51	8	Ireland	26	18
Canada	48	9	Finland	24	19
Greece	44	10	Portugal	24	20

Table 5. Top ten research areas.

Research Areas	Number of articles	Rank
Computer science	409	1
Engineering	316	2
Telecommunications	258	3
Business economics	96	4
Environmental sciences ecology	95	5
Science technology and other topics	95	6
Urban studies	87	7
Chemistry	74	8
Instruments instrumentation	72	9
Electrochemistry	63	10

4.4 Network Analysis Based on Co-citation

Recent studies have highlighted the importance of network analysis [34] in the understanding of co-citation. Thus, co-citation analysis is commonly used to gain a better understanding of the relationship between the authors; but, it can also cover other relationships including keywords and journals [34]. In this vein, our co-citation took into account the cited articles as the unit of analysis, employing VOSviewer. Therefore, we are interested in the intellectual relationships in the field [34]. Of 27251 identified authors, our threshold was 30 citations of an article; representing the minimum number of citations of a cited reference. This criterion reappeared in 40 articles, distributed in 3 clusters. For each of the 40 cited references, the total strength of the co-citation links with other cited references was calculated (Fig. 2). Besides, Table 6 shows the top 5 publications by each cluster.

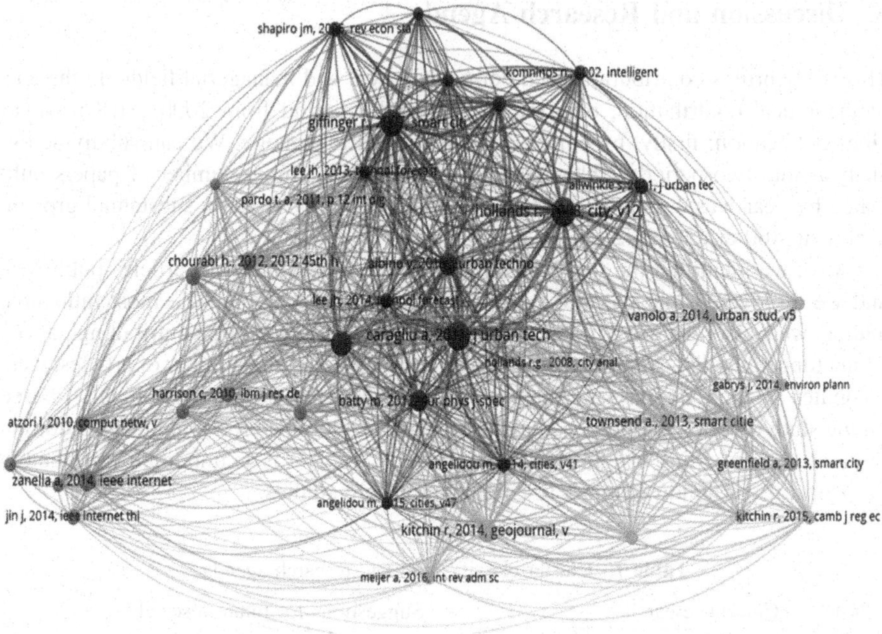

Fig. 2. Clusters based on the co-citation

Table 6. Articles organized in a cluster based on top five studies-weight citations.

Article	Cluster	Weight (Links)	Weight (Total link strength)	Weight (Citations)
[7]	1	39	849	151
[35]	1	38	750	150
[36]	1	39	709	127
[8]	1	39	618	107
[6]	1	39	521	88
[13]	2	37	210	83
[37]	2	39	341	70
[38]	2	38	271	60
[39]	2	39	264	53
[40]	2	35	174	46
[10]	3	39	544	90
[41]	3	38	492	68
[11]	3	38	441	66
[42]	3	37	368	49
[43]	3	38	293	38

5 Discussion and Research Agenda

This study brings contribution from both, theoretical and managerial fields. In the lens of theoretical contribution, our research covered a period from 2000–2018 in smart cities publication; firstly, by employing a bibliometric strategy. We can subdivide our analysis into two periods 2000–2009, in which the maximum number of papers published by year was 4, and 2010–2018, in which each year noted a substantial growth, achieving 460 articles in 2018.

Also, we identified the top 20 journals based on the number of articles published, and we discovered that the first two were open access journals. The most influential authors were also identified in the process. Regarding the countries contributing papers, China topped the list. Also, the top research areas based on the number of articles, were computer science, engineering, and telecommunications, respectively. Finally, based on the study of [27], we proposed a cluster classification (Table 7), identifying current research and providing insights for future research. Table 7 is an important contribution to theory; it can guide scholars in conducting future studies.

Table 7. Cluster classification and research agenda.

Cluster	Current research	Suggestions for future research
1	Concepts, definitions, and understanding of smart cities	Models and theories to advance the smart cities understanding taking into account the countries' particularities
2	Frameworks to describe the integration of smart cities with technologies	Frameworks to understand the effect of cutting-edge technologies (e.g., blockchain, artificial intelligence) to smart cities development
3	Smart city governance and big data analytics	Big data analytics applied to optimize the integration of people, government policies and firms

Thus, the proposed cluster classification and research agenda can generate insights for scholars and practitioners interested in gaining a deeper understanding, as well as contribute to the advancement of the field. For instance, cluster 1, has its current studies focused basically on the concepts. Also, we identified the necessity of advancing the understanding of smart cities' definitions and concepts in different countries. Example of research questions: (i) Are the six dimensions of the smart cities valid for any country? (ii) Are there differences between developing and developed economies regarding the smart cities understanding? (iii) What is the awareness level of smart cities by citizens from different countries? Considering cluster 2 that is focused on frameworks and the integration with technologies, some suggestions to advance the field could be related to frameworks that can integrate different technologies to support the firm's new operations business models. Finally, in cluster 3, there exists an interesting interplay between big data and smart city governance. Future studies could explore more in-depth models associated to citizen behaviour data, in order to support decision-makers and governance policies for the well-being of people and the promotion of the use of resources in an optimized way by the organizations.

From the managerial perspective, our study brings opportunities to managers and practitioners, as well as to government policy makers. For example, based on the top 20 countries contributing articles, we identified a gap in the unavailability of articles from emerging economies from Latin America and Africa. The lack in participation could be associated to a gap in smart cities projects and implementation in these countries. In addition, the proposed cluster classification could be a starting point for managers and practitioners to improve their awareness of smart cities, and consequently, generate insights to enable them integrate and develop projects for their businesses based on the smart cities technologies.

6 Conclusions

Based on the bibliometric approach and network analysis, this study covered a period from 2010–2018 in smart cities articles. Our study provided significant insights for scholars and practitioners interested in gaining more insights into the smart cities past and trends. In terms of the main limitations, we highlight the following: (i) we considered the keywords only in the title of the articles. Future studies can consider the search terms in the abstract, as well as in the other articles' section; (ii) we focused on the WOS database. Future studies can consider other databases such as Scopus; (iii) we developed the cluster using VOSviewer, other software can bring different results. Despite these limitations, our study provides useful insights for scholars and practitioners interested in smart cities.

References

1. United Nations: 68% of the world population projected to live in urban areas by 2050, says UN (2018). https://www.un.org/development/desa/en/news/population/2018-revision-of-world-urbanization-prospects.html
2. Manyika, J., et al.: Big Data: The Next Frontier for Innovation, Competition, and Productivity. McKinsey Global Institute (2011). https://www.mckinsey.com/business-functions/digital-mckinsey/our-insights/big-data-the-next-frontier-for-innovation
3. Queiroz, M.M., Telles, R.: Big data analytics in supply chain and logistics: an empirical approach. Int. J. Logist. Manag. **29**(2), 767–783 (2018)
4. Wamba, S.F., Akter, S., Edwards, A., Chopin, G., Gnanzou, D.: How 'big data' can make big impact: findings from a systematic review and a longitudinal case study. Int. J. Prod. Econ. **165**, 234–246 (2015)
5. Harrison, C., et al.: Foundations for smarter cities. IBM J. Res. Dev. **54**(4), 1–16 (2010)
6. Albino, V., Berardi, U., Dangelico, R.M.: Smart cities: definitions, dimensions, performance, and initiatives. J. Urban Technol. **22**(1), 1–19 (2015)
7. Caragliu, A., Del Bo, C., Nijkamp, P.: Smart cities in Europe. J. Urban Technol. **18**(2), 65–82 (2011)

8. Neirotti, P., De Marco, A., Cagliano, A.C., Mangano, G., Scorrano, F.: Current trends in smart city initiatives: some stylised facts. Cities **38**, 25–36 (2014)
9. Batty, M., et al.: Smart cities of the future. Eur. Phys. J. Spec. Top. **214**(1), 481–518 (2012)
10. Kitchin, R.: The real-time city? Big data and smart urbanism. GeoJournal **79**(1), 1–14 (2014)
11. Townsend, A.M.: Smart Cities: Big Data, Civic Hackers, and the Quest for a New Utopia. W.W. Norton & Company, New York (2013)
12. Jin, J., Gubbi, J., Marusic, S., Palaniswami, M.: An information framework for creating a smart city through Internet of Things. IEEE Internet Things J. **1**(2), 112–121 (2014)
13. Zanella, A., Bui, N., Castellani, A., Vangelista, L., Zorzi, M.: Internet of Things for smart cities. IEEE Internet Things J. **1**(1), 22–32 (2014)
14. Ismagilova, E., Hughes, L., Dwivedi, Y.K., Raman, K.R.: Smart cities: advances in research —an information systems perspective. Int. J. Inf. Manag. **47**, 88–100 (2019)
15. Lombardi, P., Giordano, S., Farouh, H., Yousef, W.: Modelling the smart city performance. Innov. Eur. J. Soc. Sci. Res. **25**(2), 137–149 (2012)
16. Albino, V., Berardi, U., Dangelico, R.M.: Smart cities: definitions, dimensions, performance, and initiatives. J. Urban Technol. **22**(1), 3–21 (2015)
17. Axelsson, K., Granath, M.: Stakeholders' stake and relation to smartness in smart city development: insights from a Swedish city planning project. Gov. Inf. Q. **35**(4), 693–702 (2018)
18. Palomo-Navarro, Á., Navío-Marco, J.: Smart city networks' governance: the Spanish smart city network case study. Telecommun. Policy **42**(10), 872–880 (2018)
19. Haarstad, H., Wathne, M.W.: Are smart city projects catalyzing urban energy sustainability? Energy Policy **129**, 918–925 (2019)
20. van den Buuse, D., Kolk, A.: An exploration of smart city approaches by international ICT firms. Technol. Forecast. Soc. Change **142**, 220–234 (2019)
21. Caragliu, A., Del Bo, C.F.: Smart innovative cities: the impact of smart city policies on urban innovation. Technol. Forecast. Soc. Change **142**, 373–383 (2019)
22. Rana, N.P., Luthra, S., Mangla, S.K., Islam, R., Roderick, S., Dwivedi, Y.K.: Barriers to the development of smart cities in Indian context. Inf. Syst. Front. **2018**, 1–23 (2018)
23. Mattoni, B., Gugliermetti, F., Bisegna, F.: A multilevel method to assess and design the renovation and integration of smart cities. Sustain. Cities Soc. **15**, 105–119 (2015)
24. Ben Letaifa, S.: How to strategize smart cities: Revealing the SMART model. J. Bus. Res. **68** (7), 1414–1419 (2015)
25. Kummitha, R.K.R., Crutzen, N.: How do we understand smart cities? An evolutionary perspective. Cities **67**, 43–52 (2017)
26. Caviggioli, F., Ughetto, E.: A bibliometric analysis of the research dealing with the impact of additive manufacturing on industry, business and society. Int. J. Prod. Econ. **208**, 254–268 (2019)
27. Mishra, D., Gunasekaran, A., Papadopoulos, T., Childe, S.J.: Big Data and supply chain management: a review and bibliometric analysis. Ann. Oper. Res. **270**(1–2), 313–336 (2018)
28. Clarivate Analytics: Web of Science (2019)
29. Liao, Y., Deschamps, F., de Loures, E.F.R., Ramos, L.F.P.: Past, present and future of Industry 4.0 - a systematic literature review and research agenda proposal. Int. J. Prod. Res. **55**(12), 3609–3629 (2017)
30. Blažun Vošner, H., Bobek, S., Sternad Zabukovšek, S., Kokol, P.: Openness and information technology: a bibliometric analysis of literature production. Kybernetes **46**(5), 750–766 (2017)

31. Shapiro, J.M.: Smart cities: quality of life, productivity, and the growth effects of human capital. Rev. Econ. Stat. **88**(2), 324–335 (2006)
32. Perera, C., Zaslavsky, A., Christen, P., Georgakopoulos, D.: Sensing as a service model for smart cities supported by Internet of Things. Trans. Emerg. Telecommun. Technol. **25**(1), 81–93 (2014)
33. Axisa, F., Schmitt, P.M., Gehin, C., Delhomme, G., McAdams, E., Dittmar, A.: Flexible technologies and smart clothing for citizen medicine, home healthcare, and disease prevention. IEEE Trans. Inf. Technol. Biomed. **9**(3), 325–336 (2005)
34. Mishra, D., Gunasekaran, A., Papadopoulos, T., Dubey, R.: Supply chain performance measures and metrics: a bibliometric study. Benchmarking: Int. J. **25**(3), 932–967 (2018)
35. Hollands, R.G.: Will the real smart city please stand up? City **12**(3), 303–320 (2008)
36. Giffinger, R., Fertner, C., Kramar, H., Kalasek, R., Pichler-Milanović, N., Meijers, E.: Smart cities – ranking of European medium-sized cities, Vienna (2007)
37. Chourabi, H., et al.: Understanding smart cities: an integrative framework. In: 2012 45th Hawaii International Conference on System Sciences, pp. 2289–2297 (2012)
38. Schaffers, H., Komninos, N., Pallot, M., Trousse, B., Nilsson, M., Oliveira, A.: Smart cities and the future Internet: towards cooperation frameworks for open innovation. In: Domingue, J., et al. (eds.) FIA 2011. LNCS, vol. 6656, pp. 431–446. Springer, Heidelberg (2011). https://doi.org/10.1007/978-3-642-20898-0_31
39. Nam, T., Pardo, T.A.: Conceptualizing smart city with dimensions of technology, people, and institutions. In: Proceedings of the 12th Annual International Digital Government Research Conference on Digital Government Innovation in Challenging Times - dg.o 2011, p. 282 (2011)
40. Atzori, L., Iera, A., Morabito, G.: The Internet of Things: a survey. Comput. Networks **54** (15), 2787–2805 (2010)
41. Vanolo, A.: Smartmentality: the smart city as disciplinary strategy. Urban Stud. **51**(5), 883–898 (2014)
42. Söderström, O., Paasche, T., Klauser, F.: Smart cities as corporate storytelling. City **18**(3), 307–320 (2014)
43. Hollands, R.G.: Critical interventions into the corporate smart city. Camb. J. Reg. Econ. Soc. **8**(1), 61–77 (2015)

Security, Privacy, Ethics and Misinformation

Authenticating Fake News: An Empirical Study in India

Gautam Prakash, Ravinder Kumar Verma(✉),
P. Vigneswara Ilavarasan, and Arpan K. Kar

Department of Management Studies, Indian Institute of Technology Delhi,
New Delhi, India
ravinderkvl@gmail.com

Abstract. Social media has become an important means for communication to promote content sharing and social networking. The usage of social media has opportunities and challenges. This article aims to highlight the ways through which individuals authenticate fake news while using social media platforms. To explore the patterns of fake news authentication on social media, online and offline surveys were conducted to get 231 responses. Social media users at the individual level authenticate fake news at two levels: internal – individual discernment and perceptiveness about news, sources and popularity of news, and external – friends and relatives, multiple external sources, formal and social spheres. This study provides insights into the usage patterns of social media platforms and ways of fake news authentication. The insights from the study might help social media platforms, governments, users and researchers.

Keywords: Social media · Fake news · Authentication of fake news

1 Introduction

The emergence of social media platforms enables the social networking of firms; individuals provide opportunities to capture the potential of social media usage. Social media enable a new mode of communication to increase social networks [1, 28]. Social media functionality impacts the following functions: sharing, presence, relationships, identity, reputation, relationships, groups and conversations [29, 30]. These functions are influenced by social media activity [2]. The usage of social media platforms poses opportunities and challenges to overcome, regarding challenges, implementation is one such challenge [1] and implementation aspects of co-evolution of social media and traditional marketing [3]. Social media provide opportunities to companies and users to connect and integrate the traditionally isolated stakeholders with each other [4]. Social media platforms have the potential to influence the users and companies to influence each other [4], and social media content can be used to predict the future by analysing the sentiments of the users [5]. Social media ecosystem provides opportunities and challenges to consider while using different platforms. In this background, fake news is a critical issue to be considered by platforms, governments, users and individuals.

Fake news is a threat not only to the company or individuals but also to the whole country [6]. Fake news is a very subjective matter. People judge the news based on

Published by Springer Nature Switzerland AG 2019
Y. Dwivedi et al. (Eds.): TDIT 2019, IFIP AICT 558, pp. 339–350, 2019.
https://doi.org/10.1007/978-3-030-20671-0_23

their belief and share it in their network. In general, fake news is fabricated news with wrong facts with a motive of deceiving or satire on someone. Social media message credibility may be influenced by any medium or delivery channel, and even the messages structure themselves [7].

There are various social media platforms available to engage people. Factors such as access to a smartphone, Internet and people interacting on social media platforms enable instant sharing of information across the world, for example, viral messages and videos. Offline news channels are moving to social media platforms to provide instant news. Social media platforms enable the news channels' content selling. Since the content flow on the Internet is free and there are limited rules and regulations available to control the content. The spread of fake news on social media platforms came into light without knowing the truth about the news, believing and sharing within their network. The shared messages are psychological, politically motivated and emotional, which influence the people who trust the content without verification. Fake news influenced the US election in 2016. People change their mind so quickly that it is very difficult to come to any conclusion. The rise in fake news makes the social media platform more powerful, which impacts government, society and individuals. Social media platforms usually do not examine the perceived credibility of social media content through its platforms [8]. With this background, this study focuses on the factors used by the users of social media platforms to authenticate social media platforms news. This article is organized as follows. Section 2 examines the literature review related to fake news and finds the gaps and Sect. 3 presents model and research question. In Sect. 4, the methodology is discussed. The fifth section presents the findings and discussion, and the final section is the conclusion.

2 Literature Review

Social media data are huge and can be categorised into various areas. The huge data and easy penetration of data across the world. Social media data availability and accessibility raise issues related to information consumption. Information consumption and perception depend on the echo effects and credibility of the information. The existence of the echo effects where the information perception is depends on the frequency of information, which generates a positive idea about the information. The credibility of the information increases when others perceive the source of information credible [9].

The youth in the Internet era are well connected to friends and relatives. They depend on social media for news, and the websites provide various discussions and opinions about the news. The individual's motivation to seek news is driven by personal interest. The youth consider social media networking sites' discussions as more authenticating means to gather news while they also gather news from mainstream news media about the concerned issues [10]. Although there is a gap in the comprehensive coverage of the news, and the youth viewpoints provide an opportunity to the traditional media to present news from different viewpoints rather than from the single objective point of view [10].

Fake news has the potential to influence election outcomes. The voters remember one or more fake news about different political candidates. The fake news divides the opinion of the voters, which has the potential to provide a winning margin to the election candidates [6].

The opinion leaders on social media influenced the perception of users/followers on news trust. Strong opinion leaders generate strong trust for the news seekers. In some cases, information shared on social media sites is perceived as more trustworthy than from direct media outlet [11]. The existence of malicious social media accounts for spreading fake news [9]. The recognition of fake news creates an interest in the practitioners to use technologies for categorization, identification and developing solutions for future projects related to fake news.

2.1 Technology and Fake News

There is enormous content generation on social media websites. To authenticate social media content requires a different approach than the traditional approach. The use of emerging technologies such as artificial intelligence, machine learning, and the network analysis approach enables a hybrid approach for fake news detection. Despite using the latest technologies, there is no straightforward solution to detect fake news [12].

Artificial intelligence is not only used to solve various issues but also has deployed to create social bots to spread fake news [13]. The social bots have been used to spread information, promote a campaign and promote ideologies on social media platforms. The social bots have been deployed to both promote right information and promote false information. The study on twitter data of US election revealed that social bots had played a key role in spreading fake news. Fake news can be stopped by targeting social bots [14]. With the help of computing, social bots can be recognized. Social media platforms enable the machine–human interactions; such interactions should be based on the authentication and recognition of the machine and human interactions to avoid false roles and spread of mistrust [13].

Fake news detection on social media can be categorized using data mining perspectives using algorithms to categorize the news and accounts as fake and real. The existence of malicious social media accounts for spread fake news [9].

Identification and verification of information on social media is a challenge for the journalist – the development of social sensor software to identify fake news based on the source and locations. Software development is based on the collaborations of social scientists, journalists and computer scientists [15].

Fake news can be categorised into serious fabrication, which is found in mainstream media, and which requires substantial efforts to collect them. The second category is large-scale hoaxes; these are creative, unique and source from multiple platforms, which require identification methods beyond text analytics. The third category is humorous news with large-scale data. The use of technologies such as big data, Natural Language Processing (NLP), LIS, journalism and fake news provides means to enable an environment for automatic detection of fake news [16].

In India, social media is used to propagate political ideologies by recruiting citizens. These are paid news where individuals are recruited, who do not belong to any political party to spread messages to their networks [17]. Fake news propagation leads to social unrest in India, for instance, cases of Muzaffarnagar riots and Dadri lynching mob. Fake news in political and economy fields influences social media networks, for instance, there was a news shared on social media platforms about GPS chips and radioactive ink in newly issued Rs. 2000 notes in India and support of United States' president to Indian political leader, these news were discussed in the mainstream news channel, which shows that mainstream news role in spreading fake news [18]. Therefore, it is critical to know the source of fake news. The source detection of misinformation and rumour in the social networks are influenced by diffusion models, network observation and centrality measures; source detection approaches have a large variation in accuracy [19]. Bhaskaran mentioned that fake news spread due to illiteracy, traditional faith in media without knowing about social media platforms' ability to manipulate and spread fake news and slacktivist convenience. Identification of fake news involves rating system, sanction against fake news spreading platforms and development of algorithms along with manual intervention [18]. It was also noted that mainstream news channels are also telecasting fake news without doing fact-finding exercise [18]. Regulatory institutions and self-regulation do not stop the fake news, while challenges lie in media training [18]. Courts in India have been receiving a petition to regulate fake news and they argued that India does not have guidelines to regulate fake news and seek court intervention to regulate fake news in India [20].

2.2 Problem Definition

Different approaches and methods have been adopted to detect fake news. There is a difference between real and fake news sources and propagation means. The source of fake news is associated with unauthenticated news source and the content of fake news changes while dispersing, whereas real news show wider dispersion without many modifications [21]. The perception about fake news differs among the individuals. The perception of individuals or groups about fake news influence on the third person is more strong than themselves or in-group members [22].

The behaviours of the individuals are different when informed and uninformed about fake news. Fake news influence individuals' behaviours to take business decisions [23]. Research in fake news on the social media domain is getting attention these days. However, to our knowledge, there are limited studies available about the approaches adopted by individuals to identify news while using social media platforms. This study is based on the approaches of individuals for authentication of social media content.

3 Model and Research Questions

3.1 Research Problem: Social Media Platform and the Problem of Fake News

There is lack of guideline and standard which enables the containment of fake news; it emerges as a threat and social media content is motivated by political, cross-border, international aspects, psychological and so on. The easy target of fake news are the common citizens, and it is common to believe news shared and read by some people without understanding the motive of the news spread.

Fake news should be managed to maintain harmony in the society and trust of people in different institutions. Hence, there is a need to manage fake news spread on social media platforms. Individuals need exposers and means to curb fake news.

3.2 Actors in Managing Fake News

Managing the fake news is not possible only by social media platforms or governments. An individual need to participate in this exercise. This should be the responsibility of all the three key stakeholders.

3.3 Conceptual Model

There are two research questions in the context of fake news; the first is related to people's way of authentication of fake news; the second is whether there is a difference between the internal and external validations by the individuals? These are illustrated as below (Fig. 1).

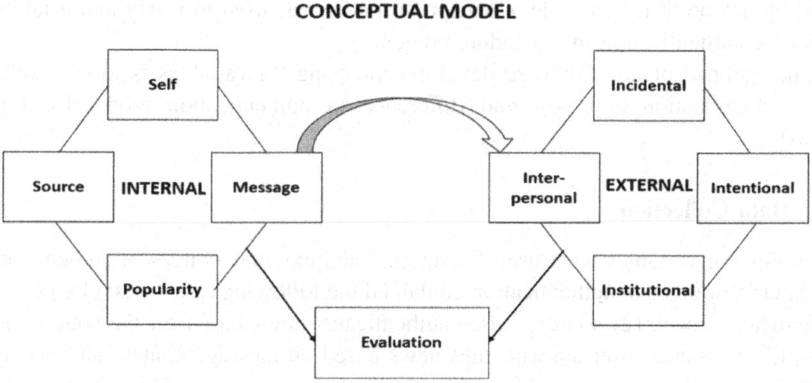

Fig. 1. Conceptual model of authentication [24]

RQ1: How do people authenticate fake news?

People, in general, authenticate through two ways for any news: internal authentication and external authentication. These ways depend on the merit of news and can be used by people to authenticate and categorize as true or fake news.

RQ2: Is there a difference in internal and external validations by the individuals?

Internal and external authentication help people authenticate the news received on social media. Now the question arises whether there is any difference in external and internal ways of authenticating. The difference between internal and external authentication is analysed using the questionnaire research tool.

4 Methodology

The study is based on the review of the existing literature for the audience act of authentication social media. A quantitative survey was conducted to analyse the audiences' fake news authentication patterns. The respondents' responses were used to analyse the factors that they used to authenticate news on social media platforms.

A survey questionnaire was constructed, which was based on constructs emerging from the literature [1, 3, 4, 11, 13, 15, 16, 25] and expert opinions. From the literature, 26 variables were identified; these variables were further divided into two categories of internal and external sources of validation. The questionnaire contained information related to age, gender, number of hours spent on social media platforms in weekdays, number of hours spent on social media platforms during holidays and regions based on urban, rural and semi-urban residence. Questions were also asked based on the different social media platforms (Facebook, WhatsApp, YouTube, Twitter, LinkedIn, Snapchat, Instagram) use and purpose (time pass, entertainment, news, exam preparation, interacting with a friend, professional reason, knowledge).

Based on the literature review to understand the authentication used by individuals, there were 26 variables considered for data collection, and this was divided into two categories – internal and external based on the empirical model. The questionnaire was based on a 5-point Likert scale. Conceptual model was used to verify and establish a model for authentication in the Indian context.

The purpose of questionnaire development using 26 variables is to capture fake news authentication approach and difference in authentication model for Indian context.

4.1 Data Collection

The following variables were used for internal and external sources of authentication. The internal sources of authentication contained the following categories: (1) self – user authenticates news, (2) source – user authenticates news based on the source of the news, (3) message – user authenticates news based on message content and (4) popularity – user authenticates news based on the popularity of news. The external sources of authentication contained the following categories: (1) incidental and interpersonal – looking for friends over social media, (2) incidental and institutional – looking for news over other media, (3) intentional and interpersonal – looking for a family member or expert views on the news and (4) intentional and institutional – looking at external sources for verification of news.

Data were collected using online and offline modes. The questionnaire was based on Likert scale. The questionnaire had the following themes: the respondent's discernment and perceptiveness, message credibility, types of news, friend and relatives, multiple and trustworthy, social sphere and the formal sphere. The online questionnaire data were collected by sharing the link on social media platforms like Facebook, WhatsApp and Messenger. The offline data were collected from an IT company. The duration of the online survey was from 30th March to 18th April 2018, and the total sample size was 231 for the final analysis of the results (Table 1).

Table 1. Demographics details (all figures in percentage)

Age (years)	20–25	26–30	31–35	36–40	41–45
Respondents	11.6	35.8	14.2	1.6	5.8
Location	Rural	Semi-urban	Urban		
	8.4	9.9	81.7		
Profession	Entrepreneurs	Private sector	Public sector	Student	Not working
	6.9	52.7	13.7	22.9	3.8

5 Findings and Discussion

The following results emerged from the analysis of the data.

5.1 Social Media Platforms' Usage

The internet use in India increased drastically in last one decade with 462 million active internet users and 430.3 million are active mobile internet users; 250 million active social media users and 230 million active mobile social media users on January 2018 [26]. Regarding time spent on social media platforms, respondents were most active WhatsApp (85%), followed by YouTube. About 83% of respondents were active on Facebook followed by LinkedIn, YouTube and WhatsApp. In terms of social media platform where users were active, WhatsApp had active users followed by Facebook and YouTube.

5.2 Emerged Model of Authentication

The analysis of fake news by the users of social media results in the following six factors after exploratory factor analysis (EFA). EFA is a good factor analysis method for identifying the underlying relationship between measured variables. Here, six factors emerged after applying the maximum likelihood extraction method with Promax using Kaiser normalization rotation method. The Pattern Matrix shows values above 0.5 for all the extracted factors. The reliability test and Cronbach's alpha value for each factor are above 0.7. These factors are as follows: popularity, self, internal sources, family and relatives, external sources and mixed external (Fig. 2).

These emerged factors are different from source questions based on the output of responses collected by Indian respondents of various locations and various professions with different age groups. Instead of the eight factors considered from source paper, a set of 26 variables are taken based on various papers and studies.

The emerged model for the authentication of fake news is influenced by the usage of social media platforms. Finally, the respondents indicated how they authenticate fake news on social media on different social media platforms using the 5-point Likert scale ranging from 1 = strongly disagree to 5 = strongly agree. Respondents' authentication is based on social media news popularity (M = 2.34, SD = 1.14). However, mostly authentication is based on seeing the news sources (M = 3.40, SD = 0.92). Respondents authenticate news on their own discernment and perceptiveness (M = 3.43, SD = 0.97). Respondents also look for their family and relative to authenticate the news (M = 2.67,

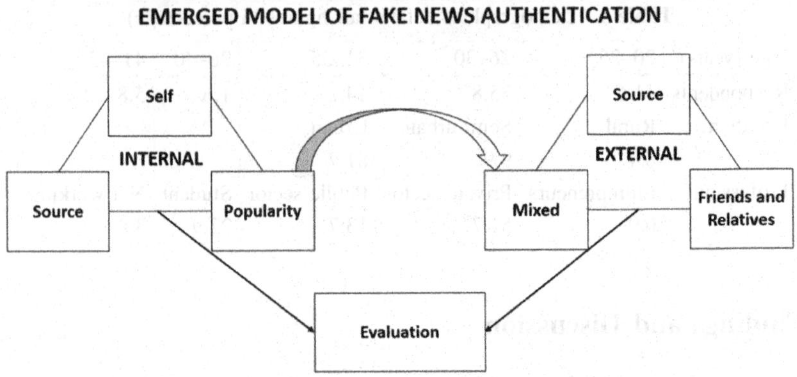

Fig. 2. Emerged model of fake news authentication

SD = 1.10). The authentication is strongly related to the external sources, and those are considered as trustworthy (M = 3.75, SD = 0.90). External validation of the fake news is also based on mixed factors such as social and formal sphere (M = 2.87, SD = 0.88).

The respondents use both internal authentication (M = 3.05, SD = 0.62) and external authentication (M = 3.10, SD = 0.70) to authenticate news on social media platforms. On comparing these two types of authentication, respondents are more oriented toward the external authentication of social media news. The response of authentication moves from internal to external with more reliability on external validation of social media news (M = 3.28, SD = 1.16).

5.3 Correlations Between the Following Factors and Social Media Usage

This section provides insights about the correlation between age and social media usage, time spent and purpose of social media usage. This section enables to highlight the following critical aspects related to the research objectives, where social media usage specifies the target groups and platforms to target for fake news authentication.

Age and Social Media Usage

There is a negative correlation between the age and the number of hours spent on social media during holiday. This means that the less the age, the more time they spend on social media platforms. Also, this is statistically significant as the significance (two-tailed) value is less than 0.05. Age and social media platform, such as Instagram, are negatively connected too in the Indian context. The teenagers' usage of Instagram is more than senior adults. This is also statistically significant as the significance (two-tailed) value is 0.01.

Age and social media platform usages purpose that 'entertainment' and 'exam preparation' are also negatively connected in the Indian context. Teenagers use social media for entertainment and exam preparation purposes than senior adults. This is also statistically significant as the significance (two-tailed) value is much less than 0.05.

Age and social media index (sum of all social media uses) are also negatively connected in the Indian context. Teenagers use social media more than senior adults. This is also statistically significant as significance (two-tailed) value is 0.005.

Duration of Social Media Usage

The number of hours on social media during weekdays is directly connected to the number of hours on social media during holidays. The mean value is around 0.65. The number of hours spent on social media during weekdays is directly connected to a purpose 'time pass' and 'news', which means people use social media for time pass and reading news during working days. However, this is a weak relationship, with the significance value (two-tailed) less than 0.05. In contrast, the number of hours spent on social media during holidays is directly connected to purposes such as 'time pass', 'entertainment', 'knowledge', 'exam prep' and 'news', which means people use social media for time pass and reading news during holidays. However, this is a weak relationship.

Social Media Platforms Usage Purpose

Facebook and news are directly connected where people use Facebook for getting the latest news. YouTube and Entrainment are directly correlated, which means that people use YouTube for their entertainment. The usage of LinkedIn is directly connected to Facebook and Twitter, which means that people also use LinkedIn while using Facebook and Twitter. However, this is a weak relationship. The use of the LinkedIn is mainly for professional reasons. Twitter is directly connected to Instagram. Many people who use Twitter also use Instagram. However, this is a weak relationship.

The usage of WhatsApp is directly connected to Instagram, which means that people using WhatsApp also use Instagram platform. The usage of WhatsApp is more for interacting with friends.

Instagram and knowledge gain are negatively correlated. People use Instagram not for gaining knowledge related to any exam preparation. However, this is a weak relationship.

5.4 Practical Implications

The study has the following practical implications for the stakeholders.

Platforms

Platforms are free for content generation, and they do not check or regulate content generation extensively. Most of the contents over social media platforms are politically motivated and are rumor, fake news and create conspiracy theory [14]. As of now, there are little regulation over online content publishing. Social media platforms allow most of the contents and share accurate and inaccurate information in the public domain. But inaccurate news is shared more frequently on social media platforms as it attracts many people in comparison to sharing of accurate news and verifying them. Fact-checking the news in general delays by 10–12 h. By the time, inaccurate news is already spread by active users. Hence, platform needs to implement fact-checking mechanism to stop the spread of inaccurate news. This provides factors to be considered while planning to implement rules and policy to curb fake news.

Governments
There are issues with the authenticity and credibility of the news on social media platforms, and in some cases, these are inaccurate and politically motivated. The fake news on social media challenge the government and might spread the rumor which highlights the inability of the government and poses a threat to the public in large. During the US election 2016, false news spread more, and people started believing it [6]. A similar thing happens in most of the countries, and the government gets destabilized.

Previously, the need to create one web-based citation database for fact-checking was discussed. This might help the government to avoid spreading fake news and take necessary steps. The patterns of social media usage emerging in this study highlight the area to focus and how to increase positive engagement with citizens.

Individuals
Individuals who are more active in social media share known person content more than the others [27]. Hence, people create networks and try to add more individuals to increase their reachability. An individual trust the shared news and share them without knowing its effects or sources. This study provides an insight into the usage and methods of authentification of the fake news at the individual level. The authentication method does not seem scientific, for instance, if one weak link in the social media network is able to enter in a network, then there are chances that fake news can still spread despite the authentification at the individual level. Such uncertainty can be removed by focusing on factors from an integrated perspective of collaborations of individuals, platforms and governments.

Managers
The implications for the managers are at personal and organizational levels. These days various managers' positions are shared on professional social media platform like LinkedIn. Organization these days look at candidate profile on social media and their information sharing patterns. Hence, managers need to restrict themselves to share any unverified information received on social media platforms. Such sharing activity can lead to job loss as organization reputation can get maligned due to their managers' action. Whereas at the organizational level, a manager can play a role to curb fake news spreading through awareness and training about the different factors of fake news spreading and complexity involved in the authentication of fake news.

6 Conclusion

Social media platforms have emerged as a good source of news. The accessibility to Internet and smartphones has enabled people in the developing countries to have various ICT services. Social media usage has become one of the preferred services. Usage of social media has opportunities and challenges. At the individual level, people are using social media platforms for various purposes such as information, social networking and entertainment.

Regarding challenges, they recognize the challenge of fake news and develop an authentication mechanism to deal with fake news. The authentication mechanism involves internal authentication and external authentication. The following factors emerged as the internal authentication: self, source and popularity; external authentication: source, mixed, friends and relatives. This article can be useful for stakeholders, especially those working on strategy building to deal with fake news for digital platforms and government. The present research has some limitation; it is based on the Indian context and have limited access to social media platforms data to incorporate in the research and future research can explore to include other factors and sub-factors of fake news authentication at different level; individual level, platforms level and government level in different social and political context.

References

1. Kaplan, A.M., Haenlein, M.: Users of the world, unite! The challenges and opportunities of Social Media. Bus. Horiz. **53**, 59–68 (2010)
2. Kietzmann, J.H., Hermkens, K., McCarthy, I.P., Silvestre, B.S.: Social media? Get serious! Understanding the functional building blocks of social media. Bus. Horiz. **54**(3), 241–251 (2011)
3. Hanna, R., Rohm, A., Crittenden, V.L.: We're all connected: the power of the social media ecosystem. Bus. Horiz. **54**(3), 265–273 (2011)
4. Mangold, W.G., Faulds, D.J.: Social media: the new hybrid element of the promotion mix. Bus. Horiz. **52**(4), 357–365 (2009)
5. Asur, S., Huberman, B.A.: Predicting the future with social media, pp. 1–8. arXiv:1003.5699v1 [cs.CY] (2010)
6. Allcott, H., Gentzkow, M.: Social media and fake news in the 2016 election. J. Econ. Perspect. **31**(2), 211–236 (2017)
7. Metzger, M.J., Flanagin, D., Eyal, A.J., Lemus, K., Mccann, R.: Credibility for the 21st century: integrating perspectives on source, message, and media credibility in the contemporary media environment. In: Communication Yearbook, vol. 27, pp. 293–335 (2003)
8. Castillo, C., Mendoza, M., Poblete, B.: Information credibility on Twitter. In IW3C2 WWW 2011, pp. 675–684 (2011)
9. Shu, K., Sliva, A., Wang, S., Tang, J., Liu, H.: Fake news detection on social media: a data mining perspective. ACM SIGKDD Explor. Newsl. **19**(1), 22–36 (2017)
10. Marchi, R.: With Facebook, blogs, and fake news, teens reject journalistic 'objectivity'. J. Commun. Inq. **36**(3), 246–262 (2012)
11. Turcotte, J., York, C., Irving, J., Scholl, R.M., Pingree, R.J.: News recommendations from social media opinion leaders: effects on media trust and information seeking. J. Comput. Commun. **20**(5), 520–535 (2015)
12. Conroy, N.J., Rubin, V.L., Chen, Y.: Automatic deception detection: methods for finding fake news. In: ASIST, pp. 1–4, November 2015
13. Ferrara, E., Varol, O., Davis, C., Menczer, F., Flammini, A.: The rise of social bots. Commun. ACM **59**(7), 9 (2014)
14. Shao, C., Ciampaglia, G.L., Varol, O., Yang, K., Flammini, A., Menczer, F.: The spread of fake news by social bots, pp. 1–16. arXiv preprint arXiv:1707.07592 (2017)
15. Schifferes, S., Newman, N., Thurman, N., Corney, D., Göker, A., Martin, C.: Identifying and verifying news through social media: developing a user-centred tool for professional journalists. Digit. Journal. **2**(3), 406–418 (2014)
16. Rubin, V.L., Chen, Y., Conroy, N.J.: Deception detection for news: three types of fake news. Proc. Assoc. Inf. Sci. Technol. **52**(1), 1–4 (2015)

17. Bradshaw, S., Howard, P.N.: Troops, trolls and troublemakers: a global inventory of organized social media manipulation, 2017.12 (2017)
18. Bhaskaran, H.: Contextualizing fake news in post-truth era: journalism education in India. Asia Pac. Media Educ. **27**(1), 41–50 (2017)
19. Shelke, S., Attar, V.: Source detection of rumor in social network – a review. Online Soc. Netw. Media **9**, 30–42 (2019)
20. Business-Standard: Petition filed before SC to put a halt to menace of fake news, March 2019
21. Jang, S.M., et al.: A computational approach for examining the roots and spreading patterns of fake news: evolution tree analysis. Comput. Hum. Behav. **84**, 103–113 (2018)
22. Jang, S.M., Kim, J.K.: Third person effects of fake news: fake news regulation and media literacy interventions. Comput. Hum. Behav. **80**, 295–302 (2018)
23. Brigida, M., Pratt, W.R.: Fake news. North Am. J. Econ. Financ. **42**, 564–573 (2017)
24. Tandoc Jr., E.C., Ling, R., Westlund, O., Duffy, A., Goh, D., Zheng Wei, L.: Audiences' acts of authentication in the age of fake news: a conceptual framework. New Media Soc. **20**(8), 2745–2763 (2018)
25. Gupta, A., Lamba, H., Kumaraguru, P., Joshi, A.: Faking sandy: characterizing and identifying fake images on Twitter during hurricane sandy. In: Proceedings of 22nd International Conference on World Wide Web, pp. 729–736 (2013)
26. Statista: Digital population in India as of January 2018 (in millions) 600. Internet Demographics Use (2019)
27. Balmas, M.: When fake news becomes real: combined exposure to multiple news sources and political attitudes of inefficacy, alienation, and cynicism. Commun. Res. **41**(3), 430–454 (2014)
28. Kapoor, K.K., Tamilmani, K., Rana, N.P., Patil, P., Dwivedi, Y.K., Nerur, S.: Advances in social media research: past, present and future. Inf. Syst. Front. **20**, 531–558 (2018)
29. Alalwan, A.A., Rana, N.P., Dwivedi, Y.K., Algharabat, R.: Social media in marketing: a review and analysis of the existing literature. Telematics Inform. **34**(7), 1177–1190 (2017)
30. Dwivedi, Y.K., Kapoor, K.K., Chen, H.: Social media marketing and advertising. Mark. Rev. **15**(3), 289–309 (2015)

Rumour Veracity Estimation with Deep Learning for Twitter

Jyoti Prakash Singh[1], Nripendra P. Rana[2(✉)], and Yogesh K. Dwivedi[2]

[1] National Institute of Technology Patna, Bihar, India
jps@nitp.ac.in
[2] School of Management, Swansea University Bay Campus, Swansea, UK
nrananp@gmail.com, ykdwivedi@gmail.com

Abstract. Twitter has become a fertile ground for rumours as information can propagate to too many people in very short time. Rumours can create panic in public and hence timely detection and blocking of rumour information is urgently required. We proposed and compare machine learning classifiers with a deep learning model using Recurrent Neural Networks for classification of tweets into rumour and non-rumour classes. A total thirteen features based on tweet text and user characteristics were given as input to machine learning classifiers. Deep learning model was trained and tested with textual features and five user characteristic features. The findings indicate that our models perform much better than machine learning based models.

Keywords: Rumour veracity · Deep learning · Twitter · Neural network · Machine learning

1 Introduction

Social media has become essential part of our day-to-day life (Alalwan et al. 2017; Alryalat et al. 2017; Dwivedi et al. 2015; Tamilmani et al. 2018; Shareef et al. 2019). Twitter (launched in July 2006) is currently one of the most popular social platforms that allows users to post any information, which is publicly visible. Each post on twitter is called tweet, which is limited in size to 280 characters. Due to short limits on tweets, users send and reads many tweets in a day. Information in the twitter diffuses very quickly through followers of a user. In a recent survey from Pew Research Centre, it is found that "two-third (67%) of Americans get news from social media". In the same survey it was also found that "about three-quarters (74%) of Twitter users get news on the site" (Shearer and Gottfried 2017).

The major reason of having an up-to-date information on Twitter is the fact that anyone can instantly post, share, and gather information. Social media data are being used to develop systems for disasters (Kumar and Singh 2019; Singh et al. 2017), location prediction of a user (Kumar et al. 2017), customer relationship management (Baabdullah et al. 2019; Kizgin et al. 2018; Kapoor et al. 2018; Shareef et al. 2019), and stock market prediction (Saumya et al. 2016). Unfortunately, the information cannot always be trusted upon (Roy et al. 2018). Some users post their tweets about

Published by Springer Nature Switzerland AG 2019
Y. Dwivedi et al. (Eds.): TDIT 2019, IFIP AICT 558, pp. 351–363, 2019.
https://doi.org/10.1007/978-3-030-20671-0_24

events without any corroboration and verification (Mendoza et al. 2010). DiFonzo and Bordia (2007) defined rumour as unverified and instrumentally relevant information statements in circulation. The open nature of Twitter is a suitable ground for rumourmongers to post and spread rumours. The rumour may result in major chaos and unpredictable reactions from involved individuals. An example of such a rumour is a tweet reporting an "Explosion at White House" in 2013. Only within three minutes, it created such a social panic that major stock indices (e.g. S&P 500 Index) dropped 14 points, and the Dow Jones Industrial Average also dropped about 145 points (Liu et al. 2018). Diffusion of negative information may cause fear and panic across people, disruption in social environments and affects the government credibility. To minimize the negative effects of rumour, it is essential to expose the falseness of information as early as possible before they can spread to larger extent.

A lot of research work across the world is being carried out to determine whether a tweet is rumour or not. In most of the literature, rumour detection is considered as a 2-class classification problem (Ma et al. 2015; Wu et al. 2015). Several features based on tweet text, propagation behaviour, user behaviour etc. are extracted to categorize a tweet into rumour and non-rumour class (Ma et al. 2015; Wu et al. 2015). The model performance of these systems depends on how accurately the features are extracted. Another group of researchers have tried to analyse the path through which the rumours are spreading on social media and used that information to differentiate rumour and non-rumour tweets (Kwon et al. 2017). The veracity or authenticity of the rumour information has also been used for tweet classification into rumour and non-rumour classes (Liang et al. 2015). The stance of the tweets whether a tweet is supporting a rumour, denying a rumour, questioning a rumour, or it is a normal comment is also being used to determine whether the tweet is rumour or non-rumour (Derczynski 2017; Enayet and El-Beltagy 2017).

In feature extraction and classification, deep learning architecture are now playing an important role. These architectures can be trained with a large amount of labelled data to learn the features directly from the data instead of extracting the features manually.

In this article, we have proposed and compared models based on machine learning as well as deep learning for rumour veracity determination. We extracted 13 features from tweet text and user characteristics to classify whether a tweet is rumour or not using different machine learning based classifiers. We compare the performance between machine learning and deep learning approaches and found that deep architecture performed better as compared to traditional machine learning approach. We utilized Long Short Term Memory (LSTM) network to exploit the deep representation of sequential data for rumour identification. Two proposed models based on the LSTM network are: (i) model using tweet text only, and (ii) model using tweet text along with user characteristics. By comparing both models, we found that textual features are sufficient to identify the rumour using an LSTM model. The main contributions of the research is proposal of deep learning based model for rumour veracity determination.

The rest of the paper is organized as follows: Sect. 2 discusses the related work; Sect. 3 represents the methodology of proposed work; Sect. 4 shows various experimental results. The results are discussed in Sect. 5 and the paper is concluded in Sect. 6.

2 Related Work

Determining the authenticity of information on social platform is a complex task. Identification of doubtful truth is very popular topic in social media. A number of researchers have worked for finding the truthfulness of information in this domain. Separating rumours information manually is not a trivial task. Hence, a number of supervised approaches have been proposed for automatic rumour identification. In this section, we present a brief description of some well-known work undertaken so far in this domain. There are two tasks where researchers have concentrated more i.e. (i) stance classification where the researchers tried to determine the stance (type) of each tweet, and (ii) veracity prediction where they determine the veracity or authenticity of rumour posts.

Oh et al. (2018) studied the acceptance of hate rumour and its consequence during a community crisis situation. They developed and tested a model using data collected from victims of a large scale (hate) rumour spread incident. Castillo et al. (2011) extracted several features, which are categorized as user-based, topic-based, content-based and propagation-based features to build a classifier. Qazvinian et al. (2011) developed a supervised approach for stance classification. In this stance, classification twitter specific rumour tweets are categorized as supporting rumour, denying rumour, questioning a rumour or neutral. They extracted several features from the time related information. According to Liang et al. (2015), the rumourmongers may have different behaviour from normal user and they investigate that replying the rumour post is different from the normal post. They proposed a user behaviour features based strategy and extracted eleven user behaviour features, which then treated as hidden representation for rumourmongers and possible rumour posts. They did their experiment with the Sina-Weibo data.

Zhao et al. (2015) explored the idea for early rumour identification. They used set of regular expressions to identify the questioning and denying tweets. Serrano et al. (2015) considered significance of time-span where they identified the difference of time between start of rumour spreading and start of anti-rumour spreading. Zubiaga et al. (2016) analysed how the rumours are diffusing on social media by utilizing the conversational posts. Using the various machine learning techniques, they explored the spreading of rumour on social media and evaluated how the users are supporting or denying a rumour to determine the veracity of a rumour. Lukasik et al. (2016) used Hawkes processes for modelling the diffusion of information on social platform in the context of stance classification. Hamidian and Diab (2016) explored the Tweet Latent Vector (TLV) approach. They proposed a TLV feature by applying the Semantic Textual Similarity (STS) model proposed by Guo and Diab (2012).

Jain et al. (2016) proposed an idea for identification of rumour source. They considered the network as undirected graph where whatever rumours are spreading on social network start from single source node with edges are connected to other nodes. We proposed a heuristic algorithm to get an estimate of the source node in as early as possible using the subgraph infected by rumour and the original graph of the network. Ma et al. (2017) developed an approach to identify rumours in social media posts using kernel learning method and propagation trees. They use the propagation tree for encoding the spread of the source tweet along with content, user and time associated with the retweeting nodes.

Zubiaga et al. (2017) explored the summarized survey of rumour detection on social media using different machine learning techniques. The survey discussed about the different approaches used for classification and detection of rumour and their performances. Srivastava et al. (2017) performed the stance classification as well as veracity prediction using cascading heuristics. By utilizing decision tree style, they trained a classifier with set of heuristics and then performance of the model is computed based on naive Bayes and winnow classifiers. Liu et al. (2017) considered the posts that had large amount of reposts and find out the difference between the rumour and non-rumour tree structure. They found that tree structure of rumour is deeper than the non-rumour and used that to separate rumour from non-rumour.

Previous approaches mostly focused on different features, which were derived from the linguistic information. However, in these approaches the performance of the system is reduced because they were limited to preserve the contextual meaning. Ma et al. (2016) proposed a recurrent neural network (RNN) based sequential approach for the veracity prediction. They counted three advantages over the traditional approaches. First, automatic feature learning capability. Second, reduction in the computation overhead. Third, capturing the semantics information. Chen et al. (2017b) explored a deep structure of neural network model, which is built on supervised classifier. They used the textual feature, which automatically learned by utilizing the different word representation techniques like pre-trained word embedding GloVe (Pennington et al. 2014).

They build a convolution neural network (CNN) for textual feature generation to preserve the contextual meaning and find the stance relationship using the source reply pairs of tweets. Rath et al. (2017) proposed a deep RNN architecture to identify the rumour spreaders by utilizing the trust. A user whose tweets are highly rated by other user is expected to have high trustworthiness score and a user who re-tweeted others tweet at high rate is expected to have high trust score and based on that score it is determined who can be possible rumour spreaders. Chen et al. (2017a) proposed a deep attention model based on recurrent neural network. Their model identifies the rumour by learning hidden sequential representation of posts. Chen et al. (2018) designed a model using recurrent neural network and auto encoder to learn the normal behaviour of individual users. They used the errors of different types of Weibo users to determine whether it is a rumour or not using self-adapting thresholds. They found that a two-layer model was performing better with an accuracy of 92.49% and F1 score of 89.16%. Lin et al. (2018) employed the LSTM and pooling operation of convolutional neural networks to build rumour identification models based on forwarding contents, spreaders and diffusion structures to detect rumours.

3 Method

3.1 Data

We have used the publically available dataset theme (Zubiaga et al. 2016) for our research work. The dataset contains rumour and non-rumour tweets and reactions on those tweets from five different events: Charlie Hebdo, Ferguson, German wings Crash, Ottawa Shooting, and Sydney Siege. Reaction is the collection of tweets replying to the source tweet. We have used 5802 source tweets, which include 1972 rumours and 3830 non-rumour tweets. The detail of the dataset is given in below in Table 1.

Table 1. Dataset with rumour and non-rumour

News	Rumor	Non-Rumor
Charlie Hebdo	22.0%	78.0%
Ferguson	24.8%	75.2%
German wings crash	50.7%	49.3%
Ottawa shooting	52.8%	47.2%
Sydney siege	42.8%	57.2%

3.2 Models

We have proposed and evaluated three models for identifying rumour veracity. The first model was a traditional machine learning based model with supervised learning setting. We used four different classifiers to train and test the machine learning model. The classifier used are (i) Support Vector Machine, (ii) k-Nearest Neighbour, (iii) Gradient Boosting and (iv) Random Forest. The second model was deep learning based model with Long Short Term Memory (LSTM) network using tweet text only. The third and final model was also deep learning based model with LSTM network but it uses user metadata along with tweet text.

3.2.1 Model 1: Machine Learning Based Model

We extracted thirteen different features from tweets contents and user characteristics to train and test the machine-learning model. The selected features are (i) Existence of question (ii) Detection of support words (iii) Detection of denial words (iv) Verified user or not (v) Number of followers (vi) Number of followees (vii) Sentiment of tweet (viii) Number of URL's (ix) Number of hashtags (x) User registered days (xi) Length of tweet text (xii) Status count (xiii) Retweet count. The first three features are derived from the contents and rest of the features are extracted from user characteristics. The complete list of features with explanation along with their sources is shown in Table 2.

The rumour veracity determination problem is framed as a supervised learning task of classifying whether a tweet is rumour or not. Four different classifiers namely support vector machines; k-nearest neighbour, gradient boosting and random forest were used to evaluate the accuracy of the proposed model.

The major problem with the machine learning models is extracting the features from data, which is given as input to the model. In case of text oriented task, most of the extracted features ignore the sequential nature of a sentence. To mitigate this problem of manual features engineering and preserving the sequential text information, deep learning models are getting popularity.

Table 2. List of different features with type and their description

Feature	Description	Type
Question existence	Whether the tweet contains question or not	Content based
Support term detection	Extraction of support word like true, truth, exactly, possible, OMG, indeed etc.	
Denial term detection	Extraction of denial terms like not true, false impossible, don't agree, shut etc.	
Verify user	Whether the user is verified user or not	User based
Number of followers	The number of users who follows an account	
Number of followees	The no of users who was followed by a post's author	
Sentiment of tweet text	Sentiment analysis decides the positivity or negativity of tweet text	
Number of URLs	The number of URL's in tweet text	
Number of hashtags	The number of hashtags in tweet text	
User registered days	The number of days since user prole was created	
Length of tweet text	The length of the tweet text	
Status count	The total number of tweets posted by user	
Retweet count	The number of times a tweet is reposted	

3.2.2 Model 2: LSTM with Tweet Text Only

Our second model was deep learning based model using LSTM network. The use of LSTM network preserves the contextual information of the text and also eliminates the need of hand-crafted features. The tweet text is embedded into a fixed size vector called embedding vector, which is given as input to the LSTM network in sequential manner. The schematic diagram of the model is given below in Fig. 1.

Word embedding is a way to represent the words into a vector to preserve the co-occurrence information of words. To get the embedding vector, we started with a bag of all unique words from the tweet text used in the experiment. The tweet text was represented by one-hot encoding vector. A look-up matrix M is created to achieve the embedding of each word w_i. We used the pre-trained look up matrix GloVe available online on nlp.stanford.edu/projects/glove/. This pre-trained matrix is used between the input layer and first hidden layer of the network to create the word embedding. The look-up matrix M contains the vector of each word, which is represented as:

$$M = \begin{bmatrix} w_{11} & w_{12} & w_{13} & \dots & w_{1d} \\ w_{21} & w_{22} & w_{23} & \dots & w_{2d} \\ \dots & & & & \\ w_{m1} & w_{m2} & w_{m3} & \dots & w_{md} \end{bmatrix} \quad (1)$$

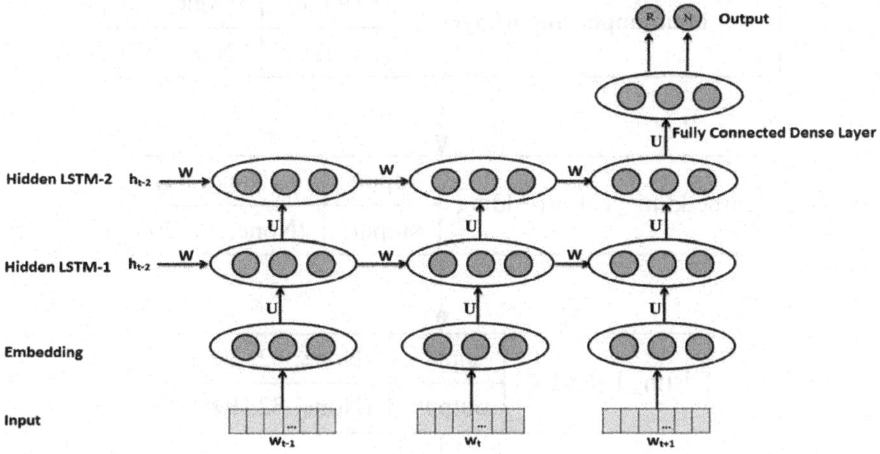

Fig. 1. Proposed LSTM module

Where, m represents total number of words and d represents the dimension to map these words. Embedding ($E(w_{1..m})$) can be represented as:

$$E(w_1..m) = e(w_1), e(w_2), e(w_3), \ldots, e(w_m) \quad (2)$$

Where $E(w_{1..m})$ denotes the embedding of all words present in a vocabulary and e (w_1), e(w_2), e(w_3),…, e(w_m) denotes the embedding of a single word.

Our model was a 2-layer LSTM network where we used 2-hidden layers with 100 neurons at each LSTM unit. A summary of the network is shown in Fig. 1. As can be seen from the figure, the input sentence length was fixed to 32 words. If the tweet has more than 32 words, then it was curtailed and only first 32 words are taken. On the other hand the short tweets are padded to make it of 32 words tweet. Each word was then embedded to a vector of length 200. The 200 length vector was scaled down to 100 length while passing through the first LSTM hidden unit. The length remains unchanged during processing by the second hidden LSTM unit. The 100 length output from LSTM unit is then passes through a dense layer, which scales it down to two outputs corresponding to rumour and non-rumour classes. In our experiment, we used 500 epochs with batch-size of 100. We used the 5-fold cross validation for training the system. The system was trained with four batch and validated with remaining one batch. We used the dropout as well recurrent-dropout at input connection and recurrent connection to the LSTM to prevent from over-fitting problem by randomly dropping some neurons in the training phase. At last, we used two neurons at dense layer for predicting whether a tweet is rumour or not? The block diagram with input/output size is shown in Fig. 2.

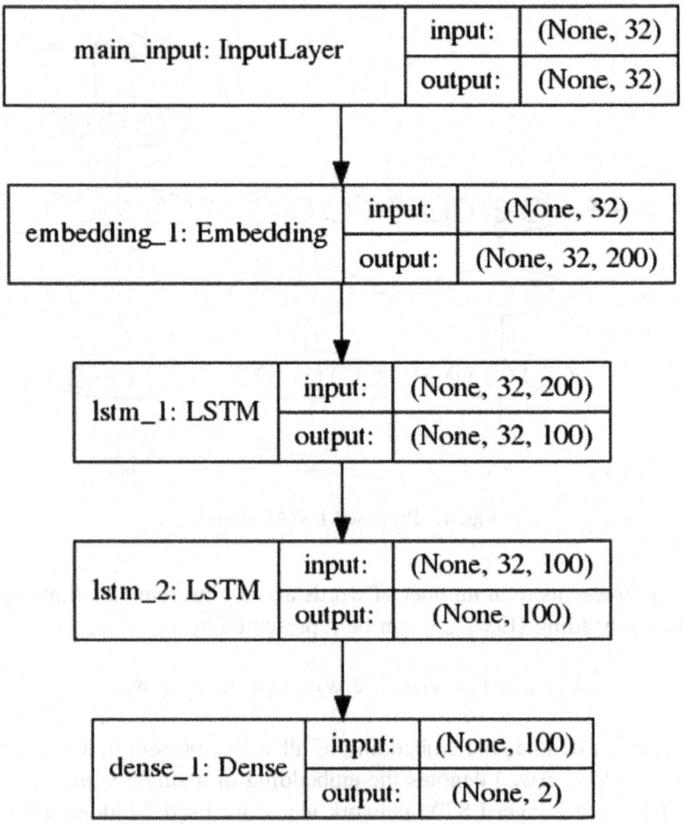

Fig. 2. LSTM with tweet text

3.2.3 Model 3: LSTM with Tweet Text and User Metadata

The user metadata like number of followers, number of followees, number of retweets, status count, verified user or not with the output of LSTM, which acts as input for the dense layer. Embedding is done as previous case, which is our third model is built by augmenting the second model to use the user information. We used a soft-max function to achieve non-linearity. At last we kept two neurons at dense layer, which is fully connected as our target was to identify whether the tweet is rumour or not.

4 Results

4.1 Result of Machine Learning Model

We performed the experiment by extracting several features, which is given in Table 2 and use them to the four different classifiers (i) SVM (ii) Gradient Boosting (iii) Random Forest (iv) k-nearest Neighbour. We normalize our dataset using Gaussian normalization and split our dataset into 3:1 for training and testing purpose.

Table 3. Performance measure of different classifiers

Classifier	Class	Precision	Recall	F1-Score
SVM	0 (Non-rumour)	0.68	0.9	0.77
	1 (Rumour)	0.64	0.3	0.41
K-Nearest neighbour	0 (Non-rumour)	0.68	0.68	0.68
	1 (Rumour)	0.51	0.51	0.51
Gradient boosting	0 (Non-rumour)	0.70	0.72	0.71
	1 (Rumour)	0.52	0.50	0.51
Random forest	0 (Non-rumour)	0.72	0.89	0.79
	1 (Rumour)	0.70	0.42	0.53

The result of SVM classifier is shown in Table 3, where our target class is class 1 or rumour and class 0 indicates non-rumour. Precision and Recall value for Class 1 were 0.64 and 0.30, which are quite low. The F1-Score for rumour class were 0.41. However, for Class 0 precision and recall and F1-score were 0.68, 0.90 and 0.77 respectively. The reason of higher performance matrices with Class 0 is the more number of data points of that class.

With k-nearest Neighbour the results are shown in Table 3. For Class 1 precision and recall value were 0.51 and 0.41 respectively. The F1-score value increased to 0.45. However, for Class 0 precision and recall and F1-score were 0.72, 0.89 and 0.79 respectively. Although there is slight increase in the performance metric, but, it is not of acceptable quality.

The result of the other two classifiers gradient boosting and random forest are tabulated in Table 3. The precision and recall value for rumour class is 0.52 and 0.50 respectively using gradient boosting. The F1-score for rumour class is improved to 0.51 and for random forest the precision and recall value for rumour class is 0.70 and 0.42. The F1-score for rumour class is improved to 0.53. These results are hardly better than a random classifier. We took these results as our benchmark to compare other two deep learning models.

4.2 Results of the LSTM Network

The average precision, recall and F1-score values for rumour class are found to be 0.77, 0.69, and 0.72 respectively, which is shown in Table 4. As compared to our baseline (Random Forest) model average precision, recall and F1-score values using deep learning approach improved by 7%, 27% and 19% respectively. We also tested our system performance by feeding text along with the user-metadata as an input but performance did not change.

Table 4. Precision, recall, and F1-Score using 2-Layer LSTM network using text

Class	Precision	Recall	F1-Score
0 (Non-rumour)	0.84	0.89	0.86
1 (Rumour)	0.77	0.69	**0.72**

5 Discussion

The major finding of the proposed research is that a 2-layer LSTM model using tweet text is performing better than machine learning based classifiers such as SVM, k-nearest neighbour, gradient boosting, and random forest. The LSTM model enhanced the performance by 35% in terms of F1-score compared to the best performing machine learning classifier (random forest). The another major finding of the research is that the tweet text itself is a good predictor of whether a tweet is rumour or not as we compared two LSTM based model using text and other metadata along with text. The model with metadata such as followers count, followees count, status count and verified status did not reported any change in the performance metric because the number of metadata parameters were very low compared to the text size. The 2-layer LSTM based model is able to identify 84% of non-rumour tweet as non-rumour and 77% of rumour related tweets are classified as rumour related. The machine learning approach using 13 different features performed very badly with best recall value of 50% with gradient boosting algorithm. Based on the result of machine learning and LSTM based model, it can be concluded that the features used for machine learning models are not relevant as well as they not preserving the contextual meaning of the tweet text.

One major theoretical implication resulting from the research is that a system with 2 layer LSTM is preferred model for rumour detection from Twitter.

One of the practical implications of our proposed system is, it is capable of identifying the rumour as soon as possible with good accuracy, which can help to take appropriate decision by the government in the situation of public panic, disruption in social order, natural disaster and terrorist attack. The main limitation of our system is that it is language dependent model. It is tested for the dataset theme, which consist of only English language tweets. Our system may not perform well for scenarios where tweets are in code mixed language.

6 Conclusion

Determining veracity of the rumour whether the Tweet is a rumour or non-rumour is critical task on Twitter. In this study for early rumour identification we explored the idea of machine learning as well deep learning approach and compare their performances. The result of this study showed the effectiveness of deep learning over machine learning regarding rumour identification. In machine learning approach we extracted several manual features from tweet contents and user meta-data information and evaluated their performance. The main limitation of the machine learning approach that it is very time-consuming process and limit to preserve the semantic representation of sequential information. On the other hand, to target the limitations of machine learning approach we used the deep learning module where our proposed LSTM model automatically learns the hidden temporal nature of tweet text which is difficult to preserve using hand-crafted features. Our deep architecture performed well over machine learning approach. The performance on detecting rumour veracity is not very high. Still accuracy of our proposed system can be improved. To know how deep learning can help in early rumour identification, more through experiments will be required. Due to overhead of data labelling, unsupervised approach can also be used.

References

Alalwan, A.A., Rana, N.P., Dwivedi, Y.K., Algharabat, R.S.: Social media in marketing: a review and analysis of the existing literature. Telematics Inform. **34**(7), 1177–1190 (2017)

Alryalat, M., Rana, N.P., Sahu, G.P., Dwivedi, Y.K., Tajvidi, M.: Use of social media in citizen-centric electronic government services: a literature analysis. Int. J. Electron. Gov. Res. **13**(3), 55–79 (2017)

Baabdullah, A.M., Rana, N.P., Alalwan, A.A., Algharabat, R., Kizgin, H., Al-Weshah, G.A.: Toward a conceptual model for examining the role of social media on social customer relationship management (SCRM) system. In: Elbanna, A., Dwivedi, Y.K., Bunker, D., Wastell, D. (eds.) TDIT 2018. IAICT, vol. 533, pp. 102–109. Springer, Cham (2019). https://doi.org/10.1007/978-3-030-04315-5_8

Castillo, C., Mendoza, M., Poblete, B.: Information credibility on twitter. In: Proceedings of the 20th International Conference on World Wide Web, pp. 675–684. ACM (2011)

Chen, T., Wu, L., Li, X., Zhang, J., Yin, H., Wang, Y.: Call attention to rumours: deep attention based recurrent neural networks for early rumour detection. arXiv preprint arXiv:1704.05973 (2017a)

Chen, W., Zhang, Y., Yeo, C.K., Lau, C.T., Lee, B.S.: Unsupervised rumor detection based on users' behaviors using neural networks. Pattern Recogn. Lett. **105**, 226–233 (2018)

Chen, Y.-C., Liu, Z.-Y., Kao, H.-Y.: IKM at SemEval-2017 task 8: convolutional neural networks for stance detection and rumour verification. In: Proceedings of the 11th International Workshop on Semantic Evaluation (SemEval-2017), pp. 465–469 (2017b)

Derczynski, L., et al.: SemEval-2017 task 8: RumourEval: determining rumour veracity and support for rumours. arXiv preprint arXiv:1704.05972 (2017)

DiFonzo, N., Bordia, P.: Rumor Psychology: Social and Organizational Approaches. American Psychological Association (2007)

Dwivedi, Y.K., Kapoor, K.K., Chen, H.: Social media marketing and advertising. Mark. Rev. **15** (3), 289–309 (2015)

Enayet, O., El-Beltagy, S.R.: NileTMRG at SemEval-2017 task 8: determining rumour and veracity support for rumours on twitter. In: Proceedings of the 11th International Workshop on Semantic Evaluation (SemEval-2017), pp. 470–474 (2017)

Guo, W., Diab, M.: A simple unsupervised latent semantics-based approach for sentence similarity. In: Proceedings of the First Joint Conference on Lexical and Computational Semantics, pp. 586–590. ACL (2012)

Hamidian, S., Diab, M.: Rumor identification and belief investigation on twitter. In: Proceedings of the 7th Workshop on Computational Approaches to Subjectivity, Sentiment and Social Media Analysis, pp. 3–8 (2016)

Jain, A., Borkar, V., Garg, D.: Fast rumour source identification via random walks. Soc. Netw. Anal. Min. **6**, 62 (2016)

Kapoor, K.K., Tamilmani, K., Rana, N.P., Patil, P., Dwivedi, Y.K., Nerur, S.: Advances in social media research: past, present and future. Inf. Syst. Front. **20**(3), 531–558 (2018)

Kizgin, H., Jamal, A., Dey, B., Rana, N.P.: The impact of social media on consumers' acculturation and purchase intentions. Inf. Syst. Front. **20**(3), 503–514 (2018)

Kumar, A., Singh, J.P.: Location reference identification from tweets during emergencies: a deep learning approach. Int. J. Disaster Risk Reduction **33**, 365–375 (2019)

Kumar, A., Singh, J.P., Rana, N.P.: Authenticity of Geo-Location and Place Name in Tweets (2017)

Kwon, S., Cha, M., Jung, K.: Rumor detection over varying time windows. PLoS ONE **12**(1), e0168344 (2017)

Liang, G., He, W., Xu, C., Chen, L., Zeng, J.: Rumor identification in microblogging systems based on user's behaviour. IEEE Trans. Comput. Soc. Syst. **2**, 99–108 (2015)

Liu, Y., Jin, X., Shen, H.: Towards early identification of online rumours based on long short-term memory networks. Inf. Process. Manage. (2018). https://doi.org/10.1016/j.ipm.2018.11.003

Liu, Y., Jin, X., Shen, H., Cheng, X.: Do rumors diffuse differently from non-rumors? A systematically empirical analysis in Sina Weibo for rumor identification. In: Kim, J., Shim, K., Cao, L., Lee, J.-G., Lin, X., Moon, Y.-S. (eds.) PAKDD 2017. LNCS (LNAI), vol. 10234, pp. 407–420. Springer, Cham (2017). https://doi.org/10.1007/978-3-319-57454-7_32

Lukasik, M., Srijith, P., Vu, D., Bontcheva, K., Zubiaga, A., Cohn, T.: Hawkes processes for continuous time sequence classification: an application to rumour stance classification in twitter. In: Proceedings of the 54th Annual Meeting of the Association for Computational Linguistics (Volume 2: Short Papers), vol. 2, pp. 393–398 (2016)

Ma, J., Gao, W., Wong, K.-F.: Detect rumours in microblog posts using propagation structure via kernel learning. In: Proceedings of the 55th Annual Meeting of the Association for Computational Linguistics (Volume 1: Long Papers), vol. 1, pp. 708–717 (2017)

Ma, J., et al.: Detecting rumours from microblogs with recurrent neural networks. In: IJCAI, pp. 3818–3824 (2016)

Ma, J., Gao, W., Wei, Z., Lu, Y., Wong, K.-F.: Detect rumours using time series of social context information on microblogging websites. In: Proceedings of the 24th ACM International on Conference on Information and knowledge Management, pp. 1751–1754. ACM (2015)

Mendoza, M., Barbara, P., Carlos, C.: Twitter under crisis: can we trust what we RT? In: Proceedings of the First Workshop on Social Media Analytics, pp. 71–79. ACM (2010)

Oh, O., Gupta, P., Agrawal, M., Rao, H.R.: ICT mediated rumour beliefs and resulting user actions during a community crisis. Gov. Inf. Q. **35**(2), 243–258 (2018)

Pennington, J., Socher, R., Manning, C.: Glove: global vectors for word representation. In: Proceedings of the 2014 Conference on Empirical Methods in Natural Language Processing (EMNLP), pp. 1532–1543 (2014)

Qazvinian, V., Rosengren, E., Radev, D.R., Mei, Q.: Rumor has it: identifying misinformation in microblogs. In: Proceedings of the Conference on Empirical Methods in Natural Language Processing, pp. 1589–1599. Association for Computational Linguistics (2011)

Rath, B., Gao, W., Ma, J., Srivastava, J.: From retweet to believability: utilizing trust to identify rumour spreaders on twitter. In: Proceedings of the 2017 IEEE/ACM International Conference on Advances in Social Networks Analysis and Mining 2017, pp. 179–186. ACM (2017)

Roy, P.K., Singh, J.P., Baabdullah, A., Kizgin, H., Rana, N.P.: Identifying reputation collectors in community question answering (CQA) sites: an exploration of the dark side of social media. Int. J. Inf. Manage. **42**, 25–35 (2018)

Saumya, S., Singh, J.P., Kumar, P.: Predicting stock movements using social network. In: Dwivedi, Y.K., et al. (eds.) I3E 2016. LNCS, vol. 9844, pp. 567–572. Springer, Cham (2016). https://doi.org/10.1007/978-3-319-45234-0_50

Serrano, E., Iglesias, C.A., Garijo, M.: A survey of twitter rumor spreading simulations. In: Núñez, M., Nguyen, N.T., Camacho, D., Trawiński, B. (eds.) ICCCI 2015. LNCS (LNAI), vol. 9329, pp. 113–122. Springer, Cham (2015). https://doi.org/10.1007/978-3-319-24069-5_11

Shareef, M.A., Mukerji, B., Dwivedi, Y.K., Rana, N.P., Islam, R.: Social media marketing: comparative effect of advertising sources. J. Retail. Consum. Serv. **46**, 58–69 (2019)

Shearer, E., Gottfried, J.: News use across social media platforms 2017. Pew Research Center, 7 (2017)

Singh, J.P., Dwivedi, Y.K., Rana, N.P., Kumar, A., Kapoor, K.K.: Event classification and location prediction from tweets during disasters. Ann. Oper. Res., 1–21 (2017)

Srivastava, A., Rehm, G., Schneider, J.M.: DFKI-DKT at SemEval-2017 task 8: rumour detection and classification using cascading heuristics. In Proceedings of the 11th International Workshop on Semantic Evaluation (SemEval-2017), pp. 486–490 (2017)

Tamilmani, K., Rana, N.P., Alryalat, M., Alkuwaiter, W., Dwivedi, Y.K.: Social media research in the context of emerging markets: an analysis of literature published in senior scholars' basket of IS journals. J. Adv. Manage. Res. (2018). https://doi.org/10.1108/JAMR-05-2017-0061

Wu, K., Yang, S., Zhu, K.Q.: False rumours detection on Sina Weibo by propagation structures. In: 2015 IEEE 31st International Conference on Data Engineering (ICDE), pp. 651–662. IEEE (2015)

Zhao, Z., Resnick, P., Mei, Q.: Enquiring minds: early detection of rumours in social media from enquiry posts. In: Proceedings of the 24th International Conference on World Wide Web, pp. 1395–1405. International World Wide Web Conferences Steering Committee (2015)

Zubiaga, A., Aker, A., Bontcheva, K., Liakata, M., Procter, R.: Detection and resolution of rumours in social media: a survey. arXiv preprint arXiv:1704.00656 (2017)

Zubiaga, A., Liakata, M., Procter, R., Hoi, G.W.S., Tolmie, P.: Analysing how people orient to and spread rumours in social media by looking at conversational threads. PloS One **11**, 1–29 (2016)

The Privacy Paradox of Utilizing the Internet of Things and Wi-Fi Tracking in Smart Cities

Krystan ten Berg(✉), Ton A. M. Spil, and Robin Effing

University of Twente, Enschede, The Netherlands
krystan.tenberg@gmail.com,
{a.a.m.spil,r.effing}@utwente.nl

Abstract. In recent years, we have seen the increase of Internet of Things (IoT) solutions, products and services. The Internet of Things will capture a large amount of data pertaining from the environment, as well as their users. The real value of collecting data will be the result of data processing and aggregation in a large-scale where new knowledge can be extracted. However, such procedures can also lead to user privacy issues. This study describes what citizens do and do not know about Wi-Fi tracking and how that knowledge affects their responses to privacy and security risks. The results of this study showed that there is a lack of awareness towards Wi-Fi tracking by people in the municipality studied. The results show that most respondents are willing to cooperate with Wi-Fi tracking, despite the fact that most people have concerns of losing control about how their data is gathered and used. This study also found that respondents indicated Wi-Fi tracking as useful and especially safety is appointed as an important benefit of Wi-Fi tracking. The results of this study confirm that privacy, trust and perceived benefits significantly influence the willingness to disclose personal information.

Keywords: Internet of Things · Privacy · Adoption of IT

1 Introduction

Control of privacy is of increasing importance (Bélanger and Crossler 2011), especially in cases of smart cities (Ismagilova et al. 2019; Hossain et al. 2016; Rana et al. 2018). The Privacy Calculus Theory (Gutierrez et al. 2019) implies that, people decide both consciously and unconsciously about the privacy they are giving up, and the benefits they receive in return (Dinev and Hart 2006). Most of the previous studies involving the privacy calculus, focused on e-commerce or services like Facebook and the behavior of the users towards data disclosure. In this study the focus lies on the privacy calculus and Wi-Fi tracking.

Earlier research, which has tried to understand consumers' attitudes towards this specific form of data collection, is often directed at student populations and on one level. This study is both important for investigating citizens attitudes towards being tracked, and for understanding how these attitudes relate to actual behavior. Van Slyke et al. (2006) introduced the concept of trust into the privacy discussion and this study includes that discussion.

Published by Springer Nature Switzerland AG 2019
Y. Dwivedi et al. (Eds.): TDIT 2019, IFIP AICT 558, pp. 364–381, 2019.
https://doi.org/10.1007/978-3-030-20671-0_25

First, the method is described followed by a structured literature review and the results of the survey are given in chapter four. Chapter five analyses these results followed by conclusions.

2 Background

The first part of the approach for this study is based on an in-depth grounded literature review of relevant studies as well as official documents of international institutions. The literature study is conducted with data bases such as Scopus, Sciencedirect, Web of science and Jstor. Keywords used to find articles related to the topic are, privacy calculus, Wi-Fi tracking, Privacy, sensing, internet of things (IOT), MAC address and Smart cities. Founded articles provide information about the concepts of smart cities, IOT and Wi-Fi tracking. For the chapters of this study, different search combinations are used. The combination "IOT AND Smart city" was used to find articles about the general description of these concepts and the link between them. From the large number of articles, the ones with the most citations where used. For the literature about Wi-Fi tracking, the key words "Mac address" AND "tracking" are used. This provided 68 results of which the most useable where selected. Furthermore, the search on the keyword phrase "privacy calculus" provided us with 324 articles. The articles with the most citations where used to describe the model of the privacy calculus used in this article. By using the key words "privacy calculus and disclosure behavior" together, 1 of 9 articles was useable for this literature review. Furthermore, the keywords "Privacy AND tracking AND Smart city" provided 19 articles, from which this research used 2 to describe privacy concerns in smart cities. "privacy concerns AND data disclosure" provide articles also usable for the chapters about privacy concerns. Some of the most cited articles where used.

2.1 Smart Cities, IOT and Wi-Fi Tracking

The Internet of Things (IoT) and Smart Cities are recent phenomena that have attracted the attention from both academia and industry. However Smart cities and The internet of things have different origins, they are moving towards each other to achieve a common goal (Perera et al. 2014). In the following chapter, the definition of a smart city will be described, followed by relevant points and problems in the context of the Internet of Things.

According to Hall et al. (2000), a smart city is a city that monitors and integrates conditions of all of its critical infrastructures, including roads, bridges, tunnels, rails, subways, airports, seaports, communications, water, power, even major buildings, can better optimize its resources, plan its preventive maintenance activities, and monitor security aspects while maximizing services to its citizens".

For a smart city initiative to be successful, urban development ICT and IOT are important building blocks in creating a smart infrastructure for managing ever increasing city population. The internet of things is one of the building blocks of a smart city. Sensing as a service model, as a solution based on IoT infrastructure has the capability to address the challenges in Smart Cities (Hollands 2008). Smart Cities will take advantage of communication and sensor capabilities integrated into the cities' infrastructures to optimize electrical, transport, and other logistical operations supporting daily life, thereby improving the quality of life for everyone (Bartoli et al. 2011). In this respect, the IoT can become the building block to realize an unified urban scale ICT platform, thus unleashing the potential of the Smart City vision (Hernández-Muñoz et al. 2011; Mulligan and Olsson 2013; Al-Dhubhani et al. 2018). So urban IoTs are designed to support the Smart City vision, because it aims at exploiting the most advanced communication technologies to support added-value services for the administration of the city and for the citizens (Zanella et al. 2014).

Because Infrastructures are a central component of the Smart City and that technology is the enabler that makes it possible, but it is the combination, connection and integration of all systems what becomes fundamental for a city being truly smart (Nam and Pardo 2011). The overall vision of the smart city needs IOT to unleash the potential of this vision. Figure 1 shows how the core components are related in this research. Smart city as an overall vision, IOT as building block to support the smart vision and Wi-Fi tracking as an application from this vision and technology. However, it must be noted that the direction of the relationship between these building blocks can be interpreted differently.

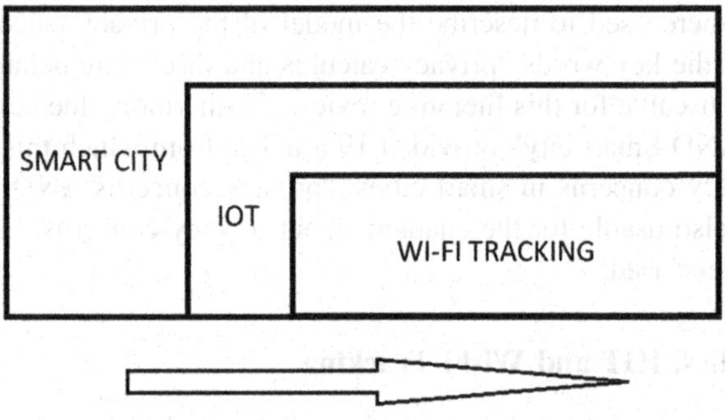

Fig. 1.

The real innovation in smart cities, comes from the Internet of Things, the ever-expanding network of sensors and devices that collect data everywhere. Atzori et al. (2010), stated that people might experience a real difficulty in understanding what IoT really means, which basic ideas stand behind this concept, and which social, economic and technical implications the full deployment of IoT will have. The Internet of Things represent an explosion of information creation, sharing, and use. This is due to greatly increased types and numbers of connected physical devices such as sensors and actuators, and systems used by people. Miorandi et al. (2012) stated that, the Internet of Things vision can provide a large set of opportunities to users, manufacturers and companies, including, e.g., environmental monitoring, health-care, inventory and product management, workplace and home support, security and surveillance. Because location information is a large component of IoT information, and concerns about its privacy are critical to widespread adoption and confidence, location privacy issues must be effectively addressed (Minch 2015). The Internet of Things is vulnerable to privacy violations. Previous research highlighted the fact that privacy could be a significant barrier to the growth of IoT (Perera et al. 2015). As more connected objects become integrated in daily lives, ensuring that people feel comfortable with IoT's impact on their privacy becomes increasingly important.

2.2 Privacy in the Internet of Things Paradox

Privacy preservation will be one of the major challenges in the development of the Internet of Things. Billions of sensor-enabled devices will be deployed for collecting fine-grained information from the environment and will share them with other devices and backend servers (Lopez et al. 2017).

Monitoring and Privacy

During the past decade, user privacy has become an important issue in networked computing environments (Lee and Kobsa 2016). The possibilities of data-gathering innovations that can underpin the smart-city framework is broad: street lights fitted with license plate readers, sensors that detect and count passing smart-phones, the presence of closed-circuit cameras in many cities etc. Many smart city technologies capture personally identifiable information (PII) and household level data about citizens – their characteristics, their location and movements, and their activities. As cities are becoming smart, people start to be increasingly aware about their surroundings, feeling more secure, but at the same time being more concerned about their privacy (Longo and Cheng 2015). Personal data is easily collected and analyzed through the use of sophisticated means of the smart-city. Mobile applications and devices are increasingly asking users to provide personal information, as well as monitoring users through behavioral tracking. Companies deploy several mesh of nodes in different area: individuals could be tracked in a large scale. Risks are higher if those localizations are correlated with other information (Demir 2013). Collected data may than be capable of linking to or identifying an individual, which raises privacy concerns (Wilson and Valecich 2012). This privacy-invasive practice is likely to increase with the proliferation of sensor devices in the upcoming era of Internet of Things. Lee and Kobsa (2017). In fact IoT and Ubiquitous technology are leading to increasing privacy as they are capturing and storing more and more information about people and their activities (Longo and Cheng 2015).

Many definitions of privacy exist in literature. Privacy is inherently difficult to reduce to a single definition that is rich enough to explain perceptions and behaviors across a range of contexts (Vasalou et al. 2015). Traditionally, privacy has been conceptualized as a right to control over information about oneself (Derikx et al. (2015). Westin (1967) defined privacy as "the claim of individuals, groups or institutions to determine for themselves when, how, and to what extent information about them is communicated to others" (as cited by Könings et al. 2016). In general terms, privacy debates acceptable practices with regards to accessing and disclosing personal and sensitive information about a person (Elwood and Leszczynski (2011).

Within this research context, privacy is mostly related to location and movement and citizens ability to control their location relevant information. According to Finn et al. (2013) privacy of location and space implies that, individuals have the right to move about in public or semi-public space without being identified, tracked or monitored. They furthermore state that, such a conception of privacy has social value. When citizens are free to move about public space without fear of identification, monitoring or tracking, they experience a sense of living in a democracy and experiencing freedom.

Wi-Fi Tracking and Privacy

In the case of monitoring and Wi-Fi tracking, location and movement privacy are most likely to be violated. Privacy of location and space is especially impacted by tracking technologies in mobile phones, cars (Derikx et al. 2015) and location based services (Krumm 2009). With the use of location based services, one of the biggest concerns is that it can be possible to compile a very detailed picture of someone's movements if they are carrying a wireless device that communicates its location to network operators. The potential for abuse of this information ranges from unsolicited advertisement from shops when a mobile user approaches, to the more serious concerns as, firms using location information on field employees to impose strict performance measures, and even dangerous or repressive, like criminals determining the right time to intrude on a subscriber's house, or an improper conviction made based on circumstantial location information (Beinat 2001; Clarke 2001) as cited by Steinfeld (2004). However, the relative success of some location-based applications implies that at least some people are comfortable with sending their location data to third parties (Krumm 2009).

Awareness

Demir (2013) concluded that people who are being surrounded by sensors embedded in their physical environment and capable of recognizing and responding to people's presence in a seamless and often invisible way, in which they are not aware of such collection, not knowing which information about them is collected, how it is being used, or with whom it may be shared down the road, will create privacy issues. Such a lack of transparency may undermine the ability of the user to effectively anticipate privacy risks associated with the collection and processing of his or her data, and subsequently take adequate countermeasures. As solution they propose to improved awareness & transparency of data practices. Users should be informed about when and how data is gathered, what kind of data is gathered, what is happening to this data and whether data might be shared with third parties. Most people are unaware that their Wi-Fi is a potential source of tracking (Demir 2013). Public Wi-Fi is incredibly convenient, but raises privacy issues for users and potential backlash for Wi-Fi providers. Wi-Fi providers gathering mobile location data, consumers are being tracked, often without they knowing it. Users' personal information is collected more passively and collectively. Users may feel less aware and in control of personal information being collected. According to Bailey (2015), are consumers willing to trade off their privacy. And one possible reason as to why consumers are willing to trade away their privacy is because they are unaware of the amount of privacy that is being lost. He furthermore stated that, even if consumers were made aware of the loss, they would still engage in privacy-sacrificing behaviors. Behavioral economists have proven that people will both underestimate their risk of harm and prefer a short-term gain to a long-term risk.

However, other studies found that, users often refuse to share their personal data with respect to time and space (Barkhuus and Dey 2003).

The Privacy Paradox

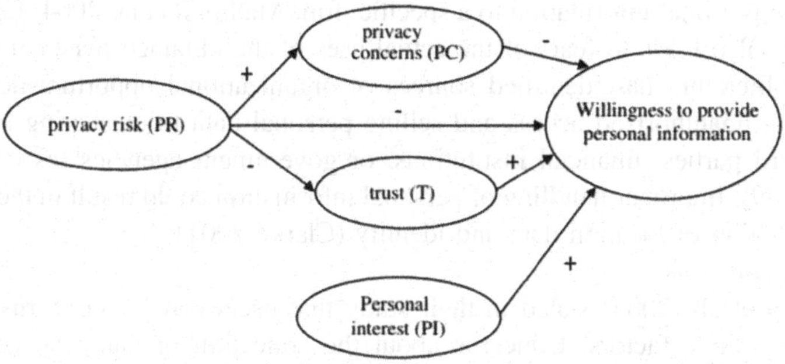

Fig. 2. Privacy calculus (Dinev and Hart 2006)

The discrepancy between actual or intended privacy related behavior and stated privacy is coined as the privacy paradox. Wilson and Valecich (2012) stated that the privacy calculus is a possible explanation for the privacy paradox. The privacy paradox is known as the discrepancy between the expressed concern and the actual behavior of users. In other words, people claim to be very worried about their privacy but do very little to protect their personal data (Barth and de Jong 2017). The calculus perspective of information privacy interprets the individual's privacy interests as an exchange where individuals disclose their personal information in return for certain benefits (Xu et al. 2009).This is consistent with the study of Dinev and Hart (2006), they addresses the trade-off between the expected costs of privacy risk beliefs and the benefits of confidence and placement beliefs on the willingness to provide personal information. According to Dinev and Hart (2006), the perceived privacy risks reduce disclosure intentions while perceived benefits of information disclosure increase intentions. An individual's unique level of general privacy will increase their context-specific perceived risk and decrease disclosure intentions. Quite often the perceived benefits outweigh the perceived risks, which eventually leads to the neglecting of privacy concerns that often results in the disclosure of information in exchange for social or economic benefit (Privacy Calculus Theory; Culnan and Armstrong 1999). Users consciously weigh the disadvantages of privacy disclosure against the perceived benefits. It would seem that users consciously resolve discrepancies between the willingness to obtain and possess something (such as downloading an app) and the simultaneous difficulties that arise in terms of unknown threats or risks (such as potential data usage by third parties (Barth and de Jong 2017).

Constructs of the Privacy Calculus

The privacy calculus model (Fig. 2) as proposed by Dinev and Hart (2006) is used in this research. The model of Dinev and hart exist of the following constructs; Risks, privacy concerns, Trust, Personal interest (benefits), and the willingness to provide personal information (in the rest of this study revered to as Attitude). The study of Barth and de Jong (2017) described the same constructs and added some more like; Awareness.

1. *Privacy risks*
   Risk beliefs in this context, is defined as the expected loss potential associated with releasing personal information to a specific firm (Malhotra et al. 2004; Lee and Rao 2007). It also leads to fears of the actual uses of the obtained personal data. Prior privacy literature has identified sources of organizational opportunistic behavior, including unauthorized access and selling personal data to or sharing information with third parties, financial institutions, or government agencies (as cited by Xu et al. 2009). Improper handling of personal information could result in the discovery and matching of location data and identity (Clarke 2001).
2. *Privacy concerns*
   Malhotra et al. (2004) stated in their study that users privacy concerns are determined by three factors: Concerns about the collection of data, the control they perceive to have over this collection, and how important they consider being aware of data collection. Furthermore, the study of Smith et al. (1996), identified four dimensions of an individual's concern about privacy, namely: Collection, Errors, Unauthorized secondary use and Improper access (as cited by Liu et al. 2014). The four factors provide a framework to explain the concerns for information privacy (Stewart and Segars 2002). That is, the likelihood of privacy breaches is expected to occur, when any of the following cases happens: (1) large amounts of personally identifiable data are being collected, (2) data are inaccurate, (3) companies use personal information for undisclosed purposes, and (4) companies fail to protect consumers' personal information (Liu et al. 2014). Furthermore the study of Fogel and Nehmad (2009) found that, general privacy concerns and identity information disclosure-concerns are of greater concern to women than men.
3. Trust
   In the case of trust, firms which implement fair information practices, and disclose these practices to their "customers" can exercise latitude in how they use personal information gathered, without risking customer defections and the other negative outcomes, they ensure that their practices are consistent with what they disclosed to their customers (Culnan and Armstrong 1999). Institutional trust refers to an individual confidence that the data – requesting stakeholders or medium will not misuse his or her data (Anderson and Agarwal 2011; Bansal and Gefen 2010; Dinev and Hart 2006) and had been found to be related to privacy concerns, risk beliefs (Malhotra et al. 2004) and intentions to disclose information (Dinev and Hart 2006). Whereas trust may not necessarily eliminate risk beliefs, Dinev and Hart (2006) argue that it can overrule their negative impact (as stated by Krasnova et al. 2012). The cumulative effects of trust and personal interests can outweigh privacy risk perception to point that it eventually leads to the disclosure of personal information (Dinev and Hart 2006).
4. Personal interests (benefits)
   Previous research about privacy from Van Zoonen (2016); Barkhuus and Dey (2003); Wirz et al. (2010) suggest that, people assess for which purpose data is used

and weigh the benefits that providing their data may offer them. When these benefits are of immediate personal relevance (medical services, commercial gain), most people are willing to share their data with the organization asking for them (e.g. Acquisti et al. 2013). Heek et al. (2015) stated in their study for example that, surveillance technologies are accepted in those locations in which crime threat is present. Users then prefer safety over privacy. User diversity is a crucial factor in this context: Women attach a higher importance to safety in general, in contrast to men, while men prefer the protection of their privacy (Heek et al. 2015).

5. Attitude
   The normalization of the collection and aggregation of data by governments raises also issues of privacy. Technologies and applications that were perceived to be creepy, have now become socially "acceptable" (Finch and Tene 2013).

However, as stated before, privacy can be considered as a tradeoff between the disclosure of personal information and service related benefits (Chorppath and Alpcan 2013; Dinev and Hart 2006; Hann et al. 2007; Laudon, 1996; Li et al., 2010; Weinberg et al. 2015). On the one hand, people become increasingly critical of the protection of their personal data, such as online or offline tracking. On the other hand, are people willing to provide a lot of privacy if there is anything about it, for example free access to a Wi-Fi network. People care about privacy, but they may care even more about convenience. People have sacrificed their privacy over the last decades, and are probably continue to do so.

This paper will provide an answer for the following research question: *To what extent are citizens of the municipality aware that they can be tracked and how can the elements of risk, concerns, trust and benefits - as used in the privacy calculus - affect their attitude to data disclosure.*

3 Results

Data Collection – Questionnaire

The second part of the study consisted of a quantitative study for better understanding citizens' views on the topic. The data required to answer the main question is collected from a survey. In this section, will be discussed how the online survey data is collected and analyzed, and what can be learned about people's privacy preferences in IOT environments. The survey was administered to broad samples of individuals from the city studied, who were asked to participate voluntarily. The time period that this survey had been administered, is between January 2018 and March 2018. The target population for this study was inhabitants of a smart-city which is utilizing Wi-Fi tracking technologies.

To ensure construct validity, scales from previous studies will be adapted wherever possible. The survey included elements taken from the privacy calculus of Dinev and Hart (2006) and Barth and de Jong (2017). The actual items were slightly adjusted from the original instruments to fit the city and Wi-Fi context of this study. Perceived risks and benefits will be adapted from Xu et al. (2009) and general privacy concerns from Malhotra et al. (2004). The concept of trust was adapted from Dinev and Hart (2004,

2006), Malhotra et al. (2004) and Westin (2001), attitudes to disclose was assessed using scales adapted from Anderson and Agarwal (2011). On top of that, demographic variables such as age and gender were included. To prevent bias towards a negative or a positive attitude, the survey questions were formulated both positive and negative, depending on the construct. The outcomes of the survey were analyzed by using the software SPSS. Measure validation for reliability was established through examining Cronbach's alpha coefficient for each construct. Relations between the different constructs were analyzed with correlation and regression analysis. Because of the relatively limited set of respondents for the analysis, a 90% confidence interval was chosen.

The total amount of respondents is 86. All responses were valid with no missing answers. The distribution of male and female respondents was N = 51 and N = 35. The Mean age was 34.56 (SD = 11.74) as shown in Table 1. For the analysis the difference between male and female and age groups are taken in to account. For the most constructs no differences were found, however for the constructs awareness and privacy differences where noted.

Table 1. Demographics

		Frequency	Percent
Valid	Male	51	59,3
	Female	35	40,7
	Total	86	100,0

	N	Minimum	Maximum	Mean	Std. Deviation
AGE	86	21	63	34,58	11,730
Valid N (listwise)	86				

The descriptive analysis shows differences in the percentage the overall knowledge of Wi-Fi tracking and Wi-Fi tracking in Enschede. Almost 25% of the respondents had not heard of Wi-Fi tracking before. And more than 45% of the respondents were not aware of the fact, that Enschede also makes use of Wi-Fi tracking. There is however a difference between the age groups <42 and >43. The elderly group respondents (>43) are more aware of the fact that, the municipality of Enschede is using Wi-Fi tracking sensors in the city to track visitors (66,7%). From the younger group only 45,9% of the respondents was aware of Wi-Fi tracking in Enschede.

Furthermore, 61,6% of the respondents indicated that they are not aware for what purposes municipalities are deploying Wi-Fi tracking sensors in cities. And more than 82% of the respondents are not aware that it is also possible that they can being tracked, without being connected to an open Wi-Fi network. What furthermore is striking is the fact that respondents of >43 are more aware of the fact that municipalities can track visitors in the city (84%) And in this age group 40% is aware of the purposes of Wi-Fi tracking. More than 54% of the respondents thinks that Wi-Fi tracking can be useful. But they also believe that the interest of the citizens are always more important that the interest of municipalities 55%.

Most respondents don't know if they will experience (some) the benefits of a better city or services, when municipalities are gathering their data with Wi-Fi tracking. But most of the respondents think that Wi-Fi tracking is useful (54,7%).

Almost all respondents have chosen safety in cities as a possible benefit of Wi-Fi tracking (86%). Furthermore, better facilities in the city are also seen as a possible benefit by 57%. Only n = 6 (7%) of the respondents thinks Wi-Fi tracking cannot provide any benefit for them at all (Table 2).

Table 2. Main benefits and usefulness

Frequencies

		Responses N	Percent of Cases
Benefits Wifi tracking[a]	Safety	74	86,0%
	Never	6	7,0%
	Offers	10	11,6%
	Facilities	49	57,0%
	Mapping	34	39,5%

a. Dichotomy group tabulated at value 1.

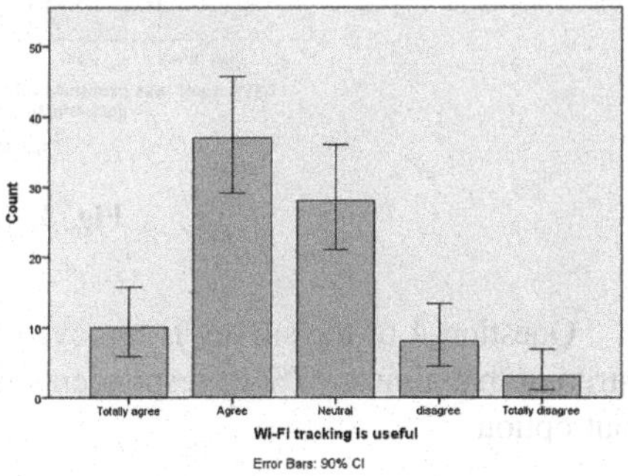

In general the respondents do trust municipalities and government to handle personal data with confidence. There is no exception between the younger group of respondents (<42 and the older group (>43). However there is a difference between males and females. Males tend to have higher trust in how municipalities handle their data and existing laws and regulation than females do.

Most respondents are indicating that the gathering of personal data comprises risks. And most respondents stated that they worry about the gathering and handling of their personal data. Possible misuse of personal data is the biggest concern of respondents (60%). The results showed that the mean scores of the privacy are higher for females than for men, indicating that the group of females tend to have more concerns regarding their privacy.

Like the concerns, more than 51% see the misuse of personal data as a (very) high risk. Actually, all the elements of risk are considered (very) high risks by respondents. Furthermore, most respondents (56%) worry that they will lose control about how their data is gathered and used. In the open comment section respondents indicated, that the possibility of their data being hacked is also a big risk.

Almost 40% of the respondents indicated that they have no or less problems with Wi-Fi tracking, when they exactly know how there data is gathered and how it will be used. Only N = 8 respondents, will still have problem with Wi-Fi tracking (Fig. 3).

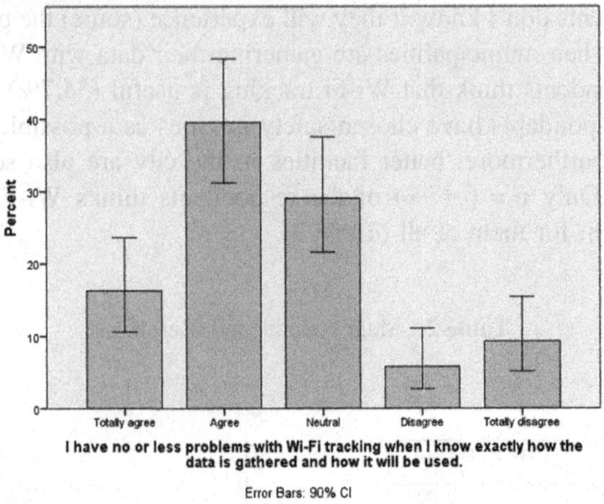

Fig. 3. Transparancy

Question 4 of the survey is removed for analyzing the correlations. However, it is striking that almost 47% of respondents indicated that they would considering the opt-out option.

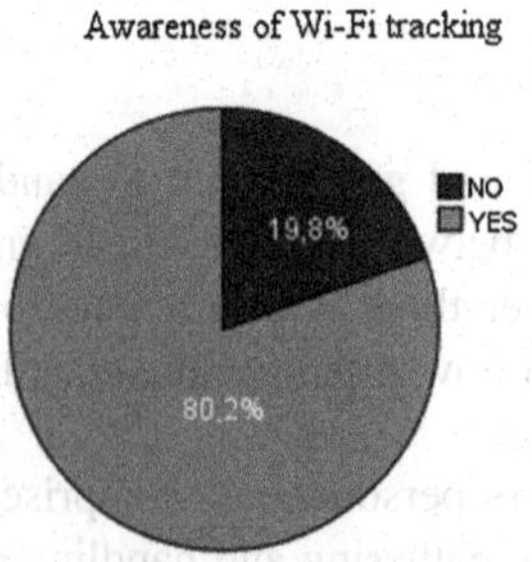

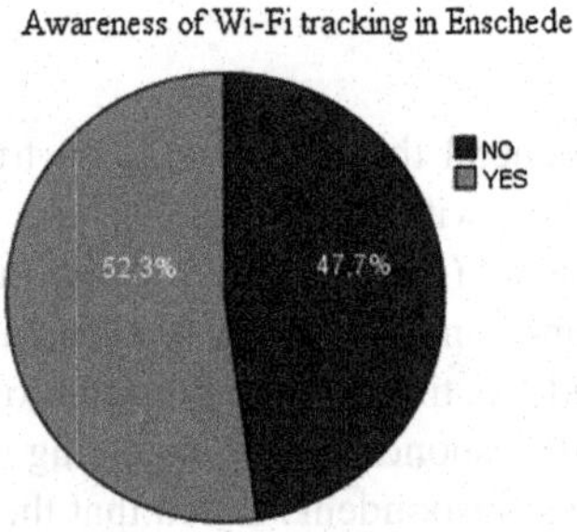

When comparing the difference between the groups who were already aware of Wi-Fi tracking and the group that was not aware, some slightly difference where found. Both groups worry about Wi-Fi tracking, but the group that is aware of Wi-Fi tracking scored a lower percentage on each question. Furthermore, the group that was not aware of Wi-Fi tracking before, tend to have a more negative outcomes when it comes to trusting municipalities and government. More that 47% of the respondents that were not aware before, think that municipalities and government don't handle their data in the right way and with confidentiality.

4 Analysis

The results showed that, more than 45% of the respondents weren't aware of the fact, that the municipality is using Wi-Fi tracking. This is consistent with Demir (2013). Wi-Fi providers gathering mobile location data, consumers are being tracked, often without them knowing it. However, the results also showed that only 25% of the respondents was not yet knowledgeable with the concept of Wi-Fi tracking. It is specially the elder group respondents, that is aware of Wi-Fi tracking in the municipality. This could be explained by the fact that at the end of last year Wi-Fi tracking was in the news. One of the companies that was in the news was CityTraffic. There were privacy concerns do to their tracking behavior (Verlaan 2016). Furthermore, studies of Demir et al. (2014) and Michael and Clarke (2013), stated that Wi-Fi tracking can provide information on human dynamics such as the peoples paths, the crowd size, the visit duration and frequency and law enforcement utilize these technologies for surveillance. So this data is extremely valuable information for many applications. However the results of this study showed that almost 62% of the respondents are not aware of the purposes of Wi-Fi tracking.

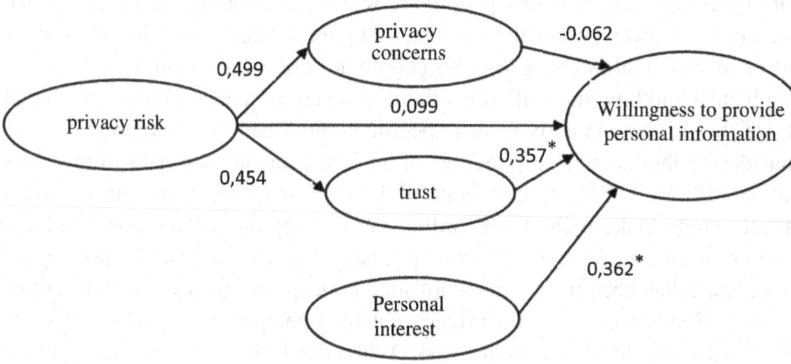

Fig. 4.

Because of the lack of knowledge about the purposes of Wi-Fi tracking, most respondents don't know if they will experience (some) benefits of a better city or services, when municipalities are gathering their data with Wi-Fi tracking. However, most of the respondents think that Wi-Fi tracking is useful (54,7%). In the case of smart cities, governments and municipals can use the knowledge extracted to make strategic decisions and future city plans (Perera et al. 2014). Only 7% of the respondents stated that none of the purposes of Wi-Fi tracking will benefit them. The results showed that almost all respondents indicated safety as an important benefit of Wi-Fi tracking (86%). This is in line with the previous research of Heek et al. (2015). They found in their study that surveillance technologies are accepted, in those locations in which crime threat is present. Users then prefer safety over privacy. Furthermore, better facilities in the city are also seen as a possible benefit by 57%. According to previous research from

Demir et al. (2014), Wi-Fi tracking can enable urban planners to manage congestion and for better adaption of public spaces to citizens. Most respondents are indicating that the gathering of personal data comprises risks. And most respondents stated that they worry about the gathering and handling of their personal data. Possible misuse of personal data is the biggest concern of the respondents (60%). The results showed that the mean scores of the privacy are higher for females than for men, indicating that the group of females tend to have more worries regarding their privacy. This is consistent with the study of Fogel and Nehmad (2009). In their research, women had significantly higher scores than men for privacy. Furthermore, Heek et al. (2017) stated that women attach a higher importance to safety in general, in contrast to men, while men prefer the protection of their privacy. Furthermore, This study shows that perceived risks, is not affecting the willingness to disclose information. No significant effect of risk and privacy on Willingness to disclose data has been found. Previous studies stated that people tend to be worried about their privacy when there is risk of sharing or the gathering of their data (Xu et al. 2009; Clarke 2001). So the results of this study are not really strange, when the analysis shows us that most of the respondents think there could be risks of losing privacy. However, despite the privacy concerns of people, the results of this study also showed that most of the respondents are willing to cooperate with municipalities when asked if they would comply. A possible reason mentioned in literature by Bailey (2015) is that people are willing to trade-off their privacy because they are not fully aware when their private data are collected and are unaware of the amount of privacy that is being lost. So people are not aware about how exactly their data can be lost and how this will affect them. As a consequence of this conclusion, the validity of the privacy paradox in this specific context can be questioned.

Considering the fact that respondents of the questionnaire see risks in the gathering of data and still are willing to cooperate with Wi-Fi tracking, there can be doubts on what level people make-tradeoffs regarding Wi-Fi tracking and the possible benefits.

Previous studies have used the term “privacy calculus” to describe privacy-related behaviors and it has become a well-established concept in privacy research. Dinev and Hart (2006) advocate the use of a privacy calculus perspective whenever data disclosure, involves some degree of privacy risk. When disclosing personal data, individuals perform a simple risk-benefit calculation before deciding whether or not to disclose their personal information and against what costs. In the privacy calculus model used in this study, the variables privacy concerns, Risks, benefits and trusting beliefs are where integrated as key predictors of willingness to disclose.

Previous studies of the privacy calculus (Dinev and Hart 2006; Barth and de Jong 2017), found that privacy concerns and risks are on the negative side of the privacy calculus, and can prevent users from disclosing information. On the positive side, are the benefits, which motivates users to disclose information. The results of this study showed that, trust and benefits are the variables with significant positive determinants in the privacy model. So, this is consistent with the prior research of Dinev and Hart (2006). The cumulative effects of trust and personal interests can outweigh privacy risk perception to point that it eventually leads to the disclosure of personal information (Dinev and Hart 2006). This study showed that almost 47% of the people are considering the opt-out option. Instead of being asked for permission, you must unsubscribe yourself from the City Traffic website so that it is not possible that municipalities or companies can track you. As mentioned before, previous research of Bosch and van Eijk (2016) suggests, that the continuous (de)activation of the phone or functionality can be a disproportionate effort. When municipalities, increasingly register Wi-Fi signals and hence peoples movements, it may not be desirable to put this responsibility entirely to the citizens.

The results of the privacy calculus furthermore showed, that risk had a very small positive, but non-significant effect on attitude, and a significant positive effect on trust as shown in Fig. 4. This is different with the previous study of Dinev and Hart (2006), who found that risks have a negative effect on trust. It could be that in general the population of this research have trust in municipalities to handle their data with care, in contrast to previous research, which focused on the trust in for example internet providers. Furthermore, some previous studies, have demonstrated that people rarely take a truly calculative approach to privacy decision making, and are often prone to take mental shortcuts instead (Acquisti and Jens Grossklags 2005; Wilson and Valacich. 2012), which could be the case in the situation of Wi-Fi tracking. The study of Dinev and Hart (2006) also showed that, the more users experience privacy concerns, the more negative their attitude will be towards tracking of every kind. This is consistent with the results in this study. The more respondents experience privacy concerns towards WI-FI tracking, the less they are willing to comply with data disclosure. The results of this study showed that, 40% of the respondents have no or less problems with Wi-Fi tracking, when they know how there data is gathered and how it will be used. Users should be informed about when and how data is gathered, what kind of data is gathered, what is happening to this data and whether data might be shared with third parties.

With the new GDPR, WI-FI tracking is bounded to specific laws and regulations as mentioned before. The result of the questionnaire showed that most of the people aren't negative on the statement, that existing laws and regulations protect their privacy. Laws and regulations are not sufficient for protecting residents, partly because of the fast moving technology society. Possible explanation for this is, that people probably don't know exactly which laws are protection their privacy, but they probably tend to have general trust that there are enough laws to protect them from possible privacy violations.

5 Conclusion

Most of the respondents are knowledgeable with Wi-Fi tracking, but almost half of the respondents are not aware of the fact that the municipality is preforming Wi-Fi tracking. Furthermore, we can conclude that the people in the municipality are not aware of the purposes of Wi-Fi tracking.

People are willing to cooperate with municipalities when asked if they would comply. Despite of the negative sentiment of Wi-Fi tracking, most of the respondents want to comply with Wi-Fi tracking. Counter wise, most people also indicate that they are considering the opt-out option.

The majority of the responders tend to have trust in municipalities to handle their data with care and are not skeptical about the protection by the law. More trust can cause people to comply with Wi-Fi tracking. Trust can overrule the negative impact of privacy risk perceptions, what will benefit municipalities. This study confirmed the previous study of Dinev and Hart (2006). The results showed that Benefits and Trust had a significant and positive effect on the Willingness to disclose data.

The final conclusion is that the adoption of IoT is influenced by the privacy calculus, it is a balance between the benefits or value of the IoT, in this case security and improved logistics, and the risks involved, in this case loss of privacy. New privacy laws requires that Wi-Fi tracking requires consent. This gives people the freedom of choice and control over their personal data. Wi-Fi tracking can make an interference in the lives of people, therefore it is important that the Wi-Fi counting must be necessary and justified.

Although the number of responders is enough to generalize, the authors note that by applying it on just one municipality might bias the results. Further study in more cities is recommended.

References

Acquisti, A., Grossklags, J.: Privacy and rationality in individual decision making. IEEE Secur. Priv. **3**(1), 26–33 (2005). https://doi.org/10.1109/MSP.2005.22

Al-Dhubhani, R., Mehmood, R., Katib, I., Algarni, A.: Location privacy in smart cities era. In: Mehmood, R., Bhaduri, B., Katib, I., Chlamtac, I. (eds.) SCITA 2017. LNICST, vol. 224, pp. 123–138. Springer, Cham (2018). https://doi.org/10.1007/978-3-319-94180-6_14

Anderson, C.L., Agarwal, R.: The digitization of healthcare: boundary risks, emotion, and consumer willingness to disclose personal health information. Inform. Syst. Res. **22**(3), 469–490 (2011)

Atzori, L., Iera, A., Morabito, G.: The Internet of Things: a survey. Comput. Netw. **54**(15), 2787–2805 (2010)

Bailey, M.W.: Seduction by technology: Why consumers opt out of privacy by buying into the Internet of Things. Tex. L. Rev. **94**, 1023 (2015)

Acquisti, A., John, L.K., Loewenstein, G.: What is privacy worth? J. Legal Stud. **42**(2), 249–274 (2013)

Bansal, G., Gefen, D.: The impact of personal dispositions on information sensitivity, privacy concern and trust in disclosing health information online. Decision Support Systems 49(2), 138–150 (2010)

Bartoli, A., Hernández-Serrano, J., Soriano, M., Dohler, M., Kountouris, A., Barthel, D.: Security and privacy in your smart city. In: Proceedings of the Barcelona Smart Cities Congress, vol. 292, December 2011

Barkhuus, L., Dey, A.K.: Location-Basedservices for mobile telephony: astudy of users'privacy concerns. In: INTERACT. Citeseer, vol. 3, pp. 702–712 (2003)

Barth, S., de Jong, M.: The privacy paradox–investigating discrepancies between expressed privacy concerns and actual online behavior–a systematic literature review. Telematics and Informatics (2017)

Bélanger, F., Crossler, R.E.: Privacy in the digital age: a review of information privacy research in information systems. MIS Q. **35**(4), 1017–1042 (2011)

Beinat, E.: Privacy and location-based services. Geo Informatics September. Belissent, J. Getting Clever About Smart Cities: New Opportunities Require New Business Models, Forrester Research, (2010)

Bosch, B.F.E., van Eijk, N.A.N.M.: Wifi-tracking in de winkel (straat): inbreuk op de privacy? Privacy Informatie **19**(251), 238–246 (2016)

Chorppath, A.K., Alpcan, T.: Trading privacy with incentives in mobile commerce: a game theoretic approach. Pervasive Mob. Comput. **4**, 598–612 (2013)

Clarke, R.: Person location and person tracking: technologies, risks and policy implications. Inform. Technol. People **14**(2), 206–231 (2001)

Culnan, M.J., Armstrong, P.K.: Information privacy concerns, procedural fairness, and impersonal trust: an empirical investigation. Organ. Sci. **10**(1), 104–115 (1999)

Demir, L., Cunche, M., Lauradoux, C.: Analysing the privacy policies of Wi-Fi trackers. In: Proceedings of the 2014 Workshop on Physical Analytics, pp. 39–44. ACM, June 2014

Demir, L.: Wi-Fi tracking: what about privacy (Doctoral dissertation, M2 SCCI Security, Cryptologyand Coding of Information-UFR IMAG) (2013)

Derikx, S., de Reuver, M., Kroesen, M., Bouwman, H.: Buying-off privacy concerns for mobility services in the Internet-of-things era. In: Proceedings of the 28th Bled eConference (2015)

Dinev, T., Hart, P.: An extended privacy calculus model for e-commerce transactions. Inform. Syst. Res. **17**(1), 61–80 (2006)

Elwood, S., Leszczynski, A.: Privacy reconsidered: New representations, data practices, and the geoweb. Geoforum **42**, 6–15 (2011)

Finch, K., Tene, O.: Welcome to the metropticon: protecting privacy in a hyperconnected town. Fordham Urb. LJ **41**, 1581 (2013)

Finn, R.L., Wright, D., Friedewald, M.: Seven types of privacy. In: Gutwirth, S., Leenes, R., de Hert, P., Poullet, Y. (eds.) European data Protection: Coming of Age, pp. 3–32. Springer, Dordrecht (2013). https://doi.org/10.1007/978-94-007-5170-5_1

Fogel, J., Nehmad, E.: Internet social network communities: risk taking, trust, and privacy concerns. Comput. Hum. Behav. **25**(1), 153–160 (2009)

Gutierrez, A., O'Leary, S., Rana, N.P., Dwivedi, Y.K., Calle, T.: Using privacy calculus theory to explore entrepreneurial directions in mobile location-based advertising: identifying intrusiveness as the critical risk factor. Comput. Hum. Behav. **95**, 295–306 (2019)

Hall, R.E., Bowerman, B., Braverman, J., Taylor, J., Todosow, H., Von Wimmersperg, U.: The vision of a smart city (No. BNL–67902; 04042). Brookhaven National Lab., Upton, NY (US) (2000)

Hann, I.H., Hui, K.L., Lee, S.Y.T., Png, I.P.: Overcoming online information privacy concerns: an information-processing theory approach. J. Manage. Inform. Syst. **24**(2), 13–42 (2007)

van Heek, J., Arning, K., Ziefle, M.: Safety and privacy perceptions in public spaces: an empirical study on user requirements for city mobility. In: Giaffreda, R., Cagáňová, D., Li, Y., Riggio, R., Voisard, A. (eds.) IoT360 2014. LNICST, vol. 151, pp. 97–103. Springer, Cham (2015). https://doi.org/10.1007/978-3-319-19743-2_15

Heek, J., Arning, K., Ziefle, M.: Where, Wherefore, and How? - contrasting two surveillance contexts according to acceptance. In Proceedings of the 6th International Conference on Smart Cities and Green ICT Systems (SMARTGREENS 2017), pp. 87–98 (2017)

Hernández-Muñoz, J.M., Vercher, J.B., Muñoz, L., Galache, José A., Presser, M., Hernández Gómez, Luis A., Pettersson, J.: Smart cities at the forefront of the future internet. In: Domingue, J., et al. (eds.) FIA 2011. LNCS, vol. 6656, pp. 447–462. Springer, Heidelberg (2011). https://doi.org/10.1007/978-3-642-20898-0_32

Hollands, R.G.: Will the real smart city please stand up? Intelligent, progressive or entrepreneurial? City **12**(3), 303–320 (2008)

Hossain, M.A., Dwivedi, Y.K., Rana, N.P.: State-of-the-art in open data research: insights from existing literature and a research Agenda. J. Organ. Comput. Electron. Commer. **26**(1–2), 14–40 (2016)

Ismagilova, E., Hughes, L., Dwivedi, Y.K., Raman, K.R.: Smart cities: Advances in research—an information systems perspective. Int. J. Inf. Manage. **47**, 88–100 (2019)
Könings, B., Schaub, F., Weber, M.: Privacy and trust in ambient intelligent environments. In: Ultes, S., Nothdurft, F., Heinroth, T., Minker, W. (eds.) Next Generation Intelligent Environments, pp. 133–164. Springer, Cham (2016). https://doi.org/10.1007/978-3-319-23452-6_4
Krasnova, H., Veltri, N.F., Günther, O.: Self-disclosure and privacy calculus on social networking sites: the role of culture. Bus. Inform. Syst. Eng. **4**(3), 127–135 (2012)
Krumm, J.: A survey of computational location privacy. Pers. Ubiquit. Comput. **13**(6), 391–399 (2009)
Lee, H., Kobsa, A.: Understanding user privacy in internet of things environments. Paper presented at the 2016 IEEE 3rd World Forum on Internet of Things, WF-IoT 2016, pp. 407–412 (2017). https://doi.org/10.1109/wf-iot.2016.7845392
Lee, J., Rao, H.R.: Perceived risks, counter-beliefs, and intentions to use anti-/counter-terrorism websites: an exploratory study of government–citizens online interactions in a turbulent environment. Decis. Support Syst. **43**(4), 1431–1449 (2007)
Liu, Z., Shan, J., Bonazzi, R., Pigneur, Y.: Privacy as a tradeoff: introducing the notion of privacy calculus for context-aware mobile applications. In: 2014 47th Hawaii International Conference on System Sciences (HICSS), pp. 1063–1072. IEEE, January 2014
Longo, S., Cheng, B.: Privacy preserving crowd estimation for safer cities. In Adjunct Proceedings of the 2015 ACM International Joint Conference on Pervasive and Ubiquitous Computing and Proceedings of the 2015 ACM International Symposium on Wearable Computers, pp. 1543–1550. ACM, September 2015
Lopez, J., Rios, R., Bao, F., Wang, G.: Evolving privacy: from sensors to the Internet of Things. Future Gener. Comput. Syst. **75**, 46–57 (2017)
Malhotra, N.K., Kim, S.S., Agarwal, J.: Internet users' information privacy concerns (IUIPC): the construct, the scale, and a causal model. Inform. Syst. Res. **15**(4), 336–355 (2004)
Michael, K., Clarke, R.: Location and tracking of mobile devices: Überveillance stalks the streets. Comput. Law Secur. Rev. **29**(3), 216–228 (2013)
Minch, R.P.: Location privacy in the Era of the Internet of Things and Big Data analytics. In: 2015 48th Hawaii International Conference on System Sciences (HICSS), pp. 1521–1530. IEEE, January 2015
Miorandi, D., Sicari, S., De Pellegrini, F., Chlamtac, I.: Internet of things: vision, applications and research challenges. Ad Hoc Netw. **10**(7), 1497–1516 (2012)
Mulligan, C., Olsson, M.: Architectural implications of smart city business models: an evolutionary perspective. IEEE Commun. Mag. **51**(6), 80–85 (2013)
Nam, T., Pardo, T.A.: Conceptualizing smart city with dimensions of technology, people, and institutions. In: Proceedings of the 12th Annual International Digital Government Research Conference: Digital Government Innovation in Challenging Times, pp. 282–291. ACM, June 2011
Perera, C., Zaslavsky, A., Christen, P., Georgakopoulos, D.: Sensing as a service model for smart cities supported by internet of things. Trans. Emerging Telecommun. Technol. **25**(1), 81–93 (2014)
Rana, N.P., Luthra, S., Mangla, S.K., Islam, R., Roderick, S., Dwivedi, Y.K.: Barriers to the development of smart cities in Indian context. Inform. Syst. Front., 1–23 (2018)
Smith, H.J., Milberg, S.J., Burke, S.J.: Information privacy: measuring individuals' concerns about organizational practices. MIS Q. **20**, 167–196 (1996)
Steinfield, C.: The development of location based services in mobile commerce. In: E-Life after the dot com bust, pp. 177–197. Physica-Verlag HD (2004)

Stewart, K.A., Segars, A.H.: An empirical examination of the concern for information privacy instrument. Inform. Syst. Res. **13**(1), 36–49 (2002)

Van Slyke, C., Shim, J.T., Johnson, R., Jiang, J.J.: Concern for information privacy and online consumer purchasing. J. Assoc. Inform. Syst. **7**(6), 16 (2006)

Vasalou, A., Joinson, A., Houghton, D.: Privacy as a fuzzy concept: a new conceptualization of privacy for practitioners. J. Assoc. Inform. Sci. Technol. **66**(5), 918–929 (2015)

Weinberg, B.D., Milne, G.R., Andonova, Y.G., Hajjat, F.M.: Internet of Things: convenience vs. privacy and secrecy. Bus. Horiz. **58**(6), 615–624 (2015)

Westin, A.F., Ruebhausen, O.M.: Privacy and Freedom, vol. 1. Atheneum, New York (1967)

Wilson, D., Valacich, J.: Unpacking the Privacy Paradox: Irrational Decision-Making within the Privacy Calculus. In: ICIS 2012 Proceedings (2012). http://aisel.aisnet.org/icis2012/proceedings/ResearchInProgress/101

Wirz, M., Roggen, D., Troster, G.: User acceptance study of a mobile system for assistance during emergency situations at large-scale events. In: 2010 3rd International Conference on Human-Centric Computing, pp. 1–6. IEEE, August 2010

Xu, H., Teo, H.H., Tan, B.C., Agarwal, R.: The role of push-pull technology in privacy calculus: the case of location-based services. J. Manage. Inform. Syst. **26**(3), 135–174 (2009)

Zanella, A., Bui, N., Castellani, A., Vangelista, L., Zorzi, M.: Internet of Things for smart cities. IEEE Internet Things J. **1**(1), 22–32 (2014)

van Zoonen, L.: Privacy concerns in smart cities. Gov. Inform. Q. **33**(3), 472–480 (2016)

The Interplay Between Privacy, Trust and Self-disclosure on Social Networking Sites

Eli Fianu[1], Kwame Simpe Ofori[2](✉), Richard Boateng[3], and George Oppong Appiagyei Ampong[4]

[1] College of Law and Management Studies, University of KwaZulu Natal, Durban, South Africa
efianu@gmail.com

[2] Department of Computer Science, Ho Technical University, Ho, Ghana
kwamesimpe@gmail.com

[3] Department of Operations and Management Information Systems, University of Ghana Business School, Accra, Ghana
richboateng@ug.edu.gh

[4] Department of Management, Ghana Technology University College, Accra, Ghana
gampong@gtuc.edu.gh

Abstract. Social Networking Sites (SNSs) have become an essential part of the daily lives of billions of people worldwide. Because SNS service providers use a revenue model that relies on data licensing (selling of user data), they share user data with other parties such as government institutions and private businesses. Sharing of user data to third parties raises several privacy concerns. Apart from privacy issues emanating from SNSs sharing user information with third parties, privacy issues may also emanate from users sharing information with SNS members. This study is motivated by the researchers' interest in investigating self-disclosure amongst Ghanaians especially from the perspective of privacy and trust primarily because of recent reports of revenge pornography and other self-disclosure related privacy violations on SNSs in Ghana. A survey was conducted on 523 students from three private universities in Ghana. Out of the 523 questionnaires administered, 452 were validated for analysis. Data collected from the survey was analyzed using the Partial Least Square approach to Structural Equation Modeling (PLS-SEM) performed on SmartPLS Version 3. Results of the study show that privacy awareness, privacy invasion experience, and privacy-seeking behavior have a significant effect on trust in SNS members. Privacy concern was found not to have a significant effect on trust in SNS members. Privacy awareness, privacy concerns, privacy invasion experience, and privacy-seeking behavior were found to have a significant effect on trust in the SNS service provider. Trust in SNS members and trust in the SNS service provider were found to have a significant effect on SNS self-disclosure. Theoretical and practical implications of the study are also discussed.

Keywords: Social Networking Sites · Privacy · Trust · Self-disclosure · Structural Equation Modelling

Y. Dwivedi et al. (Eds.): TDIT 2019, IFIP AICT 558, pp. 382–401, 2019.
https://doi.org/10.1007/978-3-030-20671-0_26

1 Introduction

Social Networking Sites (SNSs) are generally described as Internet-based applications that allow users to construct and share a personalized profile and lists of confirmed contacts with others on the site. SNSs allow users to see, browse, and communicate with their online friends as well as with friends of other users in the user's online community [1]. SNSs have become an essential part of the daily lives of billions of people worldwide [2].

Self-disclosure is a process of interaction by which a person discloses information about himself or herself to another person [3]. Self-disclosure is a predominant part of social networking because SNS users share a lot of personal information on SNSs. Due to the fast-growing popularity and usage of SNSs, there has been a tremendous rise in the information given out by SNS users [4]. Also, due to the high volumes of content shared by users on SNSs, concerns have been raised about the vulnerability of users with regards to content sharing [5].

SNSs collect and store user browsing data, personal information, as well as distributed content for an unlimited amount of time [6]. Owing to the fact that SNSs use a revenue model that relies on data licensing (selling of user data), they make user data available to other parties, including governmental agencies and business partners [5, 6]. Once user information is made available to third parties, users lose control of this information.

Apart from privacy issues emanating from SNSs sharing user information with third parties, privacy issues may also emanate from users sharing information with SNS members. SNS users fear that their posts will be exposed or abused by others [7, 8]. For users, as online social networks grow, the probability of engaging with new contacts also grows, likewise the probability of experiencing negative relationships that may give rise to social overload [9]. SNS users' private information provided during the registration for SNS accounts may become exposed to several parties, leading to possible misuse [10].

Ghana has experienced tremendous growth in SNS usage [11]. Ghana recorded a 22% annual growth of social media users from January 2017 to January 2018, the fourth highest in the world; the global growth rate was 13% [12]. In recent times, Ghana has experienced instances of revenge pornography on SNSs such as Whatsapp and Twitter. Revenge pornography is a class of online pornography that comprises of unprofessional images or videos that were home-made with the approval of those shown, but then later circulated without their approval [13]. There is an aspect of self-disclosure in revenge pornography because victims share private pictures and videos with people they initially trust.

One will expect that these incidents of revenge pornography will deter SNS users in Ghana from self-disclosing private images or videos, but more recent happenings suggest otherwise. Apart from revenge pornography, there have been several reports of other forms of self-disclosure related privacy violations on SNSs in Ghana, such as fraud-related identity theft. This study is motivated by our interest in investigating self-disclosure amongst Ghanaians, especially from the perspective of privacy and trust mostly because of recent reports of revenge pornography and other privacy violations on SNSs in Ghana.

2 Literature Review

2.1 Self-disclosure, Privacy, and Trust on SNSs

Communication Privacy Management (CPM) theory was developed by Petronio in 1991. It is a theory proposed to generate an empirical understanding of how people make decisions on disclosing and hiding private information [14]. From the perspective of CPM, self-disclosure involves the setting of rules by people when they have to decide whether to reveal or conceal personal information [15]. In effect, the individual controls the disclosure of personal information based on the rules set, and by setting privacy boundaries. Privacy boundaries can vary from fully open to fully closed [14, 16].

Fully open boundaries can be described as situations where an individual discloses information vocally or online to everybody who wants access to it. On the other hand, closed boundary individuals are sceptical about revealing information, hence, they are very careful. During interactions, people usually move between open and closed boundaries, depending on the nature of the relationship between the individuals communicating [14]. CPM proposes that individuals set privacy rules during communication; privacy rules determine what the individual will disclose or not. These privacy rules depend on several factors such as gender, cultural values, and a person's conviction about what is private or not private [14]. Privacy rules are also influenced by assessments of risk-benefits, as well as changes in situational circumstances, for instance, the changes that occur when there is a separation between couples [14]. When a couple separate, they will most likely not use the same privacy rules they had when they were a couple [14].

CPM proposes the phenomenon of boundary turbulence [14]. According to CPM, co-ownership of private information occurs when an individual shares private information with a confidant. If the two individuals who co-own the private information do not negotiate their jointly held privacy rules, there is the likelihood of "boundary turbulence", which means that there are disruptions in the way that co-owners regulate the flow of private information to third parties [14]. Boundary turbulence occurs when a co-owner deliberately destroys the synchronized boundary of privacy to reveal private information [14]. One can, therefore, deduce from CPM that the revealer places some trust in the confidant while disclosing personal information with the hope that there will not be boundary turbulence. Consequently, before an individual will share private information with a confidant, certain expectations come to play. These expectations of confidentiality and responsibility must be met before the sharing of private information. "If you meet my expectations of confidentiality and responsibility, I will share my private information with you, and vice versa" [16].

In order to prevent conflict and unwanted breaches of confidentiality, original owners of information should discuss their expectations of co-ownership of information with confidants [16]. The boundary surrounding private information should be managed by mutually negotiated and agreed-upon privacy rules [17].

SNS use for most people is fueled by their desire to be entertained and to pass time [18]. While passing time on SNSs, SNS users are entertained by the active sharing of content (images and videos) as well as synchronous interactions via instant messaging. The amount of pleasure and amusement experienced by SNS users depends on satisfactory associations and trust building. Self-disclosure on SNSs is therefore influenced by satisfactory relationships based on enjoyment, connectedness, and SNS flow experience, as well as perceived risks [18–21].

Self-disclosure in SNSs can be affected by SNS members' perceptions of the safety of their personal information with respect to the service provider [22]. Users are likely not to have a happy experience with SNS use when they have anxieties about the sharing of private information. Awareness of the credibility of a company may reduce one's privacy concerns over self-disclosure or perceived privacy risk; in other words, the more reputable the SNS provider is, the more likely it is that users will disclose personal information [23–26].

In summary, self-disclosure on SNSs is multifaceted. Self-disclosure on SNSs depends largely on user enjoyment of interactions on the SNS, perceived risks, as well as perceptions of how personal information is handled by SNS service providers [27–30].

Regarding online social networking, privacy awareness refers to a person's attention and understanding in terms of various aspects of privacy while using social media platforms [31–33]. Initial SNS studies showed that most SNS users had little knowledge of how their personal information was treated and used, however recent studies show an increase in privacy awareness among SNS users [34]. While increased privacy awareness has been found to reduce trust and information disclosure in e-commerce settings, the opposite holds true for SNSs [34]. Notwithstanding the enhanced level of privacy awareness among SNS users, activities on the SNS platforms keep increasing, which could be attributed to trust in the platforms [4].

Privacy invasion experience describes privacy violations a user might have personally experienced in the past [35]. Humor creation among friends on online social networks may lead some individuals to expose people's private information such as that which exposes their previous improper behavior, mischief, or clumsiness. This exposure may be a playful tease, but the individual whose information is exposed may be offended by the involuntary exposure. Prior privacy invasion experience negatively affects trust and further information disclosure [36].

Privacy-seeking behavior refers to the things people do to protect their information [37]. From the perspective of CPM theory, to protect one's privacy, a person would set privacy boundaries during interaction with people. Privacy boundaries are set based on trust; open when there is trust and closed when there is no trust [16]. Privacy-seeking behavior increases transactional avoidance and subsequent self-disclosure [33].

By definition, trust is the readiness to accept susceptibility based upon optimistic outlooks about another's behavior [38]. Trust theory proposes that trust, which shows a readiness to accept susceptibility based on an optimistic outlook toward another participant's imminent behavior, has a substantial effect on the behavioral intention of users of services [39]. Trust can be categorized as online or offline [40]. Online trust varies from offline trust because in an online setting, trust issues emanate from both the SNS technology and the SNS service provider. Therefore, it is difficult for internet users to keep a high level of trust for the websites. The internet is mostly viewed as a precarious territory; therefore, online trust is rather tough to achieve and sustain when compared to trust in an offline setting [40].

Interaction creates prospects for people to become acquainted, to form online communities, and to build trust [41]. Trust has been found to have a mediating effect on privacy concerns and information disclosure [42]. Self-disclosure has been a prevalent behavior of SNS users, which arguably motivated previous research to focus on the drivers and inhibitors of self-disclosure. From the perspective of a person using an SNS, ownership rules have an influence on an individual's actions with respect to trust in a "third-party disclosure" of the shared information; we co-own shared private information and so we must be responsible co-owners [43].

SNS providers must assure users of the safety of their personal information during registration for service, especially from the activities of third parties [44]. Privacy seals are issued by a third-party organization (for instance TRUSTe) to show that a site's privacy framework and processes are accredited by them. TRUSTe offers services to assist organizations to revise their privacy management procedures so that they conform to government laws and best practices. Both privacy guidelines and seals may help develop users' trust and assuage their privacy concerns [44]. Previous literature has shown that people may demonstrate more trust in websites that disclose their privacy policies [45–49]. Online trust can, therefore, be seen from the perspective of the SNS provider and SNS members.

Default SNS privacy settings allow users to see each other's profiles either through a one-on-one connection or through a closed or open user group [50]. This default setting (especially on Facebook) also implies that when for instance, A is a friend of B on the SNS, C who is a friend of B can view A's profile even though A and C are not direct friends. Thus, if users maintain the default SNS settings, they may not be aware that people who are not their friends have access to their profile (because of visibility). Consequently, users may eventually share information with people they did not intend sharing the information with. It is therefore imperative that users adjust their privacy settings in SNSs to suit their privacy rules and boundaries [51].

Unwanted privacy breaches could occur even if a user has the most restricted privacy settings [52]. For instance, with Facebook, a user's privacy is influenced by the privacy settings of their friends because if a user has restricted settings, but the friends do not have restricted settings, other people will have access to the user's information. Additionally, in cases where the user removes his/her posts from the SNS (for example Facebook), the posts may still be accessible because of the ease at which information can be saved, shared, and reposted [34]. Another issue of interest in SNSs is the activity stream. An activity stream is a thread that displays every activity of the user (e.g., posts and likes). Activity streams have raised privacy concerns among SNS users because a user might not know all the activities that are included in their activity stream. Users may also not know the people who have access to their activity stream [34]. Hence, the failure to successfully control who has access to one's information online can create discomfort for SNS users.

3 Research Model and Hypotheses Development

We develop hypotheses mainly from CPM theory and trust theory. We also refer to previous studies that have investigated the hypothesized relationships. The current study seeks to investigate three major variables namely self-disclosure, privacy and trust. Self-disclosure and privacy are inherent in CPM theory, while trust is inferred from CPM theory. To prevent parsimony while investigating these three variables, we combine CPM theory and trust theory to formulate our research model. The hypotheses are stated in the next sections.

Privacy Awareness: Based on CPM theory, we argue that awareness of the privacy structure of SNSs (especially privacy settings) allows an individual to set privacy rules when disclosing information to the SNS service provider and other SNS members. When individuals are confident that there is no likelihood of boundary turbulence, they will have trust in the SNS service provider and other SNS members. Privacy awareness, therefore, has a positive effect on trust in the SNS service provider and other SNS members. In a study to determine the impact of privacy, trust and user activity on intentions to share Facebook photos, Malik, Hiekkanen, Dhir and Nieminen [33] found that privacy awareness had a significant positive effect on trust in the Facebook platform. Facebook users with high privacy awareness tend to exhibit greater levels of trust in the service and are more active [4, 53].

In line with the findings of Malik, Hiekkanen, Dhir and Nieminen [33], O'Bien and Torres [53], and Stutzman et al. [4] we posit that:

Hypothesis 1. Privacy awareness has a significant positive effect on trust in SNS members

Hypothesis 2. Privacy awareness has a significant positive effect on trust in SNS service provider

Privacy Concern: From CPM theory we posit that privacy concern (user apprehension to disclose information) has the tendency to cause an individual to set privacy rules during interactions to prevent boundary turbulence. The higher the apprehension, the less the trust in the SNS service provider and other SNS members. Privacy concern, therefore, has a negative effect on trust in the SNS service provider and other SNS members. In the SNS setting, privacy concern is one of the key factors that affect trust in the service, as well as the intention to disclose information [53, 54]. Privacy concern has a negative influence on trust in Facebook and consequently, lower intentions to use Facebook [53]. Also, following CPM theory, we posit that privacy concern has the tendency to cause an individual to set privacy rules during interactions to prevent boundary turbulence. Privacy concern, therefore, influences trust.

In line with theory and the findings of O'Bien and Torres [53] and Proudfoot et al. [54], as well as the tenets of CPM, we posit that:

Hypothesis 3. Privacy concern has a significant negative effect on trust in SNS members

Hypothesis 4. Privacy concern has a significant negative effect on trust in SNS service provider

Privacy Invasion Experience: We posit (From CPM theory) that when one experiences privacy invasion, there is boundary turbulence which in turn affects trust. Prior privacy experience will therefore negatively influence trust in the SNS service provider and other SNS members; the greater the impact of the experience, the lesser the level of trust. Prior privacy invasion increases perceptions of online privacy risks, which in turn influences trust in SNSs, that is, trust in the SNS service provider and SNS members as well [55]. Prior experience of privacy invasion on SNSs affects trust in SNSs and motivates an individual to alter his/her privacy settings [56]. The victims of online privacy attack tend to appreciate the grave outcomes of privacy loss; their prior experience influences their trust in SNSs [57].

Therefore, in support of the above-mentioned authors and the tenets of CPM, we posit that:

Hypothesis 5. Privacy invasion experience has a significant negative effect on trust in SNS members

Hypothesis 6. Privacy invasion experience has a significant negative effect on trust in SNS service provider

Privacy-Seeking Behavior: Similar to privacy awareness, based on CPM theory, we argue that when exploring the privacy settings of the SNS allows an individual to set privacy rules when disclosing information to the SNS service provider and other SNS members. When individuals are confident that there is no likelihood of boundary turbulence, they will have trust in the SNS service provider and other SNS members. Privacy awareness, therefore, has a positive effect on trust in the SNS service provider and other SNS members. In a study to determine the impact of privacy, trust and user activity on intentions to share Facebook photos, Malik, Hiekkanen, Dhir and Nieminen [33] found that privacy-seeking behavior had a significant positive effect on Facebook usage activity. The extent to which SNS users pursue privacy protection strategies will positively affect their trust in the service and their actual activity [4, 56, 58].

In line with theory and the above findings, we posit that:

Hypothesis 7. Privacy-seeking behavior has a significant positive effect on trust in SNS members

Hypothesis 8. Privacy-seeking behavior has a significant positive effect on trust in SNS service provider

Trust in SNS Members and Trust in SNS Service Provider: Based on trust theory, we posit that an individual who trusts the SNS service provider and other SNS members is ready to accept susceptibility (based on an optimistic outlook), and therefore will be willing to disclose personal information. Furthermore, following CPM theory, we posit that when one trusts the would-be confidant, it implies the would-be confidant meets the needed expectations (of confidentiality) for self-disclosure, hence personal information is likely to be given out, and vice versa. Trust, therefore, positively influences self-disclosure. In a study on the prediction of college students' self-disclosure on Facebook, Chang and Heo [5] found that trust in Facebook had a significant positive effect on the disclosure of personal information on the platform. A study by Malik et al. [33] showed that trust positively impacts users' intentions to share photos on Facebook. Wu, Huang, Yen and Popova [49] in a study to investigate the effect of online privacy policy on consumer privacy concern and trust found out that trust has a positive impact on willingness to provide personal information.

In line with the above findings and the tenets of CPM theory, we hypothesize that:

Hypothesis 9. Trust in SNS members has a significant positive effect on self-disclosure

Hypothesis 10. Trust in SNS service provider has a significant positive effect on self-disclosure

The proposed research model is shown in Fig. 1.

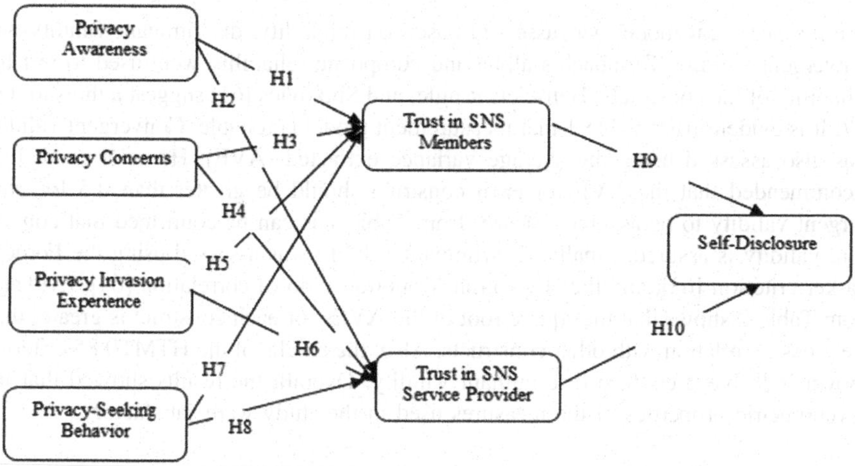

Fig. 1. The proposed research model

4 Methodology

4.1 Instrument Development, Sampling and Data Collection

In order to improve content validity, measurement items for the latent variables used in the current study were adopted from previous literature [59]. These items were however reworded to fit the context of social networking sites. Items for Privacy Awareness, Privacy Concerns and Privacy Seeking behavior were adopted from Malik et al. [33]. Privacy Invasion Experience, Trust in SNS members, Trust in SNS service provider and Self Disclosure were all measured with items derived from Cheung, Lee, and Chan [60]. All measurement items were measured using a 5-point Likert scale anchored between strongly disagree (1) and strongly agree (5). Over a five-day period, survey data was collected from 452 respondents, all of whom were students.

5 Results

Data analysis was conducted using the Partial Least Square approach to Structural Equation Modelling (PLS-SEM) performed on SmartPLS Version 3. The PLS-SEM technique is appropriate because it allows for the testing of the relationships between latent constructs in a proposed research model. The current study used the PLS approach since an initial study of the data collected revealed that the data was non-normal. Also, the PLS method is more appropriate since our model is quite new and untested.

5.1 Measurement Assessment

The measurement model was assessed based on reliability, discriminant validity and convergent validity. Cronbach's alpha and composite reliability were used to test the reliability of the constructs. Henseler, Ringle, and Sinkovics [61] suggest a threshold of 0.7. It is evident from Table 1 that measurement model is reliable. Convergent validity was also assessed using the average variance extracted (AVE), Henseler et al. [62] recommended that the AVE for each construct should be greater than 0.5 for convergent validity to be assured. Clearly from Table 1 is can be confirmed that convergent validity is assured. Finally, discriminant validity was assessed using the Fornell-Larker criterion [63], and the Heterotrait-Monotrait ratio of correlation [64]. Evidence from Table 2 shows that the square root of the AVEs for each construct is greater than the cross-correlation with other constructs. Also, the results of the HTMT0.85 criterion shown in Table 2 confirm discriminant validity. Overall, the results showed that the psychometric properties of the measures used in the study were satisfactory.

Table 1. Factor loading and reliability statistics.

	Factor loadings	A	C.R	A.V.E
PA1	**0.822**	0.912	0.932	0.695
PA2	**0.859**			
PA3	**0.880**			
PA4	**0.792**			
PA5	**0.812**			
PA6	**0.833**			
PC1	**0.914**	0.932	0.948	0.786
PC2	**0.912**			
PC3	**0.880**			
PC4	**0.828**			
PC5	**0.896**			
PIE1	**0.941**	0.870	0.939	0.885
PIE2	**0.940**			

(continued)

Table 1. (*continued*)

	Factor loadings	A	C.R	A.V.E
PSB1	**0.803**	0.826	0.882	0.652
PSB2	**0.867**			
PSB3	**0.806**			
PSB4	**0.748**			
SD1	**0.811**	0.833	0.888	0.665
SD2	**0.820**			
SD3	**0.813**			
SD4	**0.817**			
TM1	**0.832**			
TM2	**0.874**	0.929	0.944	0.738
TM3	**0.880**			
TM4	**0.868**			
TM5	**0.849**			
TM6	**0.851**			
TP1	**0.797**			
TP2	**0.860**	0.921	0.938	0.717
TP3	**0.862**			
TP4	**0.866**			
TP5	**0.846**			
TP6	**0.847**			

Table 2. Testing Discriminant Validity using the Fornell-Larcker Criterion.

	Fornell Larcker							HTMT						
	PA	PC	PIE	PSB	SD	TM	TP	PA	PC	PIE	PSB	SD	TM	TP
PA	**0.83**													
PC	−0.24	**0.89**						0.26						
PIE	−0.27	0.29	**0.94**					0.31	0.33					
PSB	0.2	0.13	−0.04	**0.81**				0.23	0.16	0.05				
SD	0.44	−0.36	−0.31	0.14	**0.82**			0.5	0.4	0.36	0.17			
TM	0.41	−0.21	−0.4	0.18	0.34	**0.86**		0.44	0.22	0.44	0.18	0.38		
TP	0.58	−0.32	−0.42	0.23	0.42	0.46	**0.85**	0.63	0.34	0.47	0.26	0.48	0.5	

Note: Square roots of average variances extracted (AVEs) shown on the first diagonal in bold

5.2 Structural Model Assessment

The structural model was assessed based on the sign, magnitude and significance of the path coefficients of each hypothesized path. The significance of the path coefficients in the structural model was tested using a bootstrap resampling technique with 5000 subsamples drawn with replacement. Results of the assessment of the structural model are shown in Table 3. Apart from the path between Privacy Concern and Trust in Members, all the paths that were earlier hypothesized were found to be significant.

About 56 per cent of the variance in the target variable (Self Disclosure) was explained by our model. To assess model fit in PLS we used the standardized root mean square residual (SRMR). The SRMR value for the model was 0.041; a value of less than 0.08 is generally considered a good fit [65]. This value indicates that the structural model exhibits a good fit.

Table 3. Hypotheses testing

Hypotheses	Path	$\hat{\beta}$	T statistics	P values	Results
H1	PA → TM	0.291	5.441	0.000	Supported
H2	PA → TP	0.445	10.528	0.000	Supported
H3	PC → TM	−0.075	1.724	0.085	Not Supported
H4	PC → TP	−0.164	4.147	0.000	Supported
H5	PIE → TM	−0.290	6.347	0.000	Supported
H6	PIE → TP	−0.245	5.776	0.000	Supported
H7	PSB → TM	0.120	2.763	0.006	Supported
H8	PSB → TP	0.149	3.464	0.001	Supported
H9	TM → SD	0.181	3.605	0.000	Supported
H10	TP → SD	0.339	6.865	0.000	Supported
Model fit					
SRMR = 0.041 R^2 = 0.56					

6 Discussions

The current study sought to investigate self-disclosure on SNSs from the perspective of trust and privacy. As mentioned earlier, the researchers treated trust as a two-dimensional variable; trust in SNS provider and trust in SNS members, mainly because the invasion of SNS users' privacy is likely to be caused by these two variables. The researchers captured privacy of the SNS user in terms of privacy awareness, privacy concerns, privacy invasion experience, and privacy-seeking behavior.

Results of the study show that privacy awareness, privacy invasion experience, and privacy-seeking behavior have a significant effect on trust in SNS members. Privacy concern was found not to have a significant effect on trust in SNS members. Privacy awareness, privacy concerns, privacy invasion experience, and privacy-seeking behavior were found to have a significant effect on trust in the SNS service provider. Trust in SNS members and trust in the SNS service provider were found to have a significant effect on SNS self-disclosure. Nine of the ten hypotheses were supported, which, significantly supports our research model.

Our study provides support for studies conducted by Malik, Hiekkanen, Dhir and Nieminen [33], O'Bien and Torres [53], and Stutzman et al. [4] which show that, in SNS settings, privacy awareness has a significant effect on trust. This finding shows that when SNS users in Ghana understand and pay attention to privacy issues, it affects the trust they have in the SNS provider as well as other SNS members. The positive relationship between privacy awareness and the trust constructs implies that when SNS users in Ghana are aware of the privacy implications of using the sites, they are likely to build more trust in the sites, that is, knowing and understanding the privacy statements and privacy settings of the SNS is likely to build trust in the SNS. Knowledge of user privacy rights and responsibilities is also likely to result in increased trust in the SNS [66]. This result also implies that SNS service providers can build more trust in SNS users if they find ingenious ways of exposing SNS users to the privacy framework of the sites.

Privacy concern was found to have a significant negative effect on trust in the SNS provider, but a non-significant effect on trust in the SNS members. This finding implies that the there is a high likelihood that Ghanaian SNS users are of the view that their concern for the manner in which their private information and information they submit on SNSs is managed does not influence their trust in SNS members, but influences their trust in the SNS provider. We argue that it is very likely that due to the influence of privacy awareness, the users may feel they are in control of the information they submit on the SNSs that may be misused by other SNS members, hence the non-significance of the influence of privacy concerns on trust in SNS members. However, due to the fact that users cannot control how their personal/private information on the SNS is used by SNS providers, a significant negative influence of privacy concerns is observed on trust in SNS provider. This finding is consistent with the findings of work done by Chang, Liu and Shen [67] who found that privacy concern has a significant negative influence on trust in using LinkedIn. Chang, Liu and Shen [67] state that because LinkedIn members mostly share their job-related information for career reasons, and the information disclosure on the site may be private between job seekers and providers or among groups with similar career interests, trust is very important for users on the site. Chang, Liu and Shen [67] also found out that for users of Facebook, there was a non-significant relationship between privacy concern and trust in using the site. Chang, Liu and Shen [67] state that relationships built on Facebook are based primarily on close friendships and acquaintances, hence, there is a less perceived risk in submitting non-confidential or non-career oriented information. This result may also explain why Ghanaian SNS users share a lot of personal content online.

Privacy invasion experience was found to have a significant negative effect on trust in SNS provider as well as trust in SNS members. This implies that SNS users in Ghana who have had prior privacy invasion experience(s) have less trust in SNSs as compared to those who have not had one. We argue that the finding in the current study is logical, and is also in line with work done by Mohamed and Hawa [57], as well as reviews made by Chen, Beaudoin and Hong [55] and Young and Quan-Haase [56] who had similar findings. We should also expect that Ghanaian SNS users who have been victims of revenge pornography would share less personal content online.

Privacy-seeking behavior was found to have a significant positive effect on trust in the SNS provider as well as trust in the SNS members. This finding implies that SNS users in Ghana who adopt strategies to protect their privacy on SNSs are likely to trust the SNSs more since they are confident their strategies will shield them from privacy risk. This finding is consistent with work by Young and Quan-Haase [56] who reported that SNS users use several privacy protection schemes in order to lessen privacy risks while still allowing them to reveal enough information to link up with colleagues and friends on Facebook. However, Malik et al. [33] found a non-significant relationship between privacy-seeking behavior and trust in a study on photo sharing on Facebook. Malik et al. [33] stated that the non-significant relationship was due to the fact that trust became negligible as users identified privacy protection strategies that they were confident will prevent privacy violations. Malik et al. [33] further state that users who vigorously involve themselves in several privacy protection schemes feel more self-assured and, thus, reveal more information and content. We, therefore, conclude that privacy protection strategies have the likelihood of making trust negligible. At the same time, privacy protection strategies can build trust in the SNS since privacy protection strategies give users confidence and help prevent privacy violations.

In line with studies by Chang and Heo [5], Malik et al. [33], and Wu, Huang, Yen and Popova [49], the current study showed that trust in SNS provider and SNS members have a significant positive effect on self-disclosure. This finding implies that the higher the levels of trust Ghanaian SNS users have in the SNS members and the SNS provider, the higher the likelihood of sharing their personal information. Previous literature also shows that trust is one of the most powerful factors that influence users' activity and readiness to give out information and content on Facebook [5]. We did not identify any study that showed a negative effect of trust on self-disclosure in the literature to enable us to do further comparative analysis. The amount of self-disclosure shown by SNS users in Ghana will thus be a reflection of the amount of trust they have in SNS service providers and other SNS members.

7 Conclusion

7.1 Theoretical Implications

This study has made contributions to growing body of literature on social media related issues [68–79]. Particularly, the current study has theoretical implications for the study of privacy, trust, and self-disclosure in the area of social media and online social networking. Not much research has been done in the area of social media and online social networking involving the quantitative analyses of the relationships between privacy, trust, and self-disclosure constructs. The current study distinguishes itself from similar previous studies because those studies have treated Trust as a one-dimensional mediating variable, for instance, Zlatolas et al. [37], Malik et al. [33], and Wu, Huang, Yen and Popova [49] (see Appendix A). The current study treats Trust as a two-dimensional mediating variable between privacy and self-disclosure. The results of the quantitative analysis of the privacy concern – trust path in the research model, that is, the significant negative effect on trust in SNS provider, but a non-significant effect on trust in SNS members, shows the multidimensional nature of the trust construct.

Practical Implications. The current study emphasizes the importance of privacy protection strategies in the use of SNSs. Most importantly, the ability of a user to adjust the privacy settings of the SNS and develop privacy protection strategies are key to the use of SNSs. It is therefore important for SNS providers to expose users to the need to adjust their privacy settings to suit their individual perceptions of risk. In our opinion, this may be better achieved if SNS providers mandatorily take users through a short tutorial on privacy settings immediately after sign-up, and also intermittently drop hints on privacy settings whilst users browse the sites.

In order to improve trust, SNS providers must assure users of the safety of their personal information during registration for service, especially from the activities of third parties. Both privacy policies and seals may help build users' trust and alleviate their privacy concern.

Also, SNS users must consciously make an effort to adjust their privacy settings to their preference to give them the needed confidence to share their personal information freely, and also have an interesting user experience.

Limitations and Directions for Further Research. Although the current study produced some interesting results that validated some theories and past research, a few limitations must be considered. First, the respondents were selected from three universities in Ghana. This sample cannot represent all SNS users. Secondly, the study used a cross-sectional design, which may not capture changes in behavior over time. A longitudinal design should be considered in future studies. Because the setting of the current study limits us from generalizing to other cultural frameworks and advanced economies, the research model could be tested in those settings. Finally, subsequent studies could investigate the moderating role of gender and age on the relationships in the model.

Appendix A

Summary of models on privacy and self-disclosure

Independent variables	Mediator variables	Dependent variables	Reference
Privacy awareness Privacy-seeking behavior Privacy concerns	Trust Activity	Sharing intentions	Malik et al. [33]
Privacy awareness Privacy social norms Privacy policy Privacy control	Privacy value Privacy concerns	Self-disclosure	Zlatolas et al. [37]
Privacy Policy Online privacy concern	Trust	Willingness to provide personal information	Wu et al. [49]

Appendix B

Research Items

Self-disclosure on SNS

SD1: I have a comprehensive profile on my favorite social networking site
SD2: I find time to keep my profile up-to-date
SD3: I keep my friends updated about what is going on in my life through my favorite social networking site
SD4: When I have something to say, I like to share it on my favorite social networking site

Trust in SNS's Service Provider

TP1: My favorite social networking site is open and receptive to the needs of its members
TP2: My favorite social networking site makes good-faith efforts to address most member concerns TP3 My favorite social networking site is also interested in the well-being of its members, not just its own
TP4: My favorite social networking site is honest in its dealings with me
TP5: My favorite social networking site keeps its commitments to its members
TP6: My favorite social networking site is trustworthy

Trust in SNS's Members

TM1: Other members on my favorite social networking site will do their best to help me
TM2: Members on my favorite social networking site care about the well-being of other member on the site
TM3: Members on my favorite social networking site are open and receptive to each other's needs TM4 Members on my favorite social networking site are honest in dealing with each other
TM5: Members on my favorite social networking site keep their promises
TM6: Other members on my favorite social networking site are trustworthy

Privacy Invasion Experience

PIE1: I have you personally been victim of what felt like an invasion of privacy on a social networking site?
PIE2: I have heard or read during the last year about the use and potential misuse of personal information about users on social networking sites?

Privacy Awareness

PA1: I have read the privacy statement of my favorite social networking site
PA2: The privacy statement of my favorite social networking site is easy to understand
PA3: The privacy settings of my favorite social networking site are easy to use
PA4: I understand all the privacy setting of my favorite social networking site
PA5: I am aware of all the appropriate actions to ensure my privacy on favorite social networking site
PA6: I am aware of my privacy rights and responsibilities on my favorite social networking site

Privacy-seeking Behavior

PSB1: Since joining this social networking site, I have changed the privacy settings multiple times PSB2: I usually keep track of my photos shared on this social networking site
PSB3: I usually delete my photos shared on this social networking site
PSB4: I usually think carefully before sharing my photos on this social networking site

Privacy Concerns

PC1: The information is share could be misused by the social networking site
PC2: The information I share on social networking sites could be accessed by third parties
PC3: The information I share on social networking sites could be misused by other use on the social networking site
PC4: The information I share on social networking sites could be seen by unwanted people
PC5: The information I share on social networking sites could reveal private information
PC6: Information I disclose on favorite social networking site could have negative consequences that I cannot foresee

References

1. Amichai-Hamburger, Y., Hayat, T.: Social networking. In: International Encyclopedia of Media Effects (2017)
2. Lenhart, A.: Teens, social media & technology overview, Washington DC (2015)
3. Ignatius, E., Kokkonen, M.: Factors contributing to verbal self-disclosure. Nord. Psychol. **59**, 362–391 (2007). https://doi.org/10.1027/1901-2276.59.4.362

4. Stutzman, F., Gross, R., Acquisti, A.: Silent listeners: the evolution of privacy and disclosure on Facebook. J. Priv. Confid. **4**, 7–41 (2012). https://doi.org/10.1145/1958824.1958880
5. Chang, C.W., Heo, J.: Visiting theories that predict college students' self-disclosure on Facebook. Comput. Hum. Behav. **30**, 79–86 (2014). https://doi.org/10.1016/j.chb.2013.07.059
6. Debatin, B., Lovejoy, J.P., Horn, A.-K., Hughes, B.N.: Facebook and online privacy: attitudes, behaviors, and unintended consequences. J. Comput. Commun. **15**, 83–108 (2009)
7. Huang, H.-Y., Chen, P.-L., Kuo, Y.-C.: Understanding the facilitators and inhibitors of individuals' social network site usage. Online Inf. Rev. **41**, 85–101 (2017). https://doi.org/10.1108/OIR-10-2015-0319
8. Zhu, Y., Bao, Z.: The role of negative network externalities in SNS fatigue. Data Technol. Appl. DTA-09-2017-0063 (2018). https://doi.org/10.1108/dta-09-2017-0063
9. Maier, C., Laumer, S., Eckhardt, A., Weitzel, T.: Giving too much social support : social overload on social networking sites, 1–18 (2014). https://doi.org/10.1057/ejis.2014.3
10. Feng, Y., Xie, W.: Teens' concern for privacy when using social networking sites: an analysis of socialization agents and relationships with privacy-protecting behaviors. Comput. Hum. Behav. **33**, 153–162 (2014)
11. Ghafla.com: Social Media Apps Ghanaians Visit The Most. http://www.ghafla.com/gh/social-media-apps-ghanaians-visit/
12. Chaffey, D.: Global Social Media Research Summary (2018). https://www.smartinsights.com/social-media-marketing/social-media-strategy/new-global-social-media-research/
13. Salter, M., Crofts, T.: Responding to revenge porn: challenges to online legal impunity. In: New Views on Pornography: Sexuality, Politics, and the Law, pp. 233–256 (2015)
14. Petronio, S., Reierson, J.: Regulating the privacy of confidentiality: grasping the complexities through communication privacy management theory. In: Afifi, T.A., Afifi, W.A. (eds.) Uncertainty, Information Management, and Disclosure Decisions: Theories and Applications, pp. 365–383. Routledge, New York (2009)
15. Frampton, B.D., Child, J.T.: Friend or not to friend: coworker Facebook friend requests as an application of communication privacy management theory. Comput. Human Behav. **29**, 2257–2264 (2013)
16. Petronio, S.: Boundaries of Privacy: Dialects of Disclosure. State University of New York Press, Albany (2002)
17. Golish, T.D.: Stepfamily communication strengths; understanding the ties that bind. Hum. Commun. Res. **29**, 41–80 (2003)
18. Special, W.P., Li-Barber, K.: Self-disclosure and student satisfaction with Facebook. Comput. Human Behav. **28**, 624–630 (2012)
19. Yoon, S.J., Han, H.E.: Experiential approach to the determinants of online word-of-mouth behavior. J. Glob. Sch. Mark. Sci. **22**, 218–234 (2012)
20. Qian, H., Scott, C.R.: Anonymity and self-disclosure on weblogs. J. Comput. Commun. **12**, 1428–1451 (2007)
21. Barth, S., de Jong, M.D.T.: The privacy paradox – investigating discrepancies between expressed privacy concerns and actual online behavior – a systematic literature review. Telemat. Inform. **34**, 1038–1058 (2017). https://doi.org/10.1016/j.tele.2017.04.013
22. Zhou, T.: The effect of network externality on mobile social network site continuance. Program **49**, 289–304 (2015). https://doi.org/10.1108/PROG-10-2014-0078
23. Myerscough, S., Lowe, B., Alpert, F.: Willingness to provide personal information online: the role of perceived privacy risk, privacy statements and brand strength. J. Website Promot. **2**, 115–140 (2008)

24. Angst, C.M., Agarwal, R.: Adoption of electronic health records in the presence of privacy concerns: the elaboration likelihood model and individual persuasion. MIS Q. **33**, 339–370 (2009)
25. Bansal, G., Zahedi, F.M., Gefen, D.: The impact of personal dispositions on information sensitivity, privacy concern and trust in disclosing health information online. Decis. Support Syst. **49**, 138–150 (2010). https://doi.org/10.1016/j.dss.2010.01.010
26. Phelps, J., Nowak, G., Ferrell, E.: Privacy concerns and consumer willingness to provide personal information. J. Publ. Policy Mark. **19**, 27–41 (2000). https://doi.org/10.1509/jppm.19.1.27.16941
27. Dinev, T., Hart, P.: An extended privacy calculus model for e-commerce transactions. Inf. Syst. Res. **17**, 61–80 (2006). https://doi.org/10.1287/isre.1060.0080
28. Culnan, M., Bies, R.: Consumer privacy: balancing economic and justice considerations. J. Soc. Issues **59**, 323–342 (2003). https://doi.org/10.1111/1540-4560.00067
29. Laufer, R., Wolfe, M.: Privacy as a concept and a social issue: a multidimensional developmental theory. J. Soc. Issues **33**, 22–42 (1977). https://doi.org/10.1111/j.1540-4560.1977.tb01880.x
30. Culnan, M.J., Armstrong, P.K.: Information privacy concerns, procedural fairness, and impersonal trust: an empirical investigation. Organ. Sci. **10**, 104–115 (1999). https://doi.org/10.1287/orsc.10.1.104
31. Rachels, J.: Why privacy is important. Philos. Publ. Aff. **4**, 323–333 (2003)
32. Jeong, Y., Kim, Y.: Privacy concerns on social networking sites: interplay among posting types, content, and audiences. Comput. Hum. Behav. **69**, 302–310 (2017). https://doi.org/10.1016/j.chb.2016.12.042
33. Malik, A., Hiekkanen, K., Dhir, A., Nieminen, M.: Impact of privacy, trust and user activity on intentions to share Facebook photos. J. Inf. Commun. Ethics Soc. **14**, 364–382 (2016). https://doi.org/10.1108/jices-06-2015-0022
34. Fox, J., Moreland, J.J.: The dark side of social networking sites: an exploration of the relational and psychological stressors associated with Facebook use and affordances. Comput. Hum. Behav. **45**, 168–176 (2015). https://doi.org/10.1016/j.chb.2014.11.083
35. Awad, K.: The personalization privacy paradox: an empirical evaluation of information transparency and the willingness to be profiled online for personalization. MIS Q. **30**, 13 (2006). https://doi.org/10.2307/25148715
36. Choi, B.C.F., Jiang, Z.J., Xiao, B., Kim, S.S.: Embarrassing exposures in online social networks: an integrated perspective of privacy invasion and relationship bonding. Inf. Syst. Res. **26**, 675–694 (2015). https://doi.org/10.1287/isre.2015.0602
37. Hölbl, M., Zlatolas, L.N., Welzer, T., Heric, M.: Privacy antecedents for SNS self-disclosure: the case of Facebook. Comput. Hum. Behav. **45**, 158–167 (2015). https://doi.org/10.1016/j.chb.2014.12.012
38. Lee, Y., Kwon, O.: Intimacy, familiarity and continuance intention: an extended expectation-confirmation model in web-based services. Electron. Commer. Res. Appl. **10**, 342–357 (2011). https://doi.org/10.1016/j.elerap.2010.11.005
39. Mayer, R.C., Davis, J.H., Schoorman, F.D.: An integrative model of organizational trust. Acad. Manag. Rev. **20**, 709–734 (1995). https://doi.org/10.5465/amr.1995.9508080335
40. Friedman, B., Khan Jr., P.H., Howe, D.C.: Trust online. Commun. ACM **43**, 34–40 (2000). https://doi.org/10.1145/355112.355120
41. Han, S., et al.: The Effect of using SNS to interpersonal relation and quality of life: focused on the moderating role of communication capability. J. Inf. Syst. **22**, 29–64 (2013)
42. Flanagin, A.J., Metzger, M.J.: Internet use in the contemporary media environment. Hum. Commun. Res. **27**, 153–181 (2001). https://doi.org/10.1093/hcr/27.1.153

43. Osatuyi, B.: Information sharing on social media sites. Comput. Hum. Behav. **29**, 2622–2631 (2013). https://doi.org/10.1016/j.chb.2013.07.001
44. Zhou, T., Li, H.: Understanding mobile SNS continuance usage in China from the perspectives of social influence and privacy concern. Comput. Hum. Behav. **37**, 283–289 (2014). https://doi.org/10.1016/j.chb.2014.05.008
45. Earp, J.B., Antón, A.I., Aiman-Smith, L., Stufflebeam, W.H.: Examining internet privacy policies within the context of user privacy values. IEEE Trans. Eng. Manag. **52**, 227–237 (2005). https://doi.org/10.1109/TEM.2005.844927
46. Eastlick, M.A., Lotz, S.L., Warrington, P.: Understanding online B-to-C relationships: an integrated model of privacy concerns, trust, and commitment. J. Bus. Res. **59**, 877–886 (2006). https://doi.org/10.1016/j.jbusres.2006.02.006
47. Galanxhi, H., Nah, F.F.-H.: Privacy issues in the era of ubiquitous commerce. Electron. Mark. **16**, 222–232 (2006). https://doi.org/10.1080/10196780600841894
48. Lwin, M.O., Wirtz, J., Stanaland, A.J.S.: The privacy dyad. Internet Res. **26**, 919–941 (2016). https://doi.org/10.1108/IntR-05-2014-0134
49. Wu, K.W., Huang, S.Y., Yen, D.C., Popova, I.: The effect of online privacy policy on consumer privacy concern and trust. Comput. Hum. Behav. **28**, 889–897 (2012). https://doi.org/10.1016/j.chb.2011.12.008
50. Zhang, Y., Fang, Y., Wei, K.K., Ramsey, E., McCole, P., Chen, H.: Repurchase intention in B2C e-commerce - a relationship quality perspective. Inf. Manag. **48**, 192–200 (2011). https://doi.org/10.1016/j.im.2011.05.003
51. Lee, S., Kim, B.G.: The impact of qualities of social network service on the continuance usage intention. Manag. Decis. **55**, 701–729 (2017). https://doi.org/10.1108/MD-10-2016-0731
52. Tan, X., Qin, L., Kim, Y., Hsu, J.: Impact of privacy concern in social networking web sites. Internet Res. **22**, 211–233 (2012). https://doi.org/10.1108/10662241211214575
53. O'Bien, D., Torres, A.: Social networking and online privacy: Facebook users' perceptions. Irish J. Manag. **31**, 63–98 (2012)
54. Proudfoot, J.G., Wilson, D., Valacich, J.S., Byrd, M.D.: Saving face on Facebook: privacy concerns, social benefits, and impression management. Behav. Inf. Technol. **37**, 16–37 (2018)
55. Chen, H., Beaudoin, C.E.: An empirical study of a social network site: exploring the effects of social capital and information disclosure. Telemat. Inform. **33**, 432–435 (2016). https://doi.org/10.1016/j.tele.2015.09.001
56. Young, A.L., Quan-Haase, A.: Privacy protection strategies on Facebook: the internet privacy paradox revisited. Inf. Commun. Soc. **16**, 479–500 (2013). https://doi.org/10.1080/1369118x.2013.777757
57. Mohamed, N., Hawa, I.: Information privacy concerns, antecedents and privacy measure use in social networking sites: evidence from Malaysia. Comput. Hum. Behav. **28**, 2366–2375 (2012). https://doi.org/10.1016/j.chb.2012.07.008
58. Acquisti, A., Brandimarte, L., Loewenstein, G.: Privacy and human behavior in the age of information. Science **347**, 509–514 (2015). https://doi.org/10.1126/science.aaa1465
59. Straub, D., Boudreau, M.-C., Gefen, D.: Validation guidelines for IS positivist research. Commun. Assoc. Inf. Syst. **13**, 63 (2004)
60. Cheung, C., Lee, Z.W.Y., Chan, T.K.H.: Self-disclosure in social networking sites: the role of perceived cost, perceived benefits and social influence. Internet Res. **25**, 279–299 (2015). https://doi.org/10.1108/IntR-09-2013-0192
61. Henseler, J., Ringle, C.M., Sinkovics, R.: The use of partial least squares path modeling in international marketing. Adv. Int. Mark. **20**, 277–319 (2009). https://doi.org/10.1108/S1474-7979(2009)0000020014

62. Henseler, J., Hubona, G., Ray, P.A.: Using PLS path modeling in new technology research: updated guidelines (2016). https://doi.org/10.1108/imds-09-2015-0382
63. Fornell, C., Larcker, D.F.: Structural equation models with unobservable variables and measurement error: algebra and statistics. J. Mark. Res. 382–388 (1981)
64. Henseler, J., Ringle, C.M., Sarstedt, M.: A new criterion for assessing discriminant validity in variance-based structural equation modeling. J. Acad. Mark. Sci. **43**, 115–135 (2014). https://doi.org/10.1007/s11747-014-0403-8
65. Hu, L., Bentler, P.M.: Cutoff criteria for fit indexes in covariance structure analysis: conventional criteria versus new alternatives. Struct. Equ. Model. Multidisc. J. **6**, 1–55 (1999)
66. Hoadley, C.M., Xu, H., Lee, J.J., Rosson, M.B.: Privacy as information access and illusory control: the case of the Facebook news feed privacy outcry. Electron. Commer. Res. Appl. **9**, 50–60 (2010). https://doi.org/10.1016/j.elerap.2009.05.001
67. Chang, S.E., Liu, A.Y., Shen, W.C.: User trust in social networking services: a comparison of Facebook and LinkedIn. Comput. Hum. Behav. **69**, 207–217 (2017). https://doi.org/10.1016/j.chb.2016.12.013
68. Kapoor, K.K., Tamilmani, K., Rana, N.P., Patil, P., Dwivedi, Y.K., Nerur, S.: Advances in social media research: past, present and future. Inf. Syst. Front. **20**(3), 531–558 (2018)
69. Aladwani, A.M., Dwivedi, Y.K.: Towards a theory of SocioCitizenry: quality anticipation, trust configuration, and approved adaptation of governmental social media. Int. J. Inf. Manag. **43**, 261–272 (2018)
70. Hossain, M.A., Dwivedi, Y.K., Chan, C., Standing, C., Olanrewaju, A.S.: Sharing political content in online social media: a planned and unplanned behaviour approach. Inf. Syst. Front. **20**(3), 485–501 (2018)
71. Shiau, W.-L., Dwivedi, Y.K., Yang, H.-S.: Co-citation and cluster analyses of extant literature on social networks. Int. J. Inf. Manag. **37**(5), 390–399 (2017)
72. Shiau, W.-L., Dwivedi, Y.K., Lai, H.-H.: Examining the core knowledge on Facebook. Int. J. Inf. Manag. **43**, 52–63 (2018)
73. Alalwan, A.A., Rana, N.P., Dwivedi, Y.K., Algharabat, R.: Social media in marketing: a review and analysis of the existing literature. Telemat. Inform. **34**(7), 1177–1190 (2017)
74. Dwivedi, Y.K., Kapoor, K.K., Chen, H.: Social media marketing and advertising. Mark. Rev. **15**(3), 289–309 (2015)
75. Rathore, A.K., Ilavarasan, P.V., Dwivedi, Y.K.: Social media content and product co-creation: an emerging paradigm. J. Enterp. Inf. Manag. **29**(1), 7–18 (2016)
76. Shareef, M.A., Mukerji, B., Dwivedi, Y.K., Rana, N.P., Islam, R.: Social media marketing: comparative effect of advertisement sources. J. Retail. Consum. Serv. **46**, 58–69 (2019)
77. Abed, S.S., Dwivedi, Y.K., Williams, M.D.: Social media as a bridge to e-commerce adoption in SMEs: a systematic literature review. Mark. Rev. **15**(1), 39–57 (2015)
78. Plume, C.J., Dwivedi, Y.K., Slade, E.L.: Social Media in the Marketing Context: A State of the Art Analysis and Future Directions. Chandos Publishing, Amsterdam (2016)
79. Dwivedi, Y.K., et al. (eds.): Social Media: The Good, the Bad, and the Ugly, vol. 9844. Springer, Heidelberg (2016). https://doi.org/10.1007/978-3-319-45234-0

A Rethink of the Nature and Value of IT Assets – Critical Realism Approach

A. Kayode Adesemowo(✉)

Nelson Mandela University, Port Elizabeth, South Africa
Kayode.adesemowo@mandela.ac.za

Abstract. In the era of fourth industrial revolution, knowledge economy and beyond, information gets increasingly prevalent and ubiquitously important. Inevitably, stakeholders' interest is increasing, which results in greater reputation risk. Do we still view IT assets in the narrowed view as we do or do we broaden our horizon? Should we not be guided by how information technology was 'coined' in the late fifties, even though the reality is that IT assets have evolved and keep evolving. More than ever before, information is now an integral part of IT assets, and IT assets must be treated and accounted for considering the critical strategic importance (of information and IT assets) to organizations. Nonetheless being ubiquitous, there is a challenge in the identification process of IT assets. There is no agreed identification metrics and common understanding on the nature, structure and mechanisms of IT assets. The impact of this challenge is that IT assets value, or benefit realization from IT assets remain underrated or risk treatments remain at risk. This research study, based on critical realism philosophy investigates the nature, structures and mechanisms of IT assets. The four domains of IT capability maturity framework was used and to an extent asset specificity, to assist with phenomena and boundaries. The study of the nature of IT assets, based on critical realism, provides better insight into dual-contrasting nature of IT assets and contributes to the discourse on assets specificity and IT assets management. The derived classification, will contribute to the areas of infonomics, information risk and IT value/diffusion.

Keywords: IT assets · Identification · Structure and mechanisms · Critical realism

1 Introduction

From time immemorial, energy is accepted to consist of potential and kinetic energies. Also, atom is seen as the smallest unit of *matter* and it consists of protons, neutrons and electron. So it seems that a number of theories and models were built on these understandings. Till date, this concept holds true. However, certain phenomena of energy and properties of *matter* cannot be explained properly with the classical theories and models of Physics. There came in quantum mechanics which allows for 'sub-atomic' level of *matter*. Yet, quantum mechanics is clouded with controversies. It took the Copenhagen convention, with its seven principles, for there to be some common understanding and a new era to begin [1]. Philosophizing about this, Bhaskar [2, p. 51]

Published by Springer Nature Switzerland AG 2019
Y. Dwivedi et al. (Eds.): TDIT 2019, IFIP AICT 558, pp. 402–414, 2019.
https://doi.org/10.1007/978-3-030-20671-0_27

cautioned against fixating on 'current state' of science without re-interrogation. It is against this backdrop, this paper investigates the nature of IT assets.

Information technology (IT), which is now synonymous and used interchangeably with information and communication technology (ICT), is a well-known concept ever since the coining of the phrase by Leavitt and Whisler [3, p. 41], in the late fifties. So it seems! This aspect will be looked into much later in this paper when exploring the nature of IT assets.

1.1 Fourth Industrial Revolution, Knowledge Economy and Beyond

Although foreseen by Leavitt and Whisler back then, knowledge economy has evolved as the economy where 'pervasive importance of knowledge and other intangibles come to the fore' [4, p. 123]. In line with this, this paper adopts the Oxford Dictionary's definition of knowledge economy as 'an economy in which growth is dependent on the quantity, quality, and accessibility of the information available, rather than the means of production' [5, p. 976].

This research study sees information and IT as essential building block of the fourth industrial revolution (4IR) era, in agreement with Lee et al. [6, p. 3], view of 4IR as the horizontal expansion of IT. They then dubbed 4IR as the second information technology (IT) revolution. Therefore, the era of 4IR, knowledge economy and beyond, call for another study of the container, processor and transmitter of information – IT assets.

1.2 Organization of the Paper

The essence, drivers and objective for the research study are presented in the next section. This include the research (critical realism) philosophical approach and the methods. The next section reviews the IT capability maturity domains and nature of IT assets. This leads to the findings and discussion on the nature, structures and mechanisms of IT assets, after which the paper concludes.

2 Research Domain

"I have always believed that scientific research is another domain where a form of optimism is essential to success ..."—Daniel Kahneman, Thinking, Fast and Slow.

2.1 Research Drivers

When considering risk, researchers' and practitioners' focus has always been on the possibility of threat to assets [7, p. 175]. However, from the theory of risk, assets of their own selves, have their own epistemic uncertainties [8, p. 463], especially from the viewpoint of subjectivity due to a lack of knowledge or when their fluctuating state is considered [9, pp. 4, 14].

This paper opined that epistemic uncertainty holds true to IT assets (and the containing intangible information assets). Hence, the need to 'unearth' IT assets in themselves.

2.2 Research Problem Statement

From the introduction and research driver, one can deduce that the nature of IT assets is one that is not 'distinct' and must be understudy in order to gain insight into it.

Therefore, in the fourth industrial economy, knowledge economy and beyond, there is a challenge in understanding the true nature of IT assets and improper understanding of the underlying intangible elements and information value.

2.3 Research Objective

The problem above indicates that organizations must have a firm understanding of the nature of IT assets if they are to properly identify IT assets, derive optimal benefits from IT assets and put proper controls over IT assets.

Hence, the primary objective (PO) of this research project is *to critically re-examine the structures and mechanism of IT assets (within information risk) in order to gain better insight into the nature of IT assets so as to derive a conceptual classification scheme for IT assets.*

In order to achieve on this, the following secondary research objectives are essential:

- RO1. To understudy and determine what are the inherent attributes of IT assets;
- RO2. To determine what classification exist for IT assets; and
- RO3. To develop a conceptual IT assets attribute classification scheme.

It is imperative that these objectives be met so that organizations are better able to identify and derive optimal benefits from their IT assets.

2.4 Research Philosophy and Methods

Framing this research work is critical realism as advocated by Bhaskar [10]. Of course, there are many contributors to critical realism as a research philosophy [11, p. 3].

Critical Realism. As a research philosophy, critical realism allows for critical investigation of a concept or theme or phenomena or research reality. In this instance, that is IT assets. Obviously, IT assets as a concept or research reality is not new as there are age-long beliefs, understanding, knowledge and praxis about them. Critical realism affords the prism to re-investigate and interrogate these beliefs and understanding within 4IR, knowledge economy and beyond. The critical review also allows for relations, conflicts and contradictions as well as commonality of knowledge [12–14].

Although IT assets (and information assets) are not natural social actors (as expected in interpretivism), the reality of the characteristics that IT assets possess, create the phenomena under which they must be studied. Hence, as expected in critical realism, traditional held beliefs about IT assets (and information assets) are being challenged, interrogated, allowing for ways to identify, highlight and possibly eliminate some of the sources of 'conflicts' or contradictions.

More so, critical realism is apt for investigating interdisciplinary concepts or reality such as IT assets (and information assets). This flows from critical realism's features of abstraction and 'retroduction' [10, p. 174], and critical realism's challenging ontological differences between physical and social realities [10, pp. 190, 384]. Hence, critical realism enables the exploring of the interplay between objects (information and IT assets) and their attributes, perceptions and realities [14].

Critical realism acknowledges empirical and actual domains which are the purview of positivist and interpretivist. However, critical realism, within the real domain, rejects linearity of causality between structures and mechanisms. Just to drill in a little bit on this, IT assets carry and process different information at different times and for different purposes. The capabilities vary based on usage, the context of use and the social agency that interacts at a particular point in time. Critical realism offers a stratified ontology that is able to take into account the alienating dichotomy autonomy of organizational systems and IT assets without denying the power that various agents (management, workers, processes, capabilities …) have to change themselves, organization culture, IT capability and resultant derived benefits or accrued value of IT assets. This is where the socio-technical identity [15] in critical reality comes into play. As such, IT assets can be interrogated as technological objects having structures and mechanisms [15], instead of being viewed as mere objects lacking in forms, specificity and interactivity. Hence, critical realism is more "incisive on epistemo-ontological questions" [11, p. 2].

Multi-method. The investigation of IT assets (and information assets) to outline the dual-contrasting nature of IT assets pose a challenge following a single approach like design science or activity theory. Critical realism by its nature allows for plurality and as such has a natural affinity for plurality of methods [14, p. 4]. The methods presented in this paper are based on the DREI (describe, 'retroduce', eliminate, identify) methodology of critical realism [16, p. 797].

Identification. Internet-based research [17, p. 292] and scoping literature review [18, 19] were used to explore, identify and interrogate the nature of IT assets. This fits in with the 'identification' and 'description' phases of critical realism [13, p. 4]. Alongside with this is the use of thematic content analysis [20, pp. 1, 4, 24] to assists with 'themes' of the nature of IT assets and classification. The international standard, ISO 22274 and IT-capability maturity framework (IT-CMF) came in handy in this instance, notably themes, taxonomy and stratified ontology.

Interviews. Flowing from the themes and stratified ontology, semi-structured based interview [21, p. 318] was used to engage with identified CxO (chief information officers, chief financial officers, IT directors, chief risk officer …). The interview sessions were not just for 'data gathering' but also part of the 'retroduction' process. The attributes, structures and mechanisms of IT assets were interrogated and validated.

Iteration and Retroduction. Many at times, a concept or phenomenon is well entrenched and/or universally understood in different field of study, but with differing viewpoints. Analogy [22, p. 12], though with its own challenges, is often used to draw inference from another field to explain or engage on a concept in a field of study. For example, the principle of coherence in quantum mechanics or optical Physics can be used to engage on the challenges of coherency in ICT for development.

Alongside analogy, argumentation, from a logical reasoning approach [23, p. 403], [24], is used in iterative step as part of the 'retroduction' step of critical realism [14, p. 3], to eliminate 'false' attributes and develop the workable classification of IT assets attributes, structures and mechanisms in this paper.

2.5 Research Domain Recap

Essential to this paper is the 'breaking down', interrogation and 'bringing back' within a context and time that take place as 'retroduction' process of iterative process of data collection and analysis, towards a set of causal mechanisms within a social structure and conditions [13, p. 3]. This is the viewpoint of critical realism as used in this paper.

This research study subscribes to the (late) Roy Bhaskar's critical realism school of thought [10, 11] and approached 'retroduction' from the eyes of reductionism [21, p. 599].

Lastly, I recap with Vandenberghe's assertion, "*critical realism is not the invention of one man, Bhaskar, but his demolition of positivism is so rigorous, radical and powerful that it makes one wonder how standard accounts of science have been able to keep the best minds captive for such a long time*" [11, p. 3].

3 Nature of IT Assets

The nature of IT assets was deconstructed and identified from literature and reasoning. This section will briefly summarize the key aspects.

3.1 IT Assets Recap

As earlier explained, the concept of IT assets has evolved ever since the coining of the phrase 'information technology' in the late fifties by Leavitt and Whisler. Nonetheless, the fundamental principle remains relevant till date. Faulkner and Runde [15] cautioned against an 'object' approach, which the author of this paper strongly opined includes IT assets. They theorized, and which can be seen from a critical realism approach, that 'object' should rather be seen and engaged as 'technological objects' or rather put 'digital objects'.

The underlying principle and IT-CMF practices and domain will now be looked at.

3.2 Leavitt and Whisler Coining of Information Technology

> *"The new technology does not yet have a single established name. We shall call it information technology. It is composed of several related parts. One includes techniques for processing large amounts of information rapidly, and it is epitomized by the high-speed computer. A second part centers around the application of statistical and mathematical methods to decision-making problems; it is represented by techniques like mathematical programing, and by methodologies like operations research. A third part is in the offing, though its applications have not yet emerged very clearly; it consists of the simulation of higher-order thinking through computer programs."*—Leavitt and Whisler, 1958

Unlike then, information technology is now pervasive and ubiquitous. So it seems! However, do we really understand information technology? If we do not, possibly we do not understand IT assets as well.

Looking at Leavitt and Whisler 'coining' statement, some attributes of IT assets are inferred. These are explored below.

Processor of large amount of information (at a rapid rate) casts our mind to the evolution of big data to what is now becoming data analytics and machine learning, (although we have had statistics, data science and neural networks with us for decades). What is evident is that enormous amounts of data as information are being processed rapidly to gain competitive advantage. Of course, this is alongside higher processing computing devices where Cloud, computing infrastructures or mobiles devices are being developed in this regard.

Application of statistical and mathematical methods to decision-making problems has been at the bedrock of operation research, management information systems and e-governments. Undoubtedly, this is not new. It was apparent in the industrial age. The 1965 'abandoned big brother' project gave an indication of what to expect from decision-making, though for governance purposes [25]. The role and place of operations research, data science/analytics, management science and e-governance in 4IR, knowledge economy and beyond might just be better left to imagination.

Simulation of higher-order thinking through computer programs is finding application in far greater domains than ever before. These span medical sciences, telecommunications, and climate changes amongst many other. The place of simulation in telecommunication is increasingly seen in the development and adoption of 5G telecommunication networks. Through simulators, artificial intelligence, and data analytics, greater inferences, forecasting, verification, and assurances are being made.

One can begin to see that a narrow view of IT assets will be a denial of reality. A more embracing view and approach is needed. The overly focus on financial and risk metrics of IT assets must be broaden so as to gain a true indication of information assets value with respect to their liability, benefit realization and value attributes [26, p. 84]. This is where the dual- contrasting nature of IT assets comes into the picture. As we gain understanding of the attributes, structures and mechanism of IT assets, we can be led to gain better insight into IT capability, IT value, as well as organizational impact (of IT assets) and IT diffusion, which are major research areas within IFIP WG8.6 [27, p. 237].

3.3 IT-CMF: IT Capability Maturity Framework Review

From principle 12 of King IV [28, p. 62], organizations must ensure that technology and information support achieving on their strategic objectives. Tillquist and Rogers [29, p. 76], rightly summarize that in fixing and determining organizations value, it is difficult to separate the "value contribution of IT assets from the context in which they operate".

An approach that has assisted is IT capability, through the purposeful, strategic application of IT across an organization [30]. Whether through asset specificity or resource-based view approach [29, p. 76], [31, p. 338], information plays an important role [32].

In brief, asset specificity relates to the identification of specific (value) contribution of IT to each facets within organizational (activities and processes) boundaries [29].

IT-CMF, built on proven management practices, provides four domains which organizational activities and processes boundaries can be structured, as depicted in Fig. 1. These attributes, structures and mechanisms of IT assets (nature) can be interrogated across the domains and boundary of an organization, so as to better identify IT assets across the organization and to apportion (carrying) values for IT assets or benefits realization of IT assets.

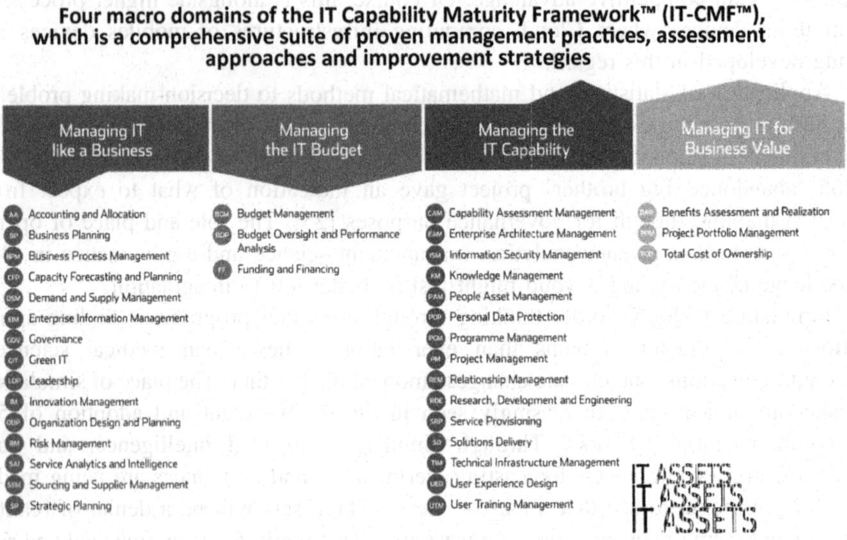

Fig. 1. The 36 critical capabilities – adapted from https://ivi.ie/it-capability-maturity-framework

In looking at the thirty-six critical capabilities of IT-CMF, due consideration was given to the IT infrastructure library – ITIL [33].

3.4 IT Capability Maturity Domains and Nature of IT Assets

Informed by the focus on service value-add and knowledge of service assets in ITIL's service assets configuration management, and the thirty-six critical capabilities of IT-CMF, as well as Leavitt and Whisler principle of IT and the exploratory scoping review, a classification system for IT assets was conceptualized. The aid used towards the conceptualization of the IT assets concept system is the ISO22274 mapping to OWL ontology available at http://tiny.cc/ITAOFIR_22274toOWL.

Through iterative refinement, the classification system was put into a graphical format that respondent can engage with. Apart from the IT concept system, respondent were encouraged to list additional elements (if any). Once respondent has 'critique' the IT assets concept system and provided their additional inputs, they are no longer at liberty to change their mind. However, they are able to and indeed they did provide rationale for their critiques and input.

The IT assets concept system grouped elements across different domains starting with 'tangible' and 'intangible'. Some of the other groupings include 'infrastructure', 'functions', 'tangible type', 'software', 'intangible information', 'intangible type', 'reputation', and 'IT capability'.

The next section presents the findings from the engagement with the respondents who are mostly CxO.

4 Findings and Discussion

4.1 Key Findings

The key finding is presented as a heat map in Fig. 2, which shows the graphical model and the contentious domains/areas. Readers are referred to the exploratory paper [34], on intangible information assets as an integral part of IT assets.

4.2 IT Assets Deconstruction: Nature, Structures and Mechanisms

The deconstruction of IT assets into elements based on the nature, structures and mechanism discovered in this project were engaged on. Some elements or domains were heavily debated upon. Some were highly contentious. The respondents are polarized on their view about what information assets are and IT assets being tangible assets.

The main areas of engagement and contentions are the concept of IT assets as distinct tangible and intangible, infrastructure functional area of use (like ERP, CRM systems), intangible type and IT capability.

4.3 Type of IT Assets: Tangible and Intangible

A key finding is that IT assets can be classified as tangible and intangible. However, as it can be observed from the heat map, there is no consensus on what exactly are tangible and what are intangible. This has cascading effect down the line.

The statement 'tangible aspect refers to things we can touch' is one of the inclination that what can be 'touched' should be tangible and what cannot should be intangible. The key recommendation is that organizations should be left to make their own decisions on what is tangible and what is intangible. Hence, in their classification system, whether for assets management or accounting or risk, there must be flexibility for organizations to make a choice.

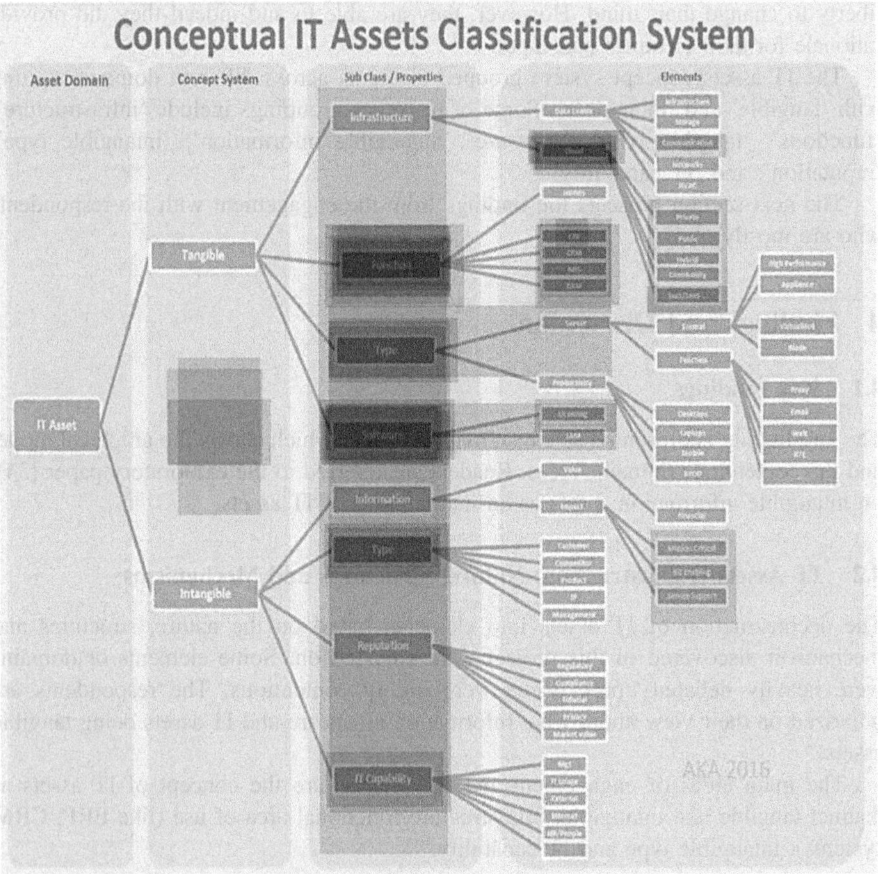

Fig. 2. Heat map representing engagement on the IT assets concept system

4.4 Type of IT Assets: Infrastructure Functional Area

Closely linked to the views on 'touch' is the concept of grouping or classifying infrastructure systems used for functional domains (line-of-business use). Whilst it is undeniable that the infrastructures are typically physical, the general view is what is termed to be the 'flip' factor, where the flip depends on how physical or function are viewed.

Systems for ERP or CRM or HRMIS or others are seen from the 'function' they provide to organizations and are considered from that functional view rather than the actual infrastructure that is in use. One suggestion is 'instead of IT function, I suggest business function'.

The other viewpoint from engagement with respondents, is that with the options of data centers, virtualization, private or public or hybrid cloud computing, infrastructure cannot simply be 'hard-defined' as physical infrastructure. This also has impact on the cost model, whether fixed cost or property, plant equipment costing approach.

Software although capable of standing as a distinct asset type should also be considered along the lines of how and where they are put to use, just like infrastructure types are considered along the line-of-business use.

4.5 Type of IT Assets: Intangible (Information) Types

The nature of information type ranging from financial to competitors information and intellectual property are classifiable as asset types. Nonetheless, how they relate to each organizations varies and must be given considerations along those lines.

4.6 Type of IT Assets: IT Capability

It is possible to group capability and impact of IT assets on an organization. The main grouping of management and strategic, IT usage, external, people are in line with the domain areas in IT-CMF. Organizations must give due considerations to the domain areas of IT-CMF, strategic intent in ITIL, and IT specificity when looking at values and benefits realization from IT assets.

4.7 Classification: Reiteration of IT Assets Structures and Mechanisms

From engagements with the CxO respondents, it is evident that the demi-regularities observed, are important in establishing the challenges faced in understanding and classifying IT asset elements. These demi-regularities have material impact on how IT assets structures, mechanisms, usage, and value would be determined, and how controls will be put in place to safeguard risk.

The demi-regularities are seen at play in the derived classification scheme for IT assets as shown in Fig. 2. The scheme has found use in an IT assets ontology for information risk [7].

4.8 Summary of Findings and Discussion

The way IT assets are treated is evidenced in how ICT investments are categorized: annual spending on hardware, software, telecommunication equipment and (internal) IT services [35, 36]. Hardware, infrastructure, telecommunication can be property, plant and equipment or fixed cost, whereas internal IT services can be fixed cost, recurring expenditure or intangibles. However, these distinct categorization no longer suffices, given the intrinsic nature, structures and mechanisms of IT assets when the multi-faceted dimensions of what IT assets consist of, composed of, context of place and use are considered. This importance of this is that IT assets can be engaged as having a carrying value, which is the financial value attribute to the IT asset and addition capability and intangible values (which are by reason of usage and the inherent attributes of IT assets. The flexibility of determining categorization as tangible and intangible is left for organizations to make.

As it was with *matter* in classical Physics, the 'hidden', non-observable, real domain of IT assets must be revisited and given due considerations in the same way *matter* was revisited and the sub-atomic nature was brought to the fore in quantum mechanics.

5 Conclusion

"Now all has been heard; here is the conclusion of the matter ..." – Ecclesiastes 12:13 NIV

The conclusion to be made in this paper stems from the starting point. Boards and directors in charge of organizations must caution against a fixed cast-in-stone view and approach to identifying, classifying, valuing, deriving benefits and managing risk of their assets, which in this instance is their IT assets.

This is done by re-interrogation based on the IT-CMF domain [37], areas and informed by their organizational strategic intent (purposeful, strategic application of IT across an organisation). This will assist in approaching IT diffusion in their organizations.

In this light, this paper addresses a very important topic: the nature, structures and mechanisms of IT assets' using critical realism philosophy approach. This is important in the identification, recognition and strategic use of IT assets.

Going forward, organizations should combine IT-CMF domain areas with the concept of asset specificity and service asset configuration management of ITIL, in approaching their IT assets, handling their IT assets and deriving benefits from their IT assets.

It is hoped that future interrogating studies will attempt to interlink reputation, information risk, accounting, IT service management, and IT diffusion. Such an approach should assist with universal definition of IT assets that will be more appropriate for the 4IR, knowledge economy and beyond. There is room to further critically examine information assets not only as intangibles [26, 34], but their common structures and mechanism with IT assets as research reality. By doing so, researchers will be re-examining the information strand of the diverse root of information technology as envisaged by Leavitt and Whisler in 1958 [3].

References

1. Wallace, P.R.: Paradox Lost: Images of the Quantum. Springer, New York (2011). https://doi.org/10.1007/978-1-4612-4014-3
2. Bhaskar, R.: A Realist Theory of Science. Routledge, Oxon, Oxford (2013)
3. Leavitt, H.J., Whisler, T.L.: Management in the 1980's. Harv. Bus. Rev. **36**, 41–48 (1958)
4. OECD: New Building Blocks for Jobs and Economic Growth : Intangible Assets as Sources of Increased Productivity and Enterprise Value. Presented at the September (2011)
5. Stevenson, A. (ed.): Oxford Dictionary of English. Oxford University Press, Oxon, Oxford (2010)

6. Lee, M., et al.: How to respond to the fourth industrial revolution, or the second information technology revolution? dynamic new combinations between technology, market, and society through open innovation. J. Open Innov. Technol. Mark. Complex. **4**, 21 (2018). https://doi.org/10.3390/joitmc4030021
7. Adesemowo, A.K., von Solms, R., Botha, R.A.: ITAOFIR: IT asset ontology for information risk in knowledge economy and beyond. In: Jahankhani, H., et al. (eds.) ICGS3 2017. CCIS, vol. 630, pp. 173–187. Springer, Cham (2016). https://doi.org/10.1007/978-3-319-51064-4_15
8. Borch, K.: The theory of risk. J. R. Stat. Soc. **29**, 432–467 (1967)
9. Aven, T., Baraldi, P., Flage, R., Zio, E.: Uncertainty in Risk Assessment. Wiley, Chichester (2014). https://doi.org/10.1002/9781118763032
10. Archer, M.S., Bhaskar, R., Collier, A., Lawson, T., Norrie, A., (eds.): Critical Realism: Essential Readings. Routledge (2013)
11. Vandenberghe, F. (ed.): What's Critical About Critical Realism?: Essays in Reconstructive Social Theory. Routledge, Oxon (2013). https://doi.org/10.4324/9780203798508. OX14 4RN
12. Oates, B.J.: Researching Information Systems and Computing. SAGE Publications, London (2006)
13. Thapa, D., Omland, H.O.: Four steps to identify mechanisms of ICT4D: a critical realism-based methodology. Electron. J. Inf. Syst. Dev. Countries **84**, e12054 (2018). https://doi.org/10.1002/isd2.12054
14. Heeks, R., Wall, P.J.: Critical realism and ICT4D research. Electron. J. Inf. Syst. Dev. Countries **84**, e12051 (2018). https://doi.org/10.1002/isd2.12051
15. Faulkner, P., Runde, J.: Technological objects, social positions, and the transformational model of social activity. MIS Q. **37**, 803–818 (2013)
16. Mingers, J., Mutch, A., Willcocks, L.: Critical realism in information systems research. MIS Q. **37**, 795–802 (2013)
17. Reips, U.-D.: Using the Internet to collect data. In: Cooper, H., Camic, P.M., Long, D.L., Panter, A.T., Rindskopf, D., Sher, K.J. (eds.) APA Handbook of Research Methods in Psychology. Research Designs: Quantitative, Qualitative, Neuropsychological, and Biological, Washington D.C., vol. 2, pp. 291–310 (2012). https://doi.org/10.1037/13620-017
18. Arksey, H., O'Malley, L.: Scoping studies: towards a methodological framework. Int. J. Soc. Res. Methodol. **8**, 19–32 (2005). https://doi.org/10.1080/1364557032000119616
19. Levac, D., Colquhoun, H., O'Brien, K.K.: Scoping studies: advancing the methodology. Implementation Sci. **5**, 69 (2010). https://doi.org/10.1186/1748-5908-5-69
20. Krippendorff, K.: Content Analysis: An Introduction to Its Methodology. SAGE Publications, Thousand Oaks (2012)
21. Saunders, M.N.K., Lewis, P., Thornhill, A.: Research Methods for Business Students. Pearson, London (2015)
22. Babbie, E.R.: The Practice of Social Research. Cengage Learning, Belmont (2012)
23. Kuechler, W., Vaishnavi, V.: A Framework for Theory Development in Design Science Research: Multiple Perspectives. J. Assoc. Inf. Syst. **13**, 395–423 (2012)
24. Walton, D.N.: Methods of Argumentation. Cambridge University Press, New York (2013). 10013
25. Chaum, D.: Security without identification: transaction systems to make big brother obsolete. Commun. ACM **28**, 1030–1044 (1985). https://doi.org/10.1145/4372.4373
26. Saunders, A., Brynjolfsson, E.: Valuing information technology related intangible assets. Manag. Inf. Syst. Q. **40**, 83–110 (2016)

27. Dwivedi, Y.K., Levine, L., Williams, M.D., Singh, M., Wastell, D.G., Bunker, D.: Toward an understanding of the evolution of IFIP WG 8.6 research. In: Pries-Heje, J., Venable, J., Bunker, D., Russo, N.L., DeGross, J.I. (eds.) TDIT 2010. IAICT, vol. 318, pp. 225–242. Springer, Heidelberg (2010). https://doi.org/10.1007/978-3-642-12113-5_14
28. Institute of Directors in Southern Africa: King IV: report on corporate governance for South Africa 2016. Institute of Directors in Southern Africa, Johannesburg, South Africa (2016)
29. Tillquist, J., Rodgers, W.: Using asset specificity and asset scope to measure the value of IT. Commun. ACM **48**, 75–80 (2005). https://doi.org/10.1145/1039539.1039542
30. Ross, J.W., Beath, C.M., Goodhue, D.L.: Develop long-term competitiveness through IT assets. MIT Sloan Manag. Rev. **38**, 31–42 (1996)
31. De Vita, G., Tekaya, A., Wang, C.L.: The many faces of asset specificity: a critical review of key theoretical perspectives. Int. J. Manag. Rev. **13**, 329–348 (2011). https://doi.org/10.1111/j.1468-2370.2010.00294.x
32. Higson, C., Dave, W.: Valuing Information as An Asset. Bucks (2010). SL7 2 EB
33. AXELOS: ITIL ® glossary and abbreviations (2011)
34. Adesemowo, A.K., Von Solms, R., Botha, R.A.: Safeguarding information as an asset: do we need a redefinition in the knowledge economy and beyond? SA J. Inf. Manag. **18**, 1–12 (2016). https://doi.org/10.4102/sajim.v18i1.706
35. Bankole, F.O., Osei-Bryson, K.-M., Brown, I.: The impact of ICT investments on human development: a regression splines analysis. J. Glob. Inf. Technol. Manag. **16**, 59–85 (2014). https://doi.org/10.1080/1097198X.2013.10845636
36. Kim, S., Poon, S., Young, R.: Issues around firm level classification of IT investment. In: Seltsikas, P., Bunker, D., Dawson, L., Indulska, M. (eds.) Proceedings of the 22nd Australiasian Conference on Information Systems ACIS 2011. p. Paper 81. Australasian Conference on Information Systems, Sydney, Australia (2011)
37. Curley, M., Kenneally, J., Carcary, M. (eds.): IT Capability Maturity Framework (IT-CMF): The Body of Knowledge Guide, 2nd edn. Van Haren Publishing, 's-Hertogenbosch (2016)

Understanding Internet Fraud: Denial of Risk Theory Perspective

Martin Offei[1(✉)], Francis Kofi Andoh-Baidoo[2], Emmanuel Ayaburi[2], and David Asamoah[3]

[1] Koforidua Technical University, P.O. Box KF 981, Koforidua, Ghana
martin.offei@ktu.edu.gh
[2] University of Texas Rio Grande Valley, 1201 W University Drive, Edinburg, TX 78539, USA
[3] Kwame Nkrumah University of Science and Technology, Kumasi, Ghana

Abstract. Internet fraud has become a global problem attracting the attention of researchers, practitioners and policy makers. Existing empirical theoretical studies on internet crimes have mostly used neutralization and deterrence theories. Despite the insights from these theories, we are still observing an increase in the number of internet crimes. We argue that Denial of Risk theory may provide new insights on internet crimes such as internet fraud. We examined how each of the three dimensions of Denial of Risk theory (scapegoating, self-confidence and comparing of risk) serve as antecedent of the intention to commit internet fraud. Using responses from 350 individuals from internet fraud hotspots, we showed that scapegoating, self-confidence and comparing of risk are positively related to intention to commit internet fraud. The study offers theoretical and practical contributions to research in the spectrum of internet fraud and the theoretical application of denial of risk in cybercrime research.

Keywords: Internet fraud · Denial of risk theory · Scapegoating · Self-confidence · Comparing of risk

1 Introduction

Cybercrime has become a global issue as it affects individuals, businesses and governments everywhere including developing economies (Chatterjee et al. 2018; Li and Cheng 2013; Shareef et al. 2018). Examples of cybercrimes include identity theft, piracy, hacking and financial fraud committed over the internet. We focus on internet fraud in this research because such crimes affect a wide audience and perpetrators are usually anonymous. Internet fraud is broadly described as crime perpetuated on the internet components such as web sites, chat rooms, and e-mail, to offer non-existent goods or services to consumers, communicating false or fraudulent representations about the schemes to consumers, or transmitting victims' funds, access devices, or other items of value to the control of the scheme's perpetrators (Kubic 2001). Internet fraud appears in diverse forms such as "skimming, Card-Not-Present (CNP), stolen credentials buyers, professional hackers/crackers, identity theft" and among others (Boyle and Walker 2016, Jegede et al. 2016a, b).

Published by Springer Nature Switzerland AG 2019
Y. Dwivedi et al. (Eds.): TDIT 2019, IFIP AICT 558, pp. 415–424, 2019.
https://doi.org/10.1007/978-3-030-20671-0_28

Most prior research have used theories such as neutralization, deterrence and motivation to extend our understanding of internet crime phenomenon (Lazarus 2018). In general, these theories assume the individual appreciate the enormity of their crime or severity of the punishment. We argue that the increasing number of internet crimes despite the recommendations from prior research is because those individuals involve do not envision any risk in their quest to defraud unsuspecting victims. This is because most individuals involved in internet crime believe they cannot be located due to the anonymity and vast size of the internet. Employing a risk perspective, this study seeks to understand the internet fraud phenomenon. Specifically, we seek to answer the following research question: What risk perception factors influence individuals who intend to commit internet fraud?

This research seeks to make theoretical and practical contributions to research in the spectrum of internet fraud by using denial of risk theory as its basis. Denial of risk theory refers to the cognitive way individuals deal with risky behaviors by rejecting the presence or effect of risk (Peretti-Watel 2003). We developed a research model to understand how risk perception influence individuals' intention to commit internet fraud using components of denial of risk theory. We collected data from 350 individuals located in internet crime hotspots on key constructs, denial of risk and intention to commit internet fraud in our model. The results of the analysis of response data offer both theoretical and practical implications. For theory, we have shown the efficacy of Denial of Risk theory in understanding burgeoning Internet fraud discourse. For practice, our study provides insights for law enforcement agencies to understand the factors that act as drivers of internet fraud.

2 Theoretical Background – Denial of Risk Theory

Denial of risk refers to cognitive ways to develop adaption to risky behaviors by rejecting the possibility of suffering any loss (Peretti-Watel 2003). The theory posits that an individual may deflect the level of risk by comparing the crime to an acceptable action they consider a crime. The theory of denial of risk has three main constructs: scapegoating, self-confidence and comparing of risk. Scapegoating is when an individual stereotype actions of others they consider harmful (them) relative to their behavior. For example, young drivers label (scapegoat) older drivers as overly cautious as a justification for their over speeding habit. Self-confidence is when an individual reject risk by distinguishing themselves from anonymous group. For instance, some drivers who overspeed justify their action by suggesting that they possess better driving abilities than an average driver on the road. Comparison-between-risk arises when an individual compares their actions with that of a group whose action are already accepted. For example, individuals who text-while-driving may deflect risk by suggesting that driving-while-using-wireless communication is equally risky as individuals in both situations are affected by the information been communicated. Denial of risk theory has been used in the criminology literature to understand why individuals commit crime such as the use of cannabis (Apostolidis et al. 2006). We argue that each of these dimensions of denial of risk theory may influence an individual's intention to commit internet fraud because of the anonymity provided by the internet.

Internet fraud involves the use of internet and related activities that violate the ethical conducts of the internet (Kubic 2001). Internet fraud is of concern globally for governments and law enforcement agencies (Grabosky 2015). Internet fraud is perpetuated by individuals or groups of individuals with different backgrounds such as needs, education and cultural idiosyncrasies (Morris and Higgins 2009). The techniques used by perpetrators of internet fraud make them believe the consequences of their actions are less harmful and sometimes beneficial to the victims (Brooks 2016). We employ the three dimensions of denial of risk to develop a conceptual model that explains intention to commit internet fraud.

3 Conceptual Model Development

Scapegoating
The scapegoat construct of the denial of risk theory deals with the propensity to label an identifiable group as taking actions that are deemed riskier (Lazarus 2018). Employing scapegoating technique results in feelings of prejudice or stigmatization toward the person or group that one has accused of committing crimes that are relatively harmful. It provides the basis for the perpetrator of the crime to deflect any risk arising from their actions, thus resulting in positive self-image (Harris and Dumas 2009; Lazarus 2018). For instance, individuals who are engaged in internet fraud feel they are not causing harm to their victims' relative to harm caused by hackers who alter or prevent victims from continuing their normal lives. For instance, some cybercriminals in developing nations have believe that criminals in western countries cause more harm to their victims than they do (Hutchings 2013). Such rationalization of the risk of committing internet fraud transforms risk into blame (Sugiura 2018). The criminals use scapegoating to absolve themselves from their criminal behavior. Thus, we posit that:

H1: *Scapegoating as a technique of denial of risk positively affects the intention to commit internet fraud*

Self-confidence
Self-confidence is the cognizance that makes one believe in their abilities to perform certain tasks without much difficulty. The self-belief in a confident person is very high and rises with more complex task such as creating situations that makes it easy to defraud another person. Self-confidence helps individuals to participate in the crimes they commit (Sigala 2017, Jegede et al. 2016a, b). Although individuals know that they are committing a crime that is punishable by law, they deny this risk by showing confidence they will not be punished. Sometimes perpetrators of internet crimes draw solidarity among themselves to increase their confidence level (Jegede et al. 2016a, b; Koay 2018). Therefore, it is posited that:

H2: *Self-confidence as a technique of denial of risk positively affect the intention to commit internet fraud*

Comparison Between Risks. Comparing of risk looks at the lesser evil perceived by the perpetuator of internet fraud. Individuals who commit internet fraud compare their activities to other crimes such as hackers or identity theft and perceive that the activities they are involved in are better evil (Choo 2011). By comparing the risk of their crimes, criminals perceive some crimes as much riskier than others.

It is reported that some individuals who are engaged in internet fraud compare the crime to other crimes such as stealing and cheating and perceive that such crimes are not less harmful when compared to what they do (Mekonnen et al. 2015). Individuals who commit internet fraud are shielded in the comfort of anonymity. Such individuals proclaim and perceive they are far away from the victims they defraud and believe that they cannot be caught or punished (McMullan and Rege 2010). Therefore, it is posited that (Fig. 1):

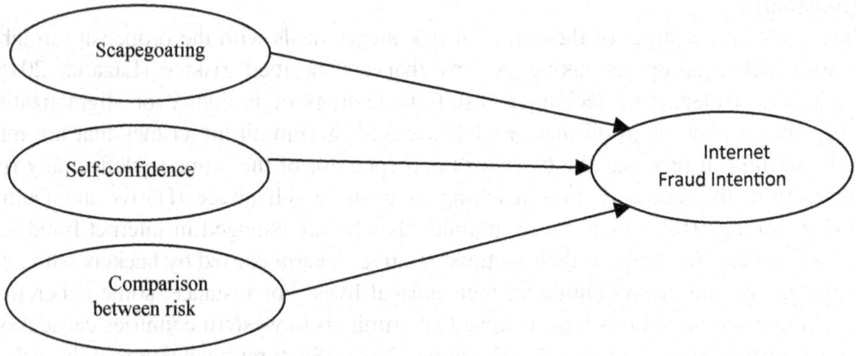

Fig. 1. Research model

H3: Comparing of risk as a technique of denial of risk positively affects the intention to commit internet fraud

4 Methodology

Measures and Sample

This study was conducted using a survey research design (Choudrie and Dwivedi 2005). The target population for this study are individuals located in alleged hotspots (internet cafes) where internet fraud originates (Odou and Bonnin 2014). Unique high unemployment in some of these regions encourages internet fraud (Smith et al. 2001; Boateng et al. 2011). Due to the heterogeneous and illegality of the phenomenon understudy, the total population of the study is not known. Our sample included 350 respondents. The sampling techniques used in this study are cluster sampling, convenient sampling, and snowball sampling approach. Cluster sampling are the regional distribution of internet fraudsters within Ghana. The clusters represented internet fraud hot spots within the selected regions (Greater Accra, Eastern, Volta, Ashanti, Central

and Western), convenient sampling was used to select a section from each cluster in the internet fraudsters' cafes. Furthermore, snowball sampling technique was used to identify other individuals suspected to be involved with internet fraud and online relationship scams.
We adopted 12 items from Peretti-Watel (2003) to measure scapegoating, self-confidence and comparing of risk. These items were used in prior study to juvenile intent to commit an illegal act -weed smokers- in France.

Our dependent variable, Internet fraud intention was operationalized as a second order construct consisting of two first order constructs (deception and fraud). The 8 items used to measure our dependent variable were adopted from (Park and Sung 2015; Siponen and Vance 2010). Details of the measures used in the study along with their loadings are presented in the appendix.

5 Results and Analysis

The Structural Equation Modeling (SEM) was used to investigate the causal paths hypothesized in this study. A two-step approach was used to analyze the data. In the first step, the covariance-based technique was used to assess the appropriateness of the measurement model. The covariance based technique was used as it minimizes the differences between the covariance of the collected sample and that of the ones predicted by the model and reproduces the covariance matrix of the observable variable. For testing the structural model, variance based partial least square (PLS) SEM was used as it maximizes the variance of the dependent variable which is explained by the independent variables.

We used the Cronbach Alpha, Composite Reliability and Average Variance Extracted (AVE) to test for reliability and validity of the constructs. Discriminant validity tests were performed to test for accuracy of the measurement items by using Fornell-Lecker Criterion and Heterotrait-Monotrait (HTMT). A HTMT is a more resilient test for discriminant validity than cross loadings. As shown in Table 1, constructs reliability are confirmed as composite reliability (CR) values for all factors were above the recommended 0.7 value threshold, indicating item consistency. The variance explained (AVE) is above the satisfactory threshold of 0.5, confirming convergent validity.

Table 1. Construct validity

	CR	AVE	CA	DorCr	DorSc	DorSg	IcifDp	Icifld
DorCr	0.833	0.625	0.842	**0.79**				
DorSc	0.878	0.705	0.724	0.214	**0.84**			
DorSg	0.874	0.699	0.790	0.222	0.971	**0.836**		
IcifDp	0.882	0.652	0.775	0.179	0.417	0.428	**0.807**	
Icifld	0.866	0.684	0.689	0.265	0.116	0.143	0.225	**0.827**

DorCr - Denial of risk-Comparing of risk, DorSc - Denial of risk-Self-confidence, DorSg - Denial of risk - Scapegoating, IcifDp - Intention to commit internet fraud-Deception, Icifld - Intention to commit internet fraud - Defraud

We conducted model robustness checks for multicollinearity. VIF values for scapegoating (2.04), self-confidence (1.937), and comparing of risk (1.5) are much less than the threshold of (VIF < 10), indicating absence of multicollinearity problem. In assessing the explanatory power, our model accounted for 58% of variance ($R^2 = 0.58$) in explaining intention to commit internet fraud.

The Adjusted R^2 (0.56) further strengthens the explanatory power as it takes into account our sample size and number of variables in our model. Summary of the hypotheses testing are shown in Table 2 and Fig. 2.

Table 2. Summary of results

	Hypothesis	Support?
H1	*Scapegoating positively affect the intention to commit internet fraud*	Supported
H2	*Self-confidence positively affect the intention to commit internet fraud*	Supported
H3	*Comparing of risk positively affect the intention to commit internet fraud*	Supported

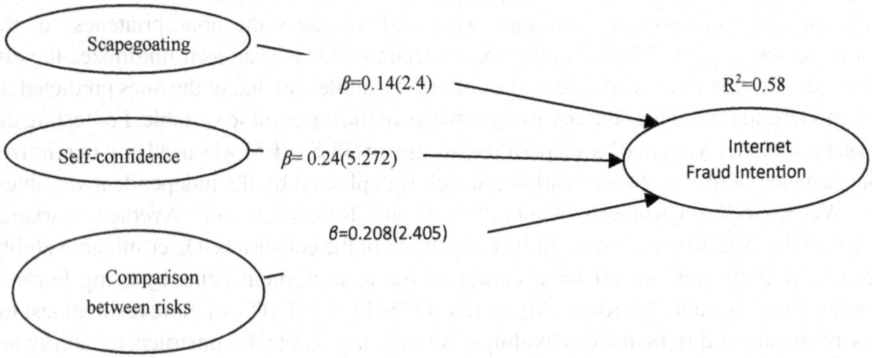

Fig. 2. Model results

As hypothesized, internet fraudsters use scapegoating to commit internet fraud ($p < 0.05$; $t = 2.44$), and hypothesis 2 supports a positive relationship between self-confidence and intention to commit internet fraud ($p < 0.05$; $t = 5.272$). Hypothesis 3 is also supported ($p < 0.05$; $t = 2.405$); comparing of risk positively influence the intention to commit internet fraud.

Discussion and Future Research Direction

Denial of risk theory refers to a mental way to deal with risk associated with deviant behaviors. Individuals who employ denial of risk attempt to reject the risk from the actions by comparing their actions to others who they deem more harmful. We used this theory as the basis to understand the intention of individuals to commit inter fraud that is regarded a harmful or unethical use of computers. We argue that internet fraudsters justify their deviant behavior by using these techniques to justify their behavior. Internet fraudsters persuade themselves they are anonymous and law enforcement are incapable of apprehending them. In societies where risk is downplayed, denial of risk theory offers an understanding of how these internet fraudsters view their risky actions by scapegoating, self-confidence and comparing of risk. This complements research on cybercrimes that have used neutralization and deterrence theory by suggesting the increase in internet fraud, a form of cybercrime, should be looked from denial of risk perspective.

The findings of the research are consistent with prior studies on denial of risk theory such as Peretti-Watel (2003) study on use of cannabis among young smokers. The publicity of arrest of individuals involve in internet fraud may have no effect on the number of internet crimes committed. One explanation is the denial of any risk through the show of self-confidence of the fraudsters to avoid getting caught. Self-confidence has the reinforcing effect as it encourages undecided individuals to engage in internet fraud. Our results show that internet fraudsters compare their crimes and are emboldened to commit internet fraud. For example, when an individual considers corruption as a form of extortion but believes society does not hold perpetrators accountable, then committing internet fraud such as credit card fraud may not be a costly crime. Thus, internet fraudsters do not consider those other crimes as different from what they do.

Our study reinforces the extensive use of comparing of risk as denial of risk technique by deviants in previous studies (Peretti-Watel 2003; Vida et al. 2012; Grabosky 2015). These internet fraudsters "see" other crimes such as, arm robbery, blood rituals, stealing from the Government as comparable to internet fraud and this perception helps them to rationalize their criminal behavior. Preventing internet fraud requires the global effort of all stakeholders including law enforcement agencies to confront it (Gottschalk and Smith 2011). The results of the study suggest that preventing internet fraud requires concerted effort to raise the level of risk associated with these crimes.

Future studies should attempt to understand how denial of risk compares with other techniques employed by individuals such as neutralization techniques who may want to commit an internet crime. Furthermore, researchers should seek to understand how age and technical experience play a role in the intention to commit internet crime.

Appendix

(See Table 3).

Table 3. Survey instrument

Item		Loading
Perceived scapegoating		
Dorsg1	Defrauding "clients" is not as bad as armed robbery	–
Dorsg2	Defrauding "clients" is not as bad as 'blood money'	0.829
Dorsg3	Defrauding "clients" is not as bad as 'Sakawa'	0.875
Dorsg4	Defrauding "clients" is not as bad as corruption	0.735
Perceived self-confidence		
Dorsc1	I feel confident in my ability to defraud "clients"	
Dorsc2	I know how to get "clients" believe in me than the average person	0.836
Dorsc3	It is not dangerous to maintain relationship with "clients" after defrauding them	0.858
Dorsc4	I have confidence in determining "clients" who are less willing to be defrauded	0.749
Perceived comparison-between-risk		
Dorcr1	Defrauding "clients" who is in relationship is no different from taking money from a spouse	–
Dorcr2	Defrauding "clients" is no different from begging for livelihood	0.813
Dorcr3	Defrauding "clients" is no different from paid workers who receive tips before they provide service	0.792
Dorcr4	Defrauding "clients" is not no different from taking money from a woman you are not sure you will marry	0.758
Intention to commit internet fraud		
Icifid1	What is the chance that you will defraud "clients"?	0.865
Icifid2	I am certain that I will defraud "clients"	0.859
Icifid3	I am likely to defraud "clients"	0.752
Icifidp1	I tell all my "clients" lies	0.785
Icifidp2	My "clients" believe the lies I tell them	0.863
Icifidp3	My "clients" don't know I am deceiving them	0.830
Icifidp4	I am crafty with my lies	0.746
Icifidp5	"Clients" needs to believe your story before you get the money	–

References

Apostolidis, T., Fieulaine, N., Simonin, L., Rolland, G.: Cannabis use, time perspective and risk perception: evidence of a moderating effect. Psychol. Health **21**(5), 571–592 (2006)

Boateng, R., Longe, O., Isabalija, R.S., Budu, J.: Sakawa - cybercrime and criminality in Ghana. J. Inf. Technol. Impact **11**(2), 85–100 (2011)

Boyle, K.M., Walker, L.S.: The neutralization and denial of sexual violence in college party subcultures. Deviant Behav. **37**(12), 1392–1410 (2016)

Brooks, G.: Explaining corruption: drifting in and out of corruption and techniques of neutralization. In: Criminology of Corruption, pp. 107–125. Palgrave Macmillan, London (2016)

Chatterjee, S., Kar, A.K., Dwivedi, Y.K., Kizgin, H.: Prevention of cybercrimes in smart cities of India: from a citizen's perspective. Inf. Technol. People (2018). https://doi.org/10.1108/ITP-05-2018-0251

Choo, K.K.R.: Cyber threat landscape faced by financial and insurance industry. Trends Issues Crime Crim. Justice **408**, 1 (2011)

Choudrie, J., Dwivedi, Y.K.: Investigating the research approaches for examining technology adoption issues. J. Res. Pract. **1**(1), 1 (2005). http://jrp.icaap.org/index.php/jrp/article/viewFile/4/7

Gottschalk, P., Smith, R.: Criminal entrepreneurship, white-collar criminality, and neutralization theory. J. Enterp. Commun.: People Places Glob. Econ. **5**(4), 300–308 (2011)

Grabosky, P.: Organized cybercrime and national security. In: Cybercrime Risks and Responses, pp. 67–80. Palgrave Macmillan, London (2015)

Harris, L.C., Dumas, A.: Online consumer misbehavior: an application of neutralization theory. Mark. Theory **9**(4), 379–402 (2009)

Hutchings, A.: Hacking and fraud: qualitative analysis of online offending and victimization. In: Global Criminology: Crime and Victimization in the Globalized Era, pp. 93–114 (2013)

Jegede, A.E., Olowookere, I.E., Elegbeleye, A.O.: Youth identity, peer influence and internet crime participation in Nigeria: a reflection. IFE Psycholog **24**(1), 37–47 (2016a)

Jegede, A.E., Oyesomi, K., Olorunyomi, B.R.: Youth crime and the organized attributes of cyber fraud in the modern technological age: a thematic review. Int. J. Soc. Sci. Hum. Rev. **6**(1), 153–164 (2016b)

Koay, K.Y.: Understanding consumers' purchase intention towards counterfeit luxury goods: an integrated model of neutralization techniques and perceived risk theory. Asia Pac. J. Mark. Logistics **30**(2), 495–516 (2018)

Kubic, T.T.: Internet Fraud Complaint Center (2001). https://archives.fbi.gov/archives/news/testimony/internet-fraud-crime-problems

Lazarus, S.: Birds of a feather flock together: the Nigerian cyber fraudsters (Yahoo Boys) and hip hop artists. Criminol. Crim. Justice Law Soc. **19**(2), 63–80 (2018)

Li, W., Cheng, L.: Effects of neutralization techniques and rational choice theory on internet abuse in the workplace. In: PACIS, p. 169 (2013)

McMullan, J.L., Rege, A.: Online crime and internet gambling. J. Gambl. Issues (24), 54–85 (2010)

Mekonnen, S., Padayachee, K., Meshesha, M.: A privacy preserving context-aware insider threat prediction and prevention model predicated on the components of the fraud diamond. In: 2015 Annual Global Online Conference on Information and Computer Technology (GOCICT), pp. 60–65. IEEE (2015)

Morris, R.G., Higgins, G.E.: Neutralizing potential and self-reported digital piracy: a multitheoretical exploration among college undergraduates. Crim. Justice Rev. **34**(2), 173–195 (2009)

Odou, P., Bonnin, G.: Consumers' neutralization strategies to counter normative pressure: the case of illegal downloading. Recherche et Applications en Marketing (English Edition), **29**(1), 103–121 (2014)

Park, J., Sung, C.: The effect of online piracy deterrence on self-control and piracy intention, PACIS, Jooyeon Park, School of Business, Yonsei University, Seoul, Korea (2015)

Peretti-Watel, P.: Neutralization theory and the denial of risk: some evidence from cannabis use among French adolescents*. Br. J. Sociol. **54**, 21–42 (2003)

Shareef, M.A., Dwivedi, Y.K., Kumar, V., Davies, G., Rana, N., Baabdullah, A.: Purchase intention in an electronic commerce environment: a trade-off between controlling measures and operational performance. Inf. Technol. People (2018). https://doi.org/10.1108/ITP-05-2018-0241

Sigala, M.: How “Bad” are you? Justification and normalisation of online deviant customer behaviour. In: Schegg, R., Stangl, B. (eds.) Information and Communication Technologies in Tourism 2017, pp. 607–622. Springer, Cham (2017). https://doi.org/10.1007/978-3-319-51168-9_44

Siponen, M., Vance, A.: Neutralization: new insights into the problem of employee information systems security policy violations. MIS Q. **34**, 487–502 (2010)

Smith, W.R., Torstensson, M., Johansson, K.: Perceived risk and fear of crime: gender differences in contextual sensitivity. Int. Rev. Victimol. **8**(2), 159–181 (2001)

Sugiura, L.: Challenging the risks in online medicine purchasing: respectable deviance. In: Respectable Deviance and Purchasing Medicine Online, pp. 101–138. Palgrave Macmillan, Cham (2018)

Vida, I., Kos Koklič, M., Kukar-Kinney, M., Penz, E.: Predicting consumer digital piracy behavior: the role of rationalization and perceived consequences. J. Res. Interact. Mark. **6**(4), 298–313 (2012)

Virtual Social Networks as Public Sphere: Relating E-government Maturity, ICT Laws, and Corruption

Jithesh Arayankalam and Satish Krishnan(✉)

Indian Institute of Management Kozhikode, Kozhikode, India
{jitheshallfpm, satishk}@iimk.ac.in

Abstract. The role of e-government in reducing corruption is an active area of research in information systems (IS). Drawing on the concept of public sphere from political science literature, we seek to explore how the diffusion of virtual social networks (VSNs) influence the relationships between e-government maturity in a country, its ICT laws and corruption. Our analyses based on publicly available archival data substantiates the (1) relationship between e-government maturity in a country and its corruption through the indirect effect of ICT laws; (2) interaction effect of VSN diffusion in a country on its e-government maturity and ICT laws; and (3) interaction effect of VSN diffusion in a country on its ICT laws and corruption. The key contribution of this research is the reestablishment of the idea of public sphere in the context of VSN diffusion, and how it affects e-government outcomes of a country.

Keywords: E-government maturity · ICT laws · Corruption · Virtual social networks diffusion · Public sphere

1 Introduction

E-government is defined as the delivery of government services using information communication technologies (ICTs) [31]; and its maturity is defined as the extent to which a government in a country has established an online presence [41]. Governments across the globe are adopting e-government by the virtue of its potential to improve the effectiveness and the efficiency in information and services delivery using ICTs [70]. With the rapid increase in the Internet usage and the arrival of new gadgets such as smartphones, society is becoming more connected than ever. As a result of this, information and services are available to the citizens in ways that couldn't have been imagined a few years ago. In this context, a deeper understanding on the impact of e-government has become much more relevant.

Extant studies on e-government can be grouped into three broad categories: (1) evolution and development; (2) adoption and implementation; and (3) impact [57]. While there are several studies related to the first two categories, research relating to the impact of e-government is scant [18]. The studies in this category focus on the benefits of e-government such as increase in citizen participation (e.g. [12, 60]), improvement in political trust (e.g. [50, 60]), better accountability (e.g. [2]), more openness (e.g. [2,

Published by Springer Nature Switzerland AG 2019
Y. Dwivedi et al. (Eds.): TDIT 2019, IFIP AICT 558, pp. 425–441, 2019.
https://doi.org/10.1007/978-3-030-20671-0_29

60]), and reduction in corruption (e.g. [4, 16, 41]), among others. In this study, we delve deeper into the relationship between e-government and corruption, defined as "the misuse of entrusted power for private gains" [59; p. 1], for two key reasons. First, the extant studies linking e-government with corruption offer contrasting results; and thus, require further inquiry. And second, the role of virtual social networks (VSNs), defined as ICT platforms that facilitate social interactions among people across the world [48], on e-government outcomes is underexplored.

While most research linking e-government and corruption deals with the direct relationship between them (e.g. [16, 41]), the possibility of an indirect effect between the two is less explored. Such an exploration is important as the extant studies offer mixed results in establishing whether or not e-government has a role in reducing corruption. For instance, studies by [4], [13], and [67], support the notion of effectiveness of e-government in combating corruption, while others (e.g. [39, 68]) question its effectiveness. This anomaly in results points to a possibility of exploring other intervening and/or moderating factors while studying the impact of e-government maturity on corruption.

One such intervening factor that may have an indirect role is ICT laws in a country. Given that privacy and security issues are one of the major concerns associated with cyberspace, they could pose a challenge for the maturity of e-government [21]. When engaging in online governmental activities, citizens fear that their sensitive information may be compromised by the government; and thus, having strong ICT based legal frameworks could enhance citizens' trust on the government [61]. While citizens' trust is identified as an important prerequisite for the success of e-government initiatives, building and restoring trust is possible only when assurance about safety from the concerns associated with engaging in online activities is incorporated in a country's ICT laws [46]. As the presence of citizens' trust has a negative effect on corruption [64], and as the poor development (or absence) of ICT laws is considered a major hurdle for the success of e-government initiatives [35], we argue that as the e-government matures in a country, its ICT laws also need to develop to deal with the challenges such as privacy and security that accompany online services. The implication of this is a possibility of an indirect relationship between e-government maturity of a country and its corruption through ICT laws. This leads us to our first research question (RQ1), which is as follows:

RQ1: *What is the relationship between e-government maturity, ICT laws, and corruption in a country?*

Another byproduct of ubiquitous connectivity is the rise of VSNs such as Facebook and Twitter, among others. As a platform for open discussion and deliberation, we argue that VSNs has the potential to be a public sphere. A public sphere is a realm of our social life where citizens can engage in political discussions and debates on common issues [24]. By mediating between the society and the government, a public sphere keeps the government accountable for its actions [24]. To qualify as a public sphere, [23] proposed three criteria namely (1) disregard for status; (2) domain of common concern; and (3) inclusivity. While disregard for status indicates that all citizens, irrespective of their status, can participate in the public sphere, domain of common concern means that citizens should be able to engage in rational discussion about affairs that concern them. And, inclusivity signifies that every citizen should be able to participate in the public sphere [23]. We argue that VSNs meets all these three criteria to be an ideal public sphere; and thus, has a potential to push the government in a country towards development of sophisticated ICT laws, and lowering corruption. This brings us to our second research question (RQ2), which is as follows:

> ***RQ2:*** *What is the role of VSN diffusion on the relationships between e-government maturity, ICT laws, and corruption in a country?*

As an attempt towards answering the aforementioned questions, we performed a cross-country analysis of 136 countries by utilizing archival data from publicly available data sources. By doing so, this research contributes to the knowledge base of e-government in three key ways. First, we identify ICT laws as an intervening variable having an indirect relationship between e-government maturity and corruption. Second, we establish the role of VSN diffusion in influencing e-government outcomes. And third, we introduce the concept of public sphere from political science literature to IS discipline by conceptualizing VSNs as public sphere, thus contributing to an inter-disciplinary research.

The rest of the paper is organized as follows. In Sect. 2, we first discuss how e-government maturity in a country is related with its ICT laws and corruption. Next, by conceptualizing VSNs as public sphere, we elaborate how the diffusion of VSNs can affect the relationships of (1) e-government maturity and ICT laws; and (2) ICT laws and corruption. In Sects. 3 and 4, we focus our efforts on research design and analyses respectively. In Sect. 5, we discuss our results, and highlight how our study contributes to the knowledge base of e-government. Finally, we conclude with a restatement of the value of our work.

2 Theory and Hypotheses

2.1 Relating E-government Maturity, ICT Laws, and Corruption

E-government maturity is defined as the extent to which a government in a country has established its online presence [41]; and this definition indicates that e-government initiatives matures and develops in stages starting from cataloging of government information to horizontal integration of different functional departments in the government, which can provide seamless services to citizens engaging in transactions with the government [42, 43, 56]. Along with other benefits such as openness and accountability, the potential of e-government in reducing corruption has been established in several studies (e.g. [1, 4, 7, 13, 16, 41, 65]). In all these studies, e-government is assumed to have a direct negative relationship with corruption indicating that when the higher is the level of e-government in a country, the lower will be its corruption. However, a handful of studies have pointed out a different viewpoint where e-government may actually increase corruption as it encourages new ways of indulging in such acts [29, 68]. These studies corroborate the views of [39] that casted doubt on the effectiveness of ICTs in reducing corruption.

These conflicting views point to a possibility of the presence of intervening factors that may influence the relationship between e-government maturity and corruption. We propose ICT laws in a country as a key intervening variable through which e-government may have an impact on corruption. ICT laws include legal mechanisms to regulate the use of ICTs within a country [62]. As security and privacy issues are major barriers to e-government initiatives [32], the poor development (or absence) of ICT laws can become a major barrier not only in the context of e-government adoption [21], but also in deriving successful outcomes from them [35]. Further, as technology in the digital age has brought in new methods of engaging in corrupt practices because of the provisions such as enhanced anonymity, the legal mechanisms to deal with these new challenges need to be strengthened [55] to minimize corrupt practices.

A well-developed ICT based legal framework has the potential to enhance citizens' trust in a country's online governmental services [49]. As citizens' trust is an important prerequisite for the success of e-government initiatives [58], building and restoring of trust is possible only when assurances about safety from the concerns associated with engaging in online activities is incorporated into the ICT based legal framework and settings of a country [46]. Further, as ICT laws has the potential to influence e-government outcomes [46] including lowering of corruption, it is logical to expect that this could happen only when a sophisticated and sound ICT based legal framework is fully developed.

Although a few studies have argued against the effectiveness of ICTs in controlling corruption (e.g. [11, 20]), it is worthy to note that a lack of proper ICT based legal framework may not allow courts to accept evidences using ICTs, which might negatively affect effective adjudication and prosecution in corruption cases [8]. The presence of effective ICT laws encourages maintenance of electronic records, facilitating identification of suspicious transactions, along with helping courts in expediting the legal processes such as prosecution [8], thus reducing corruption. A similar view is reflected in the 'Model Law' adopted by the United Nations Commission on International Trade Law, according to which admissibility of electronic messages as evidence in the courts is an important measure against fraud [62]. As authenticity of an evidence is critical in legal proceedings, authentication techniques such as digital signature can facilitate speeding up adjudication process. Thus, ICT laws, which facilitate authenticity and integrity of electronic information, can smoothen the judicial processes in deciding on corruption cases. Taken together, we argue that as e-government matures, the extent of development of ICT laws would result in minimizing corruption (see Fig. 1). Accordingly, we propose:

H_1*: *The relationship between e-government maturity in a country and its corruption is mediated by ICT laws.

2.2 Impact of Virtual Social Networks Diffusion

VSN is often interchangeably used with social media; and is defined as "a group of Internet-based applications that build on the ideological and technical foundations of

Web 2.0, and that allow the creation and exchange of user generated content" [36; p. 60]. VSN diffusion is defined as the extent to which individuals in a country use virtual social networks such as Facebook, Twitter, LinkedIn, etc. [66]. Even though VSNs have different affordances, the ability to share content publicly is something common among almost all platforms. According to [27], VSNs facilitate individuals to share and receive information regularly from their networked peers. This means that VSNs can serve as an open virtual space where individuals can engage in discussions, creating conditions for deliberative democracy [26]. One important ramification of this thought is the transformation of VSNs as public sphere.

In a public sphere, all citizens have equal access with guaranteed freedom of expression and assembly, thus encouraging opinions about affairs of general interest [24]. The original conceptualization of public sphere by Habermas included avenues of debates and discussions such as newspapers, magazines, journals, political clubs, and other meeting places where socio-political discussions were possible [23]. We extend this notion in the contemporary era of social media, and argue that VSNs are public spheres, where individuals discuss socio-political issues, among others. As mentioned earlier, there are three criteria for the formation of public sphere, namely, disregard for status, domain of common concern, and inclusivity [23]. Most VSN platforms have the potential to mimic the ideal public sphere as conceptualized by Habermas; and hence, they can be a repertoire of public demands, which have a great potential to influence government actions including framing of new laws and revamping the existing laws. Moreover, the membership on these platforms are increasing at a tremendous pace, paving the way for an increased public participation in the issues of common concern. For example, Facebook has 2.32 billion active monthly users as of December 2019 [17], making it the largest platform where people can engage in discussions and debates.

According to [9], public demand has the ability to induce and accelerate governments to make laws. For instance, the ability of VSNs to facilitate public demand, and cause government to take certain actions pertaining to public interest was witnessed during the Arab Spring revolutions [33]. In a similar instance, the power of VSNs at its zenith was noticed during the Egyptian revolution of 2011, which resulted in the ouster of President Hosni Mubarak, where the main medium of coordination and relay of information by citizens was Facebook [69]. And in 2006, using MySpace, American students pressured their government for immigration reforms [15]. Together, these instances depict how VSNs can be instrumental in pushing governments for legal reforms in a country. It can be argued that as more and more people participate on VSN platforms (i.e., when higher is the level of VSN diffusion), pressure on the government to act on public demands increases. Nevertheless, the extent of VSN diffusion varies across countries, which in turn indicates that the open participation of citizens on issues of common concern varies as well. In countries where VSN diffusion is high, more people can access VSN platforms, whereas in countries where VSN diffusion is low, such access is limited. Based on these arguments, it can be proposed that the relationship between e-government maturity and the development of ICT laws is strong when the VSN diffusion is high, whereas the relationship is weak when the VSN diffusion is low. Hence, we formally hypothesize (see Fig. 1):

***H_{2a}**: VSN diffusion in a country will have a positive moderating effect on the relationship between e-government maturity and ICT laws.*

A mere presence of ICT laws, without proper implementation, need not guarantee a reduction in corruption. One important way the proper implementation and compliance of laws can be guaranteed is through public pressure. That is, when the demand from stakeholders is strong, it puts pressure on governments to act consequently [72]. According to [10], citizens' demands affect the outcomes of law compliance, and public pressure forces the government in controlling crime [54]. Having said this, we argue that VSNs has the potential to facilitate participation of citizens in discussions and debates on public issues such as corruption, and thus, pressurize governments to act accordingly. For instance, during 2011 London riots, people used Twitter to influence government actions [47]. While VSNs has the ability to make the government more responsive to the citizens [44], the extent of VSN diffusion, as mentioned earlier, varies across countries, limiting open participation of citizens on issues of common concern. Consequently, there is a possibility of variation across countries in access to different VSN platforms. Based on these arguments, it can be proposed that the relationship between development of ICT laws and corruption is strong when the VSN diffusion is high, whereas the relationship is weak when the VSN diffusion is low. More formally, we therefore hypothesize (see Fig. 1):

***H_{2b}**: VSN diffusion in a country will have a negative moderating effect on the relationship between ICT laws and corruption.*

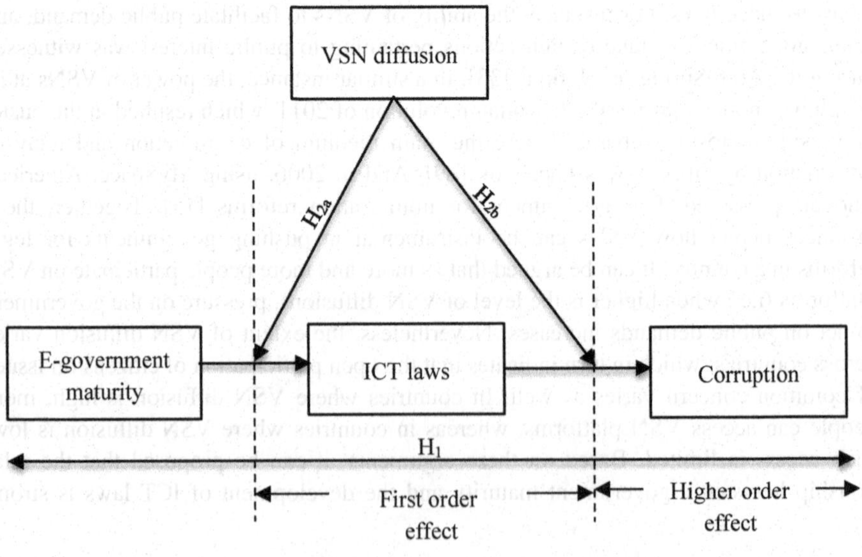

Fig. 1. Proposed model.

3 Research Design

Data to test the proposed model was obtained from the reports published by the reputed organizations such as the United Nations, World Economic Forum, Transparency International, the World Bank, etc. It is worthy to note that the research teams from these organizations followed stringent procedures and guidelines for ensuring the reliability and validity of the data. We preferred archival data as collecting primary data for several countries is constrained by the requirement of time and other resources such as money. Further, archival data has several advantages including (1) minimal common method bias [71]; (2) better reproducibility; and (3) greater generalizability [38]. Hypotheses were tested via a cross-sectional analysis of data from 136 countries. As this number is greater than the recommended value of 50 [25], we conclude that the issues pertaining to degrees of freedom in our model would be minimal.

Table 1 lists the study variables (including controls), its corresponding measures, and the sources from which the data for each variable was obtained. As the impact of e-government takes some time to show its effects [51], we considered a 2-year lag between the variables. Thus, for the variable of e-government maturity, we used data from the report published in the year 2012, and for ICT laws and corruption variables, 2014 and 2016 data were used respectively.

Table 1. Variables, measures and data sources.

Variable	Measure	Source
E-government maturity	Online Service Index	UN E-government Survey 2012 (UN, 2012)
Corruption	Corruption Perception Index	Transparency International (2016)
ICT laws	Laws relating to ICTs	Global IT Report (2016)
VSN diffusion	Use of virtual social networks	Global IT Report (2014, 2016)
Income level	GNP per capita	World Bank (2014)
Region	Region	World Bank (2014)
Internet penetration	Percentage of Internet users	International Telecommunication Union (2014)

As highlighted in the table, E-government maturity was measured using Online Service Index, the values for which were obtained from the UN E-government Survey 2012 report [63]. This index, which had been used in several past studies (e.g. [16, 73]) measured the extent of e-government in a country; and, its values ranged between 0 (low) and 1 (high). Corruption was measured using Corruption Perception Index (CPI), the scores for which were obtained from Transparency International (2016). Extant studies found CPI to have high validity (e.g. [5, 30, 34]), and its scores ranged from 0 (most corrupt) to 100 (least corrupt). For the ease of interpretation, in line with [53], we reverse coded the CPI scores. ICT laws was measured using the variable 'Laws relating to ICTs,' the data for which was taken from the Global IT Report (2016), and was captured through an Executive Opinion Survey. This variable measured the development of laws in a country relating to the use of ICTs including-commerce, digital signatures, and consumer protection, among others [66]. Its values ranged from 1 (not developed at all) to 7 (extremely well developed). VSN diffusion was measured using the variable 'Use of Virtual Social Networks,' the scores for which were taken from the WEF's Global IT reports (2014, 2016), and was used in several past studies (e.g. [40]). This variable was a measure of how widely virtual social networks are (e.g., Facebook, Twitter, LinkedIn, etc.) used in a country [66], and was captured through an Executive Opinion Survey. Its values ranged between 1 (not at all used) and 7 (used extensively). It is worthy to note that the Global IT Report (2016) contains data for VSN diffusion for the year 2014, and the Global IT report (2014) contains the data for 2012.

In addition, we controlled for the effects of several variables such as income level, region of a country, and Internet penetration. In line with extant macro level studies on corruption (e.g. [53]), we controlled for the effect of income level of a country, which is based on GNP per capita as per the World Bank's classification. World Bank classifies countries into four categories: (1) low-income (coded as 1); (2) lower-middle-income (coded as 2); (3) upper-middle-income (coded as 3); and (4) high-income (coded as 4). According to [73], corruption level varies as per the region of a country. Thus, in order to control for this effect, we accounted for the region of a country based on World Bank classification. World Bank classifies countries into 7 categories: (1) South Asia (coded as 1); (2) Europe & Central Asia (coded as 2); (3) Middle East & North Africa (coded as 3); (4) East Asia & Pacific (coded as 4); (5) Latin America & Caribbean (coded as 5); (6) Sub-Saharan Africa (coded as 6); and (7) North America (coded as 7). Lastly, as extant studies showed that Internet penetration reduces corruption (e.g. [45]), we controlled for its effects as well.

4 Analysis and Results

4.1 Descriptive Statistics and Correlations

Descriptive statistics and correlations among the study variables are shown in Table 2. As shown, in line with our initial expectations, (1) e-government maturity was negatively correlated with corruption; (2) ICT laws was negatively correlated with corruption and (3) VSN diffusion was positively correlated with both e-government maturity and ICT laws. Further, as the correlations among all the variables were below 0.8 (except for the correlations between VSN diffusion for the years 2012 and 2014), we conclude that the issues pertaining to multicollinearity would be minimal [22]. Nevertheless, we conducted variance inflation factor (VIF) test, which indicated that the VIF values were below 2 (i.e., less than the suggested cut-off of 4 [19]).

Table 2. Descriptive statistics and correlations.

Variables	M	SD	1	2	3	4	5	6	7
1. EGOV	.49	.25							
2. ICTL	3.95	.89	.71**						
3. COR	54.09	19.14	−.63**	−.75**					
4. VSN12	5.52	.70	.63**	.71**	−.62**				
5. VSN14	5.49	.70	.68**	.73**	−.62**	.90**			
6. INC	2.89	1.05	.65**	.67**	−.67**	.71**	.73**		
7. REG	3.74	1.73	−.33**	−.37**	.30**	−.36**	−.39	−.41**	
8. INT	54.5	66.29	.28**	.19**	−.25**	.35**	.37**	.39**	−.25**

Note. N = 136; M = Mean; SD = Standard deviation; ***p < 0.001 **p < 0.01 *p < 0.05 (2-tailed); EGOV: E-government maturity; ICTL: ICT laws; COR: Corruption; VSN12: VSN diffusion (2012); VSN14: VSN diffusion (2014); INC: Income level; REG: Region; INT: Internet penetration.

4.2 Hypothesis Testing

Hypotheses were tested in SPSS using Hayes' PROCESS macro, a tool to automate the analyses of mediating and moderating relationships between different variables [28]. Particularly, we used bootstrapping analysis as it is considered to be one of the powerful methods to identify mediation [52]. That is, the bootstrapping method creates a large number of sub-samples (5000 in our study) from the main sample and the parameters are estimated using these subsamples.

Regression results for the indirect effect of ICT laws on the relationship between e-government maturity and corruption are shown in Table 3. The values reported are unstandardized as it is suggested to be a better metric while reporting the results of causal models [28]. The R^2 value of 0.62 indicate that our model was effective in explaining the variance in corruption. Results in Table 4 shows that there is an indirect effect of e-government maturity on corruption through the variable of ICT laws, thus supporting hypothesis H1. It can be seen from the table that the effect is negative, indicating that as e-government in a country matured, its corruption reduced.

Table 3. Regression results for hypothesis 1.

Variables and statistics	β[a]	
	ICT laws	Corruption
EGOV	1.71***	−6.89
ICTL	–	−11.00***
INC	0.31***	−4.94***
REG	−0.05	−0.38
INT	−0.001	−0.01
R^2	0.59	0.62

Note. N = 136; ***p < 0.001 **p < 0.01 *p < 0.05 (2-tailed); [a]Regression coefficients reported are unstandardized; EGOV: E-government maturity; ICTL: ICT laws; INC: Income level; REG: Region; INT: Internet penetration.

Table 4. Indirect effect of ICT laws.

	Effect	LLCI	ULCI
ICTL	−18.80	−26.94	−4.12

Note. LLCI: Lower-level confidence interval; ULCI: Upper-level confidence interval; ICTL: ICT laws.

Next step in our analyses was to find out how this indirect relationship is influenced by VSN diffusion. Results of this analysis is shown in Table 5.

Table 5. Regression results for hypotheses 2a and 2b.

Variables and statistics	β^a	
	ICT law	Corruption
EGOV	−2.1	−8.84
ICTL	–	22.45
VSN12	0.23	–
VSN14	–	19.95***
VSN12 x EGOV	0.61**	–
VSN14 x ICTL	–	−5.67***
INC	0.15**	−5.02***
REG	−0.04	−0.2
INT	−0.002**	−0.004
R^2	0.66	0.65

Note. N = 136; ***p < 0.001 **p < 0.01 *p < 0.05 (2-tailed); [a]Regression coefficients reported are unstandardized; EGOV: E-government maturity; ICTL: ICT laws; VSN12: VSN diffusion (2012); VSN14: VSN diffusion (2014); INC: Income level; REG: Region; INT: Internet penetration.

As shown, the interaction of VSN diffusion and e-government maturity on ICT laws was positive and significant ($\beta = 0.61$; $p < 0.01$), indicating that VSN diffusion strengthens the relationship between e-government and the development of ICT laws. That is, when the VSN diffusion is high, there is a better chance that e-government maturity facilitates development of ICT laws in a country.

In a similar vein, as shown in the table, the interaction of VSN diffusion and ICT laws on corruption was negative and significant ($\beta = 5.67$; $p < 0.001$), indicating that VSN diffusion strengthens the negative relationship of ICT laws with corruption. This implies that the higher the VSN diffusion in a country, the higher is the effectiveness of its ICT laws in reducing corruption.

To further understand the role of VSN diffusion on the relationships between (1) e-government maturity and ICT laws; and (2) ICT laws and corruption, we graphed these significant interaction effects as recommended by [14], which are shown in Figs. 2 and 3 respectively. Further, we performed slope analyses as suggested by [3], the results of which are reported in Tables 6 and 7. Figure 2 shows the interaction of VSN diffusion on e-government maturity and ICT laws. As shown, when VSN diffusion was high, the significant positive relationship between e-government maturity and ICT laws was stronger in comparison to when VSN diffusion was low. Corroborating this, a simple slope analysis revealed that when VSN diffusion was high, the relationship of ICT laws with e-government maturity was positive and significant (slope = 1.83, t = 11.08; $p < 0.001$). Similarly, when VSN diffusion was low, this relationship was positive and significant (slope = 1.03; t = 38.42; $p < 0.001$). Figure 3 shows the interaction of VSN diffusion on ICT laws and corruption. As shown, when there was high VSN diffusion, the negative relationship between ICT laws and corruption was stronger. When VSN diffusion was low, this relationship was weaker. Confirming this, a simple slop analysis showed that when VSN diffusion was high, the relationship of ICT laws with corruption was negative and significant (slope = −12.64; t = −76.94; $p < 0.001$). Similarly, when VSN diffusion was low, this relationship was negative and significant (slope = −4.74; t = −177.53; $p < 0.001$). In sum, these results indicate that Hypotheses H2a and H2b were supported.

Among the three control variables, while income level was found to significantly affect ICT laws ($\beta = 0.15$; $p < 0.01$) and corruption ($\beta = -5.02$; $p < 0.001$), Internet penetration had a significant relationship with ICT laws ($\beta = -0.002$; $p < 0.01$). These findings are in line with the extant studies that have argued for the role of income and Internet penetration on corruption.

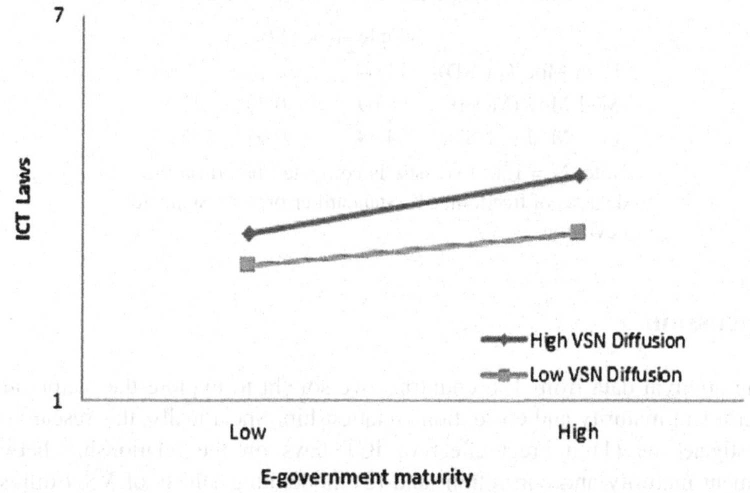

Fig. 2. Moderation effect of VSN diffusion on e-government maturity and ICT laws.

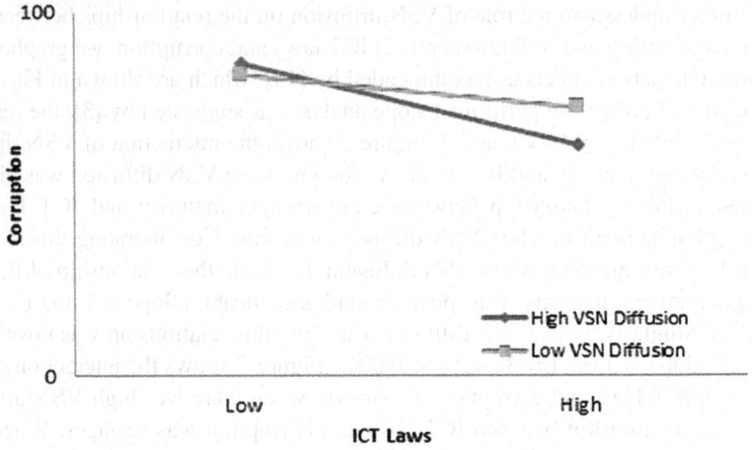

Fig. 3. Moderation effect of VSN diffusion on ICT laws and corruption.

Table 6. Slope analysis for hypothesis 2a.

	Simple slope	SE	t
High Mod (+1 SD)	1.83	0.17	11.08
Med Mod (Mean)	1.43	0.08	18.04
Low Mod (−1 SD)	1.03	0.03	38.42

Note. N = 136; t statistic is computed based on the degrees of freedom; SE: Standard error; SD: Standard deviation.

Table 7. Slope analysis for hypothesis 2b.

	Simple slope	SE	t
High Mod (+1 SD)	−12.64	0.16	−76.94
Med Mod (Mean)	−8.69	0.20	−42.52
Low Mod (−1 SD)	−4.74	0.03	−177.53

Note. N = 136; t statistic is computed based on the degrees of freedom; SE: Standard error; SD: Standard deviation.

5 Discussion

Utilizing archival data from 136 countries, we sought to explore the factors affecting "e-government maturity and corruption" relationship. Specifically, this research strived to investigate the (1) indirect effect of ICT laws on the relationship between e-government maturity and corruption; and (2) moderating effects of VSN diffusion on the relationships between e-government maturity, ICT laws, and corruption. The findings corroborate our initial argument that there could be other factors which might play a vital role in justifying the relationship of e-government maturity in a country with its corruption. Our findings indicate that when VSN diffusion is higher in a country, the extent of e-government maturity facilitates the development of ICT laws. Further, when VSN diffusion in a country is higher, better is the effectiveness of its ICT laws in reducing corruption.

Conceptualizing VSN as a public sphere, our study indicates that VSNs provides citizens a platform to connect with others, share information, voice their opinions, and achieve a common goal, which in turn are achieved by ensuring open access to all [6]. Thus, the presence of a VSN based public sphere strengthens democracy through open participation [24]. In other words, when there is a public sphere in form of VSNs, citizens have a major role in influencing their government towards development of sound ICT based laws. Further, such a public sphere, not only has the capability to complement the role of e-government in facilitating the development of sophisticated ICT laws but also has the potential to reduce corruption in a country. Taken together, in line with Srivastava's [57] value framework for assessing e-government impact, our study highlights that the impact of e-government maturity in a country on its corruption is not very direct and straightforward; rather, it is contingent on its ICT laws and VSN diffusion.

Our study contributes to the knowledge base of e-government in three key ways. Firstly, our study proposes that there could be important intervening factors between "e-government maturity and corruption" relationship, and identifies ICT laws in a country as one such intervening variable. Through this proposal, we argue that one plausible reason for the mixed findings from the extant studies on e-government and corruption could be due to the lack of focus on intervening factors. Secondly, our study acknowledges the vital role of VSNs in realizing the payoffs from e-government initiatives. By grounding the discussion on Habermasian public sphere, our study established the rediscovery of public sphere through VSNs. To elaborate further, our study is one of the first studies to conceptualize VSNs as a public sphere, and to explore the role of VSN diffusion on e-government outcomes in terms of (1) development of sound ICT based legal framework; and (2) minimizing the corruption. And lastly, our study introduces the concept of public sphere from the reference discipline of political science to information systems, thereby contributing to an inter-disciplinary research.

From a practical standpoint, our study offers several important implications for policy makers. For instance, to effectively use e-government as a tool to combat corruption our study suggests that there is a need for a comprehensive understanding of the phenomenon. That is, knowledge about intervening variables in terms of ICT laws between e-government maturity and corruption would give policy makers an idea about reducing corruption through e-government. Further, our study highlights the complementary role of VSNs for realizing the benefits from e-government initiatives.

This study is not without its limitations. First, we used archival data to arrive at the findings. Though secondary data we used in our study were from reputed sources, primary data would have enabled a better control over the definition and operationalization of variables. Second, we did not include countries such as North Korea and Hong Kong in our analyses, as the data pertaining to these countries were not available in the reports we used. Third, while we acknowledge the possible roles of other intervening factors, we limited our efforts and attention to only one variable namely, ICT laws in a country. Future research may look into other intervening variables such as administrative efficiency and governance, among others. Also, there are studies, which shows the reverse causal relationship between corruption and e-government maturity (e.g. [37]). The influence of VSN diffusion on this relationship may be explored in future research. And lastly, while our study utilized data from different years for each variable and had considered the effect lag, future research may focus on doing a longitudinal study with panel data.

6 Concluding Remarks

The relationship between e-government and corruption, though an active area of research, is underexplored and less understood. In this study, we examined the possibility of ICT laws as an intervening factor alongside the role of VSNs in influencing e-government outcomes. Specifically, our findings depict that the VSN diffusion in a country has the potential to strengthen the negative relationship of (1) e-government maturity with ICT laws; (2) ICT laws with corruption. Further, our study acknowledges the capability of VSNs in facilitating the rediscovery of public sphere as conceptualized by Habermas.

References

1. Abu-Shanab, E.A., Harb, Y.A., Al-Zoubi, S.Y.: E-government as an anti-corruption tool: citizens perceptions. Int. J. Electron. Gov. **6**(3), 232–248 (2013)
2. Ahn, M.J., Bretschneider, S.: Politics of e-government: e-government and the political control of bureaucracy. Public Adm. Rev. **71**(3), 414–424 (2011)
3. Aiken, L.S., West, S.G., Reno, R.R.: Multiple Regression: Testing and Interpreting Interactions, 1st edn. Sage Publications, Thousand Oaks (1991)
4. Banerjee, P., Chau, P.Y.K.: An evaluative framework for analysing e-government convergence capability in developing countries. Electron. Gov. Int. J. **1**(1), 29–48 (2004)
5. Barr, A., Serra, D.: Corruption and culture: an experimental analysis. J. Public Econ. **94**(11–12), 862–869 (2010)
6. Bertot, J.C., Jaeger, P.T., Grimes, J.M.: Using ICTs to create a culture of transparency: e-government and social media as openness and anti-corruption tools for societies. Gov. Inf. Q. **27**(3), 264–271 (2010)
7. Bhatnagar, S.: E-government and access to information. Glob. Corruption Rep. **2003**, 24–32 (2003)
8. Bhattacherjee, A., Shrivastava, U.: The effects of ICT use and ICT Laws on corruption: a general deterrence theory perspective. Gov. Inf. Q. **35**(4), 703–712 (2018)
9. Burstein, P.: Public opinion, demonstrations, and the passage of antidiscrimination legislation. Public Opin. Q. **43**(2), 157–172 (1979)
10. Camaj, L.: From 'window dressing' to 'door openers'? Freedom of Information legislation, public demand, and state compliance in South East Europe. Gov. Inf. Q. **33**(2), 346–357 (2016)
11. Charoensukmongkol, P., Moqbel, M.: Does investment in ICT curb or create more corruption? A cross-country analysis. Public Organ. Rev. **14**(1), 51–63 (2014)

12. Chawla, R., Bhatnagar, S.: Online delivery of land titles to rural farmers in Karnataka, India. In: Scaling Up Poverty Reduction: A Global Learning Process and Conference, pp. 25–27. The World Bank, Shanghai (2004)
13. Cho, Y.H., Choi, B.D.: E-government to combat corruption: the case of Seoul metropolitan government. Int. J. Public Adm. **27**(10), 719–735 (2004)
14. Cohen, J., Cohen, P., West, S.G., Aiken, L.S.: Applied Multiple Regression/Correlation Analysis for the Behavioral Sciences, 3rd edn. Lawrence Erlbaum Associates, New Jersey (1983)
15. Costanza-Chock, S.: The immigrant rights movement on the net: between web 2.0 and communication popular. Am. Q. **60**(3), 851–864 (2008)
16. Elbahnasawy, N.G.: E-government, internet adoption, and corruption: an empirical investigation. World Dev. **57**, 114–126 (2014)
17. Facebook Company Info. https://newsroom.fb.com/company-info. Accessed 30 Mar 2019
18. Flak, L.S., Dertz, W., Jansen, A., Krogstie, J., Spjelkavik, I., Ølnes, S.: What is the value of e-government–and how can we actually realize it? Transform. Gov.: People Process Policy **3** (3), 220–226 (2009)
19. Fox, J.: Regression Diagnostics, 1st edn. Sage Publications, Newbury Park (1991)
20. Garcia-Murillo, M.: Does a government web presence reduce perceptions of corruption? Inf. Technol. Dev. **19**(2), 151–175 (2013)
21. Gilbert, D., Balestrini, P., Littleboy, D.: Barriers and benefits in the adoption of e-government. Int. J. Public Sector Manag. **17**(4/5), 286–301 (2004)
22. Gujarati, D.N.: Basic Econometrics, 3rd edn. Tata McGraw-Hill Education, New York (2009)
23. Habermas, J.: The Structural Transformation of the Public Sphere, 1st edn. MIT Press, Cambridge (1989)
24. Habermas, J., Lennox, S., Lennox, F.: The public sphere: an encyclopedia article (1964). New German Critique **3**, 49–55 (1974)
25. Hair, J.F., Black, W.C., Babin, B.J., Anderson, R.E., Tatham, R.L.: Multivariate Data Analysis, 6th edn. Pearson Prentice Hall, Uppersaddle River (2006)
26. Halpern, D., Gibbs, J.: Social media as a catalyst for online deliberation? Exploring the affordances of Facebook and YouTube for political expression. Comput. Hum. Behav. **29**(3), 1159–1168 (2013)
27. Hampton, K.N., Lee, C., Her, E.J.: How new media affords network diversity: direct and mediated access to social capital through participation in local social settings. New Media Soc. **13**(7), 1031–1049 (2011)
28. Hayes, A.F.: Introduction to Mediation, Moderation, and Conditional Process Analysis: A Regression-Based Approach, 2nd edn. Guilford Publications, New York (2017)
29. Heeks, R.: Information technology and public sector corruption. Information Systems for Public Sector Management Working Paper No. 4 (1998)
30. Heidenheimer, A.J.: The topography of corruption: explorations in a comparative perspective. Int. Soc. Sci. J. **48**(149), 337–347 (1996)
31. Ho, A.T.: Reinventing local governments and the e-government initiative. Public Adm. Rev. **62**(4), 434–444 (2002)
32. Holden, S.H., Norris, D.F., Fletcher, P.D.: Electronic government at the local level: progress to date and future issues. Public Perform. Manag. Rev. **26**(4), 325–344 (2003)
33. Howard, P.N., Duffy, A., Freelon, D., Hussain, M.M., Mari, W., Maziad, M.: Opening closed regimes: what was the role of social media during the Arab Spring? Social Science Research Network (2011). SSRN: https://ssrn.com/abstract=2595096 or http://dx.doi.org/10.2139/ssrn.2595096
34. Husted, B.W.: Wealth, culture, and corruption. J. Int. Bus. Stud. **30**(2), 339–359 (1999)

35. Hwang, M.S., Li, C.T., Shen, J.J., Chu, Y.P.: Challenges in e-government and security of information. Inf. Secur. **15**(1), 9–20 (2004)
36. Kaplan, A.M., Haenlein, M.: Users of the world, unite! The challenges and opportunities of social media. Bus. Horiz. **53**(1), 59–68 (2010)
37. Khan, A., Krishnan, S.: Conceptualizing the impact of corruption in national institutions and national stakeholder service systems on e-government maturity. Int. J. Inf. Manag. **46**, 23–36 (2019)
38. Kiecolt, K.J., Nathan, L.E.: Secondary Analysis of Survey Data, 1st edn. Sage Publications, New Delhi (1985)
39. Kim, S., Kim, H.J., Lee, H.: An institutional analysis of an e-government system for anti-corruption: the case of OPEN. Gov. Inf. Q. **26**(1), 42–50 (2009)
40. Krishnan, S., Lymm, J.: Determinants of virtual social networks diffusion: insights from cross-country data. Comput. Hum. Behav. **54**, 691–700 (2016)
41. Krishnan, S., Teo, T.S.H., Lim, V.K.G.: Examining the relationships among e-government maturity, corruption, economic prosperity and environmental degradation: a cross-country analysis. Inf. Manag. **50**(8), 638–649 (2013)
42. Layne, K., Lee, J.: Developing fully functional e-government: a four stage model. Gov. Inf. Q. **18**(2), 122–136 (2001)
43. Lee, J.: 10 year retrospect on stage models of e-government: a qualitative meta-synthesis. Gov. Inf. Q. **27**(3), 220–230 (2010)
44. Lee, G., Kwak, Y.H.: An open government maturity model for social media-based public engagement. Gov. Inf. Q. **29**(4), 492–503 (2012)
45. Lio, M.C., Liu, M.C., Ou, Y.P.: Can the internet reduce corruption? A cross-country study based on dynamic panel data models. Gov. Inf. Q. **28**(1), 47–53 (2011)
46. Nyman-Metcalf, K.: e-Governance in law and by law. In: Kerikmäe, T. (ed.) Regulating eTechnologies in the European Union, pp. 33–51. Springer, Cham (2014). https://doi.org/10.1007/978-3-319-08117-5_3
47. Panagiotopoulos, P., Bigdeli, A.Z., Sams, S.: Citizen–government collaboration on social media: the case of Twitter in the 2011 riots in England. Gov. Inf. Q. **31**(3), 349–357 (2014)
48. Panteli, N.: Virtual social networks: a new dimension for virtuality research. In: Panteli, N. (ed.) Virtual Social Networks, pp. 1–17. Palgrave Macmillan UK, London (2009). https://doi.org/10.1057/9780230250888_1
49. Papadopoulou, P., Nikolaidou, M., Martakos, D.: What is trust in e-government? A proposed typology. In: 2010 43rd Hawaii International Conference on System Sciences, pp. 1–10. IEEE (2010)
50. Parent, M., Vandebeek, C.A., Gemino, A.C.: Building citizen trust through e-government. Gov. Inf. Q. **22**(4), 720–736 (2005)
51. Picci, L.: The quantitative evaluation of the economic impact of e-government: a structural modelling approach. Inf. Econ. Policy **18**(1), 107–123 (2006)
52. Preacher, K.J., Hayes, A.F.: Asymptotic and resampling strategies for assessing and comparing indirect effects in multiple mediator models. Behav. Res. Methods **40**(3), 879–891 (2008)
53. Robertson, C.J., Watson, A.: Corruption and change: the impact of foreign direct investment. Strateg. Manag. J. **25**(4), 385–396 (2004)
54. Shaw, M.: Crime, police and public in transitional societies. Transform. Crit. Perspect. South. Afr. **49**(1), 1–24 (2002)
55. Shelley, L.I.: Crime and corruption in the digital age. J. Int. Aff. **51**(2), 605–620 (1998)
56. Siau, K., Long, Y.: Synthesizing e-government stage models - a meta-synthesis based on meta-ethnography approach. Ind. Manag. Data Syst. **105**(3/4), 443–458 (2005)

57. Srivastava, S.C.: Is e-government providing the promised returns? A value framework for assessing e-government impact. Transform. Gov.: People Process Policy **5**(2), 107–113 (2011)
58. Teo, T.S.H., Srivastava, S.C., Jiang, L.: Trust and electronic government success: an empirical study. J. Manag. Inf. Syst. **25**(3), 99–132 (2008)
59. TI: TI Source Book (2000). https://www.transparency.org.nz/…/2000/Elements-of-a-National-Integrity-System.pdf. Accessed 30 Mar 2019
60. Tolbert, C.J., Mossberger, K.: The effects of e-government on trust and confidence in government. Public Adm. Rev. **66**(3), 354–369 (2006)
61. Turow, J., Hennessy, M.: Internet privacy and institutional trust: insights from a national survey. New Media Soc. **9**(2), 300–318 (2007)
62. UN: Information and Communication Technology Policy and Legal Issues for Central Asia (2007). http://www.unece.org/info/ece-homepage.html. Accessed 30 Mar 2019
63. UN.: The United Nations E-Government Survey (2012). https://publicadministration.un.org/egovkb/en-us/reports/un-e-government-survey-2012. Accessed 30 Mar 2019
64. Uslaner, E.M.: Trust and corruption. In: The New Institutional Economics of Corruption, pp. 90–106. Routledge (2004)
65. Von Haldenwang, C.: Electronic government (e-government) and development. Eur. J. Dev. Res. **16**(2), 417–432 (2004)
66. WEFGITR: The global information technology report 2016. World Economic Forum, vol. 1. Citeseer (2016). www3.weforum.org/docs/GITR2016/WEF_GITR_Full_Report.pdf. Accessed 30 Mar 2019
67. Welch, E.W., Wong, W.: Global information technology pressure and government accountability: the mediating effect of domestic context on website openness. J. Public Adm. Res. Theor. **11**(4), 509–539 (2001)
68. Wescott, C.G.: E-government in the Asia-pacific region. Asian J. Polit. Sci. **9**(2), 1–24 (2001)
69. Wilson, C., Dunn, A.: The Arab Spring| Digital media in the Egyptian revolution: descriptive analysis from the Tahrir data set. Int. J. Commun. **5**, 25 (2011)
70. Wimmer, M., Codagnone, C.: Roadmapping e-Government: Research Visions and Measures Towards Innovative Governments in 2020. eGovRTD2020 Project Consortium, Clusone (2007)
71. Woszczynski, A.B., Whitman, M.E.: The problem of common method variance in IS research. In: The Handbook of Information Systems Research, pp. 66–78. IGI Global (2004)
72. Yang, K., Callahan, K.: Citizen involvement efforts and bureaucratic responsiveness: participatory values, stakeholder pressures, and administrative practicality. Public Adm. Rev. **67**(2), 249–264 (2007)
73. Zhao, F.: An empirical study of cultural dimensions and e-government development: implications of the findings and strategies. Behav. Inf. Technol. **32**(3), 294–306 (2013)

Antecedents of Optimal Information Security Investment: IT Governance Mechanism and Organizational Digital Maturity

Samuel Okae[1], Francis Kofi Andoh-Baidoo[2(✉)], and Emmanuel Ayaburi[2]

[1] Nobel International Business School, Accra, Ghana
[2] University of Texas Rio Grande Valley, 1201 W University Dr, Edinburg, TX 78539, USA
francis.andohbaidoo@utrgv.edu

Abstract. Information security risk is of concern to both researchers and practitioners. In this study, we investigate the antecedents of optimal information security investment from organizational perspective using the concept of information technology governance. Specifically, we examine how board attributes including IT savviness, board duality, experience, and functional debate along with an organizational attribute, digital maturity, influence optimal information security investments. Data was collected from board members in organization to test the research model. Our results offer both theoretical and practical implications.

Keywords: Digital-maturity · Board · Dysfunctional · Duality · IT-savviness · Optimal security investment

1 Introduction

Information security incidents worldwide have attracted attention of organizations and researchers since the effects on the associated institutions are disastrous (Kozak 2005). The 2014 JPMorgan Chase data breach is a classic case of a disastrous information security incident. This attack is believed to have compromised over 83 million of the bank's accounts affecting 76 million households and 7 million businesses in the United States (Ponemon Institute 2015). Addressing information security risks demands making optimal security investments in key technologies to protect the organization. Prior studies that have examined optimal information security investments employed analytical methods (e.g., Gordon and Loeb 2002; Huang et al. 2006) with little emphasis on how organizational factors such as governance culture may play a critical role. Specifically, little is known about which attributes of organization's governing board affect how funds are allocated for security investment.

Board IT governance has been found to be critical for the success of information security programs (FFIEC 2017). Board IT governance involves the decision and strategy of board of directors in ensuring that they distribute firm resources judiciously (Heenetigala 2011). Board of directors needs to ensure resources available to the firm

Published by Springer Nature Switzerland AG 2019
Y. Dwivedi et al. (Eds.): TDIT 2019, IFIP AICT 558, pp. 442–453, 2019.
https://doi.org/10.1007/978-3-030-20671-0_30

are distributed in a manner that will yield optimal results to serve organizational aims and objectives. In deciding how firm's resources are to be distributed, the board must consider the extent to which organizational resources should be invested in critical functions such as information security. Board with inadequate information security knowledge, may ask the wrong question about IT risks and expense (Nolan and McFarlan 2005). This ultimately makes the board incapable of fulfilling their oversight responsibilities, exposing the firm to security threats. Given that the characteristics of the board are likely to affect the decisions they make, this issue bears an examination (Zahra and Pearce 1989). Thus, the purpose of the current study is to investigate which Board IT governance and organizational attributes influence optimal information security investment. We argue in this study that, having a well composed IT savvy board of directors could be one way to improve the board's decision-making regarding information security investment.

To investigate the research problem, we deploy the concept of Board IT governance (Jewer and McKay 2012), to develop a model that explicates antecedents to optional IT security investment. Data was collected from the upper level managers in the banking industry in a developing country to test the model. The financial industry is a suitable target for most hackers and cyber criminals, and the industry has experienced increased average cost of information security data breach (Mohammed 2017). The results of our analysis demonstrate that while digital maturity plays an important role in firms' decision to invest in optimal information systems not all characteristics of the board members are a good predictor of such a decision. Based on our results, we offer both theoretical and practical investments.

2 Theoretical Foundation and Hypotheses

Some scholars have studied information security investments with the focus on optimal investment. Gordon and Loeb (2002) address information security investments by building a model that helps to determine how much organizations must invest in information security. Huang et al. (2006) also developed a model for information security investments that deal with simultaneous attacks from multiple external sources. These studies employed analytical models. However, to make the necessary investment in IT, the board needs to be convinced. Several economic, strategic, technological, operational, and environmental factors inform firms' decision to invest in information security (Gordon and Loeb 2002). The economic or financial factors consider the budgetary allocations firms are ready and are able to make considering the structures at risk of being corrupted or lost if such actions are not taken to protect them in the short to long term (Johnson 2009). The organizational factors consider firms' contextual view prompting their investments in information security. The firm's organizational factors also consider operational factors that look at how existing and new IT structures will be used strategically, either exploratively or exploitatively in the protection of clients' and firms' information. The technological factors look at the technological capability of firms, the human resources available to operate and maintain information security structures when investments are made in this area (Tatsumi and Goto 2010). The environmental factors affecting investment in information security include firms' identified strengths, weaknesses, threats and identified opportunities when investment is made in information security investment. However, the human factor is considered a critical management input necessary for effective information security (Soomro et al. 2016; Chang and Ho 2006). This study investigates how a management factor, Board IT governance, influence optimal IT investment from governance perspective.

Board Information Technology Governance

Board governance makes up the integral part of corporate governance by implementing processes, relational mechanisms, and structures within the firm which allow individuals to execute their expectations in backing up IT business value (Wilkin and Chenhall 2010). Most organizations have IT governance. However, institutions with efficient governance team have set of active IT structural mechanisms such as committees, procedures and plans which are consistent in promoting actions in line with the firms' strategies and values. Board Information Technology governance refers to current and formal frameworks which provide structures to ensure that IT investment strategy is aligned with organizational strategy (Pereira and Da Silva 2012). IT governance is a structure of technologically based institutional arrangements that affects the decision-making and the framework adopted by the institutions. It emerged as a fundamental business imperative because it is key to realizing the value of IT in today's business. IT governance must consider and implement the most effective and secure structure for its effectiveness. It should adopt a defined process as any undefined actions lead to vulnerability of the system to attackers. Using Board IT governance as the theoretical basis, Jewer and McKay (2012) examine how board attributes, a governance mechanism, influence organizational strategic choice. The board attributes investigated include proportion of insiders, board size and board IT competence. In this study, we use board composition (duality, dysfunctional level of debate, and experience of board members) and IT savviness to represent proportion of insiders and board IT competence respectively. Board IT governance is the system and procedure put in place to ensure that an organization is efficient in the application of IT, in achieving the set objectives of an organization OECD (2004). IT governance considers oversight processes and the responsibilities of the management (Brisebois et al. 2007). Most organizations approach IT governance from the perspective of tool or procedures (Allen 2005). Allen (2005) argues that the likelihood of the success of IT governance procedures largely depends on certain principles. One of these identified principles is executive support. The support of the board is fundamental to the success of launching an idea in the organization. The initiatives that are adopted are often because the board can relate the IT initiative to organizational goals and appreciate how such initiative will be beneficial to the organization (OECD 2004). Another factor is the composition of the board which includes experience, duality and functional debate of the board members (Zahra and Pearce 1989).

Practical board IT governance sets apart unique assets in the firm for IT use and at the same time ensures that the organization complies with the overall principles of mission and vision. In this regard, a firm with efficient IT governance will ensure that its personnel have IT skills, IT processes, IT knowledge assets and experience. Though there is a strong argument for more board involvement in IT governance, Andriole (2009) found that boards of directors were alarmingly uninvolved in the planning or oversight of technological initiatives and were increasingly out of the loop with regards to these initiatives. The study found that because of this the various boards included in the study were missing prospects to enhance and optimize their technological investments. For IT issues, boards should be involved in decision making especially on the systems that the company uses. This study seeks to determine how IT governance structures and processes influence the relationship between board composition and information security investments. Specifically, we investigate significant organizational strategic choice, optimal security investment decision which comprises economic or financial factors considered in the budgetary allocations firms make with regard to the structures at risk of being corrupted or lost if such actions are not taken to protect them in the short to long term (Johnson 2009). Organizations with effective IT governance are likely to carve out competitive advantage regarding technological decisions (Allen 2005). According to Weill (2004), most organizations have information Technology governance. However, institutions with efficient governance team have set of active information technology structural mechanisms such as committees, procedures and plans which are consistent in promoting actions in line with the firms' strategies and values (Weill 2004).

Board's IT Savviness and Optimal Information Security Investment

Board IT savviness can be described as the level of IT knowledge possessed by board members. An IT-savvy board is considered to have enough technical knowledge regarding IT issues. This study proposes that more IT savviness of board members improves the board's understanding and appreciation of technological issue particularly in the domain of information security and would thus be able to make good information security investment decisions. Ensuring a more efficient and effective IT governance structures and information security investments would be easier if the board, who control the organization's resources and set policy, were IT savvy. Harrison et al. (1997) found that the executives' perceptions of the usefulness of IT initiatives was a major factor in their decision making. However, it can be argued that without enough level of literacy, it would be difficult for a board member to appreciate that usefulness or benefits of information security initiatives and how investing in them could assist in achieving the organizations' strategic goals. IT savviness, also referred to as IT competence (Jewer and McKay 2012), can be considered as an attribute of board members that would impact their decision making particularly regarding IT related issues. IT experience at the board level can help guide management through changes in the business environment. It would be prudent for firms to have IT-savvy members on the board to enrich boardroom discussion on IT investments (Nolan and McFarlan 2005). By asking the appropriate questions, directors can make the right decisions to improve their businesses and protect the company's integrity and brand. Thus, we posit that:

H_1: Board IT savviness has a positive effect on optimal information security investments.

Board Composition and Optimal Information Security Investment

Another board characteristic that could potentially influence members' decision making is the composition of the board. Board composition factors such as experience, duality and level of functional debate play a critical role in its governance culture (Zahra and

Pearce 1989). Our first board composition factor, Board duality, is a corporate leadership structure that merges the position of board chair and CEO. A single person holding both the Chairman and CEO role improves the value of a firm as the agency cost between the two is eliminated (Wang et al. 2019). However, CEO duality can lead to worse performance as the board cannot remove an underperforming CEO and can create an agency cost if the CEO pursues his own interest at the cost of the shareholders. Hermalin and Weisbach (1988) argue that often the context or environment that the company finds itself in will determine the extent of board duality. Their findings showed that firms tended to recruit directors from within the firm when a CEO was nearing the end of his or her tenure and often chose a new CEO from the new batch of a board member. On the other hand, their study found that when a firm or organization had had to withdraw from a market or was performing poorly, board members tended to be recruited from outside the organization. There is still debate in the literature about the effectiveness of outsider-dominated boards against insider-dominated boards. This study examines the role that duality plays in influencing the optimal information security investment.

The second component of board composition that this study will considere is the level of debate which Forbes and Milliken (1999) describe as board cohesiveness. The authors define this as the board members' ability to work with each other and their motivation to remain on the board. This refers to the level of affection or level of willingness to work together. For the purposes of this study, high levels of cohesiveness will be considered functional debate. Gabrielsson et al. (2007) argue that board members tend to make more meaningful contribution when in situations of high cohesion since they believe their inputs are valued than when faced with situations of low cohesion among the board members.

The final component of board composition considered in this study is experience. The literature generally agrees that the experience of board members is an important factor that influences the positions that board members take and the choices they make when faced with strategic and policy decisions (Westphal and Milton 2000). The experience of individual board members acts as a mix of competencies and capabilities that help in executing the governance function. Therefore, putting together we posit that:

H_{2A}: The duality of the board members has a positive effect on optimal information security investments.

H_{2B}: The level of functional debate among board members has a positive effect on optimal information security investments.

H_{2C}: The experience of the board members has a positive effect on information security investments.

Digital Maturity and Optimal Information Security Investment

Digital maturity of a firm is the degree to which the firm has used technology and its capabilities to engage its employees, enhanced its operation and develop new business (Kane et al. 2017). Digital maturity enables an organization to deploy digital innovations and to achieve enterprise-wide transformation (Kane et al. 2015). Digital maturity measures the intensity at which digital technologies are deployed in an organization and how leadership and employees are transformed through the creation of management capabilities that effectively facilitate digital transformation (Valentine and Stewart 2015). Digital maturity dictates the need to invest in innovative information technologies and build competencies in IT skills, IT knowledge and to transform business processes. An organization's digital maturity will influence how information security risks are addressed through the right information security investments even as they continue to deploy innovative technologies. Hence considering digital maturity as a valuable resource it will influence the extent to which limited resources are dedicated to information security. Thus, we posit that:

H3: The degree of digital maturity of the firm is positively related to optimal investments in information security positively.

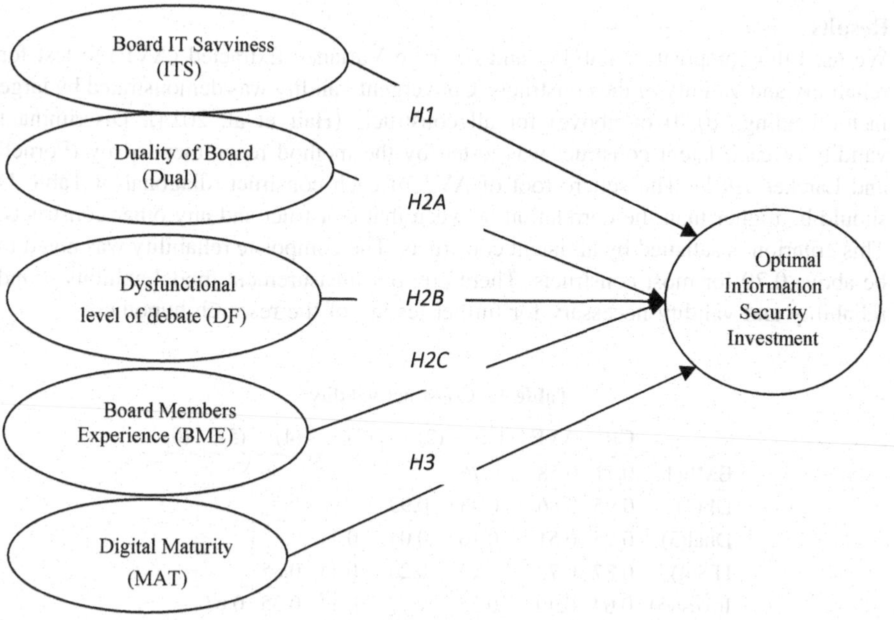

Fig. 1. Research model

3 Methodology

Measures and Sample

This study was conducted using a survey research design. The target population of the study comprises of individuals who are part of the top management team in their organization. The actions of top management are affected by decisions of board managements. These individuals have huge responsibilities in deciding how the firms' resources are utilized and are task with protecting investors. Our sample included 100 respondents. The sampling techniques used in this study are cluster sampling, convenient sampling, and snowball sampling approach. The current study used prior validated measures; Digital Maturity (MAT), Board Members Experience (BME),

Dysfunctional level of debate (DF), Duality of Board (Dual), Board IT Savviness (ITS) and optimal security investment (Massey and Dawes 2007).

Analysis

The Structural Equation Modeling (SEM) was used to investigate the casual paths hypothesized in this study. A two-step approach was used to analyze the data. In the first step, the covariance-based technique was used to assess the appropriateness of the measurement model. The covariance-based technique was used as it minimizes the differences between the covariance of the collected sample and that of the ones predicted by the model and reproduces the covariance matrix of the observable variable (Chin and Newsted 1999). For testing the structural model, Variance based partial least square (PLS) SEM was used as it maximizes the variance of the dependent variable which is explained by the independent variables (Hair et al. 2014).

Results

We used the composite reliability and Average Variance Extracted (AVE) to test for reliability and validity of the constructs. Convergent validity was demonstrated by large factor loadings (0.70 or above) for all constructs (Hair et al. 2014). Discriminant validity of each latent construct was tested by the method recommended by (Fornell and Larcker 1981). The square root of AVE of each construct (diagonal of Table 1) should be higher than the correlation between that construct and any other constructs. This criterion is satisfied by all latent constructs. The composite reliability was noted to be above 0.70 for most constructs. Therefore, our measurement model exhibits sound reliability and validity necessary for further testing of the research hypotheses.

Table 1. Construct validity

	CR	AVE	(1)	(2)	(3)	(4)	(5)	(6)
BME(1)	0.71	0.58	0.76					
DF(2)	0.95	0.86	−0.43	0.93				
Dual(3)	0.75	0.51	−0.16	0.04	0.71			
ITS(4)	0.87	0.72	0.23	−0.20	−0.11	0.85		
Invest(5)	0.64	0.40	0.35	−0.17	−0.11	0.35	0.63	
MAT(6)	0.83	0.62	0.19	−0.17	−0.04	0.34	0.35	0.78

We conducted model robustness checks for multicollinearity. VIF values for BM (1.29), DF (1.24), Dual (1.04), ITS (1.18) and MAT (1.15) were much less than the threshold of (VIF < 10), indicating absence of multicollinearity problem. In assessment of the explanatory power, our model accounted for about 25% of variance ($R^2 = 0.248$) in explaining the likelihood of making optimal decision in investing in information security in the firm. The Adjusted-R^2 (0.2018) further strengthens the explanatory power as it takes into account our sample size and number of variables in our model (Hair et al. 2014). Summary of the hypotheses testing are depicted in Table 2 and Fig. 2.

Table 2. Results

Path	Coef.	t-Stat	*P* Values	Supported?
BME -> Invest	0.271	1.988	0.047	Yes
DF -> Invest	0.031	0.247	0.805	No
Dual -> Invest	−0.035	0.246	0.806	No
ITS -> Invest	0.207	2.052	0.040	Yes
MAT -> Invest	0.234	2.093	0.037	Yes

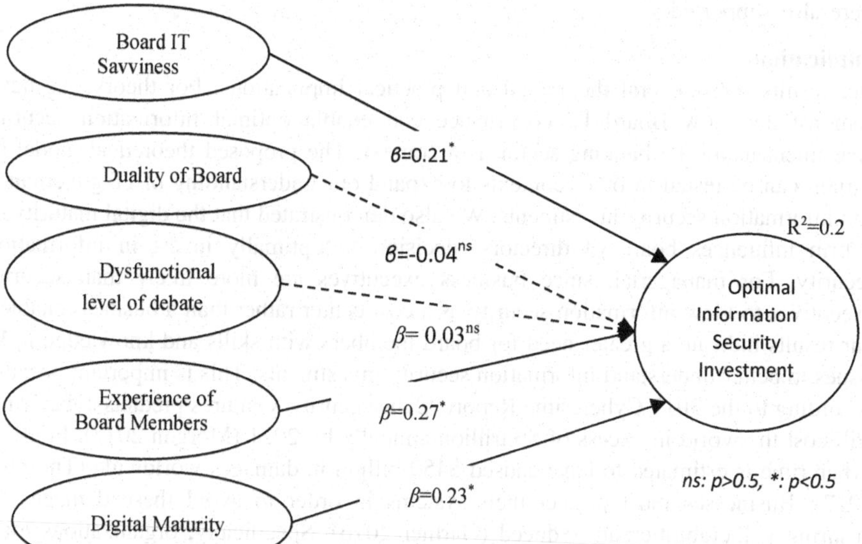

Fig. 2. Model results

As hypothesized, BME was shown to be a good predictor of optimal investment in information systems security (β = 0.27*, p < 0.05; t = 1.99), as well as the hypothesized positive relationship between ITS and MAT and optimal investment in information systems security (β = 0.21, p < 0.05; t = 2.05 and β = 0.23, p < 0.05; t = 2.09 respectively). However, no support was found for the relationship between DF and Dual, and optimal investment in information security (β = 0.03, p > 0.05; t = 0.25 and β = 0.04, p > 0.05; t = 0.25 respectively).

Discussion and Future Research Direction

The advancement of information technology (IT) has brought about rapid changes in businesses operations. However, the use of IT is associated with information risks (Dangolani 2011). Information security risk is defined in this study as the risk that arises when the firm's information assets and information systems are not protected sufficiently against various kinds of damage or loss (Straub and Welke 1998). Board of board have responsibility to provide resources to ensure that information security risks are minimized. However, to ensure the growth of businesses, corporate boards need to make concerted effort to distribute their resources judiciously. This calls for optimal information security investment. We argue that board characteristics (IT Savviness, composition) and organizational digital maturity will influence organization's optimal information security investments. Only one of the hypotheses relating the dimensions of board composition, i.e., experience was supported. Level of functional debate and duality of board members were not supported. Both IT savviness and digital maturity were also supported.

Implication

Our results offer several theoretical and practical implications. For theory, we have demonstrated how Board IT governance can enable optimal information security investment using the banking sector as a context. The proposed theoretical model or variant can be tested in other contexts to expand our understanding of IT governance and information security investments. We also demonstrated that the digital maturity of a firm influences board of directors' decision to optimally invest in information security. For managerial, since business executives are more likely than security executives to view information security as a cost center rather than a business enabler, our results indicate a greater need for board members with skills and knowledge in IT issues to better understand information security investments. This is important because according to the 2017 Cybercrime Report, Cybersecurity Ventures predicts cybercrime will cost the world in excess of $6 trillion annually by 2021 (Morgan 2017). In 2017, cybercrime is estimated to have caused $450 billion in damages worldwide (Thornton 2017). Businesses must protect their systems in order to avoid these damages by ensuring vulnerabilities are reduced (Gartner 2016). Specifically, organizations must consciously invest in various security technologies such as data loss prevention, spyware detection, removal applications and cryptographic techniques to protect systems, data and processes against technical failure, damage or attacks (Gartner 2016). Second, in general, the study highlights the need for more dialogue and information sharing between security executives, who are responsible for designing the organization's security infrastructure, and business executives who must allocate the funds to support that infrastructure. For example, in 2016, Thomson Reuters (2015) reported that the U. S. government had reserved $14 billion of its budget proposal for cybersecurity efforts to protect federal and private networks. Johnson (2009) affirms this and argues that firms invest in information security for different reasons.

Appendix: Crossloadings

	BM	DF	Dual	ITS	Invest	MAT
BME1	0.471	−0.404	−0.035	0.005	0.101	−0.020
BME2	0.969	−0.360	−0.168	0.246	0.361	0.212
DF1	−0.390	0.899	0.041	−0.201	−0.077	−0.088
DF2	−0.420	0.958	0.061	−0.215	−0.193	−0.226
DF3	−0.382	0.920	0.009	−0.132	−0.145	−0.093
DUAL1	−0.120	−0.013	0.755	−0.069	−0.078	−0.010
DUAL2	0.095	−0.136	0.557	−0.066	−0.039	0.042
DUAL4	−0.201	0.127	0.806	−0.106	−0.104	−0.076
INVEST1	0.233	−0.201	−0.128	0.309	0.778	0.286
INVEST3	0.180	−0.192	−0.275	0.031	0.310	−0.014
INVEST5	0.271	0.004	0.040	0.222	0.698	0.269
ITS2	0.166	−0.247	−0.097	0.862	0.294	0.285
ITS4	0.166	−0.194	−0.108	0.887	0.264	0.221
ITS6	0.233	−0.067	−0.090	0.797	0.314	0.342
MAT1	0.267	−0.138	−0.073	0.391	0.383	0.898
MAT3	0.105	−0.172	−0.072	0.181	0.186	0.732
MAT5	−0.045	−0.084	0.088	0.122	0.177	0.710

References

Allen, J.H.: Governing for Enterprise Security (GES), Implementation Guide: Characteristics of Effective Security Governance1, pp. 5–7. Carnegie Mellon University, USA (2005)

Andriole, S.J.: Boards of Directors and Technology Governance: The Surprising State of the Practice Boards of Directors and Technology Governance: The Surprising State of the Practice I. Boards and Technology Governance. Fortune **24**(March), 373–394 (2009)

Brisebois, R., Boyd, G., Shadid, Z.: What is IT Governance and why is it important for the IS auditor. INTOSAI IT J. **25**, 30–35 (2007)

Chang, S.E., Ho, C.B.: Organizational factors to the effectiveness of implementing information security management. Ind. Manag. Data Syst. **106**, 345–361 (2006)

Chin, W.W., Newsted, P.R.: Structural equation modeling analysis with small samples using partial least squares. Stat. Strat. Small Sample Res. **1**(1), 307–341 (1999)

Dangolani, S.K.: The impact of information technology in banking system (A case study in Bank Keshavarzi IRAN). Procedia-Soc. Behav. Sci. **30**, 13–16 (2011)

FFIEC: FFIEC Updates Cybersecurity Expectations for Boards (2017). https://www.bankinfosecurity.com/ffiec-management-booklet-a-8683. Accessed 25 Dec 2017

Forbes, D.P., Milliken, F.J.: Cognition and corporate governance: understanding boards of directors as strategic decision-making groups. Acad. Manag. Rev. **24**(3), 489–505 (1999)

Fornell, C., Larcker, D.F.: Structural equation models with unobservable variables and measurement error: algebra and statistics. J. Mark. Res. **18**, 382–388 (1981)

Gabrielsson, J., Huse, M., Minichilli, A.: Understanding the leadership role of the board chairperson through a team production approach. Int. J. Leadersh. Stud. **3**(1), 21–39 (2007)

Gartner: Magic Quadrant for Content-Aware Data Loss Prevention. G00277564, January 2016
Gordon, L.A., Loeb, M.P.: The economics of information security investment. ACM Trans. Inf. Syst. Secur. **5**(4), 438–457 (2002)
Hair Jr., J.F., Sarstedt, M., Hopkins, L., Kuppelwieser, V.G.: Partial least squares structural equation modeling (PLS-SEM) an emerging tool in business research. Eur. Bus. Rev. **26**(2), 106–121 (2014)
Harrison, D.A., Mykytyn Jr., P.P., Riemenschneider, C.K.: Executive decisions about adoption of information technology in small business: theory and empirical tests. Inf. Syst. Res. **8**(2), 171 (1997)
Heenetigala, K.: Corporate Governance Practices and Firm Performance of Listed Companies in Sri Lanka. Corporate Governance, April (2011)
Hermalin, B.E., Weisbach, M.S.: The determinants of board composition. RAND J. Econ. **19**(4), 589–606 (1988)
Huang, C.D., Hu, Q., Behara, R.S.: Economics of Information Security Investment in the Case of Simultaneous Attacks Economics of Information Security Investment in the Case of Simultaneous Attacks. Information Security (Weis 2006) (2006)
Jewer, J., McKay, K.N.: Antecedents and consequences of board IT governance: Institutional and strategic choice perspectives. J. Assoc. Inf. Syst. **13**(7), 581 (2012)
Johnson, A.M.: Business and security executives views of information security investment drivers: results from a Delphi study. J. Inf. Priv. Secur. **5**(1), 3–27 (2009)
Kane, G.C., Palmer, D., Nguyen-Phillips, A., Kiron, D., Buckley, N.: Achieving digital maturity. MIT Sloan Manag. Rev. **59**(1), 1–31 (2017)
Kane, G.C., Palmer, D., Phillips, A.N., Kiron, D.: Is your business ready for a digital future? MIT Sloan Manag. Rev. **56**(4), 37–44 (2015)
Kozak, S.: The role of information technology in the profit and cost efficiency improvements in the banking sector. J. Acad. Bus. Econ. **2**(1), 34–38 (2005)
Massey, G.R., Dawes, P.L.: The antecedents and consequence of functional and dysfunctional conflict between marketing managers and sales managers. Ind. Mark. Manag. **36**(8), 1118–1129 (2007)
Mohammed, A.A.: Ghanaian Banks Systems at Risk of Cybercrime—Cyber Security Expert (2017)
Morgan, S.: 2017 Cyber Ventures Cybercrime Report. Cybersecurity Ventures, 14 (2017)
Nolan, R., McFarlan, F.: Information technology and the board of directors. Harvard Bus. Rev. **83**(10), 96 (2005)
Organisation for Economic Co-operation and Development: OECD principles of corporate governance [Internet document] (Organisation for Economic Cooperation and Development) (2004). http://www.oecd.org/dataoecd/32/18/31557724.pdf
Pereira, R., da Silva, M.M.: IT governance implementation: The determinant factors. Commun. IBIMA **2012**, 1 (2012)
Ponemon Institute: Cost of Data Breach. Ponemon Institute, pp. 1–30, May 2015
Soomro, Z.A., Shah, M.H., Ahmed, J.: Information security management needs more holistic approach: a literature review. Int. J. Inf. Manag. **36**(2), 215–225 (2016)
Straub, D.W., Welke, R.J.: Coping with systems risk. MIS Q. **22**(404), 441–469 (1998)
Tatsumi, K., Goto, M.: Optimal timing of information security investment: a real options approach. In: Moore, T., Pym, D., Ioannidis, C. (eds.) Economics of Information Security and Privacy, pp. 211–228. Springer, Boston, MA (2010). https://doi.org/10.1007/978-1-4419-6967-5_11
Thornton, G.: Locking down the value of data Contents: Executive summary (2017)

Valentine, E., Stewart, G.: Enterprise business technology governance: three competencies to build board digital leadership capability. In: 2015 48th Hawaii International Conference on System Sciences, pp. 4513–4522. IEEE, January 2015

Wang, G., DeGhetto, K., Ellen, B.P., Lamont, B.T.: Board antecedents of CEO duality and the moderating role of country-level managerial discretion: a meta-analytic investigation. J. Manag. Stud. **56**(1), 172–202 (2019)

Weill, P.: Don't just lead, govern: how top-performing firms govern IT. MIS Q. Exec. **3**(1), 1–17 (2004)

Westphal, J.D., Milton, L.P.: How experience and network ties affect the influence of demographic minorities on corporate boards. Adm. Sci. Q. **45**(2), 366–398 (2000)

Wilkin, C.L., Chenhall, R.H.: A review of IT governance: a taxonomy to inform accounting information systems. J. Inf. Syst. **24**(2), 107–146 (2010)

Zahra, S.A., Pearce, J.A.: Boards of directors and corporate financial performance: a review and integrative model. J. Manag. **15**(2), 291–334 (1989)

Social Media and Open Computing

Social Media Presence & Usage in Indian Business Sector

Anushruti Vagrani, Jenny John, P. Vigneswara Ilavarasan, and Arpan Kumar Kar(✉)

DMS, Indian Institute of Technology, Delhi, India
anushruti.vagrani@dms.iitd.ac.in, jenny.dba@gmail.com, vignes@iitd.ac.in, arpan.kar@dmsiitd.org

Abstract. This research aims to study the interrelated concepts of adoption & usage of social media platforms and extend the discussion towards social media engagement and usage in different business sectors in India. Firms from five industries, banking, information technology, automobiles, telecommunications, and consumer goods in the Bombay Stock Exchange 500 index were selected to study the social media engagement. For all the selected firms the social media presence data was collected from Facebook, Twitter, YouTube, LinkedIn and Instagram. The study indicates a relationship between social media engagement & year-on-year sale variance; whereas different factors affecting the predictability of variance are discussed while replicating the model of corporate social media use. The paper shares implications for marketing professionals and researchers.

Keywords: Social media usage · Degree of social media usage · Social media presence score

1 Introduction

Social media has transformed the Internet from the platforms of information to platforms of influence (Alalwan et al. 2017; Dwivedi et al. 2015; Kapoor et al. 2018; Rathore et al. 2016). The huge user base on a variety of social media platforms has influenced the businesses across a variety of industries as well (Abed et al. 2015a, b; 2016). It was only a few years ago that social media was a place where consumers were speaking extensively whereas not many business firms were at a comfortable space (Kaplan and Haenlein 2010). Today firms do realize that more than just another form of media, social media can be a strategic instrument capable of transforming an organization (Nair 2011). This transition is visible across a variety of businesses that are putting efforts to integrate their business strategies with social media platforms. Social media is useful for companies to generate stakeholder dialogue and engagement as well. Thus, for better communication companies now need to consider social media platforms as well as traditional modes (Hoffman and Fodor 2010).

In this paper, we try to identify the presence of different business sectors on social media platforms. For the study, we select five different platforms namely, Facebook,

Published by Springer Nature Switzerland AG 2019
Y. Dwivedi et al. (Eds.): TDIT 2019, IFIP AICT 558, pp. 457–469, 2019.
https://doi.org/10.1007/978-3-030-20671-0_31

Twitter, YouTube, LinkedIn and Instagram. We study all the firms included in the BSE 500 index from five industries namely banking, information technology, automobiles, telecommunications and consumer goods. To measure the impact of social media, we study the relationship between year-on-year sales variance & social media engagement. While replicating the model of corporate social media use (Aichner and Jacob 2015) for the Indian companies, we use the metrics for social media applications including the number of visits, tags, page views, members/fans, impressions, incoming links, impressions-to-interactions ratio, and the average length of time visitors spend on the website.

2 Research Context

According to Statista report (Statista 2018), India has 19% the share of Internet users visiting social networking sites as on January 2018. Facebook is the leading social media networking site to share user-generated content. India is the leading country based on the number of Facebook users with 250 million users followed by United States & Brazil (Statista 2018a). The country is in the second position in terms of a number of active Twitter users with 10.1 million on monthly active users in 2018 (Statista 2018b), just below the United States. YouTube had 1.47 billion monthly active users. India ranked second with 7.13% of desktop traffic to the website as on December 2017. The United States, which ranked first had 28.35%. India still has a long way to go for the penetration & engagement to the LinkedIn Website. Photo-sharing social media mobile application Instagram is slowing gaining popularity in India.

3 Literature Review

Social media research can be driven based on roots from multiple disciplines that include information systems, social sciences, psychology, and management research. Aral, Dellarocas, and Godes, in their proposed framework for research in social media coin four activities and three levels of analysis to conceptualize social media research landscape (Aral et al. 2013). Social media and user behaviour mostly creating level 'consumers and society' is studied extensively (for instance, Boyd and Ellison 2007; Barker 2009). Adoption, motivation, personality traits of the user are mostly the focus of these studies. Researches around level 'firms and industries' are mostly implication based and draw roots from economics, marketing, strategy and social sciences. Studies suggest a significant effect of social media marketing on brand post popularity, financial, operational, corporate social performance, firm's share value, and customer equity (De Vries et al. 2012; Paniagua and Sapena 2014; Kim and Ko 2012). Researchers have been working on ways to use social media and social media data to the advantage of business decision makers (Hanna et al. 2011; He et al. 2013). In a discussion over ways to measure social media, Nair (2011) describes complexities involved with the decision on time and manner of engagement. Thomas Aichner and Frank Jacob in their paper provide a model that measures social media usage for corporates around the world on different social media platforms (Aichner and Jacob 2015). Aichner & Jacob model can help the organizations to analyze a single brand and to compare with the competitors and the industry average.

Network paradigm is often used to explain a large part of social media space. Studies including the honeycomb of social media (Kietzmann et al. 2011) suggest that it is a complex of individual traits, platform design and features, network effects and desired outcomes that drive the social media space. It is important to understand the cross-disciplinary nature and attend the complexities attached (Aral et al. 2013). The present study focuses on the level of firms and industries and attempts to understand the value derived from social media engagement in terms of year on year sales variance. The extant research indicates a paucity of research on the adoption of social media by Indian businesses (Ilavarasan 2018). Since the potential predictability of the value is subjected to a complex of variable factors, we intend to contextualize the research to the Indian market and understand social media usage through an existing matrix (Aichner and Jacob 2015) This will also help in understanding the requirement and applications of an index for social media usage.

4 Methodology and Data Preparation

We first shortlisted a suitable number of firms for the study. For these selected firms we got details about market capital and year-on-year sale variance. We also captured different parameters depicting social media presence, engagement, and usage on five selected social media platforms. To shortlist firms, we followed a study (Kaushik et al. 2017) that suggests that banking, information technology, automobiles, telecommunications and consumer goods sectors are the five sectors with highest social media score. We then looked at BSE 500 (Bombay Stock Exchange) which is an Indian stock market index that covers 500 publicly listed companies covering all major industries of the Indian Economy. BSE 500 listed firms offer a composite mix of small, medium & large capital market. Therefore, we selected firms from the BSE 500 list that fall under the five sectors namely banking, information technology, automobiles, telecommunications and consumer goods.

This gave us a total of 128 firms for analysis out of which 34 firms are banking sector, 24 are Information Technology, 22 from automobiles, 9 are telecommunications, and 39 firms are consumer goods sector. In terms of market capital, 46 firms belong to large-cap, 49 to mid-cap & 33 to small-cap. We captured market capital and year-on-year sale variance from Ace Equity platform for the month of November 2017. Data regarding social media engagement for all the selected firms were collected in the month of February 2018. The recorded parameters included account availability (1/0) for all the social media platforms, number of followers and posts for Facebook and Instagram, number of posts and tweets for Twitter, number of followers along with a number of employees and number of updates on LinkedIn, number of subscribers and number of videos for YouTube. Based on these we look at the patterns in social media presence and age. We look at social media engagement by performing a simple linear regression analysis to see the predictability of year-on-year sale variance based on social media engagement. We then discuss social media usage based on Aichner and Jacob model.

5 Analysis and Discussion

5.1 Social Media Presence

We looked at the social media presence of these 128 firms on five selected social media platforms Facebook, Twitter, YouTube, LinkedIn and Instagram. Social media accounts that were digitally integrated on the public website of the company only were taken into consideration; this ensured recording data for authentic social media accounts. Social media presence score ranged from 0 to 5 by assigning zero for non-presence and one for presence on each one of the five social media platforms. 92 out of 128 firms had a non-zero score for social media presence; i.e. they showed presence on at least one of the five selected social media platforms. We categorized the score of 0–1 as low, 2–3 as medium, and 4–5 as high. Table 1 shows the industry-wise distribution of firms in low, medium, and high social media presence score categories. The table suggests that 75% out of the firms selected under Information technology have a high social media presence score and have a presence on a variety of social media platforms. For consumer goods and Automobile sector though a larger percentage of the firms have a low social media presence.

Table 1. Industry-wise percentage of social media presence

Social media presence score	Banking (34)	Automobiles (22)	ConsGoods (39)	Info-Tech (24)	Telecom (9)
Low (0–1)	26.4%	45.4%	38.4%	12.5%	33.3%
Medium (2–3)	35.2%	22.7%	46%	12.5%	33.3%
High (4–5)	38.2%	31.8%	15.3%	75%	33.3%

Among the different social media platforms, Facebook and Twitter are most commonly used in general. Instagram is among the lesser used platforms. Table 2 shows social media platform-wise percentage of firms in different sectors considered in the study. 88% of Information technology firms have a social media presence on Twitter, Facebook and LinkedIn. In comparison the presence on Instagram is 8% only.

Table 2. Platform-wise percentage of social media presence of different sectors

Industry sectors	Social presence	Twitter	FB	YouTube	LinkedIn	Instagram
Automobile	64%	59%	55%	45%	32%	18%
Banking	76%	71%	71%	47%	47%	24%
Cons-Goods	64%	49%	56%	38%	26%	15%
Info-Tech	88%	88%	88%	75%	88%	8%
Telecom	67%	67%	67%	44%	44%	11%

5.2 Social Media Age

We looked at the social media age of the firms to understand the social media adoption pattern across different industry and sectors. Twitter and YouTube accounts provide details for joining dates on these platforms. Social media age was calculated starting from the date of joining on either of this platform (considering the earlier joining date in case of presence on both the platforms). Out of the 92 firms with non-zero SM presence score, five firms did not have accounts on either of these platforms. For the rest of the firms, Table 3 summarizes the social media age across different market capital segments. The table shows that large capital market companies were among the early adopters of the social media platform, while medium and small-scale sectors are increasingly showing a presence in later times. Till the year 2008, no small and medium market capital firm had a presence on these major social media platforms. Later years show a speedy change in a scenario with some young small and medium sector firms on different social media platforms.

Table 3. Social media age: joining period of firms from different market capital

Market capital (No. of firms on SM)	Mar '16–18	Mar '14–16	Mar '12–14	Mar '10–12	Mar '08–10	Mar '06–08
Small (33)	21	17	16	10	5	0
Medium (49)	30	24	19	14	4	0
Large (46)	36	36	31	22	11	4

Further Table 4 categorizes firms in different business sectors according to their social media age and shows that the early adoption of social media was by Banking & Information Technology sectors. Consumer goods firms are increasingly realizing and opting for different social media platforms.

Table 4. Social media age: joining period of firms from different sectors

Industry (No. of firms on SM)	Mar '16–18	Mar '14–16	Mar '12–14	Mar '10–12	Mar '08–10	Mar '06–08
Automobiles (22)	13	12	11	6	1	0
Banking (34)	24	19	14	9	3	2
Cons-Goods (39)	23	21	17	9	2	0
InfoTech (24)	21	21	20	18	12	2
Telecom (9)	6	4	4	4	2	0

5.3 Social Media Engagement

More than mere presence, the power of social media is driven by the number of people one can connect with using the platform. We explore the social media engagement of all the selected firms to explore people's response to their social media activities. When a company posts on social media, the responses in terms of 'likes', 'comments', the number of 'followers' and 'subscribers' show the extent of engagement.

$$\mathit{Social\ Media\ Engagement\ (Company)} = \frac{\sum \mathit{Number\ of\ posts/video/texts\ on\ all\ platforms}}{\sum \mathit{Number\ of\ followers/subcriber\ on\ all\ platforms}}$$

Since corporate social media engagement comes with some set objectives, measuring the output becomes important (Hanna et al. 2011). In this study, we consider output in terms of year on year sale variance. For all the selected firms from BSE500, year on year sales data was collected from AceEquity platform for November 2017. And data regarding social media engagement for all the selected firms were collected in February 2018 by recording parameters listed in previous sections. A regression analysis was done to see if there is a significant relation between social media engagement and year on year sales variance for a firm.

Ho: There is no relationship between social media engagement & year-on-year sale variance

H1: There is a relationship between social media engagement & year-on-year sale variance

Linear Regression Based on YoY Sales and Social Media Engagement Result
Simple linear regression was calculated to predict year-on-year sale variance based on social media engagement. A significant regression equation was found with ($F(1,82) = 4.578$, $p < 0.035$), with a R2 of 0.05. Null Hypothesis is rejected since p-value is less than 0.05 (Table 5). This implies a significant relationship between social media engagement & year-on-year sale variance. However, the low R2 suggests that according to this model, it is difficult to precisely predict year on year sales variance based on social media engagement.

Table 5. Regression analysis

Coefficients:	Estimate	Std. Error	t value	Pr(> |t|)
(Intercept)	1.507	3.227	0.467	0.6419
SM engagement	7.212	3.371	2.14	0.0354
Multiple R-squared: 0.05288		Adjusted R-squared: 0.04133		
F-statistic: 4.578 on 1 and 82 DF		p-value: 0.03536		

Possible reasons here can be corporate social media usage since different social media platform do not serve the same objective (For instance, YouTube could be used for product promotion videos; Twitter helps to get feedback from the customers), therefore, it is important to set the right objectives focusing on the right kind of social media platform. The next section focuses on social media usage by Indian corporates, considering their social media activities on different platforms and corresponding responses.

5.4 Social Media Usage

Thomas Aichner and Frank Jacob in their paper provide a model that measures social media usage for corporates around the world on different social media platforms (Aichner and Jacob 2015). Thirteen different types of social media including blogs, business networks, photo sharing, video sharing and social networks among others are described. All of them might not be equally relevant for all kinds of corporates based on the scope of application of the platform. Since the fast-moving world of social media is full of risks and quite demanding where consumers' reaction can make or break the brand image of the firm; corporates need to be cautious, selective and proficient while using social media. Aichner & Jacob model can help the organizations to analyze a single brand and to compare with the competitors and the industry average. We replicate the model for Indian corporates and their social media usage. Out of the five social media platforms in the study, Instagram is a platform with quite low corporate presence. Therefore, we continue with the rest of the four relatively more popular platforms Facebook, YouTube, LinkedIn & Twitter. Out of all 128 firms included in the study, three firms were selected based on highest social media presence and the highest number of followers (number of fans in case of Facebook, number of followers for Twitter, number of subscribers on YouTube & number of employees who have an account on LinkedIn).

Step 1: Social Media Monthly Active Users. An active number of users of each social media data were identified from Statista. An active user is a user who logs into the social media account, regardless of any activity done. For a platform where login is not required such as YouTube, the number of unique visitors to the platform are counted. The list in Table 6, shows the data available in April 2018.

Table 6. Monthly active users of the top 4 important social media as on April 2018

Social media name	Website	Active users/month
Facebook	www.facebook.com	2,23,40,00,000
Twitter	www.twitter.com	33,00,00,000
YouTube	www.youtube.com	1,50,00,00,000
LinkedIn	www.linkedin.com	26,00,00,000
Total		**4,32,40,00,000**

Step 2: Social Media Impact Factor. Social Media Impact Factor (SMIF) is the ratio of active users in each platform over the sum of the active users of all the social media platform included in the model. It determines the relative importance of each platform. SMIF is variable with time-based on the number of active users as well the number of platforms taken into consideration for model building. As of April 2018, the SMIF of each of the social media platform considered in the model was calculated as:

$$SMIF_{Facebook} = \frac{2,23,40,00,000}{4,32,40,00,000} = 0.52$$

$$SMIF_{Twitter} = \frac{33,00,00,000}{4,32,40,00,000} = 0.08$$

$$SMIF_{YouTube} = \frac{1,50,00,00,000}{4,32,40,00,000} = 0.35$$

$$SMIF_{LinkedIn} = \frac{26,00,00,000}{4,32,40,00,000} = 0.06$$

Step 3: Platform wise Social Media Use. Social Media Use (SMU) index depends on the type of social media and the functions offered by the platform. It is calculated based on the public information available and corresponding consumer responses. It ranges between zero to one, where zero means 'no use at all' and one means 'full use'. If the result of the equation exceeds the optimum value of one, then SMU is equal to one, that is the optimum usage. For different consumer responses, different weight is assigned that represents the degree of participation. For instance, 'comments' are given five times more weight than 'like', 'share' and 'retweets' were assigned ten times weight. Weights vary through different platforms as well. Likes & comments on YouTube are assigned 100 and 500 weights respectively.

Facebook. Table 7 shows the number of followers, posts including text, picture or video as well as average like comment & share for the three company's Facebook account. Based on these values we will calculate a constant that would be used further to estimate the SMU for Facebook. First, an average number of 'likes', 'share', and 'comments' are multiplied by their respective weights (1,5 and 10 here). Second, the sum of these three values is divided by the average number of total fans. Third, this figure is then multiplied by the average number of posts per month. Fourth, dividing the optimal value from the range of SMU (1) by this value gives us the constant. Here the constant = 1/20[{13244 + (148 * 5) + (383 * 10)}/7123333]. Then SMU for Facebook for a company can be calculated as:

$$SMU(facebook) = posts * \frac{\text{Ø 'likes' + Ø comments * 5 + Ø shares *10}}{fans} * 14.54$$

Table 7. Facebook activities of selected companies in February & March 2018

Company name	Total		Average per posting		
	Fans'	Postings	'Likes'	Comments	Shares
Bharti Airtel	1,03,60,000	63	5653	245	70
Yes Bank	73,70,000	40	1160	43	100
Axis Bank	36,40,000	18	22920	157	980
Average	71,23,333	40	13,244	148	383

Twitter. Table 8 shows the number of followers, posts as well as an average number of likes & retweet for the three selected companies.

Table 8. Twitter activities of selected companies in February and March 2018

Company name	Total		Average per posting	
	Followers	Postings	Likes	Retweets
Bharti Airtel	2430000	49	92	20
Yes Bank	3380000	1940	8	1
Axis Bank	250083	194	22	3
Average	**20,20,028**	**728**	**41**	**8**

We calculate the value for the constant in a similar way given above for Facebook. Here retweets are given weight 10. Then SMU for Twitter for a company can be calculated as:

$$SMU\left(Twitter\right) = posts * \frac{\text{Ø 'likes'} + \text{Ø retweets}*10}{followers} * 46.01$$

YouTube. Table 9 shows the number of subscribers to the channel, video uploads as well as an average number of views, likes & comments for the three selected companies.

Table 9. YouTube activities of selected companies in February and March 2018

Company	Total		Average per video		
	Subscribers	Video uploads	Views	Likes	Comments
Bharti Airtel	494584	13	1640000	124	72
Yes Bank	4410	14	164459	6	1
Axis Bank	22551	23	778508	57	8
Average	**1,73,848**	**17**	**8,60,989**	**62**	**27**

Unlike another platform where the posts are short-lived, the videos posted can be searched and watched repeatedly. Likes & comments here are assigned 100 and 500 weights respectively. Here:

$$SMU(YouTube) = videouploads * \frac{\text{Ø views} + \text{Ø likes}*100 + \text{Ø comments}*500}{subscribers} * 0.0237$$

LinkedIn. Table 10 shows the number of followers to the company profile, number of users mentioned as the employee, number of posts as well as the average number of likes & comments for the three selected companies.

Table 10. LinkedIn activities of selected companied in February and March 2018

Company name	Total			Average per post	
	Followers	Employees	Posts	Likes	Comments
Bharti Airtel	361397	39219	19	208	7
Yes Bank	227043	19085	40	153	2
Axis Bank	313565	42384	43	450	9
Average	**300668**	**33563**	**34**	**270**	**6**

For LinkedIn, a number of employees who have an account on LinkedIn is also considered along with the number of followers.

$$SMU(LinkedIn) = posts * \frac{\text{Ø likes} + \text{Ø comments}*5}{followers + employees} * 65.46$$

Social Media Use Index. Corporate Social Media Use (CSMU) index is calculated using Social Media Use (SMU) of each platform and the social media impact factor (SMIF) of the company. The company can choose one or more out of the four social media platforms here. Social media usage index of the selected platforms can be used in the following equation to calculate the Corporate Social Media Use for the firm. The equation to calculate the CSMU including all four platforms here is as follows:

$$\begin{aligned} CSMU_{company} = {} & SMU_{Facebook} * 0.52 + SMU_{Twitter} * 0.08 + SMU_{YouTube} \\ & * 0.35 + SMU_{LinkedIn} * 0.06 \end{aligned}$$

Table 11 shows the SMU for each platform as well the CSMU for all three firms Bharti Airtel, Yes Bank & Axis Bank. From, the table it can be seen that Axis Bank is using three out of four platforms in an optimum way and has the highest CSMU (0.99). Yes Bank is using the YouTube platform in an optimum way; the score for LinkedIn is close to one suggesting good use of the platform here. Bharti Airtel has scope to use social media to their potential says this segment of data.

Table 11. Corporate social media use index by Airtel, Yes Bank & Axis Bank

Description	Company name		
	Bharti Airtel	Yes Bank	Axis Bank
$SMU_{Facebook}$	0.33	0.49	> 1 = 1
$SMU_{Twitter}$	0.14	0.24	0.93
$SMU_{YouTube}$	0.53	> 1 = 1	> 1 = 1
$SMU_{LinkedIn}$	0.43	0.92	> 1 = 1
CSMU	**0.39**	**0.67**	**0.99**

6 Conclusion

The research focuses on the adoption & usage of social media platforms in different business sectors in India. It explains how in Indian market social media usage for business firms can depend on several different factors including the social media age, engagement, usage pattern, type of firm, strategy, type of social media platform, available features, target audience and content among all. Since social media is a broad, dynamic and versatile collection of platform, services and technologies, it allows varied usage and purposes for different people and businesses (Schlagwein and Hu 2017). It becomes difficult to predict a growth indicator with precision; however, a relationship between social media usage and growth indicator such as year on year sales variance is evident. We study social media presence, social media age, social media engagement and social media usage for different sector across corporate firms listed in BSE500. The collected data clearly shows that the majority of the firms are present on social media through one or the other platform. Social media age shows that large market capital firms were the early beginners on social media, and medium and small capital firms started adopting post 2008. Through social media engagement, we explore the impact of social media on year on year sales of the firm. A simple linear regression analysis suggests that social media engagement and year on year sales are related. However, the predictability of the relation here is dependent on added factors. We consider that the type and nature of the platform affect the way corporate can use social media to reach towards set objectives. To explore the usage pattern in Indian firm we replicate Aichner & Jacob model (Aichner and Jacob 2015) and find that not all corporate use different social media platforms to their optimum potential. For different firms, the SMU index suggests a degree of usage of various social media platforms.

The scope of this research includes Indian firms and business. This model can be useful to market researchers and marketing managers to compare between with the competitor as well as to understand social media usage better. For future researches, it would be relevant to classify the factors affecting social media usage for business firms and work on the model to target predictability of the growth indicators.

References

Abed, S.S., Dwivedi, Y.K., Williams, M.D.: Social media as a bridge to e-commerce adoption in SMEs: a systematic literature review. Mark. Rev. **15**(1), 39–57 (2015a)

Abed, S.S., Dwivedi, Y.K., Williams, M.D.: SMEs' adoption of e-commerce using social media in a Saudi Arabian context: a systematic literature review. Int. J. Bus. Inf. Syst. **19**(2), 159–179 (2015b)

Abed, S.S., Dwivedi, Y.K., Williams, M.D.: Social commerce as a business tool in Saudi Arabia's SMEs. Int. J. Indian Culture Bus. Manag. **13**(1), 1–19 (2016)

Aichner, T., Jacob, F.: Measuring the degree of corporate social media use. Int. J. Market Res. **57** (2), 257–276 (2015)

Alalwan, A.A., Rana, N.P., Dwivedi, Y.K., Algharabat, R.: Social media in marketing: a review and analysis of the existing literature. Telematics Inform. **34**(7), 1177–1190 (2017)

Aral, S., Dellarocas, C., Godes, D.: Introduction to the special issue—social media and business transformation: a framework for research. Inf. Syst. Res. **24**(1), 3–13 (2013)

Barker, V.: Older adolescents' motivations for social network site use: the influence of gender, group identity, and collective self-esteem. Cyberpsychology Behav. **12**(2), 209–213 (2009)

Boyd, D.M., Ellison, N.B.: Social network sites: definition, history, and scholarship. J. Comput.-Mediat. Commun. **13**(1), 210–230 (2007)

De Vries, L., Gensler, S., Leeflang, P.S.: Popularity of brand posts on brand fan pages: an investigation of the effects of social media marketing. J. Interact. Mark. **26**(2), 83–91 (2012)

Dwivedi, Y.K., Kapoor, K.K., Chen, H.: Social media marketing and advertising. Mark. Rev. **15** (3), 289–309 (2015)

Hanna, R., Rohm, A., Crittenden, V.L.: We're all connected: the power of the social media ecosystem. Bus. Horiz. **54**(3), 265–273 (2011)

He, W., Zha, S., Li, L.: Social media competitive analysis and text mining: A case study in the pizza industry. Int. J. Inf. Manag. **33**(3), 464–472 (2013)

Hoffman, D.L., Fodor, M.: Can you measure the ROI of your social media marketing? MIT Sloan Manag. Rev. **52**(1), 41 (2010)

Ilavarasan, P.V.: Social media research in and of india: a snapshot. In: Dwivedi, Y.K. (ed.) Emerging Markets from a Multidisciplinary Perspective. ATPEM, pp. 135–148. Springer, Cham (2018). https://doi.org/10.1007/978-3-319-75013-2_12

Kaplan, A.M., Haenlein, M.: Users of the world, unite! The challenges and opportunities of social media. Bus. Horiz. **53**(1), 59–68 (2010)

Kapoor, K.K., Tamilmani, K., Rana, N.P., Patil, P., Dwivedi, Y.K., Nerur, S.: Advances in social media research: past, present and future. Information Systems Frontiers **20**, 531–558 (2018)

Kaushik, B., Hemani, H., Ilavarasan, P.V.: Social media usage vs. stock prices: an analysis of Indian firms. Procedia Comput. Sci. **122**, 323–330 (2017)

Kietzmann, J.H., Hermkens, K., McCarthy, I.P., Silvestre, B.S.: Social media? Get serious! Understanding the functional building blocks of social media. Bus. Horiz. **54**(3), 241–251 (2011)

Kim, A.J., Ko, E.: Do social media marketing activities enhance customer equity? An empirical study of luxury fashion brand. J. Bus. Res. **65**(10), 1480–1486 (2012)

Nair, M.: Understanding and measuring the value of social media. J. Corp. Account. Finance **22** (3), 45–51 (2011)

Paniagua, J., Sapena, J.: Business performance and social media: Love or hate? Bus. Horiz. **57** (6), 719–728 (2014)

Rathore, A.K., Ilavarasan, P.V., Dwivedi, Y.K.: Social media content and product co-creation: an emerging paradigm. J. Enterp. Inf. Manag. **29**(1), 7–18 (2016)

Schlagwein, D., Hu, M.: How and why organisations use social media: five use types and their relation to absorptive capacity. J. Inf. Technol. **32**(2), 194–209 (2017)
Statista Number of monthly active Facebook users worldwide. https://www.statista.com/statistics/264810/number-of-monthly-active-facebook-users-worldwide/. Accessed Jan 2018
Statista Leading countries based on number of Facebook users. https://www.statista.com/statistics/268136/top-15-countries-based-on-number-of-facebook-users/. Accessed Jan 2018
Statista Leading countries based on Twitter users as of April 2018. https://www.statista.com/statistics/242606/number-of-active-twitter-users-in-selected-countries/. Accessed Jan 2018

Bright ICT and Unbounded Employment: Typology of Crowdworkers and Their Lived and Envisaged Career Trajectory in Nigeria

Ayomikun Idowu(✉) and Amany Elbanna

Royal Holloway, University of London, Egham TW20 0EX, UK
{ayomikun.idowu, amany.elbanna}@rhul.ac.uk

Abstract. Employment and work are identified as a critical area that has been impacted by advancement of ICT and is currently passing through significant changes. Hence, the Bright ICT agenda calls for researchers to focus their effort on this area that is not only in need of better understanding but also holds potential better future for many around the globe. Influenced by the widespread connectivity to the Internet and the rise of digital platforms, new ways of working such as crowdworking is rising encouraging government and International agencies to consider it an alternative route for employment that could extend employment opportunities beyond national geography and regional barriers. This qualitative study responds to Bright ICT call by exploring the lived experience of crowdworkers and how they plan and develop their future. It aims to answer the question of how crowdworkers experience this type of employment and whether they can develop their skills and organize their future? The study identifies four categories of crowdworkers and shows their practices in developing and progressing their crowdworking experience. We conceptualise these practices as a career development path and identify four career progression stages. Implications for research and practice are discussed.

Keywords: Platform employment · Crowdwork · Career development · Bright ICT · Nigeria · Crowdsourcing · Digital platforms

1 Introduction

Bright ICT represents an important initiative founded by the Association of Information Systems (AIS) that was announced in 2015 [1]. It aims to focus both research and practice on understanding the positive and negative sides of ICT and finding ways to create positive impact of ICT around the world. Work and employment are recognised as a critical area that has been impacted by the diffusion of the Internet and is currently passing through significant changes and needs better and comprehensive exploration and understanding. Hence, the Bright ICT agenda calls for researchers to focus their effort on this area which requires better understanding and also holds potentials for a better future for many around the globe [2]. Influenced by the widespread connectivity to the Internet and the rise of digital platforms, new ways of working such as crowdworking is witnessing exponential growth. Crowdwork is a new way of working which allows employers to source labour from a large group of people via digital

Published by Springer Nature Switzerland AG 2019
Y. Dwivedi et al. (Eds.): TDIT 2019, IFIP AICT 558, pp. 470–486, 2019.
https://doi.org/10.1007/978-3-030-20671-0_32

platforms [3]. It is a type of crowdsourcing where people conduct digital tasks using digital platforms as intermediaries in exchange for financial payment. In this regard, crowdsourcing presents a broader phenomenon that covers paid and non-paid digital work. Crowdsourcing offers numerous opportunities to the advantage of both employers and workers where employers reduce operating costs while workers get an opportunity to earn income [4–6]. Through platforms such as Freelancer.com, Upwork and Fiverr, individuals with the requisite skills and expertise can provide a wide range of information technology (IT) and business services to employers in remote locations [7]. Some of the services commonly provided on these platforms include image creation, graphic design, web design, app development, software testing, branding, product design, data entry, content creation, and market research [6].

Indeed, crowdworking has proliferated over the years, with individuals, small or medium enterprises being the top consumers and millennials accounting for the largest share of crowdworkers [8, 9]. Large firms have also become consumers of crowdsourcing services, a 2015 survey of the 100 Best Global Brands found that 85% of the brands had used crowdsourcing in the last decade [10]. Global research firm Gartner projected that crowdsourcing would account for 20% of all enterprise software development projects by the end of 2018 [6]. As technology advances, changing the nature and form of work by offering greater flexibility and autonomy to workers [11], crowdworking is expected to grow even more rapidly as a global phenomenon that crosses national and regional barriers, creating a global labour market. The study by Kappelman, McLean [12] revealed that challenges with IT skill shortage and retention is the second most worrisome issues with IT leaders. This brings to light the need to understand this growing group of workers and the lived experience of how they manage their lives and work in order to potentially develop a framework for hiring, motivating, retaining and developing crowdworkers.

Crowdwork is individualistic in nature without a formal structure, work teams, professional standards, and other institutional elements that characterise the traditional workplace [7, 13]. Here workers plan their lives, personal and skills development and growth independent of organisations. These aspects of work that are typically managed and monitored by traditional employers are becoming the responsibility of the individuals alone in the crowdworking model. Little we know about the possibility for crowdworkers to create and manage a career including their skills development, advancement and growth from crowdwork which is characterised by autonomy and flexibility [14]. Indeed, its vital to understand the career trajectory of individuals as it determines the life of employment, the skills developed, the occupational achievement, and the living condition of workers [15] since work is the primary means through which individuals meet their needs for survival, relatedness and self-determination [16, 17].

So far there is little understanding of how crowdworkers experience this type of employment and whether they can develop their skills, make a progression plan and find a trajectory for life development and achievement that are encompassed in a career trajectory. Therefore, this research aims to seek to understand the lived and envisaged skills and career development in crowdwork through a qualitative study examining full-time Nigerian crowdworkers, Nigeria is one of the largest countries in Africa that suffer from a significantly high unemployment rate. Government and international development agencies promote Crowdworking as holding high hopes for Nigeria in reducing unemployment and contribute to the socio-economic development of the country [18] which seem to be at odd with the short term nature of crowdwork engagements. By focusing on Nigeria, we hope to offer an in-depth understanding that could be transferred to other developing countries.

This study specifically addresses two of the main issues in the Bright ICT initiative as identified by the [2] Delphi study. Firstly, it examines how the crowdworkers in Nigeria deal with the changes in the increased adoption of the internet and other ICTs and how they design and navigate their work lives in that context. Secondly, this study sheds light on the experience of the workers' adoption of crowdwork; specifically, it focuses on how Nigerian crowdworkers live and plan their lives in this form of work. These understandings provide a foundation for identifying critical issues in crowdwork adoption and its societal and personal implication on workers lives, thereby contributing to the knowledge about dealing with and solving the inherent problems with increased adoption of ICTs and platform employment [1, 2].

The paper consists of seven sections. Following the introduction is a brief literature review, section three presents the theoretical grounding of the study, and section four details the research methodology. The results of empirical findings in section five is followed by discussions and conclusions.

2 Literature Review

2.1 Crowdsourcing and Crowdworkers

Crowdsourcing is a work model in which employers (individuals or organisations) harness the collective skills, knowledge, and expertise of a large group of people to accomplish a given task through digital platforms and remunerate them for tasks completed [4, 5, 19]. This new way of working as part of the broader digital economy is temporary and casual in nature [20]. It is a form of work initially construed to be engaged in as a hobby, as a way to earn additional income, or because of its flexibility [21]. However, due to rising unemployment and redundancy, more people are venturing into crowdwork as a full-time work [22, 23]. The absence of organisational and institutional boundaries means crowdworkers are not tied to a single, permanent employer [7] which has important implications for how they manage their work. Crowdwork encompasses a wide variety of jobs. These include IT services (e.g., software development, software testing, or web design), routine administrative tasks (e.g., data cleansing, data entry, or data processing), content development (e.g., image creation, video creation, or writing), and business services (e.g., product design, business analysis, or project management [4, 6]).

Originally, crowdworkers were misconceived as uneducated, low-skilled workers. Research finds that whereas some crowdworkers may be uneducated and low-skilled, the majority are educated and highly skilled [21]. According to Schweissguth [9], over 50% of crowdworkers held bachelors degree qualifications, and 20% had a masters degree. Most importantly, crowdworkers tend to be young knowledge workers, highly specialised and knowledgeable in their area of expertise [24, 25]. [20] analysis of four major crowdwork platforms (i.e., Freelancer.com, Fiverr, Guru.com, and

Peopleperhour) found that IT tasks such as software development account for over 50% all the crowdwork jobs posted and completed.

For so long, work has been primarily associated with organisations where employees follow particular skills development programmes and an organised career trajectory. A career trajectory, also known as a career path denotes the course and pattern of an individual's career progression during their active professional life [26, 27]. In the traditional work environment, one's career trajectory starts the moment one commences professional practice, the speed with which one advance across the career ladder is dependent on a combination of personal, social and organisational factors [28]. For instance, an individual who puts more effort at work is more likely to get a promotion. Additionally, career development is likely to be faster in an organisation that offers professional development opportunities such as continuous training [29].

Though both personal and organisational factors shape career progression in the traditional workplace, organisations play a particularly integral role. In the context of crowdwork, this element that shapes employees' career is absent [13]. Crowdwork lacks the traditional elements that shape or contribute to career advancement, such as direct employee supervision, incentives, and sanctions [7]. Though some of these management practices exist in some platforms, such as incentives and sanctions, their effectiveness is often hindered by factors such as the absence of direct supervision, invisibility of work behaviour, and the complexity of imposing sanctions [7]. For example, compared to traditional workers, crowdworkers can more easily exit without severe consequences. The unique nature of crowdsourcing has important implications for the career trajectory of crowdworkers.

Scholars and commentators have offered preliminary insight on crowdworkers skills and career development. According to [14], knowledge workers, especially software developers tend to have an individualistic orientation when it comes to career progression. Individual factors such as skills, abilities, intrinsic motivation, effort, and hard work [13] largely shape career in crowdwork. It helps crowdworkers garner up a reputation as trusted workers and, in turn, increases their chances of being awarded projects by employers. The ultimate determinant of a workers' proficiency is their reputation score, an aggregation of employers' feedbacks and platform reputation algorithms [30, 31]. On some platforms, workers with the highest score are given a label that identifies them as proven experts, which makes it easier for employers to evaluate the capability of a worker before awarding a project. Such feedback systems significantly determine how fast one's crowdwork career advances [31]. The more positive reviews one garners and the higher the reputation score, the greater their chance of winning future bids. However, despite their usefulness, feedback systems on crowdwork platforms may not necessarily be an accurate reflection of a worker's level of expertise as they may often be exaggerated [30]. Hence, beside employers' feedback, crowdwork platforms offer workers the opportunity to undergo certain tests before being awarded work, examples are general tests (e.g., language tests) and subject-specific tests (e.g., software testing and content creation tests) [31]. Other reputation systems include machine-learning models, self-assessment, and automated feedback [30]. Irrespective of the method used, the underlying aim of a reputation system is to indicate workers' level of expertise or task-proficiency status. Based on the acknowledgement of the pivotal role of platform reputation system on crowdworkers careers, [7] proposed a four-stage trajectory for crowdworkers: (1) entry-level (untrusted worker), (2) trusted worker; (3) hourly contractor, and (4) employee.

3 Theoretical Grounding

This study adopts Super's model of career development, also referred to as the life rainbow model. Developed in the 1950s and premised on human development principles, Super's model describes five stages of career development that occur as an individual: (1) growth; (2) exploration; (3) establishment; (4) maintenance; and (5) decline [32]. The tasks an individual undertakes in each stage tend to be distinct from other stages. Additionally, each stage correlates with significant events in a person's life, such as childhood, schooling, adulthood, and employment [33]. These events, according to [34], play a vital role in shaping who an individual becomes. At the core of Super's model is the argument that career development is influenced by three sets of factors: personal factors (psychological and biological), situational factors (socioeconomic and historical), and environmental factors (the labour market and employment practices) [32].

The first stage of career development according to Super's model is the growth stage. This stage starts from birth up to the age of 14 years and generally encompasses one's childhood [34]. At this stage, an individual's core occupation is school [33]. It is at this stage that the concept of self starts to develop. An individual develops interests and attitudes, socialises their needs, and starts to have a basic understanding of the world of work [32]. The exploration stage, which starts at the age of 15 years through to the age of 24 years. As a young adult, an individual attempts to understand who they are and makes a tentative career choice. Through schooling, hobbies, and work experiences, the individual gains a clearer picture of their interests and abilities as well as their place in the occupational world [33]. Based on one's tentative occupational preference, one acquires the requisite training and eventually secures a position in their preferred occupation [35].

The establishment stage is characterised by entry-level skill development and the achievement of professional stability [33, 34]. After entering one's preferred occupation, one sharpens their professional skills and abilities and pursues opportunities for further career development. By performing one's roles and responsibilities in a satisfactory manner, one solidifies their position in their professional world [36]. The fourth stage of Super's career development model is the maintenance stage. This stage starts at the age of 45 years through to the age of 64 years [34]. At this stage, the individual continually enhances their skills and abilities in an attempt to improve their career position [33]. The individual also makes attempts to explore new challenges [32]. The fifth, decline stage is characterised by reduced productivity, and at this stage, an individual starts to prepare for retirement [33]. Owing to decreased output and diminished interest in the occupational world, the individual gradually exits the workforce.

4 Methods

4.1 Research Approach and Data Collection

This qualitative study adopts an inductive interpretive research approach involving multiple data sources in explorations of understandings, accessing intricate details and produce deep insights on crowdwork and crowdworkers [37, 38]. Data sources include face-to-face interviews, website reviews, observation of crowdworkers in their workspace, informal conversations, online blogs, social media and online discussion threads. In this study, 35 Nigerian crowdworkers (23 Male, 12 females) aged between 22 and 46 years participated in a mix of 38 unstructured and semi-structured interviews in three phases of data collection. The pilot phase of unstructured interviews with six participants carried out between December 2017, and January 2018 helped to gain preliminary insight on nature of crowdwork in Nigeria, challenges, crowdworkers' experience and work practices, which also aided the development of the research design. This was followed by two interview phases between June - August 2018 and October – November 2018 with 18 and 14 in-depth semi-structured interviews. Questions at this stage were more directed towards understanding crowdworkers' feeling and aspiration for their job, experiences, career plan, and motivation, social and work practices. The nature of the interviews allowed for divergence, spontaneity which gave the researchers an opportunity to gather quality and reliable data.

The first three (3) participant were recruited through personal contacts, and subsequently, snowballing sampling employed when participants recommended other participants. Other participants were recruited from closed online groups. Participants included in the study fit the inclusion criteria that they have been involved in paid full-time crowdwork for more than two years and specialised in IT/IT services crowdwork. This is to ensure that participants have sufficient experience and knowledge in order to be able to provide reliable and valuable insights on crowdwork in Nigeria [39]. The interview was triangulated with additional data collected through informal face-to-face conversations, informal visits to workers workspace, observation of online blogs, social media groups, online discussion threads and workers profiles on crowdwork platforms.

4.2 Data Analysis

Interviews were transcribed verbatim and participants assigned pseudonym. An open and inductive approach was adopted in coding and theme development, which involves reflecting on explicit data content [40]. This approach focuses on identifying common threads that appear throughout interviews, and themes act as essential concepts that link different essential portions of the interviews together [39].

Notes of major crowdworkers' practices, experience, motivation and aspirations that were identified in the interviews were used to delve into more relevant concepts to form a better understanding and explanations of career trajectories of crowdworkers. Open coding makes it possible for concepts and themes to arise from the data in a manner that depicts the actual experiences and sentiments of the participants [40]. At this stage, each fragment and segment relevant data was captured and carefully examined for analytic interpretation. After different rounds of code generation, a comparison between different rounds of data was made, and the most useful data tested against a wide range of data. Each interview was coded to derive an emerging category that is based on sensitising concepts. Searches were made for emerging codes which were categorised into similar codes [41] and the data then used to develop the themes for in-depth and better understanding. After developing the themes, the researchers came together to review and merge the themes that overlap, confirm the themes and modify existing themes. The different categories were merged into similar themes to develop a higher order theoretical concept based on the practices, characteristics and sequential order of career progression of crowdworkers identified in the interview. This was backed up with crowdsourcing literature and theories on work career path. A theoretical representation of the themes that emerged from analysis of interviews and other data sources was hence presented in a model (see Fig. 4).

5 Research Findings

This section presents the findings on the career trajectories of crowdwork in Nigeria. It shows the different categories of crowdworkers involved in fulltime crowdwork employment and the different activities engaged in at the four stages of the different career levels of crowdwork career.

5.1 Categories of Crowdworkers

In our quest to understand the career-lifecycle and trajectories of crowdworkers, we identified four categories of people who are engaged in full-time crowdwork employment. This categorisation was based on two factors: previous employment status and previous familiarity with crowdsourcing. We established that previous familiarity with crowdwork or other crowdworkers affects career trajectory, the speed of acclimatisation, and eventual success in crowdwork endeavours. We framed this form of involvement as "Warm Start" and "Cold Start". Warm start means there is a less blunt entry into crowdworking due to previous relevant experience from which worker can draw inference upon and have a smoother start with limited pressure and time to ease into crowdwork. On the other hand, cold start involves individuals who experience a blunt entry with higher pressure, limited support, and a lack of prior experience and understanding of crowdwork before engaging in full-time crowdwork employment [42]. Based on previous employment status and previous familiarity with crowdsourcing, the four categories of crowdworkers we identified in this study are (Table 1):

Table 1. Typology of crowdworkers

	Warm start	Cold start
Previously employed	Switchers	Awakened
Previously unemployed	Early birds	Green starters

Green starters are workers who were formerly unemployed and got into crowdworking mainly as a source of income and employment. Green starters are highly driven to gain income stability and attaining the work gives them a sense of gratitude. They start from scratch and learn how to navigate the platforms.

> *"I got into crowdsourcing because of the issue of employment in the country, and one has to look for ways to make ends meet. I had to try crowdsourcing online, and do jobs for myself and make money, so no matter how difficult it is, it's more like the [only] option I have" - Blessing*

Switchers are workers who were formerly in traditional full-time employment. To supplement their income, switchers work part-time but eventually switch to full-time crowdwork. As they work part-time, switchers gain skills and knowledge of crowdwork as well as build a reputation on the platform before switching, which makes it less challenging to shift to full-time crowdwork.

> *"... was doing crowdsourcing for the extra cash, I get few jobs a month, but wasn't really doing it fulltime until I discovered that I was making the same amount doing two software work a month and from my fulltime job, so I quit my Job and moved [into crowdwork] fulltime" - Daniel*

Early birds are workers who started crowdwork when they were at the university and never bothered to get into the formal labour market (i.e., they started as students). They become crowdworkers at the age of 17–23 years. Similar to switchers, early birds are familiar with crowdsourcing before engaging in it as full-time employment. Though early birds start crowdwork earlier, they may not necessarily have worked on crowdsourcing platforms: some of them initially work with established crowdworkers. This enables them to understand crowdwork and the opportunities it presents before getting into full-time crowdwork. Based on our study, this group of workers have been around crowdworkers and have done some form of crowdwork before getting into the labour market.

> *"I learnt about crowdsourcing as a student during a 6 months internship in an IT company as part of my course. When I got there, they were actually a group of crowdworker working together as a company...they introduced me to it. When I helped with some work and got paid 20000Naira ($40), I was excited and got hooked...didn't bother looking for work after graduation" - Jude*

Awakened crowdworkers are individuals who were engaged in a supposedly formal organisation working full-time but branched out to start their own work. They might be close to crowdworkers but may not have an idea of what goes on in crowdsourcing. This category of workers has to be awakened to their environment in order to engage in crowdwork.

> *".. I was working for an employer...I noticed he actually sourced this work online...I never thought it was that possible, easy, so when I saw how he does it he told me "you can do it too, you can source this work yourself and then I won't have to be the middleman for you", so he introduced me to the first site, and then I registered there.. that's how I got to where I am today." - Aisha*

5.2 Career Trajectories of Crowdworkers

In our analysis of the career path followed by crowdworkers, we identified four stages, namely entry level (untrusted worker), mid-level (trusted professional), Veteran and post-career stage. The time spent moving through these stages differs among individuals. It was discovered that throughout the work lifecycle of crowdworkers, career stages are marked by the activities and practices they engage in rather than a specific positions or job title as in traditional employment. In other words, career stages are marked by their level of skills, capabilities, networks, practices and knowledge of the work. A career height is only reached or attained after successfully engaging in a series of systematic and progressive actions. We found that there are patterns to how an action affects the other which eventually affects the course of crowdworkers' careers. These actions include: building a reputation and social/resource networks; learning social and technology skills, and learning/skill upgrades and diversification.

Untrusted Worker: Building a Reputation and Social/Resource Networks. The algorithmic setup of crowdsourcing platforms necessitates that workers garner sufficient ratings and reputation on the platforms to be offered employment. While early bird and awakened workers have an easier time navigating and building offline support systems, switchers have an easier time building an online reputation because of their previous engagement as part-time crowdworkers. Workers starting up in crowdwork take their time to build their profiles and reputation by delivering quality products to employers. The platform reputation system is used by platform algorithms to rate crowdworkers skills, and this affects their employment potential and future crowdwork career survival. This is well articulated by Joseph below;

> *"when I started I actually focused on the quality of job I delivered to my clients, so then I wasn't after a lot of money... my goal then was to make sure I deliver a good job so that I can build the five-star profile. So then I focused on getting all my jobs done completely, and on time so that my clients would be happy with my job... now that I have been able to build a profile which is very good for me, I've been able to make a bit more money from it by getting jobs with higher pay and a lot of clients will come back and employ me too...so that's the way I was able to build my profile".*

As they build their reputation on crowdwork platforms, crowdworkers connect with networks of other workers by joining online discussion threads and social media groups. Workers also connect with crowdworkers offline, and these networks of crowdworkers play a vital role in the success of their careers both as a means of learning and as a support system when encountering challenges.

> *"You need to know other people....I'm successful in this business because of my relationship with other workers, I can easily send a message to the (social media)group if I have problem with my payment system and within minutes, I'll be able to know if everybody is also having the same problem and we can all find a way to address it...I have contact of enough crowdworkers in Lagos that we correspond regularly through text and calls to help each other and introduce to other people"- Monica*

There is constant learning throughout the career of crowdworkers, workers learn both social and technological skills. Technological skills relate to familiarising themselves with crowdsourcing platforms, understanding their interface, and learning how to bid for work. In terms of social skills, one major area of concern is the societal misunderstanding of any form of online work as fraud in Nigeria where people tend to relate online work with fraud. For switchers, learning how to transition from traditional full-time work and part-time crowdwork to full-time crowdwork is vital. The social reality of work changes because, with their previous employment, they have little course to defend their source of income in an environment that is suspicious of online work. Workers learn how to defend and project their work and how to navigate the societal perception of crowdwork. Folarin and Ola share their learning experiences;

> *"It took me some time to master how to traverse the challenges of this work, it was a long learning experience for me.... Even to the basics of how I should talk about my work in public, how to deal with employers, and what sites [platforms] I should use for what...." - Folarin*
> *"It's a learning curve, there's always something to learn...if not about the platforms, its from clients [employer], or other crowdworkers. Its important to know these things because you won't succeed in this business without knowledge of a lot of things..and they take time" - Ola*

Trusted Professional Crowdworker: Learning/Skill Upgrades and Diversification. After building networks, having a comfortable footing on the crowdwork dynamics, as well as understanding the social, technological, and economic dynamics of crowdwork, crowdworkers take the step of cementing their footings in the job. Just like any employment, in order to remain competitive and up to date, there is a need to update existing skills and learn new ones. From our study, we discovered that after mastering the necessary aspect of their new employment, crowdworkers engage in skill update and upgrade. Workers upgrade their existing skills to remain relevant. The skills that people learn are driven by what is regularly advertised on the platforms. This is similar to traditional careers where people go for additional training and certification in order to increase their career prospects.

> *"...as a crowdsource, when I see some job post online, it spurs me to go and learn those skills...I download books, watch YouTube tutorials... most of the things that I do currently as a crowdworker, I had to learn on my own by seeing that they are skills employers need" - Kingsley*

Workers learn new skills outside of their initial specialisation and fields. Some workers learn unrelated skills in order to diversify their skill set and thus expand the range of tasks they can apply for on crowdwork platforms.

> *"As a software engineer, I saw many projects where employers need people to write proposals for software development projects, I learnt it and now almost 40% of what I do is related to writing proposal and instruction guides for clients" - Ify*

Veteran Stage. At this top-most active career level, crowdworkers engage in various types of activities with varying levels of expertise and concentration and practices.

Workers with *long*-term career view of crowdwork at this stage engage in practices aimed at increasing their opportunity by increasing their expertise and offering to potential employers on the platforms. Figure 1 below shows a career crowdworkers profiles across two platforms showing the range of skills he specialises on the platforms in order to ensure his career survival.

"...decided to do this work for a long time, it's been good to me...but I need to be competitive to make enough money to so that's why I do more than one thing..[I] work on freelancer.com and Fiverr and specialise each profile on a specific area" - Daniel

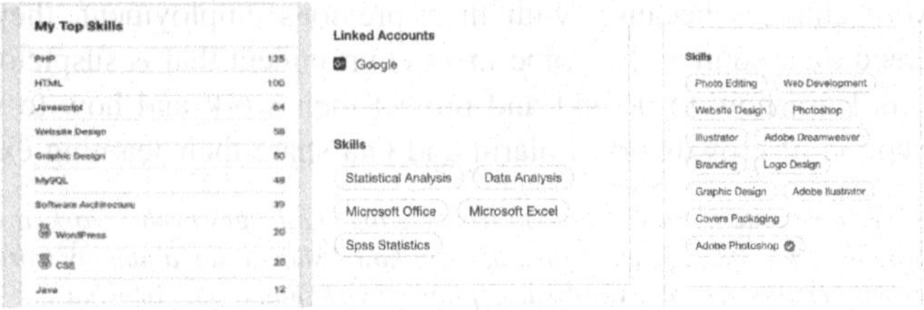

Fig. 1. A crowdworker's three profiles on two platforms

Some crowdworkers at this stage revealed they work less on tasks by leveraging their high reputation on the platform to get as many jobs as possible and then serve as intermediation by outsourcing it to workers both on and off the platform. They are more engaged in administrative tasks which involve recruiting, managing, organising and monitoring several tasks, workers, and employers at the same time (see Fig. 2). Their network of workers and relationship with employers plays a significant role in the success of this practice.

"What I do is get work on different sites and Clients [employers], negotiate payment and send the work to some of my guys [offline workers and fellow crowdworker], most times I get someone to take the Job... however if by any chance I cannot find anyone from my [offline]-contact, then I'll post it online" - Hamza

December Payments

ID	Date	Name	Amount	Payment Type	Bank	Account Number
1	02/12/2018	[redacted]	₦ 30,000.00	Bank Transfer	GTBank	[redacted]
2	02/12/2018	[redacted]	₦ 132,400.00	Bank Transfer	GTBank	[redacted]
3	05/12/2018	[redacted]	$250.00	Paypal		[redacted].com
4	05/12/2018	[redacted]	₦ 18,000.00	Bank Transfer	Access Bank	[redacted]
5	05/12/2018	[redacted]	₦ 90,000.00	Cash		
6	06/12/2018	[redacted]	₦ 200,000.00	Bank Transfer	GTBank	[redacted]
7	07/12/2018	[redacted]	₦ 45,000.00	Bank Transfer	GTBank	[redacted]
8	08/12/2018	[redacted]	₦ 20,000.00	Bank Transfer	FirstBank	[redacted]
9	10/12/2018	[redacted]	₦ 120,000.00	Bank Transfer	Access Bank	[redacted]
10	10/12/2018	[redacted]	₦ 50,000.00	Cash		[redacted]
11	10/12/2018	[redacted]	₦ 35,000.00	Bank Transfer	FirstBank	[redacted]
12	11/12/2018	[redacted]	₦ 42,300.00	Bank Transfer	Diamond Bank	[redacted]
13	17/12/2018	[redacted]	₦ 70,000.00	Bank Transfer	FCMB	[redacted]
14	17/12/2018	[redacted]	₦ 10,000.00	Bank Transfer	Zenith Bank	[redacted]
15	18/12/2018	[redacted]	₦ 100,000.00	Bank Transfer	FirstBank	[redacted]
16	26/12/2018	[redacted]	₦ 20,000.00	Bank Transfer	GTBank	[redacted]
17	27/12/2018	[redacted]	₦ 55,000.00	Bank Transfer	GTBank	[redacted]
18	30/12/2018	[redacted]	₦ 30,000.00	Bank Transfer	FirstBank	[redacted]
Total		18	₦ 1,067,950.00			

Fig. 2. A crowdworkers spreadsheet to manage payment for outsourced tasks

This career level is also one in which workers boast several years of experience in one or more fields of specialisation, they hence engage in activities by honing their skills and venturing into other knowledge areas to earn more income. Workers leverage their experience by writing books, creating blogs, and organising seminars and workshops on crowdwork. They use their experience and skills gained from crowd-work to guide others on how to navigate the complicated social, economic, and technological challenges of crowdwork. This may also take the form of mentoring new crowdworkers both online and offline. Figure 3 shows a sample blog post and a book written by a crowdworker.

Fig. 3. A blog post and book by crowdworkers

At this career stage also, some expand their horizon beyond employers on the platforms. Here crowdworkers simultaneously source for work and income both on and off the digital platforms and engaging in new business endeavours outside the platforms.

> *"... I started submitting proposals for software contracts in companies and got two(2) projects last year now, the I experience and portfolio from the work online helped a lot" - Ahmed.*

Post-crowdwork Career Plan (Exit Stage). This post active career stage of a crowdworker presents two post-crowdwork career paths identified in the study, i.e. Dream chasers and business entrepreneurs. Dream chasers are workers who plan to make enough money from crowdwork, then quit in order to follow their lifelong passion. Crowdworkers with this career goal are usually individuals who are presently earning sufficient and excess income from crowdwork.

> *"I don't think I'll be doing this work forever; I have dreams... I currently do music sometimes, when I was a student, I use to produce tracks for my friends but because I didn't have enough money to have my own production studio, I had to use my main skill, my dream is to make money from crowdsourcing and build my own studio" - Fred*

The other group, business entrepreneurs are workers who are already engaging in entrepreneurial business outside of the platform; these crowdworkers plan to expand and focus on the existing businesses they have created and quit crowdwork. By the time of exit, a crowdworker would have amassed sufficient resources to pursue other life goals.

> *"The money I'm making now, I'm using it to fund my electronic shops where I sell phones, computer, and everything electronic, so by the time I stop this job, I'll focus on it as my full-time work. I'll be a normal businessman" - Toju*

6 Discussion

This study contributes to the understanding of new types of work and employment that are brought about through the widespread use of Internet technology and the rise of digital platforms [44–50]. It addresses a critical area on the Bright ICT agenda. Hence, it aimed to understand the lived and envisaged career trajectories of crowdworkers. The study specifically intended to discover the different categories of crowdworkers and to map out the career path followed by crowdworkers. The study found that there are four categories of crowdworkers: green starters (previously unemployed individuals who venture into full time crowdwork to earn a living); switchers (individuals who abandon full time employment in other fields in favour of crowdwork); early birds (individuals who venture into crowdwork before engaging in any formal employment); and the awakened (individuals in full time employment but with no knowledge of crowdwork who require introduction to the world of crowdsourcing).

This study reveals that workers are not homogenous in terms of motivation for engaging in fulltime crowdwork employment or at what stage of their lives they start. While some start as students, others adopt crowdwork after years of traditional employment. Crowdworkers who start as students are often disinterested in formal employment after their education. The attractive rewards and independence offered by crowdwork employment [9] make this group of workers satisfied with what they do, thereby eliminating or diminishing their aspirations for formal employment. Reasons for engaging in fulltime crowdwork go beyond unemployment, or the need for flexibility into a view of lucrative income possibilities for less work when compared with traditional employment. This study reveals that owing to dissatisfaction with formal employment and the attractiveness of income from crowdwork, many young adults are leaving traditional jobs in favour of platform employment [8].

The career stages of platform workers as represented in Fig. 4 do not have a clearly defined structure; instead, they are a composition of activities engaged in and the undefined roles and practice crowdworkers engage in during their career lifecycle. The entry level is marked by self-directed professional growth through building alliances with other platform workers and connecting with the communities of other crowdworkers while also building a reputation on the platform. Workers seek connection to advance their career prospects as this helps them understand their social situatedness and how to navigate the complexity of their work. Having the required skills and top reputation on the platform may attract employers [31] but does not guarantee success beyond a certain level. Having a social connection with other crowdworkers offline has been demonstrated to be a valuable asset for a long-term successful career in platform employment, this negates the conventional wisdom of the individualistic nature of digital work [13].

The theoretical argument in this study is that in the initial stage of career development in internet-enabled work, workers' expertise, technical skills and platform reputation takes a prominent role. As workers progress, platform reputation loses its central potency while the ability to offer diverse expertise, maintain professional space, seek and exploit opportunities for growth within and outside the sphere of platform work ensures a viable career. The study shows the pivotal role that skill development

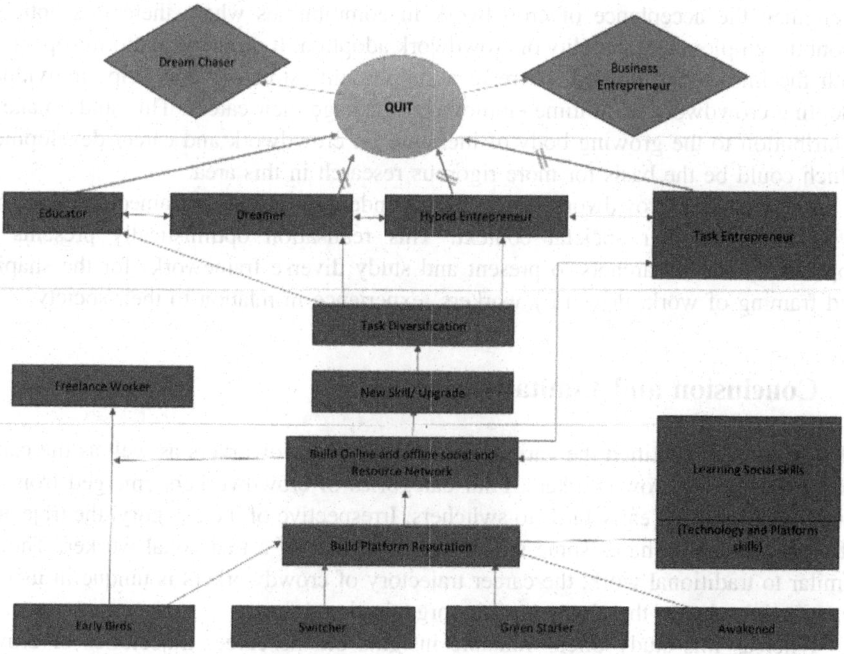

Fig. 4. The career trajectory of crowdworkers

and the diversification of skills have in ensuring income sustainability and career survival in crowdwork. This study also reveals that crowdwork and other Internet-enabled employment are not always and entirely individualistic, while by their nature they seclude workers from traditional organisational relationships, crowdworkers are able to shape their work by developing relationships with employers and forming social relationships with other crowdworkers for career survival.

This study found that crowdworkers learn new skills and attain new capabilities in order to take advantage of emerging opportunities for work in new areas and increase earnings. This findings negates the views of [42] and [43] that this form of work gives no opportunity for skill development. The findings show that crowdworkers experience becomes transferable and of economic value in the form of writing books and blogs, organising workshops, and seminars. Hence, building new and emerging economies from crowdwork, outside platforms including crowdworkers becoming employers themselves and building a work team, this empirically expands on [7] proposition on the career potential of crowdworkers being employer themselves.

Against the backdrop of fewer employment opportunities in the traditional work environment, crowdwork offers a wide range of employment opportunities for individuals with requisite skills and knowledge. For individuals already working as crowdworkers and those aspiring to join the field, this study offers valuable insights, providing a clear picture of the lived experiences of existing crowdworkers career paths and opportunities in crowdwork. Incumbent and potential crowdworkers can use this knowledge to inform their expectations of the field. It could create awareness and strengthen the acceptance of crowdwork in communities where there is scepticism about the employment viability of crowdwork adoption. It provides platforms operators with the knowledge needed to create a support infrastructure that helps individuals adopting crowdwork as fulltime employment manage their career. This study makes a contribution to the growing body of literature on crowdwork and career development which could be the basis for more rigorous research in this area.

In summation, crowdwork is heavily dependent on how it is framed and designed by workers in their societal context. This realisation optimistically presents an opportunity for researchers to present and study diverse frameworks for the shaping and framing of work, driven by workers' experience in relation to their society.

7 Conclusion and Limitations

This study has identified the various categories of crowdworkers as well as the career path followed by crowdworkers. Four categories of crowdworkers emerged from the study, ranging from early birds to switchers. Irrespective of the category, the trajectory of a crowdworker shares some similarities with that of a traditional worker. Though similar to traditional work, the career trajectory of crowdworkers is unique in its own way, mainly due to the absence of the organisational factor.

Whereas this study offers valuable insights on the career trajectories of crowdworkers in the context of Nigeria, like all qualitative research, the study provides an in-depth understanding of the lived experience of participants and is generalised to theory [37]. Hence, this research cannot claim generalisations to the entire country or other countries. More research is encouraged to examine and report on other contexts.

References

1. Lee, J.K.: Research framework for AIS grand vision of the bright ICT initiative. MIS Q. **39**(2), 3–12 (2015)
2. Lee, J., Fedorowicz, J.: Identifying issues for the bright ICT initiative: a worldwide Delphi study of is journal editors and scholars. CAIS **42**, 11 (2018)
3. Dahlander, L., Piezunka, H.: Why some crowdsourcing efforts work and others don't. Harvard Business Review (2017)
4. Kohler, T.: How to scale crowdsourcing platforms. Calif. Manag. Rev. **60**(2), 98–121 (2018)
5. Wazny, K.: "Crowdsourcing" ten years in: a review. J. Glob. Health **7**(2), 1–13 (2017)
6. Bhandari, R., et al.: How to avoid the pitfalls of IT crowdsourcing to boost speed, find talent, and reduce costs (2018). https://www.mckinsey.com/business-functions/digital-mckinsey/our-insights/how-to-avoid-the-pitfalls-of-it-crowdsourcing. Cited 20 Jan 2019
7. Kittur, A., et al.: The future of crowd work. In: Proceedings of the 2013 Conference on Computer Supported Cooperative Work. ACM (2013)
8. Deloitte. The three billion: enterprise crowdsourcing and the growing fragmentation of work. Using the crowd in enterprise (2016). https://www2.deloitte.com/content/dam/Deloitte/us/Documents/strategy/us-cons-enterprise-crowdsourcing-and-growing-fragmentation-of-work.pdf

9. Schweissguth, S.: Crowdsourcing industry trends: unique ways companies are leveraging the crowd (2014). https://www.crowdsource.com/blog/2014/05/crowdsourcing-industry-trends-unique-ways-companies-leveraging-crowd-will-impact-future-job-markets/. Cited 14 Dec 2018
10. Olenski, S.: The State of Crowdsourcing (2015). https://www.forbes.com/sites/steveolenski/2015/12/04/the-state-of-crowdsourcing/#4956b43355ee. Cited Nov 2017
11. Forman, C., King, J.L., Lyytinen, K.: Special section introduction—information, technology, and the changing nature of work. Inf. Syst. Res. **25**(4), 789–795 (2014)
12. Kappelman, L., et al.: The 2015 SIM IT issues and trends study. MIS Q. Executive **15**(1), 55–83 (2016)
13. Deng, X.N., Joshi, K.: Is Crowdsourcing a Source of Worker Empowerment or Exploitation? Understanding Crowd Workers' Perceptions of Crowdsourcing Career (2013)
14. Scholarios, D., Marks, A.: Work-life balance and the software worker. Hum. Resour. Manag. J. **14**(2), 54–74 (2004)
15. Hayward, M.D., Friedman, S., Chen, H.: Career trajectories and older men's retirement. J. Gerontol. Ser. B: Psychol. Sci. Soc. Sci. **53**(2), S91–S103 (1998)
16. Jadidian, A., Duffy, R.D.: Work volition, career decision self-efficacy, and academic satisfaction: an examination of mediators and moderators. J. Career Assess. **20**(2), 154–165 (2012)
17. Blustein, D.: The Psychology of Working: A New Perspective for Career Development, Counseling, and Public Policy. Routledge, Abingdon (2013)
18. Graham, M., Hjorth, I., Lehdonvirta, V.: Digital labour and development: impacts of global digital labour platforms and the gig economy on worker livelihoods. Transf.: Eur. Rev. Labour Res. **23**(2), 135–162 (2017)
19. Howe, J.: The rise of crowdsourcing. Wired Mag. **14**(6), 1–4 (2006)
20. Kässi, O., Lehdonvirta, V.: Online labour index: measuring the online gig economy for policy and research. Technol. Forecast. Soc. Change **137**, 241–248 (2018)
21. Mo, J., Sarkar, S., Menon, S.: Know when to run: recommendations in crowdsourcing contests (2018)
22. Hällgren, C.: Crowdsourcing identities: one way to think about young people's making of identity in conditions proposed by contemporary, digital technologies? In: 11th Annual International Conference of Education, Research and Innovation (2018)
23. Broughton, A., et al.: The experiences of individuals in the gig economy (2018)
24. Kazai, G., Kamps, J., Milic-Frayling, N.: The face of quality in crowdsourcing relevance labels: demographics, personality and labeling accuracy. In: Proceedings of the 21st ACM International Conference on Information and Knowledge Management. ACM (2012)
25. Berg, J.: Income security in the on-demand economy: findings and policy lessons from a survey of crowdworkers. Comp. Labor Law Policy J. **37**, 543 (2015)
26. Kim, K.-N.: Career trajectory in high school dropouts. Soc. Sci. J. **50**(3), 306–312 (2013)
27. Banks, M., et al.: Careers and Identities. Open University Press, Milton Keynes (1992)
28. Oriol, M.D., et al.: Understanding career trajectory: a degree alone is not enough. Int. J. Nurs. Clin. Pract. **2015**, 1–6 (2015)
29. Garwin, D.: Building a learning organization. Harvard Bus. Rev. **71**(4), 73–91 (1993)
30. Whiting, M.E., et al.: Crowd guilds: worker-led reputation and feedback on crowdsourcing platforms. In: Proceedings of the 2017 ACM Conference on Computer Supported Cooperative Work and Social Computing. ACM (2017)
31. Vakharia, D., Lease, M.: Beyond Mechanical Turk: an analysis of paid crowd work platforms. In: Proceedings of the iConference, pp. 1–17 (2015)
32. Super, D.E.: A life-span, life-space approach to career development. J. Vocat. Behav. **16**(3), 282–298 (1980)

33. Freeman, S.C.: Donald super: a perspective on career development. J. Career Dev. **19**(4), 255–264 (1993)
34. Super, D.: A theory of vocational development. Am. Psychol. **8**, 185–190 (1953)
35. Smart, R., Peterson, C.: Super's career stages and the decision to change careers. J. Vocat. Behav. **51**(3), 358–374 (1997)
36. Bingham, W.C.: Donald super: a personal view of the man and his work. Int. J. Educ. Vocat. Guidance **1**(1–2), 21–29 (2001)
37. Walsham, G.: Interpretive case studies in IS research: nature and method. Eur. J. Inf. Syst. **4**(2), 74–81 (1995)
38. Walsham, G.: Doing interpretive research. Eur. J. Inf. Syst. **15**(3), 320–330 (2006)
39. Hodkinson, P.: Grounded theory and inductive research. Res. Soc. Life **3**, 81–100 (2008)
40. Braun, V., Clarke, V., Terry, G.: Thematic analysis. In: Rohleder, P., Lyons, A.C. (eds.) Qualitative Research in Clinical and Health Psychology, pp. 95–114. Macmillan International Higher Education (2014)
41. Saldaña, J.: The Coding Manual for Qualitative Researchers. Sage, Thousand Oaks (2015)
42. Van Belle, J.P., Mudavanhu, S.: Development implications of digital economies. In: Digital Labour in Africa: A Status Report (2018)
43. Mann, L., Graham, M.: The domestic turn: business process outsourcing and the growing automation of Kenyan organisations. J. Dev. Stud. **52**(4), 530–548 (2016)
44. Alalwan, A.A., Rana, N.P., Dwivedi, Y.K., Algharabat, R.: Social media in marketing: a review and analysis of the existing literature. Telematics Inform. **34**(7), 1177–1190 (2017)
45. Abed, S.S., Dwivedi, Y.K., Williams, M.D.: Social media as a bridge to e-commerce adoption in SMEs: a systematic literature review. Mark. Rev. **15**(1), 39–57 (2015)
46. Abed, S.S., Dwivedi, Y.K., Williams, M.D.: SMEs' adoption of e-commerce using social media in a Saudi Arabian context: a systematic literature review. Int. J. Bus. Inf. Syst. **19**(2), 159–179 (2015)
47. Abed, S.S., Dwivedi, Y.K., Williams, M.D.: Social commerce as a business tool in Saudi Arabia's SMEs. Int. J. Indian Culture Bus. Manag. **13**(1), 1–19 (2016)
48. Dwivedi, Y.K., Kapoor, K.K., Chen, H.: Social media marketing and advertising. Mark. Rev. **15**(3), 289–309 (2015)
49. Kapoor, K.K., Tamilmani, K., Rana, N.P., Patil, P., Dwivedi, Y.K., Nerur, S.: Advances in social media research: past, present and future. Inf. Syst. Front. **20**, 531–558 (2018)
50. Rathore, A.K., Ilavarasan, P.V., Dwivedi, Y.K.: Social media content and product co-creation: an emerging paradigm. J. Enterp. Inf. Manag. **29**(1), 7–18 (2016)

The Role of Social Media in Citizen's Political Participation

Abreham Getachew(✉) and Tibebe Beshah

Addis Ababa University, Addis Ababa, Ethiopia
{abreham.getachew, tibebe.beshah}@aau.edu.et

Abstract. Social media is becoming important tool for political participation and engagement. Interaction in social media has a strong influence on the propensity to participate in politics. In this research, we argue that IS is in the right position to improve understanding of social media influence in political communication and participation. In this study, the role of social media for political participation is discussed and the result shows that social media plays great role in terms of replacing traditional media, facilitating political engagement, strengthening strategic collaboration as well as the potential to influence governments decisions in relation with politics. We employed qualitative research methodology and concept analysis technique to transcribe interview that can help to identify and arrange the ideas and views of interviewees. Our study explored how citizens engaged in politics through social media. Thus, the media industry, political consultants, politicians, and citizens will need to adjust their behaviors to leverage this new competitive environment abstract should summarize the contents of the paper in short terms, i.e. 150–250 words.

1 Introduction

In recent years, there is a rapid development of a new information network and information technology which is commonly known as social media. Among the different social Media sites available, the widely used sites are Facebook, LinkedIn, and Twitter, each of which are used by hundreds of millions of people (Alalwan et al. 2017; Dwivedi et al. 2015; Greenhow and Gleason 2014; Kapoor et al. 2018; Shiau et al. 2017; 2018). In past, social Medias are used for interpersonal communication and collaboration using Internet-based platforms. Based on the rapid growth of social Medias, users started to create contents on their own and express their opinion, engaged in political discussion or search for politically like-minded individuals (Dang-Xuan 2013; Dwivedi and Kapoor 2015; Grover et al. 2018; Hossain et al. 2018). Political parties feel responsible in participating political discussions with citizens when the country is democratic. Very recent phenomenon is the rise of social media as a medium for political communication. For example, In the Netherlands, during the national elections (2010), politicians with higher Social Media engagement got relatively more votes within most political parties (Effing et al. 2011).

Political participation is defined as a behavior aimed at influencing the government and affecting their political decisions (Skoric et al. 2016). Social media are also becoming an important part of the research for scholars interested in studying this new

Published by Springer Nature Switzerland AG 2019
Y. Dwivedi et al. (Eds.): TDIT 2019, IFIP AICT 558, pp. 487–496, 2019.
https://doi.org/10.1007/978-3-030-20671-0_33

political phenomenon on the role of social media and interpersonal discussion in local participation (Kim et al. 2010); the effect of social media on political participation (Stanley and weare 2004; Habermas 2006; Mcclurg 2003); the effect of digital access on the prevalence of democracy (Rhue and sundararajan 2014; Rose and Sæbø 2005); New Media and Internet Activism (Kahn and Kellner 2004); To date, Information Systems (IS) studies have investigate the role of Information system in social media use with engagement and its three sub-categories, that is, social capital, civic engagement, and political participation. (Boulianne 2015). Hofmann (2014) examine government rationale for using social media in case of Germany parliament member. Another studies (Oh et al. 2013; Wattal et al. 2010) studied social media services during large scale social movement and revolutionary political change. Studies investigating social media and its role in political and participation are fairly limited or nonexistent in the extant IS literature (Wattal et al. 2010; Maghrabi and Salam 2013).

This study observe developments in social media in the context of recent social movements and revolutionary political change occurring in many of the Middle Eastern and North African countries including Tunisia, Egypt, Lybia, Syria. In Ethiopia, the recent December 2015 ongoing Oromoprotest by students and farmers on the new master plan of Addis Ababa and around Oromia regions made headlines in the world news. This all have in common social networking. Ethiopian government blames opposition parties for facilitating and organizing the protest via Facebook. Recently Ethiopian government sent Zone nine bloggers into jail for accused of committing crime. But international organizations like Amnesty international (http://www.amnestyusa.org/news/press-releases/ethiopia-free-all-jailed-bloggers-and-journalists-before-obama-visit) describes that blogging is right and not a crime and call Ethiopian government to unconditionally release bloggers and journalists in prison and to respect freedom of speech. We can understand from this social networking becomes hot issue and starting affecting Ethiopia political system.

Identifying the theoretical implications of social media use and political participation is challenging for IS research. So it is critical for IS research to explore the role of social media for citizen's political communication and consequent revolutionary political change. These changes have significant implication for business organizations and their strategy as well as larger social and political relations. Thus, the goal of this study is to understand the role of social media for citizen's political participation and political communication. Particularly, this study will answer research question to how social media is used for citizens' political participation.

This paper will makes a number of important contributions to both research and practice. The primary contribution of this paper is to articulate a vision for and a roadmap of the productive a read for researchers to begin looking for and testing fundamental theoretical differences introduced by social media. As previous studies have shown, in the last few years social media have become an important political communication channel. It enables political institutions and citizen's to directly interact with each other. Therefore, political activities might gain more transparency and citizens might be more involved into political decision-making processes. The media industry, political consultants, politicians, and citizens will need to adjust their behaviors to leverage this new competitive environment.

2 Literature Review

Social media are new class of information technology that build on web 2.0 which support interpersonal communication and produce interactive user-generated content using Internet-based platforms (Greenhow and Gleason 2014). The quick development of social media is starting to displace traditional media and influence social and political action in which information are used to engage in participation.

The study by (Tank 2013) shown that social media has produced changes in the way people communicate than working in traditional Medias. Among the changes produced by social media, those who write and comment often use nicknames or pseudonyms. States the ability to stay unknown enabled people to overcome their psychological fear barriers to engage in a free exchange of their view (Maghrabi and Salam 2013) and sometimes it can also avoid responsibility. In addition, what is different in social media is the richness, variety and spreading speed of information as well as the society's most influential figures have merged and social media become public space.

Despite the popular adoption of social media, their application for organizational purposes, the economic impact of social media on business could exceed $1 trillion, most of which is gained from more efficient communication and collaboration within and across organizations (Greenhow and Gleason 2014). The impact of social media on and for organizations, therefore, represents an important area for information systems research.

The relatively free domain of social media creates new opportunities for citizens to become involved in politics. Political science is one area in which information system's deep understanding of the effects of technological system, creation, use and management can be great value. Social media can be classified into different categories including collaborative projects, blogs, content communities, social networking sites, virtual game worlds, and virtual social world's. The most frequently researched social medium is the social networking site is Facebook (Hofmann 2014). Political parties' perceived use Facebook to afford facilitation of direct communication to promote political interests and enable dialogue (Jenson and Dyrby 2013).

As the study is interested to explore how citizens are using social media for the political participation, studies related to social media and political communication were reviewed.

Rhue and Sundararajan (2014) examined the effects of digital access on the prevalence of democracy and its diffusion via trade, geographical and migration networks across 189 countries between 2000 and 2010. Digital access can be facilitated by both media freedom and internal political institutions, and that different digital technologies may have varying impacts while affecting diffusion via different political networks. They conclude that different forms of information technology are likely to impact democracy in different ways, perhaps mediated by different political networks.

Social media enable governments to provide the public with up-to-date information (Jaeger and Bertot 2010) since social media are close to real-time communication channels. Furthermore, Social Media is one of the fastest growing marketing platforms in the world (Coursaris et al. 2013). Although, in contrast to private sector companies, governments do not depend on selling goods, they can still 'advertise' their services and increase their reputation e.g. creating a sense of belonging among the citizens. However, until now the potentials of political discussions in social media could not be exploited sufficiently (Wattal et al. 2010).

Another study (Hofmann 2014), examined the challenges that influence governments' decision to use social media. One of the main obstacle for using social media in governments were privacy regulations or uncertainty about these regulations as well as missing personnel to maintain the social media sites. Before launching a social media site, governments observe and learn experiences of other government agencies social media activities. Social media can also be a "balancing force" to the traditional media (Lin, Bagrow and Lazer 2011).

Social media can provide an ideal environment for political expression and dissenting opinions. Other research by Skorick et al. (2012) examines the relation between social media use and perceived constraints in a semi-authoritarian system in context of the 2011 Singapore general election. The study show that if government control the traditional media there will be more production and consumption of social media content, as well as increased visits to opposition party websites and Facebook pages. This relationship is stronger for younger citizens. The interactivity of social media and their relative freedom, citizens are motivated to use social media for political content production, consumption or for information about opposition parties. In addition, Wattal et al. (2010) examine the influence of the Internet on politics, specifically, on the 2008 US election campaigning using Internet-based technologies such as Web 2.0. The study discussed how these technologies can change the nature of competition in politics and replace or complement traditional media.

Although, all of this studies are helpful, they face some limitations. Previous studies focused on the influence of social media in election result and campaigns which is a single measure and cycle in time. Therefore, it is difficult to conclude the impact of social media in political participation and discourses. Again, those previous studies examines how a particular technology or web 2.0 can change politics. Another studies are needed to conclusively demonstrate the role of these new technologies in political communication and participation.

3 Research Method

Studies examining both social media usage and political participation generally employ a qualitative based research design and observation. In keeping with this methodology convention, the researcher will conduct semi-structure interview which helps to provide flexible and to deal deeper into interviewee responses and observations. Interviewees were selected based on their potential to meet the research objective. Interview request were sent to bloggers who have many followers and most of them were show willingness and interviewed face to face and some of them responded online for our questions. Currently, Ethiopia is facing political crisis in different directions from Amhara, Oromiya and Gambela regions. Due to this some of the interviewee were fear to share their experience and beliefs confidentially.

Most of the interviewees are students in Addis Ababa University. Study by Correa et al. (2010) show that since young citizens are highly using social media since they are grew up with these digital age. 14 Students and 2 politicians are selected and interviewed since they are young's, simplicity to meet and deal with them, peoples are always fear to discuss about political issues. Addis Ababa University is located in Addis Ababa city, capital of Ethiopia. In Ethiopian history, Addis Ababa university students have a unique place in Ethiopian politics and student's movement. Semi-structured nature interview were conducted to interviewees face to face to investigate their motivation and usage of social media for political issues and participation. Each interview were takes 10–15 min in average. Each of the interview were recorded and transcribed. Concept analysis technique is applied to transcribe interview in order to identify and arrange the ideas and views of interviewees.

4 Result

In this study a total of 16 interviewee have been approached and the socio-demographic data is presented in Table 1 below.

Table 1. Socio-demographic data of the interviewee

Job of interviewee	No. of interviewee	Sex	
		Male	Female
Natural science stream student	7	4	3
Social science stream student	7	5	2
Politicians	2	2	0

The recent research work by Pew research center (Duggan et al. 2015) describes that, among the many social Media sites, the most widely used site is Facebook. Based on our observation in campuses and Internet cafe's, we can proved the same is true for Ethiopians also. Our analysis revealed four distinct themes that identify the role of social media specifically Facebook in politics.

4.1 Social Media Replacing Traditional Media Outlet

Social media are used for getting political related news leading to local traditional media such as FM radio's and TV channels. The interviewee with the code A3 share the following history

"I got news from local media and Facebook but most often I got political related news from Facebook. Thus, for political information and news, No need of going to websites, buy newspaper, radios and televisions, the only thing expected from me is login to my Facebook address and see posts"

when the student says "for political information and news, No need of going to websites, newspaper, radios and televisions, the only thing expected from me is login to my Facebook address and see posts" - both social media and the local traditional medias are used by the citizens for news sources. When we comes to politics issues, traditional media and social media is separated. For political news and information citizens are preferring social media rather than the local traditional media. When we take the phrase "No need of going to websites, buy newspaper, radios and televisions" - shows social media provides news faster and less- costly than other mediums. Other interviewee also echoed the same opinion. Facebook is a preferred news medium for political and related issues.

4.2 Social Media for Political Engagement

Social media is becoming a way of political engagement in different ways for Ethiopian citizens. One of the student code B4 relayed the following history:

"I am following many political activists in my Facebook account. I did not post political articles whether good or bad about government. Politics is not medicine. Thus, am forced to stay by liking and commenting my sentiment in others post and sometimes if the posts inspiring me much, I click the 'share' button"

Other interviewee also share the same history. The student use Social media for 'follow' political activists and get their updates. They did not post their thoughts but react the other posting by 'like' and 'comment' and also promoting or sharing other posts by using the 'share' button'. In another way, interviewee explained that Social media is created convenient environment for expressing views and thoughts about political issues. This sentiment mostly expressed by social science students. The interviewee with C3 said the following:

"I myself write and post my political thoughts about different issues in regular basis. By some means I would like my voice to be heard. You do not feel insecure to write and post political issues because one can use pseudo names for instance "Enat Hagere" ".

Students are using Facebook for participating and engaged in the political situations by posting their thoughts. It is also possible to stay unknown and post in Facebook, this helped student's to get confidence to post and share their thoughts.

4.3 Social Media for Strategic Collaboration

This is another theme of social media which is citizens building connections and strategic collaborations. Social media helps peoples to get distant families, friends may be separated for long time. The student with the code C1 speaks as follow:

"I find old friends may be from home town, previous work area in order to keep our friendship and connections. So that you can share your experience and discuss on communal issues"

When the interviewee said "I find old friends may be from home town........ discuss on communal issues". Social media is a cornerstone to strengthen connection based on their commonalities or interests.

4.4 Social Media Influence Government Action

Social media have the potential to empower people to implement and exercise political reforms in response to people need. For example the student with the code 3a said:

"You can observe the current situation in Ethiopia Oromo protest, which is organized and catalyzed by social media. Following the Protest, Ethiopian government forced to withdraw the master plan"

It is known that Ethiopian government announce the rejection of master plan which was the main reason to promo protest.

5 Discussion

Social media become a common media for political news and become replacing traditional media such as newspapers, TV channels and Radios. The interviewees agreed the overriding reason of social media for political news over traditional media is a potential to provide a simple, less-cost and real-time news and information from online user generated content. The necessary question here is why these media become different from traditional media only in politics issues. State Television called EBC (Ethiopian Broadcasting Corporation) in its 24 h transmission talk about development in daily basis siding with the ruling government. Most of the time political critic's news and issues is not transmitted in the channels. International organizations like Amnesty international and world Human right watch accuses Ethiopian government to freedom of expression. Ethiopia is one of three countries in the world with the highest number of journalists in exile (https://www.hrw.org/world-report/2015/country-chapters/ethiopia). Before Facebook is become active in Ethiopia, peoples preferred and listen radio's which broadcast from outside the country such as VOA (Voice of America) and Amharic-German radio which is broadcasting from Germany. But in nowadays, anyone can use his/her mobile or tablet to get any news from the social media. Even those traditional media are also available in social media by having Facebook pages. Anyone can get those local traditional media news as well as political activists and Diaspora based media which is always eager and interested to transit news by protesting the current Ethiopian government. Thus, Social media in Ethiopia become a preferred media outlet which can present political news from the government supporters as well as from opponent of government. The news and information broadcasting by social media are supported by multimedia like picture, video and audio. This may help peoples to enrich with adequate information and one can take the best over it.

Social movement is not individual action rather it is a collective action of peoples who have mutual interests (MaAdan 1982). Social media have the potential to build this connection. Most of the peoples and Ethiopian government also agreed that social media facilitates the current protest by using the hash tag #OromoProtest and "Say No" slogans. We observed that, those peoples in Oromia region were moving on streets by handling and shouting slogans to slogans on the web specifically Facebook. Facebook users were changed their profile picture and post the "Say No" slogans during the protest. In Protest, social media had made power to many well educated men and women to insist political and social changes in the country and become the newfangled influencer. For instance, we can notice many face book posts that were directly blaming federal polices and government in general, and videos that encourage all Oromos to stand for his right. Most of the posts have words like "we Oromos" "Stand Oromo" to call their friends worldwide to break silent and speak out against social injustice and brutality. Thus, social media used to support increased mutual understanding and collaboration in political discourse in a society. Protest activities in social media is more likely to produce a positive effect. Again, within the area of protest activities, many different kinds of activities demonstrations, boycotts and petitions are shown, making. This study shows social media plays a positive role in citizen's political participation. Ethiopian government was described that the protest is catalyzed by propaganda in social media.

The connection and collaboration may be based on ethnic group or political attitude or other interests. Which can simply lead to protests or social movement. The government was said the protest in not about political and not asking justice it is just terrorists action against our country for disturbing the peace. But after the issue become world news like Aljezira, CNN AND BBC world. The government responded that the master plan case is postponed and it is just in the discussion phase for the implementation by following the reports started out from European Union (EU) and the United States government call Ethiopian government to peacefully solve the problem. Finally, as the protest in the social media gets stronger and the protest behavior is changed time to time the government finally announce that the master plan case is rejected. Social media can have the power to change government decisions.

6 Conclusion

The relationship between information technologies and politics has begun to be explored. Previous IS researches in this area has investigated the role of social media during events like voting or crises generally ignored or very limited in the role that IS play in general politics.

This research explore to what extent social media is used by citizens for political participation and engagement. Thus, the study revealed four main distinct themes that indicates how citizens are using social media for political communication and participation, such as, social media is replacing traditional media for political news, facilitates citizens political engagement, strengthening strategic collaboration, and also social media influences government decisions. This identifies the role of social media specifically Facebook in citizens political participation. The study employed qualitative approach for understating social media role in getting political news, participation as well as strengthening connection and collaboration and also influence government actions and decision making. There is still much to learn about IS impact on e-politics. This study provide a step toward a better understating of political engagement in social media. The primary purpose of this research is to lay the base for much needed study on the role of social media in political engagement, especially, for Africa continent democracy and freedom of speech is still in the infant age. The interactions through the internet contribute to the emergence of democracy in society (Wattal et al. 2010).

Future IS researchers will investigate the bigger role of Information Systems and Technologies in politics in order to make business organizations advantageous and benefit the larger society.

References

Alalwan, A.A., Rana, N.P., Dwivedi, Y.K., Algharabat, R.: Social media in marketing: a review and analysis of the existing literature. Telemat. Inform. **34**(7), 1177–1190 (2017)

Bertot, J.C., Jaeger, P.T., Grimes, J.M.: Using ICTs to create a culture of transparency: E-government and social media as openness and anti-corruption tools for societies. Gov. Inf. Q. **27**(3), 264–271 (2010)

Boulianne, S.: Social media use and participation. A meta-analysis of current research. Inf. Commun. Soc. **18**(5), 524–538 (2015)

Correa, T., Hinsley, A.W., De Zuniga, H.G.: Who interacts on the Web?: the intersection of users' personality and social media use. Comput. Hum. Behav. **26**(2), 247–253 (2010)

Coursaris, C.K., Van Osch, W., Balogh, B.A.: A social media marketing typology: classifying brand Facebook page messages for strategic consumer engagement. In: ECIS, p. 46, June 2013

Duggan, M., Ellison, N.B., Lampe, C., Lenhart, A., Madden, M.: Social media update 2014. Pew Research Center, 19 (2015)

Dwivedi, Y.K., Kapoor, K.K., Chen, H.: Social media marketing and advertising. Mark. Rev. **15** (3), 289–309 (2015)

Dwivedi, Y.K., Kapoor, K.K.: Metamorphosis of Indian electoral campaigns: Modi's social media experiment. Int. J. Indian Cult. Bus. Manag. **11**(4), 496–516 (2015)

Effing, R., van Hillegersberg, J., Huibers, T.: Social media and political participation: are Facebook, Twitter and YouTube democratizing our political systems? In: Tambouris, E., Macintosh, A., de Bruijn, H. (eds.) ePart 2011. LNCS, vol. 6847, pp. 25–35. Springer, Heidelberg (2011). https://doi.org/10.1007/978-3-642-23333-3_3

Greenhow, C., Gleason, B.: Social scholarship: reconsidering scholarly practices in the age of social media. Br. J. Educ. Technol. **45**(3), 392–402 (2014)

Grover, P., Kar, A.K., Dwivedi, Y.K., Janssen, M.: Polarization and acculturation in US Election 2016 outcomes–Can Twitter analytics predict changes in voting preferences. Technol. Forecast. Soc. Chang. (2018). https://doi.org/10.1016/j.techfore.2018.09.009

Habermas, J.: Political communication in media society: does democracy still enjoy an epistemic dimension? The impact of normative theory on empirical research. Commun. Theory **16**(4), 411–426 (2006)

Hofmann, S.: Just because we can - governments rationale for using social media. In: Proceedings of the European Conference on Information Systems (ECIS) (2014)

Hossain, M.A., Dwivedi, Y.K., Chan, C., Standing, C., Olanrewaju, A.S.: Sharing political content in online social media: a planned and unplanned behaviour approach. Inf. Syst. Front. **20**(3), 485–501 (2018)

Jensen, T.B., Dyrby, S.: Exploring affordances of facebook as a social media platform in political campaigning. In: ECIS, p. 40 (2013)

Kahn, R., Kellner, D.: New media and internet activism: from the 'Battle of Seattle' to blogging. New Media Soc. **6**(1), 87–95 (2004)

Kapoor, K.K., Tamilmani, K., Rana, N.P., Patil, P., Dwivedi, Y.K., Nerur, S.: Advances in social media research: past, present and future. Inf. Syst. Front. **20**, 531–558 (2018)

Kim, Y., Hsu, S.H., de Zúñiga, H.G.: Influence of social media use on discussion network heterogeneity and civic engagement: the moderating role of personality traits. J. Commun. **63** (3), 498–516 (2013)

Lin, Y.R., Bagrow, J.P., Lazer, D.: More voices than ever? Quantifying media bias in networks. arXiv preprint arXiv:1111.1227 (2011)

Maghrabi, R., Salam, A.F.: Social media and citizen social movement process for political change: the case of 2011 Egyptian revolution (2013)

McClurg, S.D.: Social networks and political participation: the role of social interaction in explaining political participation. Polit. Res. Q. **56**(4), 449–464 (2003)

Oh, O., Agrawal, M., Rao, H.R.: Community intelligence and social media services: a rumor theoretic analysis of tweets during social crises. MIS Q. **37**(2), 407–426 (2013)

Rhue, L., Sundararajan, A.: Digital access, political networks and the diffusion of democracy. Soc. Netw. **36**, 40–53 (2014)

Rose, J., Sæbø, Ø.: Democracy squared: designing on-line political communities to accommodate conflicting interests. Scand. J. Inf. Syst. **17**, 5 (2005)

Shiau, W.L., Dwivedi, Y.K., Lai, H.H.: Examining the core knowledge on facebook. Int. J. Inf. Manag. **43**, 52–63 (2018)

Shiau, W.L., Dwivedi, Y.K., Yang, H.S.: Co-citation and cluster analyses of extant literature on social networks. Int. J. Inf. Manag. **37**(5), 390–399 (2017)

Skoric, M.M., Pan, J., Poor, N.D.: Social media and citizen engagement in a city-state: a study of Singapore. In: Sixth International AAAI Conference on Weblogs and Social Media, May 2012

Skoric, M.M., Zhu, Q., Goh, D., Pang, N.: Social media and citizen engagement: a meta-analytic review. New Media Soc. **18**(9), 1817–1839 (2016)

Stanley, J.W., Weare, C.: The effects of internet use on political participation evidence from an agency online discussion forum. Adm. Soc. **36**(5), 503–527 (2004)

Stieglitz, S., Dang-Xuan, L.: Social media and political communication: a social media analytics framework. Soc. Netw. Anal. Min. **3**(4), 1277–1291 (2013)

Tank, T.: Social Media - The New Power of Political Influence, Centre for European Studies, Brussels (2013)

Wattal, S., Schuff, D., Mandviwalla, M., Williams, C.B.: Web 2.0 and politics: the 2008 US presidential election and an e-politics research agenda. Mis Q., 669–688 (2010)

Development of Resilient Health Information Infrastructure in Complex, Dynamic and Resource Constrained Health Care Context

Birkinesh Woldeyohannes Lagebo(✉)

Addis Ababa University, Addis Ababa, Ethiopia
birwol2001@yahoo.com

Abstract. This research concerns the standardization strategy and organizational resilience behavior and action while designing and implementing HIS in low resource country context. Considerable IS research have been conducted to understand HIS standardization strategy and organizational resilience independently. This paper employed holistic approach, drawing up on organizational resilient and standardization literature based on interpretive case study approach, explores the process of electronic health management information system (eHMIS) design, implementation in low resource country to understand the interplay between organizational resilience and standardization strategy. The major research question guiding this study is how e-HMIS design and implementation process addressed the continuous change of health care in resource constrained context with a focus on resilience and standardization strategy.

Keywords: Implementation · e-HMIS · HIS · Resilient · Standardization · Information infrastructure

1 Introduction

Health Information System (HIS) is considered as a strategy to address the health care delivery problem through equitable health resource allocation and setting priority [33]. HIS is conceptualized differently in various IS research, a patient level data is often termed as electronic medical record (EMR); a system that handles aggregated data based on every day care provision is termed as HMIS and there are also other systems such as HRMS, Financial system, Drug and logistics system. This study concerns the health management information system (HMIS) which collects and aggregates routine data from health facility level and sends to the next higher level woreda, zonal, regional and MOH on periodic basis like on weekly, monthly, semi-annually and annual basis. Managers at various administration levels used this aggregated data for resource allocation and planning purposes. Managers at various administration levels are supposed to use this data for resource allocation and planning purposes.

Despite lack of technology, technical knowledge and skill, low economy and lack of information infrastructure in resource constrained countries, huge IT investment has been made in health care industry to reap the fruits of ICT [5]. Such IT investment in

Published by Springer Nature Switzerland AG 2019
Y. Dwivedi et al. (Eds.): TDIT 2019, IFIP AICT 558, pp. 497–512, 2019.
https://doi.org/10.1007/978-3-030-20671-0_34

low resource countries is often supported by donor agencies [33] which is susceptible for sustainable failure. However, IT investment in healthcare industry in general and in developing countries in particular does not yield the expected results [2, 3, 6, 15, 25, 58–60]. The inherent complexity and changing nature of health care is considered as a reason for viable results of IT investment in the sector in addition to various contextual challenges such as political, technological, social, resource etc.

Such inherent complexity and the continuous change of health sector challenged the developed countries HIS development and implementation efforts to produce many fragmented system which in turn require them huge investment to make it interoperable. Developing countries should take lessons from developed countries to prevent from overcrowded with multiple fragmented systems while also addressing the changing need of the sector due to the fact that e-health initiatives are still at infancy stage in developing countries.

The strategies, decision and actions taken during design and implementation will have significant impact to influence the development and evolution of [18, 21] HIS. Contemporary research is swinging in top-down and bottom-up approach to design and implement HIS in such dynamic and diversified context [37]. Some criticized the formal traditional top down approach due to the fact the approach hinders innovation in such changing world where as others justified the importance of top down approach to maintain communication and coordination amongst heterogeneous health sectors actors with considerable resource [21]. Furthermore, scholars in developing countries favor top-down approach due to the fact that many developing countries followed strict hierarchical system. However such hierarchical approach is highly criticized as it constrains innovation and generativity to address the emerging needs. Balancing standard and generativity in HIS design and implementation is the current challenge of IS research.

Contemporary research disclosed that successful HIS should constituent both stability and flexibility features to create interoperable system and also to address emergent future needs. Accordingly, IT initiatives now a days have adopted architectural and central IT governance approach in many IS design and implementation endeavor to address both stability and flexibility [21]. Recent research result extends the architectural and central IT governance approach by identifying stable and unstable system elements (ibid). For stable system elements, top-down approach has been suggested where as for unstable elements bottom up strategy. Although literatures depict how to balance generativity and stability conceptually, there are few empirical research carried out in developed countries to explicate the issue [20, 40]. Research depicts how standard enables generativity through negotiation without constraining communication and coordination [20, 21]. Such kind of empirical research is crucial to understand how to maintain a balance between standardization and generativity.

In line with these studies, drawing from organizational resilience, generativity and standardization literature, this paper seeks to contribute for this discourse by surfacing the e-HMIS implementation process in resource constrained setting. The results of the research surface key activities, strategies and decisions taken during implementation process which enable or constrain the establishment of resilient health information infrastructure. A system which has both stability and generativity feature in this paper is considered as resilient HIS.

The overall objective of this study is understanding the relationship between standardization and genrativity in e-HMIS development and implementation in Ethiopia. To realize this objective, I formulated the following major and specific research questions. :- How e-HMIS implementation process manages the continuous change of the health care context while maintaining coordination and communication? The study guided by interpretative case study using the concept of strategy and organizational resilience.

The next section is organized as follows. Section 2 discusses the theoretical foundation which is followed by research methodology in Sect. 3. Section 4 presents the research setting followed by Analysis and discussions of the study in Sect. 5. Finally conclusion will be presented in Sect. 6.

2 Theoretical Foundation

HIS requires stability and homogeneity to enable coordination and communication amongst heterogeneous health stakeholders, health programs. HIS also need variability and evolveability feature to meet the anticipated and unanticipated future needs of the sector. However, excessive variability results fragmented systems. Similarly, excessive stability can render an irreversible system [26] which is a challenge for addressing emergent needs of the industry respectively. Thus, maintaining a balance between stability and evolvability while designing and implementing HIS is a central challenge to HIS infrastructure.

2.1 Standardization Strategy

Standardization strategy is ways for developing new standards and how actors play a role, interact and change through the process of standardization. In this study eHMIS is considered as standard and strategy followed to develop and implement eHMIS. There are two major types of standardization process, top down and bottom up, in developing and implementing new standard [26]. The top-down standardization process is a formal standardization process which is characterized as stable, specification driven and often guided by standardization committee (ibid…). It is also widely used in various sectors mainly in telecommunication and engineering field. The top down standardization has four sequential stages as definition, development, implementation, diffusion and use.

On the other hand the bottom up standardization process follows evolutionary or experimental standardization approach [26]. Internet development and use is categorized under this evolutionary model which has the stages of proposed model as development, draft model which is testing and full or standard which is acceptance [1]. The existing standardization system which was initiated and used in 19th century is not appropriate to meet the complex demands of the 21st century [47]. The twenty one century standardization requires flexible standard that meets the current need. The trends of standard changes from stable to flexible due to the global process [11].

Pollock and his collegues [41] suggested generfication model which focuses on developing general software to address the interest of more users as much as possible. However this model is challenged as it requires more local appropriation [4]. Other researchers claimed flexible standards for complex technological system in such more dynamic world that changes over time [9, 26, 49]. Van den Ende et al. [49] argue that the more flexible standard is easy to adopt and more successful. Hanseth and his colleagues [26] explicate how standard can be changed easily, if it is simple and used it for many actors if it incorporates all stakeholders' interest. The simplicity emancipates from the standard definition, if the standardization process follows the top down approach, that will ended up with complex standard which is less flexible, where as if it is bottom up, it is more flexible as it is seen in internet development and use [26]. Braa and his colleagues [9] also suggest 'flexible standards strategy' for health care based on their action research done in a number of developing and middle income countries in Africa and Asia.

The recent research result has also identified three standardization strategies in relation to service innovation based on a 20 year longitudinal research in Norwegian health care development and use [21]. The identified strategies are Anticipatory, Integrated solution and Flexible Generification. The anticipatory standardization strategy characterized by top-down and specification driven is considered as the official and dominant strategy. Anticipatory standardization strategy can develop many standardization strategies which might not be feasible to implement. The remaining two, integerated solution and flexible generification strategies, are an emergent strategies [39] based on their empirical material. The integerated solution focus was on user requirements and functionality which is 'user-driven 'rather than specification driven. Thus this standardization process includes more active user involvement and designing integrated solution which satisfy the users' requirements. However, in spite of the effectiveness of the integerated solutions, it was time taking and a slow process. The third strategy is flexible generification which has focused more on developing working solutions based on users' practices and needs based on input-output legitimacy. The researchers found that flexible generification is suitable for successful HIS implementation in such turbulent area of health sector. They suggested standards to be more generic at the same time simple and flexible to adapt the changing needs of the sector [21]. Accordingly, contemporary research disclosed that successful HIS should constituent both stability and flexibility features to address the emergent future needs. IT initiatives now a days have adopted architectural and central IT governance approach in many IS design and implementation endeavor to address both stability and flexibility [21]. Recent research result extends the architectural and central IT governance approach by identifying stable and unstable system elements (ibid). For stable system elements, top-down approach has been suggested where as for unstable elements bottom up strategy.

In line with these studies, this study seeks to explore the strategies, activities; decisions that have taken during the e-HMIS implementation process to reveal its role for maintaining the balance of generitivity and standardization. In addition to the standardization strategy, literatures now a days due more attention for organizational resilient for successful HIS implementation in such changing environment [15].

2.2 Organizational Resilience

Literatures now a days due more attention for organizational resilient for successful HIS implementation in such changing environment [15]. HIS resilience consists both the stability and evolveability features [50].

The organizational resilience rooted from psychology [13] at individual level and later extensively used at organizational level [44]. Organizational resilience is suitable to explore how actors act in the process of IT implementation. According to the literatures, resilience refers to the capability of individuals, groups, or organizations to adapt quickly to changes in their environments [23, 44]. Literatures provide different definition for the organizational resilience, this study considers resilience as a process capability in overcoming barriers to change and in developing multiple sources of competitive advantages [43]. This approach has three advantages first, resilience is related to the process of change. Second, resilience is multi-faceted, rather than single quality. Thus, organizations may possess some resilient capabilities and not others. Third, in a process perspective, resilience becomes a capability that may be related to both successful and unsuccessful adoption behaviors. On one hand, resilient organizations may able to adopt an innovation and quickly recover from the interruption and return to serving its mission. On the other hand a resilient organization may able to absorb or reject an innovation without any significant change.

The concept of resilience can be used to explore how initial adopted system abandoned after certain period of time through a process point of view. In addition to this, the concept can also be used to explore the human agency adoption practice how specific and complex interactions between different levels of adoption behavior including individuals, groups and organizational unit [30].

The resilience framework can be characterized by time periods, types of systems, types of events, required system actions, and qualities that must be preserved for the system to be considered resilient [35]. In this study eight years is the time period of eHMIS implementation, the system is eHMIS, actors action is considered as needed system action, sustainable eHMIS use for data collection, reporting, analysis and use for local action is considered as qualities that must be preserved to be resilient (Fig. 1).

A knowledge of how standardization strategy influence or impede health workers, programs and public health care settings behavior and actions towards change is a vital knowledge to devise appropriate strategy that can develop organizational resilience that is capable of addressing such changes. This study seeks to investigate the relationship between standard strategy and organizational resilience. The overall objective of this study is how standard strategy influence or enhance organizational resilience and its impact on eHMIS implementation. To realize this objective, I formulated the research question as How the standardization strategy facilitates or embeds organizational resilience within public health care settings?

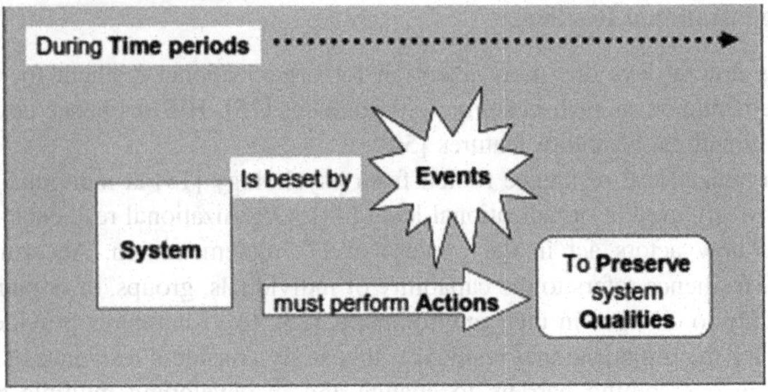

Fig. 1. Framework elements

3 Interpretive Case Study Research Methodology

The research is designed as a single case study with multiple sites involved. In this research, the case is defined as the DHIS implementation in public health care settings and allows examining relationships at different levels of analysis within the DHIS implementation context; national level, regional health bureau, zone health office, wereda health office, and health facility level. The approach will allow me to investigate the case at hand in depth to provide a rich understanding of the case. Case study research can be positivist, interpretive, or critical, depending upon the underlying philosophical assumptions of the researcher. This study will adopt interpretive approach to investigate the DHIS implementation as the study tries to understand the technical, social, cultural, organizational situations of the HIS implementation in relation health care context that various from health facility to health facility, administration level to level etc.

Interpretative understand phenomena through the meanings and interpretations that people assign to them and their understandings of the social and organizational context [52]. It thus has the potential to produce deep insights into the processes of IS development and implementation and how these influence and are influenced by the context [52].

A case study is suitable in answering questions of ‘how’ and ‘why’ [52]. It also addresses contextual and complex conditions and not just isolated variables, and rely on multiple sources of evidence [53]. Thus, case study is well suited to study the development, implementation, and use of the introduction of IT in organizational contexts [10].

The research will be designed as a single case study with multiple sites involved.

3.1 Data Collection Method

The study conducted through an in-depth review of secondary data including the organizations’ strategy documents and different rules, guidelines, registers pertinent to health service delivery and resource allocation, and official reports from the different health facilities. In addition, the majority of primary data will be collected through semi-structured interviews with key informants (such as health workers, IT technicians, persons dealing with statistics, health managers and planners), and the observation of work practices surrounding the collection, processing, use and transmission of data. Thus gathered data will be triangulated with these data collection methods.

Seventeen informants have been interviewed from the public health hierarchy (national, regional, sub city and health facility). All interviews have been conducted using recorder as well as taking notes. There are some interviewee has been interviewed twice so as to clarify and in need of additional data after transcription. Thus gathered data will be triangulated with each other. Interview took from 40 up to 60 min (Table 1).

Table 1. Details of informants

Sn	Specialization	Organization	No of respondents	No of interviews
1	HMIS Head	FMOH	1	1
2	HMIS staff	FMOH	2	2
3	HMIS head	AAHB	1	1
4	Support staff	Yeka Subcity	3	5
5	Data clerks/HIT	Health facilities	3	3
6	Health professionals	Health facility	3	3
	Total		15	20

3.2 Modes of Analysis: Hermeneutics

Hermeneutics approach is selected for the study at hand. Hermeneutics is primarily concerned with the meaning of a text or text-analogue (oral or written text). The basic question in hermeneutics is: what is the meaning of this text? [42]. Taylor says that: "Interpretation, in the sense relevant to hermeneutics, is an attempt to make clear, to make sense of an object of study. This object must, therefore, be a text, or a text-analogue, which in some way is confused, incomplete, cloudy, seemingly contradictory in one way or another, unclear. The interpretation aims to bring to light an underlying coherence or sense" [47]. Hermeneutic clarifies the different views of the organizations stakeholders which are often incomplete, cloudy and contradictory. The major objective of hermeneutic analysis is to make sense of the whole and the relationship between people, the organization and information technology. Accordingly, hermeneutics approach is followed to interpret, describe and analyze the data.

4 E-HMIS Implementation

Like any other developing countries, the introduction of ICT in Ethiopia health care setting has been facilitated by donor agencies and NGos. HIS implementation was first introduced in Ethiopia by different NGOs in different health programs in cooperation with regional health bureaus [31]. However, such varies efforts created redundancies and duplication of effort in health programs and even with in regions. Thus, in 2006, FMOH criticized such dispersed regional efforts that created fragmented systems for the country and launched HMIS reform at national level in cooperation with its partners (donors and NGOs). Comprehensive and standardized national HMIS for evidence based planning and management of health services was designed and implemented at national level [19]. The MOH partners, Tulane University and John Snow, developed and implemented two different software in different regions of the country, Tulane developed and implemented Electronic Health Management Information System (E-HMIS) in all regions except SNNPR where John snow implemented another software which does the same process data collection, process, analysis and reporting. These two systems have been in use in their respective regions till December, 2017. Having two systems with in a country created a challenge to generate a country level health report. MOH took considerable investment to integrate the reported data with two different systems at national level. Furthermore, the continuous change of health care which requires change in system, system failures required being at each site for maintenance and to incorporate changes made in the system. Such handling software maintenance and incorporate changes made in the system consumed a huge investment. Due to these problems, starting from 2015, MOH have sought solutions to address these problems. This paper focuses on e-HMIS which was working for about five years in all regions of Ethiopia till December 30, 2017.

The study will uncover the whole process of eHMIS implementation from software selection, customization, training, use and support. The study includes how the software was selected and designed, how the training and support was organized, and finally the use which includes how data is gathered first from the health facilities (clinics, health centers, and district hospitals), captured in the software, flows to the wereda, zone, the regional and the national levels. Thus, the study requires multi-level analysis which enabled an understanding of the various vertical and horizontal flows of information, resources, rules, plans, and support.

TUTAPE (Tulane University's Technical Assistance Program for Ethiopia) developed Electronic Health Management Information System Software in partnership with CDC and the Fedeeral Ministry of Health Ethiopia (FMOH) [19] using c-sharp, and sql technologies for application and database respectively. Developers used the designed standard data collection tools such as talley sheets, registers, indicators and various reports as an input to design and develop eHMIS. The system was first tested in Addis Ababa, later in eastern shoa zone of Oromia, and Tigray regions. At these testing stages, different system problems and bugs such as summation problem, report missing, and variable missing were identified for software maintenance. The software development took more than a year to deploy at sites. The software was revised three times through out its five years life time due to new users' requirement, missed indicators, reports, summation problems and so on. All these revisions required the presence of implementer at each physical point to incorporate or install the revised system.

A five day eHMIS training was given in cascading format in 21 health science colleges which were equipped with necessary equipment such as computer, projector. First, a five day master training of trainers was given for forty trainees which was conducted in Adama. Trainees from Federal Ministry of health, all regional health bureaus, and implementing partners participated in the master of training of trainees.

These master of TOT provided the EHMIS training to zonal or sub city level TOT who were expected to provide training and for zonal level users. Ultimately, end user training was given for trainees comprised of health facilities who are actually use the system for data entry, and reporting.

The initial training given for master of TOT did not enable trainers at the level providing support to end users. Thus most of the support requests were forwarded to upper level region till national level FMOH that brought a great workload on Tulane staff and also took significant period of time to get on time support. As a result, Tulane prepared and provided a 20 days troubleshooting and maintenance training for all regional and sub city HIT staff that highly minimized the support requests came to Tulane and FMOH. However, trainers did not have access to source code to continue learning about systems such as how to modify, insert new requirement including adding and modifying data element, indicator.

FMOH purchased 4000 computers, some servers to make the sites ready for system installation and use. The system was cloned in all 4,000 computers at Ministry of health and distributed to all sites including regions, zones, wereda/sub city, and health facilities found within country. However, maintenance and reinstallation required at sites due to database failure, system revision due to minor mistakes for instance missing indicators, data element and also new requirements need software installation. Thus installation consumed huge amount of time, and finance particularly when they made system revision. eHMIS had made three revision.

5 Analysis and Discussion

The analysis have been made as mentioned earlier first by interpreting the data gathered by using hermeneutics approach to come up with concepts generated from the data and establish pattern and finally map it with the standard strategy and organizational resilience concepts.

5.1 Top-Down eHMIS Strategy

The case description as shown in Sect. 5.1 has revealed how top down approach or centralized approach was followed for all eHMIS initiation, development, implementation and use. The top-down standardization process is a formal standardization process which is guided by standardization committee [21]. The HMIS steering committee chaired by FMOH, selected system developer organizations through some criteria. The top down standardization approach has been characterized as stable, and specification driven [21]. Similarly in this case, the standard data collection tools and reports, indicators were given as a specification to develop eHMIS. The centralizing approach except providing the same specification to guide the system development, it did not give a room for system developer organizations to discuss about how to develop the system. As a result both partners ended up with two different eHMIS systems with huge investment which has predominantly the same function. These two eHMIS became un-compatible at national level to prepare a national level report. Thus FMOH invested additional time, effort and finance to develop a system that can integrate and analyze a national level data and generate report. Furthermore, in order to change a single data element, data set or organizational unit, it required to change on source code which is not accessible to public organizations as well as it requires high tech knowledge and skill. Standard's simplicity depends on the approach to defining a standard, if it is top-down it is less flexible where as if it is bottom up, it is more flexible [65]. As eHMIS development followed top down approach it requires high tech knowledge and skill for system change. The top down approach which has its roots of the 19th century is not appropriate to meet the demands of the 21st century which is complex and more dynamic [49]. Similarly, eHMIS was not cope-up with highly dynamic situations of the health sector as it was stated above in the case study Sect. 5.2.1. Thus the strategy did not allow them to modify the system with existing limited system knowledge and skill. This research finding is similar to [21] anticipatory standardization strategy which is not feasible to implement or take considerable time. Researchers suggested standards to be more generic at the same time simple and flexible to adapt the changing needs of the sector [9, 11, 21]. Thus HIS managers, designers and implementers should consider the flexibility and simplicity of the standard for successful HIS design and implementation in such changing environment.

Regarding training, training was also organized at central level without making ground level assessment. This centralized training by focusing more on training specification includes training content, duration, number of trainees, training place and fund) missed key HMIS and HIT trainees in the first round master of TOT which slowed down the implementation of eHMIS. System installation and support was also organized at region level which required the presence of Tulane staff at all sites which also taken considerable time due to the vastness of the sites and the large number of support requests.

Although actors at sub city and region level had involved in many implementation activities such as conducting training, installing the software and providing support to end users, their role was limited to accompanying Tulane staff and facilitating this activity rather than discharging the activity by their own. This was mainly because system related knowledge, skills, set up files and the source code was under the control of the Tulane university. In general, the system development and implementation was primarily dominated by FMOH and Tulane University where as the public actors at region, sub city and health facility were just facilitating the implementation process. Standard's simplicity depends on the approach to defining a standard, if it is top-down it is less flexible where as if it is bottom up, it is more flexible [26].

5.2 Stakeholders Resilience Towards EHMIS

Resilience refers to the capability of individuals, groups, or organizations to adapt quickly to changes in their environments [13, 23, 35, 44]. Resilient organizations may able to adopt an innovation and quickly recover from the interruption and return to serving its mission. On the other hand a resilient organization may able to absorb or reject an innovation without any significant change. In the case at hand, FMOH, regional health bureau, Tulane University and other partner organizations including CDC, ITECH have shown considerable organizational resilient to thrive technical and organizational problem faced during implementation and to continue implementing and using the system. For instance they hired new staff to strengthen HMIS at lower levels, bought UPS, install antivirus and used various technical measures to safe the system from failure, organize extensive trouble shooting training to build lower level HIT capacity. Direction had been given to send monthly data only in eHMIS. All these actions were taken by the organizations to continue implementing and using the system. However, some of the resilient behavior was not adequate and some required significant investment, and others ended up with limiting eHMIS use to merely for data entry and reporting which missed the main goal of eHMIS which is using data for local action.

Despite all actors enthusiasm and resilient behavior towards eHMIS implementation and use, their resilient behavior was not extended eHMIS use from data entry reporting to the level of data use at all stage, enable to use local capacity for extending, modifying system and even to handle some support, rather it continued to rely on system developer organization for the day to day support issues and system changes.

5.3 The Interplay Between eHMIS Strategy and Organizational Resilient

Regardless of all public level actors enthusiasm and resilient actions towards the system as mentioned in Sect. 6.2, the centralized strategy did not extend further the created resilient action to facilitate the development and implementation of sustainable eHMIS. The administrative institutions considerable resilient action had not been extended from purchasing hardware, developing a software, organizing and conducting training and issuing rules not to the level owning system knowledge and skill, owning system source code and using eHMIS data for local action.

The top down approach did not provide suitable platform to foster learning with in public health institutions rather it centralized high level system knowledge, skill and system under the control of system developer organization. Neither the cascading training nor extensive troubleshooting training focused on limited system knowledge and skill did not allow learning and sharing deep level system knowledge and skill from system developers to public health institutions. As a result, HIT staff at various administration offices had invested unnecessary time, money and effort in surfing external resources to use such centralized knowledge and skill as it is mentioned in case description section. Second, it took considerable time to get technical support. Third, the top – down approach did not allow public HMIS and HIT staff to access the source code of the system which should have facilitated owning deep level system knowledge and skill to own system support as well as to handle system change as result the public HIT and HMIS staff heavily relied on system developer organization knowledge and skill mainly for system change. Moreover, FMOH had invested other considerable amount of money to develop and integrated data analysis tool at national level due to absence of access to source code. This finding is also in congruence with in congruence with Hanseth and Bygstad which showed how the traditional, top-down IS strategy can came up with multiple standardization, yet it was difficult to implement and slow [21]. Issuing rules not to accept paper based monthly report though enhanced the end users' eHMIS use only to the level of data entry and reporting, yet it missed the major objective of eHMIS which is using data for local action. This finding is similar to Hanseth and Bygstad [21] stated as the top-down approach merely automates the existing paper based system to computer system which is merely reduced time, not change the way HMIS was organized and use.

As described above in this analysis section, the top – down approach enabled all actors to be resilient at certain level yet not facilitated the exhibited resilient action. These resilient actions taken by all actors had also brought negative consequences. First, it required huge investment. Second it limited eHMIS to merely for data entry and reporting. Third public HIT and HMIS staff system knowledge and skill was not in a position of owning system support and modification activity rather they had been heavily relying on system developer organizations staff. Fourth the public organizations at any level did not have access to system code till the termination of eHMIS. Lastly, it missed the main objective of eHMIS development and implementation which is using generated data for local action. This finding is similar Cho et al. [15] results stated "while resilience facilitated swift and successful adoption, it also created tensions that endangered further diffusion and the long-term sustainability of the tele-health innovation" [15]. Furthermore, the strategy did not extended or foster the exhibited resilient behavior and action.

Thus, the above mentioned situations (frequent support requirement and its investment, the dynamic nature of the health care which required system revision and installation to each site, absence of system ownership to make modification, absence of the required system knowledge and skills at public HIT and HMIS staff) challenged FMOH to continue its resilient behavior towards eHMIS, rather switched to look for other better alternative. Thus despite, considerable resilient behavior was seen at all end users and public health administration offices and also partner organizations for effective implementation of eHMIS, FMOH by considering the consequences of eHMIS implementation decided to replace eHMIS with DHIS-2 which is an open source web based software.

The case analysis has vividly depicted how the top down eHMIS development and implementation strategy facilitated to develop organizational resilience with all stakeholders at certain level where as at the same time limited the organizational resilience action. This limited organization resilience action might deteriorate the developed organizational resilience through time. This interplay between eHMIS strategy and organizational resilience has shown its considerable impact on the development and implementation of sustainable eHMIS system. For instance the centralized cascading training resulted for missing key trainees, inadequate training and increases implementation cost where as the organizational resilient action of the actors 'trouble shooting and maintenance training' which was derived from the reality exhibited in institutions facilitated learning and minimizing implementation cost and time at certain level. Furthermore, the top down approach issued guideline to use merely eHMIS for data reporting though it enhanced users eHMIS use by showing resilient action by using sub city computer for data entry and reporting yet this resilient action limited the purpose of eHMIS merely to data entry and reporting. The top down strategy adopted in the case at hand case even if it created resilient action yet it was unable to facilitate the resilient action by availing more conducive environment. Thus appropriate strategy should be devised that not only to develop organizational resilient behavior and action but also fostering the organizational resilient actions by providing suitable environment. This case slightly indicated the bottom-up approach might help in developing organizational resilience and also facilitating further the organizational resilience.

6 Conclusion

The standardization strategy and resilience concept is used to understand and depict the interplay between IS implementation strategy and organizational resilience in shaping the development and implementation of eHMIS. The study identified how top-down or centralized HIS standardization strategy at the beginning created organizational resilience behavior and actions at all levels. However, the created organizational resilience behavior was not reinforced by providing system level ownership and the required system knowledge and skill. The developer organization who monopolizes the system ownership, resource and knowledge and skills did not enable them to address the users' frequent and emergent needs. It took them considerable time and resource to fix minor users' problem at lower levels. Consequently, the created organizational behavior became limited to generate the required organizational resilience behavior and actions mainly at lower levels to address the emerged users' need. Lately sub-city focused deep level training minimized the frequent users' support and helped to continue using the system. However, the negative consequences of organizational resilience and top-down strategy which requires huge running cost and time also deteriorated the upper level resilience towards the system that leads to terminate the use of eHMIS.

Thus the study by relating organizational resilience and standardization strategy depicted how their interplay shape the eHMIS design, implementation and use. The study depicts how top-down strategy is unable to create sustainable organizational resilience behavior and action to address the emerged needs of the users. Thus the research suggested for implementers to employ appropriate strategy which emphasizes both in creating and sustaining organizational resilience behavior and action that can address the emergent needs of the users at lower levels. In this case, sub city (wereda) level focused strategy produced viable results in sustaining the organizational resilience behavior and action which can address the emergent needs of users.

References

1. Abbate, J.: Inventing the Internet. MIT Press, Cambridge (1999)
2. Avgerou, C., Walsham, G.: Information Technology in Context; Studies from the Perspectives of Developing Countries. Ashgate, Hampshire (2001)
3. Avgerou, C., McGrath, K.: Power, rationality, and the art of living through socio technical change. MIS Q. **31**, 295–315 (2007)
4. Avegrou, C.: New socio-technical perspectives of is innovation in organizations. In: Larover, R.L. (eds.) ICT Innovation: Economic and Organizational Perspectives. Edward Elgar, Cheltenham (2002)
5. Avgero, C.: Information systems in developing countries: a critical research review. J. Inf. Technol. **23**, 133–146 (2008)

6. Braa, J., et al.: A study of the actual and potential usage of information and communication technology at district and provincial levels in Mozambique with a focus on the health sector. Electron. J. Inf. Syst. Dev. Countries **5**(2) (2001)
7. Braa, J., Monteiro, E., Sahay, S.: Networks of action: sustainable health information systems across developing countries. MIS Q. 337–362 (2004)
8. Braa, J., Hedberg, C.: The struggle for district-based health information systems in South Africa. Inf. Soc. **18**, 113–127 (2002)
9. Braa, J., Hanseth, O., Heywood, A., Mohammed, W., Shaw, V.: Developing health information systems in developing countries: the flexible standards strategy. MIS Q. **31**(2), 381–402 (2007)
10. Benbasat, I., et al.: The case research strategy in studies of information systems. In: Myers, M.D., Avison, D. (eds.) Qualitative Research in Information Systems: A Reader, pp. 79–99. SAGE Publications, London (2002)
11. Brunsson, N., Jacobsson, B.: The contemporary expansion of standardization. In: Brunsson, N., Jacobsson, B., (eds.) A World of Standards. Oxford University Press, New York (2002)
12. Brunsson, N., Rasche, A., Seidl, D.: The dynamics of standardization: three perspectives on standards in organization studies. Organ. Stud. **33**(5–6), 613–632 (2012)
13. Coutu, D.L.: How resilience works. Harvard Bus. Rev. **80**(5), 46–55 (2002)
14. Cho, S., Mathiassen, L., Robey, D.: Dialectics of resilience: a multi-level analysis of a telehealth innovation. J. Inf. Technol. **22**, 24–35 (2007)
15. Cho, S., Mathiassen, L., Nilsson, A.: Contextual dynamics during health information systems implementation: an event-based actor-network approach. Eur. J. Inf. Syst. **17**, 614–630 (2008)
16. Concept notes and status of ICT programmes implementation, p. 16 (2009)
17. Chandwani, R., De, R., Dwivedi, Y.K.: Telemedicine for low resource settings: exploring the generative mechanisms. Technol. Forecast. Soc. Change **127**, 177–187 (2018)
18. Dwivedi, A., Shareef, M., Simintiras, A., Lal, B., Weerakkody, V.: A generalised adoption model for services: a cross-country comparison of mobile health (m-health). Gov. Inf. Q. **33**, 174–187 (2016)
19. FMOH-Ethiopia: Health Management Information System (HMIS)/Monitoring and Evaluation (M&E) Strategic Plan for Ethiopian Health Sector. HMIS Reform Team. Federal Ministry of Health, Addis Ababa (2008)
20. Grisot, M.: Infrastructures in healthcare: the interplay between generativity and standardization. Int. J. Med. Inf. **82**(5), 170–179 (2013)
21. Hanseth, M., Bygstad, B.: Flexible generification: ICTstandardization strategies and service innovation in health care. Eur. J. Inf. Syst. **24**, 645–663 (2015)
22. Hanseth, O., Monteiro, E.: Inscribing behaviour in information infrastructure standards. Acc. Manag. Inf. Syst. **7**(4), 183–211 (1997)
23. Hamel, G., Valikangas, L.: The quest for resilience. Harvard Bus. Rev. **81**(9), 52–63 (2003)
24. Hanseth, O., Aanestad, M.: Bootstrapping networks, communities and infrastructures – on the evolution of ICT solutions in healthcare. Methods Inf. Med. **42**(4), 385–391 (2003)
25. Heeks, R.: Health information systems: failure, success and improvisation. Int. J. Med. Inf. **75**(2), 125–137 (2006)
26. Hanseth, O., Monteiro, E., Hatling, M.: Developing information infrastructure: the tension between standardization and flexibility. Sci. Technol. Hum. Values **21**(4), 407–426 (1996)
27. Herrera, A., Janczewski, L.: Modelling organizational resilience in the cloud. In: PACIS Proceedings, p. 275 (2013)
28. Hewapathirana, R., Sahay, S.: Open source adoption in health sector: understanding the stakeholder relationships in a resource constrained setting. EJISDC **81**(1), 1–21 (2017)

29. Igira, F.T.: The situatedness of work practices and organizational culture: implications for information systems innovation uptake. J. Inf. Technol. **23**(2), 79–88 (2008)
30. Klein, H., Myers, M.: A set of principles for conducting and evaluating interpretive field studies in information systems. MIS Q. **23**(1), 67–94 (1999)
31. Lagebo, B., Molla, S.: Challenges of scaling and standardization HIS implementation. MSC thesis, Faculty of Mathematics and Natural Sciences, University of Oslo (2005)
32. Liu, V., Caelli, W., Yang, Y., Lauren, M.: A test vehicle for compliance with resilience requirements in index-based e-health systems. In: PACIS Proceedings, p. 119 (2011)
33. Lippeveld, T., Sauerborn, R., Bodart, C. (eds.): Design and implementation of health (2000)
34. Lo, J., Leidner, D.: Extending the IS strategy topology: an assessment of strategy impacts on capabilities development performance. In: Thirty Third International Conference on Information Systems, Orlando (2012)
35. Mallak, L.: Putting Organizational Resilience to Work. Industrial Management IIE (1998). https://www.researchgate.net/publication/291863333. Accessed 2 Aug 2018
36. Myers, M.D., Avison, D. (eds.): Qualitative Research in Information Systems. SAGE Publications, London (2002)
37. Mekonnen, S., Sahay, S.: An institutional analysis on the dynamics of the interaction between standardizing and scaling processes: a case study from Ethiopia. Eur. J. Inf. Syst. **18**, 98 (2015)
38. Mengesha, T.: Electronic Solutions for Ethiopian Health Sector (2011)
39. Mintzbergh, H.: Patterns in strategy formation. Manag. Sci. **24**(9), 934–948 (1978)
40. Neilson, P., Hanseth, O.: Towards a design theory of usability and generativity. In: ECIS (2015)
41. Pollock, N., Williams, R., D'adderio, L.: Global software and its provenance: generification work in the production of organizational software packages. Soc. Stud. Sci. **37**(2), 254–280 (2007)
42. Radnitzky, G.: Contemporary Schools of Metascience. Scandinavian University Books, Goteborg (1970)
43. Reinmoeller, P., Baardwijk, N.V.: The link between diversity and resilience. MIT Sloan Manag. Rev. **46**(4), 61–65 (2005)
44. Riolli, L., Savicki, V.: Information system organizational resilience. Omega: Int. J. Manag. Sci. **31**(3), 227–233 (2003)
45. Sheared, S.: A frame work for system resilience discussions (2008)
46. Sahay, S., Monteiro, H., Aanstaad, M.: Toward a political perspective of integration in information systems research: the case of health information systems in India. Inf. Technol. Dev. **15**(2), 83–94 (2009)
47. Taylor-Powel, E., Renner, M.: Analyzing qualitative data. University of Wisconsin Cooperative Extension. Publication G3658-6 (2003)
48. Updegrove, A.: Breaking down trade barriers: avoiding the China syndrome. Consortium Standards Bulletin, 3 May 2004
49. Van den Ende, J., Van de Kaa, G., Den Uijl, S., De Vries, H.J.: The paradox of standard flexibility: the effects of co-evolution between standard and interorganizational network. Organ. Stud. **33**(5–6), 705–736 (2012)
50. Wareham, H., Fox, P., Lluis, J.: Technology ecosystem governance. Organ. Sci. **25**(4), 1195–1215 (2014)
51. Walsham, G., Sahay, S.: Research on information systems in developing countries: current landscape and future prospects. Inf. Technol. Dev. **12**(1), 7–24 (2006)
52. Walsham, G.: Interpretive case studies in IS research: nature and method. Eur. J. Inf. Syst. **4**(2), 74–81 (1995)
53. Yin, R.K.: Applications of Case Study Research. Sage Publications (2002)

54. Chandwani, R.K., Dwivedi, Y.K.: Telemedicine in India: current state, challenges and opportunities. Transform. Gov.: People Process Policy **9**(4), 393–400 (2015)
55. Dwivedi, Y.K., Shareef, M.A., Simintiras, A.C., Lal, B., Weerakkody, V.: A generalised adoption model for services: a cross-country comparison of mobile health (m-health). Gov. Inf. Q. **33**(1), 174–187 (2016)

Influence of Social Media Practices on the Fusion of Strategies Within Organisations

Shirumisha Kwayu[1(✉)], Banita Lal[2(✉)], and Mumin Abubakre[1(✉)]

[1] Nottingham Business School, Nottingham Trent University, Nottingham, UK
shirumisha.kwayu2014@my.ntu.ac.uk,
Mumin.abubakre@ntu.ac.uk

[2] Strategy and Management, University of Bedfordshire, Luton, UK
Banita.lal@beds.ac.uk

Abstract. Contemporary information technologies such as social media have brought into question the usefulness of the alignment perspective in understanding the role and influence of technology in organisational strategy. This has prompted some scholars to argue for a fusion view of Information Systems (IS) which sees IS as integral to business strategy. Despite the suggestion of the fusion view, there is little empirical evidence of how the fusion of strategy is realised. For instance, literature suggests that executives are struggling with how to implement social media strategy within an organisation. This paper uses the strategy as practice lens guided by the interpretivist philosophy to explore the influence of social media practices on the fusion of strategies within an organisation. The paper uses empirical evidence from the case study of a telecom organisation in Tanzania to gain theoretical insight into the role of social media in organisational strategy. This research contributes to the management literature by arguing that the fusion of strategy is achieved by the intertwinement of historical background, context, technological advances and social intent. Also, it contributes to IS literature by showing how social media extends the IS scope within an organisation while minimizing the need for organisational IT infrastructure. In practice, this research highlights the significance of informal social media practices such as WhatsApp communication in organisational processes such as knowledge sharing and customer service.

Keywords: Fusion of strategy · Digital business strategy · Social media · WhatsApp · Strategy as practice

1 Introduction

Following the rise of social media and its increasing in organisations influence (Alalwan et al. 2017; Dwivedi et al. 2015, 2016; Kapoor et al. 2018), scholars such as El Sawy (2003) suggest a new perspective - the 'fusion view of IS' - that sees Information System (IS) as embedded in, and integral to, the product and services offering of the firm. Primarily, the fusion view perceives IS strategy as the business strategy; it does not separate the two. Alignment divides them into two distinctive domains, the IT domain (IT strategy) and the business domain (business strategy). Furthermore,

Published by Springer Nature Switzerland AG 2019
Y. Dwivedi et al. (Eds.): TDIT 2019, IFIP AICT 558, pp. 513–528, 2019.
https://doi.org/10.1007/978-3-030-20671-0_35

Bharadwaj et al. (2013) and Henfridsson and Lind (2014) have argued that it is increasingly necessary to rethink the role of information technology (IT) strategy due to the intertwinement of new digital technologies and human actions. Specifically, they argue that the increasing role of digital technologies is making the alignment perspective in strategy less useful. Considering this, Bharadwaj et al. (2013) have also termed the fusion view as the Digital Business Strategy (DBS). Meanwhile, the increasing intertwinement of digital technology and human actions has led to a new conception of IS theories such as the practice perspective (e.g. Orlikowski 2000) and the sociomateriality (e.g. Cecez-Kecmanovic et al. 2014; Orlikowski 2007) perspective that seek to explain the interaction of humans and technology. Scott and Orlikowski (2014) and Huang et al. (2014), suggest that these perspectives are suitable for understanding the role of technologies such as social media, where their effect is highly integrated with human action. Thus, newer IS theories, which negate the separation of technology and human activity, are influencing a shift in thinking from the alignment perspective, which sees IT strategy and business strategy as separate domains, to that which reflects a fusion of IT and business strategy. For instance, Phillips-Wren and McKniff (2015) suggest that the concept of embeddedness can be used to study and frame the fusion of technology in an environment. Orlikowski (2000) suggests that the practice theory extends the concept of embeddedness with enactment and appropriation with emergence. Thus, practice theory, which is considered as a family of theories (Tavakoli et al. 2017) including sociomateriality (Orlikowski 2007) and strategy as practice (Jarzabkowski 2005), have concepts that are useful for studying and framing the fusion of technology with consideration of context.

Of late, IS studies on the effects of digital technologies in organisations, i.e. Huang et al. (2014), have supported the fusion view. Thus, considering that the fusion view is gaining ground in the IS field, it can be considered timely to analyze how our thinking is shifting from the alignment view to a fusion view by investigating the impact of contemporary technology within organisations. For example, the review by Kahre et al. (2017) on the shift from the alignment to fusion view suggests that future research should use different theoretical lenses to explore how DBS (fusion of strategy) is realized. Similarly, Aral et al. (2013) suggest that organisational executives are struggling with how and what broader changes in organisational structure and processes are required for implementing social media. Thus, this suggests there is a gap in understanding how the fusion of strategy is realized due to the influence of digital technologies such as social media.

Following the above, this paper aims to explore *the influence of social media practices on the fusion of strategies within organisations*. Examining social media practices will help to understand how social media is implemented within the organization and its effect on organisational structure and processes. Also, exploring social media practice will help to understand the implementation of social media hence offering an opportunity to understand the extent to which DBS is realized. Hence, the paper adopts a strategy as practice (SaP) perspective, which falls within a family of practice theory. The strategy as practice theory perceives strategy as a goal-directed activity in a situated environment (Jarzabkowski 2005). The focus of strategy as practice is on strategizing, the actual doing of strategy (Jarzabkowski and Paul Spee 2009), which emphasizes on real day-to-day activities, context, processes and content that relates to a strategic outcome (Peppard et al. 2014). Hence, the SaP lens will help us to understand the implementation of social media within an organisation while considering the context. Therefore, in a broader sense, SaP will help us understand how DBS is implemented in an organisation.

To address the aims of this research, this paper adopts an interpretivist philosophy to gather empirical evidence from a case study organisation in Tanzania. The case study organisation is a telecommunication company in Tanzania. The data was collected through semi-structured interviews with employees and managers of SIMU (a pseudonym of the company). Apart from the semi-structured interviews as primary sources of data collection, observation and documentary analysis were additional methods of gathering evidence. Further details are provided in the methodology section.

This research contributes to the management literature by arguing that the fusion of strategy is assisted by the intertwinement of historical background, context, technological advances and social intent. Also, it adds to IS literature by showing how social media extends the IS scope within an organisation while minimizing the need for organisational IT infrastructure. Furthermore, this research shows how social media practices are changing work processes which become integral to the emergent strategy of the organisation. In practice, this research demonstrates the significance of informal social media practices such as WhatsApp communication in organisational processes such as knowledge sharing and customer service.

The remainder of this paper is organised as follows: first, we discuss the literature on social media practice and value. Then follows a discussion on strategy as practice which is the theoretical lens adopted for this research. Thereafter follows the methodology section which discusses the research context, site selection and access, data collection and data analysis. Following this, we present the findings and a discussion on the implications to literature and practice. Lastly, the paper ends with concluding remarks.

2 Social Media Practice and Value

Over the last decade, social media practice has accelerated to become a mainstream practice within organisations (Pillet and Carillo 2016). For example, McKinsey & Company reported that 83% of companies in the US used social media (Braojos-Gomez et al. 2015; Culnan et al. 2010). Social media is used for various reasons in organisations. For example, Hutchings (2012) suggests that organisations can use social media as a powerful means of communicating, promoting brands and products, selling as well as increasing knowledge sharing in organisations. Likewise, Aral et al. (2013) suggest that organisations use social media for value creation. The idea of an organisation using social media for value creation and competitive advantage is defined by Piskorski (2014) as a social media strategy. A social media strategy helps an organisation to lower its cost or increase its ability to charge higher for their products and services. The strength of an organisation to leverage social media differs from one organisation to another. Braojos-Gomez et al. (2015) term this ability as social media competence, which is defined as an organisation's proficiency in using and leveraging social media for business activities. They argue that social media competence is dependent upon several factors, which include business infrastructure capability and IT infrastructure capability. These two factors specifically relate to the internal activities of an organisation and, if both are in alignment with one another, this provides an ideal environment for organisations to implement social media to obtain value successfully (Henderson and Venkatraman 1989).

Alignment refers to an organisation's ability to reconfigure internal activities and processes to cope with changing demands from the environment (Huang et al. 2014). Thus, within the context of social media, alignment is the ability of an organisation to reconfigure its internal activities and processes in response to this new technology. According to Venkatraman et al. (1993), the alignment between IT and business infrastructure is imperative for any IT investments within an organisation to gain efficiency at the operational level. Similarly, Wagner et al. (2014) suggest that achieving alignment at the operational level is vital for both IT utilisation and organisational performance within a business. Therefore, considering the above, there is a degree to which the alignment perspective can explain the role of social media in an organisation. Despite the dominance of the alignment perspective in IT strategy, and with empirical validation from various studies such as Luftman et al. (2012), it still receives substantial criticism. Chan and Reich's (2007) review of alignment highlights that the alignment research is mechanistic and fails to capture real-life. For social media, which is entangled by both social and technical elements (Scott and Orlikowski 2014), a theory that is mechanical with less consideration of social factors will be less insightful to explain how social media impacts organisations.

In addition to above criticism of alignment, Chan and Reich (2007) argue that alignment is not possible when the business strategy is unknown. Nevertheless, the recent body of literature suggests that strategy is emergent rather than planned; a strategy as practice field in IS is an example of this literature. This current literature that conceives strategy as an emergent phenomena supports Ciborra's (1994) argument that the successful application of IT is more often due to serendipity than to any formal planning. Thus, the alignment view is where strategy is designed and mostly done by management is contrary to 'strategy as practice' where strategy is emergent and done with all members of the organisation (Jarzabkowski 2005). Thus, with a collaborative technology as social media, the organisational strategy is substantively dependent on activities (practice) of its members that contribute to emergent strategy. Thus, the dynamic nature of social media, which is due to the intertwinement of social and technical elements, challenges our understanding of obtaining value from IT through aligning IT and business strategy. Hence, scholars such as El Sawy (2003), Bharadwaj et al. (2013) and Phillips-Wren and McKniff (2015) suggest adopting an extreme form of alignment, the fusion view, which sees an opportunity of seamless integration of IT and business strategy that cannot be disentangled. The fusion view, which has also been termed as a Digital Business Strategy (DBS) (Bharadwaj et al. 2013) appreciates a new logic of competitive strategy that recognizes the fused nature of IT and its central role in product development and service delivery of an organisation. Thus, this suggests a paradigmatic shift that challenges our assumption of competitive strategies, particularly with how IT value is sourced.

The fusion of IT with business practices has the potential to influence organisational strategy significantly. For instance, Huang et al. (2014) suggest that social media can shift the site of activities within an organisation; such an effect can be integral to organisational strategy and value creation. Similarly, Scott and Orlikowski (2012) suggest social media generates complex information dynamics that are forcing organisations into an unexpected direction, redrawing boundaries and shifting relationships. With such effect of social media on organisational strategy, proponents of fusion such as Bharadwaj et al. (2013) suggest the reality of traditional business strategy has changed to modular, distributed, cross-functional and global business processes that enable activity to be done across the limits of time, distance and space. Thus, with changing business dynamics that are centrally operated by these digital technologies. It is apparent that the traditional way of viewing organisations by separating the role of IT is no longer appropriate especially when considering that social media is transforming social relations inside and outside of the organisational space (Susarla et al. 2012). Hence, this signifies the value of using a fusion view in studying social media influence in an organisation as it helps to understand a reality that is dynamic and multiple.

3 Strategy as Practice

As aforementioned, the strategy as practice (SaP) perspective perceives strategy as a goal-directed activity (Jarzabkowski 2005). SaP views strategy as a situated, socially accomplished activity (ibid). Jarzabkowski (2005) continues to explain SaP as a strategy under investigation since it focuses on actions, interaction, negotiation of multiple actors and the situated context that contributes towards accomplishing the activity. Similarly, Whittington (2014) argues that SaP is concerned with how practitioners of strategy act and interact. Hence, SaP is concerned with strategizing, meaning how strategy is done, who does strategy, what they do, how they do it, what they use and what outcomes it has on shaping strategy (ibid). In this way, SaP distinguishes itself from other strategy approaches with its orientation towards 'how' a strategy emerges (Henfridsson and Lind 2014). The focus on how strategy develops positions SaP as a suitable lens for studying how the fusion of strategy in an organisation is realized, therefore making it an appropriate lens for this research.

Whittington (2014) identifies three elements of the SaP perspective that are: practitioners, practice and praxis. Practitioners are the people making strategy; they include direct practitioners (managers, consultants and employees) and indirect practitioners (policymakers and researcher). Jarzabkowski and Paul Spee (2009) classify practitioners into three groups that are: individual actors within an organisation, aggregate actors within an organisation and external actors who are conceptualised as a total; thus, its external aggregate actors. A practitioner aims to reestablish the actor in strategy research (Jarzabkowski 2005). Thus, by considering humans in strategy, SaP overcomes the weakness of other strategy approaches such as alignment which are perceived as mechanical while at the same time it appreciates strategy as a social construction.

'Practices' are defined as guidelines and routines of doing an activity (Huang et al. 2014). Leonardi (2012) claim that when IS researchers talk about technologies, they are describing practices as well. Also, practices are explained as tools and artefacts that people use in doing strategy work (Whittington 2003). Whittington (2014) suggests this is because even when improvised in praxis, technology practices tend to produce recognizable, imperfectly regular behaviors. Hence, this underscores the vital distinction which Orlikowski (2000) makes between information technology as artefact and technology in practice, which are patterns of repetitive and situated use of technology. Thus, practices as an element of SaP consider both technical and social agency.

Lastly, praxis is the flow of activities in which strategy is accomplished (Jarzabkowski 2005). It is a stream of activity that interconnects the micro action of individuals and groups with the broader institutions in which those actions are located to which they contribute (Jarzabkowski and Paul Spee 2009). Whittington (2014) explains praxis as what people do with technology in ongoing and situated activity. Also, Whittington (2014) explains the implication of praxis in research as it needs close empirical observation of how technology is used, sensitive to all adaptation and improvisation of practical life. Thus, SaP research is a useful lens for gaining insight within an organisation while producing practical insights. Therefore, by adopting the SaP lens into this research, it will help to understand how social media is implemented within an organisation hence gaining insight on how the fusion of strategy is realised.

4 Methods

Following the research aim of understanding the influence of social media practices on the fusion of strategies within an organisation led to the selection of the case study method. A case study method is a valuable method for providing an in-depth understanding into a real-life phenomenon through combining both research phenomenon and context to produce a richer understanding of context and process to which is enacted (Yin 2013). The choice of case study allows this research to dig deeper into an organisation to understand the micro-activities which constitute the life of the organisation. This case study is guided by an interpretivist philosophy, which argues that knowledge is socially constructed through language, shared meaning and consciousness (Orlikowski and Baroudi 1991). This philosophy is adopted for this research as it advocates studying a phenomenon in its natural environment enabling us to remove our predetermined views that may obscure the process of gaining new knowledge. Thus, it aims to eliminate biases. Also, the interpretivist philosophy is in line with the strategy as practice (SaP) perspective that views strategy as a social construction.

4.1 Research Context

The case study organisation is SIMU (a pseudonym). SIMU is one of the largest telecom companies in Tanzania. It has more than a thousand employees with extensive infrastructure and branches all over the country. SIMU has adopted social media within its operations making it a suitable case for this research. Furthermore, the context of Tanzania, a sub-Saharan country, provides the potential of harnessing the explanatory power of practice theory in explaining the role of IT in a developing context (Avgerou 2017). This context offers a different environment of understanding strategy in action compared to that of western developed countries which have relatively more literature. Walsham (2017) suggests that the rapid growth of ICT use in developing countries that occurred in the last decade is mostly attributed to mobile phones; prior to that, there was little literature on the use of IT in developing countries. This can suggest a difference in the use of IT due to historical path dependency as well as a different material arrangement. In addition, this suggests that literature from the developing countries context is emerging. Hence, this context provides a novel opportunity to advance the literature on strategy as practice.

4.2 Site Selection and Access

The selection of a case organisation was based on the size of the organisation and its use of social media. A large organisation was preferable as it had greater possibilities of having departments and multiple strategies within the organisation (Jarzabkowski 2005). Hence it would provide a good premise for studying the fusion of strategies within an organisation. As well as being a large organisation, the organisation supported the use of social media in its operations. Thus, following Belasen and Rufer's (2013) suggestion that high-tech industries such as telecom organisation are quicker in adopting new technology as they are faced with fast shrinking product cycle, this research opted for a telecom organisation as a valuable case.

4.3 Data Collection

The primary method used for data collection was semi-structured interviews which allowed the researcher to hear what each informant says on the topic and areas identified by the researcher (Saunders et al. 2009). The interviews were carried out with employees and managers of SIMU. The rationale for choosing managers and employees was based on the premise that strategy is something done by all members of the organisation (Jarzabkowski 2005; Golsorkhi et al. 2015). The choice of managers is based on the notion that they are the ones who oversee and make decisions regarding the use of social media, while the employees are the implementers and their actions play a significant role on emergent strategy. Twelve semi-structured interviews were conducted with members from different departments (see Table 1). Thus, the sampling was purposive. Purposive sampling is a common form of non-probability sampling that does not require a set number of participants but the researcher decides when sufficient insight is generated due to the participants' knowledge or experience (Fusch and Ness 2015). Following Guest et al. (2006), saturation was reached within the first twelve interviews while elements of meta-themes are present as early as six interviews. Also, the literature review informed the interview questions, which had three main parts: understanding the role of the informants, their use of information technology and their use of social media within the organisation. Furthermore, the research gathered complementary evidence from documents (published documents) and observation. Published documents include Tanzania Communication Regulatory Authority (TCRA)

Table 1. Interviewee profile at SIMU

No	Profile
1	CEO
2	Manager IT Operation
3	IT Staff
4	Marketing Manager
5	Marketing Staff
6	Finance Manager
7	Manager Network Development
8	Manager Product Development
9	Human Resource Head
10	Human Resource Staff
11	Regional Manager
12	Public Relation Officer Communication

annual reports and statistics, and telecoms published product information. In addition, observation was made on the telecoms activities on social media platforms.

4.4 Data Analysis

The data analysis was done using an inductive approach which collects data and explores it to extract the themes and issues that arise (Glaser and Strauss 1967). The analysis was done through structuring data using the narrative method. Coffey and Atkinson (1996) define the narrative method as an account of an experience that is told in a sequenced way, indicating a flow of related events which, when taken together, are significant for the narrator and they convey meaning to the researcher. One way of doing a narrative analysis is through creating a coherent story from the data collected during an interview. This enables the research to consider the social and organisational context where events occur (Saunders et al. 2009). After transcribing and translating the interviews from SIMU, the data was structured using the narrative method. The structuring involved summarizing the interview transcripts, coding the summaries, categorizing into clusters, displaying the themes and finally narrating. A narrative style highlights the points that were made and what they symbolize and how they spell specific issues such as organisational politics, culture and change.

5 Social Media Practice in SIMU

SIMU uses social media both for internal and external communication. For external communication, SIMU has official pages on major social media platforms such as Facebook, Twitter, Instagram and YouTube. Observation, shows social media accounts of SIMU are active with regular posting and interaction with customers. These pages are centrally controlled by the public relation office cooperating with the marketing department. SIMU uses these social media accounts to communicate with customers on their products and services as well as getting feedback from their customers. There are various reasons why social media is used in SIMU. For example, promotion of their products, i.e., selling data (internet) services, SIMU offers free usage of various social media sites without consuming customers' data allowance once they have bought a service. Social media is used for selling as many people who use the internet use social media.

The usage of social media platforms for marketing is influenced by the changing context of Tanzania which makes social media usage a strategic endeavor. The marketing manager explains how the rise of internet consumption in Tanzania created a market for their service. He states that: *'things are quite different compared to ten years ago, you could hardly find two million users of the internet, but now you have about 20 million internet users, even in rural areas people are using the internet, most of the people are using social media. So, we decided we can't be left behind we must tap this market so that they can use our service.'* Data from Tanzania Communication Regulatory Authority (TCRA) shows internet penetration in the country has increased from 5 million users (12% of the population) in 2011 to 20 million users (40% of the population) in 2016 (TCRA 2017). The primary internet providers in Tanzania are the telecom organisations. This data shows the exponential growth in the use of mobile and internet technology in Tanzania. Thus, the use of social media practice in SIMU is influenced by the increasing consumption of internet in Tanzania.

Apart from the external use of social media, which is more of a formal process within the organisation, social media (i.e. WhatsApp) is used informally for internal communication. Official communication within the company is via intranet and email communication. However, the use of WhatsApp for internal communication is a widely-held practice within SIMU. Often, SIMU employees use WhatsApp to communicate between themselves. Employees use WhatsApp groups for social and work purposes. Different groups can easily form WhatsApp groups for their objective. For example, the human resource manager explains that: *'On work, we now have WhatsApp for every department, the department has their information, and they may want to share it among themselves. For instance, it's a weekend, and there is information we need to share, WhatsApp becomes very useful in such instances.'* The WhatsApp groups can contain members of the same department and sometimes members from different departments (especially when working on a project). Also, the WhatsApp groups can have members from different levels of management or members from the same level.

Additionally, WhatsApp groups are used in assisting work processes within SIMU. Because of its wide use, it supports work processes in different ways. For example, WhatsApp is used to improve customer service. It is used in the customer registration processes. When a telecom organisation subscribes a new customer, the TCRA requires that the customer is registered before their number is activated. Sometimes, the registration process is done in the field with the sales team. Therefore, to ensure that the customer number is activated in time, they use WhatsApp to transfer information to the back office and this helps them to complete the subscription process without losing a customer due to delayed activation. Similarly, the product development manager explains how WhatsApp helps customer service as follows: *'customer service people use a lot the WhatsApp groups, especially on hosting customers' queries, because the group has everyone even if someone is at home, he or she can easily know customer's problem and offer a solution immediately. But also, when you go in the street to campaign for products, we use WhatsApp to transfer the details of the customer quickly, and they are then uploaded to the system. Because when you get the customers, you can get his information and take a photo of his ID then send it to be printed and be attached to his official forms then the customers become activated to the service. Therefore, WhatsApp is used on several official business operations.'*

The explanation of the product development manager shows how the forming of WhatsApp groups is an informal practice but is used in official business operations. It further highlights how WhatsApp is redefining where employees do work as they can address issues even when they are physically out of the organisational work space.

To understand the strategic influence of social media practice is vital to understand the organisational strategy. The CEO of SIMU is mainly in charge of the organisational strategy so is therefore a central figure in the formulation of SIMU's strategy. The CEO explains his role and strategic intent as follows: *'As the CEO of SIMU, I am expected to oversee the entire organisation strategy but also to visualize where I want to go as an organisation and put together resources including people in the sense of human capacity, financial resources, as well as other infrastructures for the benefit of the company (...) The company has not been doing so well, it has been making a loss. It's an average of 13 to 15 billion [Tanzanian Shillings (Tsh)] per year; that is the loss that we are making. And me as somebody who comes from the banking sector which is a business my first role is to turn around those figures to break even meaning that we get at a point we are not making any loss anymore but to start making profit.'* From the CEO's explanation, it is apparent that SIMU's strategic intent is to eliminate the loss and create profit. To achieve this strategic objective the CEO outlines his plan as follows: *'The firm's intention of using social media is on cutting down the cost. For example, now I told them there is no need for somebody to travel from upcountry to here. We are a technological company put on a video teleconference, video or telephone conference and then you're done. So, I am cutting down the cost. By doing that 15 billion (Tsh) loss that I am talking about it will keep on reducing until we reach a stage where we can break even.'* From the CEO's explanation, the use of social technologies is central to achieving the organisation's objectives as it can help cut cost because removing the need for travel saves time, cuts cost associated with travel such as accommodation, per diems. Thus, social technologies help to redefine the meeting practice as these move from the physical to the virtual. The CEO's view is shared amongst organisational members; for instance, the IT manager made a similar comment that: *'With Lync [skype for business], the intention is that we are in a cost-cutting phase. Previously, if you wanted to reach branch managers, you had to transport them, pay them their dues and its very costly process. But now you can plan a video conference or telephone conference using Lync'*.

Also, social media practice is associated with reducing the cost associated with stationary, marketing and surveys. For instance, the finance manager of SIMU - who has been with the organisation for 35 years - states that social media has helped SIMU to *'reduce cost on postage, from regional offices from what it was earlier on there was lots of cost on paper rims and postage.'* Likewise, the human resource officer claims that *'from the commercial side, it [social media] helps a lot the marketing in reducing cost compared to earlier expenses. Because anyone who opens Twitter sees SIMU, if someone opens Facebook sees SIMU, not like the previous Billboards.'* Equally, the social media practice is associated with the reduction of survey costs due to the quick feedback that is obtained in social media platforms. The regional manager states that: *'social media can help reduce the cost of marketing survey we are doing. You can air a question; you communicate, and people will respond. You can say you don't have enough funds, but that is an issue.'* These explanations demonstrate how different social media practices from various social media platforms support organisational strategy in multiple ways.

6 Discussion

From the findings, we learn that although strategy is an intent for the future, it is significantly influenced by the past and present conditions. The historical background of SIMU can help to explain the strategic choice of the company. For instance, the loss-making of SIMU is influencing the company to pursue a strategic vision of breaking even or profit-making, a vision that can be achieved through a cost-cutting strategy. SaP (see Jarzabkowski 2005; Orlikowski 2000) explains the cost-cutting strategy as an emerging practice. This practice emerges when path dependence is broken which then leads to adjustments. Pickering (1995) terms it as a 'mangle' of practice. This mangling of practice represents a shift in the interpretive sensibility that envisions the predefined goals of the organisation. This underscores the idea that value is always shifting and moving the target, which necessitates a change in strategic practices. The interpretive sensibility of the CEO of SIMU is to integrate the use of social media into his overall strategy of low cost through cost-cutting. Essentially, social media is central to the CEO's strategic objective of breaking even. In this way, social media practice is intertwined with the organisational objective of reducing cost.

In the absence of social media, it would be unimaginable to redefine some organisational practices such as meeting and marketing processes. This is because social media has helped members of the organization from different geographical locations to be able to collaborate and participate instantaneously. In addition, the visibility functionality enabled by videoconferencing provides an alternative to face-to-face interaction. Theoretically, this highlights the inseparability of social and material agency once they interact (Leonardi 2012). It underlines how social practices are mediated with technology. For instance, videoconferencing is a social (work) practice in SIMU, where managers virtually meet to make decisions regarding the organization. In practice, this shows how micro-activities within an organisation are related to organisational outcomes. For instance, the use of WhatsApp between staff reduces organizational expenses on communication. Thus, the apparent fact that might be overlooked for the realization of this strategy is the context and time. This social media strategy could not materialize if internet consumption and penetration were stagnant to what was five or ten years ago. The exponential growth in the use of the internet and mobile technology in Tanzania shows a change in context with time, which makes social media practice in SIMU inevitable. Thus, the empirical evidence gathered from this research contributes to literature that digital business strategy added with the intertwinement of historical background, context, technical advancement and social intents. SIMU's loss making history, the growing use of internet in Tanzania, social media applications and the need to make profit explain the digital business strategy of SIMU.

From the communication practice in SIMU, we learn about social media use and its influence on processes and structure in an organisation. The formal communication practice in SIMU is as follows: internally it is conducted through the intranet, email and Lync. Whereas for external communication, SIMU uses official accounts established on major social media platforms such as Facebook, Twitter, YouTube and Instagram. We see the emergence of WhatsApp group communication as the most used and preferred means of communication within SIMU. From a practice perspective, the rise of WhatsApp group communication could be explained as a praxis. Huang et al. (2014) explain praxis as the actual activity of creating and enacting an IS strategy, which may be like the traditional routines because of the sense-making of practitioners involved and because of unanticipated circumstances that may disrupt routine practices. From this case, we see the difference between the actual guidelines of the communication activity and the real activity of communicating. Reckwitz (2002) explains this to be the difference between practice and praxis. The emergence of these activities which take place in the organization, the praxis, are the ones that give the chance of interpretation to actors and thus they lead to social construction. The praxis here helps us to understand how strategy is done (processes and structure are enacted) because it shows the interplay between actors and practice in every communication activity that is taking place. Thus, we argue that it is this interplay between the actors and practices that affect processes and structure, consequently influencing strategy at SIMU. For example, the actual use of Lync to conduct video conferencing is one that reduces cost. Similarly, the use of social media to advertise is reducing the marketing cost. Therefore, the actual practices of social media are the ones influencing the cost-cutting strategy. Furthermore, through the practice lens, we learn about the practical use of technology in an organisation which can inform investment in IT infrastructure. For instance, the presence of widely-used WhatsApp as a means of internal communication can save SIMU on their investment on their IT infrastructure such as emails and computers because WhatsApp provides the infrastructure, thus supporting a cost-cutting strategy of the organisation. Thus, social media extends the IS scope within the organisation with less organisational IT infrastructure since it uses external infrastructure such as employees' personal phones (Kwayu et al. 2018).

The praxis influences strategy through changing work processes—for instance, the use of WhatsApp in the customer activation process. The recurring use of WhatsApp in this process implants a structure. Giddens (1989) explains a structure as what gives a social life a form and shape, but itself is not that form or shape. The emerging structures resulting from various social media practices at SIMU has the following implication. Beforehand, the emerging structures are the result of 'natural' process redesign. This emerging process performs a shift of activities by removing unnecessary processes and/or introducing new processes through the utilisation of information affordances enabled by social media. For example, similar to Treem and Leonardi's (2012) study, the social media affordances of participating and collaborating highlighted from SIMU employees' use of WhatsApp groups or Lync videoconferences; thus, enabling employees and management to perform their duties with the new processes compared to the traditional processes. One notable impact of social media use in SIMU is bringing employees together in completing tasks. The implication of this is the bundling of activities that enact new processes and organisational structures, consequently merging some strategies. For instance, through the WhatsApp group, IT personnel will collaborate with marketing personnel to accomplish a project. Through the group their relationship will be established and the group removes the structural boundaries between the IT department and marketing department. Thus, IT and marketing activities are both bundled into a group, which consequently fuses the strategies. Thus, considering that a group can contain multiple actors from different departments which have different strategies, this may lead to the fusion of various strategies. For example, people from different departments have a different perspective, but through groups which are enabled by WhatsApp, their views become fused through daily interaction and knowledge sharing, consequently increasing meta-knowledge – a knowledge of who knows what and who knows whom (Leonardi 2014) and ambient awareness (Leonardi 2015).

Lastly, the way the fusion of strategies happens is through the production of a single effect from multiple strategies within an organisation. The cost-cutting strategy of SIMU is enabled by different efforts from different strategies across the organisation. For example, the marketing strategy is exercising a cost-cutting strategy using social media. Likewise, the human resource department is also applying a cost-cutting process using social media: instead of paying allowances and dues for employees who travel, they cut those costs with teleconferences. However, when it comes to the connection of the Lync, it is conducted either by the individual or sometimes by IT members. Thus, all these efforts, which result from different strategies, have a fused effect to the overall strategy of cost-cutting: the relationship here is social media. This is consistent with Jarzabkowski (2005) highlighting the existence of multiple strategies with the organisation. From our case, we learn that social media practices are performing 'structuration' which fuses various strategies within the organisation to reflect a single strategy. Hence this contributes to the management literature on multiple strategies.

7 Conclusion

Empirical evidence from this research evidences the widespread nature of social media practice within a specific organisation. This research shows how technologies such as social media drive a digital business strategy. In respect to this, the paper contributes to the literature by arguing that the fusion of strategy is assisted by the intertwinement of historical background, context, technological advances and social intent. Second, this research contributes to IS literature by highlighting how social media extends the IS scope while minimizing the need for organisational IT infrastructure. Third, this research demonstrates how social media practices are changing work processes which become integral to the emergent strategy of the organisation. Finally, this research contributes to the literature on multiple strategies (Jarzabkowski 2005) by highlighting how organisational strategy is assisted by various strategies from different parts of the organisation. In practice, this research demonstrates the significance of informal social media practices such as WhatsApp communication in organisational processes such as knowledge sharing and customer service.

The findings of this paper were limited to one organisation; future research can benefit by comparing different cases from the same context or with a different context. This will help to increase understanding on the practices that are embedded within a context, hence contribute to concepts of embeddedness and enactment. Furthermore, future research can benefit from longitudinal data which can highlight the changing practices over time.

References

Alalwan, A.A., Rana, N.P., Dwivedi, Y.K., Algharabat, R.: Social media in marketing: a review and analysis of the existing literature. Telematics Inform. **34**(7), 1177–1190 (2017)

Aral, S., Dellarocas, C., Godes, D.: Introduction to the special issue—social media and business transformation: a framework for research. Inf. Syst. Res. **24**(1), 3–13 (2013)

Avgerou, C.: Theoretical framing of ICT4D research. In: Choudrie, J., Islam, M.S., Wahid, F., Bass, J.M., Priyatma, J.E. (eds.) ICT4D 2017. IAICT, vol. 504, pp. 10–23. Springer, Cham (2017). https://doi.org/10.1007/978-3-319-59111-7_2

Belasen, A., Rufer, R.: Innovation communication and inter-functional collaboration: a view from the competing values framework for corporate communication. In: Pfeffermann, N., Minshall, T., Mortara, L. (eds.) Strategy and Communication for Innovation, pp. 227–240. Springer, Heidelberg (2013). https://doi.org/10.1007/978-3-642-41479-4_14

Bharadwaj, A., El Sawy, O.A., Pavlou, P.A., Venkatraman, N.V.: Digital business strategy: toward a next generation of insights (2013)

Braojos-Gomez, J., Benitez-Amado, J., Llorens-Montes, F.J.: How do small firms learn to develop a social media competence? Int. J. Inf. Manage. **35**(4), 443–458 (2015)

Cecez-Kecmanovic, D., Galliers, R.D., Henfridsson, O., Newell, S., Vidgen, R.: The sociomateriality of information systems: current status, future directions. MIS Q. **38**(3), 809–830 (2014)

Chan, Y.E., Reich, B.H.: IT alignment: what have we learned? J. Inf. Technol. **22**(4), 297–315 (2007)

Ciborra, C.: The grassroots of IT and strategy. In: Ciborra, C., Jelessi, T. (eds.) Strategic Information Systems: A European Perspective, pp. 3–24. Wiley, Chichester (1994)

Coffey, A., Atkinson, P.: Making Sense of Qualitative Data: Complementary Research Strategies. Sage Publications Inc., Thousand Oaks (1996)

Culnan, M., Mchugh, P., Zubillaga, J.: How large U.S. Companies can use Twitter and other social media to gain business value. MIS Q. Exec. **9**(4), 243–259 (2010)

Dwivedi, Y.K., Kapoor, K.K., Chen, H.: Social media marketing and advertising. Mark. Rev. **15** (3), 289–309 (2015)

Dwivedi, Y.K., Shareef, M.A., Simintiras, A.C., Lal, B., Weerakkody, V.: A generalised adoption model for services: a cross-country comparison of mobile health (m-health). Gov. Inf. Q. **33**(1), 174–187 (2016)

El Sawy, O.A.: The IS Core IX: the 3 Faces of IS identity: connection, immersion, and fusion. Commun. Assoc. Inf. Syst. **12**(1), 39 (2003)

Fusch, P.I., Ness, L.R.: Are we there yet? Data saturation in qualitative research. Qual. Rep. **20** (9), 1408–1416 (2015)

Giddens, A.: Sociology. Polity Press, Cambridge (1989)

Glaser, B., Strauss, A.: The Discovery of Grounded Theory. Weidenfield & Nicolson, London (1967)

Golsorkhi, D., Rouleau, L., Seidl, D., Vaara, E. (eds.): Cambridge Handbook of Strategy as Practice, 2nd edn. Cambridge University Press, Cambridge (2015)

Guest, G., Bunce, A., Johnson, L.: How many interviews are enough? An experiment with data saturation and variability. Field Methods **18**(1), 59–82 (2006)

Henderson, J.C., Venkatraman, N.: Strategic alignment: a framework for strategic information technology management (1989)

Henfridsson, O., Lind, M.: Information systems strategizing, organizational sub-communities, and the emergence of a sustainability strategy. J. Strateg. Inf. Syst. **23**(1), 11–28 (2014)

Huang, J., Newell, S., Huang, J., Pan, S.L.: Site-shifting as the source of ambidexterity: empirical insights from the field of ticketing. J. Strateg. Inf. Syst. **23**(1), 29–44 (2014)

Hutchings, C.: Commercial use of Facebook and Twitter-risks and rewards. Comput. Fraud Secur. **2012**(6), 19–20 (2012)

Jarzabkowski, P., Paul Spee, A.: Strategy-as-practice: a review and future directions for the field. Int. J. Manag. Rev. **11**(1), 69–95 (2009)

Jarzabkowski, P.: Strategy as Practice: An Activity Based Approach. Sage, Thousand Oaks (2005)

Kahre, C., Hoffmann, D., Ahlemann, F.: Beyond business-IT alignment-digital business strategies as a paradigmatic shift: a review and research agenda (2017)

Kapoor, K.K., Tamilmani, K., Rana, N.P., Patil, P., Dwivedi, Y.K., Nerur, S.: Advances in social media research: past, present and future. Inf. Syst. Front. **20**(3), 531–558 (2018)

Kwayu, S., Lal, B., Abubakre, M.: The impact of social media on internal communications in the Tanzanian Telecom Industry. In: Dwivedi, Y.K., et al. (eds.) Emerging Markets from a Multidisciplinary Perspective. ATPEM, pp. 119–131. Springer, Cham (2018). https://doi.org/10.1007/978-3-319-75013-2_11

Leonardi, P.M.: Materiality, sociomateriality, and socio-technical systems: what do these terms mean? How are they different? Do we need them. In: Leonardi, P.M., Nardi, B.A., Kallinikos, J. (eds.) Materiality and Organizing: Social Interaction in a Technological World, p. 25. Oxford University Press, Oxford (2012)

Leonardi, P.M.: Social media, knowledge sharing, and innovation: toward a theory of communication visibility. Inf. Syst. Res. **25**(4), 796–816 (2014)

Leonardi, P.M.: Ambient awareness and knowledge acquisition: using social media to learn 'who knows what' and 'who knows whom' (2015)

Luftman, J.N., Ben-Zvi, T., Dwivedi, R., Rigoni, E.H.: IT Governance: an alignment maturity perspective. In: Business Strategy and Applications in Enterprise IT Governance, pp. 87–101 (2012)

Orlikowski, W.J., Baroudi, J.J.: Studying information technology in organizations: research approaches and assumptions. Inf. Syst. Res. **2**(1), 1–28 (1991)

Orlikowski, W.J.: Using technology and constituting structures: a practice lens for studying technology in organizations. Organ. Sci. **11**(4), 404–428 (2000)

Orlikowski, W.J.: Sociomaterial practices: exploring technology at work. Organ. Stud. **28**(9), 1435–1448 (2007)

Peppard, J., Galliers, R.D., Thorogood, A.: Information systems strategy as practice: micro strategy and strategizing for IS. J. Strategic Inf. Syst. **23**(1), 1–10 (2014)

Phillips-Wren, G., McKniff, S.: Beyond technology adoption: an embeddedness approach to reduce medication errors. J. Organ. Comput. Electron. Commer. **25**(2), 213–232 (2015)

Pickering, A.: The Mangle of Practice: Time, Agency, and Science. University of Chicago Press, Chicago (1995)

Pillet, J.C., Carillo, K.D.A.: Email-free collaboration: an exploratory study on the formation of new work habits among knowledge workers. Int. J. Inf. Manage. **36**(1), 113–125 (2016)
Piskorski, M.J.: A Social Strategy: How We Profit from Social Media. Princeton University Press, Princeton (2014)
Reckwitz, A.: The status of the "material" in theories of culture: from "social structure" to "artefacts". J. Theory Soc. Behav. **32**(2), 195–217 (2002)
Saunders, M.L., Lewis, P., Thornhill, A.: Research methods for business students (2009)
Scott, S.V., Orlikowski, W.J.: Reconfiguring relations of accountability: materialization of social media in the travel sector. Acc. Organ. Soc. **37**(1), 26–40 (2012)
Scott, S.V., Orlikowski, W.J.: Entanglements in practice: performing anonymity through social media (2014)
Susarla, A., Oh, J.H., Tan, Y.: Social networks and the diffusion of user-generated content: evidence from YouTube. Inf. Syst. Res. **23**(1), 23–41 (2012)
Tavakoli, A., Schlagwein, D., Schoder, D.: Open strategy: literature review, re-analysis of cases and conceptualisation as a practice. J. Strateg. Inf. Syst. **26**(3), 163–184 (2017)
TCRA (2017). https://www.tcra.go.tz/. Accessed 12 Dec 2017
Venkatraman, N., Henderson, J.C., Oldach, S.: Continuous strategic alignment: exploiting information technology capabilities for competitive success. Eur. Manag. J. **11**(2), 139–149 (1993)
Wagner, H., Beimborn, D., Weitzel, T.: How social capital among information technology and business units drives operational alignment and IT business value. J. Manag. Inf. Syst. **31**(1), 241–272 (2014)
Walsham, G.: ICT4D research: reflections on history and future agenda. Inf. Technol. Dev. **23**(1), 18–41 (2017)
Whittington, R.: The work of strategizing and organizing: for a practice perspective. Strateg. Organ. **1**(1), 117–125 (2003)
Whittington, R.: Information systems strategy and strategy-as-practice: a joint agenda. J. Strateg. Inf. Syst. **23**(1), 87–91 (2014)
Yin, R.K.: Case Study Research: Design and Methods. Sage Publications, Thousand Oaks (2013)

Navigating Global Online Market Places (GOMPs) – An ADR Perspective

Abayomi Baiyere(✉), Thomas Jensen, Louise Fischer, Kalina Staykova, Michael Wessel, and Jonas Hedman

Copenhagen Business School, Frederiksberg, Denmark
{aba.digi,tj.digi,lhf.digi,kss.digi,mw.digi, je.digi}@cbs.dk

Abstract. Global Online Market Places (GOMPs), such as Amazon, Alibaba, Otto, transforms ecommerce. We are moving away from a world of many ecommerce stores to a world populated by a few oligopolies. This create a new competitive situation, not only for the individual firm, but also for countries. Despite the established importance of export to a nation's economy and the proliferation of the internet today, there are still many companies grappling with taking advantage of the possibilities of e-export. This study is aimed at designing a solution and developing an intervention to mitigate the challenges faced by such companies in Denmark. This research in progress paper reports on the initial activities of the design of a platform intended to be the hub for connecting companies to multiple online market places. This paper sets the frame for the subsequent design, development and evaluation efforts as well as learnings for this research project. Our study extends the conventional view of ADR from a research approach with an organizational purview to one that is amenable to providing practically relevant solutions to national issues.

Keywords: Design science research · Platform · Online marketplaces · e-commerce

1 Introduction

In recent years, global online marketplaces (GOMPSs), have been transforming global trade. Renown examples of this are Amazon and Alibaba to mention a few. The value of export of goods and services between nations has been long established and the potential remains huge for both the companies and nations involved (Hertel and Keeney 2006). According to Porter (1990) - "A nation's competitiveness depends on the capacity of its industry to innovate and upgrade. Companies gain advantage against the world's best competitors because of pressure and challenge. They benefit from having strong domestic rivals, aggressive home-based suppliers, and demanding local customers."

GOMPs have become a potent avenue for carrying out exports today (Albaum and Duerr 2008). Despite the acclaimed value of exports and the pervasiveness of the internet and digital technologies, there are still a large number of companies that have not been able to take advantage of the opportunities of e-exports of these GOMPs.

Published by Springer Nature Switzerland AG 2019
Y. Dwivedi et al. (Eds.): TDIT 2019, IFIP AICT 558, pp. 529–535, 2019.
https://doi.org/10.1007/978-3-030-20671-0_36

According to a recent study in Denmark, only about one in ten Danish companies export digitally, while the percentage of companies taking advantage of e-export is at an average of eight percent (Christensen 2017). Due to the evolutions of technology and GOMPs in particular this premise does not hold any longer. In addition, small firms face the risk of being left behind. Therefore, from a national perspective it is critical to help firms to sell on GOMPS. We thus engage in developing a public good platform that enables firms to access and sell on GOMPs.

The paucity of companies carrying out e-export activities can be roughly traced to lack of knowledge and financial resources. We have identified some of the key challenges and this research in progress outlines a preliminary report of the planned action design research (ADR) study for mitigating against these challenges and boosting the presence of Danish companies in the e-export arena. Some of the barriers to achieving e-export stem from issues that can be classified into a class of problems for which a design outcome can provide tenable solutions. A major challenge faced by these companies stem the fact that there are multiple global online marketplaces - GOMPs. Example of GOMPs includes large ones such as Amazon and Alibaba, and a range of not so well known GOMPs such as Marktplaats and Rakuten, among many others. The challenge is that each GOMP has its own boundary resources () which further complicates this for intending companies wishing to go global. In essence, a key challenge for most companies is that they have issues in identifying and leveraging the multitude of GOMPs for e-export out there, as well as how to connect to these platforms successfully.

Additionally, this study is positioned to shift the locus of ADR studies by demonstrating that the principles of ADR approach can be useful beyond the traditional organizational context. In this study, we intend to extend the utility of ADR to demonstrate its value in the design and intervention of national issues as well by developing public goods to the benefit of society. This research in progress paper takes an ADR perspective and reports the preliminary design and intervention approach planned for helping companies minimize the barriers to e-export. The idea for the study originates from the national foundation of Danish industrial companies and an associated fund. They recognize that e-export especially business to business (B2B) is important for firms in today's competitive landscape. They found that the nation in 2016 ranked rather low compared to other nations on the share of export for B2B via on-line channels. These observations formed the background and motivation for embarking on this study.

2 Method

Our study employs the principles of ADR as articulated by Sein et al. (2010). ADR is an appropriate methodological choice in situations where the intention is to generate prescriptive design knowledge via the creation and evaluation of an IT artifact (Gregor and Hevner 2013). In contrasts with action research and design research, ADR deals with two fundamental research issues (Sein et al. 2010)). Firstly, it is a relevant approach when there is an objective to address research problems by intervening and evaluating the impact of the intervention. Secondly, it is additionally relevant when there is a need to build and evaluate an IT artifact that solves a class of problems that is typified by the issue at hand. These pivotal points in the conduct of an ADR study makes it a research approach that places emphasis on the building, intervention and evaluation of an IT artifact that is positioned to contribute both theoretical insights as well as practically relevant solutions to the actors concerned (Sein et al. 2011). Consequently, our research can be considered as an engaged scholarship (van de Ven 2007) where scholars engage with the industry to create synergies and new knowledge. ADR (Sein et al. 2011) is a recognized approach in information systems research that can be leveraged to generate useful knowledge for both practitioners and academics.

In consonance with the requirements of an ADR study, this research can be structured in four stages. Firstly, the problem formulation stage of the study gets its premise from the observed challenges of e-export by Danish companies. Our study is planned as a four years longitudinal study with support from the relevant actors for which the class of problem bears relevance. Secondly, the build, intervention and evaluation stage, is structured to involve the design and development of a platform that connects multiple GOMPs and provides seamless access to Danish companies. The emerging artifact from this process would be evaluated based on the capacity of the artifact to mitigate the highlighted challenges as well as the number of companies that can effectively begin to use the platform to exploit the benefits of e-export. Thirdly, the reflection and learning phase is structured to happen concurrently with all the other stages of the project. Considering the longitudinal nature of the project, it is expected that there will be multiple opportunities for learning and reflection during iterations across and within the ADR stages (Mullarkey and Hevner 2015). Lastly, the formalizing of learning stage is expected to follow the recommendations of van Aken (2004) to enable us abstract from the situated learning to general solution concepts that are transferrable to a class of problems. In general, our research approach for this study follows the ADR method as laid out by Sein et al. (2011), which refers to an iterative development process where knowledge and development mutually influence each other.

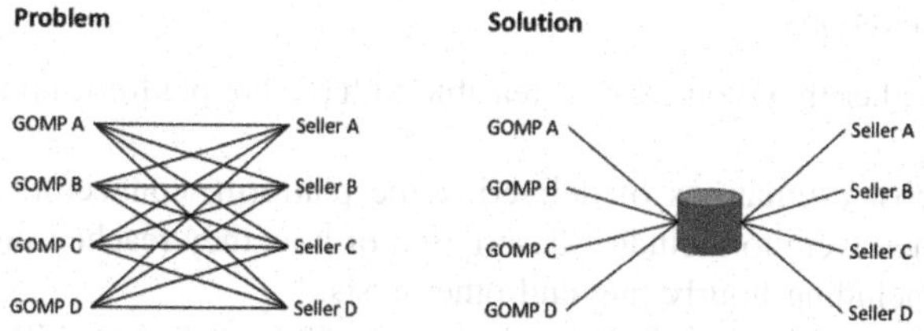

Fig. 1. Diagrammatic representation of the GOMP problem and proposed design solution

3 Intended Artifact Design (Choices and Justifications)

There are multiple intended designs, including a connector that seamlessly via APIs connect the firm's ERP system or web shops with the platform which again connect to the selected GOMPs and boundary resources, such as Open-API, SDK, documentation and tutorials. The artifact is a platform with the capacity to enable initially few firms to connect to one or more GOMPs, see Fig. 1. The intention is to gradually connect to more firms and more GOMPs after a pilot of one to three GOMPs. By year three of the project the objective is to have at least 100 firms connected with about 10 major GOMPs. Furthermore, there should be actual export activities taking place via the platform after this initiative. However, the number of ERP systems are limited to 3 which covers a relatively high share of the Danish firms.

To facilitate the individual firm's decision a range of tools are planned to be designed which included (1) decision support tool, (2) mapping of global online marketplaces, and (3) a tool to evaluate the firms maturity. The initial activity was to invite vendors that potential can deliver the platform, accordingly five vendors were invited to propose their solution and offerings. Three vendors choose to pitch their solution and offer. Each vendor received an invitation to become a partner in the platform and to pitch their candidate. They then received a description of the design and expected deliverable.

With respect to the design elements for the expected deliverable, a functioning e-export platform meeting the following design principles was requested: Synchronizing and displaying product data from Danish firms on GOMP, including connectivity to at least three GOMP, and connectivity/APIs to the top three ERP systems and the top three e-commerce systems. Furthermore, since the aim of the project is to support Danish firms, in the most efficient and effective way, the design of the platform and its connectors should be well documented based on open APIs and it should include software development kit (SDK), example code, tutorials, support, and training material. Thus, the platform and its connectors with associated documentation should be at the level that an independent IT consultant should be able to set-up the integration between Danish firms and selected GOMPs. The platform should be up and running by May 2019 and available for Danish firms. After May 2019, we foresee a process with continuous improvements, potential updates of the connectors towards the GOMP, and support to firms. By the end of the project it should have at least 100 companies selling over the e-export platform.

Additionally the vendors were asked to address the following non-design and practical considerations:

1. Indicate whether they believe it is feasible to have the platform up and running by May 2019.
2. Time and cost estimations of delivering the platform, connectors and associated material. They were to include a description of how they reached the cost and time estimates, including hourly rate and other costs.
3. Some details on experience of developing platform and open-API with some references or cases.
4. Experience of working together with universities.
5. In addition, expression of how they see the long-term survival of the platform. Or in other words its business models including its revenue sources, operating cost, and ownership after the projects ends in 2021. For instance, how much should it cost for Danish firms to enroll in the future.

Each of the three vendors delivered impressive pitches and detailed solution descriptions. The evaluation committee compared the three companies, their experiences and references, their pitches and their proposed design and solutions. There were significant variances among them both in capabilities, experiences, solutions proposed and the estimated costs. In the end one of the prototype designs with greater affinity to the design solutions identified by the research team as best fitting to address the class of problems was selected. The next phase of the study is the actual development which is expected to happen with several iterations as more knowledge is gathered and as the understanding of the problem space and its solution possibility develops. This phase is expected to be followed by a number of tests and pilot implementations to observe the extent to which the initial design assumptions hold true in addressing the issues. Some of the areas of potential improvement include:

- Identification of approach to connect to each GOMP's API and web services
- Simple and effective user interface designs to reduce complexity
- Possibility to connect via plug and play to the companies ERP systems
- Ability for participating companies to promote their products across several GOMPs with minimal effort.
- Extendability and scalability of the platform to more GOMPs
- Adaptiveness to unilateral changes of the API's and web services of GOMPs

4 Planned Evaluation Strategy

The overall evaluation criterias for the project are given by the sponsoring fund on behalf on the association of Danish industrial firms. As stipulated by the funding actor in this project, the overall success criteria for the project and the designed platform would be measured based on the following:

- Danish companies should double the volume of e-exports.
- New knowledge and new e-export tools for Danish companies.
- Reduce Danish companies' costs to begin e-exports by over 1.3 million Euros.
- 100 companies participating and should have carried out about 30 million Euros worth of transaction via the platform.
- At least 8 research publications should be published.
- At least 8 conferences, seminars and workshops should be documented.

The evaluation of the aforementioned criteria will be conducted as the project evolves over time. At the same time the success for each firm will also be evaluated. From an earlier pilot, the first firms are selling their products on the platform and accordingly metrics for the measurement of success has been developed in accordance. The first firm on the platform with connections to 5 GOMPs has been live with online e-shops online since November 1st and up to today (4 month) and therefore we have chosen to compare 01.11–01.03 2015/2016 and 2016/2017. Measured on the total of the 5 GOMPs, revenue has increased by 59.8% by the following: (1) .de: 37.5% (2) .fr: 70.2% (3) .it: 139.5% (4) .uk: −6.7% and (5) .es: 58.4%. The increase is due to the fact that the firm has gained more products online due to integration, as it has not been possible to maintain such large quantities of products in the past. In order to put the figures in perspective, it is expected that this year will be set up on a 2-digit million revenue. At the time of writing, the publication has processed more than 5,000 orders and more than 80,000 products for the firm. The results are measured on revenue through statistical tools of the GOMPs. The aim of this subsequent implementations is to have at least 100 companies and 10 major GOMPS, and to effectively monitor the increase in number of transactions. Furthermore, the evolution of the maturity of participating firms to perform e-export via GOMPs is to be assessed and a measure for that is also under development.

5 Expected Learnings/Outcomes

It is expected that the study should afford us the opportunity to abstract several theoretical and practically relevant knowledge. Chief among these possible contributions are:

- The design and development of an IT artifact (the multichannel GOMP connector platform) that faciliates e-export by mitigating the complexities of dealing with several GOMPS.
- The articulation of the key design principles that are essential and transferrable as design solutions to a class of problems regarding the design of national e-export platforms.

6 Conclusion

This research in progress study outlines the plans to solve the challenges of e-export that is limiting many Danish companies from taking full advantage of the benefits of e-export via GOMPs. The study takes its methodological premise from the principles of ADR to position its contribution as a designed artifact as well as an intervention that should collectively yield practical solutions and theoretical insights to the challenges of e-exports. We contend that it is important to study this because; (a) e-export is important in today's competitive landscape both from a nation's viewpoint as well as the respective companies perspective. (b) The problem class that this study aims to address is general and affects several nations. Hence, eliminating the barriers to achieving e-export is a pertinent research and societally relevant endeavour.

In essence, our study has the potential to address the bottleneck of companies having troubles in identifying and leveraging the multitude of e-export platforms out there. The planned study is aimed to come up with a design solution that is encapsulated in the form of a digital platform for interacting with multiple GOMPs. With this approach, it is expected that each firm does not have to set up and maintain APIs for each of the global online marketplaces which they intend to sell their markets on, thereby eliminating one of the major barrier for their attempts at e-export.

Acknowledgements. This work was carried out with the support by the "E-eksport via online markedspladser" project via a grant from the Danish Industry Foundation (grant number 2017-0165) and by the Department of Digitalization at Copenhagen Business School.

References

Albaum, G., Duerr, E.: International Marketing and Export Management. Pearson Education, London (2008)

Christensen, J.: Danish companies do not make great use of e-exports. DI Business (2017)

Davison, R., Martinsons, M.G., Kock, N.: Principles of canonical action research. Inf. Syst. J. **14**(1), 65–86 (2004)

Gregor, S., Hevner, A.R.: Positioning and presenting design science research for maximum impact. MIS Q. **37**(2), 337–355 (2013)

Hertel, T.W., Keeney, R.: What is at stake: the relative importance of import barriers, export subsidies, and domestic support. Agric. Trade Reform Doha Dev. Agenda **37** (2006)

Hevner, A.R., March, S.T., Park, J., Ram, S.: Design science in information systems research. MIS Q. **28**(1), 75–105 (2004)

Mullarkey, M.T., Hevner, A.R.: Entering action design research. In: Donnellan, B., Helfert, M., Kenneally, J., VanderMeer, D., Rothenberger, M., Winter, R. (eds.) DESRIST 2015. LNCS, vol. 9073, pp. 121–134. Springer, Cham (2015). https://doi.org/10.1007/978-3-319-18714-3_8

Sein, M.K., Henfridsson, O., Purao, S., Rossi, M., Lindgren, R.: Action design research. MIS Q. 37–56 (2011)

Van de Ven, A.H.: Engaged scholarship: a guide for organizational and social research: a guide for organizational and social research. Oxford University Press, Oxford (2007)

Van Aken, J.E.: Management research based on the paradigm of the design sciences: the quest for field-tested and grounded technological rules. J. Manag. Stud. **41**(2), 219–224 (2004)

Bright ICT: Social Media Analytics for Society and Crisis Management

Deborah Bunker[1(✉)], Stefan Stieglitz[2], Christian Ehnis[1], and Anthony Sleigh[1]

[1] University of Sydney Business School, Sydney, Australia
deborah.bunker@sydney.edu.au
[2] University of Duisburg-Essen, Duisburg, Germany

Abstract. Bright ICT promises a new era of IT adoption and use, however, in this current era of ubiquitous computing and social media platforms, we have witnessed IS users being rendered powerless in the information systems development process and professionally manipulated by large technology companies through the algorithmic structures of social networking platforms. In 1987 Markus & Bjorn-Andersen warned us of the potential of consequences of this situation which are now evident on a daily basis where data privacy is compromised, social media platform content is difficult if not impossible to manage and our political and economic systems are disrupted. This paper outlines an engaged research approach being taken by the RISE_SMA project to develop more innovative theoretical approaches and methods for analysing social media data for the assurance of social cohesion during times of crisis.

Keywords: ICT · Crisis management · Social media analytics · Engaged scholarship

1 Introduction

1.1 Eras of IT Adoption

In 2012, Hirschheim and Klein [1] wrote about the four eras of information technology (IT) adoption explaining the 40 year history of information systems and the possibility of sharing a history "that would be effective in helping to bridge the communications gap that exists between the different sub-communities that make up the discipline" [1 - p. 188]. Niederman et al. [2] further developed the ideas of Hirschheim and Klein [1] to relabel each IT adoption era to reflect the information systems development (ISD) skills orientation in each era from the "inner circle" of highly specialised IS expertise in the First Era right through to the Fourth Era "where people who previously had little engagement with information technology were suddenly power users" [2 – p. 36].

Table 1 highlights the Eras of IT Adoption and the dominant technologies in use as outlined by Hirschheim and Klein [1] and Niederman et al. [2] but it also highlights the location of ISD expertise and power/control as well as the ISD trend for each adoption era. It is interesting to note that the First and Fourth Eras reflect much the same ISD expertise and power/control which is predominantly in the hands of technology companies. It appears we have come 'full circle'.

Published by Springer Nature Switzerland AG 2019
Y. Dwivedi et al. (Eds.): TDIT 2019, IFIP AICT 558, pp. 536–552, 2019.
https://doi.org/10.1007/978-3-030-20671-0_37

Table 1. Eras of IT adoption and location of ISD power – adapted from Hirschheim and Klein [1] and Niederman et al. [2]

IT adoption ERA	Technology in use	Location of IS development expertise and power	IS development trend
First Era (mid 1960s to mid 1970s) *Computing Inner Circle*	Third generation mainframe (IBM 360); Languages (Assembler, Fortran, COBOL); Databases; Ethernet	Tech companies – high Business – low Government – low End users - none	Outsourcing (bureaux) Insourcing (vendor controlled) Proprietary networks
Second Era (mid-1970s-mid-1980s) *End User Revolution*	Minicomputers; Mid-range computers; PCs; Fifth generation computing project	Tech companies - high Business – moderate Government – moderate End users – moderate	Insourcing (vendor and organisational partnerships) Proprietary networks Personal computing
Third Era (mid-1980's to mid/late-1990s) *E-Commerce Gold Rush*	Internetworking leading to the emergence of the internet	Tech companies – low Business – high Government – high End users – moderate	Insourcing (in house developed) Proprietary networks Early internet
Fourth Era (2000 to now) *Ubiquitous Computing*	Internet age; Ubiquitous computing (laptops, netbooks, tablets, smartphones etc.); Search engines; Social media	Tech companies – high Business – low Government – low End users – low	Integrated (formal) enterprise systems Outsourcing (cloud IT service commoditisation); Commercial internet Social network (personal) computing

1.2 IFIP WG8.6 and Information Systems Development (ISD) Research

IFIP WG8.6 has the brief to "foster understanding and improve research in practice, methods, and techniques in the transfer and diffusion of information technology within systems that are developed and in the development process"[1]. Over the years, since establishment in 1993 (during the Third Era of the E-commerce Gold Rush), IFIP WG8.6 scholars have critically researched ISD practice and how it relates to adoption, diffusion, transfer and implementation of IS within society, government, organisations and on an individual level. In recent years membership of the group has been actively consolidating its scholarship in the current Fourth Era of Ubiquitous Computing.

For example, the recent working conferences 'Re-Imagining Diffusion of Information Technology and Systems: Opportunities and Risks' in 2017 at Guimaraes and 'Smart Working, Living and Organising' in 2018 in Portsmouth have taken the scholarship efforts of the group into areas such as social networks, social media, adaptive technologies, work systems, socio-technical approaches and perspectives,

[1] http://ifipwg86.wikidot.com/about-us last access 5 April 2019.

digital artifacts and boundaries, the colliding worlds of formal and self-organising systems, ICT4D, disruption and digital platforms, sharing economies, data and project governance, smart objects and systems, digital payments and security and privacy in the digital world. These new developments have reorientated our research agenda to more fulsomely consider the impact of IS and IT on society. The Working Conference to be held in June 2019 in Ghana is themed on 'Bright ICT' for societal benefit focussed on "development of relevant technologies, business models, public policies, social norms, international agreements, metrics for measuring national progress and preventing undesirable activities on the Internet"[2].

In this era of ubiquitous computing and digital disruption, however, large technology companies continue to abuse their ISD power [3] and this has an impact on Bright ICT potential. When looking at the ISD approaches to social media (SM) platforms issues such as data privacy, platform monitoring and surveillance, inability to manage platform content and disruption of political and economic systems are brought into sharp focus daily with a continuing stream of horror stories. Most recently a mass murder that occurred in Christchurch on 15th March 2019 was live streamed by the perpetrator of the murders on Facebook [4] and currently we see the Australian government is grappling with how to deal with the impact of such an action that is facilitated by a SM platform architecture [5]. SM platforms are often criticized more widely: fake news and social bots can manipulate and disturb public communication [6]. At the same time, they generate a large amount of data in real time during disasters – data that is important for the first response to such events. Also, the assurance of social cohesion during a disaster event becomes a problem when the sheer volume of messages generated means that SM messages are not able to be effectively analysed for essential information [7]. This is in part due to the communications architectures of these platforms and current limitations in the development of SM analytics software.

The development of an open and unmanaged communications platform has unforeseen consequences that are now difficult to overcome. The jinn, as they say, is out of the bottle.

On the other hand, we must acknowledge that SM channels have become important communications channels for society. Twitter, Instagram and Facebook have changed public social communication enormously. They are used by individuals as well as by political, economic and scientific players to disseminate information and messages or to find out what others think. It is imperative that we develop suitable analytics approaches that render the users of these systems more aware of their design consequences and give them the ability to develop more socially positive and "bright ICT" applications of them.

This paper discusses the outcomes of a research workshop held in Sydney on March 6th and 7th, 2019 as part of the research project "RISE_SMA – Social Media Analytics for Society and Crises". RISE_SMA is a multi-partner EU project which aims to improve data analytics methods and approaches to more effectively filter out and use relevant information in an ethical way. A key focus of the project is to involve practitioner stakeholders as research project co-creators and collaborators through the

[2] http://ugbs.ug.edu.gh/ifipwg86-2019/index.html last accessed 5 April 2019.

use of an engaged scholarship approach and research methods, so as to effectively shape analytics solutions to meet the expectations of society and crisis responders.

In this paper, we firstly discuss the awareness of power in the ISD process and what this means for SM platform providers and their users. We then go on to highlight the unforeseen consequences of SM platform developments that are a result of the professional manipulation of the ISD process by social media vendors and that result in mis-trust of SM messages and information. Next, we discuss how we might overcome these limitations through the RISE_SMA[3] project and its objective of mutual negotiation of the IS development process (in this case SM analytics) describing the project's engaged scholarship approach and live research methods to achieve this outcome. We then outline the workshop findings and conclude the paper with contributions which highlight the beginning of the fifth era of IT adoption and location of ISD power, limitations and areas of future research.

2 Awareness of Power and the Information Systems Development Process

Do the IT power users of today, as described by Niederman et al. [2] have the knowledge and understanding of information systems development to allow them sufficient power and control over the systems that they adopt and use? We would contend that currently this isn't the case. By way of example, we have seen that the development activities behind platforms like Facebook and Twitter remain secretive due to their commercial value as well as a reluctance of SM platform providers to interfere with the structure and dynamics of their platform architectures. This problem will increase even more with the new developments in artificial intelligence and machine learning.

In 1987 Markus and Bjorn-Andersen [8] wrote "The potential of consequences of IS professional power for users is simply too significant to remain unexplored" (p. 498). This statement is still as relevant now as it was in 1987. "Awareness and the perceived legitimacy of power exercise will affect users' responses to [ISD] professionals and their acceptance of the solutions they propose. Furthermore, we believe that interventions that increase this awareness will pave the way to compromises by opening up previously covert issues. This would help prevent negative consequences from power use and help achieve solutions that are acceptable to both parties" (p. 502). When both system designers and system users are aware of their power in the ISD process then *mutual negotiation* over the design and use of the system takes place. When designers are unaware, but users are aware of their power then *user resistance* to systems design and deployment occurs. When designers are aware, but users are unaware then *professional manipulation* of users by IS designers can happen but when

[3] RISE_SMA is funded by the European Union from 2019–2022, https://social-media-analytics.org/ last accessed 5 April 2019.

Table 2. Awareness of the exercise of ISD power – reproduced from Markus and Bjorn-Andersen [8]

		User awareness	
		Aware	Unaware
Designer awareness	Aware	Mutual negotiation	*Professional manipulation*
	Unaware	User resistance	Unintended influence

both are unaware of power then *unintended influence* (lack of successfully negotiated systems outcomes and opportunistic exercise of power) takes place (see Table 2).

In this era of ubiquitous computing and social media we see companies like Facebook and Twitter who are aware of their power over the ISD process and users who have been rendered unaware of this by the algorithmic structures of these platforms. This gives rise to *professional manipulation* of users by technology companies and the development of data analytics approaches which are biased towards producing profits for them and their commercial partners. But are we now seeing a shift towards a new era of ICT adoption and use? Have technology designers been largely unaware of the power of their system designs and are the general users of these systems largely unaware of their social impact?

3 The Unforeseen Consequences of Social Media Design

The unforeseen consequences (*unintended influence*) of SM platforms limit their scope for Bright ICT outcomes for society. Unforeseen consequences include: system personalisation (not mass systematisation) and the difficulty in using SM information and messages for decision making; haphazard facilitation of convergence behaviour; and enablement of anti-social behaviour. We will now discuss each of these consequences in turn.

3.1 Platforms for System Personalization not Mass Systematization

We know that SM platforms facilitate communication, collaboration and coordination of social networks when information is input to, processed by and output from a SM platform [9]. We also know that information is input and output from these platforms in many different formats, such as tweets, micro-blog posts, wiki posts, maps, etc. While these formats can work very well for personal decision-making, enhancement of social interactions, and are easily accessible on personal devices (mobile phones, pads and laptops) SM platforms and the information generated by them lack mass 'systematization' i.e. the ability to derive an optimal understanding of the 'facts at hand' for a systemic approach to decision making - such as that found in proprietary business software systems.

So, on one hand the lack of systematization is a major strength of SM platforms as they allow a relatively novice user to propagate, access, use and communicate information in a personal and relevant way. Lack of systematization does, however, also represent a major weakness of SM platforms to address common problems, as the multiple personal 'representations' of information are difficult to combine, interpret and apply to derive common analytical solutions [10]. In many instances the volume of SM information and communications often gets out of hand during a major organisational or societal event, adding further to the difficulty that organisations and governments have in interpreting and using information that is generated in this way [11].

In order for decision-making to be effectively underpinned by the use of SM, these efforts would require a minimum level of systematization of SM platforms that enables and supports the interpretation, combination and application of multiple personal 'representations' into synthesized information and processes. SM has not been designed for mass systemization and decision-making activities, however, and attempts to use it in this way can seriously backfire.

For example, enabling a SM user to upload an image of a flood can greatly enhance the effectiveness of the information they are making available to other SM users; while on the other hand, by adding the GPS coordinates of the user to the message they are uploading, (in order to systematize the information) makes the information take on extra characteristics that once interpreted by an agency may assist in rescuing the user (if they are in imminent danger) or breaching their privacy (if they are not).

3.2 Platforms Which Haphazardly Facilitate Convergence Behavior

Convergence behavior is a phenomenon that occurs during mass events like crises or protests i.e. the spontaneous and mass movement of assets, people, resources (and now information) towards the event area [12]. For instance, in the physical world, many people may converge on an event to look at it unfold [13]. In the virtual world you may use a commonly available social media platform such as Twitter, to converge on and comment on an event.

Subba and Bui [14] explain that some convergence behaviors can be expressed in both physical and virtual worlds, some in the physical world only and some in the virtual world only. They argue that all convergence behaviors i.e. physical and virtual have interaction "properties" which include:

- Local vs Global e.g. an event may be local but its impact global;
- Complementarity vs Substitutability e.g. a doctor may go online as a helper but may not necessarily substitute for a doctor at the scene;
- Formality vs Informality e.g. there is formal agency response versus informal community response;
- Legitimacy vs Illegality e.g. desirable, proper and appropriate versus illegal or morally wrong behaviors;
- Planning vs Spontaneity e.g. planned reactions versus ad hoc and emergent behaviors for example the phenomenon of "spontaneous volunteers"; and
- Centralized vs Decentralized e.g. response on the ground versus collaboration and co-operation online.

They also contend that convergence behaviors are a "double edged sword phenomena" (p. 9) as they provide additional assistance and resources to an event response, but they also bring congestion that can cause problems to manage. These behaviors are also context driven i.e. dependent on the type of event, its impact and the resilience of the community it affects, so that convergence behavior is difficult to anticipate. Event managers "have no other option but to spend time in pulling strings to manipulate the convergence process after the convergence process takes place" (p. 9).

Their conclusions focus on the initial work of Fritz and Matthewson [13] which recommended that an "initial attack on the problems of convergence requires the development of a systematic policy and programs for handling information and communications" (p. 9) as it is the characteristics of event information provision and communication that drives convergence behavior towards an event. SM platforms lack the mass systematization of proprietary business systems to coordinate and communicate information in a systemic manner. They instead produce information and communication in a haphazard, organic and disorganized way often producing emergent, persistent, undesirable and unwanted convergence behavior.

This presents a problem for any individual or organization that wishes to either communicate via, or to use information generated by SM to make decisions and negotiate outcomes in relation to an event. It is virtually impossible to authenticate the source and validate the content of SM generated information and communications, and as such, platforms generally rely on community or government agency moderation of tweets and posts for this purpose [15].

Interaction properties between convergence behavior archetypes in both physical and virtual environments are also directly impacted by the haphazard nature of SM information production and communication i.e. lack of systematization can lend an unpredictability to how people will all negotiate and interact with each other, their communities, governments, organisations and other entities both online and in the physical world, during an event.

3.3 Platforms that Enable Anti-social Behavior

While it is well known that SM platforms have greatly benefited society and individuals by enabling communication, collaboration and co-ordination activities on an unprecedented scale, due to their design and nature i.e. system personalization, they are also enablers of anti-social, narcissistic and ego centric behavior which manifests itself in activities such as propagation of false information or manipulated images, rumours (including misrepresentation of identity), bullying, harassment and coercion, privacy breaches and much more.

Online social networks and SM platforms provide an enabling platform for anti-social and narcissistic behavior as they provide an information and communications channel that is easily manipulated, controlled and personalized to project an image of an individual that may (or may not) be reflective of that individual. This notion also extends to group and convergence behavior.

This type of convergence behavior through the use of SM platforms is also in evidence all around us on a day-to-day basis through the activity of "trolling" where individuals make off-topic or inflammatory statements to provoke others and disrupt supplementary activities and discussions [16]. A study by Buckles et al. [17] highlights that SM trolls have narcissistic tendencies (as well as other negative behavioral traits). On a wider scale and at a societal level, we have also seen this type of intentional negative behavior play out in terrorist, anti-government, and political manipulation of social media platforms to cause general havoc and disruption to society [7, 12].

3.4 Social Media Distrust

We contend that these three factors, which are the unintended consequences of current SM platform ISD approaches, form a significant barrier to trust in SM platforms for society and crisis managers who wish to use them as potential information and communications platforms for Bright ICT for the common good (see Fig. 1).

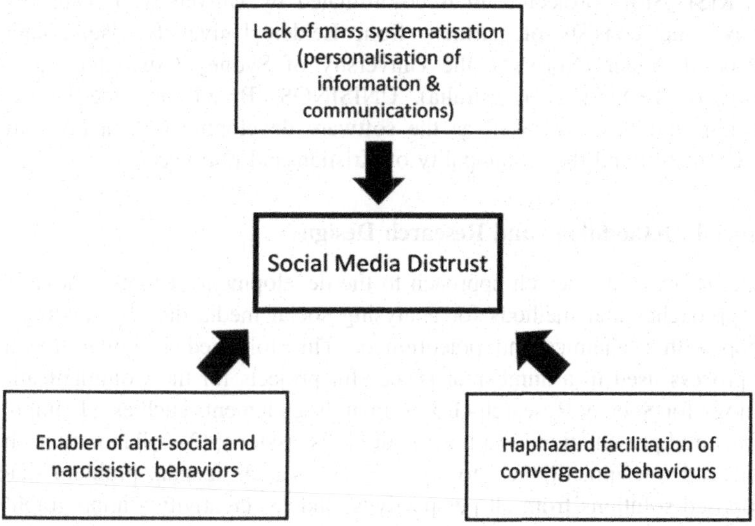

Fig. 1. Factors contributing to social media distrust

Roy Morgan Research [18] surveyed Australians and found that 47% distrusted information provided on social media platforms. Their respondents, top 5 distrust drivers were:

- Fake News/manipulation of the truth;
- False statistics/audience measurement;
- Personal information stolen & distributed;
- Anyone can make claims without any evidence; and
- News is sensationalised/becomes entertainment.

Distrust of SM platforms limits their application for Bright ICT and the associated benefits to society. This distrust is tied to the lack of mass systematisation (social media analytics) and the resulting antisocial and haphazard convergence behaviours that result. How then can we mitigate for the unintended consequences of the fourth era of ICT adoption and use so that SM technologies can more effectively produce societal benefits?

4 RISE_SMA Project Aims and Objectives

The RISE-SMA project seeks to develop more innovative theoretical approaches and methods for analysing social media data which are very important for the assurance of social cohesion during times of crisis.

The project team is tackling the project from a multi-disciplinary/academic-practitioner perspective that will define and scope the project inclusive of multiple viewpoints and which will create analytic solutions including all stakeholders in the ISD process. This will ensure effective outcomes by rendering the users of these analytics solutions aware of their power in the ISD process.

The RISE_SMA project team is co-ordinated by University of Duisburg-Essen (Germany) and consists of partners from Leiden University (Netherlands), the University of Agder (Norway), the University of Sydney (Australia), Queensland University of Technology (Australia), UNISINOS (Brazil) and the University of Padjadjaran (Indonesia) as well as the software development company Virtimo in Berlin (Germany) and the municipality of Kristiansand (Norway).

4.1 Social Methodology and Research Design

We took an engaged research approach to the development of more innovative theoretical approaches and methods for analysing social media data by holding a 2-day workshop with academics and practitioners. This followed a similar live methods design process used in a number of successful projects for the Communications and Technology for Society Research Group[4] including elements such as: (1) imprography - for structured presentations and unstructured discussions; (2) collaboration - bringing together academics/practitioners to co-create a research agenda, problem statement/s and proposed solutions from all perspectives; and (3) creativity - imprography facilitates all workshop participants to put their ideas and suggestions forward without "fear of failure" [19, 20].

During our workshop researchers/practitioners engaged with each other without taking control of the course or direction of the discussion, emphasizing and respecting the equality of experience of all participants from their own perspective "No input to the workshop is superior to any other" [20].

Our live research methods approach to workshop design differs in important aspects from other workshop methods where usually an academic research team sets the research agenda and controls the workshop structure and discussions [21]. Our approach to the workshop documented for this paper aims for the co-creation and reframing of problems and solutions by all workshop participants. Hence, it is not limited to simply analysing existing knowledge and modes of thought. Importantly, our engaged scholarship approach allows for new thinking about and deep understanding of the research area that participants i.e. academics/practitioners develop through their participation in the workshop.

[4] https://sydney.edu.au/business/our-research/research-groups/communications-and-technology-for-society.html.

Our approach also presents and re-presents the research agenda, problems and solutions in real-time; as participants work through cycles of discovery, framing and co-creation throughout the workshop. The workshop design was as follows.

Location, Date and Timing: Sydney Australia, 6th & 7th March 2019 from 10 am–4 pm.

Purpose: To develop more innovative theoretical approaches and methods for analysing social media data for the assurance of social cohesion during times of crisis.

Participants: 12 practitioner and academic participants (50/50 split) with experience in: emergency services; social media management and analytics; industry; government emergency co-ordination; geospatial information management; software development; and disaster recovery research.

Research Team: Two senior researchers, one post-doctoral researcher and three PhD candidates from Information Systems with an emphasis on IS in crisis situations and methods as they apply to data analytics.

Structure:

Day 1- Sessions

- RISE_SMA Description and Objectives - project co-ordinator and administrator (University of Duisburg Essen);
- Workshop Introduction and Outline (15 min) - project co-ordinator (University of Duisburg Essen) and team leader (University of Sydney);
- Practitioner Presentations - areas of importance for RISE_SMA - all practitioners;
- Aggregation, prioritisation and representation of practitioner areas of importance i.e. similarities, differences, systems integration issues, relationship of areas of importance to experience etc. What would a practitioner "wish list" for RISE_SMA outcomes look like? - all workshop participants; and
- Social Media Research Presentation: Issues, Trends and Future Directions – project co-ordinator (University of Duisburg Essen) and team leader (University of Sydney).

Day 2 - Sessions

- Practitioner Areas of Importance - Alignment With RISE_SMA Project Objectives i.e. what issues align, what issues don't align, why do we think this is and what should we do about it? - discussion facilitated by project co-ordinator and administrator (University of Duisburg Essen);
- Academic Presentations - Current and Future Research That Relates to RISE_SMA Objectives - all academics; and
- RISE_SMA Planning and Next Steps - all workshop participants.

Preparation: All practitioners were asked to prepare three PowerPoint slides outlining: (1) what social media means to your organisation (what do you use it for currently?); (2) key issues, problems and expectations with the use of social media in your organisation (what needs improving for the future?); and (3) your "wish list" of key outcomes for the RISE_SMA project. All academics were asked to prepare 2 PowerPoint slides outlining: (1) what research you're conducting now that relates to RISE_SMA; and (2) what you'd like to research in the future in the context of the project.

Expected Research Outcomes: The RISE_SMA project's official kick off workshop is scheduled for April 2018. In order to create a good basis for this kick-off event, the project co-ordinator (University of Duisburg-Essen) as well as research partners from Communications and Technology for Society Research Group (University of Sydney), conducted a joint workshop with practitioners from crisis social media, communications and emergency information managers to trial an engaged scholarship approach [20, 22, 23]. One goal was to firstly better understand issues surrounding the use of SM platforms for crisis communications as well as to co-create project areas of focus with both academic and practitioner team members. We utilised a "live" collaborative form of engaged scholarship i.e. workshops, so that all academic/practitioner project participants could develop insight together regarding the unforeseen consequences of SM platform, inform each other and develop a mutual understanding of research problem while formulating a focus for comprehensive and relevant analytics solutions. "We also believe that diffracting academic and professional expertise contributes to each other's development and can contribute to generating innovative ideas" [20 - p. 114].

In sum, this workshop was focussed on developing a better understanding of the problems and issues of social media use for crisis management and situational awareness purposes; and then on co-producing and framing a research agenda with all of the workshop participants.

5 Results and Discussion

The workshop gave us the opportunity to include all stakeholders in the process of project creation and agenda setting as well as identifying areas of focus for the production of useful and relevant analytics. It was facilitated by the two senior researchers on the project team and there was a planned agenda order.

This was not strictly followed so as to allow workshop participants to 'free wheel' with ideas of importance if and when they occurred out of the workshop sequence. Practitioner presentations assisted participants to better understand the problems associated with SM platform use for society and crisis management and academic presentations assisted participants to better understand what SM research trends might be important for the future.

5.1 Workshop Insights

Over the course of the 2 days of the workshop the group created an assessment of the current situation of SM platform use in crisis and emergency management. The assessment highlighted that:

- SM communications management within crisis management agencies can have many different areas of focus e.g. roles such as public information officer, warning officer, public intelligence and social media intelligence analyst are created to manage SM communications to and from the general public;

- Crisis management agencies continually improve their SM analysis procedures based on their own experiences and are often driven by a high degree of self-organisation and intrinsic motivation;
- Due to the current cost of SM analytics, government may use a combination of proprietary and open source analytics packages to work with social media information. Use of appropriate public domain tools to analyse SM communications, however, may have associated privacy issues or they may be too complex to use and/or be unsupported;
- Spread of misinformation on SM platforms is an ongoing issue i.e. people may not trust SM platforms, but they do trust their online local communities/local groups where rumours may take root and be difficult to quash;
- Moderation tools like SpreadSocial are essential to the connection of all crisis management agency pages and Twitter accounts;
- Community expectations of the efficacy and use of SM platforms for crisis information seeking and reporting must be continually managed i.e. not just during a crisis;
- Well-being of crisis agency social media officers must be continually managed i.e. negative comments especially police postings about crimes/missing people can have a deep psycho/social impact on officers dealing with these communications;
- SM analytics training for government SM managers is paramount in order to effectively gather community intelligence for situational awareness as well as how to structure outgoing information and messaging; and
- Incident control and situational awareness through SM use needs to be managed over: (a) multiple jurisdictions i.e. national, state, regional level and locally and (b) various threat types and levels.

As a result of this current assessment of SM adoption and use, the group highlighted possible research opportunities and areas. These included the co-development of analytics methods, frameworks and approaches that addressed:

- Identification, credentialing, organizing, managing, training and utilizing of digital volunteers (from all over the world) for public good;
- E-learning training modules for SM analytics approaches, frameworks and techniques;
- Automated threat analytics;
- Big data analytics (including geospatial data) i.e. more effective assessment and use of high volumes of information (text, image, video, sound) generated by SM platforms e.g. how validate and assess photos, information etc. early enough to adequately and accurately inform situational awareness;
- 24 × 7 monitoring and assessment centre capability with trained people;
- Community education regarding tools and techniques on: (1) how to upload useful crisis information, and (2) how to receive and use information e.g. how to stay cool in a heat wave;
- Creation of bots to manage and influence SM communications e.g. a ChatBot to disseminate warnings or interact with people in trouble;

- Use of geospatial information with SM data to assess crisis situations (location, spread, impact etc.), locate individuals impacted by or victims of the situation, dispatch resources to the crisis location through a multi-disciplinary approach to develop systems to combine social media with GIS data; and
- Techniques and approaches to integrate location information into SM posts as a matter of priority i.e. management of the debate over data protection vs importance of data use in crisis management.

5.2 Post Workshop Analysis of Research Notes and Workshop Materials

Post workshop, our research team (two senior researchers, one post-doctoral researcher and 3 PhD candidates) met to debrief the workshop and further synthesized and refined workshop outputs and our notes to highlight the following key areas:

Multiple research agendas for the assessment and development of social media analytics for Bright ICT in society for crisis management became evident as we analysed the workshop brainstorming and clustering activities which mainly occurred on Day 2. These research agendas included:

- Digital volunteers and systems to manage them i.e. a virtual operations support team (VOST). This agenda is of critical focus as crisis management agencies already have tried and tested systems to recruit, train and manage their existing and considerably skilled volunteer teams. Digital volunteers, whether present online or in person, can supplement agency volunteers but they present a particular challenge for crisis managers;
- Development of SM bots as a benign and useful influence on social media crisis communications; and
- Social media crisis communication for the development of situational awareness.

Multiple project areas were also identified by workshop participants to be pursued by the RISE_SMA research group which include:

- Development of 'proof of concept' training bots for crisis management SM analysis purposes - in conjunction with RISE_SMA project partners and IEERG member institutions and their student programmers;
- Organizational framework development for a VOST implementation. A possibility might be to look at matching resources/capability with demand e.g. Uber or AirBnB model could be useful but what are the limitations; and
- Creation of multiple 'fact sheets' highlighting the current 'state of the art' in plain English (and echoing the three research agendas) for consumption by practitioners and the general public on the current status of: Digital volunteers and VOST; Intelligent agents in crisis communications e.g. chatbots; and SM models for crisis communications i.e. integrated situational awareness/intelligence.

6 Contribution, Limitations and Future Research Directions

6.1 Contribution

It would seem that we are now entering a fifth era of IT adoption and use of *social influence*. This presents us with some difficult issues and unintended consequences to overcome. Users of technologies in the fourth era have been intentionally professionally manipulated in their understanding of the design architectures and choices made by technology companies, as they have had little awareness of the ISD processes behind these platforms. The technology companies, however, also seem to have been largely unaware of the utility of their system designs to disrupt society by allowing negative and socially disruptive behaviour to flourish without consequence [24]. Added to this, we are now bringing more smart sensors online, embedding more goods with computing power as well as developing and launching applications that depend on location-based services that can track individuals via GPS.

Table 3. Fifth era of IT adoption and location of ISD power

IT adoption ERA	Technology in use	Location of IS development expertise and power	IS development trend
Fifth Era (now into the future) *Social Influence*	Ubiquitous personal computing (smart phones); Search engines; Social media Smart sensors; Spatial systems; 5G communications; GPS tracking; Digital imaging; Rapid visualisation; Artificial intelligence; Satellites; Computer embedded "things" (cars, protheses, etc.)	Tech companies – low Manufacturing companies – high Data/information services – high Business – low Government – low End users – low	Cloud computing; Social networks: Location-based services; Corporate data harvesting and profiling; Shared marketing intelligence; Corporate and personal brand curation; Mass social manipulation and influencing; Embedded autonomous systems; Digital twin simulation (for design and development purposes)

Extension of work based on Hirschheim and Klein [1] and Niederman et al. [2].

This situation has ultimately led to general user distrust of SM platforms, which then impacts their usefulness for crisis communications. Development of digital volunteering and VOST organisational frameworks, targeted bot applications and appropriate SM management models and frameworks all offer potential solutions to the restoration of trust in social networking platforms and new technological developments for crisis communication purposes. As the fifth ICT adoption era of social influence gains momentum, it is of critical importance that we develop frameworks, approaches, applications and analytics to deal with the unintended consequences of the fourth era and to enable Bright ICT outcomes for society. RISE_SMA is clearly focused on this task.

6.2 Limitations

We are aware that our workshop results depend on the opinions and ideas of participating stakeholders and their operating context. The Australian setting of crisis response and management, therefore, has been the starting position for discussion of this topic. In our opinion this workshop format was quite effective, however, to identify the existing lack of knowledge and requirements for action regarding the use of SM platforms in crisis situations from both an academic perspective and practice-driven point of view.

This workshop presented us with a unique opportunity to work with practitioners to co-develop a deeper understanding of the critical issues, problems and limitations with SM use for crisis communications, management and situational awareness purposes (and hence better facilitation of the application of SM platforms to Bright ICT outcomes). It also enabled us to co-create, with experienced practitioners and researchers, a relevant data analytics research agenda and identify research projects of importance to practice for RISE_SMA to focus their efforts on.

6.3 Future Research Directions

This workshop has also enabled us to take an engaged scholarship approach and utilize a live workshop method that we had previous project success with. There is potential for this approach and method to be replicated and utilized by other RISE_SMA partner institutions at other locations to assess whether the same research agendas and potential projects might be applicable in other jurisdictions or whether there might be significant differences between jurisdictions.

An area of particular importance for the future direction of the project confirmed by our workshop participants is *identifying and defining mechanisms for organization/self-organization of digital volunteers in crisis situations via SM platforms.* SM platforms have enabled self-organizing group structures, outside of the already well established and effective volunteer teams in crisis management agencies, where individuals and communities may take an active role in a crisis through their convergence behaviour, for example as happened in the Christchurch Earthquake in 2011 with the Student Volunteer Army [25]. It is expected that new information and ideas will emerge from the RISE_SMA project on how individuals and communities organize via SM in crises and disaster scenarios, as will factors influencing the future role of SM to enable resilient communities. For instance, Taylor et al. [26] explored public SM use from January to March 2011 in Australia and New Zealand during a time where a number of natural disasters occurred. They focused in particular on the 'Cyclone Yasi Update' Facebook page, which was a community-run disaster information hub. This hub combined official information with personalized 2-way communication (which also facilitated the quashing of rumors) and orientated people to the applicable accurate sources of information. This provided "a single initial trusted point of contact for people who needed to prioritize their activities to protect themselves, rather than spend time searching for information" [26 - p. 22]. Examples such as the 'Cyclone Yasi Update' Facebook community information hub, can teach us valuable lessons about digital volunteers. Convergence behavior as it relates to the principles of self-organizing systems is a little understood topic that has the potential to make a major contribution to enhancing the use of SM to organize digital volunteers in crisis situations.

The changing nature of communities from groups of close friends and relatives to extended group members of networks, and how community dynamics are affected by SM in times of disasters, is intricately bound up with, *crisis agency organization and management practices* and *convergence behavior archetypes and their properties*. There is an urgent need to study these management practices and their interrelationship with these archetypes and their evolution in the online world. This is particularly critical if we are to better understand the interplay of convergence behaviors, information and communications personalization characteristics of SM and the enablement (or disablement) of anti-social behavior that occurs during a disaster.

References

1. Hirschheim, R., Klein, H.K.: A glorious and not-so-short history of the information systems field. J. Assoc. Inf. Syst. **13**(4), 188–235 (2012)
2. Niederman, F., Ferratt, T.W., Trauth, E.M.: On the co-evolution of information technology and information systems personnel. DATA BASE Adv. Inf. Syst. **47**(1), 29–50 (2016)
3. Wong, J.C.: Google snubs Senate hearings on election meddling, 5 September 2018. https://www.theguardian.com/technology/2018/sep/05/google-senate-hearings-facebook-twitter-russia-meddling-latest-news. Accessed 5 Apr 2019
4. Reuters World News: French Muslim group sues Facebook, YouTube over footage of Christchurch massacre, 26 March 2019. https://www.reuters.com/article/us-france-christchurch-complaint/french-muslim-group-sues-facebook-youtube-over-footage-of-christchurch-massacre-idUSKCN1R61H8. Accessed 5 Apr 2019
5. Hunter, F., Duke, J.: Facebook censured by government for failure to act on live streaming concerns, 26 March 2019. https://www.smh.com.au/politics/federal/facebook-censured-by-government-for-failure-to-act-on-livestreaming-concerns-20190326-p517sb.html. Accessed 5 Apr 2019
6. Ross, B., Pilz, L., Cabrera, B., Brachten, F., Neubaum, G., Stieglitz, S.: Are social bots a real threat? An agent-based model of the spiral of silence to analyse the impact of manipulative actors in social networks. Eur. J. Inf. Syst. (2019, forthcoming)
7. Stieglitz, S., Mirbabaie, M., Ross, B., Neuberger, C.: Social media analytics - challenges in topic discovery, data collection, and data preparation. Int. J. Inf. Manag. **39**, 156–168 (2018)
8. Markus, M.L., Bjorn-Andersen, N.: Power over users: its exercise by system professionals. Commun. ACM **30**(6), 498–504 (1987)
9. Oh, O., Agrawal, M., Rao, H.R.: Community Intelligence and social media services: a rumour theoretic analysis of tweets during social crises. MIS Q. **37**, 407–426 (2013)
10. Kroenke, D., Bunker, D., Wilson, D.: Experiencing MIS, 3rd edn. Pearson Australia, Sydney (2014)
11. Sleigh, A.: Comment by NSW Police, regarding listening for messages from inside Lindt Café, during the hostage crisis. Notes from NSW State Emergency Management, Communications Sub-committee 2nd December (2015, unpublished)
12. Mirbabaie, M., Bunker, D., Deubel, A., Stieglitz, S.: Examining convergence behaviour during crisis situations in social media - a case study on the manchester bombing 2017. In: Elbanna, A., Dwivedi, Y.K., Bunker, D., Wastell, D. (eds.) TDIT 2018. IAICT, vol. 533, pp. 60–75. Springer, Cham (2019). https://doi.org/10.1007/978-3-030-04315-5_5

13. Fritz, C.E., Mathewson, J.H.: Convergence Behavior in Disasters: A Problem in Social Control Committee on Disaster Studies. Disaster Research Group (1957)
14. Subba, R., Bui, T.: An exploration of the physical-virtual convergence behaviours in crisis situations. In: Proceedings of the 43rd Hawaii International Conference on Information Systems (2010)
15. Starbird, K., Palen, L., Hughes, A.L., Vieweg, S.: Chatter on the red: what hazards threat reveals about the social life of microblogged information. In: CSCW, Savannah, Georgia, USA, 6–10 February, pp. 241–250 (2010)
16. Golbeck, J.: Negativity and anti-social attention seeking among narcissists on Twitter: a linguistic analysis. First Monday **21**(3–7 March) (2016) http://firstmonday.org/ojs/index.php/fm/article/view/6017/5254. Accessed 15 June 2016
17. Buckles, E.E., Trapnell, P.D., Paulhus, D.L.: Trolls just want to have fun. Pers. Individ. Differ. **67**, 97–102 (2014)
18. Roy Morgan Research: Social Media deeply distrusted by Australians, 26 June 2018. http://www.roymorgan.com/findings/7640-social-media-distrusted-june-2018-201806260211. Accessed 5 Apr 2019
19. Tarr, J., Gonzalez-Polledo, E., Cornish, F.: On liveness: using arts workshops as a research method. Qual. Res. **18**, 36–52 (2018)
20. Elbanna, A., Bunker, D., Levine, L., Sleigh, A.: Emergency management in the changing world of social media: framing the research agenda with the stakeholders through engaged scholarship. Int. J. Inf. Manag. **47**, 112–120 (2019)
21. Brooks, J., Bravington, A., Rodriguez, A., King, N., Percy-Smith, B.: Using participatory research methods to facilitate wide stakeholder involvement: experiences from a community public health workshop. In: British Psychological Society Annual Conference 2016, 26th–28th April 2016, East Midlands Conference Centre (2016, unpublished)
22. Van de Ven, A.H.: Engaged Scholarship: A Guide for Organizational and Social Research: Oxford University Press on Demand (2007)
23. Van de Ven, A.H., Jing, R.: Indigenous management research in China from an engaged scholarship perspective. Manag. Organ. Rev. **8**, 123–137 (2012)
24. ABC News: New Zealand Privacy Commissioner Calls Facebook Morally Bankrupt, 9 April 2019. https://www.abc.net.au/news/2019-04-08/new-zealand-pivacy-commissioner-calls-facebook-morally-bankrupt/10982710. Accessed 9 Apr 2019
25. Bunker, D., Ehnis, C., Seltsikas, P., Levine, L.: Crisis management and social media: assuring effective information governance for long term social sustainability. In: Proceedings of the 13th Annual IEEE Conference on Technologies for Homeland Security HST 2013, Boston, United States, 14th November (2013)
26. Taylor, M., Wells, G., Howell, G., Raphael, B.: The role of social media as psychological first aid as a support to community resilience building. A Facebook study from Cyclone Yasi Update. Aust. J. Emerg. Manag. **27**(1) (2012)

Technostress Effect in Consumer Context: The Negative Effect of Following Social Media Influencers

Zainah Qasem(✉)

The School of Business Department of Marketing,
The University of Jordan, Amman, Jordan
z.qasem@ju.edu.jo

Abstract. Social media and its applications, such as social networks, have become well embedded in modern people's life. Much research has focused on the good side of social media marketing and adoption. However, very little research was devoted to study the dark-side of social media especially in out of work context. This paper is focusing on the dark side of social media in out of work context. Also utilizes the stress-strain model and social comparison theory to suggest following SMIs as potential technostressor and shopping addiction as a potential negative outcome of technostress.

Keywords: Social media · Social media influencers · Technostress

1 Introduction

Social media and its applications, such as social networks, have become well embedded in modern people's life (Alalwan et al. 2017; Dwivedi et al. 2015; Kapoor et al. 2018; Shiau et al. 2017; 2018). Over the past decade, social media have been transforming how individuals, communities, and organizations create, share, and consume information from each other and from firms (Baccarella et al. 2018). Much research focused on understanding the advantages and disadvantages of social media bring to individuals and businesses in work context (e.g. Bucher 2013; Kumar et al. 2016; Wagner 2017; Yasir et al. 2017; Stich et al. 2018). Nevertheless, little research has been conducted to understand the effects of social media out of work context.

The term "dark-side" of IT use refers to a "collection of 'negative' phenomena that are associated with the use of IT, and that have the potential to infringe the well-being of individuals, and societies" (Tarafdar et al. 2015a, p. 161).

Understanding the negative effect of social media in the personal context is very important for organizations and policymakers alike. This is due to the possibility that social media is undermining the freedoms and the well-being of the individuals and communities they serve.

The negative effect of social media on individuals outside of workplace is being increasingly reported. For example, Forest and Wood (2012) have reported that Facebook is viewed by people with low self-esteem as an appealing venue for self-disclosure. Consequently, receiving negative feedback on their disclosure can lower

Published by Springer Nature Switzerland AG 2019
Y. Dwivedi et al. (Eds.): TDIT 2019, IFIP AICT 558, pp. 553–560, 2019.
https://doi.org/10.1007/978-3-030-20671-0_38

users' happiness. Also, prolonged use of technology can lead to greater stresses and affect an individual's well-being. Thus, by understanding the negative effect of social media on individuals on their personal level is very important for policymakers to refine policies and regulations in order to protect the public.

Technostress-which refers to stress induced by information and communication technologies (Brooks et al. 2017) - was addressed by a number of studies as a negative phenomenon associated with using social media at the workplace (e.g. Tarafdar et al. 2007; Ragu-Nathan et al. 2008; Ayyagari et al. 2011). Yet, to the best of my knowledge, there is no study that focuses on identifying sources of technostress and its effect on individuals in out of work context.

In this paper, the author will follow the same stressor-strain model used in studying technostress sources and effect in the workplace to investigate one of the potential technostress sources and its effect in personal usage this is social media influencer. This paper also suggests a number of prepositions that present a potential negative outcome of adopting social networks such as Instagram.

2 Literature Review

2.1 Social Media and Social Media Influencers

Social Media "is a group of Internet-based applications that build on the ideological and technological foundations of Web 2.0, and that allow the creation and exchange of User Generated Content" (Kaplan and Haenlein 2010, p. 61). User-Generated Content, "which describes the various forms of media content created by end-users outside of a professional context and is publicly available" (Kaplan and Haenlein 2010, p. 61), is what differentiates social media from other more traditional forms of media. Social media influencer (micro-influencers) (Arora et al. 2019) are one of the content creators that are mainly found creating content on different platforms such as Instagram and snapchat.

Combley (2011) defined influencers as individuals who have the ability to induce a change in the attitudes and behaviors of others. The emergence of Web 2.0 social media has introduced a new type of influencers which is referred to as social media influencers (SMIs) (Ki 2018). SMI is described as a "third party endorser who shapes audience attitudes through blogs, tweets, and the use of other social media" (Feberg et al. 2011, p. 1).

Khamis et al. (2017) stated that SMIs (who range from unknown actresses and models, fitness trainers, friends of celebrities, and wealthy people who love luxury brands to pretty high school girls) create their own image through the practice of self-presentation on social media to attract the attention of followers. De Veirman et al. (2017) called SMI a trusted tastemaker with a solid base of fans who follow their content (published videos, images and motivational stories on social media channels such as Instagram and other social media platforms (Bolat and Gilani 2018) for entertainment or inspiration. Recently it is becoming more noticeable that SMIs shared content is focused on their luxurious life, perfect body image, and their ownership of high-end brands (Marwick 2015). Although such as postings might be considered entertaining by many followers, it can also trigger negative emotions amid ordinary people who perceive such as perfect image and luxury life as unattainable (Ki 2018). Therefore, in this paper the author we will assume SMI source stress that affect their followers negatively and investigate the outcome of this type of stress.

2.2 Technostress

Technostress is a concept that was developed in the 1980s and described mental and physiological arousal and consequent pressure caused by an inability to cope with ComputerWorld technologies in a healthy manner (Brod 1984; Lee et al. 2016). Technostress has also been described as negative attitudes, thoughts, behaviors, or physiology caused directly or indirectly by technology (Weil and Rosen 1997; Brooks et al. 2017). Further, technostress has been defined as a user's experience of stress when using technologies (Lee et al. 2016).

For clarity, this paper adopts the stressor-strain model in order to theoretically decompose the overall concept (Yan et al. 2013). Stressors are described as the source of technostress and represents any stimuli that individual is encountered with that cause a negative outcome (Ayyagari et al. 2011) in this paper we are investigating SMI as stress source. Strains are individuals' negative psychological response to stressors caused by being exposed to a specific stressor (Ayyagari et al. 2011). Stress has a broad definition that can refer to the stimuli, process, as well as outcomes (Yan et al. 2013). In this paper we will focus on two potential outcomes to stress resulting from exposure to SMIs these are shopping addiction and materialism.

2.2.1 Shopping Addiction

Research has evidence to support the existence of a relationship between stress and addiction as an outcome of stress (Brooks et al. 2017). For example, Sinha (2001) reported that that stressed out individuals tend to show vulnerability towards drug abuse. This relationship can be attributed to individuals fail to self-regulate their destructive tendencies when under stress; which results in lack of self-control (Tice et al. 2001).

Addictive behavior is a term that refers to extreme behavior that has negative consequences and characterized by a loss of control, and negative results for the individual either psychologically, physically or socially (Sussman et al. 2010; Rose and Dhandayudham 2014). Addiction is postulated to have two features. Firstly, the failure to resist the impulse behavior regardless of its negative consequences. Secondly, the existence of a period of tension followed by a relief during the act (Benson 2008).

Evidence suggests that addiction symptoms are related to technology similar to other addictive elements like drugs (Brooks et al. 2017). For example, social media may encompass some of the features that cause substance-related addictions (Kuss and Griffiths 2011). Thus, in this paper, we will investigate addiction as an outcome to social media stress.

The literature on addiction has reported that problem-based behaviors can develop in relation to both consumption and buying. Consequently, shopping was identified as a type of addiction and the number of terms has developed such as "impulsive purchasing" and shopping addiction (Baumeister 2002). In our assumption, as SMIs are showing off their luxury life. Hence, in this paper, we will investigate shopping addiction as a stress outcome that results from being exposed to SMIs.

2.2.2 Materialism

Richins and Dawson (1992) defined materialism as the importance ascribed to the ownership and acquisition of material goods in achieving major life goals or desired states. Accordingly, it is expected that individuals described as materialists will value ownership of products and will have a positive attitude and eventually the intention to own different products.

The relations between people's values such as materialism and ownership, and their emotional experiences such as stress are of key interest to many consumer researchers (Brown et al. 2016). However, there are very few published works that address the relationship between materialism and stress (Somer and Ruvio 2014). Accordingly, this paper will investigate materialism as a stress outcome that results from being exposed to SMIs.

3 Theoretical Framework

To explain the relationship between stressors (SMIs) and developing technostress in a form of negative feelings and behavior we draw on a well-known theory in psychological research, social comparison theory.

3.1 Social Comparison Theory

Social comparison theory (SCT) theorizes that individuals form opinions about their social and personal worth, and evaluate their abilities and limitations through comparing themselves to others (Festinger 1954). SCT suggests that people are continuously evaluating themselves and others across a number of domains such as attractiveness.

Research on SCT proposes that, under certain conditions, social comparison present individual with negative ideas and self-threats that can lead to negative reactions (Mussweiler and Strack 2000; Argo et al. 2006) for example, individuals who often compare themselves to other experience negative feelings such as feelings of deep dissatisfaction and envy (Chae 2018). Furthermore, SCT suggests that social comparisons will lead individuals to negatively evaluate themselves when a comparison is made against someone who is relevant or psychologically close, and when performed in an important domain (Argo et al. 2006).

SMI is very similar to their followers (some of them are even ordinary people); which makes them more relevant to their followers. Also, having these SMIs posting photos and Snaps mainly about beauty, fashion, luxury brands and lavish holidays makes them part of an important domain that people generally aspire to have and belong to but find hard to acquire and accompany (Chae 2018). As a result, it is expected that SMIs followers will start comparing their own status to SMIs', and they will develop negative feelings.

4 Research Prepositions

4.1 Social Media Influencers as a Form of Technostressor

Stressors are the reason why individuals experience technostress (Brooks et al. 2017). As SMIs are continuously posting about their luxury life, holidays, and high-end merchandise they are expected to trigger negative emotions amid ordinary people who perceive such as perfect image and luxury life as unattainable (Ki 2018). Therefore, in this paper, we propose that SMIs provokes social comparison and create stress for social media user. Therefore, they are considered a source of technostress

Proposition 1: SMIs on social media platforms are considered a stressor.

4.2 Materialism as a Strain

Mandel and Smeesters (2008) suggested that materialism may be a potential outcome of stress. Followers of SMIs on social network platforms are constantly presented with massages which glorify high brands and different product ownership as indicators of success and happiness. Thus, materialism is proposed to become a criterion to measure success. individuals, in this case, are expected to get keener on owning different products and to spend more on high brands. As a result, materialism and the need to own will become an outcome of stress.

Proposition 2: it is expected that followers of SMIs on social networks will value ownership and will develop appreciation to materialism.

4.3 Materialism as a Mediator

Richins (2004) stated that materialism is a representation of how much an individual value owning material possessions. Consequently, it is expected that individuals who holds this quality achieve emotional satisfaction through ownership. Which indicates that lack of ownership will result in a negative feeling (Belk 1987) and consequently an urge to eliminate the negative feeling.

In this paper, we postulate that appreciating materialism as a result of being exposed to SMIs will increase the stress and affect shopping addiction thus we propose that materialism will mediate the relationship between following SMIs and shopping addiction.

Proposition 3: Materialism is postulated to have a mediation relationship between following SMIs as stressors and shopping addiction as a strain.

5 Proposed Research Methodology

This research aims to study the effect of validating a number of prepositions that are related to the negative effect and behaviors related to using social media in out of work context. Therefore, the sample of this study will be followers of SMIs. Jordan comes first globally in usage of social media relative of internet users. Therefore, the sample from Jordan is expected to be a representative sample. A quantitative data collection strategy is recommended for this research as most of the proposed variables has been studied before using well-established scales. Factors will be measured using scale items adopted from previous studies. Once the data is collected, structural equation modeling (SEM) analysis will be conducted to validate the prepositions and create a conceptual model.

6 Implications to Theory and Practice

Today, everything is about Social Media which is allowing companies to engage with their customers more efficiently and at a very low cost (Kaplan and Haenlein 2010). SMIs are becoming a form of social media tools that companies use to promote for their products. Nevertheless, social media is having a noticeable negative impact on the public by undermining the freedoms and the well-being of the individuals and communities they serve. Therefore, it is very important for companies to understand the effect of their promotion tools on the public in order to remain ethical and to keep their social responsibility promise to their communities. Also, policymakers can benefit from understanding the effect of such tools in order to protect the public. This paper gives an insight into SMIs potential side effect on individuals and tries to enrich the literature of technostress by studying probing the dark-side of social media out of workplace.

References

Abidin, C.: "Aren't these just young, rich women doing vain things online?": influencer selfies as subversive frivolity. Soc. Media + Soc. **2**(2), 205 (2016)

Alalwan, A.A., Rana, N.P., Dwivedi, Y.K., Algharabat, R.: Social media in marketing: a review and analysis of the existing literature. Telemat. Inf. **34**(7), 1177–1190 (2017)

Argo, J.J., White, K., Dahl, D.W.: Social comparison theory and deception in the interpersonal exchange of consumption information. J. Consum. Res. **33**(1), 99–108 (2006)

Arndt, J., Solomon, S., Kasser, T., Kennon, M.S.: The urge to splurge: a terror management account of materialism and consumer behavior. J. Consum. Psychol. **14**, 198–212 (2004)

Arora, A., Bansal, S., Kandpal, C., Aswani, R., Dwivedi, Y.: Measuring social media influencer index-insights from facebook, Twitter and Instagram. J. Retail. Consum. Serv. **49**, 86–101 (2019)

Ayyagari, R., Grover, V., Purvis, R.: Technostress: technological antecedents and implications. MIS Q. **35**(4), 831–858 (2011)

Baccarella, C.V., Wagner, T.F., Kietzmann, J.H. McCarthy, I.P.: Social media? It's serious! Understanding the dark side of social media. Eur. Manag. J. **36**(4), 431–438 (2018)

Belk, R.W.: Material values in the comics: a content analysis of comic books featuring themes of wealth. J. Consum. Res. **14**(1), 26–42 (1987)

Bolat, E., Gilani, P.: Instagram influencers: when a special relationship with fans turns dark (2018)

Baumeister, R.F.: Yielding to temptation: self-control failure, impulsive purchasing, and consumer behavior. J. Consum. Res. **28**, 670–676 (2002)

Benson, A.L.: To Buy or Not to Buy. Trumpeter, Boston (2008)

Brod, C.: Technostress: the human cost of the computer revolution. Addison Wesley Publishing Company (1984)

Brooks, S.: Does personal social media usage affect efficiency and well-being. Comput. Hum. Behav. **46**, 26–37 (2015)

Brooks, S., Longstreet, P., Califf, C.: Social media induced technostress and its impact on internet addiction: a distraction-conflict theory perspective. AIS Trans. Hum.-Comput. Interact. **9**(2), 99–122 (2017)

Brown, K.W., Kasser, T., Ryan, R.M., Konow, J.: Materialism, spending, and affect: an event-sampling study of marketplace behavior and its affective costs. J. Happiness Stud. **17**(6), 2277–2292 (2016)

Bucher, E., Fieseler, C., Suphan, A.: The stress potential of social media in the workplace. Inf. Commun. Soc. **16**(10), 1639–1667 (2013)

Chae, J.: Explaining females' envy toward social media influencers. Media Psychol. **21**(2), 246–262 (2018)

Combley, R.: Langenscheidt standard French dictionary: French-English, EnglishFrench; [new blue headwords]: Langenscheidt (2011)

De Veirman, M., Cauberghe, V., Hudders, L.: Marketing through Instagram influencers: the impact of number of followers and product divergence on brand attitude. Int. J. Advert. **36**(5), 798–828 (2017)

Dwivedi, Y.K., Kapoor, K.K., Chen, H.: Social media marketing and advertising. Mark. Rev. **15** (3), 289–309 (2015)

Festinger, L.: A theory of social comparison processes. Hum. Relat. **7**(2), 117–140 (1954)

Freberg, K., Graham, K., McGaughey, K., Freberg, L.A.: Who are the social media influencers? A study of public perceptions of personality. Public Relat. Rev. **37**(1), 90–92 (2011)

Forest, A.L., Wood, J.V.: When social networking is not working. Psychol. Sci. **23**(3), 295–302 (2012)

Hirschman, E.C., Holbrook, M.B.: Hedonic consumption: emerging concepts, methods and propositions. J. Mark. **48**(Summer), 92–101 (1982)

Kaplan, A.M., Haenlein, M.: Users of the world, unite! The challenges and opportunities of social media. Bus. Horiz. **53**(1), 59–68 (2010)

Kapoor, K.K., Tamilmani, K., Rana, N.P., Patil, P., Dwivedi, Y.K., Nerur, S.: Advances in social media research: past, present and future. Inf. Syst. Front. **20**(3), 531–558 (2018)

Khamis, S., Ang, L., Welling, R.: Self-branding, 'micro-celebrity' and the rise of social media influencers. Celebr. Stud. **8**(2), 191–208 (2017)

Ki, C.W.: The drivers and impacts of social media influencers: the role of mimicry (2018)

Kim, Y.M., Shim, K.Y.: The influence of internet shopping mall characteristics and user traits on purchase intent. Irish Mark. Rev. **15**(2), 25–34 (2002)

Kumar, A., Bezawada, R., Rishika, R., Janakiraman, R., Kannan, P.K.: From social to sale: the effects of firm generated content in social media on customer behavior. J. Mark. **80**(1), 7e25 (2016)

Kuss, D.J., Griffiths, M.D.: Online social networking and addiction—a review of the psychological literature. Int. J. Environ. Res. Public Health **8**(9), 3528–3552 (2011)

Lee, S.B., Lee, S.C., Suh, Y.H.: Technostress from mobile communication and its impact on quality of life and productivity. Total Qual. Manag. Bus. Excell. **27**(7–8), 775–790 (2016)

Mandel, N., Smeesters, D.: The sweet escape: effects of mortality salience on consumption quantities for high- and low-self-esteem consumers. J. Consum. Res. **35**, 309–323 (2008)

Marwick, A.E.: You may know me from YouTube: (micro-) celebrity in social media. In: Marshall, P.D., Redmond, S. (eds.) A Companion to Celebrity, pp. 333–350. Wiley, Chichester (2015)

Morse, S., Gergen, K.J.: Social comparison, self-consistency, and the concept of self. J. Pers. Soc. Psychol. **16**(1), 148 (1970)

Mussweiler, T., Bodenhausen, G.V.: I know you are, but what am I? Self-evaluative consequences of judging in-group and out-group members. J. Pers. Soc. Psychol. **82**(1), 19 (2002)

Mussweiler, T., Strack, F.: Consequences of social comparison. In: Handbook of Social Comparison, pp. 253–270. Springer, Boston (2000)

Pirkkalainen, H., Salo, M.: Two decades of the dark side in the information systems basket: suggesting five areas for future research. In: ECIS 2016: Proceedings of the 24th European Conference on Information Systems, Tel Aviv, Israel, 9–11 June 2014. European Conference on Information Systems (2016)

Ragu-Nathan, T.S., Tarafdar, M., Ragu-Nathan, B.S., Tu, Q.: The consequences of technostress for end users in organizations: conceptual development and empirical validation. Inf. Syst. Res. **19**(4), 417–433 (2008)

Richins, M.L.: The material values scale: Measurement properties and development of a short form. J. Consum. Res. **31**(1), 209–219 (2004)

Richins, M.L., Dawson, S.: A consumer values orientation for materialism and its measurement: scale development and validation. J. Consum. Res. **19**(3), 303–316 (1992)

Rose, S., Dhandayudham, A.: Towards an understanding of Internet-based problem shopping behaviour: the concept of online shopping addiction and its proposed predictors. J. Behav. Addict. **3**(2), 83–89 (2014)

Shiau, W.-L., Dwivedi, Y.K., Yang, H.-S.: Co-citation and cluster analyses of extant literature on social networks. Int. J. Inf. Manag. **37**(5), 390–399 (2017)

Shiau, W.-L., Dwivedi, Y.K., Lai, H.-H.: Examining the core knowledge on Facebook. Int. J. Inf. Manage. **43**, 52–63 (2018)

Sinha, R.: How does stress increase risk of drug abuse and relapse? Psychopharmacology **158**(4), 343–359 (2001)

Sussman, S., Lisha., N., Griffiths, M. (2010). Prevalence of the addictions: a problem of the majority or the minority? Eval. Health Prof. **34**(3), 3–56

Somer, E., Ruvio, A.: The going gets tough, so let's go shopping: on materialism, coping, and consumer behaviors under traumatic stress. J. Loss Trauma **19**(5), 426–441 (2014)

Stich, J.F., Tarafdar, M., Cooper, C.L.: Electronic communication in the workplace: boon or bane? J. Organ. Effect.: People Perform. **5**(1), 98–106 (2018)

Tarafdar, M., Gupta, A., Turel, O.: Special issue on'dark side of information technology use': an introduction and a framework for research. Inf. Syst. J. **25**(3), 161–170 (2015a)

Tarafdar, M., Pullins, E.B., Ragu-Nathan, T.S.: Technostress: negative effect on performance and possible mitigations. Inf. Syst. J. **25**(2), 103–132 (2015b)

Tarafdar, M., Tu, Q., Ragu-Nathan, B.S., Ragu-Nathan, T.S.: The impact of technostress on role stress and productivity. J. Manag. Inf. Syst. **24**(1), 301–328 (2007)

The Business Dictionary (2019). http://www.businessdictionary.com/definition/shopping.html. Accessed 20 Feb 2019

Tice, D.M., Bratslavsky, E., Baumeister, R.F.: Emotional distress regulation takes precedence over impulse control: if you feel bad, do t! J. Pers. Soc. Psychol. **80**, 53–67 (2001)

Weil, M.M., Rosen, L.D.: Technostress: coping with technology@ work@ home@ play, pp. 29–32. Wiley, New York (1997)

Wills, T.A.: Downward comparison principles in social psychology. Psychol. Bull. **90**(2), 245 (1981)

Wagner, T.F.: Promoting technological innovations: towards an integration of traditional and social media communication channels. In: Meiselwitz, G. (ed.) SCSM 2017. LNCS, vol. 10282, pp. 256–273. Springer, Cham (2017). https://doi.org/10.1007/978-3-319-58559-8_22

Vaast, E., Kaganer, E.: Social media affordances and governance in the workplace: an examination of organizational policies. J. Comput. –Med. Commun. **19**(1), 78–101 (2013)

Yan, Z., Guo, X., Lee, M.K., Vogel, D.R.: A conceptual model of technology features and technostress in telemedicine communication. Inf. Technol. People **26**(3), 283–297 (2013)

Yasir, M., Adil, M., Khan, M.N., Malik, M.S., Khan, F.: Outcomes of personal social media usage in the workplace. J. Manag. Sci. **11**(3), 547–558 (2017)

Author Index

Printed in the United States
By Bookmasters